HIGH-PERFORMANCE
GRAPHICS IN C
ANIMATION AND SIMULATION

NOTES ON THE PHOTOGRAPHS

The color photographs on the front cover are examples of graphics produced by the demonstration programs included inside the book. Exposure was ¼ second at f2.8 using Kodak Ektachrome 100 Daylight color slide film. The camera was a 35mm Pentax K1000 with a 2x teleconverter (to reduce angular distortion) fitted to a 1:2 standard 50mm lens. A tripod and remote shutter cable release were used in order to minimize camera vibration. The graphics were produced by an IBM PC using an EGA (a Quadram QuadEGA ProSync). The images were displayed on an NEC Multisync monitor. The software was IBM DOS 3.20 and Microsoft QuickC 1.00.

The black and white photographs in the body of the book are halftones taken from b/w prints produced with Kodak Plus-X Pan film. Exposure was ¼ second at f2.8 and ¼ second at f3.4.

HIGH-PERFORMANCE
GRAPHICS IN C
ANIMATION AND SIMULATION

Lee Adams

Published by **Windcrest Books**

FIRST EDITION/FIRST PRINTING

Library of Congress Cataloging-in-Publication Data

Adams, Lee.

    High-performance graphics in C : animation and simulation / by Lee Adams.
       p.   cm.
    Includes 0-8306-0249-6   ISBN 0-8306-9349-1 (pbk.)
    1. C (Computer program language) 2. Computer graphics.
 I. Title.
 QA76.73.C15A32 1988
 006.6'765—dc19   88-17073
                                                  CIP

TAB BOOKS Inc. offers software for sale. For information and a catalog, please contact TAB Software Department, Blue Ridge Summit, PA 17294-0850.

Questions regarding the content of this book should be addressed to:

Windcrest Books
Division of TAB BOOKS Inc.
Blue Ridge Summit, PA 17294-0850

Ron Powers: Acquisitions Editor
David M. Harter: Manuscript Editor
Katherine Brown: Production
Jaclyn Saunders: Series Design
Doug Robson: Cover Design

NOTICES

MS-DOS, GW-BASIC, and Microsoft are registered trademarks of Microsoft Corporation. QuickC and QuickBASIC are trademarks of Microsoft Corporation.

Turbo C and Turbo BASIC are registered trademarks of Borland International, Inc.

QuadEGA+, QuadEGA ProSync, and QuadVGA are trademarks of Quadram Corporation. Quadram is a registered trademark of Quadram Corporation.

Kodak, Ektachrome, and Plus-X Pan are registered trademarks of Kodak.

Pizazz is a trademark of Application Techniques, Inc.

MetaWINDOW is a trademark of MetaGRAPHICS Software Corporation.

Essential Graphics is a trademark of Essential Graphics Inc.

TurboHALO is a trademark of Media Cybernetics and IMSI.

NEC Multisync is a trademark of NEC Home Electronics.

Sony Multiscan is a trademark of SONY Corp.

Ultrasync is a trademark of Princeton Graphic Systems. Princeton is a registered trademark of Princeton Graphic Systems.

IBM, IBM PC, IBM Personal Computer, IBM Personal Computer XT, IBM Personal Computer AT, Personal System/2, Operating System/2, and PC-DOS are registered trademarks of International Business Machines Corporation.

Aztec C is a trademark of Manx Software Systems.

Let's C is a trademark of Mark Williams Company.

CONTENTS

Acknowledgments   *xiii*

Introduction: How to Use This Book   *xv*

Summary of Program Listings   *xxi*

PART ONE — CONCEPTS

1 Concepts   3
    Graphics vs. Text   3
    Getting Started in Computer Graphics   6

2 Hardware   10
    The Graphics Adapter   10
    Graphics Modes   12
    How Graphics Adapters Work   13
    Display Memory Map   16
    Graphics Program Portability   23
    Graphics Adapter Standards   25
    Monitors   27
    Software   30

3   *Software*   31

Versatility 31
Power 32
Speed 32
Programming with C Compilers: An Overview 32
Integrated Programming Environments 33
How Integrated C Compilers Really Work 35
The Programming Cycle 36
A Typical QuickC Programming Environment 37
A Typical Turbo C Programming Environment 37
Memory Management 38
Using the Integrated Editors 39

PART TWO — TOOLS

4   *Programming Tools*   43

C Program Structure 43
C Program Control 44
C Operators 45
Loop Control in C 47
Branching Instructions in C 48
Using C Variables 49
Using C Arrays 50
Portability of C Programs 51
Communicating with Your C Compiler 51
Using BIOS Routines with C 53

5   *Graphics Tools*   56

Fundamental Graphics Functions 57
Advanced Graphics Functions 61
Graphics Syntax Incompatibilities 66

6   *How to Use Microsoft QuickC*   68

System Memory Map 68
The DOS Environment 70
The QLB Library 71
Case Study: Running a Typical C Program 73
Analysis of the Program 74
Common Error Messages 76
Creating EXE Files 77

7   *How to Use Borland TurboC*   78

System Memory Map 78
The DOS Environment 80

Case Study: Running a Typical C Program   81
Analysis of the Program   82
Common Error Messages   83
Creating EXE Files   84

PART THREE — DESIGN

8   Screen Layout: a Graphics Primer   87

Using a Drawing Template   87
From Template to Display Screen   87
The Device-Independent 640 × 480 Template   89
Fundamentals of Good Layout   90
Prototyping   98

9   How to Select Colors   99

Hardware Colors   99
Color Terminology   100
Shades, Tones, and Tints   100
Color Circles   101
Color Harmonies   101
Color Scales   103
Scales   104
Shading Matrices   106
Case Study: a Demonstration Program   108
Advanced Psychology of Color   110
Untapped Potential   111

10   Drawing on the Screen   116

Dynamic and Database Coordinates   116
Case Study: a Demonstration Program   117

11   Managing the Background Graphics   126

Sculpted Backgrounds   126
Airbrushed Backgrounds   127
Borders   130
Case Study: a Demonstration Program — Sculpted
Background   131
Case Study: a Demonstration Program — Airbrushed
Background   137

12   Using Windows and Viewports   143

Windows   143
Viewports   143
A Typical Clipping Routine for C   146

13 **Advanced Techniques for Graphics** **149**
Graphics Database 149
Saving Screen Images to Disk 150
Sound Effects 154

14 **How to Generate 3D Images** **156**
World Coordinates 156
Creating a 3D Model 157
Display Options 158
3D Formulas for Personal Computers 158
Hidden Surface Removal 159
Shading and Illumination 161
Case Study: a Demonstration Program 162

15 **Business Graphics** **170**
Case Study: a Demonstration Program in 2D 176
Case Study: a Demonstration Program in 3D 184

16 **Realistic Illustration** **195**
Styles of Illustration 195
Preparation 196
Case Study: a Demonstration Program 196

PART FOUR — FRAME ANIMATION

17 **Practical Techniques for Frame Animation** **207**
The Frame Animation Process 207
Case Study: a Utility Program 209
Optimization 211
Compatibility and Portability 211

18 **Animated Business Graphics** **212**
Case Study: Animated Business Chart 212
Analysis of the Program 213

19 **Animated Education Graphics** **222**
Preparation 222
Case Study: Animated Hovering Hummingbird 222
Analysis of the Program 223

20 **Animated Design Graphics** **235**
Case Study: a Rotating 3D Model 235
Analysis of the Program 237

PART FIVE — BITBLT ANIMATION

21 **Practical Techniques for Bitblt Animation**   **249**
Logical Operators 249
Applications for Bitblt Animation 250
Bitblt Animation Using PSET 250
Case Study: a Utility Program 256
Analysis of the Program 256

22 **Entertainment Software—the Talking Caricature**   **258**

23 **Simulation Software—the Walking Figure**   **274**

24 **Animated Education Software— Simulated Clock Face**   **285**

PART SIX — REAL-TIME ANIMATION

25 **Practical Techniques for Real-time Animation**   **299**
VGA/EGA Hidden-Page Animation 299
CGA Hidden-Page Animation 300
Two Forms of Real-time Animation 300
Dynamic Keyboard Input 300
Run-Time Performance 302
Case Study: a Utility Program 302

26 **Arcade-style Software**   **304**
Managing the Ricochets 304
Analysis of the Program 307

27 **Flight Simulation**   **314**
3D Line Clipping 316
The Demonstration Program 317
Analysis of the Program 317
Further Studies 318

APPENDICES

A **Summary of C Routines for Graphics**   **331**
Saving VGA and EGA Screen Images 331
Saving CGA Screen Images 331

Graphics Mode Configuration Module   332
Sound Effects   332
Frame Animation   332
Real-time Animation   332
Bitblt Animation   332

B   *How to Use Assembly Language*
Graphics Routines   **360**

Required Software Tools   360
The Interface to Assembly Language   361
Passing Parameters to the Subroutine   361
C Memory Models   361
Near Call vs. Far Call   361
Where to Put the OBJ File   363
Local Variables   363
Using BIOS Interrupts   364

C   *Assembly Language Routines for EGA and VGA*   **366**

D   *Assembly Language Routines for CGA*   **382**

E   *Demonstration Programs for Turbo C*   **396**

The Project File   396
How the Programs Were Adapted   396
Graphics Syntax   397
Notes on the Program Listings   397
Spurious Error Messages   399

Glossary   **497**

Index   **513**

Acknowledgments

The author extends appreciation to Quadram Corporation of Atlanta, Georgia for its generosity in providing QuadVGA+, QuadEGA ProSync, and QuadEGA graphics adapters for the author's evaluation during the preparation of the book.

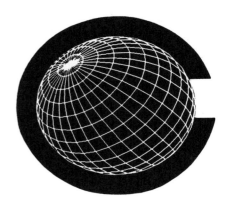

Introduction:
How to Use This Book

High-Performance Graphics in C provides you with the hands-on knowledge you need to create high-speed animation and high-performance simulations just like the ones you have admired in professional programs. Using only your personal computer and a C compiler, such as QuickC or Turbo C, you will be able to write graphics programs that rival those of packaged software. Simply stated, this book is an easy-to-follow advanced graphics text that starts where other introductory books stop.

High-Performance Graphics in C contains over 6,000 lines of valuable source code. You will learn many of the closely-guarded secrets of professional graphics programmers. Using ready-to-run program listings, you will explore the exciting topics of design, illustration, and color. You will learn the high-performance techniques of frame animation, bitblt animation, and real-time animation on your personal computer using a VGA, EGA, CGA, or MCGA graphics adapter.

The programs in this book are crafted especially for the new popular compilers: Microsoft QuickC and Borland Turbo C. These compilers possess powerful built-in graphics functions. If you are using a C compiler which does not have built-in graphics capabilities, a library of assembly language graphics routines in the appendix will get you started in the thrilling field of high-performance computer animation.

WHO SHOULD USE THIS BOOK?

If you use a personal computer and you are interested in computer graphics, then you will want to read this book. If you are a novice, then the exciting field of computer animation and simulation is waiting for you to discover. If you are an experienced programmer in C, BASIC, assembly language, or Pascal, this book will treat you to some graphics techniques that you may have thought possible only with expensive packaged software. If you are a professional programmer or software developer, you will likely learn many useful techniques for enhancing your own original programs.

If you deal with business applications, you should review Chapters 15 and 18 for information about creating and animating 2D and 3D business charts. If you deal with educational applications, you may wish to check out the animated display of the hummingbird biological sheet in Chapter 19. If you are interested in real-time animation, you should read Chapter 26 for guidance in writing arcade-style programs. Consult Chapter 27 for a look at a flight simulation prototype. If simulation software is your area of interest, you should check the walking figure in Chapter 23 and the simulated clock face in Chapter 24.

A quick review of the table of contents will convey the breadth of topics covered in this important graphics text.

ABOUT THE BOOK

High-Performance Graphics in C has been designed as a powerful learning tool. To aid the learning process, you can turn back corners of pages which interest you so that you can quickly find them again, or you can highlight portions of the text with a marker pen, or you can write your own notes into the margins of the text.

This book teaches you how to write animated graphics programs on IBM-compatible personal computers, using a modular programming environment. Because the learn-by-example approach is the most effective method of teaching, the book uses a style which is best described as here-is-how-it-is-done. Sixteen major demonstration programs are provided. Seven function prototype programs are presented.

Emphasis is placed on helping you to grasp the concepts which drive the demonstration programs. This ensures that you will find it easy to create your own original graphics programs. Using the information in this book, you will be able to create full-color programs which use bitblt animation at a blazing 43 frames per second . . . or page animation at an impressive 36 frames per second . . . or real-time animation which accepts keyboard input while it is running. Along the way, you will also learn how to generate 3D images, airbrushed backgrounds, realistic illustration, business graphics, and more.

SPECIAL FEATURES OF THE BOOK

High-Performance Graphics in C is organized in an easy to-follow format. It uses a step-one, step-two, step-three approach. Important fundamentals which are discussed near the beginning of the text become the building blocks for advanced graphics routines later in the book. Using a modular programming method, specialized subroutines are used in innovative ways to create spectacular graphics on your personal computer.

Each program listing is presented in a ready-to-run form. You will appreciate this approach if you have struggled through other C books whose programs make reference to modules and files located elsewhere in the book.

Every program listing in this book is full and complete. Simply type it in and it is ready to compile and run with QuickC or Turbo C on your IBM PC, XT, AT, PS/2, or compatible. You can use either a VGA, EGA, CGA, or MCGA graphics adapter. In fact, many of the programs contain a subroutine which ensures that the best graphics mode is used on your system. If a VGA is present, the 640×480 16-color mode is often used. If an EGA and enhanced monitor are present, the 640×350 16-color mode will be invoked. The 640×200 16-color mode is used if an EGA and standard monitor are present. If a CGA or MCGA is present, either the 640×200 2-color mode or the 320×200 4-color mode is used by the program.

All the demonstration programs are also available on disk, of course. Refer to the order coupon at the back of the book for details.

Each program listing in this book is accompanied by a photograph of an actual monitor display, so you can verify the accuracy of the animation or simulation produced on your own personal computer. A rich selection of line drawings provides the vital background information you need in order to understand the graphics concepts being used. A thorough discussion of each program gives you a modular description of the programming logic involved.

If you choose to select only topics of specific interest to your programming needs, a comprehensive table of contents at the beginning of the book and a detailed index at the end of the book can steer you to the information you need.

HOW THE BOOK IS ORGANIZED

The material is this book is organized in six sections for your easy reference.

Part One—Concepts

Part One introduces the graphics programming environment. You will learn about different hardware and software capabilities. You will discover the vast potential which exists for graphics, animation, and simulation in a wide variety of projects, including computer-aided design, computer-aided learning, analytic graphics, presentation graphics, computer-aided manufacturing, project management, business graphics, and more.

Part Two—Tools

Part Two introduces programming skills. You will learn the high-powered C statements that can be used to manage any graphics program. You will discover how to use loops, library functions, math routines, and more. You will see how to invoke the powerful graphics functions contained in QuickC and Turbo C. You will learn how to write graphics programs that will automatically adjust themselves to run on all IBM-compatible graphics adapters, including the VGA, EGA, CGA, and MCGA.

Part Three—Design

Part Three introduces the creative aspect of graphics programming. You will learn about graphic design on the computer screen. You will understand how to select the correct colors for each application. You will find out how to use halftoning to create nine shades from only a single color. You will discover how to draw on the screen using either dynamic coordinates or a database of coordinates. You will see how to manage the background graphics—airbrushed and sculptured—and how to handle viewports. The specific formulas for producing accurate 3D images are provided. You will learn how to create 2D and 3D business graphics. You will discover how to produce realistic illustrations. You will learn how easy it is to save a VGA, EGA, or CGA screen image to disk. You can experiment with sounds.

Part Four—Frame Animation

Part Four introduces the lightning-quick techniques of frame animation. You will learn how to implement this form of animation on your VGA, EGA, CGA, or MCGA graphics adapter. A case study shows you how to animate a business chart. An example of educational graphics teaches you how to animate a hovering ruby-throated hummingbird at an amazing 36 frames per second. Another case study shows you how to rotate a solid 3D model.

Part Five—Bitblt Animation

Part Five introduces bitblt animation—the technique used by many arcade-style programs. An animation prototype shows you how to animate a ricocheting ball at 43 frames per second. You will learn how to animate a talking caricature and a walking human figure. A case study teaches you how to simulate the sweep hand of an analog clock face.

Part Six—Real-time Animation

Part Six introduces the dynamic concepts of real-time animation. You will learn how easy it is to use hidden-page animation. You will see how to create a keyboard routine that permits you to control the animation while your program is running. A demonstration program teaches you how to write the process control routines used in arcade-style software. A case study of flight simulation lets you perform loops and rolls in 3D over a 16-square-grid terrain.

Appendices

The appendices provide a rich selection of vital C routines, in addition to assembly language source code for VGA, EGA, CGA, and MCGA graphics. A comprehensive glossary explains many important concepts which are unique to C graphics programming and to IBM-compatible personal computers.

WHAT YOU NEED TO USE THE BOOK

You probably already have everything you need to get the most out of this book.

Software Requirements

If you have Microsoft QuickC version 1.00 or newer, or Microsoft C version 5.0 or newer, or Borland Turbo C version 1.5 or newer, then you have all the software you need. Each of these popular C compilers has built-in graphics routines. If you are using another C compiler which does not feature built-in graphics (such as Turbo C version 1.0, for example), then you can use the library of assembly language graphics routines in the appendix to get you started in the exciting world of computer animation and simulation.

Program listings for QuickC version 1.00 and newer appear throughout the main body of the book and in Appendix A. Program listings which have been adapted for Turbo C version 1.5 and newer appear in Appendix E.

Equipment Requirements

If you have access to an IBM-compatible personal computer, then you have all the equipment you need. The programs are written for the IBM PC, the IBM Personal Computer XT, the IBM Personal Computer AT, and the IBM Personal System/2 series. Any microcomputer which is compatible with these models will run the demonstration programs.

Graphics Adapter Requirements

If you have access to an IBM-compatible graphics adapter, then you have all the graphics hardware you need. The programs in this book are written for the VGA, EGA, CGA, and MCGA graphics adapters and their compatible monitors.

If you have a color/graphics adapter (CGA) in your personal computer, then the programs will run in either the 640×200 2-color mode or the 320×200 4-color mode, depending upon the particular program.

If you have an enhanced graphics adapter (EGA) in your personal computer, then the programs will run in either the 640×350 16-color mode, the 640×200 16-color mode, or the 320×200 16-color mode, depending upon the particular program. In order to use the 640×350 mode, either an enhanced monitor such as the IBM Enhanced Color Display or a variable scanning monitor such as the NEC Multisync is required.

If you have a video graphics array (VGA) as found in the 80286- and 80386-based models of the IBM Personal System/2 series or if you have a third-party VGA-emulation board such as the QuadVGA, then the programs will run in either the 640×480 16-color mode, the 640×200 16-color mode, or the 320×200 16-color mode, depending upon the particular program.

If you are using the multicolor graphics array (MCGA) as found in 8086-based models of the IBM Personal System/2 series, then the demonstration programs will behave as if they were running on a CGA.

THE COMPANION DISK

The companion disk for this book is available in two versions: QuickC and Turbo C. Using the disk, you can begin immediately to explore the high-performance graphics routines presented in this book. Instead of typing in the program listings from the text, you simply load the program from the companion disk into your personal computer.

The companion disk is not copy-protected. You can display the source code on your monitor. You can compile and run the source code within the QuickC and Turbo C integrated editing environments. You can use the source code to create stand-alone EXE files. You can print the source code on your printer.

The companion disk for this book is a powerful graphics toolkit containing dozens of fully-tested routines that you can use to build your own high performance programs.

HOW THE DEMOS WERE CREATED

The demonstration programs in **High Performance Graphics in C** were developed on a genuine IBM PC with 640K RAM using IBM DOS 3.20, Microsoft QuickC 1.00, Borland Turbo C 1.5, an NEC Multisync monitor, and a Quadram QuadEGA ProSync graphics adapter. To ensure program portability, each program was tested using Microsoft MS-DOS 3.20 on an IBM-compatible personal computer with 640K RAM.

Each program was also tested with a Quadram QuadEGA+ graphics adapter, a Quadram QuadVGA graphics adapter, and a standard CGA graphics adapter. Monitors that were tested include an IBM Enhanced Color Display and a standard RGB color display. A variety of 8088-based and 8086-based IBM-compatible personal computers were tested.

Simply stated, the demonstration programs in this book will run on every personal computer that features IBM compatibility.

IF YOU INTEND TO ADAPT MATERIAL FROM THIS BOOK

If you intend to adapt any material from this book for your own purposes, or if you intend to use the information in this book to write commercial software, shareware, or freeware, then you should read the next three paragraphs.

The author's best efforts have been used to prepare the material which appears in this book. These efforts include the research, development, and rigorous testing of the demonstration programs to determine their effectiveness, accuracy, speed, and portability.

However, because the techniques of animation and simulation can be applied to a diverse range of projects, the author is unable to make any absolute guarantee to you that the information and program listings will solve your particular problems of design, engineering, simulation, education, business, CAD, or animation.

You will discover many powerful programming techniques in this book. If you intend to adapt the material for your own purposes, you must thoroughly test the programs before you rely upon their performance.

DO YOU NEED SPECIAL HELP?

The author welcomes questions and observations from readers, and will reply to all letters. You can write to Reader Inquiry Branch, TAB BOOKS Inc., Blue Ridge Summit, PA, 17294-0214. Allow three weeks for your correspondence to reach the author. Include a program listing or a disk if you feel it will assist in understanding your questions and comments. Provide your telephone number and area code if you wish a spoken reply.

COMING SOON

Other C books by the same author coming soon from TAB include *High-Performance Graphics in C: Computer-Aided Design* (#3059), and *High-Performance Graphics in C: Graphics Source Code* (tentative title).

Summary
of Program Listings

Each program listing in **High-Performance Graphics in C** is ready to type in and run on your IBM-compatible personal computer. In many cases, the program will automatically adjust itself to produce the best graphics possible on your system. Many programs will use the 640×480 16-color mode if a VGA is present, the 640×350 16-color mode if an EGA and enhanced monitor are present, the 640×200 16-color mode if an EGA and standard monitor are present, or the 640×200 2-color and 320×200 4-color mode if a CGA or MCGA is present.

In most instances two listings of each program are provided. One listing is compatible with Microsoft QuickC (version 1.00 and newer) and with Microsoft C (version 5.0 and newer). The other listing is compatible with Borland Turbo C (version 1.5 and newer). These compilers contain built-in graphics functions. If you are using a C compiler which does not contain a graphics library, Appendix C and Appendix D contain listings for assembly language graphics routines which you can use with your compiler.

QUICKC PROGRAM LISTINGS

These program listings for QuickC and Microsoft C are also available on the companion disk. Refer to the order coupon at the back of the book for details.

Fig. 9-13   Hues and halftones
Fig. 10-4   Illustrating with dynamic coordinates
Fig. 11-9   Sculpted background effect
Fig. 11-11   Airbrushed background effect

Fig. 14-8   How to generate a 3D image
Fig. 15-12   Business chart in 2D
Fig. 15-15   Business chart in 3D
Fig. 16-5   Realistic 2D portrait
Fig. 18-4   Animated business chart
Fig. 19-5   Animated hummingbird
Fig. 20-4   Animted rotation of 3D model
Fig. 22-4   Animated caricature
Fig. 23-5   Animated walking figure
Fig. 24-3   Animated clock face simulation
Fig. 26-8   Animated arcade-style prototype
Fig. 27-7   Animated flight simulation prototype
Fig. A-1   How to save an EGA and VGA screen image to disk
Fig. A-2   How to configure your program to run on all IBM-compatible
                     graphics adapters
Fig. A-3   How to produce sounds
Fig. A-4   How to save a CGA screen image to disk
Fig. A-5   How to produce frame animation at 14 frames per second
Fig. A-6   How to produce real-time animation
Fig. A-7   How to produce bitblt animation at 43 frames per second

TURBO C PROGRAM LISTINGS

These programs listings for Turbo C version 1.5 and newer are also available on the companion disk. Refer to the order coupon at the back of the book for details.

Fig. E-1   Hues and halftones
Fig. E-2   Illustrating with dynamic coordinates
Fig. E-3   Sculpted background effect
Fig. E-4   Airbrushed background effect
Fig. E-5   How to generate a 3D image
Fig. E-6   Business chart in 2D
Fig. E-7   Animated business chart
Fig. E-8   Animated hummingbird
Fig. E-9   Animated rotation of 3D model
Fig. E-10   Animated walking figure
Fig. E-11   Animated clock face simulation
Fig. E-12   Animated arcade-style prototype
Fig. E-13   Animated flight simulation prototype
Fig. E-14   How to configure your program to run on all IBM-compatible
                     graphics adapters
Fig. E-15   How to produce sounds
Fig. E-16   How to produce frame animation at 14 frames per second
Fig. E-17   How to produce bitblt animation at 43 frames per second

ASSEMBLY LANGUAGE LISTINGS

These program listings are designed to work with all C compilers which use near calls to invoke assembly language subroutines, but instructions are provided to modify the routines to use far calls. These valuable program listings are available only in this book.

Fig. C-1   A library of assembly language graphics routines for the
                640×200 16-color mode of the EGA and VGA
Fig. D-1   A library of assembly language graphics routines for the
                320×200 4-color mode of the CGA and MCGA

I

CONCEPTS

Graphics Programming Environment

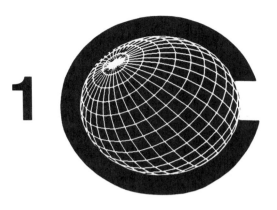

Concepts

graph-ics (graf'-iks) noun plural, noun singular—the art of making drawings, as in architecture, engineering, design, and computer images.

Graphics have become a vital component of computer programming. Of the nearly eight million IBM personal computers and compatibles in use in offices and homes around the world, a majority of those personal computers possess either VGA, EGA, or CGA graphics capability—and a growing cadre of computer users expect the programs they use to have a graphical interface. These people have found from experience that graphics can be a timesaving shortcut to learning, understanding, and mastering the software they use. Because much of this software is written in C, the C programmer who lacks graphics skills is at a disadvantage in today's highly competitive software marketplace.

An understanding of the programming algorithms behind computer graphics will provide you with the expertise you need to enhance your programs with features such as high-speed animation, high-impact illustrations, and high-performance simulations. This book strives to provide you with that understanding.

GRAPHICS VS. TEXT

Are graphics a substitute for text? The answer is no. In many instances, rather than being a substitute for text, the use of computer graphics is intended as an adjunct to text in order to further enhance a program's performance.

3

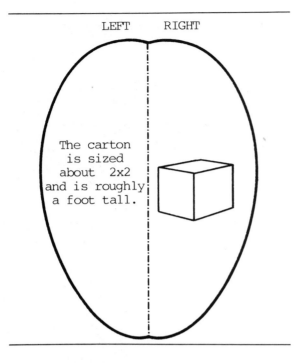

LEFT   RIGHT

The carton
is sized
about   2x2
and is roughly
a foot tall.

Fig. 1-1. The impact of graphics versus text on the left- and right-hemispheres of the human brain.

The Benefits of Using Graphics

By using both graphics and text in your programs, you can improve the quality of communication between your program and the end-user. This improvement in quality is a direct result of the physiology of the human brain. Refer to Fig. 1-1. Simply stated, the left hemisphere of the brain is responsible for interpreting text material, while the right hemisphere manages visual interpretation. Medical researchers have concluded that the left brain deals with parts and sequences of parts; the right brain deals with wholes.

Because a significant portion of the human mind remains idle if only text material is presented, your text-based program is overlooking an important channel of communication. You can use computer graphics to harness that channel.

Do Graphics Make a Difference?

Will the addition of graphics to your programs make much of a difference? Perhaps the best way to make the point is to let you decide for yourself. The material in Fig. 1-2 is presented in two different ways. The top part of Fig. 1-2 uses only text to present an idea. The lower part of the figure uses a combination of text and graphics to present the same idea. You can see for yourself how much easier it is to grasp the idea when both text and graphics are used. It is the graphics which makes the difference—and it is a big difference.

Notwithstanding the addition of graphics, the full meaning of the idea in Fig. 1-2 has not been expressed. Something is still lacking. The images are, after all, only a stationary depiction of a dynamic human activity: walking, cycling, hiking, skiing, roller skating, and running. Look at Fig. 1-2 again and imagine how powerfully the idea could be conveyed

Fig. 1-2. In many instances, a graphic image can convey information faster and easier than text.

on a computer screen if the image were animated! Imagine in your mind's eye the pumping legs of the cyclist, the measured gait of the hiker, and the flashing feet of the runner. Suddenly, the richness of the original idea has been communicated. Expressed in a more technical manner, scientific studies have shown that ease of visualization increases when animation is added to a computer-generated image.

The lesson is clear. If you want strong communication, use graphics. If you want the strongest communication possible, use animated graphics.

Where Can Graphics Be Used?

The list of software applications that use, or that could use, graphics or animated graphics is a comprehensive one. Refer to Fig. 1-3. Computer Aided Design (CAD), Computer Aided Engineering (CAE), and Computer Aided Styling (CAS) are built around computer graphics. Without computer-generated images, these software applications would simply cease to exist.

Computer Aided Learning (CAL) can be enhanced by the inclusion of graphics. Computer Aided Manufacturing (CAM) is also a candidate for graphics features. The timetables and organization structures found in project management software cry out for graphical representation. Analytic programs—both business charts and scientific graphs—

require computer graphics, animated and otherwise. Models and simulations, although often expressed as mere formulas and text data, can experience a quantum leap in performance if presented as 2D or 3D computer images. Even commonplace programs such as word processors and database managers are beginning to incorporate graphics into their displays. Entertainment software has long been known for its heavy use of graphics.

GETTING STARTED IN COMPUTER GRAPHICS

Computer graphics is a programming science in its own right, and computer animation is a specialized area with that field. Before you can produce animation on your personal computer, you must first learn how to create graphics on your personal computer. It is as simple as that.

For practical purposes, there are three types of high-speed animation available on your personal computer: frame animation, bitblt animation, and real-time animation. This book teaches you how to use C to produce all three types of animation on any IBM-compatible personal computer equipped with any IBM-compatible graphics adapter.

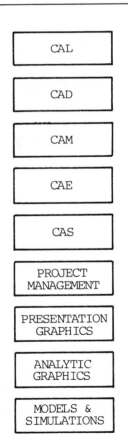

Fig. 1-3. Summary of potential applications for computer graphics and animation. The following abbreviations are used in the chart: CAL computer aided learning; CAD computer aided design; CAM computer aided manufacturing; CAE computer aided engineering; CAS computer aided styling.

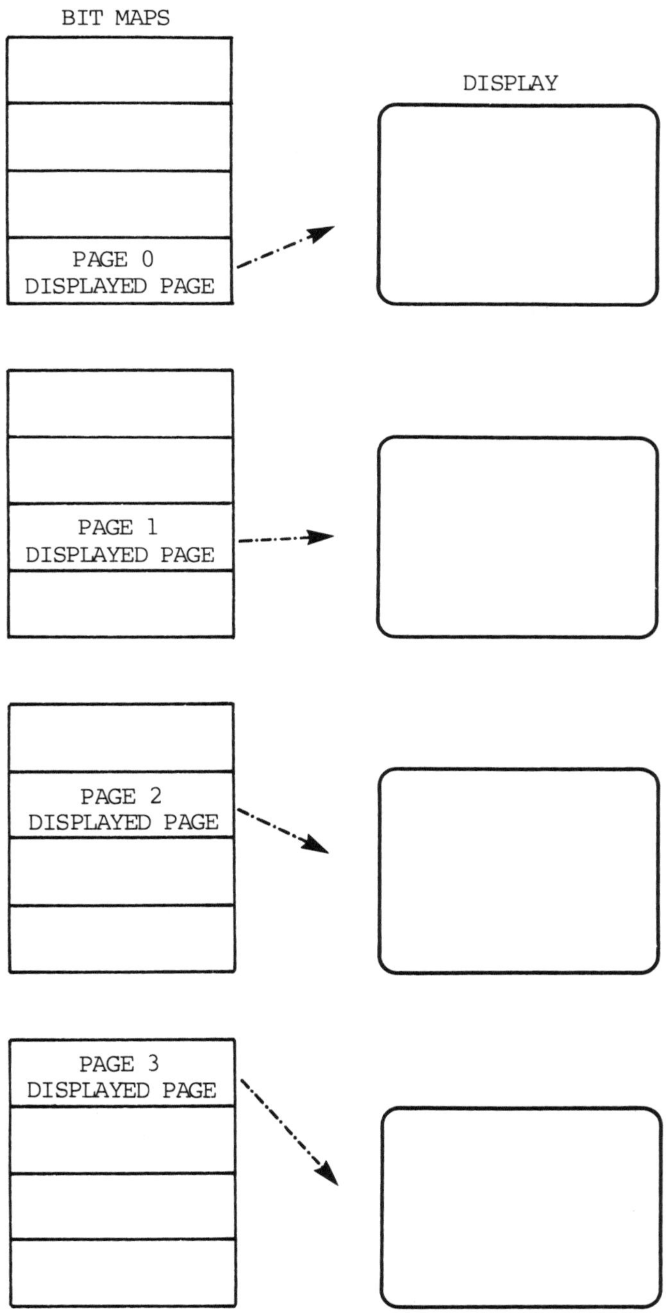

BIT MAPS

DISPLAY

PAGE 0
DISPLAYED PAGE

PAGE 1
DISPLAYED PAGE

PAGE 2
DISPLAYED PAGE

PAGE 3
DISPLAYED PAGE

Fig. 1-4. The fundamental concepts involved in frame animation.

Frame Animation

In programmer's jargon, a *page* is a screen of graphics. The page being displayed on the screen is often called the displayed page. However, a computer is capable of holding other undisplayed pages in memory. These undisplayed pages are called *frames*. Refer to Fig. 1-4. If these frames each contain a slightly different version of the same image, then animation can be created when these pages are flipped onto the screen in rapid sequence. This technique is called frame animation. Because all the graphics have been created in advance, frame animation is very fast. Speeds of 18 *fps (frames per second)* and faster are commonplace using C.

Bitblt Animation

In some cases, only a small portion of the screen needs to be animated. Refer to Fig. 1-5. If a small block of graphics is moved across the screen, then the resulting movement is called *bitblt* animation. Bitblt is an acronym for bit block transfer. Bitblt animation is also called *block graphics* and *graphic array animation*. Because only small portions of the screen are being manipulated, bitblt animation is very fast. Using C, animation speeds exceeding 30 fps are easily achievable in arcade-style animation programs.

Real-time Animation

Sometimes a program must adapt to user input while it is running. Such a program often uses real-time, *hidden page animation*. Refer to Fig. 1-6. This animation technique

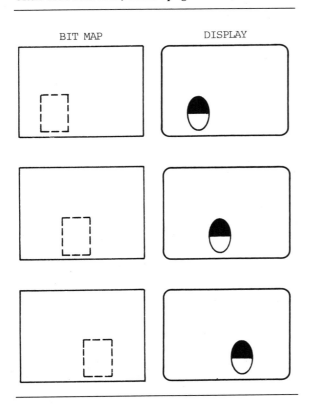

Fig. 1-5. The fundamental concepts involved in bitblt animation, some times called block animation or graphic array animation.

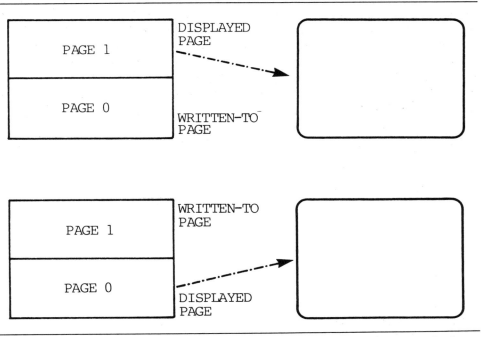

Fig. 1-6. The fundamental concept involved in real-time animation, often called ping pong animation or hidden page animation.

is also called *ping pong animation,* because it bounces back and forth between two pages. As soon as an image has been created, the computer flips it up onto the screen. While the user is looking at the new image on the screen, the computer is busy drawing the next image on a hidden page. When the next image is finished, it is flipped onto the screen, thereby creating an ongoing animation sequence. The computer is creating the graphics during the animation cycle, so the program can alter the types of images being created by accepting input from the user. But because the computer is doing two jobs at once (creating the images and animating them), the speed of real-time animation is limited by the length of time required to create each new image.

First Steps

Each of these three forms of computer animation has its strengths and weaknesses. And each of these techniques can excel when handled properly. But before you can run, you must learn how to walk. Now is a good time to look at a few important basics. The next chapter explains the graphics capabilities of IBM-compatible hardware.

 **2**

Hardware

hardware (hard-wer') noun singular—the mechanical, magnetic, and electronic design, structure, and devices of a computer.

Unlike other forms of programming, you will want to possess a good general understanding of hardware graphics capabilities if you are interested in graphics programming. At a minimum, you will want to understand the potential and the limitations of your own particular computer system. Even better, you may wish to become familiar with the broad range of graphics modes available across the entire family of IBM personal computers, graphics adapters, display monitors, and all compatibles.

Three factors control the quantity and the quality of graphics which can be generated on any particular microcomputer system. These factors are the graphics adapter, the display monitor, and the programming language. Of these three elements, the graphics adapter is the most important.

GRAPHICS QUALITY FACTOR NO. 1: THE GRAPHICS ADAPTER

The graphics adapter which is installed in your microcomputer determines the maximum graphics capabilities of your system. In general, four main types of graphics adapters are commonly used in personal computers. These graphics adapters are the VGA, the EGA, the MCGA, and the CGA. In all, these four graphics adapters can generate a diversified selection of graphics modes ranging from two colors to 256 colors, and varying from a displayable resolution of 320×200 pixels to 640×480 pixels.

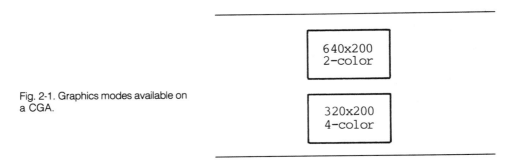

Fig. 2-1. Graphics modes available on
a CGA.

The CGA

If there is a common denominator in the world of IBM-compatible personal computers, it is the CGA—more commonly called the color/graphics adapter. Refer to Fig. 2-1. For the purpose of graphics, the CGA can generate a 320×200 4-color screen and a 640×200 2-color screen.

The notation 320×200 means 320 pixels across by 200 pixels down. A *pixel* is the smallest visual element which can be controlled on the display screen. A single pixel is usually comprised of a red dot, a green dot, and a blue dot. It is the mixing of these three colors that gives the pixel its apparent hue on the screen.

Although the CGA is a superb general-purpose graphics adapter, the coarse resolution in the 320×200 4-color mode and the severely restricted choice of colors in the 640×200 mode makes it less than ideal for advanced graphics programming. The CGA is a fine graphics adapter for learning purposes, however, and it is capable of some outstanding animation effects. Only one graphics page is available on the color/graphics adapter. Later in the book you will learn how to use C to create simulated additional graphics pages in user RAM.

The CGA is usually used with a *standard color display* monitor (SCD).

The MCGA

MCGA is an acronym for *multicolor graphics array*. The MCGA is the graphics adapter found in the 8086-based models of the IBM Personal System/2 series, such as the Model 30 and the Model 25. The name 8086 refers to the model number of the Intel microprocessor used in these systems.

The MCGA is essentially an analog superset (an extension) of the CGA. Refer to Fig. 2-2. In addition to the standard 320×200 4-color mode and the 640×200 2-color mode, the MCGA provides a 640×480 2-color mode and a 320×200 256-color mode. The 256-color mode has attracted the attention of many professional programmers and computer users.

The MCGA can be used with either an analog display monitor or a multiscanning monitor.

The EGA

EGA is an acronym for *enhanced graphics adapter*. The EGA provides the 320×200 4-color and the 640×200 2-color modes of the CGA, in addition to four EGA graphics modes: a 320×200 16-color mode, a 640×200 16-color mode, a 640×350 16-color mode,

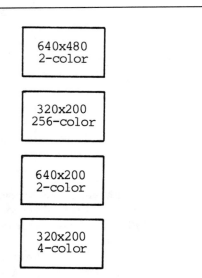

Fig. 2-2. Graphics modes available on an MCGA.

and a 640×350 2-color mode. Refer to Fig. 2-3. Multiple graphics pages are available on the EGA.

The EGA can be used with either a standard color display monitor (SCD) or with an *enhanced color display* (ECD). An ECD is required in order to generate the 640×350 modes, because an SCD can display a maximum of only 200 lines.

The VGA

If there is a graphics standard in the world of IBM personal computers and compatibles, it is the VGA. The VGA is the *video graphics array* found on the 80286-based and the 80386-based models of the IBM Personal System/2 series, such as the Model 50, Model 60, and Model 80. 80286 and 80386 are the names of the Intel microprocessors found in these systems.

The VGA provides all the modes of EGA, CGA, and MCGA graphics, as well as one additional graphics mode: the 640×480 16-color mode. Refer to Fig. 2-4. Like the EGA, multiple graphics pages are available on the VGA.

The VGA requires either an analog display monitor or a multiscanning monitor.

Third-party VGAs are often capable of working with standard color display monitors and enhanced color displays, in addition to analog display monitors and multiscanning monitors.

GRAPHICS MODES

Figure 2-5 illustrates the rich range of graphics modes recognized by IBM. The CGA and EGA modes are digital in composition (the screen images are produced by a series of electronic pulses which are either on or off). The MCGA and VGA modes are analog in composition (the images are produced by a series of electronic pulses which can be varied in intensity, ranging from fully on to fully off and anywhere in between).

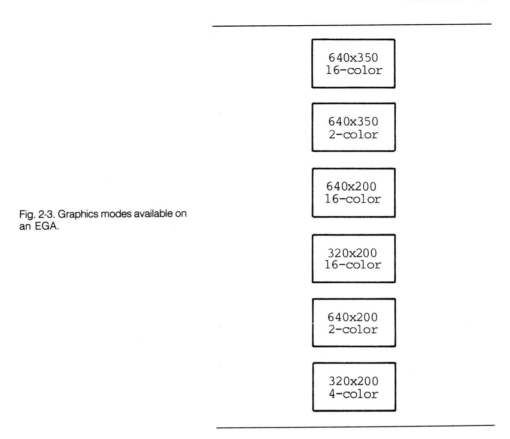

Fig. 2-3. Graphics modes available on an EGA.

Graphics adapters operating in a digital mode require a TTL monitor. TTL is an acronym for *transistor-to-transistor logic*. The SCD and the ECD are TTL monitors. Graphics adapters operating in an analog mode require an analog monitor or a multiscanning monitor. The IBM 8512 PS/2 Display is an analog monitor. The NEC Multisync and the Princeton Ultrasync are multiscanning monitors.

HOW GRAPHICS ADAPTERS WORK

The manner in which the display memory is organized, and the manner in which the hardware displays that memory on the screen, is different for CGA, EGA, and VGA modes. CGA graphics adapters use multibit-per-pixel display memory. VGA and EGA graphics adapters use multiplane-per-pixel display memory.

Multiplane-per-pixel Display Memory

The VGA and EGA use a strategy based upon *multiplane-per-pixel* graphics (mpp). Refer to Fig. 2-6. Four separate graphics images are stored in display memory. Each image is called a *bit plane*. Each bit plane stores the complete image as one of the four primary color codes used by the VGA and EGA: red, green, blue, and (in the case of the EGA) intensity level.

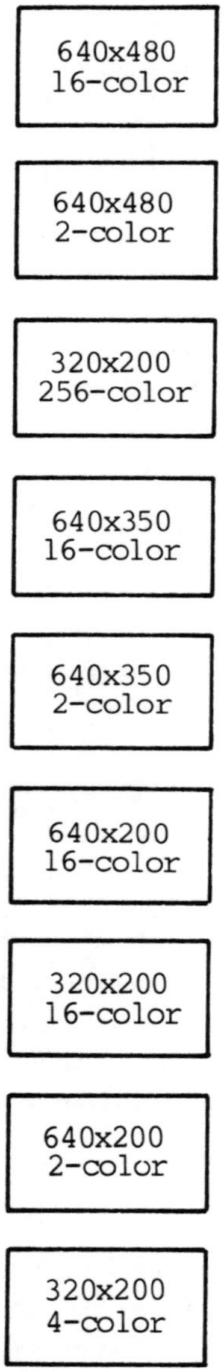

```
640x480
16-color
```

```
640x480
2-color
```

```
320x200
256-color
```

```
640x350
16-color
```

Fig. 2-4. Graphics modes available on a VGA.

```
640x350
2-color
```

```
640x200
16-color
```

```
320x200
16-color
```

```
640x200
2-color
```

```
320x200
4-color
```

The display controller of the VGA and EGA simultaneously reads the corresponding bits from all four bit planes and uses the aggregate to determine which of 16 available colors should be displayed at that location on the display screen. Because each bit plane can exhibit a 0 or a 1 value at a particular point, adding all four bit planes together yields a range of 0000 binary to 1111 binary (or a range from 0 to 15: 16 choices). In concept, you can think of the four bit planes as being sandwiched together by the graphics adapter in order to yield the full-color display image you see on the monitor.

MODE	RESOLUTION	ADAPTER	MONITOR	BUFFER	MEMORY	BPP	TEXT
04	320x200 4-color	VGA,EGA,CGA,MCGA	PS/2,VS,ECD,SCD	16,000	2 banks	2	40x25
06	640x200 2-color	VGA,EGA,CGA,MCGA	PS/2,VS,ECD,SCD	16,000	2 banks	1	80x25
0D	320x200 16-color	VGA,EGA	PS/2,VS,ECD,SCD	32,000	4 planes	4	40x25
0E	640x200 16-color	VGA,EGA	PS/2,VS,ECD,SCD	64,000	4 planes	4	80x25
0F	640x350 2-color	VGA,EGA	PS/2,VS,ECD	28,000	2 planes	2	80x25
10	640x350 16-color	VGA,EGA	PS/2,VS,ECD	112,000	4 planes	4	80x25
11	640x480 2-color	VGA,MCGA	PS/2,VS	38,400	2 planes	2	80x30
12	640x480 16-color	VGA	PS/2,VS	153,600	4 planes	4	80x30
13	320x200 256-color	VGA,MCGA	PS/2,VS	64,000	4 planes	8	40x25
--	640x480 256-color	8514/A	PS/2,VS	307,200	4 planes	8	--
--	1024x768 256-color	8514/A	8514	786,432	4 planes	8	--

Fig. 2-5. IBM-compatible graphics modes and the required adapters, monitors, and memory. The following abbreviations are used in the chart: VGA video graphics array, EGA enhanced graphics adapter, CGA color/graphics adapter, MCGA multicolor graphics array, PS/2 analog monitor, VS variable scan monitor, ECD enhanced color display, SCD standard color display.

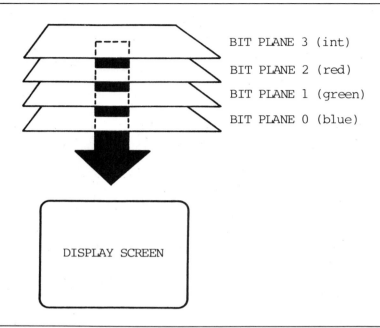

BIT PLANE 3 (int)

BIT PLANE 2 (red)

BIT PLANE 1 (green)

BIT PLANE 0 (blue)

DISPLAY SCREEN

Fig. 2-6. Multiplane-per-pixel mapping is used in the enhanced modes of the VGA and EGA: 320×200 16-color, 640×200 16-color, 640×350 16-color, 640×480 16-color, and 320×200 256-color.

The *hue* (color) which is associated with each of those 16 choices is determined by the display controller hardware. On the EGA (which uses a digital system) the hardware plots each red, green, and blue dot on the screen as either off, normal intensity on, or high intensity on. On the VGA (which uses an analog system) the hardware plots each red, green, and blue dot on the screen at a brightness which can vary anywhere between fully on and fully off. The visual mixture of these tiny red, green, and blue triplets on the screen is what produces the apparent range of hues on the monitor. The theory of color mixing is discussed in more detail in Chapter 9.

Multibit-per-pixel Display Memory

The CGA uses a strategy called *multibit-per-pixel* display memory (mbp). Refer to Fig. 2-7. Only a single bit plane is used, commonly called a *bit map*. For 320×200 4-color graphics, two bits per pixel are required. This is because two bits can express four different color attributes: 00, 01, 10, and 11. Therefore, one byte in the bit map controls four pixels on the display screen. For the 640×200 2-color mode, one bit per pixel is required because a single bit can express two different color attributes: 0 and 1 (off and on).

DISPLAY MEMORY MAP

256K of memory has been set aside for display purposes on IBM personal computers and compatibles. The location of this block of memory is fixed at address A0000 hex. Refer to Fig. 2-8. Whether or not a particular graphics adapter uses all of this 256K, the entire

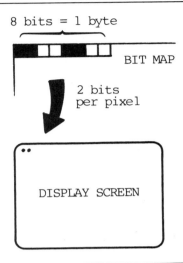

Fig. 2-7. Multibit-per-pixel mapping is used for the 320×200 4-color mode of the CGA and MCGA.

block is reserved for graphics purposes. It is interesting to note that A0000 hex is 640K, which is the top of user RAM on IBM PC, XT, AT, and compatibles. On the IBM Personal System/2 series a full megabyte (1000K) of user RAM is available. The extra 360K is located above FFFFF hex (refer to Fig. 2-8) and does not corrupt the display memory block.

The layout of the 256K display memory block is depicted in Fig. 2-9. If a color/graphics adapter is present, it uses 16K of memory beginning at address B8000 hex (736K). If a VGA or EGA graphics adapter is present, its display memory begins at A0000 hex (640K). An EGA with 256K of display memory will use all the memory reserved for graphics. An EGA with 64K, such as IBM's EGA, will only use one quarter of the memory actually reserved for display purposes. A VGA always contains 256K of display memory.

The 16K of display memory found on a CGA is depicted in Fig. 2-10. The first 8000 bytes of display memory are used to house the even raster lines of the image (lines 0 through 198). The second 8000 bytes of display memory contain the odd raster lines (1 through 199). This layout is a result of hardware idiosyncracies built into the CGA in an effort to reduce screen flicker caused by the slow operating speeds of the adapter and its monitors. Neither the VGA nor the EGA modes use this odd-even methodology, adopting instead a simple left to right, top to bottom memory map which corresponds directly to the pixels on the screen.

It is interesting to note that a VGA or EGA which is running in either the 320×200 4-color CGA mode or the 640×200 2-color CGA mode will use the 16K of memory at B8000 hex.

640×200 16-color Mode

The multiplane-per-pixel strategy used by the VGA and EGA in the 640×200 16-color mode is represented in Fig. 2-11. In the 640×200 16-color mode, four graphics pages are available, but they are not contiguous. The graphics adapter provides 16384 bytes of storage per bit plane, even though each bit plane requires 16000 bytes. The extra 384 bytes between each bit plane is unused.

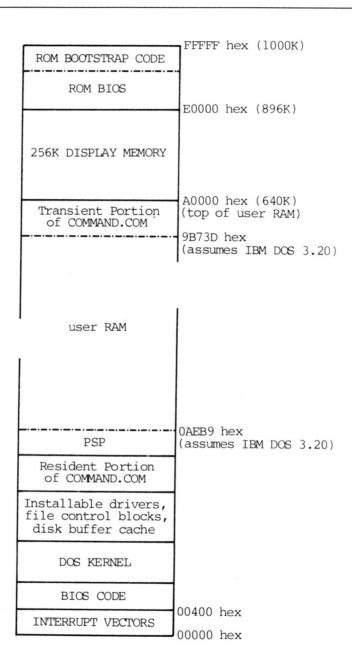

Fig. 2-8. System memory map for IBM and IBM-compatible personal computers. Extended user RAM, if installed, is located at memory addresses beyond FFFFF hex.

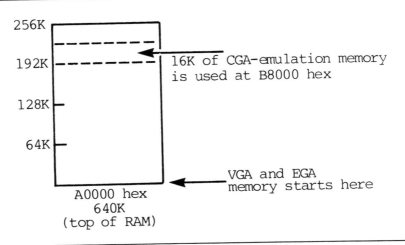

Fig. 2-9. Display memory of a VGA and EGA graphics adapter.

Fig. 2-10. Display memory of a CGA. Total buffer memory is 16K (16384 bytes). Because each bank requires only 8000 bytes, two areas of 192 bytes each are unused.

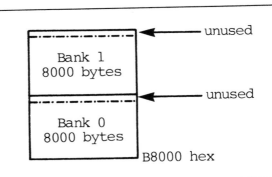

The first 64K of VGA and EGA display memory holds only bit plane 0 of each of the four graphics pages. The next bit plane for each page is found in the next 64K segment of memory. It is interesting to note that only the first 64K segment of display memory can be directly accessed by your program; you must use the latching registers of the VGA and EGA to write graphics to the bit planes which reside in the higher segments. Versions of C which support the EGA perform this latching for you, of course. This addressability applies to all VGA and EGA modes.

Because four pages are available in the 640×200 16-color mode on VGA and EGA graphics adapters, this mode supports a full range of animation techniques, including frame animation, bitblt animation, and real-time hidden page animation.

640×350 16-color Mode

Figure 2-12 illustrates the display memory map for a VGA or EGA using the 640×350 16-color mode. Because each bit plane requires 28000 bytes of memory, only two pages

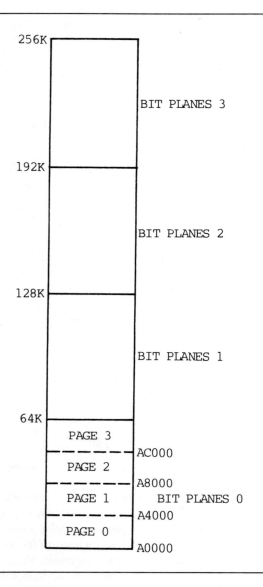

Fig. 2-11. Memory map of a VGA or EGA using the 640×200 16-color mode. Four pages are available.

are available. A full screen of data (comprised of four bit planes) requires 112000 bytes of storage.

Because two pages are available, animation techniques available in the 640×350 16-color mode include frame animation, bitblt animation, and real-time hidden page animation.

320×200 256-color Mode

The display memory map of a VGA running in the 640×480 16-color mode is shown in Fig. 2-13. Only one graphics page is available, because each bit plane requires 38400 bytes of storage. A screenful of data (four bit planes) requires 153600 bytes of storage.

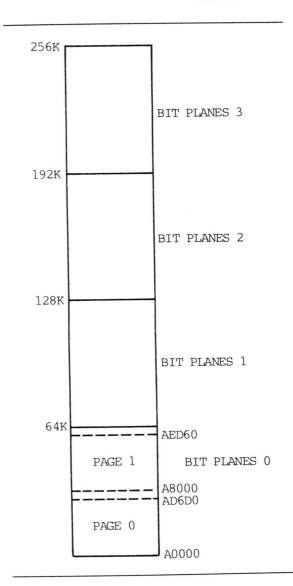

Fig. 2-12. Memory map of a VGA or EGA using the 640×350 16-color mode. Two pages are available.

Animation techniques which are useful in the 640×480 16-colors mode include bitblt animation and any real-time animation which does not require a hidden page (such as arcade-style animation, for example).

320×200 16-color Mode

Figure 2-14 illustrates the display memory map for a VGA or EGA using the 320×200 16-color mode. Because each bit plane requires only 8000 bytes of storage, eight pages are available. A full screen image (comprised of four bit planes) requires 32000 bytes of storage.

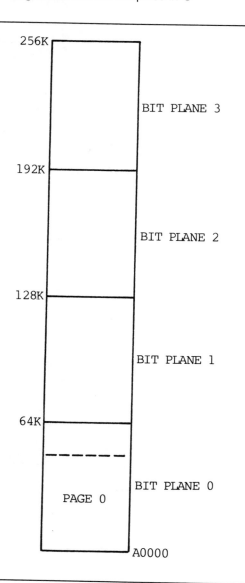

256K

BIT PLANE 3

192K

BIT PLANE 2

Fig. 2-13. Memory map of a VGA using the 640×480 16-color mode. Eight pages are available.

128K

BIT PLANE 1

64K

BIT PLANE 0

PAGE 0

A0000

Because eight pages are available, the technique of frame animation is most productive in the 320×200 16-color mode. The techniques of bitblt animation and real-time hidden page animation are also available.

640×480 16-color Mode

The display memory map of a VGA or MCGA running in the 320×200 256-color mode is shown in Fig. 2-15. This mode employs a slightly modified bit-to-pixel mapping strategy than the other multiplane-per-pixel graphics modes and is able to store a bit plane in only 16000 bytes. A screenful of data requires 64000 bytes of storage allowing four display pages.

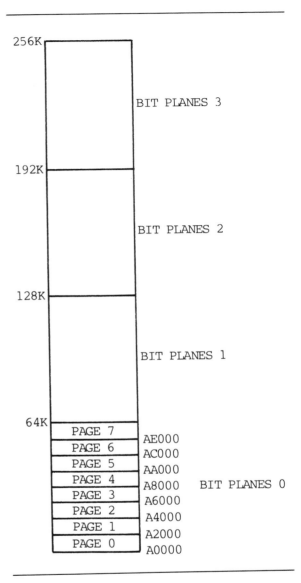

Fig. 2-14. Memory map of a VGA or EGA using the 320×200 16-color mode. Eight pages are available.

The 320×200 256-color mode can support the techniques of frame animation, bitblt animation, and real-time hidden page animation.

GRAPHICS PROGRAM PORTABILITY

Graphics program portability refers to the capability of a graphics program to be used by a variety of different hardware and software configurations. Clearly, if a graphics program is written for the 640×480 16-color mode of the VGA, it will not function correctly in the 640×350 mode or the 640×200 mode or the 320×200 mode. As a C graphics

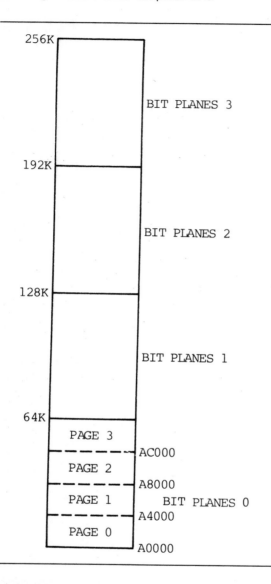

Fig. 2-15. Memory map of a VGA using the 320×200 256-color mode. Four pages are available.

programmer, you likely want your programs to be compatible with different graphics adapters and monitors.

By using graphics routines that are not explicitly linked to any particular graphics mode, your programs can be made *device-independent*. That means they will run in different graphics modes, and that means they will run on different graphics adapters and monitors, and that means wider circulation and a broader market for your graphics programs.

Many of the program listings in this book use a configuration module that sets up the best graphics mode possible on the graphics adapter and monitor being used with the microcomputer. The graphics instructions in many of the demonstration programs are based on an imaginary 640×480 screen. During program execution these graphics instructions are filtered through a special subroutine which scales the instructions to fit whatever screen mode is being used by the program, no matter whether it is the 640×480 or the 640×350 or the 640×200 or the 320×200 screen. (The imaginary 640×480 screen, called a device-independent screen template, is discussed in detail in Chapter 8.)

GRAPHICS ADAPTER STANDARDS

The microcomputer industry generally adheres to graphics standards which have been established by IBM, but more graphics adapters are purchased from manufacturers other than IBM. The EGA and VGA provide an illuminating example of how third-party manufacturers such as Quadram Corporation, Video Seven, AST Research, Paradise Systems, Sigma Designs, Tecmar, Tseng Laboratories, and others, have adopted and expanded the capabilities of a graphics adapter originally introduced by IBM.

Case Study: Quadram Corporation

Quadram Corporation is a typical example of a third-party manufacturer who provides graphics adapters for use in IBM-compatible personal computers. Quadram's range of products has kept pace with the graphics standards endorsed by IBM.

QuadEGA+

The QuadEGA+ is a full-function EGA card with 256K display memory. Refer to Fig. 2-16. The QuadEGA+ is 100% compatible at the hardware level and 100% compatible

Fig. 2-16. The QuadEGA+ graphics adapter from Quadram Corporation offers IBM EGA compatibility.

at the BIOS level with a genuine IBM EGA. The 256K standard display memory is typical of third-party EGAs; it is four times the 64K provided on the IBM EGA.

The QuadEGA+ can generate the 320×200 4-color mode and the 640×200 2-color mode of the CGA, in addition to the EGA graphics mode: the 320×200 16-color mode, the 640×200 16-color mode, the 640×350 16-color mode, and the 640×350 2-color mode. As an added feature, the QuadEGA+ also provides emulation of the IBM Monochrome Text Adapter (MA) and the Hercules Graphics Adapter (HGA).

The QuadEGA+ provides eight graphics pages in the 320×200 16-color mode, four graphics pages in the 640×200 16-color mode, and two pages in the 640×350 mode. The QuadEGA+ is a half-length card that uses digital technology. It comes with an installation guide and operating instructions.

QuadEGA ProSync

The QuadEGA ProSync produced by Quadram Corporation is an enhancement of the QuadEGA+. Refer to Fig. 2-17. In addition to the modes found on the QuadEGA+, the ProSync offers a 640×480 16-color mode and a 752×410 16-color mode.

The QuadEGA ProSync is a half-length card that uses digital technology. It comes with an installation guide and operating instructions.

Fig. 2-17. The QuadEGA ProSync graphics adapter from Quadram Corporation offers IBM EGA compatibility plus selected higher resolution modes.

QuadVGA

The QuadVGA graphics adapter from Quadram Corporation offers full VGA compatibility at the BIOS level. It provides all the graphics modes of the CGA and EGA, as well as the 640×480 2-color mode and the 320×200 256-color mode of the MCGA. It also provides the 640×480 16-color VGA mode. Refer to Fig. 2-18.

The QuadVGA is equipped with both digital and analog output sockets so you can use it with either a standard color display monitor, an enhanced color display, a multiscanning monitor, or an analog monitor. The MCGA and VGA graphics modes require the use of either an analog monitor or a multiscanning monitor.

The QuadVGA is a half-length card that is capable of using either digital or analog technology. It comes with an installation guide and operating instructions.

GRAPHICS QUALITY FACTOR NO. 2: MONITORS

The graphics adapter, the display monitor, and the programming language each play a role in determining the quantity and the quality of graphics that can be produced. Of these three factors, the monitor is second in importance only to the graphics adapter. The display monitor which is connected to a particular graphics adapter will provide a physical limitation on the output of the graphics adapter.

Fig. 2-18. The QuadVGA from Quadram Corporation offers IBM VGA compatibility.

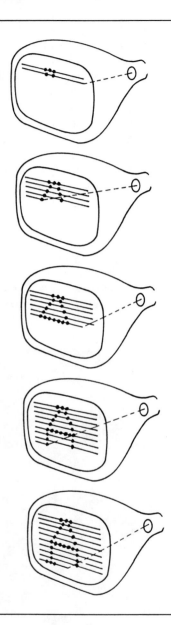

Fig. 2-19. The fundamental concepts of a raster display, which is the technology used in most personal computer monitors.

There are four main types of display monitors being used with IBM-compatible personal computers. These are the standard color display (SCD), the enhanced color display (ECD), the analog display, and the multiscanning (variable frequency) display.

Each of these four types of monitors uses the raster technology depicted in Fig. 2-19. Simply stated, the electronic guns of the cathode ray tube are continually scanning the light-sensitive phosphors on the tube from left to right, top to bottom. (Each scanned line is called a *raster line*). By turning on and turning off the guns at appropriate times, the phosphors are lit. Before the excited phosphors can fade, the guns again scan the screen. The number of times that the entire screen is scanned by the guns is called the refresh rate.

Standard Color Display

The SCD provides a maximum screen resolution of 640×200 pixels and it can simultaneously display 16 different colors. These are the same 16 default colors which are are available on the EGA, VGA, and MCGA graphics adapters. Refer to Fig. 2-20. If a standard color display is used with a CGA, both the 320×200 4-color mode and the 640×200 2-color mode can be displayed. If a standard color display is used with an EGA, the additional 320×200 16-color mode and the 640×200 16-color mode can be displayed. (The 640×350 16-color mode cannot be displayed on a standard color display because only 200 raster lines are available on the SCD.) The standard color display cannot be used with either VGA or MCGA graphics adapters, although some third-party VGAs will drive an SCD in the TTL mode.

Enhanced Color Display

The ECD provides a maximum screen resolution of 640×350 pixels and it can display a maximum of 16 simultaneous colors. However, unlike the SCD, the ECD can choose those 16 displayable colors from a palette of 64 colors when the 640×350 16-color mode is being used. If an enhanced color display is used with a CGA graphics adapter only the 320×200 4-color mode and the 640×200 2-color mode can be displayed. If an enhanced color display is used with an EGA graphics adapter, the additional modes of 320×200 16-color, 640×200 16-color, and 640×350 16-color can be displayed. The IBM Enhanced Color Display is an example of an ECD.

Analog Display

Whereas the SCD and the ECD use digital technology to display colors, analog displays like those found on the IBM Personal System/2 series of microcomputers use a continuously variable signal capable of generating more colors—and capable of generating more subtle gradations between those colors.

When used with a VGA, an analog display can display all the CGA and EGA graphics modes. In addition, a 320×200 256-color mode can be displayed, as well as a 640×480

Fig. 2-20. The standard palette of 16 colors available on IBM-compatible graphics adapters.

0	black	8	gray
1	blue	9	int. blue
2	green	10	int. green
3	cyan	11	int. cyan
4	red	12	int. red
5	magenta	13	int. magenta
6	brown	14	yellow
7	white	15	int. white

16-color mode and a 640×480 2-color mode. The 256 colors and 16 colors of these analog modes can be selected from a total palette of more than 256,000 colors. An example of an analog display is the IBM 8512 PS/2 Color Display.

Variable Frequency Displays

Multiscanning variable frequency displays offer the best of both worlds. They can display digital video signals and analog video signals. The prefix ''multi'' used by some manufacturers refers to the ability of the monitor to scan the variable output signal of the graphics adapter to determine which graphics mode is being used. Monitors such as the NEC Multisync, the Sony Multiscan, and the Princeton Ultrasync can display all of the EGA, CGA, MCGA, and VGA modes in digital or analog mode as the situation requires. They can also display non-standard modes such as the 752×410 16-color mode of the QuadEGA ProSync graphics adapter.

GRAPHICS QUALITY FACTOR NO. 3: SOFTWARE

You have seen the roles played by the first two factors: the graphics adapter and the monitor. The third factor which influences the quantity and the quality of graphics is the programming language, and it is the topic of the next chapter.

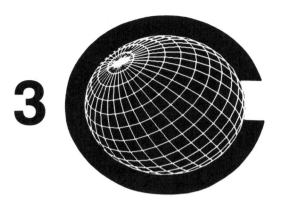

3

Software

software (soft'-wer) noun singular—1. the programs, data, and routines for use in a digital computer, as distinguished from the physical components; 2. generic term for computer programs.

The software—or programming language—that you choose to use for graphics programming has a strong impact on how easy or how difficult your programming tasks will be. C offers three advantages to graphics programmers: versatility, power, and speed. All three features are vital to graphics programs.

C ADVANTAGE NO. 1: VERSATILITY

Because of C's versatility in memory management and process control, it is a wise choice for graphics programming.

Memory management is important because graphic images are stored as blocks of data in memory and because the numeric values used to plot those graphic images are often stored as databases in memory.

C's versatility in memory management includes the ability to organize the computer's memory in different ways in order to meet the needs of different types of graphics programs. Some programs use large amounts of data and a relatively small module of executable code. Other programs involve large modules of executable code and use very little numeric data. C can accommodate both of these environmental needs.

C's versatility in memory management also includes the ability to quickly move the contents of one block of memory to another block. This ability is vital for some forms of animation where page moves are involved or where graphic arrays are used.

Process control is important because graphics programs often branch to subroutines, often employ loops and counters, and often accept keyboard input. C's process control instructions are rich and varied, as discussed in Chapter 4.

C ADVANTAGE NO. 2: POWER

C's power is a direct result of its aggregate combination of low-level, middle-level, and high-level language characteristics.

A *low-level language* is a programming language whose syntax closely correlates to the operation of the computer's internal hardware registers. A low-level language is often said to function at the bit level. A low-level language offers awesome raw power to a programmer, but often at the expense of hard-to-understand source code. If you are using a low-level language such as assembly language, your programs can do anything that the hardware can do, which is usually pretty substantial.

A *middle-level language* provides a set of instructions that bear a moderate resemblance to the actual workings of the registers, but that also feature macro-like instructions that can move blocks of data and so forth. A middle-level language is often said to be a byte-oriented language. The source code for a middle-level language, such as Pascal, for example, is easier to read than the source code for a low-level language, but it is still far removed from text.

A *high-level language* usually uses syntax that closely resembles english. The instructions in a high-level language are routine-oriented. One instruction will cause the computer to perform a series of middle-level and low-level functions. BASICA is a good example of a high-level language. Although a high-level language offers ease of use, the quid pro quo power usually suffer. You are, after all, limited to the instructions which the author of the language has provided—and because the routines behind the instructions must often handle a number of different situations, they are rarely optimized for any one particular situation.

C offers an assortment of instructions which fall into all three programming categories: low-level, middle-level, and high-level. This regime offers many advantages to the graphics programmer, especially when many of the instructions are graphics-oriented, as they are in QuickC and in Turbo C (version 1.5 and newer).

C ADVANTAGE NO. 3: SPEED

C produces fast-running code because of its close relationship with assembly language. C offers a variety of specialized subroutines (called functions by C programmers)—and specialization means speed, which is often vital to graphics programs. In addition, C's close relationship with assembly language means that it is a straightforward task to use C in combination with high-speed assembly language subroutines if optimum performance is needed.

PROGRAMMING WITH C COMPILERS: AN OVERVIEW

The use of a C compiler to create graphics programs always involves four steps. Refer to Fig. 3-1. First, you must create the source code. Second, the compiler translates this source code into an OBJ file of machine language instructions which the computer hardware will understand. Third, the linker creates an EXE file by attaching to your program other

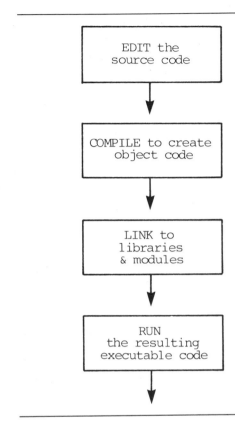

Fig. 3-1. The four conceptual phases of creating programs with a C compiler.

previously-created subroutines which you program requires at run-time. Fourth, the resulting file is executed by the computer.

During this four-stage process it is often all too easy to lose sight of the objective, which is to produce fast-running, reasonably sized programs in a moderate amount of time. During the programming process, you are continually faced with the productivity options presented in Fig. 3-2.

Any graphics program can be optimized for the fastest performance possible and at the same time occupy very little space in memory. This, in fact, would be the ideal program. The cost in programmer's labor to create such a program, however, balloons out of proportion.

Of the other three options shown in Fig. 3-2, the execution time priority model is usually favored by graphics programmers who use C. Especially for animated programs, fast execution time is vital. Provided that the program size and the hours of programmer's labor are not astronomical, this productivity model is a good choice.

INTEGRATED PROGRAMMING ENVIRONMENTS

QuickC and Turbo C are integrated programming environments. Each provides you with the capability to perform a number of related operations during your programming sessions.

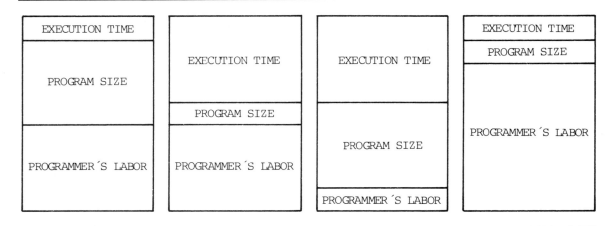

Fig. 3-2. The productivity profile choices which face a C programmer.

First, both QuickC and Turbo C provide powerful and versatile text editors which can be used to write and edit your source code.

Second, both QuickC and Turbo C provide a built-in compiler and linker to create the finished EXE file. In the case of QuickC this EXE program is stored in memory. In the case of Turbo C this EXE program is written to disk as an EXE file.

Third, both QuickC and Turbo C provide an environment where you can execute your program, observe its performance, and then return directly to the editor. In the case of QuickC, the EXE program is simply executed from memory. In the case of Turbo C, the EXE file is first downloaded from disk and then executed.

Other C compilers, such as Microsoft C version 4.00, for example, are command-line compilers. A command-line compiler requires that you operate from the DOS command-line prompt. This means that you must first load your text editor before you can create or edit your source code. You must then return to DOS in order to give the compiler its marching orders. Once the compiler has created the OBJ file, you must again use the DOS command-line to give instructions to the linker. Finally, in order to run the program, you invoke it from DOS. When the program finishes running, you are returned to the DOS prompt.

Because of the added work and increased delays imposed by command-line compilers, integrated compilers such as QuickC and Turbo C are more suitable for graphics programming, where feedback is important. Both QuickC and Turbo C can quickly compile, link, and run your program and then return you to the editing mode. In effect, you never leave the integrated programming environment. Prototyping is made much easier.

Many command-line C compilers are provided without a graphics library, unlike QuickC and Turbo C, which contain built-in graphics capabilities. C compilers which lack built-in graphics features must be enhanced with third-party graphics libraries such as MetaWindow, Essential Graphics, or TurboHALO, or other packages. All of these excellent add-on libraries entail additional out-of-pocket expense, which is often substantial. Alternatively, you can write your own graphics routines in assembly language. If you are using a C compiler which does not include graphics routines, refer to Appendix C and to Appendix D for a selection of assembly language subroutines.

HOW INTEGRATED C COMPILERS REALLY WORK

The diagram in Fig. 3-3 illustrates what happens during a typical compile/link session. This process is similar for all C compilers, whether integrated-environment C compilers or command-line C compilers.

Step one is the edit phase. You use a text editor to write the C source code. If you are using QuickC or Turbo C, you generally use the built-in editor. If you are using another C compiler, you can use any text editor or word processor which can create ASCII text files.

Step two is the compilation phase. The C compiler first inserts any other C source code modules which you have requested by your use of the #include directive. It then translates the entire source code into machine code, also called object code. This object code is stored as a file with the filename extension OBJ. Turbo C actually writes the OBJ file to disk; QuickC merely stores it temporarily in RAM during the compilation process.

Step three is the link phase. The linker attaches other, previously-created, routines to your OBJ code. These other routines can include subroutines (functions) which reside in

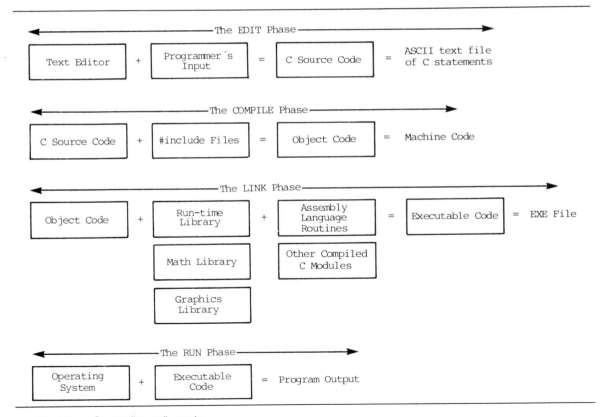

Fig. 3-3. How a C compiler really works.

the run-time library, math library, or graphics library provided with the compiler. These other routines can also be comprised of assembly language routines which you have previously created or other C modules which you have previously compiled into OBJ form. The linker binds all these modules together in order to create the executable program, often stored on disk as a file with the filename extension EXE.

Step four is the run-time phase. An EXE file can be run from the DOS command line. If QuickC or Turbo C is being used, the EXE program can be invoked directly from the editor. In this instance, control is returned back to the integrated environment of the editor when the EXE program is finished running. Control is returned to DOS if a command-line C compiler is being used, however.

THE PROGRAMMING CYCLE

The development of any C graphics program involves the methodology depicted in Fig. 3-4. The larger the project, the more likely these steps will be formal steps made in writing. The more experienced the programmer, the more likely these steps will be formal steps made in writing. In small projects, however, many of these steps are informal, spontaneous, and often performed at the subconscious level.

Simply stated, the *concept* is an idea: an expression of the raison d'etre for the program. The concept states in a single sentence what the program is going to do. The *specific features* are the actual functions performed by the program, usually visible to the end-user at run-time. The *logic flowchart* is a thumbnail sketch of how the various subroutines in the program are tied together. The *pseudocode* is a description, in english-like statements, of how important sections of the code will perform certain functions. The *source code* is simply the pseudocode

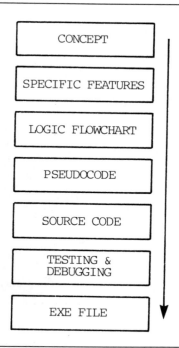

Fig. 3-4. The programming cycle from concept to finished program.

stated in C syntax, ready for the compiler. *Testing and debugging* is the running, revising, and re-running cycle. The *EXE file* is, of course, the finished file on the distribution disk.

A TYPICAL QuickC PROGRAMMING ENVIRONMENT

A typical QuickC programming environment for a two-drive system using Microsoft QuickC is shown in Fig. 3-5. First, the microcomputer is started using the DOS boot disk in drive A. Next, the QuickC program disk containing QB.EXE is placed in drive A. The companion disk for **High Performance Graphics in C** or your own source files disk is placed in drive B. The QuickC editor is invoked from the QuickC program disk in drive A. Finally, the disk containing #include files is placed in drive A, from where QuickC will fetch these files if required during the compilation process.

The source files disk in drive B must contain a special QLB file (discussed in more detail in Chapter 6). This QLB file is loaded into the top of RAM memory when QuickC is first invoked. The graphics routines which actually draw the images on the screen are contained in this QLB library.

A TYPICAL Turbo C PROGRAMMING ENVIRONMENT

A typical programming environment for a two-drive system using Turbo C is shown in Fig. 3-6. First, the microcomputer is started using a DOS boot disk in drive A. Then,

boot with DOS disk
in drive A

Fig. 3-5. The QuickC programming environment on a personal computer with two floppy disk drives.

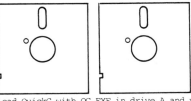

load QuickC with QC.EXE in drive A and your user´s disk
containing the QLB file in drive B

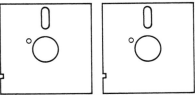

program with #include files disk in drive A
and your user´s disk containing QLB file and
your source code files in drive B

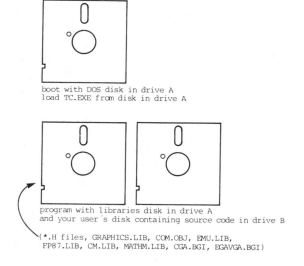

boot with DOS disk in drive A
load TC.EXE from disk in drive A

program with libraries disk in drive A
and your user's disk containing source code in drive B

(*.H files, GRAPHICS.LIB, COM.OBJ, EMU.LIB,
FP87.LIB, CM.LIB, MATHM.LIB, CGA.BGI, EGAVGA.BGI)

Fig. 3-6. The Turbo C programming environment on a personal computer with two floppy disk drives.

the Turbo C program disk containing TC.EXE is placed in drive A and the Turbo C editor is invoked. Next, the companion disk for this book or your own disk of source files is placed in drive B. The libraries disk containing the #include files, the graphics library, math libraries, and run-time libraries is placed in drive A, from where these various routines will be fetched by Turbo C during the compilation phase. (Refer to Chapter 7 for a detailed discussion of setting up a graphics programming environment with Turbo C.)

MEMORY MANAGEMENT

As you learned earlier in this chapter, C is capable of supporting different types of memory environments for graphics programs. These memory environments are called *memory models*. Two common memory models are shown in Fig. 3-7. Other models are also available.

The *medium memory model* provides for a maximum of 64K of data, a maximum of 64K of stack space, and unlimited executable code size. (The default start-up stack size for QuickC is 2K; for Turbo C it is 4K. Both these default conditions are ample for almost all graphics programs.) QuickC can only be operated in the medium model mode. Later in the book you will learn how to overcome the 64K limit on data when using memory-intensive graphics arrays to produce bitblt animation. Turbo C can be (and should be) configured via its menu system to operate in the medium model mode.

The *compact memory model* limits executable code to 64K of memory, but permits unlimited data. The maximum stack size is, again, 64K. This memory model is useful for specialized graphics programs (such as CAD) which require a lot of data. Turbo C can be configured via its menu system to run in the compact model mode. If you are using QuickC, however, you must switch to the command-line version of the compiler if you wish to use any memory model other than the medium memory model.

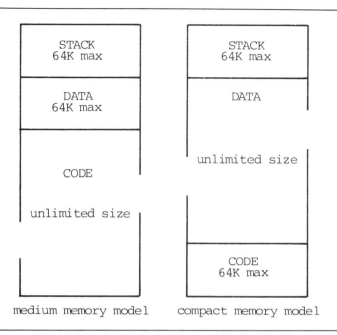

Fig. 3-7. Memory models useful for C graphics programming. Only the medium model can be used with QuickC. Turbo C uses the small model by default, but can be reconfigured to use other models. (Compact memory model shown here only for reference.)

USING THE INTEGRATED EDITORS

Both QuickC and Turbo C provide powerful text editors. Each compiler package offers text editing commands to delete blocks of text, move blocks of text, copy blocks of text, delete individual lines, and merge blocks of source code from disk. These versatile functions should not be overlooked, and it is a wise C programmer who takes the time to master the block-oriented capabilities of the text editor being used.

When you are writing your own original C graphics programs, you may wish to use subroutines that you have already written for other programs. Rather than rewriting these subroutines or retyping them, a lot of time and effort can be saved by simply fetching them from disk and merging them into your current source code.

II

TOOLS

Programming Skills

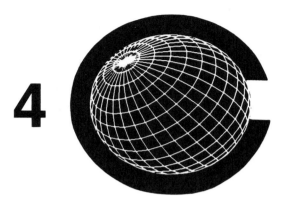

4

Programming Tools

The programming tools that C offers to the graphics programmer are rich and diversified. It is important to realize, however, what is needed, not an encyclopedic knowledge of all C's instructions, but rather a thorough understanding of how to use the more limited range of C instructions which are specific to graphics output. An ability to use a modest number of C instructions with great dexterity is more useful than an ability to use every instruction offered by C—but with only moderate skill. In graphics programming it is quality, not quantity, that counts.

C PROGRAM STRUCTURE

The chart in Fig. 4-1 illustrates how all C programs are organized. Every C program has a master routine, also called the main routine, main module, executive module, and executive routine. All these names refer to what C programmers called **main( )**.

The parentheses ( ) are important. Every **main( )** routine and every subroutine in C is designated by the routine's name, followed by a set of parentheses. A hypothetical subroutine named **sort_it**, for example, would be coded as **sort_it( )**. If values are being passed to a subroutine, then those variables or constants are placed into the parentheses. Suppose you needed to provide three values to **sort_it( )** for sorting, then you might call the subroutine with the instruction **sort_it(8,3,11);**, thereby passing the values of 8 and 3 and 11 to the subroutine. The semi-colon is merely C's way of ending an instruction.

The **main( )** routine is the starting point of every C program. It is also the ending point. When the **main( )** routine is finished executing, the C program ends. As Fig. 4-1 shows, the **main( )** routine calls upon specialized subroutines to help it accomplish a va-

43

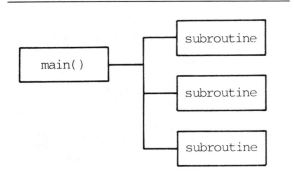

Fig. 4-1. The fundamental conceptual structure of all C programs.

riety of tasks. Although there is no physical constraint preventing you from simply writing all the tasks into the **main( )** routine, it is easier to understand a C program which uses subroutines.

C programmers often call subroutines "functions." Because each subroutine is a module, this style of programming is described as *modular*. As the program listings in this book will demonstrate, modular programming provides powerful advantages to the graphics programmer.

Although all C programs are structured according to the organizational chart depicted in Fig. 4-1, graphics programs are by their very nature different from other C programs. That difference is primarily centered around program control characteristics of graphics programs.

C PROGRAM CONTROL

Program control refers to the run-time activities of a C program. It refers to "what happens next" while a program is running. A good graphics program actually contains three different kinds of program control, each working hand-in-hand with the others. Each of these three varieties of program code can occur in the **main( )** routine and in subroutines. Each form of program control code can occur alone or it can occur alongside the other kinds of program control code. (Code is used here to mean program instructions.)

The three forms of program control code are: process control code, math code, and graphics code. To become a skilled C graphics programmer, it is important that you understand what is contributed to the program by each of these distinctly separate kinds of code.

Process Control Code

Process control code includes such things as **if/then** decision-making instructions, **for/next** loops, keyboard input, and code that calls subroutines (functions). Process control code is the backbone of the C graphics program.

Math Code

Math control code performs arithmetic and mathematical manipulations on numbers. Those numbers can be constants or variables, and the numeric values of those constants or variables can be expressed as integers or floating-point numbers. Math code is often vital to C graphics programming because so much of graphics relies upon figuring out where to draw lines. The 3D cube which is created by the demonstration program in Chapter 14 relies heavily upon math code.

Graphics Code

Graphics control code is comprised of the C instructions which actually produce graphics output. For example, a line is created on the screen by the **__lineto(x,y)** instruction in QuickC and by the **lineto(x,y)** instruction in Turbo C. A circle can be constructed by the **__ellipse(__GBORDER,x1,y1,x2,y2)** instruction of QuickC and by Turbo C's **circle(x,y,radius)** instruction. Graphics code is usually invoked after the process control code and the math code have performed their work.

In order for each of these three forms of program control code to operate, the C programming language provides a rich assortment of operators.

C OPERATORS

The operators provided by C that are useful for graphics programming include arithmetic operators, relational operators, assignment operators, logical operators, and mathematical operators. These operators are the building blocks which are used to construct the **main( )** routine and the subroutines of C graphics programs. Not all C operators are described here, only those important for C graphics programming. A full list can be found in your C user's manual.

Arithmetic Operators

The arithmetic operators provided by C are depicted in Fig. 4-2. If you have programmed in another language, you are likely already familiar with these fundamental addition, subtraction, multiplication, and division operators.

Relational Operators

The relational operators provided by C are shown in Fig. 4-3. It is important to note that the > -greater-than-or-equal-to operator and the < -less-than-or-equal-to operator must

Fig. 4-2. Arithmetic operators useful for C graphics programming.

```
+    addition
-    subtraction
*    multiplication
/    division
```

Fig. 4-3. Relational operators useful for C graphics programming.

```
>    greater than...
<    less than...
>=   greater than or equal to...
<=   less than or equal to...
==   equal to...
!=   not equal to...
```

be written in exactly that format. Care should also be taken when using the equal-to relational operator, = =. Do not confuse the = = equal-to operator with the = assignment operator, which means "assign a new value to this variable."

Assignment Operators

The assignment operators provided by C are illustrated in Fig. 4-4. The + + increment operator simply increases a variable by a unit of 1. Similarly, the − − decrement operator decreases a variable by a unit of 1. These two assignment operators are especially useful in loops that must stop after a certain number of repetitions. This kind of loop is often used in animation programs.

Note the distinction between the = operator in Fig. 4-4 and the = = operator in Fig. 4-3. The = operator is used to assign a new value to the variable. If a variable named **this__value** equals 3, for example, the instruction **this__value**=7 assigns the value 7 to the variable **this__value**. The variable **this__value** is now equal to 7. However, the = = operator is used to test the value of **this__value**. The instruction: **if (this__value**= =7) tests to determine if **this__value** equals 7. It does not alter the value of the variable; it merely checks to see what the value is.

Logical Operators

Logical operators provided by C, which are useful for graphics programming, are depicted in Fig. 4-5.

Mathematical Operators

Mathematical functions provided by C which are useful for graphics programming are depicted in Fig. 4-6. These functions are not actual operators, but are subroutines (functions) provided in the library which accompanies most C compilers. The **SIN( )** and **COS( )** functions are used to calculate the sine and cosine of angles. These functions are

```
++   increment
--   decrement
=    assign new value to...
```

Fig. 4-4. Assignment operators useful for C graphics programming.

```
&&   AND
||   OR
!    NOT
```

Fig. 4-5. Logical operators useful for C graphics programming.

```
SIN();    sine of...
COS();    cosine of...
SQRT();   square root of...
ABS();    absolute value of...
```

Fig. 4-6. Mathematical functions useful for C graphics programming.

useful for 3D graphics, including the flight simulation prototype provided in Chapter 27. The **SQRT( )** function calculates the square root of a number, which is helpful in certain types of adversarial games programming. The **ABS( )** function strips off the sign of a number and returns the absolute value of the number. Both 620 and −620 would be transformed into 620 by **ABS( )**, for example. The **ABS( )** function is useful for animated adversaries.

LOOP CONTROL IN C

Loops are blocks of process control code which repeat until a certain condition is met. Loops—especially endless loops—are used in many C animation programs.

The for/next Instruction

The **for/next** instruction provided by C is shown in Fig. 4-7. The three parameters inside the parentheses are used to control the qualitative and quantitative aspects of the loop.

The first parameter defines the starting value of the counter to be used by the loop. In Fig. 4-7 the counter is the variable **t1**, whose initial value is set to 1.

The second parameter defines the condition which will cause the loop to stop executing. In Fig. 4-7 the condition is **t1 < =10**. This means that the loop will continue to repeat while the variable **t1** is less than or equal to 10. As soon as **t1** is greater than 10 the loop will cease executing.

The third parameter inside the parentheses defines how the counter will react during each pass through the loop. In Fig. 4-7, the statement **t1 + +** uses the + + increment operator to indicate that the counter will be incremented by a unit of 1 on each pass through the loop.

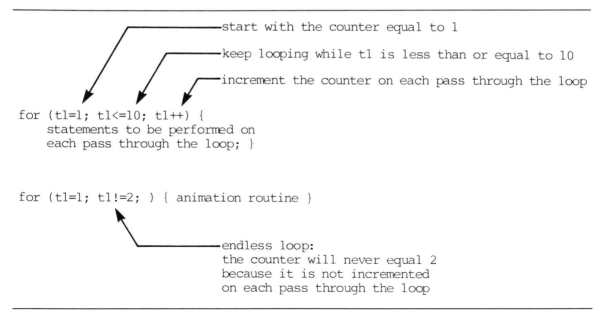

```
                              start with the counter equal to 1

                              keep looping while t1 is less than or equal to 10

                              increment the counter on each pass through the loop

for (tl=1; tl<=10; tl++) {
    statements to be performed on
    each pass through the loop; }


for (tl=1; tl!=2; ) { animation routine }


                              endless loop:
                              the counter will never equal 2
                              because it is not incremented
                              on each pass through the loop
```

Fig. 4-7. The for/next instruction is used to control processing loops in C graphics programs.

By inspecting all three parameters inside the parentheses of Fig. 4-7, you can see that the loop will execute for 10 iterations, because the counter begins at 1 and increments by a value of 1 on each pass through the loop, thereby causing the loop to stop when the counter exceeds 10.

It is interesting to note that an endless loop can be created by the for/next instruction, also illustrated in Fig. 4-7. The instruction: **for(t1=1;t1!=2;)** tells the program that the counter will start at 1, that the loop will continue while **t1** does not equal 2, and that the counter will not be incremented or decremented on each pass through the loop. Because the counter never changes, the loop will repeat forever (because **t1** will never be incremented to a value of 2).

The goto Instruction

Figure 4-8 illustrates a common use for the much-maligned **goto** instruction. By inserting an address label at the beginning of a loop, you simply use a **goto** instruction to cause the program to keep looping back to the label. This method for creating an infinite loop produces code which runs slightly faster than a **for/next** loop, because the microprocessor does not have to perform any calculations or comparisons to determine if the loop should keep repeating. This is one of the few occasions in C programming where the use of a **goto** instruction is justified (and, indeed, desirable).

BRANCHING INSTRUCTIONS IN C

The **if/then** instruction is an important decision-making component of process control code in C graphics programs. Refer to the examples in Fig. 4-9. Simply stated, the **if/then** instruction operates on the basis that if a specified condition is met then a specified block of instructions will be executed. If the specified condition is not met, then the specified block of instructions will not be executed, and the program will continue with the next instruction after the **if/then** block of instructions.

A few things are worth noting here. First, if more than one instruction is to be performed by the **if/then** decision, then the group of instructions must be enclosed in braces, as shown in Fig. 4-9. These braces tell C that all the instructions contained inside the brace are to be considered as a single block of code. If you refer back to Fig. 4-7, you

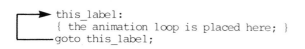

Fig. 4-8. The much-maligned goto instruction is useful for animation loops, especially in real-time animation, where run-time speed is vital.

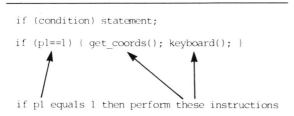

Fig. 4-9. The if/then/else instruction is used to control program flow at run-time in C graphics programming.

Fig. 4-10. Both these statements accomplish the same task. If both sxa and sxb are less than min—x, then the return instruction will be executed.

```
if ((sxa<min_x) && (sxb<min_x) return;

if (sxa<min_x)  if (sxb<min_x) return;
```

will see that the group of instructions to be executed during a loop must also be bounded by braces. (Throughout this book, ( ) are referred to as parentheses, [ ] are called brackets, and { } are referred to as braces. Parentheses are used in conjunction with subroutine names. Brackets are used to access numeric arrays. Braces are used to designate blocks of code.)

Second, it is important to remember to use the = = operator and not the = operator when testing for a value. For example, the statement **if(p1 = =1)** is correct, but the statement **if(p1 =1)** is incorrect and will produce erratic and unpredictable results when the program is running.

Third, it is possible to simultaneously test for a variety of conditions when you are using the **if/then** instruction. Each of the examples provided in Fig. 4-10 check to see if both **sxa** and **sxb** are less than the variable **min—x**. The first example uses the **&&** logical operator; the second example uses nested **if/then** statements. Both methods produce the same result, but the nesting approach is sometimes easier to read and understand. (The 2D line-clipping routine provided later in the book uses nested **if/then** statements.)

USING C VARIABLES

A variable is a numeric value which can change during program execution. In hardware terms, a variable is simply a memory address which is used to hold a numeric value. The value of the variable is altered by writing a new numeric value into memory at its address.

A constant is a numeric value which cannot change during program execution. You can use actual numbers to represent constants, or you can use C's **#define** directive to declare a variable as a constant. When so declared, the value of the variable cannot—and does not—change during program execution.

The nature of a C variable is called its *type*. Figure 4-11 depicts C variable types. Only the kinds of C variables useful for graphics programming are shown in Fig. 4-11. Refer to your C user's manual for a broader discussion.

Char–A variable of type *char* is stored in a single byte of memory. Most C compilers by default assume that a char variable is signed, which means it can range in value from −128 to +127. A variable of type *unsigned char* can range from 0 to 255. Char variables are often used to hold the ASCII values of alphanumeric characters, although they are also useful for storing small integers.

Int–A variable of type *int* is stored in two bytes of memory. It is considered to be signed. Another name for variables of type int is *short*. A variable of type int can hold integer values from −32,768 to +32,767. A variable of type *unsigned short* can hold numeric integer values ranging from 0 to 65,535. (An *integer* is a whole number. Integers contain neither fractions nor decimal points.)

Long–Because of the limited range of numbers which can be expressed as type int, C provides a longer integer variety called type *long*. Variables of type long occupy four bytes of memory and can hold values ranging from −2,147,483,648 to +2,147,483,647.

TYPE	MEMORY REQUIRED	RANGE	USEFULNESS
char	1 byte	-128 to 127	used to represent ASCII characters, small numbers
unsigned char	1 byte	0 to 255	used to represent ASCII characters, small numbers
int (short)	2 bytes	-32,768 to 32,767	used to represent whole numbers
unsigned short	2 bytes	0 to 65,535	used to represent positive whole numbers
long	4 bytes	-2,147,483,648 to 2,147,483,647	used to represent large whole numbers
float	4 bytes	3.4E-38 to 3.4E+38	used to represent real numbers

Fig. 4-11. Numeric variables useful for C graphics programming.

Float–Floating-point numbers are numbers which contain a decimal point. In C, these numbers can be stored in variables of type *float,* which occupy four bytes of memory. A floating-point number is also called a *real number.* These values are stored in memory in a form of scientific notation called *exponential* notation. Variables of type float can hold values ranging from the smallest: 3.4E−38 to the largest: 3.4E+38. 3.4E38 is 340,000,000,000,000,000,000,000,000,000,000,000,000. Although floating-point numbers can be extremely large, they are only accurate to the first six digits.

USING C ARRAYS

A numeric array is simply a group of sets. Arrays are useful for storing graphics databases in memory. Databases are useful for storing the various screen coordinates to be used by the graphics program.

The array which is created by the sample code in Fig. 4-12 is composed of four sets of two elements each. Note how the brackets are used to identify the dimensions of the array, and how braces are used to contain the actual contents of the array.

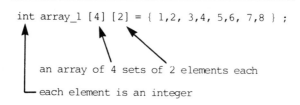

```
int array_1 [4] [2] = { 1,2, 3,4, 5,6, 7,8 } ;
```

an array of 4 sets of 2 elements each

each element is an integer

Fig. 4-12. Numeric arrays are useful as drawing coordinate databases for C graphics programs. At run-time the program retrieves the array elements from the array as required.

Arrays in C can contain variables of type char, int, or float, but you cannot mix variables of different types within the same array. (If you wish to use array-like objects that contain variables of different types, you must use an object of type struct, discussed later.) As some of the demonstration programs in this book will show, arrays are a powerful tool for dealing with screen coordinates.

PORTABILITY OF C PROGRAMS

An essential quality of the C programming language is its portability. Portability refers to a program's ability to run on different computer hardware using different operating systems and different C compilers. But because computer graphics is so hardware-dependent, program portability should receive special attention from C graphics programmers.

Graphics Portability

The process control instructions of a C graphics program can be used in order to make the program compatible with a wide range of different graphics adapters and monitors. Because many graphics instructions (discussed in the next chapter) return a certain value if the instruction fails, you can use **if/then** instructions to make program flow decisions based upon the success or failure of the graphics instruction.

If you attempt to invoke a specific screen mode and the attempt fails, you can use an **if/then** instruction to invoke a different screen mode. This tactic is useful in finding out which graphics modes are compatible with the installed hardware. Refer to Fig. 4-13. All of the program listings in this book and all of the demonstration programs on the companion disk use a configuration routine that sets up the best graphics mode permitted by the hardware. The configuration routine adheres to the logic depicted in Fig. 4-13.

This approach to program portability ensures the widest market possible for your original C graphics programs. (A more detailed analysis of a graphics configuration module suitable for QuickC is offered in Chapter 6. A configuration module suitable for Turbo C is provided in Chapter 7.)

Syntax Portability

Notwithstanding the industry-wide standards to which many C compilers aspire, trivial discrepancies exist in language syntax. The QuickC and Turbo C compilers are no exception. Refer to Fig. 4-14 for an overview of process control syntax incompatibilities which were encountered during the creation of the demonstration programs for this book. A chart of graphics syntax differences is presented in the next chapter.

Fortunately, the actual output of these process control instructions is identical in both QuickC and Turbo C; only the syntax in inconsistent. If you are using a C compiler other than QuickC or Turbo C, you will want to review your user's manual in order to determine if any other language syntax differences exist between your compiler and the program listings featured in this book.

COMMUNICATING WITH YOUR C COMPILER

In general, C compilers expect to receive their marching orders from the programmer in a consistent manner. Figure 4-15 illustrates the writing tools that most C compilers

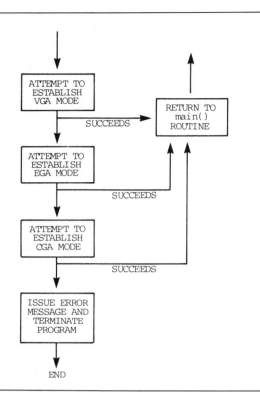

Fig. 4-13. Error trapping can be used to ensure that a C graphics program will perform correctly on either a VGA, EGA, or CGA graphics adapter.

expect programmers to use when crafting the program source code. Braces are used to mark blocks of instructions which are to be considered a single entity by the compiler. Semi-colons are used to signify a statement (instruction). Brackets are used to access the contents of arrays. The /* */ combination is used to mark off comments which are to be ignored by the compiler. Spaces, tabs, carriage returns, and line feeds are likewise ignored by the compiler, thereby making it easy for you to format your source code in an easy-to-read manner (using plenty of tabs and indentations, for example).

On a broader level, C compilers expect the source code to adhere to the generic layout shown in Fig. 4-16. This layout consists of five important elements.

First, directives such as **#include** and **#define** are used to instruct the compiler to insert source code from other files and to define certain variables as constants.

Second, pragmas are occasionally used to instruct the compiler to add specialized code which checks *pointers* (memory addresses) for legality and which checks for *stack overflow* (out of memory conditions).

Third, all subroutines which the program code creates and subsequently calls are declared, and all variables used by the program are declared with respect to their type. It is good programming practice to assign a value to each variable at this time.

Fourth, the **main( )** routine is provided.

Fifth, the various subroutine (functions) contained in the program are provided.

A graphics programmer who adheres to these fundamentals will enjoy a reliable level of communication with the compiler.

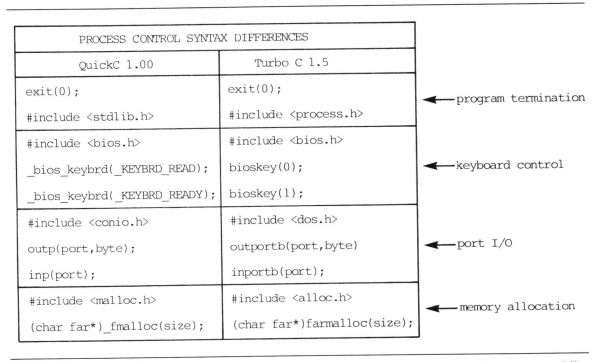

PROCESS CONTROL SYNTAX DIFFERENCES	
QuickC 1.00	Turbo C 1.5
exit(0); #include <stdlib.h>	exit(0); #include <process.h>

#include <bios.h>
 	
_bios_keybrd(_KEYBRD_READ);
 	
_bios_keybrd(_KEYBRD_READY);
	#include <bios.h>
	
	bioskey(0);
	
	bioskey(1);

#include <conio.h>
 	
outp(port,byte);
 	
inp(port);
	#include <dos.h>
	
	outportb(port,byte)
	
	inportb(port);

#include <malloc.h> (char far*)_fmalloc(size);	#include <alloc.h> (char far*)farmalloc(size);

program termination

keyboard control

port I/O

memory allocation

Fig. 4-14. Among C instructions useful for graphics programming, there are only four minor areas of syntax incompatibility between QuickC and Turbo C.

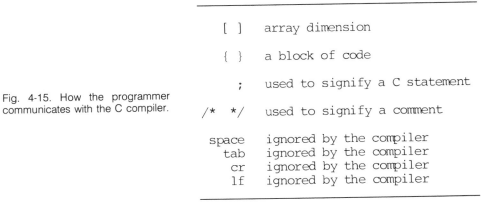

Fig. 4-15. How the programmer communicates with the C compiler.

```
[ ]      array dimension

{ }      a block of code

  ;      used to signify a C statement

/*  */   used to signify a comment

space    ignored by the compiler
  tab    ignored by the compiler
   cr    ignored by the compiler
   lf    ignored by the compiler
```

USING BIOS ROUTINES WITH C

C compilers provide an array-like variable of a type called struct which enables easy access to the code contained in the ROM BIOS routines. These BIOS routines can be used to fetch keystrokes from the keyboard, to write pixels to the display screen, and other functions.

The example shown in Fig. 4-17 manipulates the contents of a struct named REGS in order to call BIOS interrupt 16 hex, which fetches a keystroke from the keyboard buff-

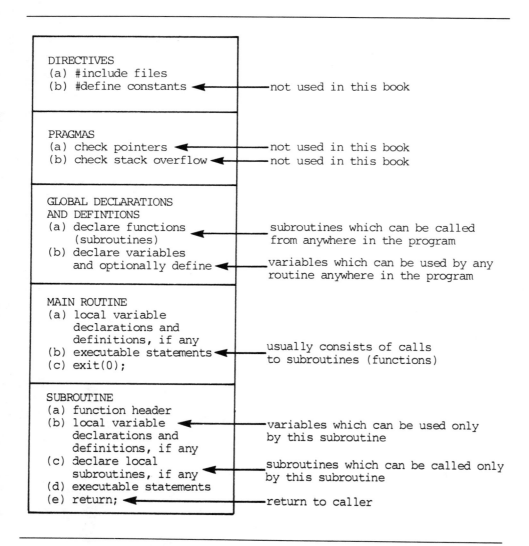

Fig. 4-16. The fundamental layout of a C program.

```
union REGS regs;
regs.h.ah=0;
return int86(0x16,&regs,&regs);
```

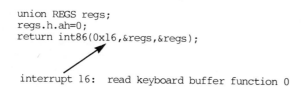

interrupt 16: read keyboard buffer function 0

Fig. 4-17. Using BIOS routines from
C programs.

er. This programming tactic will be described in further detail later in the text. For now it is important to note how the **regs.h.ah** instruction assigns a value to the ah register by using the decimal method of addressing the contents of the struct object. Objects of type struct can contain variables of different types (unlike arrays, which can only contain variables of the same type). Using the syntax: **regs.h.bh**, for example, you could assign a value to be placed into the bh register.

Refer to your DOS Technical Reference or to any good book about DOS programming for a list of available BIOS functions and DOS functions.

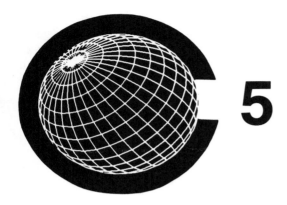

5

Graphics Tools

The most efficient way to create high-performance C graphics programs is to use a C compiler that offers built-in graphics routines. A powerful and fully developed library of such routines is provided with Microsoft QuickC version 1.00 and newer, with Microsoft C version 5.00 and newer, and with Borland Turbo C version 1.5 and newer. The program listings in **High Performance Graphics in C** and the demonstration programs on the companion disk are compatible with these versions of QuickC, Microsoft C, and Turbo C.

If you prefer to use a C compiler that does not offer built-in graphics functions, you can choose from three programming alternatives. First, you can use C itself to write graphics routines. Because of its powerful memory-management abilities, and because of its versatile bit-manipulation capabilities, C can easily handle all the low level work which is required in order to create graphics routines. However, using C to build these routines will result in run-time performance which is unacceptably slow. When it comes to graphics programs, faster is better.

Second, you can purchase a graphics library from a third-party manufacturer such as MetaWINDOW, TurboHALO, or Essential Graphics. These add-on graphics functions are, typically, extremely powerful and versatile. However, serious issues of compatibility, cost, and distribution licensing fees are raised.

Third, you can write your own assembly language graphics drivers. If you possess the requisite expertise, this alternative can yield specialized routines that do exactly what you want. (If you do not have the expertise, you can use the assembly language subroutines presented in Appendix C and Appendix D to get you started in C graphics programming.)

Clearly, the most trouble-free way to explore the exciting world of computer graphics is to use a C compiler that contains built-in graphics routines, such as QuickC or Turbo C.

FUNDAMENTAL GRAPHICS FUNCTIONS

The toolkit of graphics routines that you need in order to begin writing graphics programs is neither large nor unwieldly. In fact, the fundamental toolkit is surprisingly small (and surprisingly powerful). Only five fundamental graphics functions are essential to get started. These are:

(a) the ability to establish a graphics screen mode
(b) the ability to clear the screen
(c) the ability to draw lines
(d) the ability to fill areas with color
(e) the ability to place alphanumeric (text) material onto the graphics screen
(f) the ability to return to the default text mode.

Any graphics functions beyond these can be considered advanced functions.

Establishing the Graphics Mode

The VGA, EGA, and CGA graphics adapters can support a rich and varied range of graphics screen modes. Refer to Fig. 5-1. QuickC uses the __**setvideomode** instruction

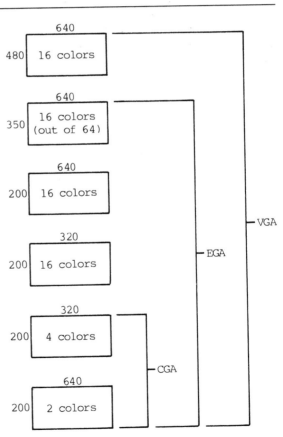

Fig. 5-1. The screen modes used for the demonstration programs in this book. Other available modes include the 320×200 256-color mode, the 640×480 2-color mode, and the 640×350 2-color mode.

to invoke a graphics mode. Turbo C sets the graphics mode by using the **initgraph** instruction.

If you are using QuickC, you can use __setvideomode(__VRES16COLOR) to invoke the 640×480 16-color mode of the VGA; or __setvideomode(__ERESCOLOR) to establish the 640×350 16-color mode of the VGA and EGA; or __setvideomode (__HRES16COLOR) to set up the 640×200 16-color mode of the VGA and EGA; or setvideomode(__MRES16COLOR) to invoke the 320×200 16-color mode of the VGA and EGA; or __setvideomode(__MRES4COLOR) to call up the 320×200 4-color mode of the VGA, EGA, and CGA; or __setvideomode(__HRESBW) to establish the 640×200 2-color mode of the VGA, EGA, and CGA.

If you are using Turbo C, you can use **initgraph(VGAHI)** to set up the 640×480 16-color mode of the VGA; or **initgraph(EGAHI)** to establish the 640×350 16-color mode of the VGA and EGA; or **initgraph(EGALO)** to invoke the 640×200 16-color mode of the VGA and EGA; or **initgraph(CGAC3)** to call up the 320×200 4-color mode of the VGA, EGA, and CGA; or **initgraph(CGAHI)** to establish the 640×200 2-color mode of the VGA, EGA, and CGA. (Note that Turbo C version 1.5 does not support the 320×200 16-color mode of the VGA and EGA.)

If the necessary graphics adapter and monitor are not present, then both QuickC and Turbo C will simply return an error code. Chapter 6 and Chapter 7 show how to use this error code to make your graphics programs compatible with any graphics adapter.

Once you have established a graphics mode, you generally create graphics on the screen by using xy coordinates. Using the 640×200 mode, for example, **x** can range from 0 to 639 and **y** can range from 0 to 199. The center of the screen would be described as 319,99. The horizontal **x** coordinate is always listed first and the vertical **y** coordinate is always listed second.

Clearing the Screen

Surprisingly, the most important tool in any graphics programmer's toolkit is the ability to clear the screen. After all, you must have a clean canvas on which to draw.

If you are using QuickC, you can use the __clearscreen (__GCLEARSCREEN) instruction to blank the graphics screen. Provided that you have not tampered with any palette settings, the screen will be set to black. If you are using Turbo C, you can employ the **cleardevice( )** instruction to blank the graphics screen.

Drawing Lines

The ability to draw simple lines on the screen gives you other capabilities, as illustrated in Fig. 5-2. Polylines are simply a collection of connected lines. Dashed lines and dotted lines are simply lines which have been drawn in a particular style. Polygons and other shapes are merely groups of lines. Even circles, ellipses, and arcs can be constructed from (very short) lines.

If you are using QuickC, you can draw a line by using the __lineto(x,y) instruction. You would prepare for this instruction by using the __setcolor instruction to define the active drawing color and by using the __moveto instruction to establish the starting point for the line. If you are using Turbo C, you can draw a line by using the **lineto(x,y)** instruction. Again, you would prepare the system by using the **setcolor** and **moveto** instructions.

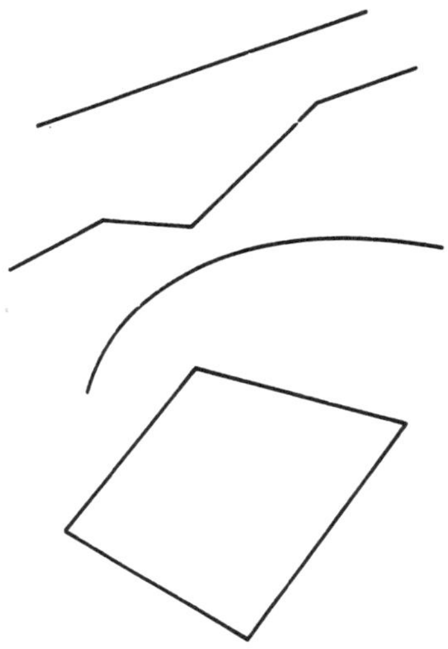

Fig. 5-2. Using simple line functions. From top to bottom: line, polyline, curve constructed of short line segments, polygon constructed of simple lines.

Suppose you wished to draw a line from the center of the 640×200 screen to the lower right corner of the screen. Using QuickC, you could use the instructions: **__moveto(319,99); __lineto(639,199);**. If you were using Turbo C, you would use the instruction: **moveto(319,99); lineto(639,199);**. (Remember, the semi-colon is C's way of completing an instruction.)

Area Fill

The graphics function which fills an area with color is called *area fill, floodfill,* or *painting*. Area fill functions usually operate by defining a seed point as a start point and then filling the area with a color until a particular boundary color is encountered. Refer to Fig. 5-3. Unpredictable results occur when you attempt to fill an area which is not completely circumscribed by the boundary.

If you are using QuickC, then you can invoke area fill by using the **__floodfill(x,y,edge)** function. If you are using Turbo C, then you would employ the **floodfill(x,y,edge)** function. In both instances, the area fill begins at the screen point described by the xy coordinates and continues in all directions until a pixel containing the color of variable "edge" is encountered.

Writing Text on the Graphics Screen

If you are using QuickC or Turbo C, then you can place alphanumerics onto the graphics screen in a manner similar to that employed by the text modes. Unfortunately, QuickC and Turbo C use different approaches to this function.

If you are using QuickC, then the location of the text to be displayed is described by rows and columns, as shown in Fig. 5-4. In the 640×200 and 640×350 modes, 80 characters can be displayed on each of 25 rows. In the 640×480 mode, 80 characters can be displayed on each of 30 rows. Suppose, for example, you wished to display the

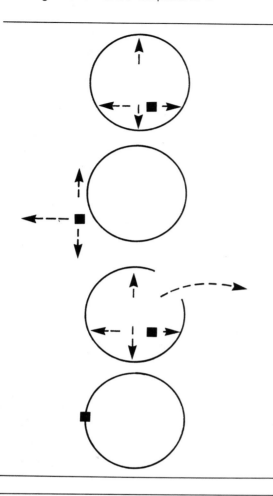

Fig. 5-3. Fundamental concepts of area fill. If the seed point is located inside a closed polygon, the area will be filled up to the specified boundary color. If the seed point is located outside a closed polygon, the interior of the polygon remains unfilled. If the polygon is not fully closed, the area fill will spill out and corrupt other areas of the screen. If the seed point is located on a pixel of the boundary color, no area fill will occur.

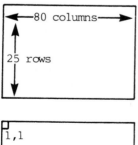

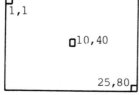

Fig. 5-4. Text coordinates for graphics modes which support 80-column alphanumerics. QuickC specifies text location as a pair of row/column coordinates, where row ranges from 1 to 25 and column ranges from 1 to 80.

customary "Hello" expression while your program was using the 640×200 mode. (C programming tradition says that your first C program should say "Hello" on the screen.) First you would tell QuickC what color to use for the text by using the **_settextcolor (color)** instruction. Then you would use the **_settextposition(row,column)** instruction to identify the location of the first text character. The column parameter can range from 1 to 80 across; the row parameter can range from 1 to 25 down. Finally, you would use the **_outtext("Hello")** instruction to write the alphanumerics to the graphics screen.

If you are using Turbo C, then the location of the text to be displayed is described by xy graphics coordinates. In the 640×200/350/480 modes, a maximum of 80 characters can be displayed across the screen. A maximum of 25 characters can be printed from top to bottom in the 640×200 and 640×350 modes. In the 640×480 mode, 80 characters can be printed on each of a maximum of 30 rows. Remember that the starting position of the text is identified as an xy coordinate when using Turbo C. Suppose that you wished to display the customary "Hello" expression while your program was using the 640×200 mode. First you would tell Turbo C what color to use for the text by using the **setcolor(color)** instruction (which also defines the active graphics color). Then you would use the **moveto(x,y)** instruction to identify the location of the first text character. The **x** parameter can range from 0 to 639 across; the **y** parameter can range from 0 to 199, or from 0 to 349, or from 0 to 479, depending upon the screen mode. Finally, you would use the **outtext("Hello")** instruction to write the alphanumerics to the graphics screen.

Note that QuickC overwrites the existing screen graphics when text is written to a graphics mode, displaying each character as a colored alphanumeric on a black field. Turbo C, on the other hand, superimposes the text over the existing screen graphics, allowing the background graphics to show through.

Returning to the Text Mode

Your graphics program must gracefully return to the text mode (or to the default mode in which it originally found the computer) after completing its tasks. In its broadest form, every C graphics program follows the rule depicted by Fig. 5-5: program start-up occurs in the default text mode; graphics output occurs in the chosen graphics screen mode; program shut-down occurs back in the default text mode.

If you are using QuickC, you can return to the original text mode by using the instruction: **_setvideomode(_DEFAULTMODE)**. If you are using Turbo C, you would use the instruction: **restorecrtmode( )**.

ADVANCED GRAPHICS FUNCTIONS

Five advanced graphics functions will serve to round out the toolkit of the serious graphics programmer. These five functions are:

(a) halftoning
(b) line dithering
(c) page copying
(d) the ability to draw graphics on a hidden page
(e) block graphics.

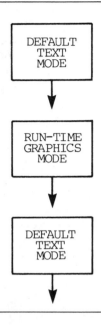

Fig. 5-5. The first task in graphics program development is the ability to establish the appropriate screen mode for graphics output and then to gracefully return to the default text mode before terminating the program.

Halftoning

Halftoning refers to the technique of creating patterns. The technical name for this procedure is *bit tiling*. As Fig. 5-6 illustrates, different levels of shading can be created by the halftoning process. If only every second pixel is turned on during an area fill function, for example, a 50% shade will have been created. If only every fourth pixel is turned on, a 25% shade will result. As you can see, halftoning gives you the capability to create many new colors from the standard palette of colors provided by your graphics adapter.

If you are using QuickC, you can define the halftoning pattern (also called a mask) by the __setfillmask instruction. This mask definition process will be discussed further when color theory is presented in Chapter 9. If you are using Turbo C, you can set the halftone pattern with the **setfillpattern** instruction.

Using QuickC, you simply use the **standard __floodfill** instruction to fill an area with the halftone pattern. Using Turbo C, you employ the **floodfill** instruction to fill a polygon or the **bar(x1,y1,x2,y2)** instruction to create and fill a rectangle.

Line Dithering

Line dithering is also called *line styling*. *Line dithering* refers to the style of dots and dashes used to draw a line. By default, both QuickC and Turbo C draw lines as solid entities, but both can be customized to create different line dithering effects, which are especially useful for 3D graphics, as Fig. 5-7 shows.

If you are using QuickC, you can use the __**setlinestyle(style)** instruction to define the pattern to be used when the line is drawn. The ''style'' parameter is a four-digit hexadecimal number which corresponds to the pixel pattern of the line. Suppose, for example, that you wish to draw a line where only every second pixel was drawn. The dotted line would be represented by the pixel pattern 10101010 10101010, which is AAAA

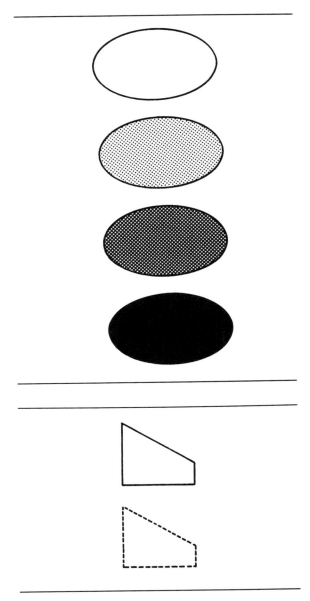

Fig. 5-6. Halftoning on VGA, EGA, CGA, and CGA graphics adapters. From top: solid area fill, 30% area fill, 60% area fill, solid area fill.

Fig. 5-7. Fundamental concepts of line dithering (line styling). The lines which comprise a polygon can be matched to the halftone area fill, thereby creating a planar surface.

hex. You would set this as the style by __**setlinestyle(Oxaaaa)**. C uses the notation **Ox** to denote a hexadecimal number. If you are using Turbo C, you would initialize this line pattern by the instruction: **setlinestyle(USERBITLINE,Oxaaaa,NORM__WIDTH)**.

Page Copying

As you learned in Chapter 2, more than one graphics page is available on VGA and EGA graphics adapters. Some animation programs operate by quickly moving the image from one page to another. This movement is called *page copying* and is conceptually

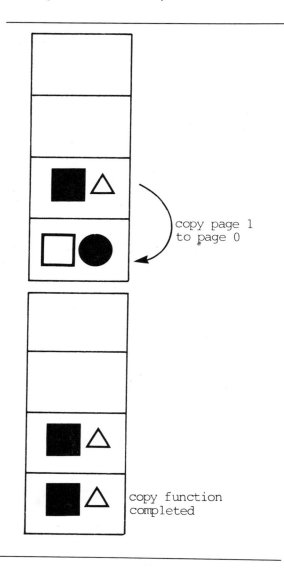

copy page 1
to page 0

copy function
completed

Fig. 5-8. The page copy function. On VGA and EGA graphics adapters, multiple pages are located in the adapter's display memory (usually 256K). When a CGA is used, additional pages can be stored in user RAM, the number of pages being limited only by available RAM.

portrayed in Fig. 5-8. Even CGAs can employ page copying by setting up simulated graphics pages in user RAM.

Although neither QuickC nor Turbo C offer a built-in graphics page-copying function, it is a relatively straightforward task to write such a subroutine in C. Chapter 17 provides a page copy routine for C during the discussion of frame animation techniques.

Drawing on a Hidden Page

Because both VGAs and EGAs offer numerous graphics pages, it is not necessary to draw graphics on the same page that is being displayed on the monitor. By drawing on a hidden page, as depicted in Fig. 5-9, you can present your end-user with completed

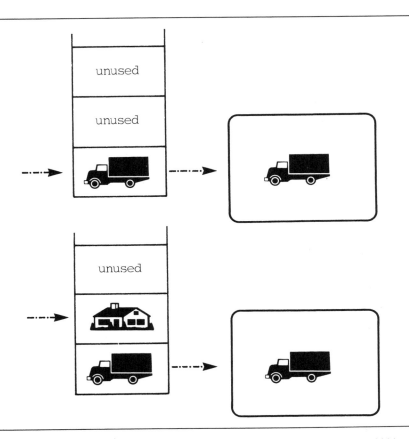

Fig. 5-9. Top: the CPU draws graphics on the visible page. Bottom: graphics output is sent to a hidden page.

images, rather than allowing the actual drawing process to be observed. The ability to draw on a hidden page also gives you the capability to create real-time animation as discussed in Chapter 2.

If you are using QuickC, the **__setactivepage** instruction is used to determine which page is written to by subsequent graphics instructions. The instruction: **__setvisualpage** determines which page is displayed on the monitor by the hardware. When using Turbo C, the **setactivepage** instruction sets the written-to page and the **setvisualpage** sets the displayed page.

Even CGAs, which carry only enough display memory for a single page, can use hidden-page drawing by setting aside an area in user RAM for use as a simulated graphics page. The assembly language graphics routines provided for the CGA in Appendix D use this methodology.

Block Graphics

Bitblt animation uses *block graphics* to move graphical entities across the screen. Refer to Fig. 5-10. In some other programming languages this is known as *graphic array animation.* In essence, the bytes which make up the block on the screen are saved in memory

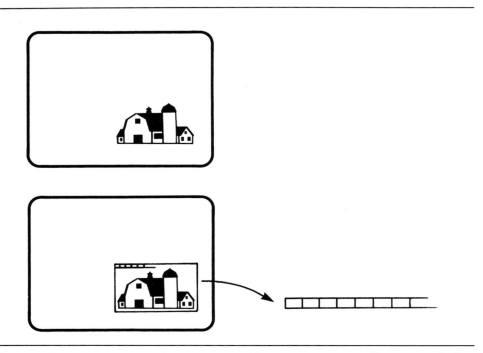

Fig. 5-10. Blocks of the graphics bit ap can be stored in memory as an array. The array can be later mapped onto the screen at any legal location.

as a single-dimensional array. A small header at the beginning of the array tells C how many bytes wide the block graphic is and how many rows deep it is. Using this information, the program can then place the array back onto the display screen at any location. (Technically speaking, it does not place the array onto the display screen, it writes the array into display memory on the graphics adapter.) Bitblt techniques can produce many spectacular high-speed effects, primarily due to the different logical operators which can be used to control the way in which each byte is written back onto the screen. If you are using QuickC, then you can store a block graphic in an array in user RAM by using the __**getimage** instruction. The array is placed back onto the screen by using the __**putimage** instruction. Turbo C uses the **getimage** and **putimage** instructions. In both cases, a simple algorithm is used to tell the computer how to calculate how large the array must be in order to hold all the graphics data for the block being stored. Chapter 21 provides a more detailed discussion when bitblt animation is introduced.

GRAPHICS SYNTAX INCOMPATIBILITIES

Although both QuickC and Turbo C each offer many powerful and versatile built-in graphics functions, the two systems are, for all intent and purposes, completely incompatible. In many instances, the instructions are remarkably similar—sometimes differing by only a single character. Yet even a single character can spell total incompatibility, and "near enough" only counts in hand grenades and horseshoes, neither of which is used in computer graphics programming.

SUMMARY OF GRAPHICS SYNTAX DIFFERENCES	
QuickC 1.00	Turbo C 1.5
#include <graph.h>	#include <graphics.h>
_setvideomode(_VRES16COLOR);	initgraph(&graphics_adapter, &graphics_mode);
_setvideomode(_DEFAULTMODE);	restorecrtmode();
_clearscreen(_GCLEARSCREEN); _setcolor(clr);	cleardevice(); setcolor(clr);
_setlinestyle(0xffff)	setlinestyle(USERBIT_LINE, 0xffff,NORM_WIDTH);
_setfillmask(fill_50); _setfillmask(NULL);	setfillpattern(fill_50,clr); setfillstyle(SOLID_FILL,clr);

_moveto(x,y);
_lineto(x,y);
_setpixel(x,y);
	moveto(x,y);
	lineto(x,y);
	putpixel(x,y,clr);

_rectangle(_GBORDER,x1,y1,x2,y2); _rectangle(_GFILLINTERIOR, x1,y1,x2,y2);	rectangle(x1,y1,x2,y2); bar(x1,y1,x2,y2);
_ellipse(_GBORDER,x1,y1,x2,y2); _ellipse(_GFILLINTERIOR, x1,y1,x2,y2);	circle(x,y,radius); ---
_floodfill(x,y,edge);	floodfill(x,y,edge);
_setactivepage(pagenum); _setvisualpage(pagenum);	setactivepage(pagenum); setvisualpage(pagenum);
name=(char far*)_fmalloc ((unsigned int)_imagesize (x1,y1,x2,y2));	name=(char far*)farmalloc ((unsigned long)imagesize (x1,y1,x2,y2));
_getimage(x1,y1,x2,y2,name);	getimage(x1,y1,x2,y2,name);
_putimage(x1,y1,name,_GPSET); _GAND _GOR _GXOR	putimage(x1,y1,name,COPY_PUT); AND_PUT OR_PUT XOR_PUT

_settextcolor(clr);
_settextposition(row,col);
_outtext("Hello.");
	setcolor(clr);
	moveto(x,y);
	outtext("Hello.");
	outtext(x,y,"Hello.");

Fig.5-11.Summary of graphics syntax differences between Microsoft QuickC and Borland Turbo C 1.5.

Figure 5-11 summarizes the graphics instructions available in Microsoft QuickC version 1.00 and in Borland Turbo C version 1.5. (This chart was used to convert the demonstration programs in this book from one compiler to another. By using Fig. 5-11 in concert with the compatibility chart provided in Chapter 4, you can readily convert any of your own original graphics programs from QuickC to Turbo C, or from Turbo C to QuickC.)

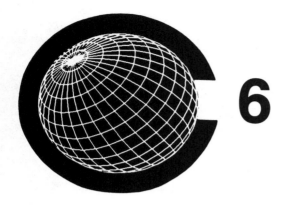

How to Use
Microsoft QuickC

The integrated programming environment provided by Microsoft QuickC is an effective and efficient tool for creating high-performance graphics programs. After you have configured your computer system to work with QuickC, using a graphics function is no more difficult than using a built-in C instruction. Configuring your system usually means telling QuickC where to find the various files that it needs during compilation, linking, and execution of your C program.

SYSTEM MEMORY MAP

A typical memory map of the QuickC programming environment is shown in Fig. 6-1. If your computer has less than 640K of user RAM, the amount of free memory shown in Fig. 6-1 will be compressed, but the diagram will otherwise remain as depicted.

The lowest portion of memory is occupied by assorted interrupt vectors, BIOS code, DOS kernel code, file control blocks, and the resident part of DOS COMMAND.COM. A part of COMMAND.COM called the transient portion is actually loaded into high memory, where it is often overwritten by application programs. DOS needs this transient code to interpret your keyboard instructions. When you return to DOS from an application program DOS first checks to see that the transient portion is intact. If it is not, then DOS asks you to ''Insert Disk containing COMMAND.COM'' before it can continue.

When DOS loads QuickC (the QC.EXE file), it first constructs a *program segment prefix* (PSP) which contains information about the file being loaded: the length of file, the parameters passed to it on the DOS command line, and so on. It is interesting to note

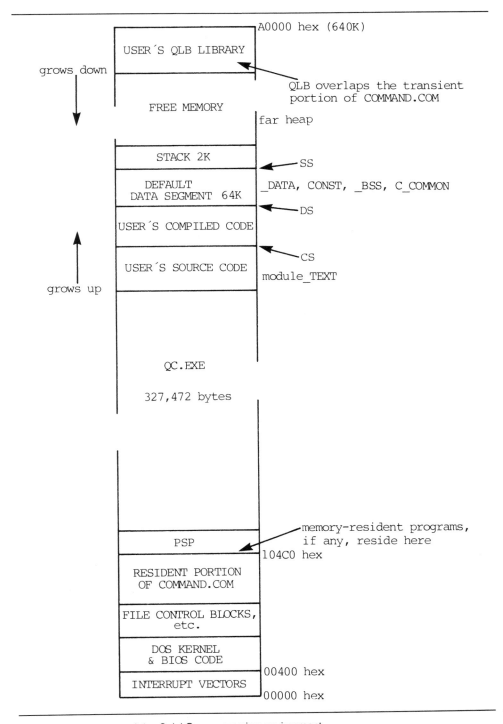

Fig. 6-1. Memory map of the QuickC programming environment.

that (as Fig. 6-1 illustrates) any memory-resident programs which are present are loaded by DOS into the memory block just above the resident portion of COMMAND.COM. If you are using a memory-resident (TSR) graphics print program such as Pizazz, for example, DOS would place it just above COMMAND.COM.

After QuickC has been loaded by DOS, QuickC establishes a text buffer in the block of memory immediately above QuickC itself. This is where your source code resides. If you load in a C program from disk, it goes here. If you use the QuickC editor to type in a C program, it goes here.

When you instruct QuickC to compile your C source code, it translates the text into machine code which is placed immediately above the text buffer in memory. This portion of memory is the code segment; the CS segment register points here. Although each code module cannot exceed a maximum size of 64K bytes, QuickC permits as many code modules as memory will allow. Theoretically (but not in practice), your executable code could be one megabyte (1000K) in size.

The *data segment* (DS) is located in memory immediately above the code segment. Various strings and variables are stored here. QuickC limits your data to 64K bytes maximum.

The stack which your C program will use during run-time is located just above the data segment. By default, QuickC sets up a run-time stack of 2K for your program. This size is adequate for virtually all graphics programs and animation programs, although QuickC allows you to increase the stack size if you wish. (Refer to the QuickC user's manual for more on stack size allocation.)

If your C program uses the functions contained in QuickC's graphics library, then you must place these functions into a memory-resident QLB library, which must be loaded into high memory where your compiled code can find it. The QLB library overwrites the transient portion of DOS COMMAND.COM, as discussed earlier. A discussion of how to create and load this QLB library appears later in this chapter.

As your C source code grows in size, the text buffer, the code segment, the data segment, and the stack segment grow upward. As you add more graphics functions to your QLB library, the QLB module grows downward. The memory between these two growing blocks is called *free memory,* also known as the *far heap.* The far heap can be used to store graphic arrays and other data, if you wish, thereby overcoming the 64K limitation of the default data segment.

THE DOS ENVIRONMENT

QuickC uses DOS to read and write disk files. Before you load QuickC, you must tell DOS where to find the various source files, OBJ files, and linking tools that QuickC needs. You would normally do this at the time you start your computer.

A typical AUTOEXEC.BAT file is depicted in Fig. 6-2. When you first start your computer with DOS, the instructions contained in the AUTOEXEC.BAT file are performed. Even before that, however, the system configures itself according to any CONFIG.SYS file found on the boot disk. (See Fig. 6-2. QuickC requires that a minimum number of files and buffers be available for its use.)

The AUTOEXEC.BAT file in Fig. 6-2 informs DOS that any libraries and include files which it might need can be found in drive A. (If you are using a hard disk, you would change this to drive C.) This frees up drive B for your own C source files.

```
AUTOEXEC.BAT file:

ECHO OFF
CLS
DATE
TIME
SET PATH=A:;
SET LIB=A:;
SET INCLUDE=A:\INCLUDE;
CLS
VER
ECHO Operating environment set for QuickC:
ECHO      PATH=A:
ECHO      LIB=A:
ECHO      INCLUDE=A:\INCLUDE
ECHO      files=15
ECHO      buffers=10


CONFIG.SYS file:

files=15
buffers=10
```

Fig. 6-2. A typical AUTOEXEC.BAT file to control the boot process in preparation for a QuickC programming session.

If you are using a computer with two 5.25-inch disk drives, you can use the AUTOEXEC.BAT file and the CONFIG.SYS file shown in Fig. 6-2. You must create these files yourself using the COPY CON instruction of DOS. At the DOS prompt, simply type COPY CON A:AUTOEXEC.BAT and then type in the instructions you want included in the AUTOEXEC.BAT file. When you are finished, press the F6 key and then press ENTER to tell DOS you are done. To create other files from the DOS prompt, simply change either the drive letter or the program name in the COPY CON A:AUTOEXEC.BAT sequence. To create a CONFIG.SYS file on your hard disk, for example, you would type COPY CON C:CONFIG.SYS. You may wish to refer to your DOS manual if you have never done this before.

THE QLB LIBRARY

The machine code for the graphics functions which your C program uses is contained in a memory-resident module called the *QLB file,* also known as a *QLB library.* Microsoft calls this a Quicklibrary. You can place as many (or as few) graphics functions as you wish into your QLB file. You can also place other non-graphics functions into the QLB file.

The QLB file method is used by Microsoft because not every C instruction is present inside the QuickC integrated programming environment. So if you write programs that use advanced functions (such as graphics functions), or if you write programs that use less familiar C instructions such as **sin( )** or **sqrt( )**, then you simply supplement QuickC's built-in routines by putting the additional desired routines into a memory-resident QLB module.

The QLB file that was used during the creation of the demonstration programs for this book is shown in Fig. 6-3. You use the QuickC editor to write this file. Simply type in the name of each function that you want QuickC to place into the QLB library.

```
#include <graph.h>
#include <math.h>
#include <stdlib.h>
#include <conio.h>
#include <bios.h>

main(){
_setvideomode();_getvideoconfig();
_setcolor();
_setlinestyle();_setfillmask();
_moveto();_lineto();_rectangle();
_setpixel();_ellipse();
_imagesize();_getimage();_putimage();
_floodfill();_clearscreen();
_setvisualpage();_setactivepage();
_settextposition();_settextcolor();
_outtext();
sin();cos();outp();inp();
_bios_keybrd();
}
```

Fig. 6-3. The contents of a graphics-oriented QLB file.

In step-by-step form, here is how to create a QLB library:

1. Use the QuickC editor to write a C source program. This C source program simply contains the name of each function that you want to include in the QLB library. Be certain that you also type in the **#include** files that are needed by these functions. You will be right on the mark if you type in the text, as shown in Fig. 6-3, because this was the QLB file used to create the demonstration programs in the book.

2. Press the ALT key to position the menu bar cursor on the File menu. Press ENTER to pull down the File menu. Scroll down and select the function marked as Save As. . .

3. Type in the filename GRFX.C (or some other name you might prefer). Then press the TAB key to move to the *OK* prompt and press ENTER to save the file. You should always save your original C program before you compile it, and you should always use the filename extension .C when you are saving a C source file.

4. Next, press the ALT key to return to the menu bar. Select the **Run** menu and scroll down to the **Compile. . .** selection. Press ENTER and a dialog box will appear with the cursor sitting on the **Level 1 Warning Level** option. Use the TAB key to move the cursor over to the **Output Options** area. Then use the UP-ARROW key to select the **Obj** option. Press TAB until you reach the **Compile File** selection and then press the SPACEBAR. QuickC will translate your C source code into machine code and place it onto the disk in drive B as an OBJ file. (If you are using a hard drive, QuickC will place the OBJ file onto drive C.)

5. Exit QuickC and return to DOS.

6. Place a disk containing the files QUICKLIB.OBJ (provided with the QuickC package) and your freshly created OBJ file into drive B. Place a disk containing LINK.EXE, MLIBCE.LIB, and GRAPHICS.LIB into drive A. These files are provided in the QuickC package. You are going to use LINK to combine the required functions from MLIBCE.LIB and GRAPHICS.LIB into your QLB file.

7. Ensure that drive B is the default drive. The DOS prompt should be **B>**. If it is **A>**, change it by typing B: and then pressing ENTER. (If you are using a hard drive, you should use drive C.)

8. To create the QLB file, type the following:

A:LINK QUICKLIB.OBJ + GRFX.OBJ, GRFX.QLB,,/Q;

and then press ENTER. If you have named your C source file something other than GRFX, change the filenames accordingly. The punctuation is important; be careful when typing in this instruction.

9. When LINK has finished creating your QLB library, it will store it on the disk in drive B and the DOS prompt will return to the screen. Copy the resulting QLB file onto the disk where you keep your C source files. This is the disk that you would normally keep in drive B while you are programming with QuickC. When QuickC is initially loaded, it checks drive B to see if a QLB file is present.

The memory-resident QLB library is invoked by designating it on the command line when you first load QuickC. If your QLB file is named GRFX.QLB, for example, you would load QuickC from DOS by using the following syntax:

A>B:
B>A:QC /lGRFX.QLB

Although QuickC does not actually actually load all of the memory-resident QLB library at this time, it sets up certain memory locations and addresses in readiness for future use of the QLB module.

CASE STUDY: RUNNING A TYPICAL C PROGRAM

Appendix A contains a program listing named func-002.c. This program invokes the highest graphics mode permitted by the hardware. The algorithm which is used in func-002.c can be used to make your original C graphics programs run on any IBM-compatible graphics adapter. If a VGA is present, then the program sets up the 640×480 16-color mode. If an EGA and enhanced color display or multiscanning monitor are present, the 640×350 16-color mode is used. If an EGA and standard monitor are installed, the 640×200 16-color mode is invoked. If a CGA or an MCGA is present, the 320×200 4-color mode is used.

Because of the importance of this program listing for portability purposes, it is a good candidate for your first QuickC graphics experiment. Here, in detail, is how to create and run a graphics program with the integrated programming environment of QuickC. This discussion assumes that you are using two 5.25-inch disk drives. (Everything will occur on drive C if you are using a hard disk.)

1. Insert your DOS boot disk into drive A. Ensure that the AUTOEXEC.BAT and CONFIG.SYS files shown in Fig. 6-2 are on the boot disk.

2. Turn on your monitor. Turn on your computer. Enter the date and time if requested.

3. When the DOS prompt appears, remove the boot disk from drive A.

4. Insert the disk containing your QLB file into drive B. If you are typing in the programs from the book, this is the disk where you will be saving them. If you have the companion disk for this book, you should copy func-002.c from the companion disk onto the disk that you will be using in drive B. Alternatively, you can copy your QLB file onto the companion disk.

5. Place the QuickC program disk (which contains QC.EXE) into drive A.

6. Set the default drive to B by typing B: and then pressing ENTER. The DOS prompt ''B>'' should appear (unless you are using a hard disk as drive C).

7. Load QuickC (and portions of the QLB file) by typing the following:

A:QC /lGRFX.QLB

8. When the QuickC screen appears, remove the QuickC program disk from drive A. Insert a disk that contains the #include files provided in the QuickC package.

9. If you are using the companion disk, go to step 11. If you are typing in the listings from the book, go to step 10.

10. Type in the program listing named func-002.c from Appendix A. Use the **Save As . . .** option of the **File** menu to save the program to disk. Go to step 12.

11. Use the **Open . . .** option of the **File** menu to load func-002.c from disk.

12. Hold down the SHIFT key while you press F5. This tells QuickC to compile and run the program that is currently in memory. As you watch the line numbers flashing by during compilation, you can see QuickC loading the various #include files mentioned in func-002.c. Immediately before running the program, QuickC loads the full QLB module into high memory and links its addresses to the compiled C code in the code segment (refer to Fig. 6-1).

13. When QuickC transfers control to the C program, the appropriate graphics mode is activated and a text label identifies which mode has been used. Press any key to stop the program and to return to the QuickC editor.

AN ANALYSIS OF THE PROGRAM

You may wish to refer to the program listing for func-002.c in Appendix A as you read this section.

Before any code appears in the listing, a comment section appears, denoted by the /* symbols. This commentary describes the purpose of the program, compatibility issues, and so on.

Next, the **#include** directives are used to instruct the QuickC compiler to merge other source code files into the program at this point. These **#include** files, customarily bearing the filename extension .H, are simply definitions of variables that are used by some of the C instructions that appear later in the program. These definitions are called *declarations* by C programmers.

The declarations section of the source code appears next. First, the **struct** instruction is used to identify an area in memory which contains assorted video definitions used by your program at run-time. Second, the variables used by the program are declared as either integers or floating-point values. Numeric values are assigned to the variables. (This is called *initializing* a variable.) Finally, the subroutines (functions) which are part of the program are named. The mnemonic ''void'' which is prefixed to each subroutine declaration means that no value is returned to the caller by the subroutine. The parameter ''void'' which is suffixed to each subroutine declaration means that the subroutine does not expect to receive any parameters from the caller.

Next is the **main( )** routine. The first act performed by this routine is to call a subroutine named **graphics_setup( )**. This subroutine is the graphics compatibility module that comprises the nuts and bolts of the program. A more detailed discussion of **graphics_setup( )** is presented later in this chapter.

After returning to the **main( )** routine, a built-in QuickC function named **_getvideoconfig( )** is called. This function stores the various graphics parameters of your computer system, including the default mode (so QuickC knows which screen mode to re-install when your graphics program is finished executing).

Next, the **main( )** routine calls upon a subroutine named **keyboard( )** to wait for any key to be pressed. When a key is struck, control returns to the **main( )** routine, which then calls **quit_pgm( )** to gracefully terminate the program and to return to QuickC. You can see how **quit_pgm( )** uses the **_clearscreen( )** and **_setvideomode( )** instructions to return to the pre-existing screen mode before ending the program.

The subroutine named **graphics_setup( )** checks the hardware and then sets up the best graphics mode that is permitted by the graphics adapter and monitor. You can see that there are five labels in this subroutine. They are **VGA_mode:**, **EGA_ECD_mode:**, **EGA_SCD_modes:**, **CGA_mode:**, and **abort_message:**. The code in **VGA_mode** sets up the 640×480 16-color mode of the VGA. The code in **EGA_ECD_mode** sets up the 640×350 16-color mode supported by an EGA and enhanced color display or multiscanning monitor. The code in **EGA_SCD_mode** invokes the 640×200 16-color display supported by an EGA when a standard color display is present. The code in **CGA_mode** invokes the 320×200 4-color mode of the CGA and MCGA.

Look at the first instruction in **VGA_mode**. When the **_setvideomode( )** instruction is used, it returns a value other than zero if its operation was successful. So if **_setvideomode( )** returns a value of zero, then it failed to invoke the 640×480 16-color mode, probably because the existing graphics hardware does not support that graphics mode. In this instance, the instruction ''**goto EGA_ECD_mode**'' tries the next best graphics mode. Each module in turn tries to set up a graphics mode. If successful, program control is passed back to the **main( )** routine. If unsuccessful, program control passes to the next module, which attempts to set up a lower-resolution graphics mode.

If all attempts to set up a graphics mode fail, program control eventually falls through to the module named **abort_message**. This routine simply displays an error message and terminates the program.

The advantages of the **graphics_setup( )** subroutine are numerous. First, you can see how any graphics program could use this module to establish the best graphics mode permitted by the graphics adapter and monitor. This means that your original C graphics programs can run on any IBM-compatible graphics adapter and monitor. Second, each module inside **graphics_setup( )** can use specialized text and specialized variables which are unique to the graphics mode being used. The text which is displayed in each graphics mode invoked by **func-002.c** is a good example of this specialization. The variables **x_res** and **y_res** also vary, depending upon which graphics mode is invoked. These variables are used to ensure that all xy screen coordinates are accurate, no matter which graphics mode is being used. A universal template which uses these device-independent world coordinates is discussed in detail in Chapter 8.

The variable **mode__flag** is simply an indicator of which graphics mode is being used by the program. This will come in handy during some of the other demonstration programs in this book, especially when different graphics adapters require different algorithms for animation.

COMMON ERROR MESSAGES

Whenever you are writing your own original C programs, typing the program listings from **High Performance Graphics in C** or using the companion disk, you will eventually encounter error messages from QuickC. These error messages are often confusing and difficult to interpret because the compiler has been fooled by the source code.

The chart in Fig. 6-4 lists typical error messages. It is important to understand that error messages are most often caused by lines of code which precede the actual error message, not by the line which appeared to generate the error message. Missing braces and brackets are often the culprit.

There are a few errors in logic syntax which the compiler will not catch for you. If your program calls a subroutine but the subroutine never seems to execute, you may have neglected to use "( )" when you called the subroutine. If you wish to call a subroutine named **quit__pgm**, for example, you call it thus: **quit__pgm( );**. Even though no parameters are passed, you must still use the parentheses (inside which the parameters would be placed). Remember that the semi-colon is used to indicate the end of an individual instruction.

new line in constant	you neglected to add the closing " quotation mark to an _outtext instruction
cannot load user-define library	your QLB file must be present on disk at compile time and again at run-time
missing ´;´ before type ´void´	you probably forgot the final } brace of a loop or the final } brace of the preceding function (subroutine)
null pointer assignment	your program may be writing over the contents of your QLB library in RAM. You may wish to reboot before continuing.
´setcolor´: redefinition	your probably used an extra } brace on a previous statement
´bios keybrd´: unresolved external	you neglected to place the appropriate C library function into your memory-resident QLB file
syntax error: ´int constant´	you probably neglected to use a required comma between elements of an array declaration.

Fig. 6-4. Common error messages encountered during development of QuickC graphics programs.

If all possible variations of an **if/then** instruction seem to be executing, you have likely used the = operator when the == operator should be used. If, for example, you want to test if **x1** equals 9, the instruction to use is **(x1==9)**. Refer to Chapter 4 for a further discussion of C operators.

After working with C graphics programs for a time, you will find the same error messages cropping up over and over again. The compiler will quickly condition your responses and you will find yourself getting better at tracking down the bug (usually hiding in a line preceding the line which caused the error message).

CREATING EXE FILES

Creating a finished EXE file with QuickC is not a difficult task. An EXE file can be run directly from the DOS prompt.

First, use QuickC to produce an OBJ file. Then return to DOS. Place a disk containing LINK.EXE, MLIBCE.LIB, and GRAPHICS.LIB into drive A. Place the disk containing your OBJ file into drive B. After ensuring that drive B is the default drive, type in the following line at the DOS prompt:

A:LINK filename.OBJ, filename.EXE, NUL.MAP, MLIBCE.LIB

Insert the actual name of your OBJ file where the pseudonym ''filename'' has been used in the above example, of course. The linker will create an EXE file named ''filename.EXE'' by using the machine code routines contained in the library MLIBCE.LIB and GRAPHICS.LIB. The resulting EXE file is a stand-alone file which requires no other modules at run-time.

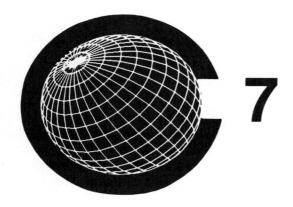

How to Use Borland Turbo C

The integrated programming environment provided by Borland Turbo C version 1.5 and newer makes the development of high-performance graphics programs an easily manageable task. After you have configured your computer system to work with Turbo C, using a graphics function is just like using any other built-in C instruction. Configuring your system usually means telling Turbo C where to find the various files that it needs during compilation, linking, and execution of your C program.

SYSTEM MEMORY MAP

A typical memory map of the Turbo C programming environment is shown in Fig. 7-1. If your computer has less than 640K of user RAM, the amount of free memory shown in Fig. 7-1 will be reduced, but the chart will remain the same in all other respects.

The lowest portion of memory is occupied by assorted interrupt vectors, BIOS code, DOS kernel code, file control blocks, and the resident part of DOS COMMAND.COM. A part of COMMAND.COM called the transient portion is actually loaded into high memory, where it is often overwritten by application programs. DOS needs this transient code to interpret your keyboard instructions. When you return to DOS from an application program DOS first checks to see that the transient portion is intact. If it is not, then DOS asks you to ''Insert Disk containing COMMAND.COM'' before it can continue.

When DOS loads Turbo C (the TC.EXE file), it first constructs a program segment prefix (PSP) which contains information about the file being loaded: the length of the file, the parameters passed to it on the DOS command line, and so on. It is interesting to note that (as Fig. 7-1 illustrates) any memory-resident programs which are present are loaded

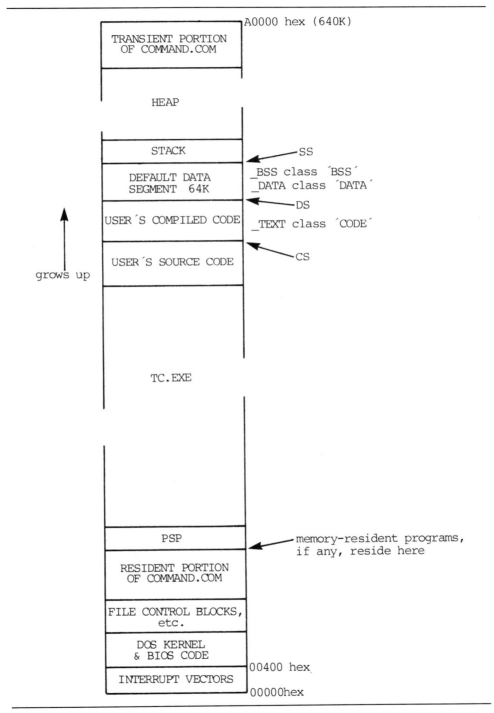

Fig. 7-1. Memory map of the Turbo C programming environment.

by DOS into the memory block just above the resident portion of COMMAND.COM. If you are using a memory-resident graphics print program such as Pizazz, for example, then DOS would place it just above COMMAND.COM. Memory-resident programs are often called TSR programs (terminate and stay resident).

After Turbo C has been loaded by DOS, Turbo C builds a text buffer in the block of memory immediately above Turbo C itself. This is where your source code resides. If you load in a C program from disk, then it is placed here. If you use the Turbo C editor to type in a C program, then it goes here.

When you use the ALT+R keys to instruct Turbo C to compile and run your C source code, it first merges any source files indicated by the **#include** directive, and then translates the resulting text into machine code which is stored on disk as an OBJ file. Next, Turbo C links the OBJ file to the various libraries which contain the C routines used by your program. The linker stores the resulting EXE file on disk.

To run the finished program, Turbo C loads the program from disk into the block of memory immediately above the text buffer. The first portion of this memory is the code segment; the CS segment register points here. Although each code module cannot exceed a maximum size of 64K bytes, Turbo C permits as many code modules as memory will allow (when you are using the medium memory model).

The *data segment* (DS) is located in memory immediately above the code segment. Various strings and variables are stored here. Turbo C limits your data to 64K bytes maximum when you are using the medium memory model.

The stack which your C program will use during run-time is located just above the data segment (and is in fact considered by Turbo C to be a part of the 64K data segment). By default, Turbo C sets up a run-time stack of 4K for your program. This size is adequate for virtually all graphics programs and animation programs, although Turbo C allows you to increase the stack size if you wish. (Refer to the Turbo C user's manual for more on stack size allocation using the **__stklen** variable.)

If your C program uses the functions contained in Turbo C's graphics library, then you must place the file GRAPHICS.LIB on the same disk which contains the include files and other C library files. If you are using the medium memory model, then the disk would normally contain all the **#include** files with the filename extension .H, as well as GRAPHICS.LIB, COM.OBJ, EMU.LIB, FP87.LIB, MATHM.LIB, CM.LIB, CGA.BGI, and EGAVGA.BGI.

As your C source code grows in size, the text buffer and the memory used by the EXE file grow upward. The memory being squeezed by these two growing blocks is called *free memory,* also known as the *far heap.* The far heap can be used to store graphic arrays and other data (including simulated graphics pages), if you wish, thereby overcoming the 64K limitation of the default data segment.

THE DOS ENVIRONMENT

Turbo C uses DOS to read and write disk files. Before you use Turbo C, you must tell DOS where to find the various source files, OBJ files, and linking tools that Turbo C needs. You would normally do this by using Turbo C's menus.

If you are using a computer with two 5.25-inch disk drives, here is how to set up Turbo C. When you first load Turbo C, use the right-arrow key to move the menu bar cursor to the **Options** menu. Press ENTER to pull down the **Options** menu. Use the DOWN-

ARROW key to scroll down to the **Directories** selection. Press ENTER and a dialog box will appear. Set the **Include** directories to A:, set the **Libraries** directions to A:, and set the **Turbo C** directory to A:. Set the **Output** directory to B:. While you are programming with Turbo C, the compiler will now look in drive A for **#include** files and libraries; it will store in drive A any OBJ files and EXE files that it creates. (If you are using a hard disk, you would set all these options to drive C.)

In addition, your boot disk should contain a CONFIG.SYS file which establishes the proper DOS environment for Turbo C. If you are using a system with two 5.25-inch disk drives, then you can build a CONFIG.SYS file from the DOS prompt. Type COPY CON A:CONFIG.SYS and then press ENTER. Type files=20 and press ENTER. Type buffers=10 and press ENTER. Press F6 and then press ENTER. DOS will save the CONFIG.SYS file on the disk in drive A.

CASE STUDY: RUNNING A TYPICAL C PROGRAM

Appendix E contains a program listing named **func−002.c**. This program invokes the highest graphics mode permitted by the hardware. The algorithm which is used in **func−002.c** can be used to make your original C graphics programs run on any IBM-compatible graphics adapter. If a VGA is present, the program sets up the 640×480 16-color mode. If an EGA and an enhanced color display or a multiscanning monitor are present, the 640×350 16-color mode is used. If an EGA and a standard monitor are installed, the 640×200 16-color mode is invoked. If a CGA or an MCGA is present, the 320×200 4-color mode is used.

Because of the importance of this program listing for portability purposes, it is a good candidate for your first Turbo C graphics experiment. Here in detail is how to create and run a graphics program with the integrated programming environment of Turbo C. This discussion assumes that you are using two 5.25-inch disk drives. (Everything will occur on drive C if you are using a hard disk.)

1. Insert your DOS boot disk into drive A. Ensure that the CONFIG.SYS file discussed earlier is on the boot disk.

2. Turn on your monitor. Turn on your computer. Enter the date and time if requested.

3. When the **DOS** prompt appears, if the Turbo C program file (TC.EXE) is not on the boot disk, remove the boot disk from drive A.

4. Insert the disk containing your source files into drive B. If you are typing in the programs from the book, then save them on this disk. If you have the companion disk for the book, you should copy **func−002.c** from the companion disk onto the disk that you will be using in drive B. Alternatively, you can use the companion disk in drive B, although it is good programming practice never to use the original disk.

5. Place the Turbo C program disk (which contains TC.EXE) into drive A. If the file TC.EXE is on your boot disk, then it is already loaded in drive A.

6. Load Turbo C by typing the following:

    A:TC

7. When the Turbo C screen appears, remove the Turbo C program disk from drive A. Insert a disk that contains the **#include** files provided in the Turbo C package. If you

are using the medium memory model for programming, then that disk should contain the following files: all the **#include** files (with the filename extension .H), GRAPHICS.LIB, COM.OBJ, EMU.LIB, FP87.LIB, MATHM.LIB, CM.LIB, CGA.BGI (graphics drivers for the CGA), and EGAVGA.BGI (graphics drivers for the EGA and VGA).

8. Create a Project list that tells Turbo C that you will be using routines from GRAPHICS.LIB in your program. First, select the **Edit** mode from the main menu bar. Type GRAPHICS.LIB and press ENTER. Type B:FUNC−002.C and press ENTER. Then press F10 to return to the main menu bar. Select the Files menu. Choose the Write To option and save the file as B:FUNC−002.PRJ. Next, pull down the Project menu and choose the Project Name selection. When the dialog box appears, type in the project filename B:FUNC−002.PRJ.

9. If you are using the companion disk, then go to step 11. If you are typing in the listings from the book, then go to step 10.

10. Type in the program listing named func−002.c from Appendix E. Use the Write To option of the File menu to save the program to disk. Go to step 12.

11. Use the Load option of the File menu to load **func−002.c** from disk.

12. Hold down the ALT key while you press R. This tells Turbo C to compile and run the program that is currently in memory. As you watch the context prompts flashing by during compilation, you can see Turbo C loading the various **#include** files mentioned in **func−002.c**, creating and writing to disk the OBJ file, and linking in all the required modules to create the EXE file. Immediately before running the program, Turbo C loads the full EXE module into memory (refer to Fig. 7-1) and then loads in the appropriate graphics driver (either CGA.BGI or EGAVGA.BGI).

13. When Turbo C transfers control to the C program, the appropriate graphics mode is activated and a text label identifies which mode has been used. Press any key to stop the program and to return to the Turbo C editor.

ANALYSIS OF THE PROGRAM

You may wish to refer to the program listing for **func−002.c** in Appendix E as you read this section.

Before any code appears in the listing, a comment section appears, denoted by the /* symbols. This commentary describes the purpose of the program, compatibility issues, and so on.

Next, the **#include** directives are used to instruct the Turbo C compiler to merge other source code files into the program at this point. These **#include** files, customarily bearing the filename extension .H, are simply definitions of variables that are used by some of the C instructions which appear later in the program. These definitions are called *declarations* by C programmers.

The declarations section of the source code appears next. First, the variables used by the program are declared as either integers or floating-point values. Numeric values are assigned to the variables. (This is called initializing a variable.) Second, the subroutine (functions) which are part of the program are named. The mnemonic "void" which is prefixed to each subroutine declaration means that no value is returned to the caller by the subroutine. The parameter "void" which is suffixed to each subroutine declaration means that the subroutine does not expect to receive any parameters from the caller.

Next comes the **main( )** routine. The first act performed by this routine is to call a subroutine named **graphics__setup( )**. This subroutine is the graphics compatibility module which comprises the main purpose of the program. A more detailed discussion of **graphics__setup( )** is presented later in this chapter.

Next, the **main( )** routine calls upon a subroutine named **keyboard( )** to wait for any key to be pressed. When a key is struck, control returns to the **main( )** routine, which then calls **quit__pgm( )** to gracefully terminate the program and to return to Turbo C. You can see how **quit__pgm( )** uses the **__cleardevice( )** and **__restorecrtmode( )** instructions to return to the pre-existing screen mode before ending the program.

The subroutine named **graphics__setup( )** checks the hardware and then sets up the best graphics mode which is permitted by the graphics adapter and monitor. You can see that there are six labels in this subroutine. They are **VGA__mode: EGA__ECD__mode:**, **EGA__SCD__mode:**, **CGA__mode:**, **MCGA__mode:**, and **abort__message:**. The code in **VGA__mode** sets up the 640×480 16-color mode of the VGA. The code in **EGA__ECD__mode** sets up the 640×350 16-color mode supported by the EGA and enhanced color display or multiscanning monitor. The code in **EGA__SCD__mode** invokes the 640×200 16-color display supported by an EGA when a standard color display is presented. The code in **CGA__mode** invokes the 320×200 4-color mode of the CGA. The code in **MCGA__mode** initializes the 320×200 4-color mode of the MCGA.

Look at the first block of code in **graphics__setup( )**. The **detectgraph( )** instruction is used in order to detect which graphics adapter and monitor are present. A series of **if/then** instructions is used to branch to the appropriate label, based upon the results returned by the **detectgraph( )** function. If no IBM-compatible graphics adapter was found, the the program flow falls through to the **goto abort__message** instruction, which gracefully terminates the program.

There are a number of advantages to the **graphics__setup( )** subroutine. First, you can see how any graphics program could use this module to establish the best graphics mode permitted by the graphics adapter and monitor. This means that your original C graphics programs can run on any IBM-compatible graphics adapter and monitor. Second, each module inside **graphics__setup( )** can use specialized text and specialized variables which are unique to the graphics mode being used. The text which is displayed in each graphics mode invoked by **func−002.c** is a good example of this specialization. The variables **x__res** and **y__res** also change, depending upon which graphics mode is invoked. These variables are used to ensure that all xy screen coordinates are accurate, no matter which graphics mode is being used. A universal template which uses these device-independent world coordinates is discussed in detail in Chapter 8.

The variable **mode__flag** is simply an indicator of which graphics mode is being used by the program. This will come in handy during some of the other demonstration programs in this book, especially when different graphics adapters require different algorithms for animation.

COMMON ERROR MESSAGES

Whether you are writing your own original C programs, typing in the program listings from **High Performance Graphics in C**, or using the companion disk, you will eventually encounter error messages from Turbo C. These error messages are often confusing and difficult to interpret because the compiler itself has often been fooled by the source code.

Warning: unreachable code	you are likely using a goto to force an animation loop. Ignore the warning.
Declaration syntax error	you might have forgotten the final */ from the previous comment
Statement missing ; in function...	you omitted the ; semicolon from a previous statement
Warning: unreachable code in function main	the main( ) routine probably contains an animation loop which uses goto. Ignore the warning.

Fig. 7-2. Common error messages encountered during development of Turbo C graphics programs.

The chart in Fig. 7-2 lists typical error messages. It is important to understand that error messages are most often caused by lines of code which precede the actual error message, not by the line which appeared to generate the error message. Missing braces and brackets are often the culprit.

There are a few errors in logic syntax which the Turbo C compiler will not catch for you. If your program calls a subroutine but the subroutine never seems to execute, you may have neglected to use "( )" when you called the subroutine. If you wish to call a subroutine named **quit_pgm**, for example, you call it as **quit_pgm( );**. Even though no parameters are being passed to the subroutine, you must still use the parentheses (inside which the parameters would be placed). Remember that the semi-colon is used to indicate the end of an individual instruction.

If all possible variations of an **if/then** instruction seem to be executing, you have likely used the = operator when the == operator should be used. If, for example, you want to test if **x1** equals 9, the instruction to use is (**x1**==**9**). Refer to Chapter 4 for a further discussion of C operators.

If you occasionally use **goto** instructions in your C graphics programs, Turbo C will often generate a spurious warning message: **unreachable code.** Because high-performance animation routines often use the **goto** instruction to force an infinite loop, this warning message can safely be ignored in those circumstances. The following demonstration programs from this book will generate a warning message during compilation which can be ignored: TC-014.C, TC-016.C, TC-017.C, and FUNC-007.C.

CREATING EXE FILES

Turbo C automatically creates an EXE file and saves it on the output disk whenever you ask Turbo C to compile your C program. An EXE file can be run directly from the DOS prompt.

III

DESIGN

Graphics
Creativity

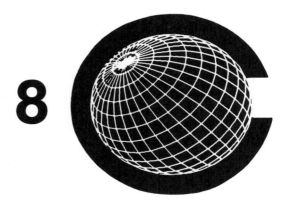

8

Screen Layout:
A Graphics Primer

In the field of computer graphics, *layout* refers to the manner in which graphical material is organized on the display screen. Stated with more precision, layout refers to the position, color, and size of various graphic elements.

USING A DRAWING TEMPLATE

In many instances, the most efficient way to compose a strong, balanced layout on the display screen is to use a drawing template. As illustrated in Fig. 8-1, a drawing template (also called a screen template) is simply a grid, usually drawn on a sheet of paper, which corresponds to the addressable area of the display screen. It is important to note that the addressable area is seldom as large as the whole screen.

To create a drawing template, first draw a rectangle whose ratio of width to height is four to three (4:3). Alternatively, use a tape measure to actually measure the addressable area of your particular monitor. For example, you might invoke the 640×200 mode, draw a rectangle whose upper left corner is 0,0 and whose lower right corner is 639,199, and then measure the dimensions of the resulting graphic. You could even place a sheet of tracing paper over the screen and transfer the dimensions that way, if you wished. The important thing is to acquire a rectangle of 4:3 ratio on a sheet of paper.

Next, use a ruler to notch a series of tick marks along the horizontal and vertical axes of the rectangle. These tick marks are then used to draw a grid.

FROM TEMPLATE TO DISPLAY SCREEN

Figure 8-2 shows the evolution of a typical computer graphic. First, a quick sketch of the desired shape is drawn on the template. This preliminary drawing is called a *thumbnail*

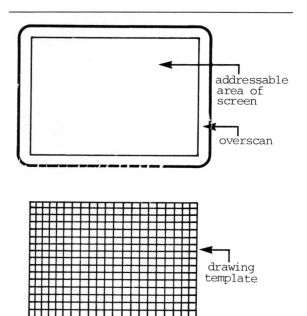

Fig. 8-1. The drawing template corresponds to the addressable portion of the display screen.

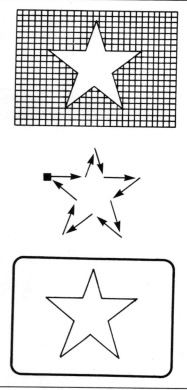

Fig. 8-2. Top: a preliminary drawing on a grid template provides the xy coordinates. Center: the drawing strategy used by the C program. Bottom: the resultant display image.

sketch by professional artists. You can make this first prototype as simple or as extravagant as you wish.

Next, the programmer decides upon an algorithm which could be used by the program to draw the image. In the instance described in Fig. 8-2, a simple polyline will get the job done. If you are using QuickC, this is the **__line to(x,y)** instruction; if you are using Turbo C, it is the **line to(x,y)** instruction.

The line starts at an arbitrary vertex and merely moves from point to point around the shape until the graphic has been outlined. Finally, the standard area fill function provided by both QuickC and Turbo C can be used to color the image.

Many of the program listings in **High Performance Graphics in C** and many of the demonstration programs in the companion disk for this book started out as simple thumbnail sketches on a blank sheet of paper. (The animated hummingbird from Chapter 19 evolved from a ballpoint pen sketch on a slip of paper being used as a bookmark.) A more detailed sketch on a drawing template made it easy to identify the xy screen coordinates which would be required by a C program in order to generate an image on the display screen.

THE DEVICE-INDEPENDENT 640×480 TEMPLATE

Although you can create your drawing template grid to match any screen mode you prefer, there is a better approach. Rather than setting up a 640×350 grid, or a 640×200 grid, or a 320×200 grid, you can ensure that your original C graphics programs will be fully portable to all IBM-compatible graphics adapters if you employ a grid whose ratio is 4:3.

The 640:480 ratio is identical to the 4:3 ratio used by the addressable area of all screen modes. Because the integrity of the ratio is preserved, a square sized 100×100 on a 640×480 template, for example, will appear as a square. In contrast, a rectangle sized 100×100 will produce a tall, narrow image on the 640×200 screen.

By using 640×480 xy coordinates to define your graphic, you can use a simple windowing routine to convert these coordinates to any IBM-compatible graphics screen. Figure 8-3 shows the simple mathematics required to map the 640×480 xy coordinates to either the 640×480 VGA screen, the 640×350 VGA/EGA screen, the 640×200 VGA/EGA/CGA/MCGA screen, or the 320×200 VGA/EGA CGA/MCGA screen.

Because the xy coordinates of the 640×480 drawing template are not intended to correspond directly to any particular screen mode, they are device-independent. That is, they are not dependent upon any one particular graphics adapter. It is a mere coincidence that the 640×480 template uses the same coordinate as the highest VGA mode. It would be just as easy to use a 1280×960 device-independent drawing template, of course. It is the 4:3 ratio that is important.

Many of the program listings in this book use world coordinates which are derived from a device-independent 640×480 drawing template. The ratio formulas depicted in Fig. 8-3 are included in each program listing as a specialized subroutine named **coords( )**. At program start-up the compatibility module, which was first presented in Chapter 6 for QuickC and Chapter 7 for Turbo C, assigns the horizontal and vertical screen resolution to the variables **x__res** and **y__res**. Before a point is plotted on the display screen, the xy coordinates of the point are filtered through the window mapping subroutine, thereby ensuring that the program will function correctly no matter which graphics adapter you are using.

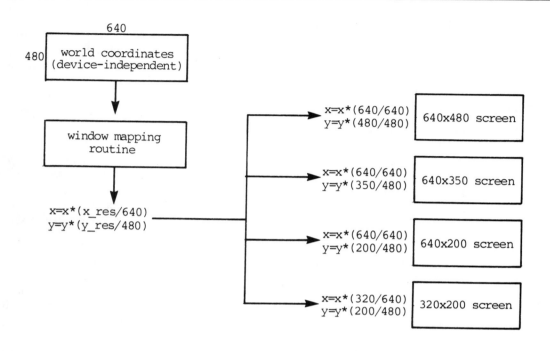

Fig. 8-3. Simple ratio formulas are used to map the device-independent world coordinates of the 640×480 template to the device-dependent dimensions of the screen mode currently in effect.

FUNDAMENTALS OF GOOD LAYOUT

As an aspiring C graphics programmer, you will want to understand some of the fundamental concepts of layout. An overview of the more important rules of layout is presented here for your ready reference.

Visual Center

The visual center of the display screen is the position that "looks like" the center of the screen. However, as Fig. 8-4 illustrates, the visual center of a display screen is not the same as the physical center. What appears to the human eye as the center of the screen is in reality located slightly above the actual physical center.

If you wish a graphic to appear centered, you should position it slightly above the physical center of the display screen.

Center of Interest

The center of interest is the portion of the display screen that receives most of the viewer's attention, as illustrated in Fig. 8-5. Under normal circumstances, this area is built around the visual center of the screen. Your graphic images will be more powerful if you keep the most important elements of your composition located in this center of interest "hot zone."

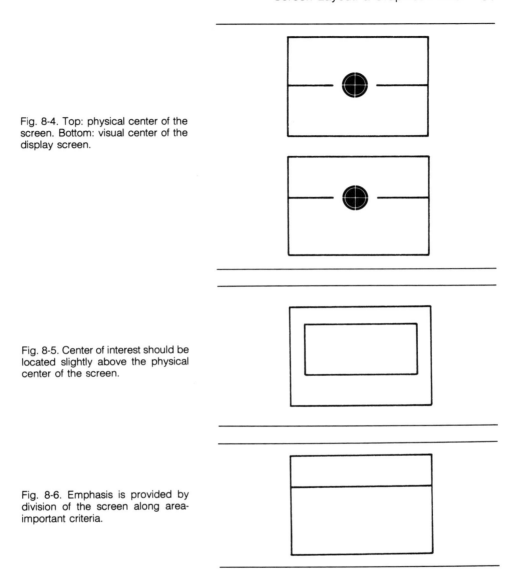

Fig. 8-4. Top: physical center of the screen. Bottom: visual center of the display screen.

Fig. 8-5. Center of interest should be located slightly above the physical center of the screen.

Fig. 8-6. Emphasis is provided by division of the screen along area-important criteria.

Dividing the Screen for Emphasis

How you divide the screen helps to provide emphasis. Refer to Fig. 8-6. Generally, the more space you provide for a graphic, the more emphasis the graphic receives. The viewer responds to this layout emphasis by paying more attention to the emphasized area. Any screen image can be made more powerful if one element is emphasized over all other elements present in the composition.

Ambiguity

As Fig. 8-7 shows, ambiguous shapes are frustrating to the viewer. Simply stated, the viewer does not know for certain which shape you have intended to draw. Did you

Fig. 8-7. Ambiguous shapes are frustrating to the viewer. In the instance illustrated here, the ellipse should be either an obvious circle or an obvious oval. An oval which is almost a true circle is ambiguous.

intend an ellipse or a true circle? Did you mean a square or a rectangle? If you intend to draw an ellipse, make it an obvious ellipse, not an almost-circle.

Visual Balance

Good layout appears balanced. It does not appear top heavy—about to fall over. The most effective way to balance a composition is through stacking, as Fig. 8-8 illustrates. By centering the graphical elements on the display screen, and by ensuring that the largest elements are nearest the bottom of the screen, a well-balanced layout will result. Even if you cannot seem to get the hang of good layout, you will not go wrong if you remember to stack your graphic elements.

Using Layout for Emphasis

If a number of graphical elements appear in your drawing, you can use layout to emphasize the important elements and to de-emphasize the less important elements. Refer to Fig. 8-9.

You can use position to emphasize one element. Simply position the element apart from the other elements. You can use size to emphasize one element. Simply make it larger than the other elements, and keep the other elements approximately the same size. You can use color to emphasize one element. Simply make its color different from the other elements, which should all share the same color, if possible.

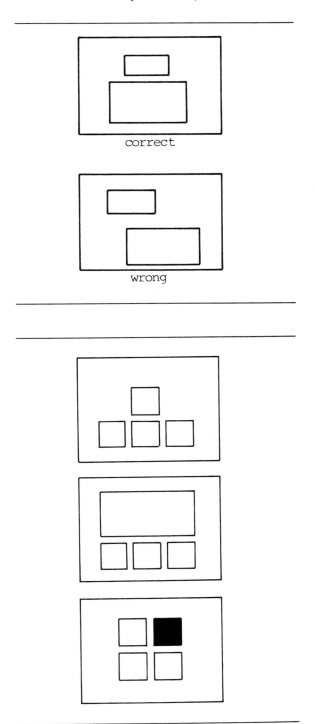

Fig. 8-8. The concept of visual balance and stacking.

Fig. 8-9. Three methods of providing emphasis. Top: emphasizing with layout. Center: emphasizing with size. Bottom: emphasizing with color or contrast.

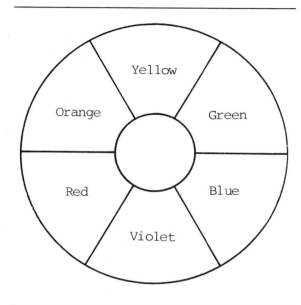

Fig. 8-10. The conceptual color wheel. Mixing two hues will produce the hue which lays halfway between them.

Using Color Wisely

Although many artistically creative individuals will maintain that the correct use of color is largely a matter of innate talent, there is in fact a strong body of scientific knowledge which proscribes the proper use of color in computer graphics. Of the primary hues shown in Fig. 8-10, for example, certain colors produce certain psychological effects. Certain combinations of hues go well together and others do not. And certain combinations (called harmonies) produce certain emotional effects. Figure 8-11 provides an introduction to color harmony. Chapter 9 will provide a more detailed discussion of the important influence of color on computer graphics.

Avoiding Layout Ambiguity

More often than not, the difference between a good layout and an amateurish attempt is line ambiguity. As the illustration in Fig. 8-12 shows, the juxtaposition of two graphical elements can be either definitive or ambiguous. If a single line can be interpreted as belonging to both or either of two different elements, then the layout is defective. The ambiguity which is present in such a layout will seriously impede the ability of the image to communicate to the viewer.

Good Text Layout

The two most useful methods for arranging text material are depicted in Fig. 8-13. Text that is centered is most useful for headings, title pages, captions, and so on. Alphanumeric characters which are lined up at the left margin are said to be flush left. Research has shown that this is the most effective layout for bodymatter material, because the ragged right side of the material helps the human eye keep its place as it gets ready to scan to the beginning of the next line. Text bodymatter which is lined up on both the

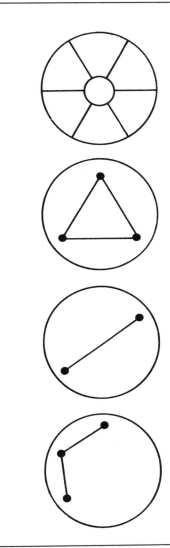

Fig. 8-11. Concepts of color harmony. From top: color wheel, triadic harmony, direct harmony, analogous harmony.

left and the right margins may look better balanced as a block, but it is more difficult to read. Typesetters and graphic artists called bodymatter which is lined up on both margins *"justified"*; they call bodymatter which is lined upon the left margin *"ragged right"*; they call body matter which is lined up on the right margin *"ragged left."*

Using Contrast

Strong contrast means strong impact. Refer to Fig. 8-14. If you cannot use size or position to achieve the emphasis you want, you can use contrast. A pure white graphic adjacent to a pure black graphic provides strong impact. Pure red or pure blue against either white or black is also powerful and effective. On the other hand, if your goal is

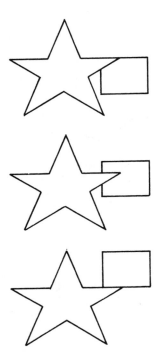

Fig. 8-12. Avoidance of ambiguity between two adjacent graphical
elements.

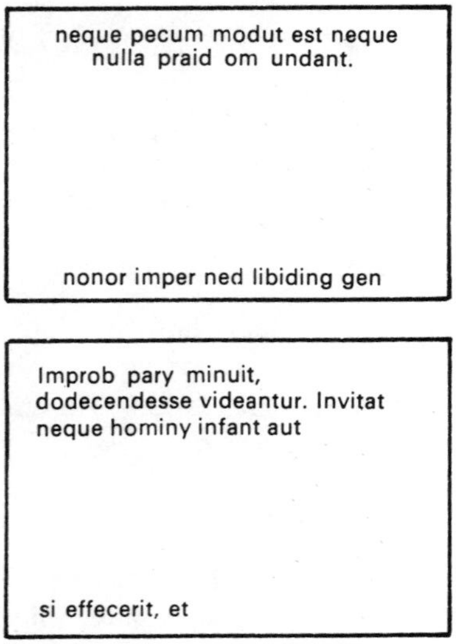

neque pecum modut est neque
nulla praid om undant.

nonor imper ned libiding gen

Improb pary minuit,
dodecendesse videantur. Invitat
neque hominy infant aut

si effecerit, et

Fig. 8-13. Layout of text on the
graphics screen. Top: using centered
lines. Bottom: using flush left lines
(also called ragged right).

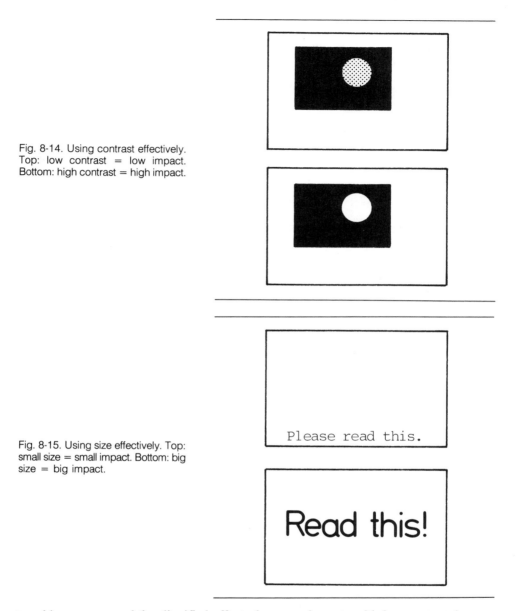

Fig. 8-14. Using contrast effectively. Top: low contrast = low impact. Bottom: high contrast = high impact.

Fig. 8-15. Using size effectively. Top: small size = small impact. Bottom: big size = big impact.

to achieve a more subtle, dignified effect, then use elements with low contrast in your graphic images. Light blue against a medium gray is an example of low contrast.

Text Size

The impact of text is more a factor of size than of position on the display screen. As Fig. 8-15 shows, text size can mean the difference between a shouted order and a whispered request. Most C programs would normally strike a chord somewhere between these two extremes.

Combining Text with Graphics

If you combine text with graphics on the display screen, most viewers will look at the graphics first. It makes sense, therefore, to position the graphics near the visual center of the screen. Text which is used as a heading should be placed near the top of the screen if the graphics are powerful; the heading should run across the center of the screen if the graphics are intended as background material. Text which is used as a caption or as an explanation of the graphic would normally be placed along the bottom of the screen. It is interesting to note that market research has shown that readers and viewers direct their gaze to layout elements in the following order of priority: 1. pictures and drawings, 2. captions, 3. headings, and 4. bodymatter. You may wish to keep this in mind as you design your screens.

PROTOTYPING

Even professional artists—both commercial artists and fine artists—have a difficult time producing a perfect layout on the very first attempt. These experienced professionals have learned that good layout is often a result of trial and error. As a C graphics programmer, a willingness to keep experimenting until it looks right is your ticket to successful layouts. You won't often go wrong if you first draw a quick thumbnail sketch and then tinker with it until it appears balanced. The time you spend on the thumbnail sketch will save you many hours of programming time later.

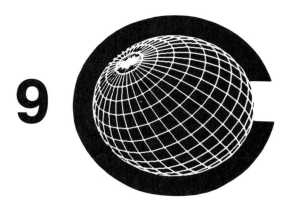

9

How to Select Colors

The VGA, EGA, CGA, and MCGA graphics adapters found in IBM-compatible personal computers are capable of generating an impressive palette of colors. But to make the most efficient use of this palette, an understanding of color theory is essential. As you will discover in this chapter, the incredible potential of computer color graphics has barely been touched upon by existing software.

HARDWARE COLORS

The standard palette found on all IBM-compatible graphics adapters is shown in Fig. 9-1. These 16 colors are the default colors of the 640×480 16-color mode of the VGA, the 640×350 16-color mode of the EGA, the 640×200 16-color modes of the EGA, the 320×200 16-color mode of the EGA, and the text modes. The standard palette for the four colors of the 320×200 4-color CGA mode is depicted in Fig. 9-2.

The numbers from 0 to 15 which are used to call colors are not the same as the colors themselves. The color code found in a C drawing instruction is more properly known as a color attribute, or a software color. As Chapter 2 explains, each software color is assigned a hardware color. On an EGA using the 640×350 16-color mode, this hardware color is selected from a total hardware palette of 64 colors, although only 16 may be displayed simultaneously on the screen. On a VGA using the 640×480 16-color mode, this hardware color is selected from a total hardware palette of over 65,000 colors, although only 16 may be shown simultaneously. On an EGA using the 640×200 16-color mode or the 320×200 16-color mode, the hardware color is selected from a total hardware palette of only 16 colors (although all 16 can be shown simultaneously, of course).

0	black	8	gray
1	blue	9	int. blue
2	green	10	int. green
3	cyan	11	int. cyan
4	red	12	int. red
5	magenta	13	int. magenta
6	brown	14	yellow
7	white	15	int. white

Fig. 9-1. The standard graphics palette of hardware colors available on IBM-compatible VGA and EGA graphics adapters.

0	black	2	magenta
1	cyan	3	white

Fig. 9-2. The standard graphics palette of hardware colors available on a CGA using the 320×200 4-color mode.

COLOR TERMINOLOGY

When professionals speak about color, they use specific terminology. Chromatic colors are those colors which have a hue in them. Refer to Fig. 9-3. Red is a hue; yellow is a hue; green is a hue. Achromatic colors are those colors which are neutral: white, gray, and black. Achromatic colors have no hue in them.

It is important to understand the difference between hue, value, and chroma.

A *hue* distinguishes one chromatic color from another. Hues find their most effective use in color wheels, as shown in Fig. 9-4, which can be used to create other forms of colors intended to produce particular emotional effects, psychological effects, and visual impact. Using a color wheel takes all the guesswork out of color. Hues fall into two broad categories: warm hues and cool hues. The warm hues are red, yellow, orange, and so on. The cool hues are in the green and blue portions of the color wheel.

Value refers to the apparent lightness or darkness of a color. *Chroma* refers to the relative grayness or purity of a color. For example, orange has strong chroma, but tan has weak chroma. Chroma is also called *intensity* or *saturation*.

SHADES, TONES, AND TINTS

Shades are formed by mixing pure colors with black. Brown, maroon, and olive are shades. *Tones* are formed by mixing pure colors with gray. Tan and beige are tones. *Tints* are formed by mixing pure colors with white. Pink, lavender, and peach are tints.

Shades, tones, and tints created from the same warm hue are markedly different. For example, pink (a tint) is decidedly unlike red (the original hue); brown (a shade) is unlike orange (the original hue). On the other hand, shades, tones, and tints created from the same cool hue tend to remain essentially the same types of colors. A green tint and a green shade still look a lot like the original pure green hue.

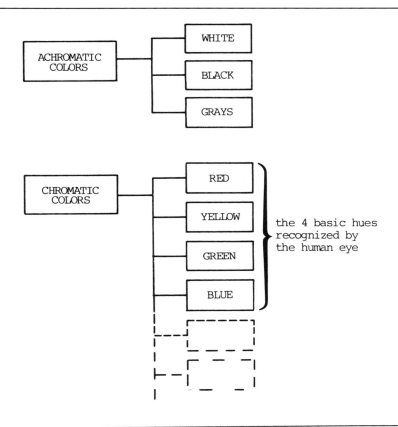

Fig. 9-3. Achromatic colors have no hues in them and are comprised on white, black, and grays. Chromatic colors have a pure hue or a mixed hue in them.

COLOR CIRCLES

The color wheel shown in Fig. 9-4 is derived from a standard color circle. A color circle is created by the four basic hues which are recognized by the human eye: red, yellow, green, and blue. Using the physics of light—which is the same mechanism used by the glowing pixels on your computer monitor—the basic hues of red/blue/green can be intermixed to form all the other pure colors shown on the color wheel in Fig. 9-4. This is why computer monitors are often called RGB displays. They use red, green, and blue phosphor dots to create the full range of colors.

COLOR HARMONIES

Certain combinations of colors in a layout will produce certain psychological effects and emotional effects. These combinations of colors are called *harmonies,* and are shown in Figs. 9-5, 9-6, and 9-7.

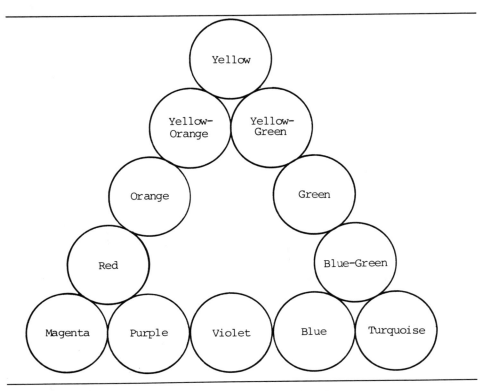

Fig. 9-4. The color wheel, used to interpret harmonies and color schemes.

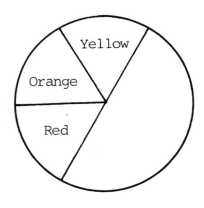

Fig. 9-5. The red-orange-yellow combination of hues is a typical analogous harmony.

Analogous Harmony

An *analogous harmony* is a combination of hues which are adjacent to each other on the color wheel. Analogous harmonies produce a psychological effect which corresponds to the warm or cool hues used in the harmony. An analogous color scheme consisting of either blue, red, or green hues is perceived as being direct and frank. More subtlety

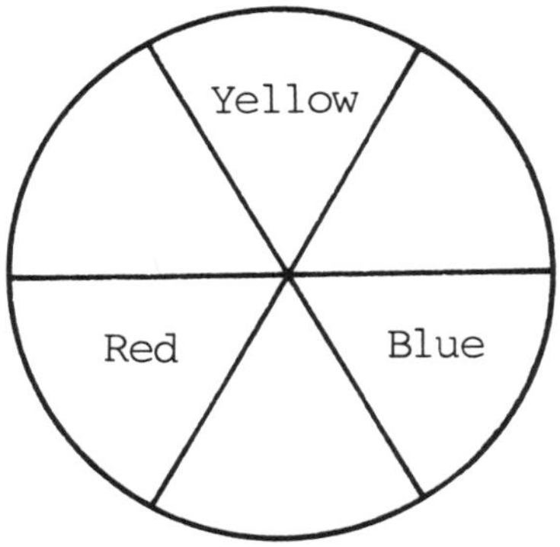

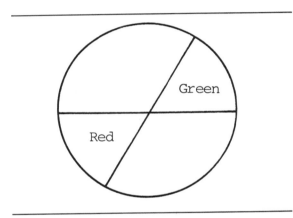

Fig. 9-6. The red-yellow-blue combination of hues is a typical triadic harmony—also called a split-compliment harmony.

Fig. 9-7. The red-green combination of colors is a typical direct harmony.

and elegance is formed by analogous harmonies which are based upon colors such as orange, violet, yellow-green, and so on.

Complementary Harmonies

Complementary harmonies fall into two categories: direct harmony and split-complement harmony. A *direct* harmony is a combination of colors which are directly opposite each other on the color wheel. An example of a direct harmony is the red-green combination. Direct harmonies tend to produce strong impact.

Split-complement harmonies are formed by combining colors which are positioned as a triangle on the color wheel. Split-complement harmony schemes are also called *triadic* harmonies. The red-yellow-blue combination is a split-complement harmony. The magenta-yellow-turquoise scheme tends to be perceived as primitive. The red-yellow/green-blue scheme is perceived as gaudy. The purple-yellow/orange-blue/green scheme is perceived as suitable. The orange-green-violet split-complement is perceived as delicate.

COLOR SCALES

A single hue can be mixed with differing quantities of pure white and pure black to produce an unlimited number of shades, tones, and tints. The color equation chart shown

A mathematical description of color mixing formulas for tints, shades, and tones, expressed as a percentage of Color/White/Black.

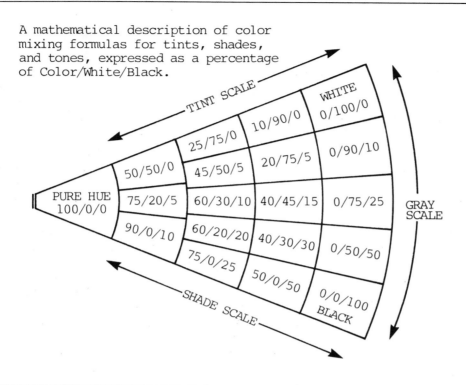

Fig. 9-8. Color equation chart, representing the tint scale, shade scale, gray scale, and tone scale. Color equations take the natural visual order of color and reduce it to mathematical equations.

in Fig. 9-8 is the same methodology used by household paint manufacturers and textile mills to precisely control the colors they use in their products.

The mixtures that fall between the pure hue and pure white, form a tint scale. The mixtures that fall between the pure hue and pure black, form a shade scale. The mixtures that fall between pure white and pure black are grays. The mixtures formed by the pure hue as it migrates to various positions along that gray scale are called tones. Figure 9-9 illustrates this concept in its simplest form. Figure 9-8 depicts the precise mixing formulas used by this scientific approach to the creation of shades, tones, and tints.

SCALES

The human eye can recognize nine distinct shades of gray between pure white and pure black. This scale is depicted in Fig. 9-10. The halftoning capabilities of QuickC and Turbo C make it possible for the C graphics programmer to mimic this gray scale on the display screen. Even the dark-to-light scales of other hues can be created on the screen, including the blues, greens, reds, cyans, magentas, and browns of the standard 16-color IBM-compatible palette discussed earlier. This means that the standard hues found in the 16-color palette can be expanded to a palette of over 149 shades (23 shades each of 8 different hues minus duplication), all of which can be shown simultaneously on the screen.

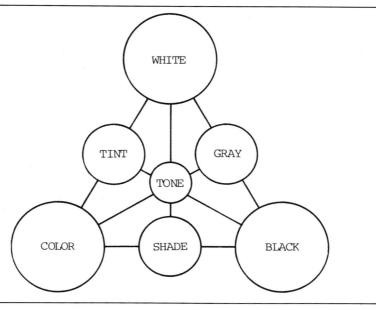

Fig. 9-9. Color chart in concept only, minus the color equation formulas. Also known as the tint-shade-tone subtraction model.

Fig. 9-10. The human eye can recognize nine distinct shades of gray between pure white and pure black.

| | MIXTURE | |
	white	black
BLACK	0%	100%
1	15%	85%
2	35%	65%
3	50%	50%
4	65%	35%
5	75%	25%
6	85%	15%
7	90%	10%
8	95%	5%
9	98%	2%
WHITE	100%	0%

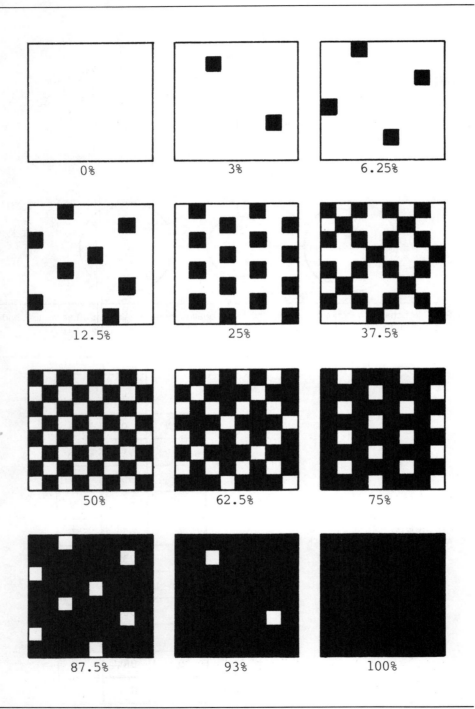

Fig. 9-11. A set of 8×8 matrices can be used to create a range of halftones for any two hardware colors.

If different hues are intermixed (different percentages of green and blue, for example), over 2,400 different mixed colors can be created and displayed simultaneously in any 16-color screen mode.

SHADING MATRICES

Figure 9-11 shows a set of 8×8 matrices which can create a full range of halftones between any two hardware colors when using an IBM-compatible graphics adapter such as a VGA, EGA, CGA, or MCGA.

Both QuickC and Turbo C use a halftoning strategy which describes an area on the display screen sized eight pixels by eight pixels. The 25% halftone shown in Fig. 9-11, for example, is coded thus:

First, determine the bit by bit nature of the first horizontal row. The second and the sixth pixel are turned on, so the bit code is 01000100. This is the same as the decimal number 68.

Next, determine the bit pattern used by the second row. It is 00010001, which is decimal number 17.

Because these two horizontal patterns are repeated for the rest of the 8×8 matrix, the string of numbers which would describe the bit pattern (tiling mask) for the 25% halftone pattern is 68, 17, 68, 17, 68, 17, 68, 17.

To enable your C compiler to paint these patterns when using area fill, you first declare a numeric array holding this string of numbers. You would use the following syntax, for example:

char fill__25[ ] = {68,17,68,17,68,17,68,17};

The array is named **fill__25**, but you can use any name you wish.

If you are using QuickC, you would activate this fill mask with the following instruction:

__setfillmask(fill__25);

The halftone would be applied using the active drawing color.

If you are using Turbo C, you would use the following instruction:

setfillpattern(fill__25,color);

where the variable named **color** contains a number from 0 to 15, which is the color to be applied using the halftone pattern.

Any subsequent use of QuickC's **__floodfill** or of Turbo C's **floodfill** instruction would cause the area fill to be performed using the halftone pattern defined in the array named **fill__25**.

It is important to note that QuickC and Turbo C use different algorithms in their halftoning routines. QuickC sets only those pixels which are defined as "on" in the pixel pattern. The background graphics—the pre-existing image—is left otherwise unaltered. Turbo C, on the other hand, overwrites and obliterates the background. TurboC's halftone pattern is always applied as a mixture of colored pixels and black pixels.

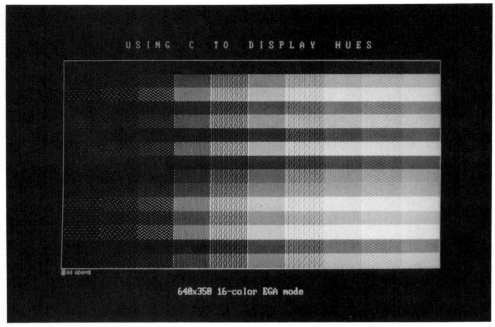

Fig. 9-12(a). The VGA and EGA video display produced by the demonstration program in Fig. 9-13.

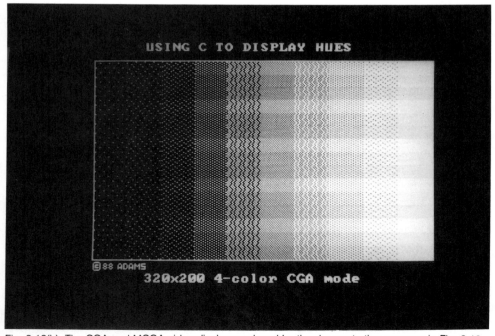

Fig. 9-12(b). The CGA and MCGA video display produced by the demonstration program in Fig. 9-13.

CASE STUDY: A DEMONSTRATION PROGRAM

The photograph in Fig. 9-12(a) shows the video output of the demonstration program listed in Fig. 9-13 when used with the VGA or EGA. The photograph in Fig. 9-12(b) shows the video output of the demonstration program listed in Fig. 9-13 when used with a CGA or MCGA. Figure 9-13 contains the QuickC version of the program; for a Turbo C version of the program refer to Fig. E-1 in Appendix E. If you are using the companion disk for this book you can load program QC-002.C with QuickC; load program TC-002.C with Turbo C.

This demonstration program uses the scientific scale theorem depicted in Fig. 9-10 and the set of 8×8 matrices shown in Fig. 9-11 to create 150 different halftones, displayed simultaneously on your monitor. The resulting halftones are very effective in the higher resolution graphics modes, including the 640×480 16-color mode of the VGA, the 640×350 16-color mode of the VGA/EGA, and the 640×200 16-color mode of the VGA/EGA. The image is less convincing when lower resolution modes are used, including the 320×200 4-color mode of the CGA/MCGA and the 320×200 16-color mode of the VGA/EGA. You can see how the pixel pattern becomes somewhat overbearing in the low resolution modes, whereas the halftone pattern is blended together more smoothly by the high resolution modes.

Although the demonstration program in Fig. 9-13 (and Fig. E-1) is only an introductory example of halftoning, it is clear that this technique can be used to create all the shades, tones, and tints discussed earlier. This means that you, the C graphics programmer, can exercise precise control over the display screen if you choose.

The **INCLUDE FILES** section of the program listing asks the C compiler to merge the appropriate header files into the source code. These header files simply declare variables which are used in the BIOS call for the keyboard input, the text display routines, and the graphics functions.

The **DECLARATIONS** section of the program listing defines all the numeric values which are later used to create the halftone patterns. The arrays are composed of the numeric codes first introduced in Fig. 9-11.

The source code next declares the subroutines which have been created in the program listing. Note, for example the declaration for the subroutine named **notice( )**. The first use of the word **void** tells you that the subroutine does not return any result to the caller. The contents of the appended parentheses tell you that the subroutine named **notice( )** expects the caller to pass on to it two floating-point values. All the other subroutines declared in this section of the source code neither return any value nor expect to receive any values from the caller.

The **DECLARATIONS** section next declares and initializes the variable used in the program. By declaring these variables at this point in the source code, they can be used by all routines of the program.

The **main( )** routine appears next. First, **main( )** calls the subroutine named **graphics_setup( )** to initialize the highest graphics mode permitted by the hardware. If you have a VGA, this program runs in the 640×480 16-color mode. If you have an EGA and an enhanced monitor, this program runs in the 640×350 16-color mode. If you have an EGA and a standard color display, this monitor runs in the 640×200 16-color mode. If you have a CGA or MCGA, this program runs in the 320×200 4-color mode.

Note how the **main( )** routine calls a subroutine named **halftone_swatch( )**. This subroutine sets the halftone mask to the appropriate pattern and fills the interior of the rectangle. The subroutine creates ten shades in the color that has been established in the **main( )** routine. By calling this subroutine 15 times, the software colors ranging from 1 to 15 can be displayed against a black background.

After the graphics have been completed, the **main( )** routine calls a subroutine named **keyboard( )**. This subroutine uses the BIOS to check for the presence of the ESC keystroke in the keyboard buffer. The ESC keystroke is ASCII code 27. In simple terms, the subroutine merely keeps looping while the keystroke is not equal to ASCII code 27 (the != operator). As soon as ASCII 27 is discovered, the subroutine passes control back to the **main( )** routine, which calls **quit_pgm( )** to gracefully end the program.

The subroutine named **quit_pgm( )** clears the screen, restores the original screen mode, and then returns to the **main( )** routine. By convention, when C encounters the final instruction in a **main( )** routine, it ends the program. A more professional way to terminate this program would be to add the instruction, **exit(0);**, to the subroutine named **quit_pgm.**

ADVANCED PSYCHOLOGY OF COLOR

You may be surprised to learn that any given hue can be manipulated on your computer screen to produce a wide variety of different psychological effects. The technique used is the same scientific approach used by artists who have been properly schooled in color theory.

For example, the same red hue can be manipulated to produce the following different visual effects:

- filmy, like a misty fog
- transparent, like tinted glass
- luminous, like a traffic light
- lustrous, like silk
- metallic, like colored foil
- iridescent, like a pearl

Law of Field Size

It is the Law of Field Size that makes possible these transformations of perception. Simply stated, the background against which the red hue is shown will influence the eye's perception of the quality of the red hue. In all the examples described above, it is not the red hue which changes on the computer screen, it is the background.

A dark field (composed of shades) simulates dim illumination and produces lustrous effects. A light field (composed of tints) simulates bright illumination and produces a chromatic mist effect. A grayish field (composed of tones) simulates mist and distance, and produces iridescent effects.

A few specific examples will demonstrate how this advanced technique works.

Lustrous Effects

For example, suppose you want the red hue to appear lustrous, like the shine of fine silk. You could achieve this by having the background graphics composed of shades (pure hues mixed with varying percentages of pure black). Now, any pure hue (the red) will appear exceptionally brilliant by comparison.

Iridescent Effects

Suppose you wanted the red hue to appear iridescent, like the subtle inherent glow of an opal or a pearl. In nature, this iridescence is actually caused by diffraction of light rays. By keeping the background on the computer screen grayish in tone, the eye will be deceived into perceiving mistiness and uniformly reduced chroma. The pure red hue will appear to glow in an iridescent manner.

UNTAPPED POTENTIAL

Clearly, the amazing potential of the VGA and EGA graphics adapters has barely been touched by existing software. By studying the demonstration program in this chapter—and by adding your own additional halftone patterns—you can begin to explore the exciting field of color theory. For the purposes of this book, however, it is time to move on to other discussions.

Fig. 9-13. Program listing for hues, tones, and shades—QuickC version. VGA/EGA/CGA/CGA compatible. For Turbo C version, consult Appendix E.

```
/*_____


                              qc-002.c


        Function:  This program displays the versatile range of
        colors available on VGA, EGA, and CGA graphics adapters.

        Compatibility:  Supports all graphics adapters and monitors.
        The software uses the 640x480 16-color mode if a VGA is
        present, the 640x350 16-color mode if an EGA and enhanced
        monitor are present, the 640x200 16-color mode if an EGA and
        standard monitor are present, and the 320x200 4-color mode
        if a CGA is present.

        Copyright 1988 Lee Adams and TAB BOOKS Inc.



        _____


                    I N C L U D E    F I L E S           */

        #include <dos.h>                    /* supports the BIOS call */
        #include <stdio.h>             /* supports the printf function */
        #include <graph.h>          /* supports the graphics functions */

        /*_____


                      D E C L A R A T I O N S            */

        struct videoconfig vc;              /* table of video parameters */
```

```
char fill_3[ ]={0,32,0,0,0,2,0,0};                    /*    3% fill */
char fill_6[ ]={32,0,2,0,128,0,8,0};                  /* 6.25% fill */
char fill_12[ ]={32,2,128,8,32,2,128,8};              /* 12.5% fill */
char fill_25[ ]={68,17,68,17,68,17,68,17};            /*   25% fill */
char fill_37[ ]={146,41,148,73,164,73,146,73};        /* 37.5% fill */
char fill_50[ ]={85,170,85,170,85,170,85,170};        /*   50% fill */
char fill_62[ ]={109,214,107,182,91,182,109,182};     /* 62.5% fill */
char fill_75[ ]={187,238,187,238,187,238,187,238};    /*   75% fill */
char fill_87[ ]={223,253,127,247,223,253,127,247};    /* 87.5% fill */

                   /* declare global subroutines */
void keyboard(void);void quit_pgm(void);void halftone_swatch(void);
void notice(float x,float y);void graphics_setup(void);

                   /* declare global variables */
float x,y,h,v,xl,vl;float sxl,syl,sx2,sy2;
int C0=0,Cl=1,C2=2,C3=3,C4=4,C5=5,C6=6,C7=7,C8=8,C9=9,C10=10,
    Cl1=11,Cl2=12,Cl3=13,Cl4=14,Cl5=15,mode_flag=0;
float x_res,y_res;

/*_____


                M A I N    R O U T I N E                      */

main(){
graphics_setup();                        /* establish graphics mode */
_getvideoconfig(&vc);                    /* initialize video table */

_setcolor(C8);halftone_swatch();
x=xl;y=y+vl;_setcolor(C7);halftone_swatch();
x=xl;y=y+vl;_setcolor(Cl5);halftone_swatch();
x=xl;y=y+vl;_setcolor(Cl);halftone_swatch();
x=xl;y=y+vl;_setcolor(C9);halftone_swatch();
x=xl;y=y+vl;_setcolor(C6);halftone_swatch();
x=xl;y=y+vl;_setcolor(Cl4);halftone_swatch();
x=xl;y=y+vl;_setcolor(C4);halftone_swatch();
x=xl;y=y+vl;_setcolor(Cl2);halftone_swatch();
x=xl;y=y+vl;_setcolor(C5);halftone_swatch();
x=xl;y=y+vl;_setcolor(Cl3);halftone_swatch();
x=xl;y=y+vl;_setcolor(C3);halftone_swatch();
x=xl;y=y+vl;_setcolor(Cl1);halftone_swatch();
x=xl;y=y+vl;_setcolor(C2);halftone_swatch();
x=xl;y=y+vl;_setcolor(Cl0);halftone_swatch();
_setcolor(C7);_rectangle(_GBORDER,sxl,syl,sx2,sy2);

notice(sxl+1,sy2+2);                                      /* notice */

keyboard();                      /* wait for user to press <Esc> */
quit_pgm();                      /* end the program gracefully */
}

/*_____


         SUBROUTINE: DRAW HALFTONE SWATCHES                   */

void halftone_swatch(void){
```

```
_setfillmask(fill_3);_rectangle(_GFILLINTERIOR,x,y,x+h,y+v);
x=x+h;_setfillmask(fill_6);_rectangle(_GFILLINTERIOR,x,y,x+h,y+v);
x=x+h;_setfillmask(fill_12);_rectangle(_GFILLINTERIOR,x,y,x+h,y+v);
x=x+h;_setfillmask(fill_25);_rectangle(_GFILLINTERIOR,x,y,x+h,y+v);
x=x+h;_setfillmask(fill_37);_rectangle(_GFILLINTERIOR,x,y,x+h,y+v);
x=x+h;_setfillmask(fill_50);_rectangle(_GFILLINTERIOR,x,y,x+h,y+v);
x=x+h;_setfillmask(fill_62);_rectangle(_GFILLINTERIOR,x,y,x+h,y+v);
x=x+h;_setfillmask(fill_75);_rectangle(_GFILLINTERIOR,x,y,x+h,y+v);
x=x+h;_setfillmask(fill_87);_rectangle(_GFILLINTERIOR,x,y,x+h,y+v);
x=x+h;_setfillmask(NULL);_rectangle(_GFILLINTERIOR,x,y,x+h,y+v);
return;}

/*_____


            SUBROUTINE: CHECK THE KEYBOARD BUFFER            */

void keyboard(void){
union u_type {int a;char b[3];} keystroke;
int get_keystroke(void);            /* declare a local subroutine */

do keystroke.a=get_keystroke();
while (keystroke.b[0]!=27);          /* return if <Esc> is pressed */
}

/*          LOCAL SUBROUTINE: RETRIEVE ONE KEYSTROKE          */

int get_keystroke(void){
union REGS regs;regs.h.ah=0;return int86(0x16,&regs,&regs);}

/*_____


            SUBROUTINE: GRACEFUL EXIT FROM THE PROGRAM            */

void quit_pgm(void){
_clearscreen(_GCLEARSCREEN);_setvideomode(_DEFAULTMODE);}

/*_____


            SUBROUTINE: VGA/EGA/CGA compatibility module

    This subroutine invokes the highest-resolution graphics mode
    which is permitted by the hardware.  The 640x480 16-color mode
    is established if a VGA is present.  The 640x350 16-color mode
    is established if an EGA is being used with an enhanced color
    display monitor or a multiscanning monitor.  The 640x200
    16-color mode is established if an EGA is being used with a
    standard color monitor.  The 320x200 4-color mode is invoked
    if a CGA is present.                                        */

void graphics_setup(void){

VGA_mode:
if (_setvideomode(_VRES16COLOR)==0) {goto EGA_ECD_mode;}
else {x_res=640;y_res=480;mode_flag=1;x=19;y=39;h=60;v=24;x1=19;
      v1=25;sx1=18;sy1=38;sx2=620;sy2=414;
```

```
        _settextcolor(7);_settextposition(30,27);
        _outtext("640x480 16-color VGA mode");
        _settextposition(1,16);
        _outtext("U S I N G    C    T O    D I S P L A Y    H U E S");
        return;}

EGA_ECD_mode:                      .
if (_setvideomode(_ERESCOLOR)==0) {goto EGA_SCD_mode;}
else {x_res=640;y_res=350;mode_flag=2;x=19;y=28;h=60;v=18;xl=19;
        vl=19;sxl=18;syl=27;sx2=620;sy2=313;
        _settextcolor(7);_settextposition(25,27);
        _outtext("640x350 16-color EGA mode");
        _settextposition(1,16);
        _outtext("U S I N G    C    T O    D I S P L A Y     H U E S")
        return;}

EGA_SCD_mode:
if (_setvideomode(_HRES16COLOR)==0) {goto CGA_mode;}
else {x_res=640;y_res=200;C0=0;mode_flag=3;x=19;y=16;h=60;v=10;
        xl=19;vl=11;sxl=18;syl=15;sx2=620;sy2=181;
        _settextcolor(7);_settextposition(25,27);
        _outtext("640x200 16-color EGA mode");
        _settextposition(1,16);
        _outtext("U S I N G    C    T O    D I S P L A Y     H U E S");
        return;}

CGA_mode:
if (_setvideomode(_MRES4COLOR)==0) {goto abort_message;}
else {x_res=320;y_res=200;C0=0;Cl=3;C2=1;C3=2;C4=1;C5=3,C6=2;C7=1;
        C8=3;C9=1;Cl0=2;Cl1=3;Cl2=2;Cl3=1;Cl4=3;Cl5=2;mode_flag=4;
        x=16;y=16;h=30;v=10;xl=10;vl=11;sxl=9;syl=15;sx2=310;sy2=181;
        _settextcolor(3);_settextposition(25,8);
        _outtext("320x200 4-color CGA mode");
        _settextposition(1,8);_outtext("USING C TO DISPLAY HUES");
        return;}

abort_message:
printf("\n\nUnable to proceed.\n");
printf("Requires VGA, EGA, or CGA adapter\n");
printf("   with appropriate monitor.\n");
printf("Please refer to the book.\n\n");
exit(0);
}

/*_____


                SUBROUTINE: Copyright Notice
     This subroutine displays the standard copyright notice.
     If you are typing in this program from the book you can
     safely omit this subroutine, provided that you also remove
     the instruction "notice()" from the main routine.        */

int copyright[][3]={0x7c00,0x0000,0x0000,0x8231,
0x819c,0x645e,0xba4a,0x4252,0x96d0,0xa231,0x8252,0x955e,0xba4a,
0x43d2,0xf442,0x8231,0x825c,0x945e,0x7c00,0x0000,0x0000};
void notice(float x, float y){
int a,b,c; int tl=0;
for (tl=0;tl<=6;tl++){a=copyright[tl][0];b=copyright[tl][1];
```

```
c=copyright[tl][2];_setlinestyle(a);_moveto(x,y);_lineto(x+15,y);
_setlinestyle(b);_moveto(x+16,y);_lineto(x+31,y);_setlinestyle(c);
_moveto(x+32,y);_lineto(x+47,y);y=y+1;};_setlinestyle(0xFFFF);
return;}
```

/*_____

                        End of source code   */

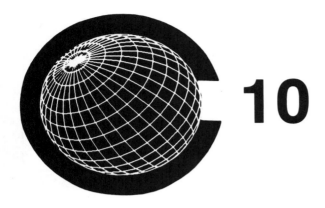 **10**

Drawing on the Screen

There are two methods for drawing on the display screen—the dynamic coordinates methods and the database coordinates method. Both approaches use the xy coordinates derived from a template drawing, as shown in Fig. 10-1. If a 640×480 device-independent template grid is used, the resulting xy coordinates must be filtered through a windowing routine before they can be plotted on the display screen, but the program will be capable of running on any IBM-compatible graphics adapter. The concept of a device-independent template was discussed in Chapters 5, 6, and 7.

Dynamic and Database Coordinates

Using dynamic coordinates means specifying the xy screen coordinates with the C drawing instruction, for example **line to(319,199)**. Because the xy screen coordinates are bundled with the drawing instruction, it is difficult to create loops which can handle repetitive drawing processes. Using dynamic coordinates enables the C programmer to develop a working prototype very quickly.

Using database coordinates means storing all the xy screen coordinates in a database (usually an array in RAM). While the drawing process is underway, the program fetches the xy screen coordinates it requires from the database. Because no xy screen coordinates are actually coded alongside the drawing instructions, it is possible to write loops for repetitive drawing processes. On each pass through the loop the program retrieves another set of xy screen coordinates from the database.

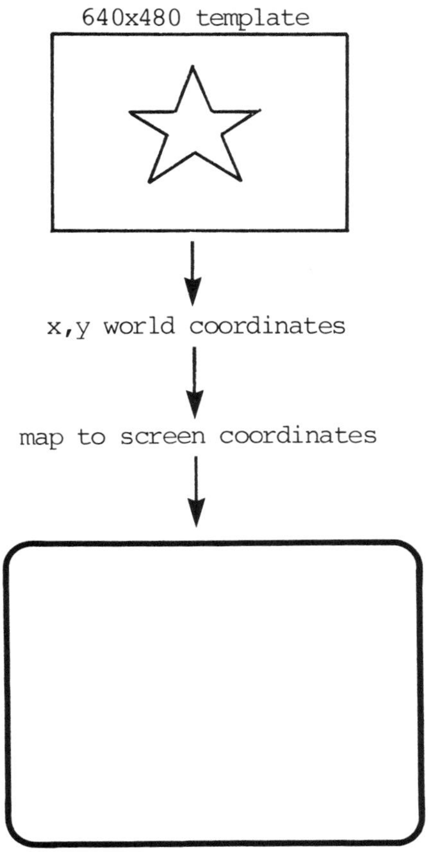

640x480 template

x,y world coordinates

map to screen coordinates

Fig. 10-1. The xy drawing coordinates can be derived from the template. A simple window mapping formula will yield the appropriate sx sy screen coordinates for the current graphics mode.

CASE STUDY: A DEMONSTRATION PROGRAM

A demonstration program will serve to provide a working example of how dynamic coordinates can be used to create sophisticated graphics on the display screen.

The line drawing in Fig. 10-2 is taken from the original pencil sketch used to prepare the demonstration program for this chapter. The sketch was prepared over a 640×480 grid, making it possible to determine the set of xy world coordinates that would describe the various graphical elements in the drawing.

By inspecting Fig. 10-2, you can begin to formulate an algorithm for producing the image on the display screen. First, the program might use area fill to create the solid background field. Then, a solid black rectangle could be created, representing the shadow which is cast by the graphic (called a *dropshadow* by professional artists and graphic designers). A solid, colored square might next be drawn, and finally a polyline might be used to draw the silhouette of the star, which could be filled with the appropriate color.

The photograph in Fig. 10-3 shows the video output of the demonstration program in Fig. 10-4. The program listing in Fig. 10-4 is the QuickC version. If you are using Turbo C, then use the listing provided in Fig. E-2 of Appendix E. If you have the companion

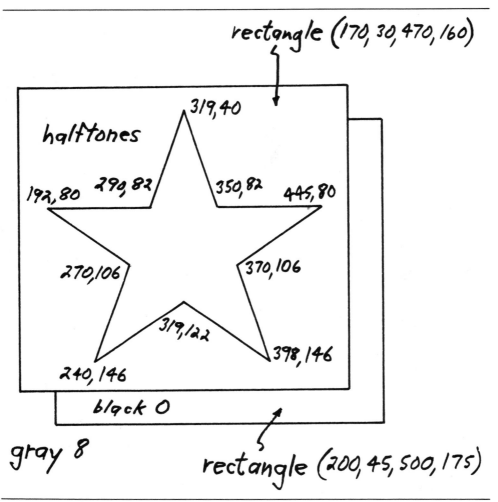

rectangle (170, 30, 470, 160)

halftones

319,40

192,80   290,82   350,82   445,80

270,106   370,106

319,122

240,146   398,146

black 0

gray 8   rectangle (200, 45, 500, 175)

Fig. 10-2. The original sketch used to derive the xy coordinates used by the demonstration program in Fig. 10-4.

disk for this book, then load the program named QC-003.C if you are using QuickC, or load the program named TC-003.C if you are using Turbo C.

The demonstration program will run on all IBM-compatible graphics adapters. If you are using a VGA, then the program will run in the 640×480 16-color mode. If you are using an EGA with an enhanced monitor, then the program will run in the 640×350 16-color mode. If you are using an EGA with a standard color display, then the program will run in the 640×200 16-color mode. If you are using a CGA or MCGA, then the program runs in the 320×200 4-color mode.

Program Flow

The conceptual program flow for the demonstration program is depicted in Fig. 10-5. This generic format will prevail for all the demonstration programs in this book.

Fig. 10-3. The video display produced by the demonstration program in Fig. 10-4.

First, the program source code uses **#include** directives to identify which header files are to be merged into the code by the compiler. Next, the area fill codes, global subroutines, and global variables are declared.

The **main( )** routine first called upon the **graphics__setup( )** subroutine to establish the highest graphics mode which is permitted by the hardware. Next, the graphical elements are drawn on the screen. Before each xy point is plotted on the screen, however, the windowing subroutine named **cords( )** is called to map the point to fit whichever graphics mode has been set up by the **graphics__setup( )** subroutine.

After the image has been completed, the **main( )** routine calls a keyboard subroutine to wait for input from the user. When this arrives, via a keystroke, the **main( )** routine calls a final subroutine to tidy up and to return to the original text mode.

Analysis of the Program

Note how the first major block of code in the **main( )** routine uses the rectangle function to create the background, then the dropshadow, and finally the colored block graphic. The next block of code adds the airbrushed effect to the block graphic. (An explanation of this algorithm is presented in the next chapter; it is not necessary to understand the airbrush procedure yet.)

The third major block of code in the **main( )** routine draws the star. Observe how the **sx** and **sy** screen coordinates are first defined according to the pencil sketch, then the **coords( )** subroutine is called to map these 640×480 coordinates to fit whichever screen mode is in effect. Finally, the **line to** instruction is used to plot the resulting **sx** and **sy** points onto the display screen.

The keyboard subroutine which follows the **main( )** routine in the program listing is the same subroutine used in the demonstration program in the previous chapter.

The compatibility module in this program listing is the same subroutine discussed in previous chapters. Note how each block of code in the compatibility module defines the **x__res** and **y__res** variables as the screen mode is initialized. These **x__res** and **y__res** variables are used by the mapping subroutine, **coords( )**.

Fig. 10-4. Program listing for a 2D illustration using dynamic coordinates—QuickC version. VGA/EGA/CGA/CGA compatible. For Turbo C version, consult Appendix E.

```
/*_____

                          qc-003.c

    Function:  This program demonstrates how to draw on the
    screen using dynamic coordinates.

    Compatibility:  Supports all graphics adapters and monitors.
    The software uses the 640x480 16-color mode if a VGA is
    present, the 640x350 16-color mode if an EGA and enhanced
    monitor are present, the 640x200 16-color mode if an EGA and
    standard monitor are present, and the 320x200 4-color mode
    if a CGA is present.

    Remarks:  Refer to the book for guidance in preparing a
    template and for instruction in design techniques.

    Copyright 1988 Lee Adams and TAB BOOKS Inc.

    _____


               I N C L U D E    F I L E S              */

#include <dos.h>                      /* supports the BIOS call */
#include <stdio.h>               /* supports the printf function */
#include <graph.h>           /* supports the graphics functions */

/*_____


               D E C L A R A T I O N S                 */

struct videoconfig vc;              /* table of video parameters */

char fill_3[ ]={0,32,0,0,0,2,0,0};              /*    3% fill */
char fill_6[ ]={32,0,2,0,128,0,8,0};            /* 6.25% fill */
char fill_12[ ]={32,2,128,8,32,2,128,8};        /* 12.5% fill */
char fill_25[ ]={68,17,68,17,68,17,68,17};      /*   25% fill */
char fill_37[ ]={146,41,148,73,164,73,146,73};  /* 37.5% fill */
char fill_50[ ]={85,170,85,170,85,170,85,170};  /*   50% fill */
char fill_62[ ]={109,214,107,182,91,182,109,182}; /* 62.5% fill */
```

```
char fill_75[]={187,238,187,238,187,238,187,238};  /*   75% fill */
char fill_87[]={223,253,127,247,223,253,127,247};  /* 87.5% fill */

                  /* declare global subroutines */
void keyboard(void);void quit_pgm(void);
void notice(float x, float y);
void graphics_setup(void);void coords(void);

float sx=0,sy=0;                      /* screen display coordinates */

float x_res=0,y_res=0;                /* dimensions of screen */
int C0=0,Cl=1,C2=2,C3=3,C4=4,C5=5,C6=6,C7=7,C8=8,C9=9,C10=10,
Cll=11,C12=12,C13=13,C14=14,C15=15,mode_flag=0;
float sxl=0,syl=0,sx2=0,sy2=0;

/*_____


                  M A I N    R O U T I N E                    */

main(){
graphics_setup();                    /* establish graphics mode */
_getvideoconfig(&vc);                /* initialize video table */

_setcolor(C7);_setfillmask(fill_25);
sx=0;sy=24;coords();sxl=sx;syl=sy;
sx=639;sy=454;coords();sx2=sx;sy2=sy;
_rectangle(_GFILLINTERIOR,sxl,syl,sx2,sy2)    /* draw background */
_setfillmask(NULL);_setcolor(C0);
sx=200;sy=108;coords();sxl=sx;syl=sy;
sx=500;sy=420;coords();sx2=sx;sy2=sy;
_rectangle(_GFILLINTERIOR,sxl,syl,sx2,sy2);        /* dropshadow */
_setcolor(C9);
sx=170;sy=72;coords();sxl=sx;syl=sy;
sx=470;sy=384;coords();sx2=sx;sy2=sy;
_rectangle(_GFILLINTERIOR,sxl,syl,sx2,sy2); /* the block graphic */

_setcolor(Cl);            /* add halftoning to the block graphic */
sx=170;sy=72;coords();sxl=sx;syl=sy;
sx=470;sy=98;coords();sx2=sx;sy2=sy;
_setfillmask(fill_6);_rectangle(_GFILLINTERIOR,sxl,syl,sx2,sy2);
sx=170;sy=98;coords();sxl=sx;syl=sy;
sx=470;sy=132;coords();sx2=sx;sy2=sy;
_setfillmask(fill_12);_rectangle(_GFILLINTERIOR,sxl,syl,sx2,sy2);
sx=170;sy=132;coords();sxl=sx;syl=sy;
sx=470;sy=168;coords();sx2=sx;sy2=sy;
_setfillmask(fill_25);_rectangle(_GFILLINTERIOR,sxl,syl,sx2,sy2);
sx=170;sy=168;coords();sxl=sx;syl=sy;
sx=470;sy=204;coords();sx2=sx;sy2=sy;
_setfillmask(fill_37);_rectangle(_GFILLINTERIOR,sxl,syl,sx2,sy2);
sx=170;sy=204;coords();sxl=sx;syl=sy;
sx=470;sy=240;coords();sx2=sx;sy2=sy;
_setfillmask(fill_50);_rectangle(_GFILLINTERIOR,sxl,syl,sx2,sy2);
sx=170;sy=240;coords();sxl=sx;syl=sy;
sx=470;sy=276;coords();sx2=sx;sy2=sy;
```

```
_setfillmask(fill_62);_rectangle(_GFILLINTERIOR,sxl,syl,sx2,sy2);
sx=170;sy=276;coords();sxl=sx;syl=sy;
sx=470;sy=312;coords();sx2=sx;sy2=sy;
_setfillmask(fill_75);_rectangle(_GFILLINTERIOR,sxl,syl,sx2,sy2);
sx=170;sy=312;coords();sxl=sx;syl=sy;
sx=470;sy=348;coords();sx2=sx;sy2=sy;
_setfillmask(fill_87);_rectangle(_GFILLINTERIOR,sxl,syl,sx2,sy2);
sx=170;sy=348;coords();sxl=sx;syl=sy;
sx=470;sy=384;coords();sx2=sx;sy2=sy;
_setfillmask(NULL);_rectangle(_GFILLINTERIOR,sxl,syl,sx2,sy2);

_setcolor(C7);                                    /* draw the star */
sx=319;sy=96;coords();_moveto(sx,sy);
sx=350;sy=192;coords();_lineto(sx,sy);
sx=445;sy=192;coords();_lineto(sx,sy);
sx=370;sy=254;coords();_lineto(sx,sy);
sx=398;sy=350;coords();_lineto(sx,sy);
sx=319;sy=293;coords();_lineto(sx,sy);
sx=240;sy=350;coords();_lineto(sx,sy);
sx=270;sy=254;coords();_lineto(sx,sy);
sx=192;sy=192;coords();_lineto(sx,sy);
sx=290;sy=192;coords();_lineto(sx,sy);
sx=319;sy=96;coords();_lineto(sx,sy);
sx=319;sy=238;coords();_floodfill(sx,sy,C7);

sx=0;sy=0;coords();notice(sx,sy);                          /* notice */

keyboard();                        /* wait for user to press <Esc> */
quit_pgm();                          /* end the program gracefully */
}

/*_____


              SUBROUTINE: CHECK THE KEYBOARD BUFFER              */

void keyboard(void){
union u_type {int a;char b[3];} keystroke;
int get_keystroke(void);          /* declare a local subroutine */

do keystroke.a=get_keystroke();
while (keystroke.b[0]!=27);        /* return if <Esc> is pressed */
}

/*          LOCAL SUBROUTINE: RETRIEVE ONE KEYSTROKE              */

int get_keystroke(void){
union REGS regs;regs.h.ah=0;return int86(0x16,&regs,&regs);}

/*_____


              SUBROUTINE: GRACEFUL EXIT FROM THE PROGRAM         */

void quit_pgm(void){
```

```
        _clearscreen(_GCLEARSCREEN);_setvideomode(_DEFAULTMODE);}
```

```
/*_____


                    SUBROUTINE: VGA/EGA/CGA compatibility module

        This subroutine invokes the highest-resolution graphics mode
        which is permitted by the hardware.  The 640x480 16-color mode
        is established if a VGA is present.  The 640x350 16-color mode
        is established if an EGA is being used with an enhanced color
        display monitor or a multiscanning monitor.  The 640x200
        16-color mode is established if an EGA is being used with a
        standard color monitor.  The 320x200 4-color mode is invoked
        if a CGA is present.                                          */

void graphics_setup(void){

VGA_mode:
if (_setvideomode(_VRES16COLOR)==0) {goto EGA_ECD_mode;}
else {x_res=640;y_res=480;C0=0;C1=1;C2=2;C3=3;C4=4;C5=5,C6=6;C7=7;
      C8=8;C9=9;C10=10;C11=11;C12=12;C13=13;C14=14;C15=15;
      mode_flag=1;
      _settextcolor(7);_settextposition(30,1);
      _outtext("640x480 16-color VGA mode.");
      return;}

EGA_ECD_mode:
if (_setvideomode(_ERESCOLOR)==0) {goto EGA_SCD_mode;}
else {x_res=640;y_res=350;C0=0;C1=1;C2=2;C3=3;C4=4;C5=5,C6=6;C7=7;
      C8=8;C9=9;C10=10;C11=11;C12=12;C13=13;C14=14;C15=15;
      mode_flag=2;
      _settextcolor(7);_settextposition(25,1);
      _outtext("640x350 16-color EGA mode.");
      return;}

EGA_SCD_mode:
if (_setvideomode(_HRES16COLOR)==0) {goto CGA_mode;}
else {x_res=640;y_res=200;C0=0;C1=1;C2=2;C3=3;C4=4;C5=5,C6=6;C7=7;
      C8=8;C9=9;C10=10;C11=11;C12=12;C13=13;C14=14;C15=15;
      mode_flag=3;
      _settextcolor(7);_settextposition(25,1);
      _outtext("640x200 16-color EGA mode.");
      return;}

CGA_mode:
if (_setvideomode(_MRES4COLOR)==0) {goto abort_message;}
else {x_res=320;y_res=200;C0=0;C1=1;C2=1;C3=1;C4=1;C5=1,C6=1;C7=3;
      C8=1;C9=0;C10=1;C11=1;C12=1;C13=2;C14=1;C15=3;
      mode_flag=4;
      _settextcolor(3);_settextposition(25,1);
      _outtext("320x200 4-color CGA mode.");
      return;}
```

```
abort_message:
printf("\n\nUnable to proceed.\n");
printf("Requires VGA, EGA, or CGA adapter\n");
printf("   with appropriate monitor.\n");
printf("Please refer to the book.\n\n");
exit(0);
}
```

```
/*_____

                SUBROUTINE: coords()

    This subroutine accepts sx,sy device-independent display
    coordinates and returns sx,sy device-dependent screen
    coordinates scaled to fit the 640x480, 640x350, 640x200, or
    320x200 screen, depending upon the graphics mode being used. */

void coords(void){
sx=sx*(x_res/640);sy=sy*(y_res/480);return;}
```

```
/*_____


                SUBROUTINE: Copyright Notice
    This subroutine displays the standard copyright notice.
    If you are typing in this program from the book you can
    safely omit this subroutine, provided that you also remove
    the instruction "notice()" from the main routine.          */

int copyright[][3]={0x7c00,0x0000,0x0000,0x8231,
0x819c,0x645e,0xba4a,0x4252,0x96d0,0xa231,0x8252,0x955e,0xba4a,
0x43d2,0xf442,0x8231,0x825c,0x945e,0x7c00,0x0000,0x0000};

void notice(float x, float y){
int a,b,c; int tl=0;
for (tl=0;tl<=6;tl++){a=copyright[tl][0];b=copyright[tl][1];
c=copyright[tl][2];_setlinestyle(a);_moveto(x,y);_lineto(x+15,y);
_setlinestyle(b);_moveto(x+16,y);_lineto(x+31,y);_setlinestyle(c);
_moveto(x+32,y);_lineto(x+47,y);y=y+1;};_setlinestyle(0xFFFF);
return;}
```

```
/*_____


                End of source code                          */
```

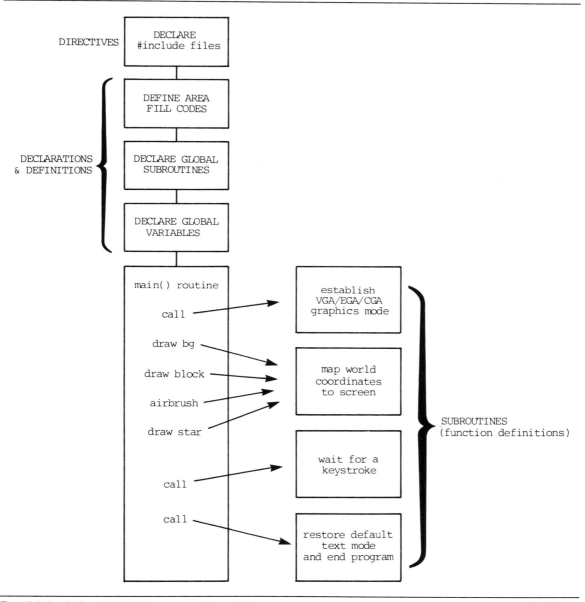

Fig. 10-5. Logic flowchart for the program listing in Fig. 10-4.

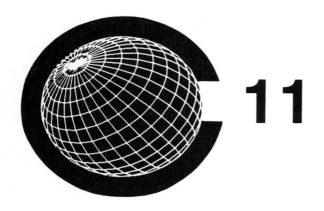

Managing the
Background Graphics

In many instances when creating computer graphics, the background is as important as the foreground. Because all graphical elements are relative—including color, size, shape, and contrast—the quality of the background graphics has a strong influence on the perceived quality of the foreground graphics.

For most purposes, the background of the screen can be considered to be the addressable area of the display monitor. Refer to Fig. 11-1. If the monitor is correctly adjusted, this background field will exhibit a horizontal to vertical ratio of 4:3. A varient of different design schemes can be used to make this background rectangle an important component of the overall screen design.

SCULPTED BACKGROUNDS

Contrast can be used to make backgrounds appear three-dimensional or sculpted in appearance. As Fig. 11-2 illustrates, dark graphics provide the illusion of shadow, while lighter graphics give the illusion of strong sunlight. This contrast often fools the eye into perceiving depth on a flat display screen.

If you are using a VGA or EGA graphics adapter, you can select from intense white (15), normal white (7), and the intense hues (9, 10, 11, 12, 13, and 14) to draw the portions of your background which simulate bright light conditions. For the shadow areas, use black (0) or gray (8). For the remainder of the background use any of the normal intensity hues (1, 2, 3, 4, 5, and 6). If you are using a CGA, you will create the shadow areas with black (0), the highlight areas with white (3), and the remainder of the background with color 1 or 2.

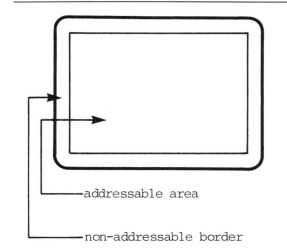

Fig. 11-1. Addressable portions of the graphics screen.

addressable area

non-addressable border

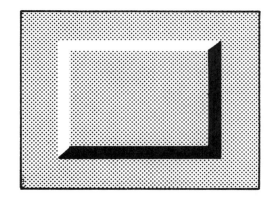

Fig. 11-2. Levels of contrast can be used to simulate a sculpted background.

AIRBRUSHED BACKGROUNDS

Using the halftoning techniques introduced in earlier chapters, you can easily create a background which appears airbrushed, whereby the color of the background shifts delicately from the top of the background to the bottom.

As Fig. 11-3 shows, the halftone area fill is simply a collection of 8×8 pixel matrices. After the pattern mask has been defined by your C program (see Chapter 9), the **floodfill** instruction of QuickC and Turbo C uses the halftone pattern whenever an area fill is requested.

By choosing different halftone percentages for different parts of the screen, as shown in Fig. 11-4, a gradation in color can be produced. This gradation can range from a 6% pattern to a full 100% pattern.

If you are using Turbo C, the halftone pattern overwrites any existing background, thereby providing a halftone which is always expressed as colored pixels against a black

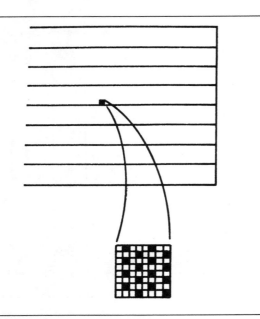

Fig. 11-3. Halftone area fill is used to create airbrushed backgrounds.

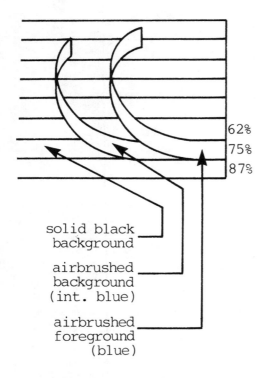

62%
75%
87%

solid black
background

airbrushed
background
(int. blue)

airbrushed
foreground
(blue)

Fig. 11-4. Blue hardware color 1 and blue hardware color 9 are mixed to produce a subtle airbrushed effect.

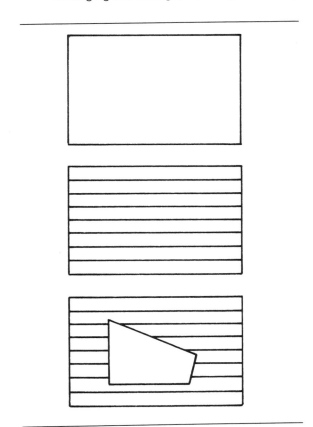

Fig. 11-5. Using airbrushed backgrounds with other foreground graphics. From top: Step One — black screen; Step Two — apply airbrushing; Step Three — use non-conflicting colors to draw the foreground graphic.

field. This provides a dramatic airbrushed background, with plenty of contrast between the top and bottom of the screen.

If you are using QuickC, the halftone pattern sets only those pixels which have been defined by the mask. This means you can invoke more subtle effects that rely upon the existing background as well as the halftone mask to produce an airbrushed effect. For example, if the existing background is intense blue (color 9) and the halftoning is performed in normal blue (color 1), the result is a very delicate shift of colors on the display screen.

Figure 11-5 shows the three-step procedure for generating full color graphics against an airbrushed background. It is essential that the foreground graphic be drawn in colors which are not found in the background graphic, otherwise area fill routines will act erratically. This is because the boundary color (your drawing color) already appears in the background graphics.

If you must use a foreground graphic with colors which have already been used by the airbrushed background, you can use a key matte to ensure that the foreground graphic is drawn correctly. First, draw a silhouette of your foreground image in a color which is not used in the background. Then, use black area fill to blank the interior of this matte. Finally, redraw the silhouette (or other portions) of the foreground graphic in the preferred colors. Because none of the background airbrushing appears in the foreground graphic, the area fill routines will now function correctly.

BORDERS

Rather than using the entire addressable area of the display screen as the background, you can use a smaller area to create the background. In many cases, this will result in a border effect. The designs shown in Fig. 11-6 have been found to produce a visual impact on computer screens.

The standard frame border illustrated in Fig. 11-6 is simply a rectangle or a square. The important thing to remember is to carefully center your foreground graphic inside the frame border. The border can consist of an outline, or it can be a filled rectangle. An effective variation of this border style is the round-cornered border.

The breakout border shown in Fig. 11-6 is an advanced technique based upon the standard round-cornered border. This style serves to make the foreground graphic appear very important and dynamic, because it appears to be "breaking out" of the bounds which circumscribe it.

The elliptical border depicted in Fig. 11-6 can be constructed as either a circle or an oval—either as outline or filled. A powerful derivation of the elliptical border is the bull's eye border. If analogous harmonies (such as yellow-orange-red) are used to fill the concentric rings, the bull's eye border can create a strong visual impact. As Fig. 11-7 shows, even rectangular borders can benefit from the bull's eye theorem, especially when

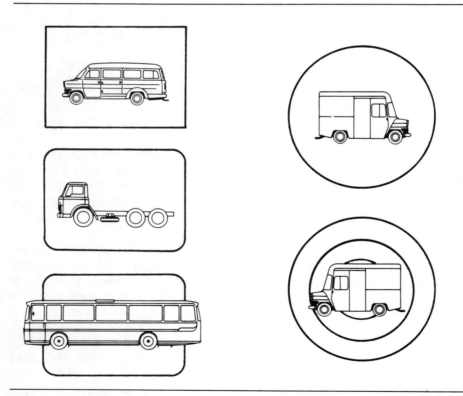

Fig. 11-6. From top left, standard frame border, round-cornered border, breakout border, elliptical border, bull's eye border.

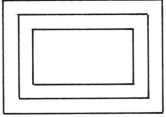

two area fills of the same hue
(ie hardware color 2 green
and hardware color 10 int. green)

Fig. 11-7. Chromatic strategies for
solid filled borders.

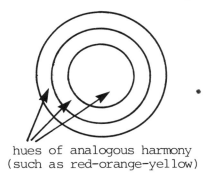

hues of analogous harmony
(such as red-orange-yellow)

analogous color schemes are used. (Refer to Chapter 9 for a detailed discussion of color theory.)

CASE STUDY: A DEMONSTRATION PROGRAM—SCULPTED BACKGROUND

The photograph in Fig. 11-8 depicts the video output of the demonstration program in Fig. 11-9. The program generates a sculpted background using the contrast techniques discussed in this chapter. The program listing in Fig. 11-9 is the QuickC version. If you are using Turbo C, use the program listing provided in Fig. E-3 of Appendix E. If you have the companion disk for this book, load program QC-004.C if you are using QuickC and load program TC-004.C if you are using Turbo C.

This demonstration program supports all IBM-compatible graphics adapters. If you are using a VGA, the program runs in the 640×480 16-color mode. If you are using an EGA with an enhanced monitor, the program will run in the 640×350 16-color mode. If you are using an EGA and a standard color display, the program will use the 640×200 16-color mode. If you are using a CGA or MCGA, the program runs in the 320×200 4-color mode.

Note the compatibility module in the source code. As each different screen mode is initialized, the variables which are used by the drawing loop in the **main( )** routine are initialized.

The **main( )** routine is built around two major blocks of graphics instructions. The first block draws the background graphic. Variable names like **bg**, **shadow**, and **hilite**

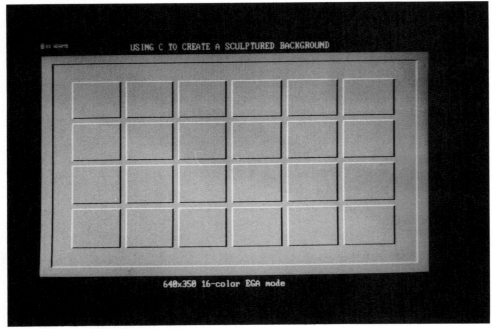

Fig. 11-8. The video display produced by the demonstration program in Fig. 11-9.

have been used to make the logic easy to follow. The second block of graphics instructions is a powerful loop which draws four rows of six sculpted rectangles. For each rectangle, first the top highlight line is drawn, then the shadow lines are drawn down the right side and across the bottom, and finally the final highlight line is drawn up the left side, thereby completing the illusion.

To make this program easier to understand, you may wish to tinker with the values assigned to the **t** and **t1** counters in the drawing loop. It is also interesting to experiment with the various starting positions and displacement factors defined in the compatibility module.

You can force this program to use a lower resolution screen mode, if you wish. Suppose you are using a VGA or EGA and you want to see how the graphics would appear on a CGA. If you are using QuickC, simply edit the first line in the compatibility module to read as follows:

void graphics__setup(void){ goto CGA__mode;

If you are using Turbo C, simply change the appropriate **if/then** instruction by adding the **goto** instruction. If, for example, you are using an EGA and an enhanced monitor, the resulting line would be as follows:

if (graphics__mode==EGAHI) goto CGA__mode;

Fig. 11-9. Program listing for sculpted background—QuickC version. VGA/EGA/CGA/MCGA compatible. For Turbo C version, consult Appendix E.

```
/*_____

                          qc-004.c

    Function:  This program demonstrates how to simulate a
    sculptured background graphic.

    Compatibility:  Supports all graphics adapters and monitors.
    The software uses the 640x480 16-color mode if a VGA is
    present, the 640x350 16-color mode if an EGA and enhanced
    monitor are present, the 640x200 16-color mode if an EGA and
    standard monitor are present, and the 320x200 4-color mode
    if a CGA is present.

    Remarks:  By altering two variables in the declarations
    module you can try out different color combinations.
    The brightness control and the contrast control on your
    monitor have a strong effect on the image's appearance.

    Copyright 1988 Lee Adams and TAB BOOKS Inc.

    _____


                 I N C L U D E   F I L E S             */

#include <dos.h>                        /* supports the DOS call */
#include <stdio.h>              /* supports the printf function */
#include <graph.h>           /* supports the graphics functions */

/*_____


                 D E C L A R A T I O N S               */

struct videoconfig vc;

void keyboard(void);              /* declare global subroutines */
void quit_pgm(void);
void graphics_setup(void);void coords(void);
void notice (float x, float y);

                                   /* declare global variables */
float sx=0,sy=0,x_res=0,y_res=0,sx1=0,sy1=0,sx2=0,sy2=0;
int C0=0,C1=1,C2=2,C3=3,C4=4,C5=5,C6=6,C7=7,C8=8,C9=9,C10=10,
    C11=11,C12=12,C13=13,C14=14,C15=15,mode_flag=0;
int t=1,t1=1;                           /* counters for loops */
float x=52,y=32,x1=52,h1=80,v1=30,h2=81,v2=31,h3=90,v3=35;
int bg=2,shadow=0,hilite=10;

/*_____
```

```
                    M A I N     R O U T I N E                    */
main(){
graphics_setup();                       /* establish graphics mode */
_getvideoconfig(&vc);                   /* initialize video table */

bg=C2;shadow=C0;hilite=C10;
_setcolor(bg);
sx=0;sy=24;coords();sx1=sx;sy1=sy;
sx=639;sy=454;coords();sx2=sx;sy2=sy;
_rectangle(_GFILLINTERIOR,sx1,sy1,sx2,sy2);      /* bg */
sx=619;sy=41;coords();_moveto(sx,sy);_setcolor(hilite);
sx=619;sy=437;coords();_lineto(sx,sy);
sx=620;sy=41;coords();_moveto(sx,sy);
sx=620;sy=437;coords();_lineto(sx,sy);
sx=19;sy=437;coords();_lineto(sx,sy);
_setcolor(shadow);sx=19;sy=41;coords();_lineto(sx,sy);
sx=20;sy=437;coords();_moveto(sx,sy);
sx=20;sy=41;coords();_lineto(sx,sy);
sx=620;sy=41;coords();_lineto(sx,sy);

for (tl=1;tl<=4;tl++){           /* loop for 4 rows of pedestals */
   for (t=1;t<=6;t++){    /* nested loop for 6 pedestals per row */
   _moveto(x,y);_setcolor(hilite);_lineto(x+hl,y);
   _setcolor(shadow);_moveto(x+hl,y+1);_lineto(x+hl,y+vl);
   _moveto(x+h2,y+1);_lineto(x+h2,y+vl);_lineto(x,y+vl);
   _setcolor(hilite);_lineto(x,y);_moveto(x+1,y+vl);
   _lineto(x+1,y);x=x+h3;};   /* reposition x for next pedestal */
x=xl;y=y+v3;};                 /* reposition x,y for next row */

_setcolor(C7);notice(0,0);                          /* notice */
keyboard();                    /* wait for user to press <Esc> */
quit_pgm();                    /* end the program gracefully */
}
/*_____


                 SUBROUTINE: CHECK THE KEYBOARD BUFFER          */

void keyboard(void){
union u_type {int a;char b[3];} keystroke;
int get_keystroke(void);             /* declare a local subroutine */

do keystroke.a=get_keystroke();
while (keystroke.b[0]!=27);        /* return if <Esc> is pressed */
}

/*          LOCAL SUBROUTINE: RETRIEVE ONE KEYSTROKE            */

int get_keystroke(void){
union REGS regs;regs.h.ah=0;return int86(0x16,&regs,&regs);}

/*_____
```

```
                 SUBROUTINE: GRACEFUL EXIT FROM THE PROGRAM              */

void quit_pgm(void){
_clearscreen(_GCLEARSCREEN);_setvideomode(_DEFAULTMODE);}

/*_____


                 SUBROUTINE: VGA/EGA/CGA compatibility module

     This subroutine invokes the highest-resolution graphics mode
     which is permitted by the hardware.  The 640x480 16-color mode
     is established if a VGA is present.  The 640x350 16-color mode
     is established if an EGA is being used with an enhanced color
     display monitor or a multiscanning monitor.  The 640x200
     16-color mode is established if an EGA is being used with a
     standard color monitor.  The 320x200 4-color mode is invoked
     if a CGA is present.                                             */

void graphics_setup(void){

VGA_mode:
if (_setvideomode(_VRES16COLOR)==0) {goto EGA_ECD_mode;}
else {x_res=640;y_res=480;mode_flag=1;
x=52;y=77;xl=52;       /* upper left starting position */
hl=80;vl=72;           /* horizontal & vertical displacement */
h2=81;v2=73;                   /* thickness displacement */
h3=90;         /* horizontal distance between each pedestal */
v3=84;    /* vertical distance between each row of pedestals */
_settextcolor(7);_settextposition(30,27);
_outtext("640x480 16-color VGA mode");
_settextposition(1,20);
_outtext("USING C TO CREATE A SCULPTURED BACKGROUND");
return;}

EGA_ECD_mode:
if (_setvideomode(_ERESCOLOR)==0) {goto EGA_SCD_mode;}
else {x_res=640;y_res=350;mode_flag=2;
x=52;y=56;xl=52;       /* upper left starting position */
hl=80;vl=53;           /* horizontal & vertical displacement */
h2=81;v2=54;                   /* thickness displacement */
h3=90;         /* horizontal distance between each pedestal */
v3=61;    /* vertical distance between each row of pedestals */
_settextcolor(7);_settextposition(25,27);
_outtext("640x350 16-color EGA mode");

_settextposition(1,20);
_outtext("USING C TO CREATE A SCULPTURED BACKGROUND");
return;}

EGA_SCD_mode:
if (_setvideomode(_HRES16COLOR)==0) {goto CGA_mode;}
else {x_res=640;y_res=200;mode_flag=3;
x=52;y=32;xl=52;       /* upper left starting position */
```

```
hl=80;vl=30;        /* horizontal & vertical displacement */
h2=81;v2=31;                  /* thickness displacement */
h3=90;          /* horizontal distance between each pedestal */
v3=35;      /* vertical distance between each row of pedestals */
_settextcolor(7);_settextposition(25,27);
_outtext("640x200 16-color EGA mode");
_settextposition(1,20);
_outtext("USING C TO CREATE A SCULPTURED BACKGROUND");
return;}


CGA_mode:
if (_setvideomode(_MRES4COLOR)==0) {goto abort_message;}
else {x_res=320;y_res=200;C0=0;C2=2;Cl0=3;mode_flag=4;
x=26;y=32;xl=26;      /* upper left starting position */
hl=40;vl=30;        /* horizontal & vertical displacement */
h2=41;v2=31;                  /* thickness displacement */
h3=45;          /* horizontal distance between each pedestal */
v3=35;      /* vertical distance between each row of pedestals */
_settextcolor(3);_settextposition(25,9);
_outtext("320x200 4-color CGA mode");
_settextposition(1,11);
_outtext("SCULPTURED BACKGROUND");
return;}


abort_message:
printf("\n\nUnable to proceed.\n");
printf("Requires VGA, EGA, or CGA adapter\n");
printf("   with appropriate monitor.\n");
printf("Please refer to the book.\n\n");
exit(0);
}
/*_____


                    SUBROUTINE: coords()

    This subroutine accepts sx,sy device-independent display
    coordinates and returns sx,sy device-dependent screen
    coordinates scaled to fit the 640x480, 640x350, 640x200, or
    320x200 screen, depending upon the graphics mode being used. */

void coords(void){
sx=sx*(x_res/640);sy=sy*(y_res/480);return;}


/*_____



                    SUBROUTINE: Copyright Notice
    This subroutine displays the standard copyright notice.
    If you are typing in this program from the book you can
    safely omit this subroutine, provided that you also remove
    the instruction "notice()" from the main routine.          */

int copyright[][3]={0x7c00,0x0000,0x0000,0x8231,
0x819c,0x645e,0xba4a,0x4252,0x96d0,0xa231,0x8252,0x955e,0xba4a,
```

```
0x43d2,0xf442,0x8231,0x825c,0x945e,0x7c00,0x0000,0x0000};

void notice(float x, float y){
int a,b,c; int tl=0;
for (tl=0;tl<=6;tl++){a=copyright[tl][0];b=copyright[tl][1];
c=copyright[tl][2];_setlinestyle(a);_moveto(x,y);_lineto(x+15,y);
_setlinestyle(b);_moveto(x+16,y);_lineto(x+31,y);_setlinestyle(c);
_moveto(x+32,y);_lineto(x+47,y);y=y+1;};_setlinestyle(0xFFFF);
return;}

/*_____


                        End of source code                     */
```

CASE STUDY: DEMONSTRATION PROGRAM—AIRBRUSHED BACKGROUND

The photograph in Fig. 11-10 depicts the video output of the demonstration program in Fig. 11-11. The program generates an airbrushed background using the halftoning techniques discussed in this chapter and in previous chapters. The program listing in Fig. 11-11 is the QuickC version. If you are using Turbo C, use the program listing provided in Fig. E-4 of Appendix E. If you have the companion disk for this book, load program QC-005.C if you are using QuickC and load program TC-005.C if you are using Turbo C.

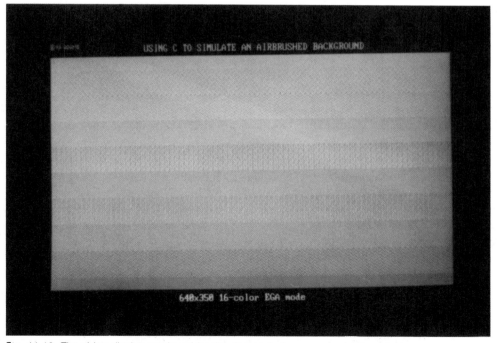

Fig. 11-10. The video display produced by the demonstration program in Fig. 11-11.

This demonstration program supports all IBM-compatible graphics adapters. If you are using a VGA, the program runs in the 640×480 16-color mode. If you are using an EGA with an enhanced monitor, the program will run in the 640×350 16-color mode. If you are using an EGA and a standard color display, the program will use the 640×200 16-color mode. If you are using a CGA or MCGA, the program runs in the 320×200 4-color mode.

The workhorse of this program is the **main( )** routine. Note how the rectangle instruction is used repeatedly with different **sx, sy** screen coordinates and with different halftone masks in order to create the airbrushed effect from the top of the screen to the bottom.

As the program draws the airbrushed background, it calls upon the subroutine named **coords( )** to ensure that the graphics are being plotted correctly for whichever graphics mode has been initialized during program start-up. Note how the screen coordinate values are assigned to **sx** and **sy** before calling **coords( )**. Note how the resulting coordinates are then assigned to either **sx1** and **sy1** or to **sx2** and **sy2**, which are the defining corners of the rectangle. The original **sx** and **sy** coordinates are derived from a device-independent 640×480 template, of course.

This demonstration program produces markedly different results, depending upon whether QuickC or Turbo C is used. Because QuickC superimposes the halftone pattern over the existing graphics, subtle and delicate airbrushed effects can be created by mixing colors. Turbo C, on the other hand, always overwrites the existing background, producing a halftone pattern consisting of colored pixels against a black field. The airbrushed background produced by the Turbo C version of this demonstration program is much more dramatic and exhibits higher contrast than the QuickC version, which appears delicate in comparison.

Even the CGA is capable of producing airbrushed backgrounds. If you are using a VGA or EGA, you can adjust the compatibility module to force the demonstration program to run in the 320×200 4-color mode of the CGA. A simple **goto** instruction will do the trick.

Fig. 11-11. Program listing for airbrushed background—QuickC version. VGA/EGA/CGA/CGA compatible. For Turbo C version, consult Appendix E.

```
/*

                              qc-005.c

  Function:  This program demonstrates how to simulate an
  airbrushed background.

  Compatibility:  Supports all graphics adapters and monitors.
  The software uses the 640x480 16-color mode is a VGA is
  present, the 640x350 16-color mode if an EGA and enhanced
  monitor are present, the 640x200 16-color mode if an EGA and
  standard monitor are present, and the 320x200 4-color mode
  if a CGA is present.

  Remarks:  By altering two variables in the declarations
  module you can try out different foreground and background
  color combinations.
```

```
                    I N C L U D E     F I L E S                    */

#include <dos.h>                         /* supports the BIOS call */
#include <stdio.h>                   /* supports the printf function */
#include <graph.h>              /* supports the graphics functions */

/*_____


                    D E C L A R A T I O N S                    */

struct videoconfig vc;

char fill_3[ ]={0,32,0,0,0,2,0,0};                    /*    3% fill */
char fill_6[ ]={32,0,2,0,128,0,8,0};                  /* 6.25% fill */
char fill_12[ ]={32,2,128,8,32,2,128,8};              /* 12.5% fill */
char fill_25[ ]={68,17,68,17,68,17,68,17};            /*   25% fill */
char fill_37[ ]={146,41,148,73,164,73,146,73};        /* 37.5% fill */
char fill_50[ ]={85,170,85,170,85,170,85,170};        /*   50% fill */
char fill_62[ ]={109,214,107,182,91,182,109,182};     /* 62.5% fill */
char fill_75[ ]={187,238,187,238,187,238,187,238};    /*   75% fill */
char fill_87[ ]={223,253,127,247,223,253,127,247};    /* 87.5% fill */

void keyboard(void);void quit_pgm(void);void graphics_setup(void);
void coords(void);void notice(float x,float y);

float sx=0,sy=0,sxl=0,syl=0,sx2=0,sy2=0,x_res=0,y_res=0;
int C0=0,Cl=1,C2=2,C3=3,C4=4,C5=5,C6=6,C7=7,C8=8,C9=9,C10=10,
    Cll=11,C12=12,C13=13,C14=14,C15=15,mode_flag=0;
int fg,bg;                        /* foreground & background colors */

/*_____


                    M A I N    R O U T I N E                    */

main(){
graphics_setup();                     /* establish graphics mode */
_getvideoconfig(&vc);                 /* initialize video table */

fg=Cl;bg=C9;                   /* set foreground, background hue */
sx=0;sy=24;coords();sxl=sx;syl=sy;
sx=639;sy=454;coords();sx2=sx;sy2=sy;
_setcolor(bg);_rectangle(_GFILLINTERIOR,sxl,syl,sx2,sy2);

_setcolor(fg);                        /* ready to begin halftoning */

_setfillmask(fill_6);sx=0;sy=48;coords();sxl=sx;syl=sy;
```

```
sx=639;sy=96;coords();sx2=sx;sy2=sy;
_rectangle(_GFILLINTERIOR,sxl,syl,sx2,sy2);
_setfillmask(fill_12);sx=0;coords();sxl=sx;syl=sy2+1;
sx=639;sy=144;coords();sx2=sx;sy2=sy;
_rectangle(_GFILLINTERIOR,sxl,syl,sx2,sy2);
_setfillmask(fill_25);sx=0;coords();sxl=sx;syl=sy2+1;
sx=639;sy=192;coords();sx2=sx;sy2=sy;
_rectangle(_GFILLINTERIOR,sxl,syl,sx2,sy2);
_setfillmask(fill_37);sx=0;coords();sxl=sx;syl=sy2+1;
sx=639;sy=240;coords();sx2=sx;sy2=sy;
_rectangle(_GFILLINTERIOR,sxl,syl,sx2,sy2);
_setfillmask(fill_50);sx=0;coords();sxl=sx;syl=sy2+1;
sx=639;sy=288;coords();sx2=sx;sy2=sy;
_rectangle(_GFILLINTERIOR,sxl,syl,sx2,sy2);
_setfillmask(fill_62);sx=0;coords();sxl=sx;syl=sy2+1;
sx=639;sy=336;coords();sx2=sx;sy2=sy;
_rectangle(_GFILLINTERIOR,sxl,syl,sx2,sy2);
_setfillmask(fill_75);sx=0;coords();sxl=sx;syl=sy2+1;
sx=639;sy=384;coords();sx2=sx;sy2=sy;
_rectangle(_GFILLINTERIOR,sxl,syl,sx2,sy2);
_setfillmask(fill_87);sx=0;coords();sxl=sx;syl=sy2+1;
sx=639;sy=432;coords();sx2=sx;sy2=sy;
_rectangle(_GFILLINTERIOR,sxl,syl,sx2,sy2);
_setfillmask(NULL);sx=0;coords();sxl=sx;syl=sy2+1;
sx=639;sy=454;coords();sx2=sx;sy2=sy;
_rectangle(_GFILLINTERIOR,sxl,syl,sx2,sy2);

_setcolor(C7);notice(0,0);                          /* notice */
keyboard();                   /* wait for user to press <Esc> */
quit_pgm();                      /* end the program gracefully */
}
/*_____


             SUBROUTINE: CHECK THE KEYBOARD BUFFER            */

void keyboard(void){
union u_type {int a;char b[3];} keystroke;
int get_keystroke(void);          /* declare a local subroutine */

do keystroke.a=get_keystroke();
while (keystroke.b[0]!=27);       /* return if <Esc> is pressed */
}

/*          LOCAL SUBROUTINE: RETRIEVE ONE KEYSTROKE          */

int get_keystroke(void){
union REGS regs;regs.h.ah=0;return int86(0x16,&regs,&regs);}

/*_____


          SUBROUTINE: GRACEFUL EXIT FROM THE PROGRAM          */
```

```
void quit_pgm(void){
_clearscreen(_GCLEARSCREEN);_setvideomode(_DEFAULTMODE);}

/*_____


              SUBROUTINE: VGA/EGA/CGA compatibility module

    This subroutine invokes the highest-resolution graphics mode
    which is permitted by the hardware.  The 640x480 16-color mode
    is established if a VGA is present.  The 640x350 16-color mode
    is established if an EGA is being used with an enhanced color
    display monitor or a multiscanning monitor.  The 640x200
    16-color mode is established if an EGA is being used with a
    standard color monitor.  The 320x200 4-color mode is invoked
    if a CGA is present.                                        */

void graphics_setup(void){

VGA_mode:
if (_setvideomode(_VRES16COLOR)==0) {goto EGA_ECD_mode;}
else {x_res=640;y_res=480;mode_flag=1;
      _settextcolor(7);_settextposition(30,27);
      _outtext("640x480 16-color VGA mode");
      _settextposition(1,20);
      _outtext("USING C TO SIMULATE AN AIRBRUSHED BACKGROUND");
      return;}

EGA_ECD_mode:
if (_setvideomode(_ERESCOLOR)==0) {goto EGA_SCD_mode;}
else {x_res=640;y_res=350;mode_flag=2;
      _settextcolor(7);_settextposition(25,27);
      _outtext("640x350 16-color EGA mode");
      _settextposition(1,20);
      _outtext("USING C TO SIMULATE AN AIRBRUSHED BACKGROUND");
      return;}

EGA_SCD_mode:
if (_setvideomode(_HRES16COLOR)==0) {goto CGA_mode;}
else {x_res=640;y_res=200;mode_flag=3;
      _settextcolor(7);_settextposition(25,27);
      _outtext("640x200 16-color EGA mode");
      _settextposition(1,20);
      _outtext("USING C TO SIMULATE AN AIRBRUSHED BACKGROUND");
      return;}

CGA_mode:
if (_setvideomode(_MRES4COLOR)==0) {goto abort_message;}
else {x_res=320;y_res=200;C0=0;C1=1;C7=3;C9=3;mode_flag=4;
      _settextcolor(3);_settextposition(25,9);
      _outtext("320x200 4-color CGA mode");
      _settextposition(1,11);
      _outtext("AIRBRUSHED BACKGROUND");
      return;}
```

```
abort_message:
printf("\n\nUnable to proceed.\n");
printf("Requires VGA, EGA, or CGA adapter\n");
printf("   with appropriate monitor.\n");
printf("Please refer to the book.\n\n");
exit(0);
}
```

```
/*_____
```

                    SUBROUTINE: coords()

    This subroutine accepts sx,sy device-independent display
    coordinates and returns sx,sy device-dependent screen
    coordinates scaled to fit the 640x480, 640x350, 640x200, or
    320x200 screen, depending upon the graphics mode being used. */

```
void coords(void){
sx=sx*(x_res/640);sy=sy*(y_res/480);return;}
```

```
/*_____
```

                    SUBROUTINE: Copyright Notice

    This subroutine displays the standard copyright notice.
    If you are typing in this program from the book you can
    safely omit this subroutine, provided that you also remove
    the instruction "notice()" from the main routine.   */

```
int copyright[][3]={0x7c00,0x0000,0x0000,0x8231,
0x819c,0x645e,0xba4a,0x4252,0x96d0,0xa231,0x8252,0x955e,0xba4a,
0x43d2,0xf442,0x8231,0x825c,0x945e,0x7c00,0x0000,0x0000};
```

```
void notice(float x, float y){
int a,b,c; int tl=0;
for (tl=0;tl<=6;tl++){a=copyright[tl][0];b=copyright[tl][1];
c=copyright[tl][2];_setlinestyle(a);_moveto(x,y);_lineto(x+15,y);
_setlinestyle(b);_moveto(x+16,y);_lineto(x+31,y);_setlinestyle(c);
_moveto(x+32,y);_lineto(x+47,y);y=y+1;};_setlinestyle(0xFFFF);
return;}
```

```
/*_____
```

                    End of source code   */

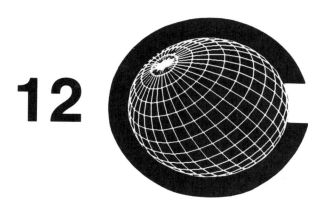

12

Using Windows
and Viewports

No matter which graphics screen mode you are using, you are not restricted to pencil sketches or graphics databases that fit neatly into the screen's horizontal and vertical coordinates. By using window mapping and viewports, you can achieve considerable versatility within a single screen mode, using either the 640×480 16-color mode, the 640×350 16-color mode, the 640×200 16-color mode, the 320×200 16-color mode, the 640×200 2-color mode, or the 320×200 4-color mode.

WINDOWS

Windowing refers to scaling a set of world coordinates to fit the screen coordinates. Refer to Fig. 12-1. Window mapping normally is used to make a larger drawing fit onto the smaller screen. Every graphical element which appears in the original image will also appear on the screen, although usually reduced in size.

Windowing is a scaling procedure, where the scaling factor is a simple ratio. As the code fragment in Fig. 12-2 shows, the math involved is not complicated. The code fragment shown here is the basis for the windowing routine used in many of the demonstration programs in this book. The algorithm is straightforward: divide the horizontal screen resolution by the horizontal resolution of the world coordinates to get the scaling factor for the x coordinates, and divide the vertical screen resolution by the vertical resolution of the world coordinates to get the scaling factor for the y coordinates.

VIEWPORTS

Whereas windows are scaling routines, viewports are clipping routines. Refer to Fig. 12-3. A windowing routine will map an entire image to fit the display screen. A viewport

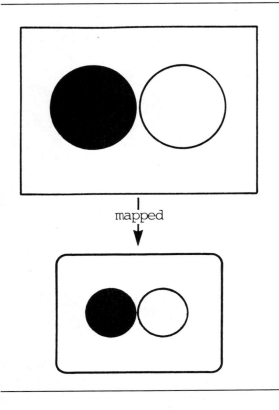

mapped

Fig. 12-1. A world coordinate database mapped to the existing display screen.

$$sx = sx * (x\_res / window\_x\_res)$$

$$sy = sy * (y\_res / window\_y\_res)$$

Fig. 12-2. Window mapping routine. Different sized windows can be mapped to the display screen (x_res, y_res) by adjusting the size of the window in the world coordinates database (window_x_res, window_y_res).

routine will not reduce the original image, but will rather clip portions of the image which do not fit the screen. Full screen viewports clip at the edges of the screen.

In addition, viewports can be defined for any portion of the screen (called a *subset* of the screen). Subset viewports will clip to the edges of the viewport, not to the edge of the screen itself. The effects produced by a typical line-clipping algorithm are shown in Fig. 12-4.

Provided that the database that holds the drawing coordinates has been properly constructed, a viewport routine could easily provide a full 360-degree view of a landscape, as suggested by Fig. 12-5. Imagine a long, narrow drawing where the two ends contain duplicate images. The drawing coordinates on this sketch might range from (0,0) to (5000,199), for example. By adjusting the clipping limits of the viewport routine, you could easily draw a series of images which panned along the database. This technique is sometimes called "*roaming* through a database."

Fig. 12-3. A world coordinate database clipped to the existing display screen.

clipped

Fig. 12-4. The effects of clipping.

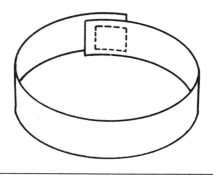

Fig. 12-5. A properly-structured database of world coordinates can provide a full 360 degree panoramic view by varying the scope of the window mapping routine.

A TYPICAL CLIPPING ROUTINE FOR C

The code fragment in Fig. 12-6 is an efficient line-clipping routine which will clip any line to fit the display screen. The program logic for this viewport algorithm is presented in Fig. 12-7. The algorithm first checks to see of the line to be clipped is completely hidden. If both endpoints of the line are positioned to the right of the screen's maximum x coordinate, for example, then the line will be invisible and no clipping is required. The algorithm next compares the endpoints of the line with the top, bottom, left, and right edges of screen. Any segments of the line which must be clipped are "pushed" to the edge of the screen by trigonometry.

```
void viewport(void){
if (sxa>sxb) {temp_swap=sxa;sxa=sxb;sxb=temp_swap;
              temp_swap=sya;sya=syb;syb=temp_swap;};
if (sxa<minx) if (sxb<minx) return;
if (sxa>maxx) if (sxb>maxx) return;
if (sya<miny) if (syb<miny) return;
if (sya>maxy) if (syb>maxy) return;
if (sxa<minx) {{c=(syb-sya)/(sxb-sxa)*(sxb-minx);   /* push right */
               sxa=minx;sya=syb-c;};
              if (sya<miny) if (syb<miny) return;
              if (sya>maxy) if (syb>maxy) return;
              };
if (sxb>maxx) {{c=(syb-sya)/(sxb-sxa)*(maxx-sxa);   /* push left */
               sxb=maxx;syb=sya+c;};
              if (sya<miny) if (syb<miny) return;
              if (sya>maxy) if (syb>maxy) return;
              };
if (sya>syb) {temp_swap=sya;sya=syb;syb=temp_swap;
              temp_swap=sxa;sxa=sxb;sxb=temp_swap;};
if (sya<miny) {c=(sxb-sxa)/(syb-sya)*(syb-miny);    /* push down */
               sxa=sxb-c;sya=miny;};
if (syb>maxy) {c=(sxb-sxa)/(syb-sya)*(maxy-sya);    /* push up */
               sxb=sxa+c;syb=maxy;};
return;}
```

Fig. 12-6. Line-clipping algorithm.

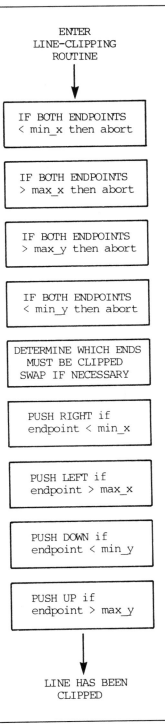

Fig. 12-7. Logic flowchart for a typical line-clipping routine using C.

The variables **minx, maxx, miny,** and **maxy** refer to the minimum and maximum x and y values which are permitted in any particular screen mode. If the 640×200 mode were being used, **minx** would be 0, **maxx** would be 639, **miny** would be 0, and **maxy** would be 199. These variables would normally be defined in the compatibility module when it initializes the particular screen mode.

The routine shown in Fig. 12-6 is very useful for 3D graphics, where the model being drawn occasionally exceeds the edges of the display screen. The 3D demonstration program in Chapter 14 uses this clipping routine. The 3D flight simulation prototype in Chapter 27 also uses this routine.

Note the nested **if/then** instruction in the clipping routine. They have been written this way to make the source code easier to read. Professional C graphics programmers would write:

if (sya < miny) && (syb < miny) return;

instead of:

if (sya < miny) if (syb < miny) return;

13

Advanced Techniques for Graphics

In addition to the graphics functions provided by QuickC and Turbo C, there are a number of advanced techniques useful for graphics programming in general and for animation programming in particular. These advanced skills include graphics database management, the ability to store screen images on disk, and sound effects.

GRAPHICS DATABASE

The most efficient manner for the C graphics programmer to manage a graphics database is by using a numeric array. Refer to Fig. 13-1. Because an array is essentially a collection of sets, its format is ideal for storage of xy screen coordinates.

To establish a two-dimensional array capable of holding ten sets of horizontal-vertical screen coordinates, for example, you might use the following declaration in your C graphics program:

int this_array [10] [2] = { 21,64 42,8, 309,99, 100,199, 244,244, 84,147, 62,4, 319,50, 281,81, 0,0 };

Note that the first set of xy coordinates in this array, the values 21 and 64, are addressed in the following manner. To retrieve the value 21 from the array you would write:

x = this_array[0][0];

```
int array_1 [ ] [2] = { 1,2, 3,4, 5,6 } ;
```

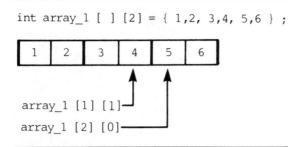

Fig. 13-1. Storage of array elements in memory.

To retrieve the value 64 from the array you would write:

y = this_array[0][1];

The first element in the array is addressed as [0][0] because numbering starts at zero, not at one. To retrieve the last set of xy coordinates in the array, you would write:

x = this_array[9][0]; y = this_array[9][1];

Each set in the array is called a *record*. Each member of a set is called a *field*. In more general terms, each value that is stored in an array is called an *element* of the array. In the example above, **this_array** consists of ten records, with two fields in each record. The array contains 20 elements in all.

The use of graphics databases is helpful when complex drawings are being created on the screen, because many graphics instructions can be coded as loops. On each pass through the drawing loop a new set of xy coordinates can be fetched from the database. The 3D demonstration program in the next chapter uses a database of xyz coordinates during the drawing process.

SAVING SCREEN IMAGES TO DISK

Because screen images are composed of little more than a block of bytes in memory, it is possible to save screen images to disk by saving the appropriate memory block to disk. C provides a number of powerful memory-move instructions which make this task relatively easy.

When using a VGA or EGA, for example, the multiplane-per-pixel mapping strategy of the graphics adapter requires you to save each bit plane separately. To do this, you must manipulate the VGA/EGA internal registers which control the read/write operations of the bit planes. Refer to Fig. 13-2.

The CGA, on the other hand, uses only a single bit plane, although it is broken into two separate banks of memory, as discussed in Chapter 2. However, as Fig. 13-3 shows, the entire block of display memory used by the CGA can be saved in one fell swoop.

How to Save VGA and EGA Screen Images

Appendix A contains a number of utility programs which are useful for saving screen images to disk and for retrieving previously saved screen images from disk. The program

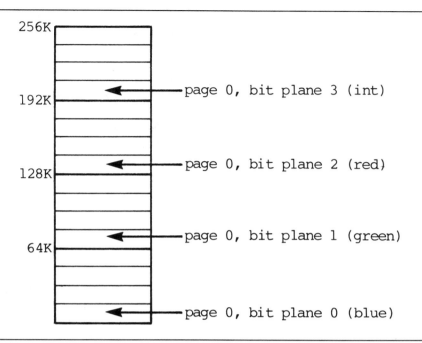

Fig. 13-2. When saving a VGA or EGA image to disk, each bit plane must be captured individually by manipulating the internal registers of the VGA/EGA controller.

Fig. 13-3. When saving a CGA image to disk, programmers will often save 16,384 bytes of contiguous memory (which includes two unused portions of memory totalling 384 bytes).

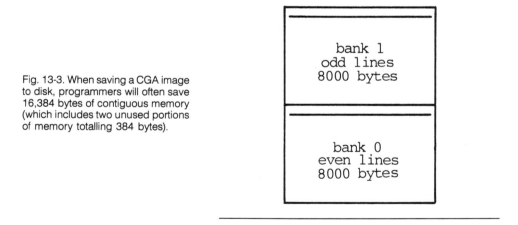

listing in Fig. A-1 can be used to save a VGA or EGA screen image to disk. The program will run in either the 640×480 16-color mode, the 640×360 16-color mode, or the 640×200 16-color mode, depending upon which graphics adapter and monitor is installed in your computer system.

The demonstration program in Fig. A-1 first draws four colored square on the screen a red, green, blue, and white solids, Next, the program saves the four bit planes of

VGA/EGA display memory onto the disk in drive B. Each bit plane is saved as a separate file on disk. The program then clears the screen and retrieves the images from disk, placing them back into the appropriate bit planes of the graphics adapter.

Note how the value of the variable named **plane_length** is defined in the compatibility module when the graphics screen mode is first initialized. Each screen mode uses bit planes of different length, of course. Each bit plane of the 640×480 16-color mode requires 38,400 bytes of storage. Each bit plane of the 640×350 16-color mode requires 28,000 bytes of storage. Each bit plane of the 640×200 16-color mode requires 16,000 bytes of storage.

To calculate the length of a bit plane in a particular mode, use the following algorithm:

((x resolution * y resolution) * bits-per-pixel) /8 =
total-bytes-required

total-bytes-required / 4 = bytes-per-bit-plane

Here is how the subroutine named **savescrn( )** actually saves a screen image to disk. First, the **segread** instruction is used to determine the segment address being used by C to store data during program execution. The instruction: **segment=segregs.ds** is the code that actually moves the address in the ds data segment register into the variable named **segment**.

Next, the program determines the offset address of the array named **image_buffer**, which is located somewhere in the data segment. This array was declared at program start-up to be large enough to hold any of the three possible screen modes which might be used by the program. (Refer back to the **DECLARATIONS** section of the source code for the instruction, **char image_buffer[38400];**).

The array named **image_buffer** is required because C cannot move the data directly from the display adapter's memory to disk. The data must first be moved from the display adapter memory to use RAM, and then saved from user RAM to disk.

Next, the demonstration program uses the **fopen** instruction to open a file named B:IMAGE1.BLU. This first file will deal with the contents of the blue bit plane. The parameter **wb**, which is appended to the **fopen** instruction tells C that the file is to be opened as a binary file for writing.

Next, the **outp** instruction is used to manipulate the internal registers of the VGA/EGA graphics controller in order to read only bit plane 0 (which is the blue bit plane). The hex numbers used for these instructions was gleaned from the IBM EGA Technical Reference. The values, however, work correctly in all VGA and EGA multiplane graphics modes.

The **movedata** instruction is then used to move the contents of the bit plane from the display adapter memory to a buffer in user RAM (the array named **image_buffer**). The **movedata** instruction takes the following form:

movedata (sourceseg, sourceoffset, targetseg, targetoffset, length);

where **sourceseq** is the source segment address, **sourceoffset** is the source offset address, **targetseg** is the target segment address, **targetoffset** is the target offset address, and **length** is the size in bytes of the memory block which is to be moved by the **movedata** instruction.

By referring back to Chapter 2 you can determine that the address of bit plane 0, page 0, on a VGA or EGA is A000:0000 hex.

After the block of data has been moved into the buffer in user RAM, the **fwrite** instruction is employed to write the data to a disk file. By inspecting the source code in Fig. A-1 you can see how the variables **image__file**, **plane__length**, and **image__buffer** are used to control the manner in which **fwrite** operates.

Finally, the **fclose** instruction is used to close the file. The first bit plane has been saved on disk. The same procedure is used in turn for the remaining three bit planes.

The algorithm is then reversed for use in the subroutine named **loadscrn( )**, which retrieves the image files from disk and redisplays the image on the screen. The subroutine first loads the contents of an image file into the buffer in user RAM, from where the data is transferred up onto the display adapter's memory. Again, the **outp** instruction is used to manipulate the internal registers of the VGA/EGA graphics controller so that only the required bit plane is being written to. Note the parameter **rb**, which is appended to the **fopen** instruction. This tells C that the file is to be opened for a binary read.

The code provided in the utility program in Fig. A-1 can be used in any of your original C graphics programs which are intended to run on VGA or EGA graphics adapters. In its current form, the demonstration program can save either the 640×480 16-color VGA mode, the 640×350 16-color VGA/EGA mode, or the 640×200 16-color VGA/EGA mode. You could, however, easily modify the routines to save the 320×200 16-color VGA/EGA mode and the 320×200 256-color VGA/EGA/MCGA mode. The length of a single bitplane in the 320×200 16-color mode is 8000 bytes (4 bits-per-pixel). The length of a single bit plane in the 320×200 256-color mode is 16000 bytes (8 bits-per-pixel). If you are going to be working in the 256-color mode, you may wish to consider acquiring a copy of the IBM VGA Technical Reference manual, because this mode uses a modified mapping strategy.

Note that the algorithm used to save VGA and EGA multiplane screen modes will not work correctly if used with CGA modes.

How to Save CGA Screen Images

The program listing in Fig. A-2 in Appendix A demonstrates how to save a CGA screen image to disk. The algorithm which is used in this utility program will work with either the 320×200 4-color mode or the 640×200 2-color mode of the CGA and MCGA.

Here is how the subroutine named **savescrn( )** actually saves a screen image to disk. First, the **segread** instruction is used to determine the segment address being used by C to store data during program execution. The instruction: **segment=segregs.ds** is the code that actually moves the value in the ds data segment register into the variable named **segment**.

Next, the program determines the offset address of the array named **image__buffer**, which is located somewhere in the data segment. This array was declared at program start-up to be large enough to hold the contents of the CGA display buffer: 16384 bytes. (Refer back to the **DECLARATIONS** section of the source code for the instruction, **char image__buffer[16384];**).

The array named **image__buffer** is required because C cannot move the data directly from the display adapter's memory to disk. The data must first be moved from the display adapter memory to user RAM, and then saved from user RAM to disk.

Next, the demonstration program uses the **fopen** instruction to open a file named B:IMAGE1.BIN. The parameter; **wb**, which is appended to the **fopen** instruction tells C that the file is to be opened as a binary file for writing.

The **movedata** instruction is then used to move the contents of the display memory to a buffer in user RAM (the array named **image__buffer**). The **movedata** instruction takes the following form:

movedata (sourceseg, sourceoffset, targetseg, targetoffset, length);

where **sourceseq** is the source segment address, **sourceoffset** is the source offset address, **targetseg** is the target segment address, **targetoffset** is the target offset address, and **length** is the size in bytes of the memory block which is to be moved by the **movedata** instruction. by referring back to Chapter 2 you can determine that the address of CGA display memory is B800:0000 hex. (Even VGA and EGA graphics adapters which are using a CGA screen mode use the B800:0000 address.)

After the block of data has been moved into the buffer in user RAM, the **fwrite** instruction is employed to write the data to a disk file. By inspecting the source code in Fig. A-2 you can see how the variables **image__file**, **plane__length**, and **image__buffer** are used to control the manner in which **fwrite** operates.

Finally, the **fclose** instruction is used to close the file.

The algorithm is then reversed for use in the subroutine named **loadscrn( )**, which retrieves the image file from disk and redisplays the image on the screen. The subroutine first loads the contents of an image file into the buffer in user RAM, from where the data is transferred up onto the display adapter's memory. Note the parameter: **rb**, appended to the **fopen** instruction, which tells C to open the file for binary reading.

SOUND EFFECTS

Graphics programs generally, and animated programs in particular, can benefit from the addition of sound effects. The animated arcade-style demonstration program in Chapter 26, for example, uses a sound effect on each occasion when the speeding ball ricochets off a barrier.

The utility program listing presented in Fig. A-3 of Appendix A demonstrates how to control the sound chip of your computer. Fig. A-3 contains the QuickC version of the utility program. If you are using Turbo C, use instead the program listing in Fig. E-15 of Appendix E.

The sound effect generated by the utility program follows the format depicted in Fig. 13-4. First, a series of short bursts creates a rising arpeggio. Next, a falling arpeggio is generated. Finally, a steady monotone announces the end of the demonstration.

The cornerstone of this utility program is the subroutine named **sound( )**. (If you are using Turbo C, this subroutine is named **noise( )**, because Turbo C already contains a built-in function named **sound( )**.)

The **sound( )** subroutine expects to receive two values from the caller: the frequency of the sound, expressed in hertz, and the duration of the sound, expressed as the iteration counter for a loop. Here is how the subroutine works.

First, the **if/then** instruction is used to test if the hertz value is within the range of 40 hertz to 4660 hertz. This range should be ample for all C graphics applications, because the audible range of human hearing is from 40 to 2400 hertz.

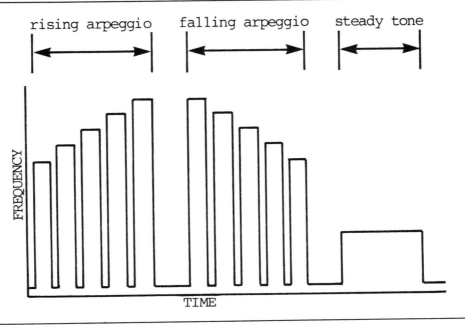

Fig. 13-4. Schematic representation of the sounds produced by the utility program in Fig. A-3.

Next, simple division provides the count value which must be passed to the hardware's sound chip. The **outp** instruction is used to send this count value as two bytes through port 42 hex.

Next, the existing values at port 61 are saved before the port is manipulated in order to turn on the computer's speaker. A **for/next** loop is used to wait for the appropriate length of time before restoring the port to its original condition. The **for/next** loop uses the count value which was passed to the subroutine by the caller.

In its current form, the subroutine turns off the speaker after it has generated the sound. This means that any sounds you create are separated by moments of silence. If you wished to create integrated sounds, such as sirens, for example, you would want to modify the program so that the speaker was left on until the different pitches had been generated through the sound speaker.

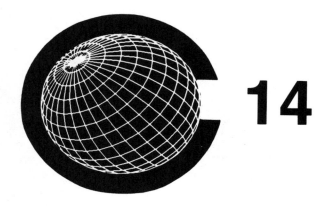

14

How to Generate 3D Images

Graphics programs which can generate 3D models—whether as wire-frame models or as fully-shaded models—are well within your reach as a C graphics programmer. The 3D perspective formulas and halftone shading algorithms which look so spectacular on graphics workstations are easily adapted to work on your personal computer. All that is required is an understanding of the programming concepts involved in 3D graphics.

This chapter presents a condensed overview of important 3D concepts, algorithms, and formulas. For a more detailed discussion of solid modeling with computer-controlled shading using BASIC see my book: *HIGH-PERFORMANCE INTERACTIVE GRAPHICS: MODELING, RENDERING, & ANIMATING FOR IBM PCs AND COMPATIBLES* (#2879), available through your favorite bookstore or order direct from TAB Books Inc.

Real objects possess the three dimensions of height, width, and depth. An image displayed on a microcomputer screen which simulates the height, width, and depth of the object is said to be *three-dimensional*, or 3D. In computer graphics, a 3D image is often called a *3D model*. The generation of a 3D model is called *modeling*. The application of shading, highlights, textures, and shadows is called *rendering*.

WORLD COORDINATES

The fundamental shape of the model which you wish to display is expressed as xyz coordinates. Refer to Fig. 14-1. The three dimensions of *height, width,* and *depth* can be defined by using a coordinate axis system. The x axis is often used to represent the up-down dimensions; the z axis is used to represent near-far dimensions. The viewpoint of you, the viewer, is located at position 0,0,0, as illustrated in Fig. 14-1.

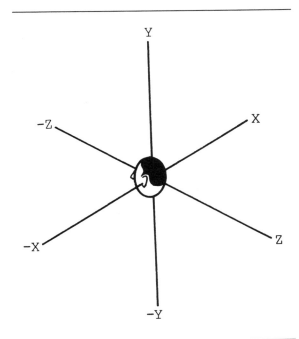

Fig. 14-1. The location of the viewpoint in a 3D coordinate system.

Three sets of coordinates are used during the 3D modeling process. Refer to Fig. 14-2. The world coordinates are the true shape of the model in the 3D axis system. The view coordinates describe the position of the model after it has been rotated and moved to an appropriate location for viewing. The display coordinates are the xy coordinates used to draw the model on the microcomputer's 2D display screen.

CREATING A 3D MODEL

The first step in modeling an object is to define the *world coordinates* of the object. Refer to Fig. 14-3. These world coordinates describe the fundamental shape or design of the model. World coordinates are also called *absolute* coordinates, *cartesian* coordinates, and *model space* coordinates. The xyz axis represents the real world, independent of your program and independent of your personal computer. The xyz coordinates of the model are often termed *device-independent* coordinates.

The second step in modeling an object is to spin the object and move it to an appropriate viewing position. Spinning the object is called *rotation*. Moving the object is called *translation*. Refer to Fig. 14-3. The rotation formulas are based upon matrix mathematics, expressed as sine and cosine algebra in the formulas used with your personal computer. The translation formulas are based upon simple addition and subtraction. The xyz coordinates for various points which describe the model after rotation and translation are called *view coordinates,* because this is how the model would be viewed by an imaginary viewer within the 3D axis system.

The third step in modeling an object is to display it on the screen. The formulas which convert the xyz coordinates to xy display coordinate are called *projection formulas.*

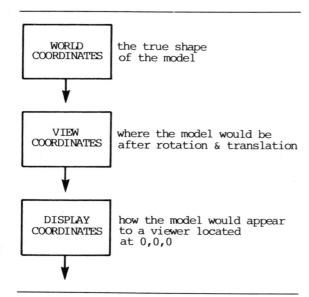

Fig. 14-2. The migration of xyz world coordinates (device-independent)to the display screen as sx sy display coordinates (device-dependent).

DISPLAY OPTIONS

A number of different 3D displays can be created from the world coordinates of an object. Refer to Fig.14-4. The simplest image is the transparent wire-frame model. This is the type of model generated by the demonstration program in this chapter. The shape of the model is accurate, but no subroutines are provided to remove surfaces which should be hidden from view.

Solid models are 3D images which have been subjected to hidden surface removal. The formulas which calculate whether a particular surface is hidden from view are usually based upon plane equation formulas.

Fully-shaded models are solid models that have been shaded using bit tiling area fill patterns to represent different levels of brightness on the surface of the model. The formulas to calculate levels of illumination are usually based upon surface normals.

3D FORMULAS FOR PERSONAL COMPUTERS

The code fragment in Fig. 14-5 gives you complete control over the creation, rotation, translation, and display of a 3D model on your personal computer using C.

The formulas first perform the yaw, roll, and pitch rotations to the xyz world coordinates which you have defined for the model. The **sr** and **cr** variables in the formulas are sine and cosine values of the appropriate angles, expressed as radians (6.28319 radians equals 360 degrees).

The formulas then perform the translation adjustments. During this process, the rotated model is moved left or right, up or down, or nearer or farther relative to the viewing position (at 0,0,0). To change the position of a model, it is the model itself that is always moved; the viewpoint remains constant.

Figure 14-6 shows how the three concepts of yaw, roll, and pitch fit into the 3D axis system. Yaw changes the compass heading of the model. Roll tilts the model clockwise or counterclockwise. Pitch tilts the model towards you or away from you.

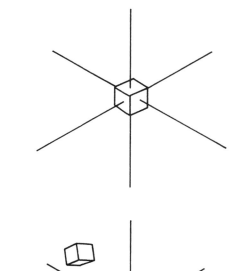

Fig. 14-3. The rotation-translation-projection sequence. Top: xyz world coordinates. Center: xyz view coordinates. Bottom: sx sy display coordinates.

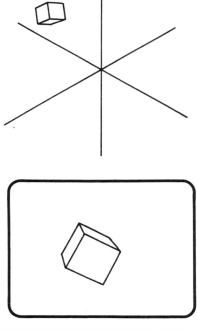

The last function provided by the 3D formulas is *projection*. Simple geometry is used to translate the 3D xyz view coordinates into 2D xy display coordinates which the microcomputer can plot onto the screen.

HIDDEN SURFACE REMOVAL

The plane equation method of hidden surface removal uses vector mathematics to determine if a particular surface is visible or hidden from view. The plane equation method first determines the orientation of a plane in 3D space by comparing at least three of

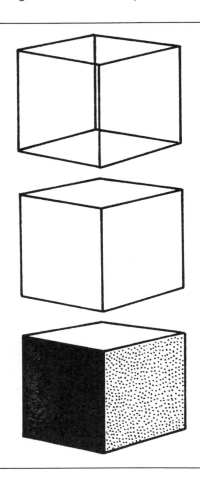

Fig. 14-4. From top: transparent wire-frame model, solid model with hidden surfaces removed, shaded solid model.

```
void calc_3d(void){
x=(-1)*x;xa=cr1*x-sr1*z;za=sr1*x+cr1*z;x=cr2*xa+sr2*y;
ya=cr2*y-sr2*xa;z=cr3*za-sr3*ya;y=sr3*za+cr3*ya;x=x+mx;y=y+my;
z=z+mz;sx=d*x/z;sy=d*y/z;return;}
```

Fig. 14-5. Standard 3D rotation-translation-projection formulas for C programs.

its vertices. A *vertex* is a corner of the plane. Then, by comparing the orientation of the plane to the position of the viewpoint (at 0,0,0), the plane equation routine can discern if the surface of the plane is visible to the viewer or not.

The plane equation method provides a bullet-proof method for drawing solid models which are convex polygons. For more complex 3D models, where an extension or protrusion may obscure from view another portion of the model, it is important to construct the nearest portion of the model last. This ensures that the nearer parts of the 3D model will correctly hide the more distant parts of the model.

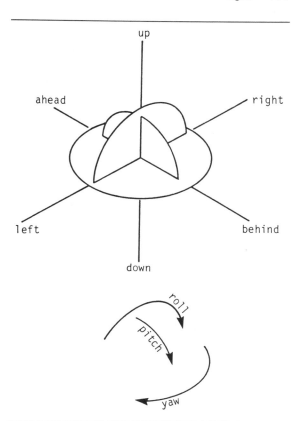

Fig. 14-6. The yaw, roll, and pitch planes in the 3D environment.

SHADING AND ILLUMINATION

Computer images begin to breathe with a life of their own when rendering techniques are used to add illumination and shading. The shading is applied using halftone shading techniques, based upon the bit tiling capabilities of C introduced in Chapter 5. The algorithm which determines the style of halftone shading to be applied to a particular surface is based upon vector mathematics.

The brightness of a surface is determined by its orientation relative to the light source. Specifically, the angle between the rays of light and the surface perpendicular will determine how bright the surface will appear to the viewer. This is often referred to as Lambert's Cosine Law, named after a mathematician. The surface perpendicular is a line (vector) coming out from the flat surface at a 90 degree angle to the surface. The surface perpendicular is often called a *surface normal.*

A typical shading subroutine does three things. First, it calculates the illumination level of the surface, expressing the brightness as an integer in a range of typically 1 to 20. Second, it chooses an area fill pattern based on this level of brightness. The strings for the bit tiling pattern would have already been defined in another part of the program. Third, it assigns a linestyling pattern which can be used to outline the filled area in a manner that closely matches the area fill halftone pattern. This outlining is called line dithering. (For a complete discussion of computer-controlled shading capabilities for the VGA, EGA,

CGA, and MCGA, consult my book, *HIGH-PERFORMANCE INTERACTIVE GRAPHICS: MODELING, RENDERING, & ANIMATING FOR IBM PCs AND COMPATIBLES* (#2879), available through your favorite bookstore or order direct from TAB Books Inc.)

CASE STUDY: A DEMONSTRATION PROGRAM

The photograph in Fig. 14-7 shows the image which is produced by the demonstration program in Fig. 14-8. The program listing in Fig.14-8 is the QuickC version; if you are using Turbo C you should use instead the program listing in Fig. E-5 of Appendix E. If you are using the companion disk for this book, load program QC-006.C if you are using QuickC. and load program TC-006.C if you are using Turbo C.

The demonstration program creates a 3D cube, drawn in accurate perspective. Depending upon which graphics adapter and monitor you have installed in your personal computer, the program will run in either the 640×480 16-color mode, the 640×350 16-color mode, the 640×200 16-color mode, or the 320×200 4-color mode.

An important addition to the **INCLUDE FILES** section of this source code is the **#include <math.h>** directive. This header file contains definitions which support the sine and cosine functions necessary for 3D computer graphics. Note, also, the substantial number of variables which are initialized by the **DECLARATIONS** section. (You may wish to experiment with different values for **d**, which affects angular distortion, or for **mz**, which affects the viewer's distance from the 3D model.)

Of particular note is the array named **array1** which is loaded with xyz coordinates during program compilation. Because the cube to be drawn is sized 60×60×60 units,

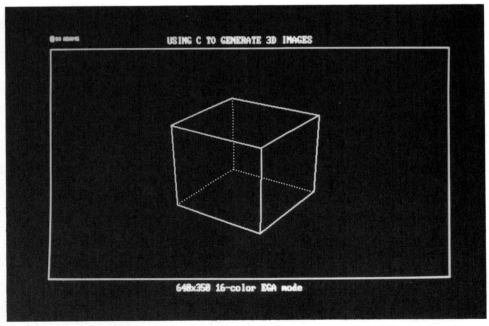

Fig. 14-7. The video display produced by the demonstration program in Fig. 14-8.

and because the cube is located at the center of the world coordinate system (0,0,0), the corners of the cube are located at plus or minus 30, as the case may be.

The first important subroutine to be called by the **main( )** routine is named **rotation( )**. This routine calculates the rotation factors by applying sine and cosine to the viewing angles.

The next important activity of the **main( )** routine is the **for/next** loop which draws the six surfaces of the 3D cube. Note how the variable named **p1** is used to point into the array as the loop is executed. The **setlinestyle** instructions are used to draw the back edges of the cube as dashed lines, thereby making the cube easier to perceive as 3D.

The drawing loop calls a subroutine named **calc_3d( )**, which contains the standard 3D formulas introduced earlier in this chapter. Then a subroutine named **window( )** is called in order to map the coordinates onto the screen. This algorithm is a simple derivation of the windowing formula introduced in Chapter 12. Note the use of **sx+399** and **sy+299** to move the range of the world coordinates into the range of the screen's coordinates. This is required because the coordinates from the 3D model expect 0,0 to be at the center of the subroutine named **viewport( )** is called. This is the same subroutine which was presented in Chapter 12.

This program listing can be used as a template for creating other programs that deal with 3D images. By using the halftone patterns presented in Chapter 5 and Chapter 9 you can create very realistic solid models.

Fig. 14-8. Program listing for a 3D model—QuickC version. VGA/EGA/CGA/MCGA compatible. For Turbo C version, consult Appendix E.

```
/*_____

                            qc-006.c

       Function:  This program demonstrates how to create accurate
       3D images on the display screen.

       Compatibility:  Supports all graphics adapters and monitors.
       The software uses the 640x480 16-color mode if a VGA is
       present, the 640x350 16-color mode if an EGA and enhanced
       monitor are present, the 640x200 16-color mode if an EGA and
       standard monitor are present, and the 320x200 4-color mode
       if a CGA is present.

       Remarks:  In addition to the standard 3D perspective formulas,
       versatile viewport and line-clipping routines are provided.

       Copyright 1988 Lee Adams and TAB BOOKS Inc.

       _____


                       I N C L U D E   F I L E S            */

#include <dos.h>                    /* supports the BIOS call */
#include <stdio.h>               /* supports the printf function */
#include <graph.h>             /* supports the graphics functions */
```

```c
#include <math.h>        /* supports sine and cosine functions */

/*_____


                    D E C L A R A T I O N S              */

struct videoconfig vc;


                /* declare global variables */
float x=0.0,y=0.0,z=0.0;                    /* world coordinates */
float sx=0.0,sy=0.0;          /* output of 3D perspective formulas */
float xa=0.0,ya=0.0,za=0.0;    /* temporary values in 3D formulas */
float sxa=0.0,sya=0.0,sxb=0.0,syb=0.0;        /* 2D line endpoints */
float sxs=0.0,sys=0.0;      /* temp storage of 2D line startpoint */
float temp_swap=0.0;                  /* used for variable swaps */
float d=1200.0;                     /* angular perspective factor */
double r1=5.68319;                    /* yaw angle in radians */
double r2=6.28319;                    /* roll angle in radians */
double r3=5.79778;                    /* pitch angle in radians */
double sr1=0.0,sr2=0.0,sr3=0.0;        /* sine rotation factors */
double cr1=0.0,cr2=0.0,cr3=0.0;      /* cosine rotation factors */
float mx=0.0,my=0.0,mz=-350.0;         /* viewpoint position */
int maxx=638,minx=1,maxy=198,miny=1;      /* clipping viewport */

float screen_x=639,screen_y=199;    /* dimensions of screen mode */
float c=0.0;                     /* used in line-clipping routine */
float rx=0.0,ry=0.0;    /* scaling values used in mapping routine */
int t1=0,t2=0;                            /* loop counters */
int p1=0;                                 /* array indexer */


        /* database of xyz cartesian world coordinates for 3D cube */
int array1[][3]={
30,-30,30, 30,-30,-30, -30,-30,-30, -30,-30,30, 30,-30,30,
30,30,-30, -30,30,-30, -30,-30,-30, 30,-30,-30, 30,30,-30,
-30,30,-30, -30,30,30, -30,-30,30, -30,-30,-30, -30,30,-30,
-30,30,30, 30,30,30, 30,-30,30, -30,-30,30, -30,30,30,
30,30,30, 30,30,-30, 30,-30,-30, 30,-30,30, 30,30,30,
-30,30,-30, 30,30,-30, 30,30,30, -30,30,30, -30,30,-30};

int C0=0,C1=1,C2=2,C3=3,C4=4,C5=5,C6=7,C7=7,C8=8,C9=9,C10=10,
    C11=11,C12=12,C13=13,C14=14,C15=15,mode_flag=0;
float sx1,sy1,sx2,sy2;
float x_res,y_res;


                /* declare global subroutines */
void keyboard(void);void quit_pgm(void);void calc_3d(void);
void rotation(void);void window(void);void viewport(void);
void graphics_setup(void);void coords(void);
void notice(float x,float y);

/*_____
```

```
                    M A I N    R O U T I N E                    */
main(){
graphics_setup();                          /* establish graphics mode */
_getvideoconfig(&vc);                      /* initialize video table */

_setcolor(C7);sx=0;sy=24;coords();sx1=sx;sy1=sy;
sx=638;sy=455;coords();sx2=sx;sy2=sy;
_rectangle(_GBORDER,sx1,sy1,sx2,sy2);

rotation();        /* calculate yaw, roll, pitch rotation factors */
for (t2=1;t2<=6;t2++)                  /* draw 6 sides of the cube */
  {if (t2<4) _setlinestyle(0x8888); else _setlinestyle(0xffff);
  x=array1[pl][0];y=array1[pl][1];z=array1[pl][2];
  calc_3d();window();sxa=sx;sya=sy;
  for (tl=1;tl<=4;tl++)
    {pl++;
    x=array1[pl][0];y=array1[pl][1];z=array1[pl][2];
    calc_3d();window();sxs=sx;sys=sy;sxb=sx;syb=sy;
    viewport();_moveto(sxa,sya);_lineto(sxb,syb);
    sxa=sxs;sya=sys;};
  pl++;};
notice(0,0);
keyboard();                        /* wait for user to press <Esc> */
quit_pgm();}                       /* end the program gracefully */
```

```
/*_____



             SUBROUTINE: CALCULATE SIN, COS FACTORS
    Enter with r1,r2,r3 viewing angles for yaw, roll, pitch
    expressed in radians (0.0 through 6.28319).  Returns sine
    and cosine factors.                                        */

void rotation(void){
sr1=sin(r1);sr2=sin(r2);sr3=sin(r3);cr1=cos(r1);cr2=cos(r2);
cr3=cos(r3);return;}
```

```
/*_____



                SUBROUTINE: STANDARD 3D FORMULAS
    Enter with x,y,z cartesian world coordinates.  Returns sx,sy
    cartesian display coordinates.  Returns x,y,z cartesian view
    coordinates.                                               */

void calc_3d(void){
x=(-1)*x;xa=cr1*x-sr1*z;za=sr1*x+cr1*z;x=cr2*xa+sr2*y;
ya=cr2*y-sr2*xa;z=cr3*za-sr3*ya;y=sr3*za+cr3*ya;x=x+mx;y=y+my;
z=z+mz;sx=d*x/z;sy=d*y/z;return;}
```

```
/*_____
```

```
         SUBROUTINE: MAP CARTESIAN COORDS TO PHYSICAL SCREEN COORDS
         Enter with sx,sy cartesian display coordinates.  Returns sx,sy
         unclipped physical display coordinates.                      */

void window(void){
sx=sx+399;sy=sy+299;rx=screen_x/799;ry=screen_y/599;sx=sx*rx;
sy=sy*ry;return;}

/*_____




                    SUBROUTINE: 2D LINE-CLIPPING
         Enter with sxa,sya and sxb,syb endpoints of line to be
         clipped.  Returns display coordinates for line clipped to
         fit physical screen viewport defined by minx,miny and
         maxx,maxy.                                                   */

void viewport(void){

if (sxa>sxb) {temp_swap=sxa;sxa=sxb;sxb=temp_swap;
                temp_swap=sya;sya=syb;syb=temp_swap;};
if (sxa<minx) if (sxb<minx) return;
if (sxa>maxx) if (sxb>maxx) return;
if (sya<miny) if (syb<miny) return;
if (sya>maxy) if (syb>maxy) return;
if (sxa<minx) {{c=(syb-sya)/(sxb-sxa)*(sxb-minx);  /* push right */
                sxa=minx;sya=syb-c;};
                if (sya<miny) if (syb<miny) return;
                if (sya>maxy) if (syb>maxy) return;
                };
if (sxb>maxx) {{c=(syb-sya)/(sxb-sxa)*(maxx-sxa);   /* push left */
                sxb=maxx;syb=sya+c;};
                if (sya<miny) if (syb<miny) return;
                if (sya>maxy) if (syb>maxy) return;
                };
if (sya>syb) {temp_swap=sya;sya=syb;syb=temp_swap;
                temp_swap=sxa;sxa=sxb;sxb=temp_swap;};
if (sya<miny) {c=(sxb-sxa)/(syb-sya)*(syb-miny);    /* push down */
                sxa=sxb-c;sya=miny;};
if (syb>maxy) {c=(sxb-sxa)/(syb-sya)*(maxy-sya);      /* push up */
                sxb=sxa+c;syb=maxy;};
return;}

/*_____


                                                      .

                 SUBROUTINE: CHECK THE KEYBOARD BUFFER          */

void keyboard(void){
union u_type {int a;char b[3];} keystroke;
int get_keystroke(void);              /* declare a local subroutine */

do keystroke.a=get_keystroke();
while (keystroke.b[0]!=27);            /* return if <Esc> is pressed */
```

```
}
/*              LOCAL SUBROUTINE: RETRIEVE ONE KEYSTROKE              */

int get_keystroke(void){
union REGS regs;regs.h.ah=0;return int86(0x16,&regs,&regs);}

/*_____


               SUBROUTINE: GRACEFUL EXIT FROM THE PROGRAM           */

void quit_pgm(void){
_clearscreen(_GCLEARSCREEN);_setvideomode(_DEFAULTMODE);}

/*_____

               SUBROUTINE: VGA/EGA/CGA compatibility module

    This subroutine invokes the highest-resolution graphics mode
    which is permitted by the hardware.  The 640x480 16-color mode
    is established if a VGA is present.  The 640x350 16-color mode
    is established if an EGA is being used with an enhanced color
    display monitor or a multiscanning monitor.  The 640x200
    16-color mode is established if an EGA is being used with a
    standard color monitor.  The 320x200 4-color mode is invoked
    if a CGA is present.                                            */

void graphics_setup(void){

VGA_mode:
if (_setvideomode(_VRES16COLOR)==0) {goto EGA_ECD_mode;}
else {x_res=640;y_res=480;mode_flag=1;
      maxx=638;minx=1;maxy=478;miny=1;screen_x=639;screen_y=479;
      _settextcolor(7);_settextposition(30,27);
      _outtext("640x480 16-color VGA mode");
      _settextposition(1,25);
      _outtext("USING C TO GENERATE 3D IMAGES");
      return;}

EGA_ECD_mode:
if (_setvideomode(_ERESCOLOR)==0) {goto EGA_SCD_mode;}
else {x_res=640;y_res=350;mode_flag=2;
      maxx=638;minx=1;maxy=348;miny=1;screen_x=639;screen_y=349;
      _settextcolor(7);_settextposition(25,27);
      _outtext("640x350 16-color EGA mode");
      _settextposition(1,25);
      _outtext("USING C TO GENERATE 3D IMAGES");
      return;}

EGA_SCD_mode:
if (_setvideomode(_HRES16COLOR)==0) {goto CGA_mode;}
else {x_res=640;y_res=200;mode_flag=3;
      maxx=638;minx=1;maxy=198;miny=1;screen_x=639;screen_y=199;
```

```
        _settextcolor(7);_settextposition(25,27);
        _outtext("640x200 16-color EGA mode");
        _settextposition(1,25);
        _outtext("USING C TO GENERATE 3D IMAGES");
        return;}

CGA_mode:
if (_setvideomode(_MRES4COLOR)==0) {goto abort_message;}
else {x_res=320;y_res=200;C7=3;
        mode_flag=4;
        maxx=318;minx=1;maxy=198;miny=1;screen_x=319;screen_y=199;
        _settextcolor(3);_settextposition(25,9);
        _outtext("320x200 4-color CGA mode");
        _settextposition(1,16);
        _outtext("3D IMAGES");
        return;}

abort_message:
printf("\n\nUnable to proceed.\n");
printf("Requires VGA, EGA, or CGA adapter\n");
printf("   with appropriate monitor.\n");
printf("Please refer to the book.\n\n");
exit(0);
}
```

```
/*_____
```

SUBROUTINE: coords()

This subroutine accepts sx,sy device-independent display
coordinates and returns sx,sy device-dependent screen
coordinates scaled to fit the 640x480, 640x350, 640x200, or
320x200 screen, depending upon the graphics mode being used. */

```
void coords(void){
sx=sx*(x_res/640);sy=sy*(y_res/480);return;}
```

```
/*_____
```

SUBROUTINE: Copyright Notice
This subroutine displays the standard copyright notice.
If you are typing in this program from the book you can
safely omit this subroutine, provided that you also remove
the instruction "notice()" from the main routine.   */

```
int copyright[][3]={0x7c00,0x0000,0x0000,0x8231,
0x819c,0x645e,0xba4a,0x4252,0x96d0,0xa231,0x8252,0x955e,0xba4a,
0x43d2,0xf442,0x8231,0x825c,0x945e,0x7c00,0x0000,0x0000};

void notice(float x, float y){
int a,b,c; int tl=0;
for (tl=0;tl<=6;tl++){a=copyright[tl][0];b=copyright[tl][1];
c=copyright[tl][2];_setlinestyle(a);_moveto(x,y);_lineto(x+15,y);
```

```
_setlinestyle(b);_moveto(x+16,y);_lineto(x+31,y);_setlinestyle(c);
_moveto(x+32,y);_lineto(x+47,y);y=y+1;};_setlinestyle(0xFFFF);
return;}
```

/*_____

                        End of source code   */

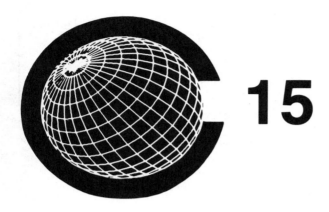

15

Business Graphics

Because computer graphics can enhance the communicative content of a business analysis program, more and more software is using graphical charts to get the message across. Even animation can play a pivotal role in business graphics, especially in the case of before-and-after charts.

As a C graphics programmer, you will want to be familiar with some fundamental concepts of business graphics. Although a wide variety of different chart styles are available for you to use in your original C graphics programs, it is all too easy to overlook the reason why graphics are being used in the first place: to communicate information.

Simplicity

As Fig. 15-1 illustrates, business charts should be kept simple and to the point. Too much information can easily overwhelm the viewer. The best charts typically compare only two components. If your business chart begins to look confusing, it is best to break up the material into separate charts, rather than burdening a single chart with too many elements.

Emphasis

In many business charts, it is important for one element to be emphasized as the center of interest or as more important than the other elements in the chart. Refer to Fig. 15-2. This emphasis can be achieved in two ways. First, you can position the important element away from the other elements. This technique is especially useful when a pie chart is being used. Second, you can use a different color to differentiate the important element

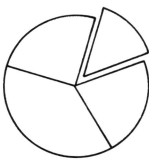

Fig. 15-1. Business charts must be kept simple in order to avoid overwhelming the viewer.

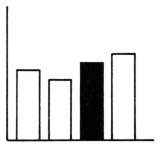

Fig. 15-2. Emphasis can be achieved by position (top example) or by color and contrast (bottom example).

from the other elements in the chart. This approach is useful when bar charts are being employed.

Grouping

Some business charts compare groups of elements, as shown in Fig. 15-3. In this instance, the elements being compared should be positioned very close to each other. The resulting groups should be separated by a reasonable amount of space from other groups. If spacing is not enough to make the purpose of the chart obvious to the viewer, you may wish to use color to tie together the individual elements within each group.

Spacing

Poor spacing is the most common cause of unprofessional-looking charts. As Fig. 15-4 shows, the elements of the chart should fill the available space, using the concepts of layout introduced in Chapter 8. Keep in mind that larger elements often mean that you have the opportunity to add color to each element, giving a richer look to the graphic. Small, thin elements tend to look less appealing to the viewer.

Scale

Next to color, the most important influence on psychological impact is scale. Refer to Fig. 15-5. Any business chart can be made to appear more dramatic by shortening one of the axes. Clearly, most businesses are interested in long-term steady growth and would not benefit from the radical image produced by a shortened scale. On the other hand, if your goal is to convince management that quick action is required because of some changes in the marketplace or poor company performance, then a tighter scale may be exactly what your business chart needs.

To indicate scale on a business chart, two approaches are most commonly used: tick marks and grid lines. When using grid lines, as depicted in Fig. 15-6, it is important to avoid cluttering the graphic. If you are using a VGA or EGA, where 16 colors are available, you would be well advised to draw the grid lines in a color that clearly differentiates them from the other elements in the chart. A dark gray is often the best choice of color for use as a grid. Tick marks, on the other hand, can be used on nearly any axis and will

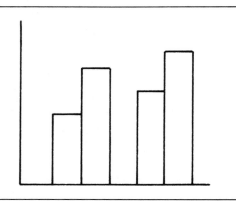

Fig. 15-3. Business chrts can achieve unity of related elements by spacing, position, and color.

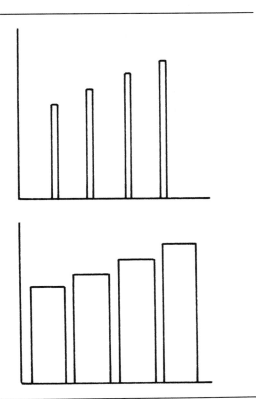

Fig. 15-4. Spacing considerations in business graphics. Top: improper spacing. Bottom: improved spacing.

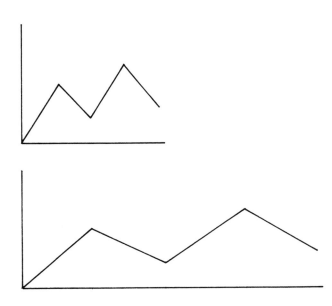

Fig. 15-5. Scale can alter the impact of the psychological same set of statistics.

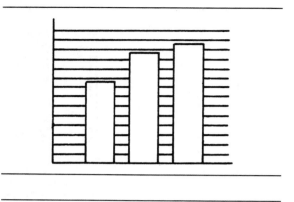

Fig. 15-6. Grid lines, if not overused, can assist in perception of relative values in the chart.

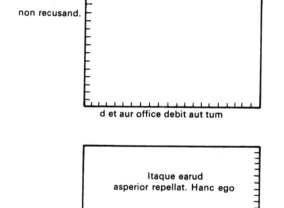

non recusand.

d et aur office debit aut tum

Fig. 15-7. Placement of labels and tick marks.

Itaque earud
asperior repellat. Hanc ego

seldom cause any layout difficulties, as illustrated in Fig. 15-7. The use of tick marks to indicate scale also makes it easier to add labels and captions to the business chart, because the background has been left free of distracting material.

Types of Bar Charts

Although pie charts can be an effective means for communicating business information, as shown earlier in Fig. 15-2, most computer programs use bar charts for business analytic graphics. Surprisingly, a wide variety of bar chart styles are available for your use, as shown in Fig. 15-8. A single-column bar chart, which compares individual columns, can be either vertical or horizontal in layout. A two-column bar chart is often used when groups of elements are being compared.

A 100% column bar chart, also illustrated in Fig. 15-8, is helpful when you are attempting to show how various elements form a whole. The use of different colors to represent different elements of the column is essential.

A deviation column chart shows how individual elements deviate from a benchmark or a norm. Deviation charts are often used when elements can move in either a positive direction or a negative direction. The animated revenue chart in Chapter 18 uses a deviation column chart.

A range column chart is useful when individual elements tend to exhibit a range of values, although this type of graphic lends itself to animation for better communication of the chart's contents.

3D bar charts, like the prototype shown in Fig. 15-9, can be very dramatic. Care must be taken, however, to avoid ambiguities often caused by the 3D process. Because 3D solids can obscure material which is located behind them, it is vital that the layout be kept simple and that labels be generously used.

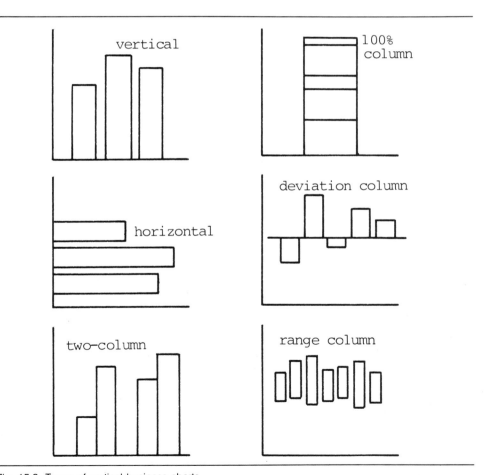

Fig. 15-8. Types of vertical business charts.

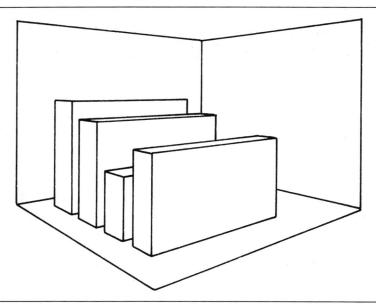

Fig. 15-9. A 3D bar chart.

CASE STUDY: A DEMONSTRATION PROGRAM IN 2D

Figure 15-10 depicts the original pencil sketch from which the demonstration program was developed. The photograph in Fig. 15-11 shows the image produced by the demonstration program in Fig. 15-12.

The program listing in Fig. 15-12 is for QuickC. If you are using Turbo C you should use instead the program listing in Fig. E-6 of Appendix E. If you are using the companion disk for this book, you can load program QC-007.C if you are using QuickC, and you can load program TC-007.C if you are using Turbo C.

The demonstration program uses the 640×350 16-color mode if a VGA is present or if an EGA and enhanced monitor are present. The 640×200 16-color mode is used if an EGA and standard color display are present. If a CGA or MCGA is present, the program uses the 640×200 2-color mode. (This program can be easily adapted for the 640×480 16-color mode if you have a VGA. However, the 80×30 text resolution of the 640×480 mode means that 30 lines of text are available, whereas 25 lines of text are used in the 640×350 and 640×200 modes. Because of the importance of binding the text to the graphical elements of the chart, you will need to change some of the row/column coordinates for text positioning if you decide to run this program in the 640×480 16-color mode on your VGA.)

This program consists of three main components: the airbrushed background effect, the bar graphics, and the text labels. The airbrushed background is created by the first block of code in the **main( )** routine. This halftoning technique is the same as presented in earlier chapters. Note how the horizontal axis and vertical axis of the chart are drawn in a color which contrasts with the background airbrushing.

The labels for the business chart are created using C's built-in instructions. If you are using QuickC, the **_settextposition** instruction is used to set the row/column position

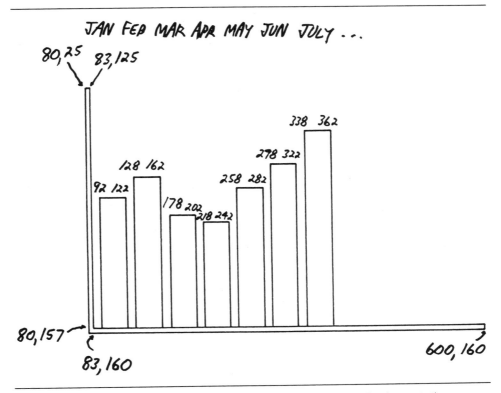

Fig. 15-10. Original template drawing used to obtain screen coordinates for the demonstration program in Fig. 15-12.

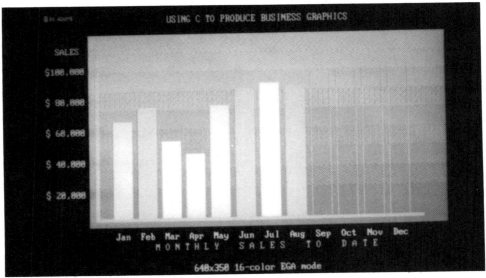

Fig. 15-11. The video display produced by the demonstration program in Fig. 15-12.

before the **__outtext** instruction is used to write the text material to the screen. If you are using Turbo C, the **moveto** instruction is used to set the row/column position before the **outtext** instruction writes the alphanumerics to the screen. QuickC uses the **__settextcolor** instruction to define the color of the alphanumeric characters being written to the screen; Turbo C uses the **setcolor** instruction (which also defines the active color for graphics).

The final block of code in the **main( )** routine draws the bar graphics, using the **rectangle** instruction. In QuickC, this instruction takes the form of **__rectangle (style,x1,y1,x2,y2)**, where **style** indicates whether the rectangle is to be outlined or filled. In Turbo C, the instruction takes the form of **bar(x1,y1,x2,y2)**, where the graphic is automatically filled using the area fill pattern defined earlier by a **setfillstyle** instruction.

The subroutine which pauses and waits for the viewer to strike a key is the same routine used by previous demonstration programs. The compatibility module and the windowing subroutine are also familiar pieces of code.

You may wish to experiment with the visual impact of this business graph by deleting the block of code in **main( )** which creates the background airbrushed graphic. Although the deletion makes the chart simpler and more dramatic, the level of professionalism is reduced.

Fig. 15-12. Program listing for 2D bar chart—QuickC version. VGA/EGA/CGA/MCGA compatible. For Turbo C version, consult Appendix E.

```
/*_____


                            qc-007.c

        Function:  This program demonstrates how to produce high-impact
        business graphics.

        Compatibility:  Supports all graphics adapters and monitors.
        The software uses the 640x350 16-color mode if a VGA is
        present or if an EGA and enhanced monitor are present,
        the 640x200 16-color mode if an EGA and standard monitor are
        present, and the 640x200 2-color mode if a CGA is present.

        Remarks:  Refer to the book.

        Copyright 1988 Lee Adams and TAB BOOKS Inc.


        _____


                    I N C L U D E    F I L E S              */

#include <dos.h>                       /* supports the BIOS call */
#include <stdio.h>              /* supports the printf function */
#include <graph.h>        /* supports the graphics functions */

  /*_____
```

```
                  D E C L A R A T I O N S                          */

struct videoconfig vc;

char fill_3[]={0,32,0,0,0,2,0,0};                    /*    3% fill */
char fill_6[]={32,0,2,0,128,0,8,0};                  /* 6.25% fill */
char fill_12[]={32,2,128,8,32,2,128,8};              /* 12.5% fill */
char fill_25[]={68,17,68,17,68,17,68,17};            /*   25% fill */
char fill_37[]={146,41,148,73,164,73,146,73};        /* 37.5% fill */
char fill_50[]={85,170,85,170,85,170,85,170};        /*   50% fill */
char fill_62[]={109,214,107,182,91,182,109,182};     /* 62.5% fill */
char fill_75[]={187,238,187,238,187,238,187,238};    /*   75% fill */
char fill_87[]={223,253,127,247,223,253,127,247};    /* 87.5% fill */

void keyboard(void);void quit_pgm(void);
void notice(float x,float y);
void coords(void);void graphics_setup(void);

int fg=1;                                    /* foreground color */
int bg=9;                                    /* background color */

float sx,sy,sx1,sy1,sx2,sy2;
float sybase;
float x_res,y_res;
int C0=0,C1=1,C2=2,C3=3,C4=4,C5=5,C6=6,C7=7,C8=8,C9=9,C10=10,
    C11=11,C12=12,C13=13,C14=14,C15=15,mode_flag=0;

/*_____


                  M A I N    R O U T I N E                       */

main(){
graphics_setup();                       /* establish graphics mode */
_getvideoconfig(&vc);                   /* initialize video table */

fg=C1;bg=C9;

              /* draw the background */
_setcolor(bg);
sx=70;sy=38;coords();sx1=sx;sy1=sy;
sx=639;sy=396;coords();sx2=sx;sy2=sy;
_rectangle(_GFILLINTERIOR,sx1,sy1,sx2,sy2);_setcolor(fg);
_setfillmask(fill_6);
sx=70;sy=38;coords();sx1=sx;sy1=sy;
sx=639;sy=72;coords();sx2=sx;sy2=sy;
_rectangle(_GFILLINTERIOR,sx1,sy1,sx2,sy2);
_setfillmask(fill_12);
sx=70;coords();sx1=sx;sy1=sy2+1;
sx=639;sy=108;coords();sx2=sx;sy2=sy;
_rectangle(_GFILLINTERIOR,sx1,sy1,sx2,sy2);
_setfillmask(fill_25);
sx=70;coords();sx1=sx;sy1=sy2+1;
```

```
sx=639;sy=144;coords();sx2=sx;sy2=sy;
_rectangle(_GFILLINTERIOR,sxl,syl,sx2,sy2);
_setfillmask(fill_37);
sx=70;coords();sxl=sx;syl=sy2+1;
sx=639;sy=180;coords();sx2=sx;sy2=sy;
_rectangle(_GFILLINTERIOR,sxl,syl,sx2,sy2);
_setfillmask(fill_50);
sx=70;coords();sxl=sx;syl=sy2+1;
sx=639;sy=216;coords();sx2=sx;sy2=sy;
_rectangle(_GFILLINTERIOR,sxl,syl,sx2,sy2);
_setfillmask(fill_62);
sx=70;coords();sxl=sx;syl=sy2+1;
sx=639;sy=252;coords();sx2=sx;sy2=sy;
_rectangle(_GFILLINTERIOR,sxl,syl,sx2,sy2);
_setfillmask(fill_75);
sx=70;coords();sxl=sx;syl=sy2+1;
sx=639;sy=288;coords();sx2=sx;sy2=sy;
_rectangle(_GFILLINTERIOR,sxl,syl,sx2,sy2);
_setfillmask(fill_87);
sx=70;coords();sxl=sx;syl=sy2+1;
sx=639;sy=324;coords();sx2=sx;sy2=sy;
_rectangle(_GFILLINTERIOR,sxl,syl,sx2,sy2);
_setfillmask(NULL);
sx=70;coords();sxl=sx;syl=sy2+1;
sx=639;sy=396;coords();sx2=sx;sy2=sy;
_rectangle(_GFILLINTERIOR,sxl,syl,sx2,sy2);

                /* draw the axis display */
if (mode_flag==4) C7=0;
_setcolor(C7);
sx=80;sy=60;coords();sxl=sx;syl=sy;
sx=85;sy=384;coords();sx2=sx;sy2=sy;
_rectangle(_GFILLINTERIOR,sxl,syl,sx2,sy2);
sx=80;sy=380;coords();sxl=sx;syl=sy;sybase=sy-1;
sx=600;sy=384;coords();sx2=sx;sy2=sy;
_rectangle(_GFILLINTERIOR,sxl,syl,sx2,sy2);

                /* display the text labels */
if (mode_flag==4) C7=1;
_settextcolor(C7);_settextposition(22,15);
_outtext("Jan Feb Mar Apr May Jun Jul Aug Sep Oct Nov Dec");
_settextcolor(Cl2);_settextposition(23,23);
_outtext("M O N T H L Y    S A L E S    T O    D A T E");
_settextcolor(C7);_settextposition(4,3);_outtext("SALES");
_settextposition(6,1);_outtext("$100,000");
_settextposition(9,1);_outtext("$ 80,000");
_settextposition(12,1);_outtext("$ 60,000");
_settextposition(15,1);_outtext("$ 40,000");
_settextposition(18,1);_outtext("$ 20,000");

                /* draw the monthly levels */
_setcolor(Cl4);
sx=108;sy=204;coords();sxl=sx;syl=sy;
```

```
sx=138;coords();sx2=sx;sy2=sybase;
_rectangle(_GFILLINTERIOR,sx1,sy1,sx2,sy2);
_setcolor(C10);
sx=148;sy=178;coords();sx1=sx;sy1=sy;
sx=178;coords();sx2=sx;sy2=sybase;
_rectangle(_GFILLINTERIOR,sx1,sy1,sx2,sy2);
_setcolor(C11);
sx=188;sy=240;coords();sx1=sx;sy1=sy;
sx=218;coords();sx2=sx;sy2=sybase;
_rectangle(_GFILLINTERIOR,sx1,sy1,sx2,sy2);
_setcolor(C13);
sx=228;sy=264;coords();sx1=sx;sy1=sy;
sx=258;coords();sx2=sx;sy2=sybase;
_rectangle(_GFILLINTERIOR,sx1,sy1,sx2,sy2);
_setcolor(C14);
sx=268;sy=175;coords();sx1=sx;sy1=sy;
sx=298;coords();sx2=sx;sy2=sybase;
_rectangle(_GFILLINTERIOR,sx1,sy1,sx2,sy2);
_setcolor(C10);
sx=308;sy=144;coords();sx1=sx;sy1=sy;
sx=338;coords();sx2=sx;sy2=sybase;
_rectangle(_GFILLINTERIOR,sx1,sy1,sx2,sy2);
_setcolor(C11);
sx=348;sy=134;coords();sx1=sx;sy1=sy;
sx=378;coords();sx2=sx;sy2=sybase;
_rectangle(_GFILLINTERIOR,sx1,sy1,sx2,sy2);
if (mode_flag==4) C7=0;
_setcolor(C7);
sx=388;sy=139;coords();sx1=sx;sy1=sy;
sx=418;coords();sx2=sx;sy2=sybase;
_rectangle(_GFILLINTERIOR,sx1,sy1,sx2,sy2);
if (mode_flag==4) C7=1;
_setcolor(C7);
sx=428;sy=115;coords();sx1=sx;sy1=sy;
sx=458;coords();sx2=sx;sy2=sybase+1;
_rectangle(_GBORDER,sx1,sy1,sx2,sy2);
sx=468;sy=110;coords();sx1=sx;sy1=sy;
sx=498;coords();sx2=sx;sy2=sybase+1;
_rectangle(_GBORDER,sx1,sy1,sx2,sy2);
sx=508;sy=106;coords();sx1=sx;sy1=sy;
sx=538;coords();sx2=sx;sy2=sybase+1;
_rectangle(_GBORDER,sx1,sy1,sx2,sy2);
sx=548;sy=101;coords();sx1=sx;sy1=sy;
sx=578;coords();sx2=sx;sy2=sybase+1;
_rectangle(_GBORDER,sx1,sy1,sx2,sy2);

if (mode_flag==4) C7=1;
_setcolor(C7);notice(0,0);
keyboard();                       /* wait for user to press <Esc> */
quit_pgm();                       /* end the program gracefully */
}
/*_____
```

```
                    SUBROUTINE: CHECK THE KEYBOARD BUFFER              */

void keyboard(void){
union u_type {int a;char b[3];} keystroke;
int get_keystroke(void);              /* declare a local subroutine */

do keystroke.a=get_keystroke();
while (keystroke.b[0]!=27);           /* return if <Esc> is pressed */
}

/*            LOCAL SUBROUTINE: RETRIEVE ONE KEYSTROKE                 */

int get_keystroke(void){
union REGS regs;regs.h.ah=0;return int86(0x16,&regs,&regs);}

/*_____


                    SUBROUTINE: GRACEFUL EXIT FROM THE PROGRAM        */

void quit_pgm(void){
_clearscreen(_GCLEARSCREEN);_setvideomode(_DEFAULTMODE);}

/*_____


                    SUBROUTINE: VGA/EGA/CGA compatibility module
```

This subroutine invokes the highest-resolution graphics mode
which is permitted by the hardware. The 640x350 16-color mode
is established if a VGA is present. The 640x350 16-color mode
is established if an EGA is being used with an enhanced color
display monitor or a multiscanning monitor. The 640x200
16-color mode is established if an EGA is being used with a
standard color monitor. The 640x200 2-color mode is invoked
if a CGA is present.   */

```
void graphics_setup(void){

EGA_ECD_mode:
if (_setvideomode(_ERESCOLOR)==0) {goto EGA_SCD_mode;}
else {x_res=640;y_res=350;mode_flag=2;
      _settextcolor(7);_settextposition(25,31);
      _outtext("640x350 16-color EGA mode");
      _settextposition(1,26);
      _outtext("USING C TO PRODUCE BUSINESS GRAPHICS");
      return;}

EGA_SCD_mode:
if (_setvideomode(_HRES16COLOR)==0) {goto CGA_mode;}
else {x_res=640;y_res=200;mode_flag=3;
      _settextcolor(7);_settextposition(25,31);
      _outtext("640x200 16-color EGA mode");
      _settextposition(1,26);
```

```
        _outtext("USING C TO PRODUCE BUSINESS GRAPHICS");
        return;}

CGA_mode:
if (_setvideomode(_HRESBW)==0) {goto abort_message;}
else {x_res=640;y_res=200;C0=0;C1=1;C2=1;C3=1;C4=1;C5=1,C6=1;C7=3;
        C8=1;C9=0;C10=0;C11=0;C12=1;C13=0;C14=0;C15=0;mode_flag=4;
        _settextcolor(1);_settextposition(25,31);
        _outtext("640x200 2-color CGA mode");
        _settextposition(1,26);
        _outtext("USING C TO PRODUCE BUSINESS GRAPHICS");
        return;}
abort_message:
printf("\n\nUnable to proceed.\n");
printf("Requires VGA, EGA, or CGA adapter\n");
printf("   with appropriate monitor.\n");
printf("Please refer to the book.\n\n");
exit(0);
}
/*_____

                    SUBROUTINE: coords()

    This subroutine accepts sx,sy device-independent display
    coordinates and returns sx,sy device-dependent screen
    coordinates scaled to fit the 640x480, 640x350, 640x200, or
    320x200 screen, depending upon the graphics mode being used. */

void coords(void){
sx=sx*(x_res/640);sy=sy*(y_res/480);return;}

/*_____

                 SUBROUTINE: Copyright Notice

    This subroutine displays the standard copyright notice.
    If you are typing in this program from the book you can
    safely omit this subroutine, provided that you also remove
    the instruction "notice()" from the main routine.           */

int copyright[][3]={0x7c00,0x0000,0x0000,0x8231,
0x819c,0x645e,0xba4a,0x4252,0x96d0,0xa231,0x8252,0x955e,0xba4a,
0x43d2,0xf442,0x8231,0x825c,0x945e,0x7c00,0x0000,0x0000};

void notice(float x, float y){
int a,b,c; int tl=0;
for (tl=0;tl<=6;tl++){a=copyright[tl][0];b=copyright[tl][1];
c=copyright[tl][2];_setlinestyle(a);_moveto(x,y);_lineto(x+15,y);
_setlinestyle(b);_moveto(x+16,y);_lineto(x+31,y);_setlinestyle(c);
_moveto(x+32,y);_lineto(x+47,y);y=y+1;};_setlinestyle(0xFFFF);
return;}

/*_____

                    End of source code                    */
```

CASE STUDY: A DEMONSTRATION PROGRAM IN 3D

Figure 15-13 shows the original pencil sketch used to create the 3D business chart demonstration program in Fig. 15-15. The image produced by this program is presented in Fig. 15-14.

The program listing in Fig. 15-15 is compatible with QuickC. If you are using the companion disk for this book, you can load the program named QC-008.C.

The demonstration program supports all IBM-compatible graphics adapters. If you are using a VGA, the program runs in the 640×480 16-color mode. If you are using an EGA with an enhanced monitor, the program uses the 640×350 16-color mode. The 640×200 16-color mode is used if an EGA and standard color display are installed. If you are using a CGA or MCGA, then the program initializes the 320×200 4-color mode.

As the photograph in Fig. 15-14 clearly indicates, this program is equally effective on VGA, EGA, CGA, and MCGA graphics adapters. The essential ingredient of this graphic is the careful use of halftoning to enhance the three-dimensional qualities of the image.

The foundation of this program is the database located in the DECLARATIONS section of the source code. By referring back to the original thumbnail sketch in Fig. 15-13, you

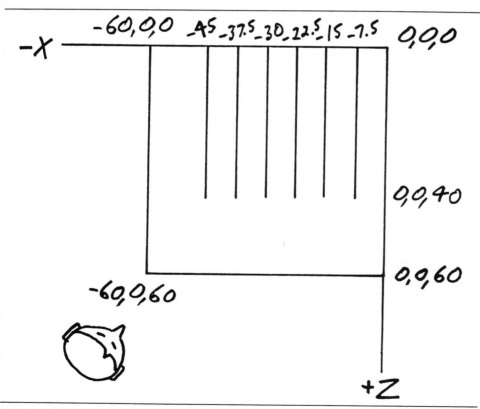

Fig. 15-13. Original template drawing used to obtain the xyz world coordinates for the 3D business chart in Fig. 15-15.

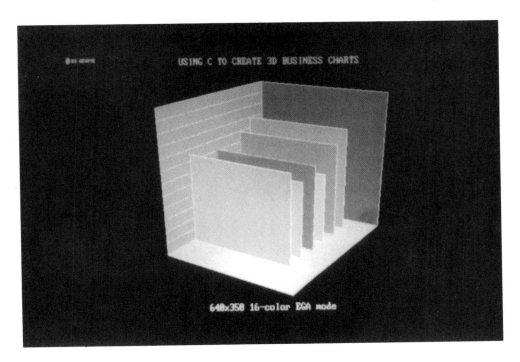

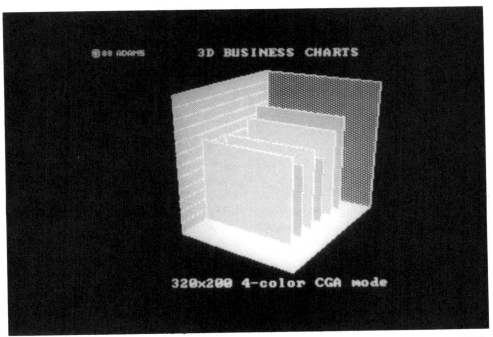

Fig. 15-14. The video display produced by the demonstration program in Fig. 15-15. Top: VGA/EGA. Bottom: CGA.

can see how the xyz coordinates were derived. Note how even the seed points for area fill must be expressed as three-dimensional xyz coordinates. The program draws six bars; you can alter the height of a bar by modifying the y coordinate in the third and fourth sets of xyz coordinates for each bar. The first bar in the database, for example, is expressed as:

$$-8,0,0, \quad -8,0,40, \quad -8,45,40, \quad -8,45,0 \quad -8,20,20$$

This bar is 45 units high in the 3D environment. Suppose you wished to make it only 35 units high. You would change the line to read as follows:

$$-8,0,0, \quad -8,0,40, \quad -8,35,40, \quad -8,35,0, \quad -8,20,20$$

The last set of xyz triplets is the seed point for the area fill.

At the beginning of the **main( )** routine, note how a key matte color has been defined. Because each 3D bar is drawn in front of previously-drawn material, the bar must first be drawn and filled in a unique color to make a hole for the new graphic. As this program executes, you can see the key matte being drawn before the final version of the bar is created.

The 3D subroutines used by this program are identical to those which were presented in Chapter 14. An important addition, however, is the subroutine named **polygon( )**. This subroutine automates the task of drawing a four-sided polygon in a 3D environment.

Note how the **main( )** routine calls a subroutine named **get_coords( )** to retrieve the appropriate xyz values from the database on each occasion before **polygon( )** is called. The subroutine **get_coords( )** is very careful to increment the pointer into the database array whenever it retrieves a set of xyz coordinates. The instruction **p1++** gets the job done.

You can experiment with the angular positioning of the 3D business chart by modifying the variable named **r1** in the DECLARATIONS section. The **r1/r2/r3** variables define the yaw, roll, and pitch of the image. These angles are expressed in radians. 0 radians equals 0 degrees, which is north. 1.57079 equals 90 degrees, which is east. 3.14159 equals 180 degrees, which is south. 4.71239 equals 270 degrees, which is west. 6.28319 radians is the same as 0 radians, and is north. Trying changing **r1** from .98319 to .78319.

This demonstration program is structured in a manner that allows it to be used to display a wide variety of 3D business charts. After you have grasped the relationship between the database array (in the **DECLARATIONS** section) and the subroutine which retrieves xyz coordinates from the database, you can easily adapt this program for your own purposes. Any program intended to run on a VGA in the 640×480 16-color mode should address the issue of the 80×30 text resolution, of course. The other EGA and CGA modes usually use an 80×25 resolution for text matter.

Fig. 15-15. Program listing for a 3D business chart. QuickC version. VGA/EGA/CGA/MCGA compatible.

```
/*_____

                          qc-008.c

   Function:  This program demonstrates how to create 3D
   business graphics.

   Compatibility:  Supports all graphics adapters and monitors.
   The software uses the 640x480 16-color mode if a VGA is
   present, the 640x350 16-color mode if an EGA and enhanced
   monitor are present, the 640x200 16-color mode if an EGA and
   standard monitor are present, and the 320x200 4-color mode
   if a CGA is present.

   Remarks:  3D business charts can often introduce ambiguities
   into the quantities being compared.  Refer to the book for
   further guidance.

   Copyright 1988 Lee Adams and TAB BOOKS Inc.

   _____



                INCLUDE    FILES              */

#include <dos.h>                    /* supports the BIOS call */
#include <stdio.h>             /* supports the printf function */
#include <graph.h>           /* supports the graphics functions */
#include <math.h>          /* supports sine and cosine functions */


/*_____



                DECLARATIONS                  */

struct videoconfig vc;

                    /* declare global variables */
float x=0.0,y=0.0,z=0.0;                   /* world coordinates */
float sx=0.0,sy=0.0;            /* output of 3D perspective formulas */
float xa=0.0,ya=0.0,za=0.0;     /* temporary values in 3D formulas */
float sxa=0.0,sya=0.0,sxb=0.0,syb=0.0;       /* 2D line endpoints */
float sxs=0.0,sys=0.0;         /* temp storage of 2D line startpoint */
float sx1=0.0,sx2=0.0,sx3=0.0,sx4=0.0,sxf=0.0; /* polygon coords */
float sy1=0.0,sy2=0.0,sy3=0.0,sy4=0.0,syf=0.0; /* polygon coords */
float temp_swap=0.0;                   /* used for variable swaps */
float d=1200.0;                    /* angular perspective factor */
double r1=.98319;                      /* yaw angle in radians */
double r2=6.28319;                     /* roll angle in radians */
double r3=5.89778;                     /* pitch angle in radians */
double sr1=0.0,sr2=0.0,sr3=0.0;        /* sine rotation factors */
```

```
double crl=0.0,cr2=0.0,cr3=0.0;          /* cosine rotation factors */
float mx=0.0,my=-10.0,mz=-250.0;              /* viewpoint position */
int maxx=638,minx=1,maxy=198,miny=1;          /* clipping viewport */
float screen_x=639,screen_y=199;     /* dimensions of screen mode */
float c=0.0;                        /* used in line-clipping routine */
float rx=0.0,ry=0.0;      /* scaling values used in mapping routine */
int tl=0,t2=0;                                     /* loop counters */
int pl=0;                                          /* array indexer */
int EDGE=7;                                /* boundary color for fill */
int FILL=1;                                           /* fill color */
int KEY_MATTE=6;                                 /* key matte color */
int BACKGROUND=0;                         /* clean background color */

int C0=0,Cl=1,C2=2,C3=3,C4=4,C5=5,C6=6,C7=7,C8=8,C9=9,C10=10,
    Cl1=11,C12=12,C13=13,Cl4=14,C15=15,mode_flag=0;
float x_res,y_res;

               /* define dithering codes for halftoning */
char fill_3[ ]={0,32,0,0,0,2,0,0}; char fill_6[ ]={32,0,2,0,128,0,
8,0}; char fill_12[ ]={32,2,128,8,32,2,128,8}; char fill_25[ ]={68,
17,68,17,68,17,68,17}; char fill_37[ ]={146,41,148,73,164,73,146,
73}; char fill_50[ ]={85,170,85,170,85,170,85,170}; char fill_62[ ]=
{109,214,107,182,91,182,109,182}; char fill_75[ ]={187,238,187,238,
187,238,187,238}; char fill_87[ ]={223,253,127,247,223,253,127,247};

               /* database of xyz cartesian world coordinates */
int arrayl[ ][3]={
0,0,0, -60,0,0, -60,0,50, 0,0,50, 0,0,0,                 /* pedestal */
0,0,0, -60,0,0, -60,60,0, 0,60,0, 0,0,0,            /* left backdrop */
0,0,0, 0,0,50, 0,60,50, 0,60,0, 0,0,0,             /* right backdrop */
-30,30,0, 0,30,30, -30,0,30,                       /* area fill seeds */
-60,5,0, 0,5,0, -60,10,0, 0,10,0, -60,15,0, 0,15,0,       /* scale */
-60,20,0, 0,20,0, -60,25,0, 0,25,0, -60,30,0, 0,30,0,
-60,35,0, 0,35,0, -60,40,0, 0,40,0, -60,45,0, 0,45,0,
-60,50,0, 0,50,0, -60,55,0, 0,55,0,
-8,0,0, -8,0,40, -8,45,40, -8,45,0, -8,20,20,             /* bars */
-15,0,0, -15,0,40, -15,40,40, -15,40,0, -15,20,20,
-23,0,0, -23,0,40, -23,30,40, -23,30,0, -23,20,20,
-30,0,0, -30,0,40, -30,36,40, -30,36,0, -30,20,20,
-38,0,0, -38,0,40, -38,32,40, -38,32,0, -38,10,20,
-45,0,0, -45,0,40, -45,38,40, -45,38,0, -45,10,20};


               /* declare global subroutines */
void keyboard(void);void quit_pgm(void);void calc_3d(void);
void rotation(void);void window(void);void viewport(void);
void get_coords(void);void polygon(void);void coords(void);
void notice (float x,float y);void graphics_setup(void);

/*_____

                    M A I N   R O U T I N E                    */

main(){
graphics_setup();                       /* establish graphics mode */
```

```
_getvideoconfig(&vc);                        /* initialize video table */

EDGE=C7;FILL=C1;KEY_MATTE=C6;BACKGROUND=C0;
_setcolor(C7);

rotation();          /* calculate yaw, roll, pitch rotation factors */

for (t2=1;t2<=3;t2++){                            /* draw the backdrops */
  get_coords();calc_3d();window();sxa=sx;sya=sy;
  for (t1=1;t1<=4;t1++)
    {get_coords();calc_3d();window();sxs=sx;sys=sy;sxb=sx;syb=sy;
     viewport();_moveto(sxa,sya);_lineto(sxb,syb);sxa=sxs;sya=sys;};
  };

get_coords();calc_3d();window();                    /* apply halftoning */
_setfillmask(fill_50);_floodfill(sx,sy,C7);
get_coords();calc_3d();window();
_setfillmask(fill_25);_floodfill(sx,sy,C7);
get_coords();calc_3d();window();
_setfillmask(NULL);_floodfill(sx,sy,C7);

for (t1=1;t1<=11;t1++){                            /* draw scale markers */
  get_coords();calc_3d();window();sxa=sx;sya=sy;
  get_coords();calc_3d();window();sxb=sx;syb=sy;
  viewport();_moveto(sxa,sya);_lineto(sxb,syb);};

                             /* draw the sales performance blocks */
for (t1=1;t1<=6;t1++){
  if (t1==1) {EDGE=C9;FILL=C9;}
  if (t1==2) {EDGE=C10;FILL=C10;}
  if (t1==3) {EDGE=C11;FILL=C11;}
  if (t1==4) {EDGE=C12;FILL=C12;}
  if (t1==5) {EDGE=C13;FILL=C13;}
  if (t1==6) {EDGE=C14;FILL=C14;}
  get_coords();calc_3d();window();sx1=sx;sy1=sy;
  get_coords();calc_3d();window();sx2=sx;sy2=sy;
  get_coords();calc_3d();window();sx3=sx;sy3=sy;
  get_coords();calc_3d();window();sx4=sx;sy4=sy;
  get_coords();calc_3d();window();sxf=sx;syf=sy;
  polygon();
  _setcolor(FILL);_setfillmask(fill_50);_floodfill(sxf,syf,EDGE);
  };

_setcolor(C7);notice(0,0);
keyboard();                          /* wait for user to press <Esc> */
quit_pgm();}                          /* end the program gracefully */

/*_____
```

SUBROUTINE: DRAW 3D POLYGON
This subroutine uses a unique fill color to prepare a
polygon ready for halftoning. Enter with sx1,sy1...
sxf,syf unclipped display coordinates. Enter with

```
      KEY_MATTE color, EDGE color, BACKGROUND color.              */

void polygon(void){
_setfillmask(NULL);_setlinestyle(0xffff);_setcolor(KEY_MATTE);
sxa=sx1;sya=sy1;sxb=sx2;syb=sy2;viewport();
_moveto(sxa,sya);_lineto(sxb,syb);
sxa=sx2;sya=sy2;sxb=sx3;syb=sy3;viewport();
_moveto(sxa,sya);_lineto(sxb,syb);
sxa=sx3;sya=sy3;sxb=sx4;syb=sy4;viewport();
_moveto(sxa,sya);_lineto(sxb,syb);
sxa=sx4;sya=sy4;sxb=sx1;syb=sy1;viewport();
_moveto(sxa,sya);_lineto(sxb,syb);_floodfill(sxf,syf,KEY_MATTE);
_setcolor(EDGE);
sxa=sx1;sya=sy1;sxb=sx2;syb=sy2;viewport();
_moveto(sxa,sya);_lineto(sxb,syb);
sxa=sx2;sya=sy2;sxb=sx3;syb=sy3;viewport();
_moveto(sxa,sya);_lineto(sxb,syb);
sxa=sx3;sya=sy3;sxb=sx4;syb=sy4;viewport();
_moveto(sxa,sya);_lineto(sxb,syb);
sxa=sx4;sya=sy4;sxb=sx1;syb=sy1;viewport();
_moveto(sxa,sya);_lineto(sxb,syb);
_setcolor(BACKGROUND);_floodfill(sxf,syf,EDGE);
return;}
```

```
/*_____


   SUBROUTINE: RETRIEVE xyz WORLD COORDINATES FROM DATABASE
   This subroutine retrieves a set of xyz cartresian world
   coordinates from the database.  The index pointer is
   automatically incremented.                              */

void get_coords(void){
x=array1[pl][0];y=array1[pl][1];z=array1[pl][2];pl++;return;}
```

```
/*_____


            SUBROUTINE: CALCULATE SIN, COS FACTORS
   Enter with r1,r2,r3 viewing angles for yaw, roll, pitch
   expressed in radians 0.0 through 6.28319.  Returns sine
   and cosine factors.                                     */

void rotation(void){
sr1=sin(r1);sr2=sin(r2);sr3=sin(r3);cr1=cos(r1);cr2=cos(r2);
cr3=cos(r3);return;}
```

```
/*_____
.

            SUBROUTINE: STANDARD 3D FORMULAS
   Enter with x,y,z cartesian world coordinates.  Returns sx,sy
```

cartesian display coordinates. Returns x,y,z cartesian view
coordinates.   */

```
void calc_3d(void){
x=(-1)*x;xa=cr1*x-sr1*z;za=sr1*x+cr1*z;x=cr2*xa+sr2*y;
ya=cr2*y-sr2*xa;z=cr3*za-sr3*ya;y=sr3*za+cr3*ya;x=x+mx;y=y+my;
z=z+mz;sx=d*x/z;sy=d*y/z;return;}
```

/*_____

    SUBROUTINE: MAP CARTESIAN COORDS TO PHYSICAL SCREEN COORDS
    Enter with sx,sy cartesian display coordinates derived from
    world coordinate space -399,-299 to 400,300. Returns sx,sy
    unclipped physical display coordinates.   */

```
void window(void){
sx=sx+399;sy=sy+299;rx=screen_x/799;ry=screen_y/599;sx=sx*rx;
sy=sy*ry;return;}
```

/*_____

                    SUBROUTINE: 2D LINE-CLIPPING
    Enter with sxa,sya and sxb,syb endpoints of line to be
    clipped. Returns display coordinates for line clipped to
    fit physical screen viewport defined by minx,miny and
    maxx,maxy.   */

```
void viewport(void){
if (sxa>sxb) {temp_swap=sxa;sxa=sxb;sxb=temp_swap;
             temp_swap=sya;sya=syb;syb=temp_swap;};
if (sxa<minx) if (sxb<minx) return;
if (sxa>maxx) if (sxb>maxx) return;
if (sya<miny) if (syb<miny) return;
if (sya>maxy) if (syb>maxy) return;
if (sxa<minx) {{c=(syb-sya)/(sxb-sxa)*(sxb-minx);  /* push right */
             sxa=minx;sya=syb-c;};
             if (sya<miny) if (syb<miny) return;
             if (sya>maxy) if (syb>maxy) return;
             };
if (sxb>maxx) {{c=(syb-sya)/(sxb-sxa)*(maxx-sxa);  /* push left */
             sxb=maxx;syb=sya+c;};
             if (sya<miny) if (syb<miny) return;
             if (sya>maxy) if (syb>maxy) return;
             };
if (sya>syb) {temp_swap=sya;sya=syb;syb=temp_swap;
             temp_swap=sxa;sxa=sxb;sxb=temp_swap;};
if (sya<miny) {c=(sxb-sxa)/(syb-sya)*(syb-miny);   /* push down */
             sxa=sxb-c;sya=miny;};
if (syb>maxy) {c=(sxb-sxa)/(syb-sya)*(maxy-sya);   /* push up */
             sxb=sxa+c;syb=maxy;};
return;}
```

```
/*_____

              SUBROUTINE: CHECK THE KEYBOARD BUFFER            */

void keyboard(void){
union u_type {int a;char b[3];} keystroke;
int get_keystroke(void);           /* declare a local subroutine */

do keystroke.a=get_keystroke();
while (keystroke.b[0]!=27);         /* return if <Esc> is pressed */
}

/*          LOCAL SUBROUTINE: RETRIEVE ONE KEYSTROKE            */

int get_keystroke(void){
union REGS regs;regs.h.ah=0;return int86(0x16,&regs,&regs);}

/*_____


              SUBROUTINE: GRACEFUL EXIT FROM THE PROGRAM        */

void quit_pgm(void){
_clearscreen(_GCLEARSCREEN);_setvideomode(_DEFAULTMODE);}

/*_____


              SUBROUTINE: VGA/EGA/CGA compatibility module
```

This subroutine invokes the highest-resolution graphics mode
which is permitted by the hardware. The 640x480 16-color mode
is established if a VGA is present. The 640x350 16-color mode
is established if an EGA is being used with an enhanced color
display monitor or a multiscanning monitor. The 640x200
16-color mode is established if an EGA is being used with a
standard color monitor. The 320x200 4-color mode is invoked
if a CGA is present.   */

```
void graphics_setup(void){

VGA_mode:
if (_setvideomode(_VRES16COLOR)==0) {goto EGA_ECD_mode;}
else {x_res=640;y_res=480;mode_flag=1;
      maxx=638;minx=1;maxy=478;miny=1;       /* clipping viewport */
      screen_x=639;screen_y=479;     /* dimensions of screen mode */
      x_res=640;y_res=480;           /* resolution of screen mode */
      _settextcolor(7);_settextposition(30,30);
      _outtext("640x480 16-color VGA mode");
      _settextposition(1,24);
      _outtext("USING C TO CREATE 3D BUSINESS CHARTS");
      return;}

EGA_ECD_mode:
```

```
if (_setvideomode(_ERESCOLOR)==0) {goto EGA_SCD_mode;}
else {x_res=640;y_res=350;mode_flag=2;
     maxx=638;minx=1;maxy=348;miny=1;        /* clipping viewport */
     screen_x=639;screen_y=349;      /* dimensions of screen mode */
     x_res=640;y_res=350;            /* resolution of screen mode */
     _settextcolor(7);_settextposition(25,30);
     _outtext("640x350 16-color EGA mode");
     _settextposition(1,24);
     _outtext("USING C TO CREATE 3D BUSINESS CHARTS");
     return;}

EGA_SCD_mode:
if (_setvideomode(_HRES16COLOR)==0) {goto CGA_mode;}
else {x_res=640;y_res=200;mode_flag=3;
     maxx=638;minx=1;maxy=198;miny=1;        /* clipping viewport */
     screen_x=639;screen_y=199;      /* dimensions of screen mode */
     x_res=640;y_res=200;            /* resolution of screen mode */
     _settextcolor(7);_settextposition(25,30);
     _outtext("640x200 16-color EGA mode");
     _settextposition(1,24);
     _outtext("USING C TO CREATE 3D BUSINESS CHARTS");
     return;}

CGA_mode:
if (_setvideomode(_MRES4COLOR)==0) {goto abort_message;}
else {x_res=320;y_res=200;C0=0;Cl=3;C6=2;C7=3;
     C9=1;C10=3;C11=1;C12=3;C13=1;C14=3;
     mode_flag=4;
     maxx=318;minx=1;maxy=198;miny=1;        /* clipping viewport */
     screen_x=319;screen_y=199;      /* dimensions of screen mode */
     x_res=320;y_res=200;            /* resolution of screen mode */
     _settextcolor(3);_settextposition(25,10);
     _outtext("320x200 4-color CGA mode");
     _settextposition(1,13);
     _outtext("3D BUSINESS CHARTS");
     return;}

abort_message:
printf("\n\nUnable to proceed.\n");
printf("Requires VGA, EGA, or CGA adapter\n");
printf("   with appropriate monitor.\n");
printf("Please refer to the book.\n\n");
exit(0);
}

/*_____

            SUBROUTINE: coords()

   This subroutine accepts sx,sy device-independent display
   coordinates and returns sx,sy device-dependent screen
   coordinates scaled to fit the 640x480, 640x350, 640x200, or
   320x200 screen, depending upon the graphics mode being used. */
```

```
void coords(void){
sx=sx*(x_res/640);sy=sy*(y_res/480);return;}

/*_____


                    SUBROUTINE: Copyright Notice
        This subroutine displays the standard copyright notice.
        If you are typing in this program from the book you can
        safely omit this subroutine, provided that you also remove
        the instruction "notice()" from the main routine.          */

int copyright[][3]={0x7c00,0x0000,0x0000,0x8231,
0x819c,0x645e,0xba4a,0x4252,0x96d0,0xa231,0x8252,0x955e,0xba4a,
0x43d2,0xf442,0x8231,0x825c,0x945e,0x7c00,0x0000,0x0000};

void notice(float x, float y){
int a,b,c; int tl=0;
for (tl=0;tl<=6;tl++){a=copyright[tl][0];b=copyright[tl][1];
c=copyright[tl][2];_setlinestyle(a);_moveto(x,y);_lineto(x+15,y);
_setlinestyle(b);_moveto(x+16,y);_lineto(x+31,y);_setlinestyle(c);
_moveto(x+32,y);_lineto(x+47,y);y=y+1;};_setlinestyle(0xFFFF);
return;}

/*_____


                        End of source code               */
```

16

Realistic Illustration

Both QuickC and Turbo C are capable of generating realistic illustrations, especially when using the higher resolution screen modes. As shown in Fig. 16-1, a line thickness is actually limited by a resolution of three pixels, because a space is needed on each side of the line in order to separate it from other graphical elements on the display screen. This three-pixel regime means that the 320×200 graphics modes are for the most part less than adequate for the purposes of realistic graphics (except the 320×200 256-color mode, which can compensate for the lack of resolution by increased color differentiation between graphical elements).

If you are using a VGA, the best screen choice for displaying the detailed elements which are required by realistic illustration is the 640×480 16-color mode. If you are using an EGA with an enhanced monitor, you should use the 640×350 16-color mode. If you are using an EGA with a standard color display, you should use the 640×200 16-color mode. If you are using a CGA, you should use the 640×200 2-color mode.

STYLES OF ILLUSTRATION

As a C graphics programmer, a variety of time-proven drawing styles are available for your use, including line drawing, stipple drawing, and contrast drawing. Refer to Fig. 16-2. *Line drawings* use simple lines to describe the various edges of the subject matter. *Stipple drawings* rely upon points and dots to simulate the highlight and shadow areas of the subject matter. (In fine art circles, this technique is called *pointilism*.) *Contrast drawings* use broad areas of black and white to simulate the contrast between highlight areas and shadow areas found in the subject matter.

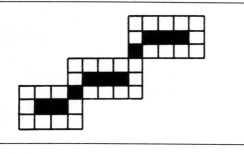

Fig. 16-1. Actual minimum required resolution is a three-pixel horizontal and vertical distance, because two lines placed adjacent to each other become a single fat line.

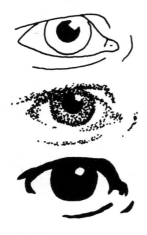

Fig. 16-2. A variety of drawing techniques are available for realistic illustration on computer screens. Top: line drawing. Center: stippled drawing. Bottom: contrast drawing.

PREPARATION

Figure 16-3 depicts the original sketch which was used to create the demonstration program in this chapter. From this sketch were derived the xy screen coordinates which make up the image on the computer screen. The xy coordinates are stored in a database array in the C program.

In most cases it is essential for the C programmer to work from a sketch on paper. Much time can be saved and the trial and error component of the programming cycle can be reduced dramatically if the glitches are corrected at the pencil sketch stage, rather than at the computer keyboard. It is far easier to erase and redraw a line on paper than it is to compile, run, edit, recompile, and rerun a program over and over again until you get the xy coordinates exactly right.

CASE STUDY: A DEMONSTRATION PROGRAM

The photograph in Fig. 16-4 shows the image produced by the demonstration program in Fig. 16-5. The program listing in Fig. 16-5 is compatible with QuickC. If you are using the companion disk for this book, you can load the program named QC-009.C.

The demonstration program supports all IBM-compatible graphics adapters. If you are using a VGA, the program runs in the 640×480 16-color mode. If you are using an

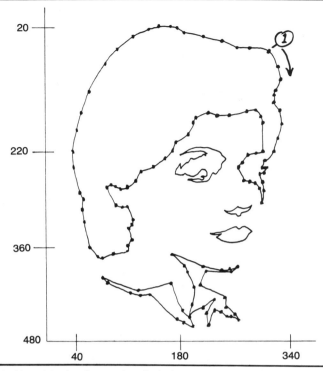

Fig. 16-3. The original template drawing used to obtain the xy coordinates for the demonstration program in Fig. 16-5.

Fig. 16-4. The video display produced by the demonstration program in Fig. 16-5.

EGA and an enhanced monitor, the program runs in the 640×350 16-color mode. If you are using an EGA and a standard color display, the program runs in the 640×200 16-color mode. If you are using a CGA or MCGA, the program initializes the 640×200 2-color mode.

Six arrays in the **DECLARATIONS** section of the source code are used to build the database for this graphics program. Separate arrays are used to hold the xy coordinates for the mouth, nose, hair, eyes, chin, and collar. By reviewing the **main( )** routine, you can see how the **p1** variable is used to point into the database arrays. Note how **p1** is incremented after fetching each set of xy coordinates, thereby leaving **p1** pointed at the next set of xy coordinates.

The **main( )** routine relies heavily upon polylines to create the realistic illustration. The **for/next** loop concept is used in combination with QuickC's **___line to** instruction to draw a series of connected lines. These connected lines make up the actual illustration. Before any line is drawn, however, the **main( )** routine calls upon the subroutine named **coords( )** to map the coordinates to fit whichever screen mode is in effect.

If you intend to write original C programs to create realistic illustrations, you need two personal attributes: talent and perseverance. Artistic talent is essential in order to produce good artwork, and there is no substitute for talent, unfortunately. Perseverance is needed in order to cope with the large numbers of xy coordinates in the database. In many cases, the larger the database the better the drawing.

Fig. 16-5. Program listing for a realistic illustration—QuickC version. VGA/EGA/CGA/MCGA compatible.

```
/*_____


                              qc-009.c


    Function:  This program demonstrates how to create realistic
    illustrations using database screen coordinates.

    Compatibility:  Supports all graphics adapters and monitors.
    The software uses the 640x480 16-color mode if a VGA is
    present, the 640x350 16-color mode if an EGA and enhanced
    monitor are present, the 640x200 16-color mode if an EGA and
    standard monitor are present, and the 640x200 2-color mode
    if a CGA is present.

    Remarks:  Refer to the book.

    Copyright 1988 Lee Adams and TAB BOOKS Inc.


    _____


              I N C L U D E    F I L E S              */

#include <dos.h>                      /* supports the BIOS call */
#include <stdio.h>             /* supports the printf function */
#include <graph.h>          /* supports the graphics functions */
```

```
/*_____


                        D E C L A R A T I O N S                    */

struct videoconfig vc;

void keyboard(void);void quit_pgm(void);
void notice(float x,float y);
void coords(void);void graphics_setup(void);

float sx,sy,sx1,sy1,sx2,sy2;
float x_res,y_res;
int C0=0,C1=1,C2=2,C3=3,C4=4,C5=5,C6=6,C7=7,C8=8,C9=9,C10=10,
    C11=11,C12=12,C13=13,C14=14,C15=15,mode_flag=0;

int t1=1;                            /* counter for drawing loops */
int p1=0;                            /* index pointer into arrays */

int array1[][2]={                         /* xy coordinates for mouth */
    265,321, 270,325, 277,321, 283,325, 288,330, 286,333,
    283,335, 281,340, 275,345, 270,347, 260,346, 250,342,
    243,339, 250,339, 259,335, 240,335, 235,332, 232,333,
    233,329, 240,330, 248,329, 265,321, 270,330};
int array2[][2]={                          /* xy coordinates for nose */
    288,290, 284,299, 275,300, 272,305, 269,303, 266,300,
    260,301, 255,300, 251,298, 260,299, 268,290, 272,290,
    280,294, 285,292, 288,290, 270,295};

int array3[][2]={                          /* xy coordinates for hair */
    310,42,  322,62,  325,75,  330,88,  325,106, 320,112,
    320,120, 319,126, 332,150, 328,178, 320,200, 318,211,
    310,219, 305,220, 302,228, 311,229, 307,237, 300,240,
    302,245, 305,257, 307,262, 308,272, 306,280, 303,283,
    303,270, 300,257, 292,252, 286,250, 280,248, 275,245,
    272,228, 285,210, 295,205, 300,204, 305,204, 303,198,
    303,180, 302,152, 296,140, 288,145, 275,148, 250,149,
    235,142, 212,150, 208,166, 204,178, 195,185, 186,190,
    184,200, 179,210, 171,220, 155,232, 147,238, 138,238,
    128,255, 125,260, 116,262, 103,260, 98,260,  92,261,
    100,271, 102,280, 105,280, 109,290, 115,289, 122,288,
    131,322, 126,311, 126,321, 122,328, 127,338, 129,341,
    121,354, 121,360, 114,365, 105,362, 99,367,  88,372,
    80,368,  70,355,  64,320,  60,288,  61,280,  55,265,
    48,218,  50,190,  50,180,  52,168,  62,130,  68,112,
    80,89,   88,79,   90,68,   95,60,   104,50,  112,42,
    133,22,  138,20,  165,11,  170,13,  180,10,  187,12,
    200,20,  215,24,  245,30,  255,35,  261,36,  268,42,
    278,44,  292,45,  300,41,  310,42,  180,100};

int array4[][2]={                          /* xy coordinates for eye */
    189,212, 205,201, 220,199, 232,201, 240,201, 250,206,
    255,211, 254,218, 246,223, 248,232, 240,240, 234,241,
```

```
            221,244, 229,240, 229,238, 227,232, 224,231, 220,231,
            220,238, 215,242, 211,243, 205,242, 200,238, 199,241,
            190,240, 185,237, 193,223, 194,230, 198,225, 205,221,
            207,218, 215,218, 225,210, 231,209, 222,205, 206,206,
            189,212, 230,220};

int array5[][2]={                        /* xy coordinates for chin */
            182,363, 225,385, 240,390, 257,390, 270,388, 275,392,
            257,394, 240,393, 229,391, 220,415, 234,420, 246,425,
            255,432, 257,447, 270,465, 260,462, 239,450, 231,472,
            231,458, 241,432, 205,460, 214,430, 214,420, 201,386,
            182,363, 225,430};

int array6[][2]={                        /* xy coordinates for collar */
             88,402, 135,422, 181,410, 186,435, 216,465, 213,477,
            200,475, 152,428, 144,432, 100,410,  88,402, 170,425};

/*_____


                    M A I N    R O U T I N E                      */


main(){
graphics_setup();                         /* establish graphics mode */
_getvideoconfig(&vc);                     /* initialize video table */
_setcolor(C7);_setfillmask(NULL);


                    /* draw the white canvas */
sx=0;sy=0;coords();sx1=sx;sy1=sy;
sx=399;sy=479;coords();sx2=sx;sy2=sy;
_rectangle(_GFILLINTERIOR,sx1,sy1,sx2,sy2);
_setcolor(C0);sx=5;sy=462;coords();notice(sx,sy);       /* notice */
_setcolor(C0);                            /* set drawing color to black */


                    /* draw the subject's mouth */
pl=0;
sx=array1[pl][0];sy=array1[pl][1];pl++;coords();_moveto(sx,sy);
for (tl=1;tl<=21;tl++){
    sx=array1[pl][0];sy=array1[pl][1];pl++;
    coords();_lineto(sx,sy);};
sx=array1[pl][0];sy=array1[pl][1];coords();_floodfill(sx,sy,C0);


                    /* draw the subject's nose */
pl=0;
sx=array2[pl][0];sy=array2[pl][1];pl++;coords();_moveto(sx,sy);
for (tl=1;tl<=14;tl++){
    sx=array2[pl][0];sy=array2[pl][1];pl++;
    coords();_lineto(sx,sy);};
sx=array2[pl][0];sy=array2[pl][1];coords();_floodfill(sx,sy,C0);
```

```
                    /* draw the subject's hair and left eye */
pl=0;
sx=array3[pl][0];sy=array3[pl][1];pl++;coords();_moveto(sx,sy);
for (tl=1;tl<=111;tl++){
    sx=array3[pl][0];sy=array3[pl][1];pl++;
    coords();_lineto(sx,sy);};
sx=array3[pl][0];sy=array3[pl][1];coords();_floodfill(sx,sy,C0);


                    /* draw the subject's right eye */
pl=0;
sx=array4[pl][0];sy=array4[pl][1];pl++;coords();_moveto(sx,sy);
for (tl=1;tl<=36;tl++){
    sx=array4[pl][0];sy=array4[pl][1];pl++;
    coords();_lineto(sx,sy);};
sx=array4[pl][0];sy=array4[pl][1];coords();_floodfill(sx,sy,C0);


                    /* draw the subject's chin */
pl=0;
sx=array5[pl][0];sy=array5[pl][1];pl++;coords();_moveto(sx,sy);
for (tl=1;tl<=24;tl++){
    sx=array5[pl][0];sy=array5[pl][1];pl++;
    coords();_lineto(sx,sy);};
sx=array5[pl][0];sy=array5[pl][1];coords();_floodfill(sx,sy,C0);


                    /* draw the subject's collar */
pl=0;
sx=array6[pl][0];sy=array6[pl][1];pl++;coords();_moveto(sx,sy);
for (tl=1;tl<=10;tl++){
    sx=array6[pl][0];sy=array6[pl][1];pl++;
    coords();_lineto(sx,sy);};
sx=array6[pl][0];sy=array6[pl][1];coords();_floodfill(sx,sy,C0);


                    /* add highlight trim for eyes, etc. */
_setcolor(C7);                          /* set drawing color to white */
sx=213;sy=233;coords();_setpixel(sx,sy);
sx=214;sy=233;coords();_setpixel(sx,sy);
sx=213;sy=234;coords();_setpixel(sx,sy);
sx=214;sy=234;coords();_setpixel(sx,sy);
sx=202;sy=228;coords();_moveto(sx,sy);
sx=210;sy=226;coords();_lineto(sx,sy);
sx=220,sy=226;coords();_lineto(sx,sy);
sx=223;sy=228;coords();_lineto(sx,sy);


keyboard();                             /* wait for user to press <Esc> */
quit_pgm();                             /* end the program gracefully */
}
/*_____
```

```
                    SUBROUTINE: CHECK THE KEYBOARD BUFFER                */

void keyboard(void){
union u_type {int a;char b[3];} keystroke;
int get_keystroke(void);              /* declare a local subroutine */

do keystroke.a=get_keystroke();
while (keystroke.b[0]!=27);           /* return if <Esc> is pressed */
}

/*            LOCAL SUBROUTINE: RETRIEVE ONE KEYSTROKE                  */

int get_keystroke(void){
union REGS regs;regs.h.ah=0;return int86(0x16,&regs,&regs);}
/*_____


            SUBROUTINE: GRACEFUL EXIT FROM THE PROGRAM               */

void quit_pgm(void){
_clearscreen(_GCLEARSCREEN);_setvideomode(_DEFAULTMODE);}

/*_____


            SUBROUTINE: VGA/EGA/CGA compatibility module
```

This subroutine invokes the highest-resolution graphics mode
which is permitted by the hardware. The 640x480 16-color mode
is established if a VGA is present. The 640x350 16-color mode
is established if an EGA is being used with an enhanced color
display monitor or a multiscanning monitor. The 640x200
16-color mode is established if an EGA is being used with a
standard color monitor. The 640x200 2-color mode is invoked
if a CGA is present.   */

```
void graphics_setup(void){

VGA_mode:
if (_setvideomode(_VRES16COLOR)==0) {goto EGA_ECD_mode;}
else {x_res=640;y_res=480;mode_flag=1;
     _settextcolor(7);_settextposition(30,54);
     _outtext("640x480 16-color VGA mode");
     _settextcolor(12);_settextposition(13,58);
     _outtext("USING C TO CREATE");
     _settextposition(14,55);
     _outtext("REALISTIC ILLUSTRATIONS");
     _settextcolor(7);
     return;}

EGA_ECD_mode:
if (_setvideomode(_ERESCOLOR)==0) {goto EGA_SCD_mode;}
else {x_res=640;y_res=350;mode_flag=2;
```

```
        _settextcolor(7);_settextposition(25,54);
        _outtext("640x350 16-color EGA mode");
        _settextcolor(12);_settextposition(13,58);
        _outtext("USING C TO CREATE");
        _settextposition(14,55);
        _outtext("REALISTIC ILLUSTRATIONS");
        _settextcolor(7);
        return;}

EGA_SCD_mode:
if (_setvideomode(_HRES16COLOR)==0) {goto CGA_mode;}
else {x_res=640;y_res=200;mode_flag=3;

        _settextcolor(7);_settextposition(25,54);
        _outtext("640x200 16-color EGA mode");
        _settextcolor(12);_settextposition(13,58);
        _outtext("USING C TO CREATE");
        _settextposition(14,55);
        _outtext("REALISTIC ILLUSTRATIONS");
        _settextcolor(7);
        return;}

CGA_mode:
if (_setvideomode(_HRESBW)==0) {goto abort_message;}
else {x_res=640;y_res=200;C0=0;C1=1;C2=1;C3=1;C4=1;C5=1,C6=1;C7=1;
        C8=1;C9=1;C10=1;C11=1;C12=1;C13=1;C14=1;C15=1;mode_flag=4;
        _settextcolor(1);_settextposition(25,54);
        _outtext("640x200 2-color CGA mode");
        _settextposition(13,58);
        _outtext("USING C TO CREATE");
        _settextposition(14,55);
        _outtext("REALISTIC ILLUSTRATIONS");
        return;}

abort_message:
printf("\n\nUnable to proceed.\n");
printf("Requires VGA, EGA, or CGA adapter\n");
printf("   with appropriate monitor.\n");
printf("Please refer to the book.\n\n");
exit(0);
}

/*_____

                    SUBROUTINE: coords()

   This subroutine accepts sx,sy device-independent display
   coordinates and returns sx,sy device-dependent screen
   coordinates scaled to fit the 640x480, 640x350, 640x200, or
   320x200 screen, depending upon the graphics mode being used. */

void coords(void){
sx=sx*(x_res/640);sy=sy*(y_res/480);return;}
/*_____
```

```
                    SUBROUTINE: Copyright Notice

      This subroutine displays the standard copyright notice.
      If you are typing in this program from the book you can
      safely omit this subroutine, provided that you also remove
      the instruction "notice()" from the main routine.          */

int copyright[][3]={0x7c00,0x0000,0x0000,0x8231,
0x819c,0x645e,0xba4a,0x4252,0x96d0,0xa231,0x8252,0x955e,0xba4a,
0x43d2,0xf442,0x8231,0x825c,0x945e,0x7c00,0x0000,0x0000};

void notice(float x, float y){
int a,b,c; int tl=0;
for (tl=0;tl<=6;tl++){a=copyright[tl][0];b=copyright[tl][1];
c=copyright[tl][2];_setlinestyle(a);_moveto(x,y);_lineto(x+15,y);
_setlinestyle(b);_moveto(x+16,y);_lineto(x+31,y);_setlinestyle(c);
_moveto(x+32,y);_lineto(x+47,y);y=y+1;};_setlinestyle(0xFFFF);
return;}

/*_____



                    End of source code                          */
```

IV

FRAME ANIMATION

Lightning-Quick Techniques

17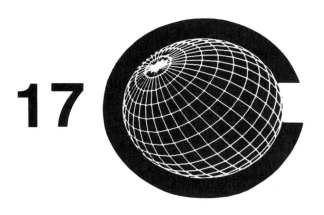

Practical Techniques
for Frame Animation

Frame animation produces the fastest-running animation on IBM-compatible personal computers. Because the images to be animated have been created in advance, the computer can concentrate all of its processing power on the animation procedure itself. Animation rates of 30 frames per second (fps) and faster are easily achieved, even when using the slow-running 4.77 Mhz 8088-based models of the IBM family. Frame animation is called *page* animation by Microsoft.

A *frame* is a block of memory which contains the data for a screenful of graphics. Another name for frame is page. The page which is being displayed on the screen is called the *display page*. The other pages are hidden. The page to which the computer is sending graphics is called the *active page*. If a hidden page is being written to, it is called a *hidden, written-to page*.

THE FRAME ANIMATION PROCESS

Figure 17-1 summarizes the essential components of frame animation. On a VGA or EGA using the 640×200 16-color mode, four graphics pages are available. (Refer to Chapter 2 for a detailed discussion of graphics adapters.) On a CGA, which carries only enough display memory for a single page, this limitation can be overcome by storing the other graphics pages in user RAM.

The first step in creating frame animation is to create the images on the frames. One way to do this is to simply draw the graphics directly onto the appropriate pages. To direct QuickC to draw on PAGE 2, for example, you would use the instruction: **__setactivepage(2);**. To direct Turbo C to draw on page 2, you would use the instruction

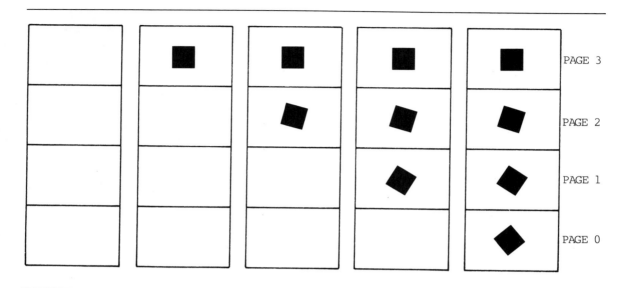

Fig. 17-1. The frame creation process. A: content of graphics pages at program start-up. B: first version is stored in page 3. C: second version is stored in page 2. D: third version is stored in page 1. E: fourth version is stored in page 0. After all frames have been loaded, the system is ready to begin the frame animation loop.

setactivepage(2). This method of using hidden, written-to-pages ia a graceful way of setting up the environment for frame animation, because the viewer does not witness this drawing process. You can leave PAGE 0 on the display screen while your program is busy at work behind the scenes drawing on pages 1, 2, and 3.

The other way to create the images for the frames is to use a *memory move*. You draw directly on the display page. First, draw the image for page 3. When it is complete, move the image from page 0 to page 3. Then, draw the image for page 2. When it is complete, move the data from page 0 to page 2.

Neither QuickC nor Turbo C provides a page copying function as a part of the built-in graphics library, but it is a simple task to create such a routine using C itself. (This shortcoming is very interesting, considering how powerful C is in memory management, and considering that many versions of the much-maligned programming language, BASIC, contain built-in page copying functions.)

If you are using a CGA, it is mandatory that you use the page copying method for setting up the pages for frame animation. Each image is drawn on the CGA's display memory and then moved to a simulated page in user RAM.

After all of the individual frames have been created, you can use a single instruction from either QuickC or Turbo C to animate the images if you are using a VGA or EGA graphics adapter. QuickC uses the **_setvisualpage** instruction; Turbo C uses the **setvisualpage** instruction. By using this instruction to rapidly view the different graphics pages in sequence, you can deceive the human eye into perceiving motion. The real trick, of course, lies in the graphical content of the images themselves. They must be slight variations of what is essentially the same drawing.

If you are using a CGA graphics adapter, you must use a memory move subroutine to quickly move the simulated pages back onto the CGA display memory. By moving these pages onto the screen in sequence, animation will be created.

CASE STUDY: A UTILITY PROGRAM

A modest utility program will serve to demonstrate the fundamental processes of frame animation on the VGA, EGA, and CGA.

The drawing in Fig. 17-2 shows the animation produced by the utility program in Fig. A-5 of Appendix A. The program listing in Fig. A-5 is for QuickC; if you are using Turbo C you should use instead the program listing in Fig. E-16 of Appendix E. If you have the companion disk for this book you can load the program named FUNC-005.C.

The program runs in the 640×200 16-color mode if it is used with a VGA or EGA. The program runs in the 640×200 2-color mode if a CGA or MCGA is present.

Figure 17-3 shows the memory locations of the four graphics pages which are used by the demonstration program when a VGA or EGA is installed. The 640×200 16-color mode is used because four pages are available in this mode.

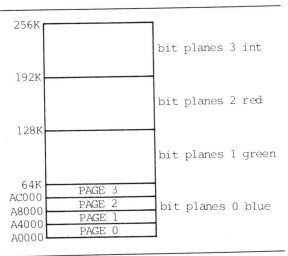

Fig. 17-2. The perceived movement produced by the frame animation utility listing in Fig. A-5.

Fig. 17-3. The locations of the available pages on a VGA or EGA running in the 640×200 16-color mode.

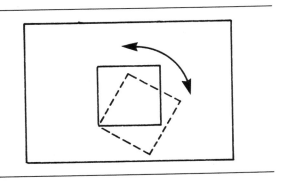

If you are using a CGA, these pages are stored in user RAM, as depicted by Fig. 17-4. The memory addresses used for these four buffers are very important, because the computer system will hang if any of the run-time EXE code is overwritten or if any of the compiler code is overwritten. Note the unused memory at the top of RAM, where the transient portion of DOS's COMMAND.COM is located. The memory map depicted in Fig. 17-4 will function correctly when either QuickC or Turbo C is used with a personal computer carrying 640K of user RAM. Refer to Chapter 3 for detailed memory maps showing the key milepost addresses used by the compiler and your source code.

This program is actually two programs in one. One set of animation subroutines is used when the program is running on a VGA or EGA. Another, totally different, set of subroutines is used when the program is running on a CGA.

The first important thing to note is the **#include<memory.h>** directive in the

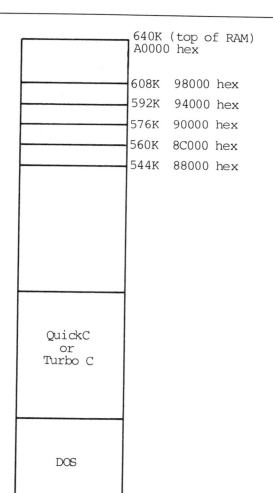

Fig. 17-4. The locations of the simulated graphics pages in user RAM when a CGA graphics adapter is used for frame animation.

INCLUDE FILES section. (QuickC uses **memory.h**; Turbo C requires **mem.h.**) This header file contains assorted variable definitions which support the memory moves used in the program.

The **main( )** routine performs two important tasks. First, it creates the four frames and stores them in the appropriate pages, using the value of **mode_flag** to decide which method to use in order to create and store the frames. Second, it transfers control to the appropriate animation subroutine.

The subroutine named **animVGAEGA( )** manages the frame animation if a VGA or EGA is being used. Because the reassignment of the display page is so quick, a **for/next** loop must be used between each new frame to slow down the animation rate to a realistic speed. By displaying the four pages in sequence, the square which has been drawn by the program seems to rotate back and forth.

The subroutine named **animCGA( )** manages the frame animation if the program is running on a CGA. The subroutine calls another subroutine named **pagemove( )** to rapidly move the frames from their buffers in user RAM up onto the CGA's display memory. The **pagemove( )** subroutine simply uses C's **movedata** instruction to perform the memory move. The source and target addresses are those as depicted in Fig. 17-4, of course.

Whether you are using a VGA, EGA, CGA, or MCGA, you may find it instructive to tinker with the timing delays in **animVGAEGA( )** and **animCGA( )**. This utility program is set up to run at a pleasing speed when used on a genuine IBM PC running at 4.77 Mhz. If you are using an AT-compatible or a PS/2, you may wish to slow down the animation rate, because these computers use a much faster internal clock rate. By making the **t2 < =** expression compare itself against a larger number you can slow down the animation rate.

This program is also interesting because it uses built-in keyboard functions. If you are using Turbo C, the **bioskey( )** instruction is used to test if a keystroke is waiting in the keyboard buffer. If you are using QuickC, the **_bios_keybrd( )** instruction is used to check for a keystroke. If no keystroke is waiting to be read, the program loops back to the animation manager. If a key has been pressed, the program branches to **quit_pgm( )**, which gracefully terminates the program.

OPTIMIZATION

Although the **movedata( )** instruction is a reliable way of copying pages from one buffer to another, you would likely want to use a short assembly language subroutine if you were writing a program for distribution. When this utility program runs on a CGA, the odd-even banks of the CGA can be detected by the human eye during the animation process. A suitable assembly language subroutine capable of performing lightning-quick page moves (in less than $\frac{1}{18}$th of a second) can be found in the assembly language graphics drivers provided in the appendices.

COMPATIBILITY AND PORTABILITY

Clearly, if frame animation is being performed with a VGA or EGA, there are no portability problems, mainly because the display memory found on the graphics adapter is part of a hardware standard. However, if a CGA is being used, you must exercise caution in your selection of memory addresses for the simulated graphics pages in user RAM. In many cases, you must know beforehand the amount of user RAM present on the CGA-equipped computer.

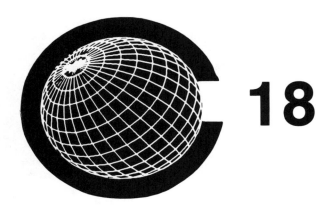

18

Animated
Business Graphics

Animated business charts are an effective way to represent business growth and change. They provide an especially powerful visual method of depicting before-and-after scenarios for business.

The line drawing shown in Fig. 18-1 is the original sketch from which the demonstration program in this chapter was developed. The graphic is a deviation bar chart which illustrates a company's income statement. By animating this analytic chart, you can show the change in sales from the beginning of a particular reporting period to the end of the time period. And after the briefing, you can present each executive who attended the meeting with a graphics printout, as shown in Fig. 18-2. It is the animation, however, that will leave an indelible impression on your audience.

CASE STUDY: ANIMATED BUSINESS CHART

The photograph in Fig. 18-3 shows one of the frames generated by the demonstration program provided in Fig. 18-4. The program listing in Fig. 18-4 is the QuickC version; if you are using Turbo C you should use instead the program listing presented in Fig. E-7 of Appendix E. If you are using the companion disk for this book, you can load QC-010.C if you are using QuickC; load TC-010.C if you are using Turbo C.

This animated demonstration program supports all IBM-compatible graphics adapters. If a VGA or EGA is present, the program uses the 640×200 16-color mode. If a CGA or MCGA is installed, the program uses the 640×200 2-color mode.

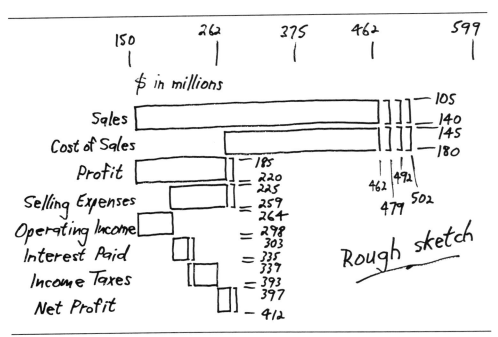

Fig. 18-1. The original template drawing used to obtain xy coordinates for the frame animation demonstration program in Fig. 18-4.

ANALYSIS OF THE PROGRAM

This program adheres to the format introduced in the previous chapter. The only substantive difference between the frame animation utility program presented in Chapter 17 and the demonstration program in this chapter is the complexity of the image being animated.

As you watch the program execute, you first see four different versions of the deviation chart being created. A version is drawn; the screen is blanked; another version is drawn. Next, after a momentary pause, the animation cycle begins. Each individual bar on the deviation chart moves smoothly between its position at the start of the business time period and its position at the end of the business reporting period. The chart is animated for 20 cycles—a total of 120 frames—and the program then terminates by gracefully returning you to QuickC or Turbo C, as the case may be.

The **main( )** routine contains four blocks of code. Each block defines the position of the bars of the chart (denoted by **x2,x3**, and so on) before calling the subroutine named **blocks( )** to draw the bars. In the QuickC version, the **_rectangle( )** instruction is used to generate each bar on the business chart. In the Turbo C version, the **bar( )** instruction is used.

Note the abbreviated compatibility module in the source code. The differentiation between graphics adapters is only relevant for EGA/VGA versus CGA. The 640×200 16-color mode must be used on both the VGA and EGA because four frames (graphics pages) are required by this animated program. If a CGA is being used, the four frames are stored assimulated graphics pages in user RAM.

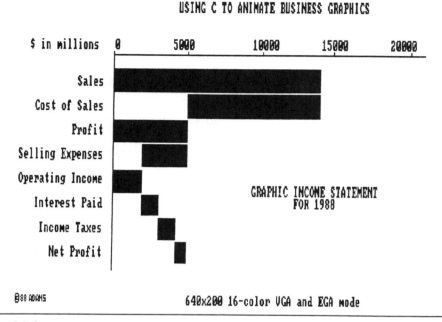

Fig. 18-2. Screen capture utilities can be used to produce printed copies of business graphics generated using C.

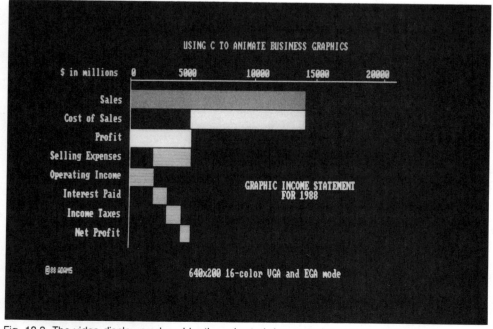

Fig. 18-3. The video display produced by the animated demonstration program in Fig. 18-4.

Fig. 18-4. Program listing for an animated business chart (income statement using deviation graph)—
QuickC version. VGA/EGA/CGA/MCGA compatible. For Turbo C version, consult Appendix E.

```
/*_____

                        qc-010.c

   Function:  This program demonstrates how to animate business
   charts by using the high speed techniques of frame animation.

   Compatibility:  Supports all graphics adapters and monitors.
   The software uses the 640x200 16-color mode if a VGA or an
   EGA is present.  The 640x200 2-color mode is used if a
   CGA is present.

   Remarks:  The 640x200 16-color mode is used with the VGA and
   EGA because four graphics pages are required by this animated
   program.  Only one page is available in the VGA's 640x480
   16-color mode.  Only two pages are available in the EGA's
   640x350 16-color mode.  Eight pages are available in the
   320x200 16-color mode, but the large size of the alphanumerics
   tends to restrict the usefulness of that mode.

   If a CGA is present, the extra graphics pages required by
   this program are stored in user RAM, where care must be taken
   in order to avoid overwriting the C compiler, the user's
   source code, or the operating system.

   Copyright 1988 Lee Adams and TAB BOOKS Inc.


   _____


                I N C L U D E    F I L E S              */

#include <stdio.h>            /* supports the printf function */
#include <graph.h>        /* supports the graphics functions */
#include <stdlib.h>         /* supports the exit() function */
#include <memory.h>              /* supports memory moves */

   /*_____


                D E C L A R A T I O N S                 */

struct videoconfig vc;

void keyboard(void);void quit_pgm(void);
void notice(float x,float y);
void coords(void);void graphics_setup(void);
void scales(void);void labels(void);void blocks(void);

void animVGAEGA(void);                   /* EGA and VGA only */
void animCGA(void);                           /* CGA only */
```

```
void pagemove(unsigned source,unsigned target);      /* CGA only */

float sx,sy,sx1,sy1,sx2,sy2;float x_res,y_res;
int C0=0,C1=1,C2=2,C3=3,C4=4,C5=5,C6=6,C7=7,C8=8,C9=9,C10=10,
    C11=11,C12=12,C13=13,C14=14,C15=15,mode_flag=0;
int t1=1,t2=2;

            /* coordinates for analytic graphics */
float x1=151,x2=262,x3=194,x4=219,x5=245,x6=462;
float y1=105,y2=140,y3=145,y4=180,y5=185,y6=220,
      y7=225,y8=259,y9=264,y10=298,y11=303,y12=335,
      y13=339,y14=373,y15=377,y16=410;

/*_____


                MAIN   ROUTINE                         */
main(){
graphics_setup();                       /* establish graphics mode */
_getvideoconfig(&vc);                   /* initialize video table */


   if (mode_flag==3)                            /* if VGA or EGA */
     {_setvisualpage(0);_setactivepage(0);};
_clearscreen(_GCLEARSCREEN);
scales();                          /* create the scale for the chart */
labels();                          /* create the alphanumeric labels */
_setcolor(C3);sx=5;sy=460;coords();notice(sx,sy);      /* notice */
blocks();                               /* draw the analytic graphics */
   if (mode_flag==4) {pagemove(0xB800,0x8800);}        /* if CGA */


   if (mode_flag==3)                            /* if VGA or EGA */
     {_setvisualpage(1);_setactivepage(1);};
_clearscreen(_GCLEARSCREEN);
x6=479;x2=265;x3=192;x4=218;
scales();                          /* create the scale for the chart */
labels();                          /* create the alphanumeric labels */
_setcolor(C3);sx=5;sy=460;coords();notice(sx,sy);      /* notice */
blocks();                               /* draw the analytic graphics */
   if (mode_flag==4) {pagemove(0xB800,0x8C00);}        /* if CGA */


   if (mode_flag==3)                            /* if VGA or EGA */
     {_setvisualpage(2);_setactivepage(2);};
_clearscreen(_GCLEARSCREEN);
x6=492;x2=268;x3=190;x4=217;
scales();                          /* create the scale for the chart */
labels();                          /* create the alphanumeric labels */
_setcolor(C3);sx=5;sy=460;coords();notice(sx,sy);      /* notice */
blocks();                               /* draw the analytic graphics */
   if (mode_flag==4) {pagemove(0xB800,0x9000);}        /* if CGA */
```

```
        if (mode_flag==3)                              /* if VGA or EGA */
        {_setvisualpage(3);_setactivepage(3);};
_clearscreen(_GCLEARSCREEN);
x6=502;x2=271;x3=188;x4=216;
scales();                              /* create the scale for the chart */
labels();                              /* create the alphanumeric labels */
_setcolor(C3);sx=5;sy=460;coords();notice(sx,sy);       /* notice */
blocks();                              /* draw the analytic graphics */
        if (mode_flag==4) {pagemove(0xB800,0x9400);}        /* if CGA */
        if (mode_flag==3) {_setvisualpage(0);_setactivepage(0);};


for (t1=1;t1<=30000;t1++);                    /* pause before animating */
if (mode_flag==3) animVGAEGA();       /* animation for VGA and EGA */
if (mode_flag==4) animCGA();                    /* animation for CGA */

quit_pgm();}                             /* end the program gracefully */

/*_____


        SUBROUTINE: frame animation manager for VGA and EGA        */

void animVGAEGA(void){
for (t1=1;t1<=20;t1++){     /* animate 20 cycles of 6 frames each */
    _setvisualpage(1);for (t2=1;t2<=6000;t2++);
    _setvisualpage(2);for (t2=1;t2<=6000;t2++);
    _setvisualpage(3);for (t2=1;t2<=30000;t2++);
    _setvisualpage(2);for (t2=1;t2<=6000;t2++);
    _setvisualpage(1);for (t2=1;t2<=6000;t2++);
    _setvisualpage(0);for (t2=1;t2<=30000;t2++);};
_setactivepage(0);_setvisualpage(0);
return;}

/*_____


        SUBROUTINE: frame animation manager for CGA        */

void animCGA(void){
for (t1=1;t1<=20;t1++){     /* animate 20 cycles of 6 frames each */
    pagemove(0x8C00,0xB800);for (t2=1;t2<=6000;t2++);
    pagemove(0x9000,0xB800);for (t2=1;t2<=6000;t2++);
    pagemove(0x9400,0xB800);for (t2=1;t2<=30000;t2++);
    pagemove(0x9000,0xB800);for (t2=1;t2<=6000;t2++);
    pagemove(0x8C00,0xB800);for (t2=1;t2<=6000;t2++);
    pagemove(0x8800,0xB800);for (t2=1;t2<=30000;t2++);};
    return;}

/*_____


        SUBROUTINE: pagemove for CGA
This subroutine is called during the graphics drawing process
```

in order to store the frames in user RAM. This subroutine is
also called during the frame animation process in order to
flip the previously-stored pages onto the CGA display buffer
at B8000 hex.   */

```
void pagemove(unsigned source, unsigned target){
movedata(source,0x0000,target,0x0000,16000);
return;}
```

```
/*_____


                    SUBROUTINE: draw the scales            */
void scales(void){
_setcolor(C7);
sx=150;sy=420;coords();_moveto(sx,sy);
sx=150;sy=82;coords();_lineto(sx,sy);
sx=620;sy=82;coords();_lineto(sx,sy);

sx=150;sy=82;coords();_moveto(sx,sy);
sx=150;sy=78;coords();_lineto(sx,sy);
sx=262;sy=82;coords();_moveto(sx,sy);
sx=262;sy=78;coords();_lineto(sx,sy);
sx=375;sy=82;coords();_moveto(sx,sy);
sx=375;sy=78;coords();_lineto(sx,sy);
sx=482;sy=82;coords();_moveto(sx,sy);
sx=482;sy=78;coords();_lineto(sx,sy);
sx=599;sy=82;coords();_moveto(sx,sy);
sx=599;sy=78;coords();_lineto(sx,sy);
return;}
```

```
/*_____


                 SUBROUTINE: alphanumeric labels           */
void labels(void){

_settextcolor(C3);_settextposition(25,34);
if (mode_flag==3) {_outtext("640x200 16-color VGA and EGA mode");}
        if (mode_flag==4) {_outtext("640x200 2-color CGA mode");}
_settextposition(1,32);
_outtext("USING C TO ANIMATE BUSINESS GRAPHICS");
_settextcolor(C7);
_settextposition(4,4);_outtext("$ in millions");
_settextposition(7,13);_outtext("Sales");
_settextposition(9,5);_outtext("Cost of Sales");
_settextposition(11,12);_outtext("Profit");
_settextposition(13,2);_outtext("Selling Expenses");
_settextposition(15,2);_outtext("Operating Income");
_settextposition(17,5);_outtext("Interest Paid");
_settextposition(19,6);_outtext("Income Taxes");
```

```
_settextposition(21,8);_outtext("Net Profit");
_settextposition(4,20);_outtext("0");
_settextposition(4,31);_outtext("5000");
_settextposition(4,46);_outtext("10000");
_settextposition(4,59);_outtext("15000");
_settextposition(4,72);_outtext("20000");
_settextposition(16,46);_outtext("GRAPHIC INCOME STATEMENT");
_settextposition(17,54);_outtext("FOR 1988");
return;}

/*_____


                SUBROUTINE: draw the analytic graphics         */

void blocks(void){
_setfillmask(NULL);                 /* use solid pattern for areafill */

_setcolor(C4);
sx=x1;sy=y1;coords();sx1=sx;sy1=sy;
sx=x6;sy=y2;coords();sx2=sx;sy2=sy;
_rectangle(_GFILLINTERIOR,sx1,sy1,sx2,sy2);            /* sales */

_setcolor(C7);
sx=x2;sy=y3;coords();sx1=sx;sy1=sy;
sx=x6;sy=y4;coords();sx2=sx;sy2=sy;
_rectangle(_GFILLINTERIOR,sx1,sy1,sx2,sy2);      /* cost of sales */

_setcolor(C7);
sx=x1;sy=y5;coords();sx1=sx;sy1=sy;
sx=x2;sy=y6;coords();sx2=sx;sy2=sy;
_rectangle(_GFILLINTERIOR,sx1,sy1,sx2,sy2);            /* profit */

_setcolor(C1);
sx=x3;sy=y7;coords();sx1=sx;sy1=sy;
sx=x2;sy=y8;coords();sx2=sx;sy2=sy;
_rectangle(_GFILLINTERIOR,sx1,sy1,sx2,sy2);  /* selling expenses */

_setcolor(C1);
sx=x1;sy=y9;coords();sx1=sx;sy1=sy;
sx=x3;sy=y10;coords();sx2=sx;sy2=sy;
_rectangle(_GFILLINTERIOR,sx1,sy1,sx2,sy2);  /* operating income */
_setcolor(C2);
sx=x3;sy=y11;coords();sx1=sx;sy1=sy;
sx=x4;sy=y12;coords();sx2=sx;sy2=sy;
_rectangle(_GFILLINTERIOR,sx1,sy1,sx2,sy2);      /* interest paid */

_setcolor(C2);
sx=x4;sy=y13;coords();sx1=sx;sy1=sy;
sx=x5;sy=y14;coords();sx2=sx;sy2=sy;
_rectangle(_GFILLINTERIOR,sx1,sy1,sx2,sy2);       /* income taxes */

_setcolor(C2);
sx=x5;sy=y15;coords();sx1=sx;sy1=sy;
```

```
sx=x2;sy=y16;coords();sx2=sx;sy2=sy;
_rectangle(_GFILLINTERIOR,sx1,sy1,sx2,sy2);          /* net profit */

_setcolor(C7);return;}
```

```
/*_____


          SUBROUTINE: GRACEFUL EXIT FROM THE PROGRAM          */

void quit_pgm(void){
_clearscreen(_GCLEARSCREEN);_setvideomode(_DEFAULTMODE);
exit(0);}
```

```
/*_____


          SUBROUTINE: VGA/EGA/CGA compatibility module          */

void graphics_setup(void){

VGA_EGA_mode:
if (_setvideomode(_HRES16COLOR)==0) {goto CGA_mode;}
else {x_res=640;y_res=200;mode_flag=3;
      return;}

CGA_mode:
if (_setvideomode(_HRESBW)==0) {goto abort_message;}
else {x_res=640;y_res=200;mode_flag=4;
      C0=0,C1=1,C2=1,C3=1,C4=1,C5=1,C6=1,C7=1,C8=1,C9=1,C10=1,
      C11=1,C12=1,C13=1,C14=1,C15=1;
      return;}

abort_message:
printf("\n\nUnable to proceed.\n");
printf("Requires VGA or EGA adapter\n");
printf("   with appropriate monitor.\n");
printf("Please refer to the book.\n\n");
exit(0);
}
```

```
/*_____

                   SUBROUTINE: coords()
   This subroutine accepts sx,sy device-independent display
   coordinates and returns sx,sy device-dependent screen
   coordinates scaled to fit the 640x480, 640x350, 640x200, or
   320x200 screen, depending upon the graphics mode being used. */

void coords(void){
sx=sx*(x_res/640);sy=sy*(y_res/480);return;}
```

```
/*_____
```

```
                    SUBROUTINE: Copyright Notice
     This subroutine displays the standard copyright notice.
     If you are typing in this program from the book you can
     safely omit this subroutine, provided that you also remove
     the instruction "notice()" from the main routine.          */

int copyright[][3]={0x7c00,0x0000,0x0000,0x8231,
0x819c,0x645e,0xba4a,0x4252,0x96d0,0xa231,0x8252,0x955e,0xba4a,
0x43d2,0xf442,0x8231,0x825c,0x945e,0x7c00,0x0000,0x0000};

void notice(float x, float y){
int a,b,c; int tl=0;
for (tl=0;tl<=6;tl++){a=copyright[tl][0];b=copyright[tl][1];
c=copyright[tl][2];_setlinestyle(a);_moveto(x,y);_lineto(x+15,y);
_setlinestyle(b);_moveto(x+16,y);_lineto(x+31,y);_setlinestyle(c);
_moveto(x+32,y);_lineto(x+47,y);y=y+1;};_setlinestyle(0xFFFF);
return;}

/*_____


                    End of source code                         */
```

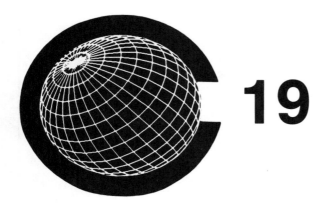 **19**

Animated
Educational Graphics

Computer animation is a powerful medium for teaching. In many instances, the essence of an item under discussion is not so much what it is, but what it does. Animation can simulate the movement inherent in many entities. As Chapter 1 explained, understanding and perception improve if movement is added to a computer image.

A biology class can benefit from an animated presentation of a hummingbird, for example. As Fig. 19-1 shows, only four frames are required to reasonably depict the full hovering cycle of the hummingbird. By smoothly displaying PAGEs 0 to 3 and then PAGEs 3 to 0, the full wingbeat cycle of the hummingbird can be simulated. And because frame animation can produce such lightning-quick speeds, the simulation can become extremely realistic indeed.

PREPARATION

The line drawing in Fig. 19-2 shows the original sketches from which the demonstration program in this chapter was developed. The wings of the hummingbird have been sketched in four different positions, although the torso and head remain stationary.

In order to preserve the authenticity of the work, frequent reference was made to a biology text whose photographs of the Ruby-throated Hummingbird (Archilochus colubris) formed the basis for the preliminary sketch.

CASE STUDY: ANIMATED HOVERING HUMMINGBIRD

The photograph in Fig. 19-3 shows a single frame from the animated demonstration program presented in Fig. 19-5. The photograph in Fig. 19-4 is an exposure which clearly shows all four frames of the animation cycle.

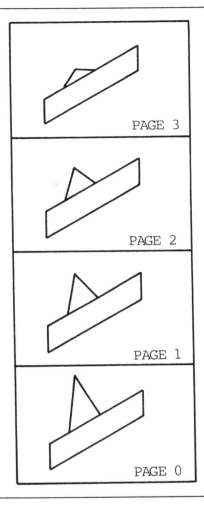

Fig. 19-1. The four versions of the hummingbird and their conceptual locations in memory.

The program listing in Fig. 19-5 is the QuickC version. If you are using Turbo C you should use instead the program listing presented in Fig. E-B of Appendix E. If you have the companion disk for this book you can load QC-011.C if you are using QuickC, or you can load TC-011.C if you are using Turbo C.

The program supports all IBM-compatible graphics adapters. If a VGA or EGA is present, the animation runs in the 640×200 16-color mode. If a CGA or MCGA is present, the program uses the 640×200 2-color mode.

The program first creates the four frames for the cycle, then animates the four pages at 36 frames per second (on a 4.77 MHz IBM PC using an EGA).

ANALYSIS OF THE PROGRAM

The program adheres to the principles introduced in the utility program in Chapter 17. Note the substantial database arrays in the DECLARATIONS section, which contain

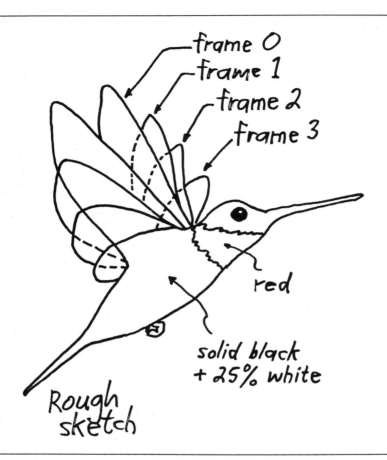

—frame 0
—frame 1
—frame 2
—frame 3

red

solid black
+ 25% white

Rough
sketch

Fig. 19-2. The original template drawing used to obtain the xy coordinates for the four versions of the hovering hummingbird.

the numerous xy screen coordinates required to create the various versions of the hummingbird. The polyline is the primary tool for generating the drawing on the screen.

The **main( )** routine calls upon a subroutine named **draw__bird( )** to draw each frame. Note how **draw__bird( )** jumps to a different block of code within itself, depending upon which frame is being drawn. Although the torso and head of the hummingbird are uniform for all four frames, different wing positions are needed for each version. Note how the **p1** variable is used to point into the database array while the xy coordinates are being retrieved. It is important to increment **p1** after each fetch in order to ensure that it is pointing at the next element in the array.

The VGA/EGA animation manager is contained in the subroutine named **animVGAEGA( )**. The CGA animation manager is contained in the subroutine named **animCGA( )**. During the animation process, both managers send the program branching to a subroutine named **keyboard( )**, which checks to determine if any keystrokes are waiting in the keyboard buffer. If none are present, the program loops back to the animation manager. If, on the other hand, the viewer has pressed a key, program control is transferred

Fig. 19-3. A single frame from the video display produced by the animated demonstration program in Fig. 19-5.

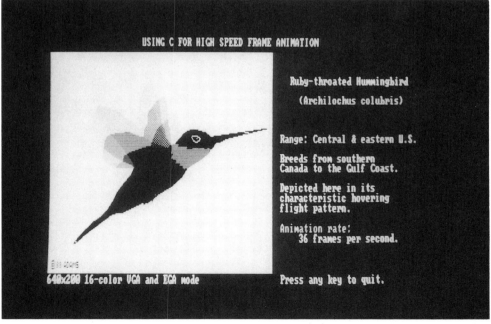

Fig. 19-4. A composite image showing all four frames from the video display produced by the animated demonstration program in Fig. 19-5.

to a subroutine named **quit_pgm**, which gracefully terminates the program. If the animation managers did not call for the keyboard check, then the program would be stranded inside an endless loop.

Of particular interest is the blazing speed at which this animated program runs. 36 frames per second on a VGA or EGA is certainly nothing to scoff at. And even 10 frames per second on a CGA is respectable.

The speed of the animation is controlled by two factors: the internal clock rate of your computer's microprocessor and the animation timing loop itself. If you are using a computer which runs faster than an IBM PC (4.77 MHz), the animation will appear more natural if you slow it down a bit. The following instruction in the animation managers is the piece of code which adds the delay between each frame:

for (t2=1;t2<=1000;t2++);

Simply stated, the computer pauses for the length of time it takes to count from 1 to 1000. You may wish to change each of these **for/next** instructions to read as follows:

for (t2=1;t2<=12500;t2++);

Be sure to change all six occurrences of the **for/next** loop in the animation manager. If you wish to see the fastest speeds possible, remove all the delay loops from the animation cycle.

If you are using a VGA or EGA, the animation runs smoothly and looks very professional. If you are using a CGA, however, the odd/even nature of the CGA's display memory is obvious as the frames are being transferred to the screen. If you were writing your own original C graphics programs for distribution, you would want to use an assembly language routine for the memory moves, as discussed in Chapter 17. The odd and even banks of the CGA are discussed in Chapter 2.

Fig. 19-5. Program listing for an animated biological display—QuickC version. VGA/EGA/CGA/MCGA compatible. For Turbo C version, consult Appendix E.

```
/*

                             qc-011.c

     Function:  This program demonstrates high speed frame
     animation of a hovering hummingbird.  The software takes
     the format of a scientific presentation graphic.

     Compatibility:  Supports all graphics adapters and monitors.
     The software uses the 640x200 16-color mode if a VGA or an
     EGA is present.  The 640x200 2-color mode is used if a
     CGA is present.

     Remarks:  The speed of the microprocessor has a dramatic
     effect upon the required animation speed.  The current
     delay loops in the animation routines are suited for a
     standard 8088 CPU running at 4.77 MHz as found on an IBM PC.
```

If your personal computer runs faster, you may wish to add
longer delays in the animation routines. Refer to the book.

Copyright 1988 Lee Adams and TAB BOOKS Inc.

```
                      I N C L U D E    F I L E S              */

#include <stdio.h>              /* supports the printf function */
#include <graph.h>              /* supports the graphics functions */
#include <stdlib.h>             /* supports the exit() function */
#include <memory.h>             /* supports memory moves */
#include <bios.h>               /* supports read of keyboard buffer */

/*_____


                      D E C L A R A T I O N S              */

struct videoconfig vc;

void keyboard(void);void quit_pgm(void);
void notice(float x,float y);void coords(void);
void graphics_setup(void);void labels(void);void draw_bird(void);

void animVGAEGA(void);                       /* EGA and VGA only */
void animCGA(void);                          /* CGA only */
void pagemove(unsigned source,unsigned target);    /* CGA only */

int frame=0,t1=1,t2=2;
float sx,sy,sx1,sy1,sx2,sy2;float x_res,y_res;
int C0=0,C1=1,C2=2,C3=3,C4=4,C5=5,C6=6,C7=7,C8=8,C9=9,C10=10,
    C11=11,C12=12,C13=13,C14=14,C15=15,mode_flag=0;
char fill_75[]={187,238,187,238,187,238,187,238};

int p1=0;                                    /* pointer into arrays */
int array1[][2]={                            /* xy coordinates for body */
    205,219, 208,218, 212,214, 218,212, 221,208, 229,197,
    232,192, 241,187, 250,183, 258,183, 265,185, 273,189,
    282,198, 377,180, 376,182, 310,200, 297,207, 289,211,
    286,217, 282,221, 278,230, 269,238, 256,248, 249,253,
    240,261, 235,269, 231,278, 228,280, 214,294, 199,304,
    188,310, 181,317, 177,324, 176,321, 169,328, 168,325,
    162,330, 162,326, 135,340, 126,345, 120,345, 111,346,
    106,349,  58,390,  49,399,  42,405,  42,402,  51,391,
     74,364,  87,353,  99,339, 107,324, 114,309, 127,289,
    138,274, 146,259};

int array2[][2]={        /* xy coordinates for near wing, frame 0 */
    146,259, 143,246, 136,234, 128,221, 110,199,  98,184,
     88,169,  79,144,  76,136,  74,118,  73, 98,  69, 72,
```

```
      74, 69,  80, 71,  86, 74, 107,101, 119,112, 124,118,
     143,139, 154,154, 161,166, 166,171, 181,188, 187,195,
     193,200, 197,209, 205,219, 179,259};

int array3[][2]={            /* xy coordinates for far wing, frame 0 */
     119,112, 118, 99, 118, 87, 121, 59, 121, 52, 126, 49,
     134, 47, 139, 62, 146, 73, 154, 88, 174,129, 187,170,
     194,184, 199,197, 207,209, 212,214, 139, 99};

int array4[][2]={                      /* xy coordinates for eye */
     248,199, 250,196, 258,195, 261,197, 263,200, 261,204,
     258,207, 252,205, 250,203, 248,199, 257,200};

int array5[][2]={            /* xy coordinates for throat markings */
     212,214, 218,212, 224,212, 222,217, 239,217, 237,219,
     245,222, 259,219, 258,222, 269,220, 268,224, 278,220,
     278,224, 282,221, 278,230, 269,238, 256,248, 249,253,
     240,261, 240,258, 234,261, 234,257, 232,258, 232,253,
     226,252, 227,249, 219,248, 222,244, 219,242, 220,240,
     211,238, 214,230, 211,228, 212,214, 239,239};

int array6[][2]={            /* xy coordinates for near wing, frame 1 */
     146,259, 140,250, 129,245, 109,234,  92,219,  82,209,
      77,193,  73,179,  74,159,  78,146,  84,136,  96,138,
     119,147, 129,157, 140,165, 152,178, 159,184, 175,199,
     189,210, 194,213, 205,219,  85,179};

int array7[][2]={            /* xy coordinates for far wing, frame 1 */
     152,178, 151,156, 151,137, 154,121, 156,113, 164, 98,
     166, 89, 170, 84, 178, 93, 180,100, 185,107, 188,127,
     191,148, 193,169, 197,179, 202,199, 212,214, 177,119};

int array8[][2]={            /* xy coordinates for near wing, frame 2 */
     146,259, 119,258, 104,253,  98,249,  93,241,  90,237,
      90,228,  94,204,  97,198, 106,193, 124,190, 137,189,
     151,195, 163,199, 175,208, 205,219, 109,242};

int array9[][2]={            /* xy coordinates for far wing, frame 2 */
     163,199, 163,184, 169,171, 169,152, 173,144, 178,138,
     187,127, 194,119, 199,118, 202,125, 203,134, 204,162,
     207,179, 209,195, 210,207, 212,214, 199,139};

int array10[][2]={           /* xy coordinates for near wing, frame 3 */
     146,259, 137,270, 124,277, 118,277, 114,276, 111,269,
     112,260, 114,258, 125,246, 127,237, 139,228, 163,219,
     174,218, 179,218, 191,219, 205,219, 119,269};

int array11[][2]={           /* xy coordinates for far wing, frame 3 */
     174,218, 178,203, 185,185, 192,177, 199,169, 211,160,
     224,157, 227,161, 227,169, 226,177, 224,188, 217,205,
     212,214, 219,179};

/*_____
```

```
                    M A I N   R O U T I N E                   */

main(){
graphics_setup();                      /* establish graphics mode */
_getvideoconfig(&vc);                  /* initialize video table */
_setcolor(C7);_settextcolor(C7);

if (mode_flag==3) {_setvisualpage(0);_setactivepage(0);};
_clearscreen(_GCLEARSCREEN);
frame=0;                                      /* set the frame flag */
labels();                         /* create the alphanumeric labels */
draw_bird();                                    /* draw the graphics */
if (mode_flag==4) {pagemove(0xB800,0x8800);}         /* if CGA */

if (mode_flag==3) {_setvisualpage(1);_setactivepage(1);};
_clearscreen(_GCLEARSCREEN);
frame=1;                                      /* set the frame flag */
labels();                         /* create the alphanumeric labels */
draw_bird();                                    /* draw the graphics */
if (mode_flag==4) {pagemove(0xB800,0x8C00);}         /* if CGA */

if (mode_flag==3) {_setvisualpage(2);_setactivepage(2);};
_clearscreen(_GCLEARSCREEN);
frame=2;                                      /* set the frame flag */
labels();                         /* create the alphanumeric labels */
draw_bird();                                    /* draw the graphics */
if (mode_flag==4) {pagemove(0xB800,0x9000);}         /* if CGA */
if (mode_flag==3) {_setvisualpage(3);_setactivepage(3);};
_clearscreen(_GCLEARSCREEN);
frame=3;                                      /* set the frame flag */
labels();                         /* create the alphanumeric labels */
draw_bird();                                    /* draw the graphics */
if (mode_flag==4) {pagemove(0xB800,0x9400);};        /* if CGA */

if (mode_flag==3) {_setvisualpage(0);_setactivepage(0);};
if (mode_flag==4) {pagemove(0x8800,0xB800);};

for (t1=1;t1<=30000;t1++);              /* pause before animating */
if (mode_flag==3) animVGAEGA();     /* animation for VGA and EGA */
if (mode_flag==4) animCGA();               /* animation for CGA */

quit_pgm();}                      /* end the program gracefully */

/*_____

        SUBROUTINE: frame animation manager for VGA and EGA       */

void animVGAEGA(void){
for (t1=1;t1!=2; ){                    /* animate for endless loop */
    _setvisualpage(1);for (t2=1;t2<=1000;t2++);
    _setvisualpage(2);for (t2=1;t2<=1000;t2++);
    _setvisualpage(3);for (t2=1;t2<=1000;t2++);keyboard();
    _setvisualpage(2);for (t2=1;t2<=1000;t2++);
```

```
   _setvisualpage(1);for (t2=1;t2<=1000;t2++);
   _setvisualpage(0);for (t2=1;t2<=1000;t2++);keyboard();};
return;}
```

/*_____

                SUBROUTINE: frame animation manager for CGA   */

```
void animCGA(void){
for (tl=1;tl!=2; ){                          /* animate for endless loop */
    pagemove(0x8C00,0xB800);for (t2=1;t2<=1000;t2++);
    pagemove(0x9000,0xB800);for (t2=1;t2<=1000;t2++);
    pagemove(0x9400,0xB800);for (t2=1;t2<=1000;t2++);keyboard();
    pagemove(0x9000,0xB800);for (t2=1;t2<=1000;t2++);
    pagemove(0x8C00,0xB800);for (t2=1;t2<=1000;t2++);
    pagemove(0x8800,0xB800);for (t2=1;t2<=1000;t2++);keyboard();};
    return;}
```

/*_____

                  SUBROUTINE: pagemove for CGA

    This subroutine flips a graphics page from the screen buffer
    into RAM or from RAM to the screen buffer.   */

```
void pagemove(unsigned source, unsigned target){
movedata(source,0x0000,target,0x0000,16000);return;}
```

/*_____

                SUBROUTINE: display the alphanumeric labels   */

```
void labels(void){
_settextcolor(C7);_settextposition(25,1);
if (mode_flag==3) {_outtext("640x200 16-color VGA and EGA mode");}
if (mode_flag==4) {_outtext("640x200 2-color CGA mode");}
_settextposition(1,21);
_outtext("USING C FOR HIGH SPEED FRAME ANIMATION");
_settextposition(25,51);_outtext("Press any key to quit.");
_settextcolor(C14);_settextposition(5,53);
_outtext("Ruby-throated Hummingbird");
_settextcolor(C7);
_settextposition(7,55);
_outtext("(Archilochus colubris)");
_settextposition(11,51);
_outtext("Range: Central & eastern U.S.");
_settextposition(13,51);_outtext("Breeds from southern");
_settextposition(14,51);_outtext("Canada to the Gulf Coast.");
_settextposition(16,51);_outtext("Depicted here in its");
_settextposition(17,51);_outtext("characteristic hovering");
_settextposition(18,51);_outtext("flight pattern.");
```

```
_settextcolor(C12);
_settextposition(20,51);_outtext("Animation rate:");
_settextcolor(C7);
_settextposition(21,51);
if (mode_flag==3) {
    _outtext("     36 frames per second.");}
if (mode_flag==4) {
    _outtext("     10 frames per second.");}
return;}

/*_____


                  SUBROUTINE: draw the graphics                  */

void draw_bird(void){

_setcolor(C7);_setfillmask(NULL);
sx=0;sy=30;coords();sx1=sx;sy1=sy;
sx=385;sy=458;coords();sx2=sx;sy2=sy;
_rectangle(_GFILLINTERIOR,sx1,sy1,sx2,sy2);

_setcolor(C0);

pl=0;                                  /* draw the hummingbird´s body */
sx=array1[pl][0];sy=array1[pl][1];pl++;coords();_moveto(sx,sy);
for (tl=1;tl<=55;tl++){
    sx=array1[pl][0];sy=array1[pl][1];pl++;
    coords();_lineto(sx,sy);};

if (frame==0) {
pl=0;                                  /* draw near wings for frame 0 */
sx=array2[pl][0];sy=array2[pl][1];pl++;coords();_moveto(sx,sy);
for (tl=1;tl<=26;tl++){
    sx=array2[pl][0];sy=array2[pl][1];pl++;
    coords();_lineto(sx,sy);};
sx=array2[pl][0];sy=array2[pl][1];coords();_floodfill(sx,sy,C0);
pl=0;_setfillmask(fill_75);
sx=array3[pl][0];sy=array3[pl][1];pl++;coords();_moveto(sx,sy);
for (tl=1;tl<=15;tl++){
    sx=array3[pl][0];sy=array3[pl][1];pl++;
    coords();_lineto(sx,sy);};
sx=array3[pl][0];sy=array3[pl][1];coords();_floodfill(sx,sy,C0);
_setfillmask(NULL);}

if (frame==1) {
pl=0;                                  /* draw near wings for frame 1 */
sx=array6[pl][0];sy=array6[pl][1];pl++;coords();_moveto(sx,sy);
for (tl=1;tl<=20;tl++){
    sx=array6[pl][0];sy=array6[pl][1];pl++;
    coords();_lineto(sx,sy);};
sx=array6[pl][0];sy=array6[pl][1];coords();_floodfill(sx,sy,C0);
pl=0;_setfillmask(fill_75);
sx=array7[pl][0];sy=array7[pl][1];pl++;coords();_moveto(sx,sy);
```

```
for (tl=1;tl<=16;tl++){
    sx=array7[pl][0];sy=array7[pl][1];pl++;
    coords();_lineto(sx,sy);};
sx=array7[pl][0];sy=array7[pl][1];coords();_floodfill(sx,sy,C0);
_setfillmask(NULL);}

if (frame==2) {
pl=0;                               /* draw near wings for frame 2 */
sx=array8[pl][0];sy=array8[pl][1];pl++;coords();_moveto(sx,sy);
for (tl=1;tl<=15;tl++){
    sx=array8[pl][0];sy=array8[pl][1];pl++;
    coords();_lineto(sx,sy);};
sx=array8[pl][0];sy=array8[pl][1];coords();_floodfill(sx,sy,C0);
pl=0;_setfillmask(fill_75);
sx=array9[pl][0];sy=array9[pl][1];pl++;coords();_moveto(sx,sy);
for (tl=1;tl<=15;tl++){
    sx=array9[pl][0];sy=array9[pl][1];pl++;
    coords();_lineto(sx,sy);};
sx=array9[pl][0];sy=array9[pl][1];coords();_floodfill(sx,sy,C0);

_setfillmask(NULL);}

if (frame==3) {
pl=0;                               /* draw near wings for frame 3 */
sx=array10[pl][0];sy=array10[pl][1];pl++;coords();_moveto(sx,sy);
for (tl=1;tl<=15;tl++){
    sx=array10[pl][0];sy=array10[pl][1];pl++;
    coords();_lineto(sx,sy);};
sx=array10[pl][0];sy=array10[pl][1];coords();_floodfill(sx,sy,C0);
pl=0;_setfillmask(fill_75);
sx=array11[pl][0];sy=array11[pl][1];pl++;coords();_moveto(sx,sy);
for (tl=1;tl<=12;tl++){
    sx=array11[pl][0];sy=array11[pl][1];pl++;
    coords();_lineto(sx,sy);};
sx=array11[pl][0];sy=array11[pl][1];coords();_floodfill(sx,sy,C0);
_setfillmask(NULL);}

_setcolor(C7);
pl=0;                               /* draw the hummingbird's eye */
sx=array4[pl][0];sy=array4[pl][1];pl++;coords();_moveto(sx,sy);
for (tl=1;tl<=9;tl++){
    sx=array4[pl][0];sy=array4[pl][1];pl++;
    coords();_lineto(sx,sy);};
sx=array4[pl][0];sy=array4[pl][1];coords();_setpixel(sx,sy);

_setcolor(C4);_setfillmask(NULL);
pl=0;                               /* draw the throat markings */
sx=array5[pl][0];sy=array5[pl][1];pl++;coords();_moveto(sx,sy);
for (tl=1;tl<=33;tl++){
    sx=array5[pl][0];sy=array5[pl][1];pl++;
    coords();_lineto(sx,sy);};
sx=array5[pl][0];sy=array5[pl][1];coords();_floodfill(sx,sy,C4);

_setcolor(C0);sx=5;sy=436;coords();notice(sx,sy);      /* notice */
```

```
_setcolor(C7);return;}

/*_____


              SUBROUTINE: press any key to quit                */
void keyboard(void){
if (_bios_keybrd(_KEYBRD_READY)==0) return; else quit_pgm();}

/*_____


          SUBROUTINE: GRACEFUL EXIT FROM THE PROGRAM          */
void quit_pgm(void){
if (mode_flag==3) {_setvisualpage(0);_setactivepage(0);};

_clearscreen(_GCLEARSCREEN);_setvideomode(_DEFAULTMODE);exit(0);}

/*_____


          SUBROUTINE: VGA/EGA/CGA compatibility module          */
void graphics_setup(void){

VGA_EGA_mode:
if (_setvideomode(_HRES16COLOR)==0) {goto CGA_mode;}
else {x_res=640;y_res=200;mode_flag=3;
      return;}

CGA_mode:
if (_setvideomode(_HRESBW)==0) {goto abort_message;}
else {x_res=640;y_res=200;mode_flag=4;
      C0=0,Cl=1,C2=1,C3=1,C4=0,C5=1,C6=1,C7=1,C8=1,C9=1,C10=1,
      Cl1=1,Cl2=1,Cl3=1,Cl4=1,Cl5=1;
      return;}

abort_message:
printf("\n\nUnable to proceed.\n");
printf("Requires VGA, EGA, or CGA adapter\n");
printf("   with appropriate monitor.\n");
printf("Please refer to the book.\n\n");exit(0);}

/*_____

              SUBROUTINE: coords()
   This subroutine accepts sx,sy device-independent display
   coordinates and returns sx,sy device-dependent screen
   coordinates scaled to fit the 640x480, 640x350, 640x200, or
   320x200 screen, depending upon the graphics mode being used. */

void coords(void){sx=sx*(x_res/640);sy=sy*(y_res/480);return;}
```

```
/*_____


                    SUBROUTINE: Copyright Notice
        This subroutine displays the standard copyright notice.
        If you are typing in this program from the book you can
        safely omit this subroutine, provided that you also remove
        the instruction "notice()" from the main routine.        */

int copyright[][3]={0x7c00,0x0000,0x0000,0x8231,
0x819c,0x645e,0xba4a,0x4252,0x96d0,0xa231,0x8252,0x955e,0xba4a,
0x43d2,0xf442,0x8231,0x825c,0x945e,0x7c00,0x0000,0x0000};

void notice(float x, float y){


int a,b,c; int tl=0;
for (tl=0;tl<=6;tl++){a=copyright[tl][0];b=copyright[tl][1];
c=copyright[tl][2];_setlinestyle(a);_moveto(x,y);_lineto(x+15,y);
_setlinestyle(b);_moveto(x+16,y);_lineto(x+31,y);_setlinestyle(c);
_moveto(x+32,y);_lineto(x+47,y);y=y+1;};_setlinestyle(0xFFFF);
return;}


/*_____


                    End of source code                        */
```

20

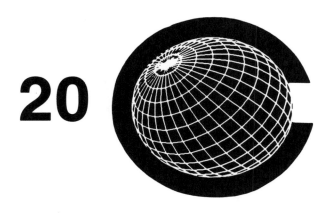

Animated Design Graphics

The programming techniques of frame animation are especially useful if 3D solid models are to be animated. Because 3D objects typically take a lot of processing time to draw, frame animation excels because of its separation of drawing time from animating time. No matter how long it took to create the frames, the microprocessor can devote 100% of its computing power to managing the animation cycle when frame animation is used.

Even complex models like the entity illustrated in Fig. 20-1 can be subjected to high-speed frame animation using C. By storing four views (different rotations) of the 3D model in separate graphics pages, as shown in Fig. 20-2, the computer's microprocessor can devote its full attention to the animation process.

The model shown in Fig. 20-1 is simply a series of cleverly arranged four-sided polygons, not much different in concept from the polygons used by the 3D business chart demonstration program in Chapter 15. By sorting the polygons so that the farthest parts are drawn first, the nearer parts which are drawn last will hide appropriate portions of the farther objects. This is how the eye perceives the model in real life, of course. Note how the drawing scheme has been planned so that it is not necessary to draw the surfaces of the model which would be completely hidden from view.

Each version of the model is drawn at a slightly different yaw angle and pitch angle. Later, when the animation cycle is operating, the 3D solid model appears to be rotating itself in order to give you an opportunity to better see how it is constructed.

CASE STUDY: A ROTATING 3D MODEL

The photograph in Fig. 20-3 shows the image produced by the animated demonstration program presented in Fig. 20-4. The program listing in Fig. 20-4 is the QuickC version.

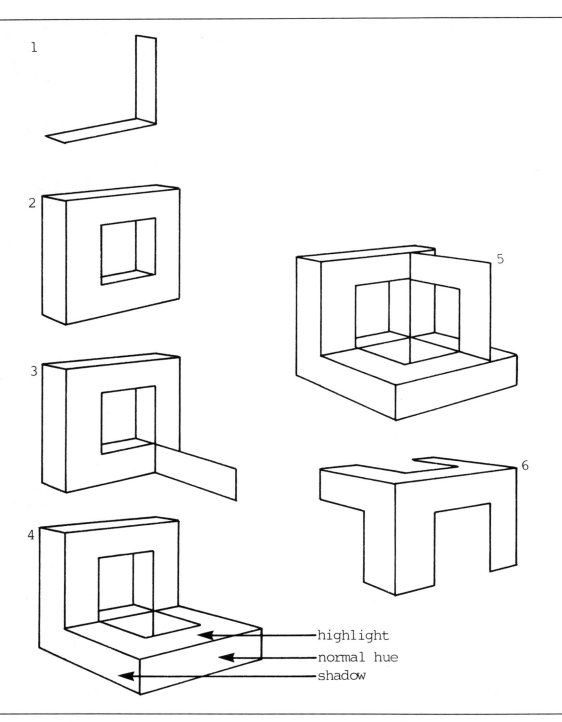

1

2

3

4

5

6

highlight

normal hue

shadow

Fig. 20-1. The six modeling steps used to create the 3D solid model produced by the animated demonstrated program in Fig. 20-4.

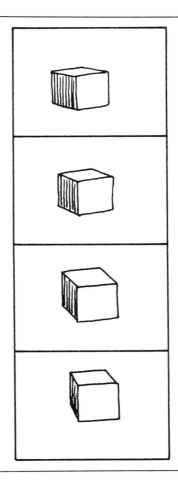

Fig. 20-2. The four versions of the animated 3D model stored in pages.

If you are using Turbo C, you should use the program listing in Fig. E-9 from Appendix E. If you are using the companion disk to this book you can load QC-012.C if you are using QuickC and you can load TC-012.C if you are using Turbo C.

The program provides support for VGA and EGA graphics adapters. The four graphics pages available in the 640×200 16-color mode are used.

As you watch the program execute, you can see how a key matte template is used to punch out a hole for each surface which is drawn. This key matte methodology was introduced in Chapter 14. Without it, the area fill routines would fail because of conflicting background colors.

ANALYSIS OF THE PROGRAM

The most important coding element in this program is the angle adjustments made by the **main( )** routine. Note how **r1**, **r2**, and **r3** are redefined on each occasion before **main( )** calls upon **draw—object( )** to create the next version of the 3D model. The variable **r1**, for example, is incremented by .08727 radians, which is 5 degrees. If you wished

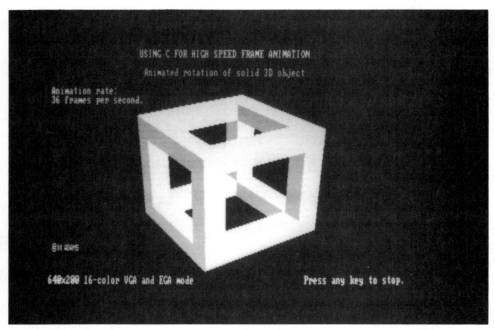

Fig. 20-3. The video display produced by the animated demonstration program in Fig. 20-4. The first frame of the animation sequence is shown here.

to modify the program to rotate the model by only 1 degree between frames, you could change the appropriate lines in **main( )** to read: **r1=r1+.017453**.

Note how the subroutine named **draw_object( )** calls upon a subroutine named **draw_poly( )** to help it create each individual four-sided polygon. The **draw_poly( )** subroutine, in turn, calls upon a number of 3D-oriented subroutines to accomplish the task. These 3D-oriented subroutines are the same algorithms which were presented in Chapter 14 under the topic, How To Generate 3D Images. The model is drawn using white, intense blue, and normal blue, in order to simulate the highlight and shadow areas of a solid object. Color theory is discussed in detail in Chapters 8 and 9.

The compatibility module is responsible only for checking if a VGA or EGA is present. If so, the 640×200 16-color mode is initialized. If not, then the program jumps to the label, **abort_message:**, and gracefully terminates the program with an error message.

You can readily adapt this demonstration program to draw a variety of solid 3D models. Simply delete the database arrays and add your own coordinate database. Then modify the **draw_object( )** subroutine to draw your particular 3D model.

Fig. 20-4. Program listing for animated rotation of 3D model—QuickC version. VGA/EGA/CGA/MCGA compatible. For Turbo C version, consult Appendix E.

```
/*_____


                            qc-012.c

   Function:  This program demonstrates high speed frame
   animation of a 3D shaded object.  Visual perception of the
   model is improved by the rotation of the model, which
   enhances the three dimensional effect.

   Compatibility:  Supports VGA and EGA graphics adapters and
   monitors.  The software uses the 640x200 16-color mode.

   Remarks:  The speed of the microprocessor has a dramatic
   effect upon the required animation speed.  Refer to the book.

   Copyright 1988 Lee Adams and TAB BOOKS Inc.

   _____


                   I N C L U D E    F I L E S              */

#include <stdio.h>            /* supports the printf function */
#include <graph.h>           /* supports the graphics functions */
#include <stdlib.h>           /* supports the exit() function */
#include <memory.h>              /* supports memory moves */
#include <bios.h>          /* supports read of keyboard buffer */
#include <math.h>       /* supports the sine and cosine functions */

/*_____


                   D E C L A R A T I O N S                 */

struct videoconfig vc;          /* QuickC's video data table */

void keyboard(void);void quit_pgm(void);
void notice(float x,float y);void coords(void);
void graphics_setup(void);void labels(void);void draw_object(void);
void calc_3d(void);void rotation(void);void window(void);
void line_clip(void);void get_coords(void);void draw_poly(void);
void animVGAEGA(void);

int t1=1,t2=2,t3=1;                      /* loop counters */
float x_res,y_res;      /* used by compatibility mapping routine */
int C0=0,C1=1,C2=2,C3=3,C4=4,C5=5,C6=6,C7=7,C8=8,C9=9,C10=10,
    C11=11,C12=12,C13=13,C14=14,C15=15,mode_flag=0;    /* colors */
int CLR,CLR1,CLR2,CLR3,EDGE;

int p1=0,p2=0;                        /* pointer into arrays */
float x=0.0,y=0.0,z=0.0;                 /* world coordinates */
```

```
float sx=0.0,sy=0.0;            /* output of 3D perspective formulas */
float xa=0.0,ya=0.0,za=0.0;    /* temporary values in 3D formulas */
float sxa=0.0,sya=0.0,sxb=0.0,syb=0.0;      /* 2D line endpoints */
float sxs=0.0,sys=0.0;      /* temp storage of 2D line startpoint */
float temp_swap=0.0;                /* used for variable swaps */
float d=1200.0;                  /* angular perspective factor */
double rl=.48539;                  /* yaw angle in radians */
double r2=6.28319;                  /* roll angle in radians */
double r3=5.79778;                  /* pitch angle in radians */
double srl=0.0,sr2=0.0,sr3=0.0;      /* sine rotation factors */
double crl=0.0,cr2=0.0,cr3=0.0;    /* cosine rotation factors */
float mx=0.0,my=-5.0,mz=-250.0;          /* viewpoint position */
int maxx=638,minx=1,maxy=198,miny=1;      /* clipping viewport */
float c=0.0;                    /* used in line-clipping routine */
float screen_x=639,screen_y=199;    /* dimensions of screen mode */
float rx=0.0,ry=0.0;    /* scaling values used in mapping routine */


            /* database of xyz world coordinates */
int array_xyz[][3]={
20,-20,-30, 20,20,-30, 20,20,-20, 20,-20,-20, 20,-20,-30, 20,0,-25,
20,-20,-30, -20,-20,-30, -20,-20,-20, 20,-20,-20, 20,-20,-30, 0,-20,-25,


-30,30,-30, 30,30,-30, 30,30,-20, -30,30,-20, -30,30,-30, 0,30,-25,
-30,30,-30, -30,30,-20, -30,-30,-20, -30,-30,-30, -30,30,-30, -30,0,-25,
-30,30,-20, 30,30,-20, 30,20,-20, -30,20,-20, -30,30,-20, 0,25,-20,
30,30,-20, 30,-30,-20, 20,-30,-20, 20,30,-20, 30,30,-20, 25,0,-20,
30,-30,-20, -30,-30,-20, -30,-20,-20, 30,-20,-20, 30,-30,-20, 0,-25,-20,
-30,-30,-20, -30,30,-20, -20,30,-20, -20,-30,-20, -30,-30,-20, -25,0,-20,


20,-30,-20, 20,-20,-20, 20,-20,20, 20,-30,20, 20,-30,-20, 20,-25,0,


-30,-30,30, -30,-20,30, 30,-20,30, 30,-30,30, -30,-30,30, 0,-25,30,
-30,-30,-30, -30,-20,-30, -30,-20,30, -30,-30,30, -30,-30,-30, -30,-25,0,
-30,-20,-20, -20,-20,-20, -20,-20,30, -30,-20,30, -30,-20,-20, -25,-20,0,
30,-20,-20, 30,-20,30, 20,-20,30, 20,-20,-20, 30,-20,-20, 25,-20,0,
-30,-20,30, -30,-20,20, 30,-20,20, 30,-20,30, -30,-20,30, 0,-20,25,


20,30,-20, 20,30,30, 20,20,30, 20,20,-20, 20,30,-20, 20,25,0,
20,30,30, 20,-20,30, 20,-20,20, 20,30,20, 20,30,30, 20,0,25,


-30,30,-30, -20,30,-30, -20,30,30, -30,30,30, -30,30,-30, -25,30,0,
20,30,-30, 30,30,-30, 30,30,30, 20,30,30, 20,30,-30, 25,30,0,
-30,30,30, -30,30,20, 30,30,20, 30,30,30, -30,30,30, 0,30,25,


-30,-30,30, -30,30,30, -20,30,30, -20,-30,30, -30,-30,30, -25,0,30,
20,-30,30, 20,30,30, 30,30,30, 30,-30,30, 20,-30,30, 25,0,30,
-30,30,30, 30,30,30, 30,20,30, -30,20,30, -30,30,30, 0,25,30,
-30,20,-30, -30,30,-30, -30,30,30, -30,20,30, -30,20,-30, -30,25,0,
-30,-30,20, -30,30,20, -30,30,30, -30,-30,30, -30,-30,20, -30,0,25};

/*_____
```

```
                    M A I N   R O U T I N E                    */

main(){
graphics_setup();                        /* establish graphics mode */
_getvideoconfig(&vc);                    /* initialize video table */

CLR1=C7;CLR2=C9;CLR3=C1;EDGE=C1;   /* color scheme for rendering */

_setvisualpage(0);_setactivepage(0);
_clearscreen(_GCLEARSCREEN);
r1=.58539;r2=6.28319;r3=5.79778;labels();draw_object();

_setvisualpage(1);_setactivepage(1);
_clearscreen(_GCLEARSCREEN);
r1=r1+.08727;r2=6.28319;r3=r3+.04363;labels();draw_object();

_setvisualpage(2);_setactivepage(2);
_clearscreen(_GCLEARSCREEN);
r1=r1+.08727;r2=6.28319;r3=r3+.04363;labels();draw_object();

_setvisualpage(3);_setactivepage(3);
_clearscreen(_GCLEARSCREEN);
r1=r1+.08727;r2=6.28319;r3=r3+.04363;labels();draw_object();

_setvisualpage(0);_setactivepage(0);          /* reset to frame 0 */
for (t1=1;t1<=30000;t1++);                           /* pause */
animVGAEGA();                           /* animation for VGA and EGA */
quit_pgm();}                            /* end the program gracefully */

/*_____


            SUBROUTINE: display the alphanumeric labels          */

void labels(void){
_settextcolor(C7);_settextposition(25,1);
_outtext("640x200 16-color VGA and EGA mode");
_settextposition(1,21);
_outtext("USING C FOR HIGH SPEED FRAME ANIMATION");
_settextposition(25,58);_outtext("Press any key to stop.");
_settextcolor(C12);_settextposition(3,22);
_outtext("Animated rotation of solid 3D object");
_settextcolor(C7);_settextposition(5,1);_outtext("Animation rate:");
_settextposition(6,1);_outtext("36 frames per second.");
_settextcolor(C7);return;}

/*_____

            SUBROUTINE: draw the graphics                        */

void draw_object(void){

rotation();          /* recalculate sine and cosine rotation factors */
p1=0;                                   /* reset array index pointer */
```

```
CLR=CLR3;EDGE=CLR3;draw_poly();                              /* step one */
CLR=CLR1;EDGE=CLR1;draw_poly();

draw_poly();                                                 /* step two */
CLR=CLR3;EDGE=CLR3;draw_poly();
CLR=CLR2;EDGE=CLR2;for (t3=1;t3<=4;t3++){draw_poly();}

CLR=CLR3;EDGE=CLR3;draw_poly();                            /* step three */

CLR=CLR2;EDGE=CLR2;draw_poly();                             /* step four */
CLR=CLR3;EDGE=CLR3;draw_poly();
CLR=CLR1;EDGE=CLR1;for (t3=1;t3<=3;t3++){draw_poly();}

CLR=CLR3;EDGE=CLR3;for (t3=1;t3<=2;t3++)                    /* step five */
                   {draw_poly();}

CLR=CLR1;EDGE=CLR1;for (t3=1;t3<=3;t3++)                     /* step six */
                   {draw_poly();}
CLR=CLR2;EDGE=CLR2;for (t3=1;t3<=3;t3++){draw_poly();}
CLR=CLR3;EDGE=CLR3;for (t3=1;t3<=2;t3++){draw_poly();}

_setcolor(C7);sx=5;sy=400;coords();notice(sx,sy);return;}

/*_____


              SUBROUTINE: draw and fill polygon in 3D space        */

void draw_poly(void){

_setcolor(Cl3);                          /* set the key matte color */
get_coords();          /* retrieve xyz vertex coords from database */
calc_3d();                /* 3D rotation, translation, projection */
window();               /* map display coords to fit 4:3 screen */
sxa=sx;sya=sy;                                /* line start point */
for (tl=1;tl<=4;tl++){                       /* draw 4 lines in 3D */
    get_coords();    /* retrieve xyz vertex coords from database */
    calc_3d();             /* 3D rotation, translation, projection */
    window();             /* map display coords to fit 4:3 screen */
    sxs=sx;sys=sy;sxb=sx;syb=sy;   /* line is sxa,sya to sxb,syb */
    line_clip();                   /* clip line to screen edges */
    _moveto(sxa,sya);_lineto(sxb,syb);   /* draw the line in 3D */
    sxa=sxs;sya=sys;                  /* define next start point */
    }                                     /* repeat until done */
get_coords();      /* retrieve xyz area fill coords from database */
calc_3d();window();_floodfill(sx,sy,Cl3);              /* area fill */

_setcolor(CLR);EDGE=CLR;pl=pl-6;            /* reset index pointer */
get_coords();calc_3d();window();sxa=sx;sya=sy;
for (tl=1;tl<=4;tl++){
    get_coords();calc_3d();window();sxs=sx;sys=sy;sxb=sx;syb=sy;
    line_clip();_moveto(sxa,sya);_lineto(sxb,syb);
    sxa=sxs;sya=sys;}
```

```
get_coords();calc_3d();window();_floodfill(sx,sy,EDGE);

return;}                                         /* return to caller */

/*_____


         SUBROUTINE: frame animation manager for VGA and EGA      */

void animVGAEGA(void){
for (t1=1;t1!=2; ){                        /* animate for endless loop */
    _setvisualpage(1);for (t2=1;t2<=1500;t2++);
    _setvisualpage(2);for (t2=1;t2<=1500;t2++);
    _setvisualpage(3);for (t2=1;t2<=30000;t2++);keyboard();
    _setvisualpage(2);for (t2=1;t2<=1500;t2++);
    _setvisualpage(1);for (t2=1;t2<=1500;t2++);
    _setvisualpage(0);for (t2=1;t2<=30000;t2++);keyboard();
    _setvisualpage(1);for (t2=1;t2<=2500;t2++);
    _setvisualpage(2);for (t2=1;t2<=2500;t2++);
    _setvisualpage(3);for (t2=1;t2<=30000;t2++);keyboard();
    _setvisualpage(2);for (t2=1;t2<=2500;t2++);
    _setvisualpage(1);for (t2=1;t2<=2500;t2++);
    _setvisualpage(0);for (t2=1;t2<=30000;t2++);keyboard();};
return;}

/*_____


    SUBROUTINE: RETRIEVE xyz WORLD COORDINATES FROM DATABASE
    This subroutine retrieves a set of xyz cartresian world
    coordinates from the database.  The index pointer is
    automatically incremented.                                 */

void get_coords(void){
x=array_xyz[pl][0];y=array_xyz[pl][1];z=array_xyz[pl][2];
pl++;return;}

/*_____


              SUBROUTINE: CALCULATE SIN, COS FACTORS
    Enter with r1,r2,r3 viewing angles for yaw, roll, pitch
    expressed in radians 0.0 through 6.28319.  Returns sine
    and cosine factors.                                        */

void rotation(void){
sr1=sin(r1);sr2=sin(r2);sr3=sin(r3);cr1=cos(r1);cr2=cos(r2);
cr3=cos(r3);return;}

/*_____


              SUBROUTINE: STANDARD 3D FORMULAS
    Enter with x,y,z cartesian world coordinates.  Returns sx,sy
```

cartesian display coordinates. Returns x,y,z cartesian view
coordinates.   */

```
void calc_3d(void){
x=(-1)*x;xa=crl*x-srl*z;za=srl*x+crl*z;x=cr2*xa+sr2*y;
ya=cr2*y-sr2*xa;z=cr3*za-sr3*ya;y=sr3*za+cr3*ya;x=x+mx;y=y+my;
z=z+mz;sx=d*x/z;sy=d*y/z;return;}
```

/*_____

    SUBROUTINE: MAP CARTESIAN COORDS TO PHYSICAL SCREEN COORDS
    Enter with sx,sy cartesian display coordinates derived from
    world coordinate space -399,-299 to 400,300. Returns sx,sy
    unclipped physical display coordinates.   */

```
void window(void){
sx=sx+399;sy=sy+299;rx=screen_x/799;ry=screen_y/599;sx=sx*rx;
sy=sy*ry;return;}
```

/*_____

                    SUBROUTINE: 2D LINE-CLIPPING
    Enter with sxa,sya and sxb,syb endpoints of line to be
    clipped. Returns display coordinates for line clipped to
    fit physical screen viewport defined by minx,miny and
    maxx,maxy.   */

```
void line_clip(void){
if (sxa>sxb) {temp_swap=sxa;sxa=sxb;sxb=temp_swap;
              temp_swap=sya;sya=syb;syb=temp_swap;};
if (sxa<minx) if (sxb<minx) return;
if (sxa>maxx) if (sxb>maxx) return;
if (sya<miny) if (syb<miny) return;
if (sya>maxy) if (syb>maxy) return;
if (sxa<minx) {{c=(syb-sya)/(sxb-sxa)*(sxb-minx);  /* push right */
              sxa=minx;sya=syb-c;};
              if (sya<miny) if (syb<miny) return;
              if (sya>maxy) if (syb>maxy) return;
              };
if (sxb>maxx) {{c=(syb-sya)/(sxb-sxa)*(maxx-sxa);  /* push left */
              sxb=maxx;syb=sya+c;};
              if (sya<miny) if (syb<miny) return;
              if (sya>maxy) if (syb>maxy) return;
              };
if (sya>syb) {temp_swap=sya;sya=syb;syb=temp_swap;
              temp_swap=sxa;sxa=sxb;sxb=temp_swap;};
if (sya<miny) {c=(sxb-sxa)/(syb-sya)*(syb-miny);   /* push down */
              sxa=sxb-c;sya=miny;};
if (syb>maxy) {c=(sxb-sxa)/(syb-sya)*(maxy-sya);   /* push up */
              sxb=sxa+c;syb=maxy;};
return;}
```

```
/*_____

                SUBROUTINE: press any key to quit                 */

void keyboard(void){
if (_bios_keybrd(_KEYBRD_READY)==0) return; else quit_pgm();}

/*_____

            SUBROUTINE: GRACEFUL EXIT FROM THE PROGRAM            */

void quit_pgm(void){
if (mode_flag==3) {_setvisualpage(0);_setactivepage(0);};
_clearscreen(_GCLEARSCREEN);_setvideomode(_DEFAULTMODE);exit(0);}

/*_____

            SUBROUTINE: VGA/EGA/CGA compatibility module          */

void graphics_setup(void){

VGA_EGA_mode:
if (_setvideomode(_HRES16COLOR)==0) {goto abort_message;}
else {x_res=640;y_res=200;mode_flag=3;
      maxx=638;minx=1;maxy=198;miny=1;        /* clipping viewport */
      screen_x=639;screen_y=199;              /* dimensions of screen */
      x_res=640;y_res=200;                    /* resolution of screen */
      return;}

abort_message:
printf("\n\nUnable to proceed.\n");
printf("Requires VGA or EGA adapter\n");
printf("    with appropriate monitor.\n");

printf("Please refer to the book.\n\n");exit(0);}

/*_____
                    SUBROUTINE: coords()
    This subroutine accepts sx,sy 640x480 device-independent
    display coordinates and returns sx,sy device-dependent screen
    coordinates scaled to fit the 640x480, 640x350, 640x200, or
    320x200 screen, depending upon the graphics mode being used. */

void coords(void){sx=sx*(x_res/640);sy=sy*(y_res/480);return;}

/*_____

                SUBROUTINE: Copyright Notice
    This subroutine displays the standard copyright notice.
```

```
      If you are typing in this program from the book you can
      safely omit this subroutine, provided that you also remove
      the instruction "notice()" from the main routine.          */

int copyright[][3]={0x7c00,0x0000,0x0000,0x8231,
0x819c,0x645e,0xba4a,0x4252,0x96d0,0xa231,0x8252,0x955e,0xba4a,
0x43d2,0xf442,0x8231,0x825c,0x945e,0x7c00,0x0000,0x0000};

void notice(float x, float y){
int a,b,c; int tl=0;
for (tl=0;tl<=6;tl++){a=copyright[tl][0];b=copyright[tl][1];
c=copyright[tl][2];_setlinestyle(a);_moveto(x,y);_lineto(x+15,y);
_setlinestyle(b);_moveto(x+16,y);_lineto(x+31,y);_setlinestyle(c);
_moveto(x+32,y);_lineto(x+47,y);y=y+1;};_setlinestyle(0xFFFF);
return;}

/*_____


                   End of source code                    */
```

V

BITBLT ANIMATION

Versatility In Motion

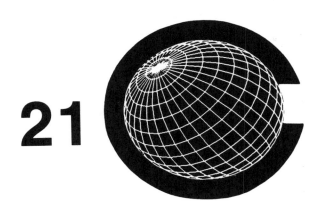

21

Practical Techniques
for Bitblt Animation

Bitblt animation uses a pre-drawn graphic block to move an image across the computer screen. This rectangular block of display memory is called a *graphic array* or a *software sprite*. Bitblt is an acronym for *bit block transfer*. Bitblt animation is also known as graphic array animation, software sprite animation, and arcade animation. Microsoft calls it *snapshot* animation.

You can think of the display buffer as simply a large array in memory. The display buffer (or graphics page) is really just a database that defines the screen image. As Fig. 21-1 shows, parts of the database which correspond to individual screen lines can be saved as an array in user RAM. A small header at the beginning of the array is used to store the length of the array, the number of records (lines), and the length of each line. When the array is written back to the screen, the data in the array is actually inserted back into the database which makes up the screen image.

LOGICAL OPERATORS

The manner in which these bytes are inserted back into the screen buffer will determine the graphical image which results. Refer to Fig. 21-2. The most common method is to simply overwrite any existing bytes in the screen buffer, using the PSET logical operator in conjunction with the appropriate QuickC or Turbo C graphics instruction that "put" the array on the screen.

The XOR logical operator is especially useful for graphics cursors, because XORing an array twice onto the same location will restore the pre-existing screen background to its initial condition. Combinations of XOR, OR, and AND operators can be cleverly

249

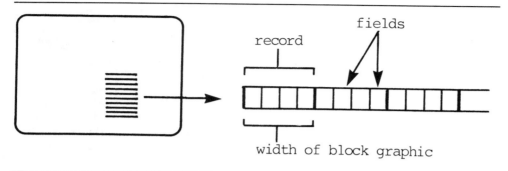

Fig. 21-1. Storage of a block graphic in RAM as an array.

arranged to permit you to install a random-shaped multicolored object against a multicolor background without corrupting either image.

The visual effects produced by the PSET, XOR, OR, and AND logical operators are presented in Fig. 21-3. Compare this with the bit-wise analysis provided in Fig. 21-2.

APPLICATIONS FOR BITBLT ANIMATION

The ability of graphic arrays to deal with blocks of image gives the C programmer considerable graphics capability. If the size of the array is kept reasonably small, C can place the image onto the screen extremely quickly, thereby opening the door for high-speed arcade-style animation programming. The utility program discussed later in this chapter is capable of animating a ricocheting ball at speeds faster than the 60 Hz refresh rate of the display monitor.

Even larger, slower-running, graphic arrays are useful for C graphics programming. As shown in Fig. 21-4, the use of graphic arrays can make pull-down menus very easy to manage. A utility array can save the portion of the screen which will be obliterated by the pull-down menu. Then the pull-down menu, which is itself a pre-drawn image in a graphic array, is written to the screen. When the user is finished with the menu, the utility array is written back to the screen, thereby restoring the screen to its original pristine condition.

Because bitblt animation deals only with portions of the screen—and not with the screen as a whole—graphic array animation techniques are often the best choice for simulations. Complex backgrounds can be used because they can be created in advance. Complex graphic arrays can likewise be created because they are produced in advance. The microprocessor concerns itself only with calculating the next position at which to install the graphic block. The drawing component has been separated from the animation component of the program.

BITBLT ANIMATION USING PSET

Figure 21-5 illustrates the fundamental concept of bitblt animation using the PSET logical operator. First, the image to be animated is drawn and saved in a graphic array in user RAM. Second, the background over which the object is to be animated is created. Third, the first occurrence of the object is installed on the screen (the graphic array is written to the screen buffer). Fourth, subsequent installations of the graphic array are slightly

	COLOR IN + ARRAY	COLOR ON = SCREEN	RESULTING COLOR
PSET	0	0	0
	0	1	0
	1	0	1
	1	1	1
XOR	0	0	0
	0	1	1
	1	0	1
	1	1	0
OR	0	0	0
	0	1	1
	1	0	1
	1	1	1
AND	0	0	0
	0	1	0
	1	0	0
	1	1	1

Fig. 21-2. The effect of different logical operators on bitblt animation ("putting" a graphic array onto the screen).

offset, thereby creating the illusion of movement while simultaneously overwriting previous versions of the object. Because C needs to write only one array to the screen for each frame of the animation cycle, bitblt animation using PSET is very quick. It is so fast that it can often be performed on-screen, with no need to hide the write from the viewer.

It is sometimes necessary to perform the bitblt installation on a hidden page, and then transfer the finished results to the display page, especially when other logical operators

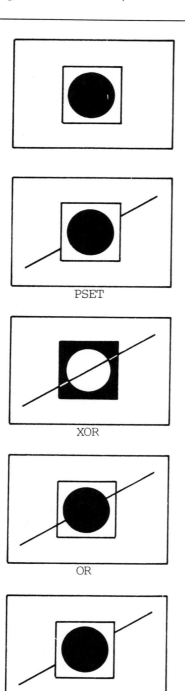

Fig. 21-3. Graphical effect of different logical operators on bitblt installation.

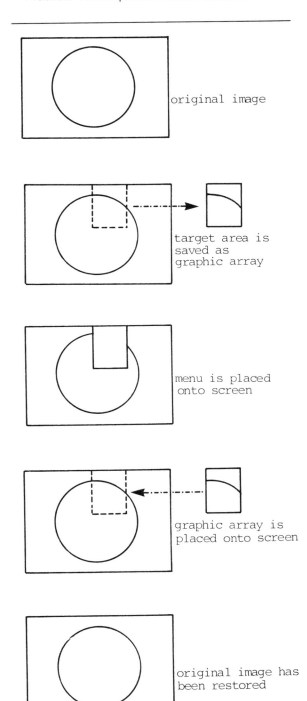

Fig. 21-4. Menu management made easy using graphic arrays.

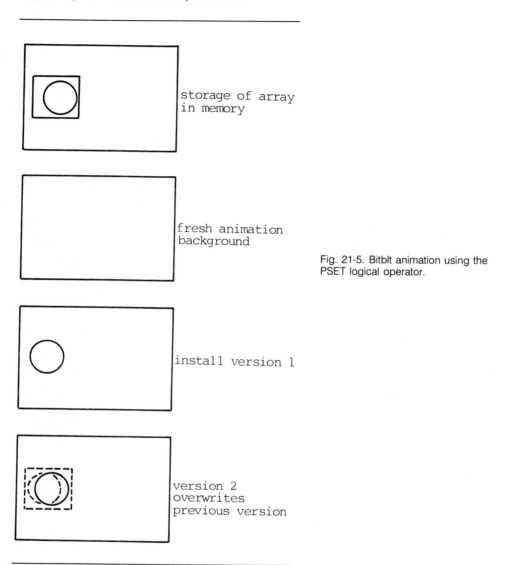

storage of array
in memory

fresh animation
background

Fig. 21-5. Bitblt animation using the
PSET logical operator.

install version 1

version 2
overwrites
previous version

are being used or when the object being animated is large. As illustrated in Fig. 21-6, you can use a combination of OR and XOR to place a multicolored, random-shaped object against a multicolored background. The first graphic array which is written over the background is essentially a key matte which punches a hole in readiness for the next array. The second graphic array is actually a bit-by-bit reversal of the desired image against a black background. By XORing this reversed image onto the screen, the true colors of the object can be created while none of the background which surrounds the object in the array is transferred to the display buffer.

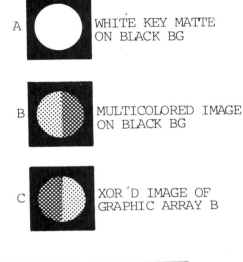

A WHITE KEY MATTE
   ON BLACK BG

B MULTICOLORED IMAGE
   ON BLACK BG

C XOR´D IMAGE OF
   GRAPHIC ARRAY B

Fig. 21-6. Using a combination of
logical operators to place a random-
shaped multicolor graphic array
against a multicolor background.

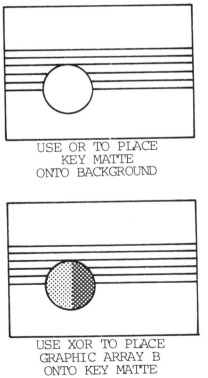

USE OR TO PLACE
KEY MATTE
ONTO BACKGROUND

USE XOR TO PLACE
GRAPHIC ARRAY B
ONTO KEY MATTE

CASE STUDY: A UTILITY PROGRAM

The program listing in Fig. A-7 of Appendix A is the QuickC version of a utility program that demonstrates an arcade-style animation sequence running at 43 frames per second. The Turbo C version of this program listing is contained in Fig. E-17 of Appendix E. If you are using the companion disk for this book, you can load the program named FUNC-007.C.

The program animates a small ball which ricochets at a realistic angle of deflection whenever the ball strikes one of the surfaces of the rectangle that encloses it.

The demonstration utility program supports all IBM-compatible graphics adapters. By default it uses the 640×200 2-color mode of the CGA. This mode produces the fastest bitblt animation possible, because only one bit is needed to define the color of each pixel on the display screen. If you are using a VGA or EGA, however, you can remove the appropriate line in the configuration module and the program will animate using the 640×200 16-color mode. Because four bits are needed to define the color of each pixel in this mode, the animation runs considerably slower than the monochrome mode.

ANALYSIS OF THE PROGRAM

It is interesting to note how the program saves the graphic array in user RAM. If you are using QuickC, the instructions which calculate the size of RAM required and which then allocate space from the far heap are:

(char far*)__fmalloc((unsigned int)__imagesize(x1,y1,x2,y2);

If you are using Turbo C, the instructions are:

(char far*)farmalloc((unsigned long)imagesize(x1,y1,x2,y2));

The **imagesize** instruction is a built-in routine of the C graphics library that calculates the number of bytes required to store an array outlined by the rectangle defined by **x1**, **y1** and **x2,y2**. The **__fmalloc** or **farmalloc** instruction, as the case may be, simply allocates a block of memory in the far heap large enough to hold the block which has been calculated by the **imagesize** function. If you are using QuickC, the **__getimage** instruction will save the image from the screen to the area of memory set aside by **__fmalloc.** If you are using Turbo C, the **getimage** instruction will save the image to the memory allocated by **farmalloc.**

The instruction that writes the graphic array back to the screen is **__putimage** (if you are using QuickC) or **putimage** (if you are using Turbo C).

Note the bitblt animation manager, which is located in the **main( )** routine. The four **if/then** statements are used to test whether the animated ball has struck either the left, right, top, or bottom boundaries of the rectangular playing field. The next line uses the variables named **sxmove** and **symove** to alter the position at which the next graphic array will be installed.

This utility program contains all the essential ingredients that you would require to write virtually any bitblt animation program. And because of the ability of bitblt animation to add movement to objects of diverse size and colors, this technique gives you considerable versatility as a C graphics programmer, as the demonstration programs in the next three chapters will demonstrate.

You may be interested to see how the run-time speed of this utility program will be affected by multiple logical operators (if you were installing a multicolor object against a multicolor background, for example). You can simulate this condition by adding the following line just before the existing **putimage** instruction in the bitblt animation manager. If you are using QuickC, add:

_putimage(sx,sy,gr_array1,_GPSET);

If you are using Turbo C, add:

putimage(sx,sy,gr_array1,COPY_PUT);

 **22**

Entertainment Software

The line drawing shown in Fig. 22-1 is the original sketch used to develop the animated demonstration program in this chapter. The caricature's mouth moves as if it were talking and the forehead creases shift up and down at apparently random intervals.

Despite the sophisticated animation produced by this program, very few graphic arrays are required. Refer to Fig. 22-2. Only three versions of the mouth are used. By varying the timing and the sequence of the mouth arrays, the semi-random nature of speaking can be visually simulated. Only one version of the forehead creases is used. This single array is simply written to the screen at different locations in order to simulate a furrowing forehead.

The photograph in Fig. 22-3 shows one frame from the video display produced by the animated demonstration program in Fig. 22-4. The program listing in Fig. 22-4 is for QuickC. If you are using the companion disk for this book, you can load the program named QC-013.C.

The program supports all IBM-compatible graphics adapters. If a VGA or an EGA is present, the program uses the 640×200 16-color mode. If a CGA or MCGA is present, the program starts up in the 640×200 2-color mode.

Because of the complexity of the caricature's facial features, the database arrays in the **DECLARATION** section are relatively lengthy. Many of the details—particularly around the eyes of the caricature—are essential to the visual impression created by this program. You could leave out many facial characteristics, but the quality of the image would suffer accordingly.

The sections of code which create the airbrushed background and the bull's eye border have been thoroughly discussed in previous chapters. Of particular interest, however,

Fig. 22-1. Original template drawing of the caricature to be animated.

Fig. 22-2. Three versions of the caricature's mouth are saved in RAM as graphic arrays.

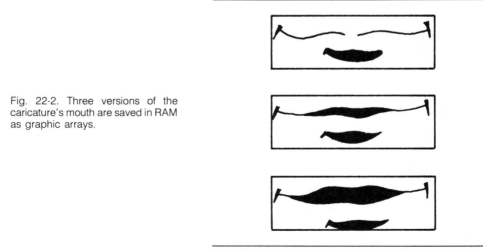

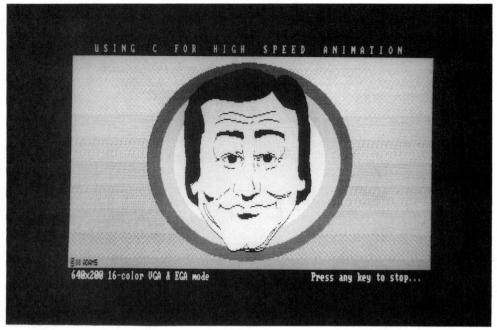

Fig. 22-3. The video display produced by the animated demonstration program in Fig. 22-4.

is the subroutine named **caricature( )**, which draws the caricature's fundamental shape. Note how numerous **for/next** counting loops have been used to eliminate much of the tedium of drawing the image on the screen. On each pass through a **for/next** loop the **p1** variable, which points at array elements, is incremented.

The subroutine named **save__arrays( )** is responsible for creating and saving the graphic arrays which will be used later for bitblt animation. First, the forehead and the existing mouth array created by **caricature( )** are saved. Next, the second version of the mouth is drawn and then saved in an array. Then the third version is drawn and saved. Finally, the first array is written back to the screen in order to restore the original image in preparation for the animation cycle.

The bitblt animation manager is built into the **main( )** routine. A **for/next** instruction is left open-ended to ensure an infinite loop. Note how much of the loop has been written out in longhand in order to simulate the semi-random nature of human speech. The **t2** timing delay has been occasionally altered, and the sequence and number of arrays written to the screen have been varied. You could delete much of this code and use instead one loop consisting of a single animation cycle, but the resulting animation would look too repetitive to seem realistic. It is essential that the semi-randomness of a human-like caricature be mimicked by the software.

The shapes of the mouth used in the different version arrays are of equal importance. As the line drawing in Fig. 22-1 clearly shows, some artistic skill is necessary for advanced C animation.

Fig. 22-4. Program listing for animated caricature. QuickC version. VGA/EGA/CGA/MCGA compatible.

```
/*_____

                            qc-013.c

       Function:  This program demonstrates high speed animation of
       a talking caricature using bitblt animation techniques.

       Compatibility:  Supports all graphics adapters and monitors.
       The software uses the 640x200 16-color mode if a VGA or an
       EGA is present.  The 640x200 2-color mode is used if a
       CGA is present.

       Remarks:  The screen resolution and number of available
       colors have a dramatic effect upon the animation speed.
       Refer to the book.

       Copyright 1988 Lee Adams and TAB BOOKS Inc.

       _____


                     I N C L U D E    F I L E S              */

#include <stdio.h>             /* supports the printf function */
#include <graph.h>            /* supports the graphics functions */
#include <stdlib.h>           /* supports the exit() function */
#include <bios.h>           /* supports read of keyboard buffer */
#include <malloc.h>              /* supports memory allocation */

   /*_____


                     D E C L A R A T I O N S             */

struct videoconfig vc;

void keyboard(void);void quit_pgm(void);
void notice(float x,float y);void coords(void);
void graphics_setup(void);void background(void);
void caricature(void);void save_arrays(void);

int t1=1,t2=2;                               /* loop counters */
float x_res,y_res;           /* used during automatic configuration */
int C0=0,C1=1,C2=2,C3=3,C4=4,C5=5,C6=6,C7=7,C8=8,C9=9,C10=10,
    C11=11,C12=12,C13=13,C14=14,C15=15;
float sx=0,sy=0,sx1=0,sy1=0,sx2=0,sy2=0;
int fg=1,bg=9;                     /* foreground & background colors */

char fill_3[]={0,32,0,0,0,2,0,0};            /*    3% fill */
char fill_6[]={32,0,2,0,128,0,8,0};          /* 6.25% fill */
char fill_12[]={32,2,128,8,32,2,128,8};      /* 12.5% fill */
```

```
char fill_25[ ]={68,17,68,17,68,17,68,17};             /*    25% fill */
char fill_37[ ]={146,41,148,73,164,73,146,73};         /* 37.5% fill */
char fill_50[ ]={85,170,85,170,85,170,85,170};         /*    50% fill */
char fill_62[ ]={109,214,107,182,91,182,109,182};      /* 62.5% fill */
char fill_75[ ]={187,238,187,238,187,238,187,238};     /*    75% fill */
char fill_87[ ]={223,253,127,247,223,253,127,247};     /* 87.5% fill */


                          /* graphic arrays will be stored in far heap */
char far *mouth_array0;char far *mouth_array1;
char far *mouth_array2;char far *fhead_array;

int p1=0;                      /* pointer into database arrays */
int hair[ ][2]={                        /* xy coordinates for hair */
    231,138, 219,134, 211,130, 208,125, 206,120, 206,113,
    205,110, 206,106, 207,98,  205,93,  203,80,  203,76,
    202,68,  203,58,  209,52,  211,46,  221,42,  231,36,
    240,33,  252,30,  280,25,  300,22,  312,20,  319,20,
    326,21,  335,21,  341,23,  359,26,  368,30,  369,28,
    374,26,  386,26,  391,27,  400,30,  409,36,  415,42,
    420,50,  422,54,  422,58,  423,64,  426,68,  427,77,
    426,100, 427,104, 429,114, 430,118, 428,126, 423,129,
    420,132, 412,134, 408,136, 403,136, 405,130, 406,124,
    410,125, 414,125, 419,123, 420,120, 420,116, 414,113,
    415,116, 410,114, 408,112, 407,108, 407,105, 408,98,
    407,78,  406,66,  404,61,  400,55,  390,54,  380,52,
    374,48,  368,45,  363,41,  360,39,  355,42,  345,45,
    332,47,  319,48,  306,49,  290,48,  276,47,  263,46,
    251,47,  242,49,  237,51,  232,53,  240,68,  240,75,
    238,76,  235,77,  233,87,  232,96,  234,111, 232,114,
    230,116, 228,118, 228,116, 218,121, 220,118, 215,120,
    218,125, 221,128, 225,129, 228,127, 230,125, 230,131,
    231,135, 231,138, 320,35};

int jaw[ ][2]={                             /* xy coordinates for jaw */
    231,138, 235,142, 246,150, 252,154, 260,158, 270,162,
    277,165, 286,172, 290,174, 298,175, 307,174, 315,174,
    320,175, 331,175, 340,175, 347,174, 351,172, 359,166,
    366,162, 375,156, 387,150, 394,145, 400,140, 403,136,
    320,100};

int left_eyebrow[ ][2]={        /* xy coordinates for left eyebrow */
    259,83,  263,77,  270,75,  278,75,  284,74,  290,75,
    300,74,  309,75,  310,77,  311,80,  309,81,  305,79,
    295,78,  281,77,  266,78,  259,83,  300,76};

int right_eyebrow[ ][2]={      /* xy coordinates for right eyebrow */
    332,80,  330,78,  330,75,  334,74,  350,73,  360,73,
    371,74,  381,76,  383,82,  380,79,  373,77,  365,76,
    346,77,  340,79,  332,80,  350,75};

int nose[ ][2]={                          /* xy coordinates for nose */
    296,119, 295,122, 294,124, 295,126,
    298,128, 302,128, 304,129,
```

```
        327,116,  330,124,  332,123,  327,116,
        340,118,  341,122,  341,125,  340,127,  330,128,  324,130,
        316,130,  311,128,  308,128,  310,131,  315,133,  320,133,
        327,132,  332,129,  340,127,  320,131};

int left_cheek[][2]={                  /* xy coordinates for left cheek */
        240,126,  250,130,  255,131,  259,131,  258,133,  252,134,
        248,133,  240,126,  253,132,
        264,132,  267,132,  270,131,  273,129,  277,128,  288,123};

int right_cheek[][2]={                 /* xy coordinates for right cheek */
        353,125,  366,128,  375,129,  380,129,  385,128,  386,130,
        378,131,  368,130,  358,127,  353,125,  380,130,
        388,128,  396,126,  389,130,  388,128,  399,124,  400,123,
        400,127,  395,131,  393,133,  391,136};

int left_crease[][2]={                 /* xy coordinates for left crease */
        244,136,  248,141,  255,146,  268,154,  273,157,  253,148,
        246,144,  242,140,  240,136,  244,136};

int jaw_crease[][2]={                  /* xy coordinates for jaw details */
        307,173,  310,173,  373,153,  378,151,
        312,173,  316,171,  319,169,  321,172,  332,173,  341,171,
        349,168,  360,160,  371,155,  358,164,  348,172,  340,173,
        333,174,  321,173,  315,173,  312,173,};

int eyes[][2]={                             /* xy coordinates for eyes */
        286,100,  284,98,   284,96,   286,95,   292,94,   298,95,
        299,97,   299,99,   298,100,  295,101,  286,101,  290,97,
        293,96,
        348,100,  346,98,   346,96,   348,95,   352,94,   358,94,
        360,95,   361,97,   360,99,   358,100,  348,100,  355,97,
        355,96};

int eyelids[][2]={                        /* xy coordinates for eyelids */
        278,100,  274,98,   280,97,   286,95,   292,94,   298,95,
        304,96,   307,97,   309,98,   309,99,   306,100,
        340,99,   335,99,   335,97,   340,97,   348,95,   352,94,
        358,94,   360,95,   366,96,   369,98,   366,100};

int near_eyes[][2]={                   /* assorted creases near the eyes */
        277,104,  282,105,  288,106,  290,106,  296,106,  308,104,
        311,101,  329,102,  330,105,  331,107,  332,108,  335,102,
        339,104,  352,107,  357,106,  360,106,  367,105,  369,103};

int sinus[][2]={                                     /* sinus creases */
        330,99,   329,96,   329,94,   331,95,   336,95,   347,94,
        333,96,   330,99,   333,95,
        312,99,   310,97,   305,95,   297,92,   304,92,   308,93,
        309,90,   311,95,   312,99,   334,96,
        330,92,   330,90,   309,88,   307,86};

int ulids[][2]={                               /* details above eyes */
        354,92,   360,93,   366,94,   370,97,   376,96,   380,94,
```

```
         382,92,   383,88,   288,93,   281,94,   275,95,   271,97,
         372,98,   380,97,   372,99,   376,100,  268,98,   262,97,
         268,99,   262,100,  260,95,   258,92,   258,88};

int forehead[][2]={          /* xy coordinates for forehead array */
         260,68,   271,65,   285,64,   295,65,   306,66,   312,67,
         318,67,   323,67,   328,66,   337,66,   350,64,   360,64,
         370,65,   373,66,   267,62,   270,60,   291,58,   300,59,
         308,60,   317,62,   325,62,   341,60,   354,58,   367,57};

int mouth0[][2]={            /* xy coordinates for mouth array 0 */
         268,140,  270,136,  273,137,  268,140,  370,139,  368,135,
         370,134,  370,139,  270,137,  282,140,  289,140,  295,138,
         306,137,  309,138,  314,139,  324,139,  331,138,  338,137,
         345,137,  352,138,  360,137,  366,136,  369,135,
         302,144,  310,145,  316,144,  326,144,  330,145,  335,145,
         340,144,  335,146,  326,147,  320,148,  311,148,  306,147,
         302,145,  302,144,  320,146};

int mouth1[][2]={            /* xy coordinates for mouth array 1 */
         268,140,  270,136,  273,137,  268,140,  370,139,  368,135,
         370,134,  370,139,
         270,137,  282,140,  287,140,  294,139,  300,137,  306,136,
         310,136,  320,137,  330,136,  340,137,  352,138,  360,137,
         366,136,  369,135,  352,138,  346,138,  340,139,  328,140,
         318,140,  305,139,  295,139,  287,140,  320,138,
         302,146,  310,147,  316,146,  326,146,  330,147,  335,147,
         340,146,  335,148,  326,149,  320,150,  311,150,  306,149,
         302,147,  302,146,  320,148};

int mouth2[][2]={            /* xy coordinates for mouth array 2 */
         268,140,  270,136,  273,137,  268,140,  370,139,  368,135,
         370,134,  370,139,
         270,137,  277,138,  281,139,  290,138,  296,137,  302,136,
         309,135,  312,135,  321,136,  330,135,  340,136,  352,137,
         360,137,  369,135,  360,137,  344,139,  340,140,  331,142,
         320,141,  315,140,  307,140,  295,141,  286,140,  281,139,
         320,140,
         304,148,  312,149,  318,148,  328,148,  332,149,  337,149,
         342,148,  337,150,  328,151,  322,152,  313,152,  308,151,
         304,149,  304,148,  322,150};


/*_____

                    M A I N   R O U T I N E                    */

main(){
graphics_setup();                    /* establish graphics mode */
_getvideoconfig(&vc);                /* initialize video table */
_setcolor(C7);_settextcolor(C7);

fg=C1;bg=C9;background();        /* create the airbrushed background */
caricature();                        /* draw the caricature face */
```

```
save_arrays();                          /* create and save graphic arrays */
for (t1=1;t1!=2; ){                          /* animate for endless loop */
   _putimage(265,133,mouth_array1,_GPSET);for (t2=1;t2<=2000;t2++);
   _putimage(265,133,mouth_array2,_GPSET);for (t2=1;t2<=2000;t2++);
   _putimage(265,133,mouth_array1,_GPSET);for (t2=1;t2<=2000;t2++);
   _putimage(265,133,mouth_array0,_GPSET);for (t2=1;t2<=2000;t2++);
   keyboard();
   _putimage(265,133,mouth_array1,_GPSET);for (t2=1;t2<=2000;t2++);
   _putimage(265,133,mouth_array0,_GPSET);for (t2=1;t2<=2000;t2++);
   _putimage(265,133,mouth_array1,_GPSET);for (t2=1;t2<=2000;t2++);
   _putimage(265,133,mouth_array2,_GPSET);for (t2=1;t2<=2000;t2++);
   _putimage(265,133,mouth_array1,_GPSET);for (t2=1;t2<=2000;t2++);
   _putimage(265,133,mouth_array0,_GPSET);for (t2=1;t2<=2000;t2++);
   keyboard();_putimage(258,55,fhead_array,_GPSET);
   _putimage(265,133,mouth_array1,_GPSET);for (t2=1;t2<=2000;t2++);
   _putimage(265,133,mouth_array2,_GPSET);for (t2=1;t2<=2000;t2++);
   _putimage(265,133,mouth_array1,_GPSET);for (t2=1;t2<=2000;t2++);
   _putimage(265,133,mouth_array2,_GPSET);for (t2=1;t2<=2000;t2++);
   _putimage(265,133,mouth_array1,_GPSET);for (t2=1;t2<=2000;t2++);
   _putimage(265,133,mouth_array0,_GPSET);for (t2=1;t2<=2000;t2++);
   keyboard();
   _putimage(265,133,mouth_array1,_GPSET);for (t2=1;t2<=1000;t2++);
   _putimage(265,133,mouth_array2,_GPSET);for (t2=1;t2<=1000;t2++);
   _putimage(265,133,mouth_array1,_GPSET);for (t2=1;t2<=1000;t2++);
   _putimage(265,133,mouth_array0,_GPSET);for (t2=1;t2<=1000;t2++);
   keyboard();
   _putimage(265,133,mouth_array1,_GPSET);for (t2=1;t2<=1000;t2++);
   _putimage(265,133,mouth_array0,_GPSET);for (t2=1;t2<=1000;t2++);
   _putimage(265,133,mouth_array1,_GPSET);for (t2=1;t2<=1000;t2++);
   _putimage(265,133,mouth_array2,_GPSET);for (t2=1;t2<=1000;t2++);
   _putimage(265,133,mouth_array1,_GPSET);for (t2=1;t2<=1000;t2++);
   _putimage(265,133,mouth_array0,_GPSET);for (t2=1;t2<=1000;t2++);
   keyboard();_putimage(258,56,fhead_array,_GPSET);
   _putimage(265,133,mouth_array1,_GPSET);for (t2=1;t2<=1000;t2++);
   _putimage(265,133,mouth_array2,_GPSET);for (t2=1;t2<=1000;t2++);
   _putimage(265,133,mouth_array1,_GPSET);for (t2=1;t2<=1000;t2++);
   _putimage(265,133,mouth_array2,_GPSET);for (t2=1;t2<=1000;t2++);
   _putimage(265,133,mouth_array1,_GPSET);for (t2=1;t2<=1000;t2++);
   _putimage(265,133,mouth_array0,_GPSET);for (t2=1;t2<=1000;t2++);
   };
quit_pgm();}                             /* end the program gracefully */

/*_____


            SUBROUTINE: create & save graphic arrays              */

void save_arrays(void){
                                        /* save the forehead array */
fhead_array=(char far *)_fmalloc((unsigned int)
_imagesize(258,56,376,70));_getimage(258,56,376,70,fhead_array);

                                     /* save the existing mouth array */
```

```
mouth_array0=(char far *)_fmalloc((unsigned int)
_imagesize(265,133,383,152));_getimage(265,133,383,152,mouth_array0);

pl=0;                         /* draw the details in mouth array 1 */
_setcolor(C7);_rectangle(_GFILLINTERIOR,266,133,373,152);
_setcolor(C0);
sx=mouth1[pl][0];sy=mouth1[pl][1];pl++;_moveto(sx,sy);
for (tl=1;tl<=3;tl++){
    sx=mouth1[pl][0];sy=mouth1[pl][1];pl++;
    _lineto(sx,sy);};
sx=mouth1[pl][0];sy=mouth1[pl][1];pl++;_moveto(sx,sy);
for (tl=1;tl<=3;tl++){
    sx=mouth1[pl][0];sy=mouth1[pl][1];pl++;
    _lineto(sx,sy);};
sx=mouth1[pl][0];sy=mouth1[pl][1];pl++;_moveto(sx,sy);
for (tl=1;tl<=21;tl++){
    sx=mouth1[pl][0];sy=mouth1[pl][1];pl++;
    _lineto(sx,sy);};
sx=mouth1[pl][0];sy=mouth1[pl][1];pl++;_floodfill(sx,sy,C0);
sx=mouth1[pl][0];sy=mouth1[pl][1];pl++;_moveto(sx,sy);
for (tl=1;tl<=13;tl++){
    sx=mouth1[pl][0];sy=mouth1[pl][1];pl++;
    _lineto(sx,sy);};
sx=mouth1[pl][0];sy=mouth1[pl][1];pl++;_floodfill(sx,sy,C0);
mouth_array1=(char far *)_fmalloc((unsigned int)
_imagesize(265,133,383,152));_getimage(265,133,383,152,mouth_array1);

pl=0;                         /* draw the details in mouth array 2 */
_setcolor(C7);_rectangle(_GFILLINTERIOR,266,133,373,152);
_setcolor(C0);
sx=mouth2[pl][0];sy=mouth2[pl][1];pl++;_moveto(sx,sy);
for (tl=1;tl<=3;tl++){
    sx=mouth2[pl][0];sy=mouth2[pl][1];pl++;
    _lineto(sx,sy);};
sx=mouth2[pl][0];sy=mouth2[pl][1];pl++;_moveto(sx,sy);
for (tl=1;tl<=3;tl++){
    sx=mouth2[pl][0];sy=mouth2[pl][1];pl++;
    _lineto(sx,sy);};
sx=mouth2[pl][0];sy=mouth2[pl][1];pl++;_moveto(sx,sy);
for (tl=1;tl<=23;tl++){
    sx=mouth2[pl][0];sy=mouth2[pl][1];pl++;
    _lineto(sx,sy);};
sx=mouth2[pl][0];sy=mouth2[pl][1];pl++;_floodfill(sx,sy,C0);
sx=mouth2[pl][0];sy=mouth2[pl][1];pl++;_moveto(sx,sy);
for (tl=1;tl<=13;tl++){
    sx=mouth2[pl][0];sy=mouth2[pl][1];pl++;
    _lineto(sx,sy);};
sx=mouth2[pl][0];sy=mouth2[pl][1];pl++;_floodfill(sx,sy,C0);
mouth_array2=(char far *)_fmalloc((unsigned int)
_imagesize(265,133,383,152));_getimage(265,133,383,152,mouth_array2);

_putimage(265,133,mouth_array0,_GPSET); /* restore mouth array 0 */

return;}
```

```
/*_____


                SUBROUTINE: draw the caricature                */

void caricature(void){

_setcolor(C0);
pl=0;                                      /* draw the hair outline */
sx=hair[pl][0];sy=hair[pl][1];pl++;_moveto(sx,sy);
for (tl=1;tl<=109;tl++){
    sx=hair[pl][0];sy=hair[pl][1];pl++;_lineto(sx,sy);};
sx=hair[pl][0];sy=hair[pl][1];
_floodfill(sx,sy,C0);_setcolor(C0);

pl=0;                                      /* draw the jaw outline */
sx=jaw[pl][0];sy=jaw[pl][1];pl++;_moveto(sx,sy);
for (tl=1;tl<=23;tl++){
    sx=jaw[pl][0];sy=jaw[pl][1];pl++;_lineto(sx,sy);};
sx=jaw[pl][0];sy=jaw[pl][1];
_setcolor(C7);_floodfill(sx,sy,C0);_setcolor(C0);

pl=0;                                      /* draw the left eyebrow */
sx=left_eyebrow[pl][0];sy=left_eyebrow[pl][1];pl++;_moveto(sx,sy);
for (tl=1;tl<=15;tl++){
    sx=left_eyebrow[pl][0];sy=left_eyebrow[pl][1];pl++;
    _lineto(sx,sy);};
sx=left_eyebrow[pl][0];sy=left_eyebrow[pl][1];_floodfill(sx,sy,C0);

pl=0;                                      /* draw the right eyebrow */
sx=right_eyebrow[pl][0];sy=right_eyebrow[pl][1];pl++;_moveto(sx,sy);
for (tl=1;tl<=14;tl++){
    sx=right_eyebrow[pl][0];sy=right_eyebrow[pl][1];pl++;

    _lineto(sx,sy);};
sx=right_eyebrow[pl][0];sy=right_eyebrow[pl][1];
_floodfill(sx,sy,C0);

pl=0;                                          /* draw the nose */
sx=nose[pl][0];sy=nose[pl][1];pl++;_moveto(sx,sy);
for (tl=1;tl<=3;tl++){
    sx=nose[pl][0];sy=nose[pl][1];pl++;
    _lineto(sx,sy);};
sx=nose[pl][0];sy=nose[pl][1];pl++;_moveto(sx,sy);
for (tl=1;tl<=2;tl++){
    sx=nose[pl][0];sy=nose[pl][1];pl++;
    _lineto(sx,sy);};
sx=nose[pl][0];sy=nose[pl][1];pl++;_moveto(sx,sy);
for (tl=1;tl<=3;tl++){
    sx=nose[pl][0];sy=nose[pl][1];pl++;
    _lineto(sx,sy);};
sx=nose[pl][0];sy=nose[pl][1];pl++;_moveto(sx,sy);
for (tl=1;tl<=14;tl++){
    sx=nose[pl][0];sy=nose[pl][1];pl++;
```

```
    _lineto(sx,sy);};
sx=nose[pl][0];sy=nose[pl][1];
_floodfill(sx,sy,C0);

pl=0;                                /* draw the left cheek */
sx=left_cheek[pl][0];sy=left_cheek[pl][1];pl++;_moveto(sx,sy);
for (tl=1;tl<=7;tl++){
    sx=left_cheek[pl][0];sy=left_cheek[pl][1];pl++;
    _lineto(sx,sy);};
sx=left_cheek[pl][0];sy=left_cheek[pl][1];pl++;
_floodfill(sx,sy,C0);
for (tl=1;tl<=3;tl++){
    sx=left_cheek[pl][0];sy=left_cheek[pl][1];pl++;_moveto(sx,sy);
    sx=left_cheek[pl][0];sy=left_cheek[pl][1];pl++;
    _lineto(sx,sy);};

pl=0;                                /* draw the right cheek */
sx=right_cheek[pl][0];sy=right_cheek[pl][1];pl++;_moveto(sx,sy);
for (tl=1;tl<=9;tl++){
    sx=right_cheek[pl][0];sy=right_cheek[pl][1];pl++;
    _lineto(sx,sy);};
sx=right_cheek[pl][0];sy=right_cheek[pl][1];pl++;
_floodfill(sx,sy,C0);
sx=right_cheek[pl][0];sy=right_cheek[pl][1];pl++;_moveto(sx,sy);
for (tl=1;tl<=3;tl++){
    sx=right_cheek[pl][0];sy=right_cheek[pl][1];pl++;
    _lineto(sx,sy);};
for (tl=1;tl<=3;tl++){
    sx=left_cheek[pl][0];sy=left_cheek[pl][1];pl++;_moveto(sx,sy);
    sx=left_cheek[pl][0];sy=left_cheek[pl][1];pl++;
    _lineto(sx,sy);};
pl=0;                                /* draw the left crease */
sx=left_crease[pl][0];sy=left_crease[pl][1];pl++;_moveto(sx,sy);
for (tl=1;tl<=9;tl++){
    sx=left_crease[pl][0];sy=left_crease[pl][1];pl++;
    _lineto(sx,sy);};

pl=0;                                /* draw the jaw details */
for (tl=1;tl<=2;tl++){
    sx=jaw_crease[pl][0];sy=jaw_crease[pl][1];pl++;_moveto(sx,sy);
    sx=jaw_crease[pl][0];sy=jaw_crease[pl][1];pl++;
    _lineto(sx,sy);};
sx=jaw_crease[pl][0];sy=jaw_crease[pl][1];pl++;_moveto(sx,sy);
for (tl=1;tl<=15;tl++){
    sx=jaw_crease[pl][0];sy=jaw_crease[pl][1];pl++;
    _lineto(sx,sy);};

pl=0;                                /* draw the eyes */
_setcolor(Cl);
sx=eyes[pl][0];sy=eyes[pl][1];pl++;_moveto(sx,sy);
for (tl=1;tl<=10;tl++){
    sx=eyes[pl][0];sy=eyes[pl][1];pl++;
    _lineto(sx,sy);};
```

```
sx=eyes[pl][0];sy=eyes[pl][1];pl++;
_floodfill(sx,sy,Cl);_setcolor(C7);
sx=eyes[pl][0];sy=eyes[pl][1];pl++;_setpixel(sx,sy);
_setcolor(Cl);
sx=eyes[pl][0];sy=eyes[pl][1];pl++;_moveto(sx,sy);
for (tl=1;tl<=10;tl++){
    sx=eyes[pl][0];sy=eyes[pl][1];pl++;
    _lineto(sx,sy);};
sx=eyes[pl][0];sy=eyes[pl][1];pl++;
_floodfill(sx,sy,Cl);_setcolor(C7);
sx=eyes[pl][0];sy=eyes[pl][1];pl++;_setpixel(sx,sy);
_setcolor(C0);

pl=0;                                   /* draw the eyelids */
for (t2=1;t2<=2;t2++){
    sx=eyelids[pl][0];sy=eyelids[pl][1];pl++;_moveto(sx,sy);
    for (tl=1;tl<=10;tl++){
        sx=eyelids[pl][0];sy=eyelids[pl][1];pl++;
        _lineto(sx,sy);};
    };

pl=0;                          /* draw the creases near the eyes */
sx=near_eyes[pl][0];sy=near_eyes[pl][1];pl++;_moveto(sx,sy);
for (tl=1;tl<=2;tl++){
    sx=near_eyes[pl][0];sy=near_eyes[pl][1];pl++;
    _lineto(sx,sy);};
for (tl=1;tl<=6;tl++){
    sx=near_eyes[pl][0];sy=near_eyes[pl][1];pl++;_moveto(sx,sy);
    sx=near_eyes[pl][0];sy=near_eyes[pl][1];pl++;
    _lineto(sx,sy);};
sx=near_eyes[pl][0];sy=near_eyes[pl][1];pl++;_moveto(sx,sy);
for (tl=1;tl<=2;tl++){
    sx=near_eyes[pl][0];sy=near_eyes[pl][1];pl++;
    _lineto(sx,sy);};

pl=0;                                     /* draw the sinuses */
sx=sinus[pl][0];sy=sinus[pl][1];pl++;_moveto(sx,sy);
for (tl=1;tl<=7;tl++){
    sx=sinus[pl][0];sy=sinus[pl][1];pl++;_lineto(sx,sy);};
sx=sinus[pl][0];sy=sinus[pl][1];pl++;_floodfill(sx,sy,C0);
sx=sinus[pl][0];sy=sinus[pl][1];pl++;_moveto(sx,sy);
for (tl=1;tl<=8;tl++){
    sx=sinus[pl][0];sy=sinus[pl][1];pl++;_lineto(sx,sy);};
sx=sinus[pl][0];sy=sinus[pl][1];pl++;_floodfill(sx,sy,C0);
for (tl=1;tl<=2;tl++){
    sx=sinus[pl][0];sy=sinus[pl][1];pl++;_moveto(sx,sy);
    sx=sinus[pl][0];sy=sinus[pl][1];pl++;
    _lineto(sx,sy);};
pl=0;                          /* draw the details above the eyes */
for (t2=1;t2<=3;t2++){
    sx=ulids[pl][0];sy=ulids[pl][1];pl++;_moveto(sx,sy);
    for (tl=1;tl<=3;tl++){
        sx=ulids[pl][0];sy=ulids[pl][1];pl++;
```

```
        _lineto(sx,sy);};
    };
for (tl=1;tl<=4;tl++){
    sx=ulids[pl][0];sy=ulids[pl][1];pl++;_moveto(sx,sy);
    sx=ulids[pl][0];sy=ulids[pl][1];pl++;_lineto(sx,sy);};
sx=ulids[pl][0];sy=ulids[pl][1];pl++;_moveto(sx,sy);
for (tl=1;tl<=2;tl++){
    sx=ulids[pl][0];sy=ulids[pl][1];pl++;
    _lineto(sx,sy);};

pl=0;                       /* draw the details in the forehead array */
sx=forehead[pl][0];sy=forehead[pl][1];pl++;_moveto(sx,sy);
for (tl=1;tl<=6;tl++){
    sx=forehead[pl][0];sy=forehead[pl][1];pl++;
    _lineto(sx,sy);};
sx=forehead[pl][0];sy=forehead[pl][1];pl++;_moveto(sx,sy);
sx=forehead[pl][0];sy=forehead[pl][1];pl++;_lineto(sx,sy);
sx=forehead[pl][0];sy=forehead[pl][1];pl++;_moveto(sx,sy);
for (tl=1;tl<=4;tl++){
    sx=forehead[pl][0];sy=forehead[pl][1];pl++;
    _lineto(sx,sy);};
sx=forehead[pl][0];sy=forehead[pl][1];pl++;_moveto(sx,sy);
for (tl=1;tl<=9;tl++){
    sx=forehead[pl][0];sy=forehead[pl][1];pl++;
    _lineto(sx,sy);};


pl=0;                       /* draw the details in mouth array 0 */
sx=mouth0[pl][0];sy=mouth0[pl][1];pl++;_moveto(sx,sy);
for (tl=1;tl<=3;tl++){
    sx=mouth0[pl][0];sy=mouth0[pl][1];pl++;
    _lineto(sx,sy);};
sx=mouth0[pl][0];sy=mouth0[pl][1];pl++;_moveto(sx,sy);
for (tl=1;tl<=3;tl++){
    sx=mouth0[pl][0];sy=mouth0[pl][1];pl++;
    _lineto(sx,sy);};
sx=mouth0[pl][0];sy=mouth0[pl][1];pl++;_moveto(sx,sy);
for (tl=1;tl<=6;tl++){
    sx=mouth0[pl][0];sy=mouth0[pl][1];pl++;
    _lineto(sx,sy);};
sx=mouth0[pl][0];sy=mouth0[pl][1];pl++;_moveto(sx,sy);
for (tl=1;tl<=7;tl++){
    sx=mouth0[pl][0];sy=mouth0[pl][1];pl++;
    _lineto(sx,sy);};
sx=mouth0[pl][0];sy=mouth0[pl][1];pl++;_moveto(sx,sy);
for (tl=1;tl<=13;tl++){
    sx=mouth0[pl][0];sy=mouth0[pl][1];pl++;
    _lineto(sx,sy);};
sx=mouth0[pl][0];sy=mouth0[pl][1];pl++;_floodfill(sx,sy,C0);

return;}

/*_____
```

```
                    SUBROUTINE: airbrushed background              */

void background(void){
sx=0;sy=24;coords();sxl=sx;syl=sy;
sx=639;sy=454;coords();sx2=sx;sy2=sy;
_setcolor(bg);_rectangle(_GFILLINTERIOR,sxl,syl,sx2,sy2);
_setcolor(fg);                          /* ready to begin halftoning */
_setfillmask(fill_6);sx=0;sy=48;coords();sxl=sx;syl=sy;
sx=639;sy=96;coords();sx2=sx;sy2=sy;
_rectangle(_GFILLINTERIOR,sxl,syl,sx2,sy2);
_setfillmask(fill_12);sx=0;coords();sxl=sx;syl=sy2+1;
sx=639;sy=144;coords();sx2=sx;sy2=sy;
_rectangle(_GFILLINTERIOR,sxl,syl,sx2,sy2);
_setfillmask(fill_25);sx=0;coords();sxl=sx;syl=sy2+1;
sx=639;sy=192;coords();sx2=sx;sy2=sy;
_rectangle(_GFILLINTERIOR,sxl,syl,sx2,sy2);
_setfillmask(fill_37);sx=0;coords();sxl=sx;syl=sy2+1;
sx=639;sy=240;coords();sx2=sx;sy2=sy;
_rectangle(_GFILLINTERIOR,sxl,syl,sx2,sy2);
_setfillmask(fill_50);sx=0;coords();sxl=sx;syl=sy2+1;
sx=639;sy=288;coords();sx2=sx;sy2=sy;
_rectangle(_GFILLINTERIOR,sxl,syl,sx2,sy2);
_setfillmask(fill_62);sx=0;coords();sxl=sx;syl=sy2+1;
sx=639;sy=336;coords();sx2=sx;sy2=sy;
_rectangle(_GFILLINTERIOR,sxl,syl,sx2,sy2);
_setfillmask(fill_75);sx=0;coords();sxl=sx;syl=sy2+1;
sx=639;sy=384;coords();sx2=sx;sy2=sy;
_rectangle(_GFILLINTERIOR,sxl,syl,sx2,sy2);
_setfillmask(fill_87);sx=0;coords();sxl=sx;syl=sy2+1;
sx=639;sy=432;coords();sx2=sx;sy2=sy;
_rectangle(_GFILLINTERIOR,sxl,syl,sx2,sy2);
_setfillmask(NULL);sx=0;coords();sxl=sx;syl=sy2+1;
sx=639;sy=454;coords();sx2=sx;sy2=sy;
_rectangle(_GFILLINTERIOR,sxl,syl,sx2,sy2);
_setcolor(C0);notice(5,182);            /* standard copyright notice */

                                        /* draw the bull's eye graphic */
_setcolor(C4);_ellipse(_GFILLINTERIOR,136,15,503,184);
_setcolor(C12);_ellipse(_GFILLINTERIOR,160,27,480,173);
_setcolor(C14);_ellipse(_GFILLINTERIOR,185,39,454,161);
_setfillmask(fill_50);_setcolor(C12);
_floodfill(320,100,C12);_setcolor(C7);_setfillmask(NULL);

return;}

/*_____
                    SUBROUTINE: press any key to quit              */

void keyboard(void){
if (_bios_keybrd(_KEYBRD_READY)==0) return; else quit_pgm();}

/*_____
```

```
                SUBROUTINE: GRACEFUL EXIT FROM THE PROGRAM          */

  void quit_pgm(void){
  _clearscreen(_GCLEARSCREEN);_setvideomode(_DEFAULTMODE);exit(0);}

  /*_____


                SUBROUTINE: VGA/EGA/CGA compatibility module          */

  void graphics_setup(void){

  VGA_EGA_mode:
  if (_setvideomode(_HRES16COLOR)==0) {goto CGA_mode;}
  else {x_res=640;y_res=200;
      _settextposition(1,6);_settextcolor(C7);
      _outtext("U S I N G    C    F O R    H I G H    ");
      _outtext("S P E E D    A N I M A T I O N");
      _settextposition(25,2);
      _outtext("640x200 16-color VGA & EGA mode");
      _settextposition(25,55);
      _outtext("Press any key to stop...");
  return;}

  CGA_mode:
  if (_setvideomode(_HRESBW)==0) {goto abort_message;}
  else {x_res=640;y_res=200;
      C0=0,C1=0,C2=0,C3=0,C4=1,C5=0,C6=0,C7=1,C8=0,C9=0,C10=0,
      C11=0,C12=1,C13=0,C14=1,C15=1;
      _settextposition(1,6);
      _outtext("U S I N G    C    F O R    H I G H    ");
      _outtext("S P E E D    A N I M A T I O N");
      _settextposition(25,2);
      _outtext("640x200 16-color CGA mode");
      _settextposition(25,55);
      _outtext("Press any key to stop...");
  return;}

  abort_message:
  printf("\n\nUnable to proceed.\n");
  printf("Requires VGA, EGA, or CGA adapter\n");
  printf("   with appropriate monitor.\n");
  printf("Please refer to the book.\n\n");exit(0);}

  /*_____


                    SUBROUTINE: coords()
    This subroutine accepts sx,sy device-independent display
    coordinates and returns sx,sy device-dependent screen
    coordinates scaled to fit the 640x480, 640x350, 640x200, or
    320x200 screen, depending upon the graphics mode being used. */

  void coords(void){sx=sx*(x_res/640);sy=sy*(y_res/480);return;}
```

```
/*_____

                SUBROUTINE: Copyright Notice
   This subroutine displays the standard copyright notice.
   If you are typing in this program from the book you can
   safely omit this subroutine, provided that you also remove
   the instruction "notice()" from the main routine.        */

int copyright[][3]={0x7c00,0x0000,0x0000,0x8231,
0x819c,0x645e,0xba4a,0x4252,0x96d0,0xa231,0x8252,0x955e,0xba4a,
0x43d2,0xf442,0x8231,0x825c,0x945e,0x7c00,0x0000,0x0000};

void notice(float x, float y){

int a,b,c; int tl=0;
for (tl=0;tl<=6;tl++){a=copyright[tl][0];b=copyright[tl][1];
c=copyright[tl][2];_setlinestyle(a);_moveto(x,y);_lineto(x+15,y);
_setlinestyle(b);_moveto(x+16,y);_lineto(x+31,y);_setlinestyle(c);
_moveto(x+32,y);_lineto(x+47,y);y=y+1;};_setlinestyle(0xFFFF);
return;}

/*_____


                     End of source code                    */
```

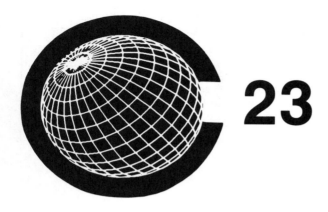 **23**

Simulation Software

This chapter presents a demonstration program which simulates the movements of a human-like figure walking across the display screen. The stickperson lifts and moves each leg in a realistic fashion, and swings its arms in a natural support of the gait.

The line drawing in Fig. 23-1 is the sketch used to develop the demonstration program. Seven versions of the walking figure are needed. More versions would be required except for the fact that only half the gait is actually depicted by the program. As the animation is running the left and right legs become interchangeable and the viewer's eye is deceived into believing that each leg follows a complete cycle.

During animation, each graphic array is placed onto the screen slightly to the left of the previous array, as shown in Fig. 23-2. This ensures that movement will be perceived and that the previous array will be completely overwritten. The size of the rectangular array which contains each version of the walking figure has been arranged to provide for this cover-up.

Despite the coarse resolution of the image (see Fig. 23-3), the simulation is very convincing. The positioning of the arms and legs is the critical factor, of course. The seven versions of the walking figure were drawn on individual sheets of paper and then flipped by thumb to test for accuracy before being coded into the source code. It was much easier to use an eraser and pencil to make the necessary adjustments at the sketching stage then it would have been to fumble with the database of xy coordinates in the C source code.

The photograph in Fig. 23-4 shows one frame from the video image produced by the animated demonstration program in Fig. 23-5. The program listing in Fig. 23-5 is the QuickC version. If you are using Turbo C, you should instead use the program listing

Fig. 23-1. The seven versions of the walking figure that will be animated by the demonstration program in Fig. 23-5.

contained in Fig. E-10 of Appendix E. If you are using the companion disk for this book you can load QC-014.C if you are using QuickC, and you can load TC-014.C if you are using Turbo C.

The demonstration program supports all IBM-compatible graphics adapters. If a VGA or EGA is present, the animation runs in the 320×200 16-color mode. If a CGA or MCGA is present, the program uses the 320×200 4-color mode. If Turbo C is being used, the demonstration program always uses the 320×200 4-color mode, no matter which graphics adapter is installed, because Turbo C 1.5 does not support the 320×200 16-color mode.

Note the animation loop contained in the **main( )** routine. The seven-version cycle is repeated 18 times by the **for/next** loop. This causes the humanoid figure to walk completely across the display screen. When the stickperson reaches the far edge of the screen, the program refreshes the background image and installs the array back over on the right side of the screen. The animation routine continues until you strike any key.

As you watch the animation sequence running, you can observe how the blue sky and green grass are not corrupted by the array. In fact, the array includes a patch of sky and terrain which exactly matches the background, allowing the array to be written to the screen using **PSET**.

The **main( )** routine calls upon a subroutine named **save_arrays( )** to create the seven different versions of the walking stickperson and save them as arrays in user RAM. Note the **for/next** drawing loops and the **p1** pointer used in this subroutine.

After the stickperson arrays have been saved, the **main( )** routine calls a subroutine named **draw_bg( )** to create the background image: a blue sky and a patch of green grass. Then **main( )** enters the animation loop.

The essence of this animated simulation is the preparation which went into the preliminary pencil sketches. Without this hard work, the simulation would not seem

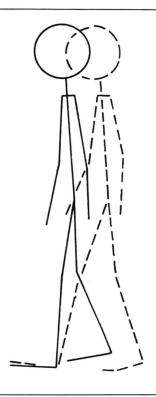

Fig. 23-2. Each array is placed on the screen slightly to the left of the previous array.

realistic. The positioning of each array during the animation cycle was achieved by trial and error, as was the **t1 < =18** instruction.

Note that the animation manager contains no delay routines. The relatively large size of the arrays being used means that C takes a noticeable length of time to write each array to the screen. If you watch the animation carefully, you can detect a slight ripple as each array is installed. This is caused by C's habit of writing the array from top to bottom on the display screen. As the array is being written you are actually seeing a walking stickperson composed of part of the new array and part of the old array.

If you are compiling this demonstration program using Turbo C, you can safely ignore the warning message generated by the compiler. Turbo C assumes that every time you use a **goto** instruction you are making some portions of the code "unreachable". The **goto** instruction is a valuable tool for C graphics programmers, especially in the creation of optimized endless loops.

USING C FOR HIGH SPEED ANIMATION

320x200 4-color VGA and EGA mode
Press any key to stop

Fig. 23-3. Dot-matrix print-out of the image produced by the animated demonstration program in Fig. 23-5.

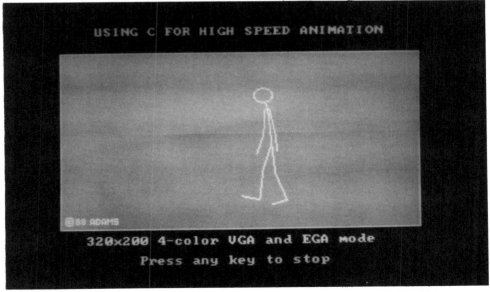

Fig. 23-4. The video display produced by the animated demonstration program in Fig. 23-5.

Fig. 23-5. Program listing for an animated figure—QuickC version. VGA/EGA/CGA/MCGA compatible. For Turbo C version, consult Appendix E.

```
/*_____

                              qc-014.c

      Function:  This program demonstrates high speed animation of
      a walking human figure using bitblt animation techniques.

      Compatibility:  Supports all graphics adapters and monitors.
      If a VGA or EGA is present, the 320x200 16-color mode is
      used.  The software uses the 320x200 4-color mode if a CGA
      is present.

      Remarks:  Refer to the book.

      Copyright 1988 Lee Adams and TAB BOOKS Inc.

      _____


                   I N C L U D E    F I L E S              */

#include <stdio.h>              /* supports the printf function */
#include <graph.h>          /* supports the graphics functions */
#include <stdlib.h>            /* supports the exit() function */
#include <bios.h>         /* supports read of keyboard buffer */
#include <malloc.h>           /* supports memory allocation */

/*_____


                   D E C L A R A T I O N S                 */

struct videoconfig vc;

void keyboard(void);void quit_pgm(void);
void notice(float x,float y);void graphics_setup(void);
void save_arrays(void);void draw_bg(void);

int t1=1,t2=2;                                  /* loop counters */
int C0=0,C1=1,C2=2,C3=3,C4=4,C5=5,C6=6,C7=7,C8=8,C9=9,C10=10,
    C11=11,C12=12,C13=13,C14=14,C15=15;
float sx=0,sy=0,sx1=0,sy1=0,sx2=0,sy2=0;
int x=252,x1=-2;

                  /* graphic arrays will be stored in far heap */
char far *A1;char far *A2;char far *A3;char far *A4;
char far *A5;char far *A6;char far *A7;

int p1=0;                          /* pointer into database arrays */

int draw_A1[][2]={                  /* xy coordinates for frame 1 */
```

```
               155,53,  171,65,  165,66,  167,72,  170,100, 144,143,
               159,146, 162,122, 170,100, 173,125, 183,147, 173,150,
               170,150, 157,108, 163,92,  164,72,  168,71,  173,90,
               175,106};

int draw_A2[][2]={                       /* xy coordinates for frame 2 */
               155,53,  171,65,  165,66,  167,72,  170,100, 141,144,
               154,146, 161,122, 170,100, 176,125, 186,146, 177,150,
               172,150, 153,107, 162,93,  164,72,  168,71,  175,90,
               178,107};

int draw_A3[][2]={                       /* xy coordinates for frame 3 */
               155,53,  171,65,  165,66,  167,72,  170,100, 145,146,
               159,148, 164,125, 170,100, 175,124, 183,146, 176,150,
               172,150, 158,107, 163,93,  164,72,  168,71,  173,89,
               174,105};

int draw_A4[][2]={                       /* xy coordinates for frame 4 */
               155,53,  171,65,  165,66,  167,72,  170,100, 153,149,
               168,150, 168,123, 170,100, 173,123, 183,144, 170,147,
               162,109, 165,91,  164,72,  168,71,  172,89,  175,106};

int draw_A5[][2]={                       /* xy coordinates for frame 5 */
               155,53,  171,65,  165,66,  167,72,  170,100, 155,150,
               170,150, 168,122, 170,100, 169,122, 176,143, 160,146,
               166,108, 167,90,  164,72,  168,71,  170,90,  171,108};

int draw_A6[][2]={                       /* xy coordinates for frame 6 */
               155,53,  171,65,  165,66,  167,72,  170,100, 158,144,
               172,142, 165,122, 170,100, 170,122, 175,150, 162,150,
               162,108, 167,91,  164,72,  168,71,  171,89,  174,106};

int draw_A7[][2]={                       /* xy coordinates for frame 7 */
               155,53,  171,65,  165,66,  167,72,  170,100, 148,143,
               161,145, 163,122, 170,100, 172,124, 178,148, 163,150,
               158,110, 164,92,  164,72,  168,71,  172,89,  175,107};


/*_____


                   M A I N   R O U T I N E                      */

main(){
graphics_setup();                        /* establish graphics mode */
_getvideoconfig(&vc);                    /* initialize video table */

save_arrays();                   /* create and save graphic arrays */
draw_bg();                                /* draw the background */
_settextposition(10,7);_outtext("Ready to begin animation...");
for (tl=1;tl<=30000;tl++);                              /* pause */
for (tl=1;tl<=30000;tl++);                              /* pause */
draw_bg();
```

```
animation_loop:
for (t1=1;t1<=18;t1++){
    _putimage(x,50,A1,_GPSET);x=x+x1;
    for (t2=1;t2<=1000;t2++);keyboard();
    _putimage(x,50,A2,_GPSET);x=x+x1;
    for (t2=1;t2<=1000;t2++);keyboard();
    _putimage(x,50,A3,_GPSET);x=x+x1;
    for (t2=1;t2<=1000;t2++);keyboard();
    _putimage(x,50,A4,_GPSET);x=x+x1;
    for (t2=1;t2<=1000;t2++);keyboard();
    _putimage(x,50,A5,_GPSET);x=x+x1;
    for (t2=1;t2<=1000;t2++);keyboard();
    _putimage(x,50,A6,_GPSET);x=x+x1;
    for (t2=1;t2<=1000;t2++);keyboard();
    _putimage(x,50,A7,_GPSET);x=x+x1;
    for (t2=1;t2<=1000;t2++);};
x=252;
for (t2=1;t2<=30000;t2++);keyboard();
for (t2=1;t2<=30000;t2++);keyboard();
draw_bg();
goto animation_loop;                         /* infinite loop */

quit_pgm();}                         /* end the program gracefully */

/*_____


                 SUBROUTINE: create & save graphic arrays          */

void save_arrays(void){

_setcolor(C1);_rectangle(_GFILLINTERIOR,140,50,190,90);
_setcolor(C2);_rectangle(_GFILLINTERIOR,140,91,190,150);
_setcolor(C7);pl=0;
sx1=draw_A1[pl][0];sy1=draw_A1[pl][1];pl++;
sx2=draw_A1[pl][0];sy2=draw_A1[pl][1];pl++;
_ellipse(_GBORDER,sx1,sy1,sx2,sy2);
sx=draw_A1[pl][0];sy=draw_A1[pl][1];pl++;_moveto(sx,sy);
for (t1=1;t1<=2;t1++){
    sx=draw_A1[pl][0];sy=draw_A1[pl][1];pl++;_lineto(sx,sy);};
sx=draw_A1[pl][0];sy=draw_A1[pl][1];pl++;_moveto(sx,sy);
for (t1=1;t1<=7;t1++){
    sx=draw_A1[pl][0];sy=draw_A1[pl][1];pl++;_lineto(sx,sy);};
sx=draw_A1[pl][0];sy=draw_A1[pl][1];pl++;_moveto(sx,sy);
for (t1=1;t1<=5;t1++){
    sx=draw_A1[pl][0];sy=draw_A1[pl][1];pl++;_lineto(sx,sy);};
A1=(char far *)_fmalloc((unsigned int)
_imagesize(140,50,190,150));     /* calculate memory requirements */
_getimage(140,50,190,150,A1);             /* save array in memory */

_setcolor(C1);_rectangle(_GFILLINTERIOR,140,50,190,90);
_setcolor(C2);_rectangle(_GFILLINTERIOR,140,91,190,150);
_setcolor(C7);pl=0;
sx1=draw_A2[pl][0];sy1=draw_A2[pl][1];pl++;
```

```
sx2=draw_A2[pl][0];sy2=draw_A2[pl][1];pl++;
_ellipse(_GBORDER,sxl,syl,sx2,sy2);
sx=draw_A2[pl][0];sy=draw_A2[pl][1];pl++;_moveto(sx,sy);
for (tl=1;tl<=2;tl++){
    sx=draw_A2[pl][0];sy=draw_A2[pl][1];pl++;_lineto(sx,sy);};
sx=draw_A2[pl][0];sy=draw_A2[pl][1];pl++;_moveto(sx,sy);
for (tl=1;tl<=7;tl++){
    sx=draw_A2[pl][0];sy=draw_A2[pl][1];pl++;_lineto(sx,sy);};
sx=draw_A2[pl][0];sy=draw_A2[pl][1];pl++;_moveto(sx,sy);
for (tl=1;tl<=5;tl++){
    sx=draw_A2[pl][0];sy=draw_A2[pl][1];pl++;_lineto(sx,sy);};
A2=(char far *)_fmalloc((unsigned int)
_imagesize(140,50,190,150));     /* calculate memory requirements */
_getimage(140,50,190,150,A2);                /* save array in memory */

_setcolor(Cl);_rectangle(_GFILLINTERIOR,140,50,190,90);
_setcolor(C2);_rectangle(_GFILLINTERIOR,140,91,190,150);
_setcolor(C7);pl=0;
sxl=draw_A3[pl][0];syl=draw_A3[pl][1];pl++;
sx2=draw_A3[pl][0];sy2=draw_A3[pl][1];pl++;
_ellipse(_GBORDER,sxl,syl,sx2,sy2);
sx=draw_A3[pl][0];sy=draw_A3[pl][1];pl++;_moveto(sx,sy);
for (tl=1;tl<=2;tl++){
    sx=draw_A3[pl][0];sy=draw_A3[pl][1];pl++;_lineto(sx,sy);};
sx=draw_A3[pl][0];sy=draw_A3[pl][1];pl++;_moveto(sx,sy);
for (tl=1;tl<=7;tl++){
    sx=draw_A3[pl][0];sy=draw_A3[pl][1];pl++;_lineto(sx,sy);};
sx=draw_A3[pl][0];sy=draw_A3[pl][1];pl++;_moveto(sx,sy);
for (tl=1;tl<=5;tl++){
    sx=draw_A3[pl][0];sy=draw_A3[pl][1];pl++;_lineto(sx,sy);};
A3=(char far *)_fmalloc((unsigned int)
_imagesize(140,50,190,150));     /* calculate memory requirements */
_getimage(140,50,190,150,A3);                /* save array in memory */

_setcolor(Cl);_rectangle(_GFILLINTERIOR,140,50,190,90);
_setcolor(C2);_rectangle(_GFILLINTERIOR,140,91,190,150);
_setcolor(C7);pl=0;
sxl=draw_A4[pl][0];syl=draw_A4[pl][1];pl++;
sx2=draw_A4[pl][0];sy2=draw_A4[pl][1];pl++;
_ellipse(_GBORDER,sxl,syl,sx2,sy2);
sx=draw_A4[pl][0];sy=draw_A4[pl][1];pl++;_moveto(sx,sy);
for (tl=1;tl<=2;tl++){
    sx=draw_A4[pl][0];sy=draw_A4[pl][1];pl++;_lineto(sx,sy);};
sx=draw_A4[pl][0];sy=draw_A4[pl][1];pl++;_moveto(sx,sy);
for (tl=1;tl<=6;tl++){
    sx=draw_A4[pl][0];sy=draw_A4[pl][1];pl++;_lineto(sx,sy);};
sx=draw_A4[pl][0];sy=draw_A4[pl][1];pl++;_moveto(sx,sy);
for (tl=1;tl<=5;tl++){
    sx=draw_A4[pl][0];sy=draw_A4[pl][1];pl++;_lineto(sx,sy);};
A4=(char far *)_fmalloc((unsigned int)
_imagesize(140,50,190,150));     /* calculate memory requirements */
_getimage(140,50,190,150,A4);                /* save array in memory */

_setcolor(Cl);_rectangle(_GFILLINTERIOR,140,50,190,90);
```

```
_setcolor(C2);_rectangle(_GFILLINTERIOR,140,91,190,150);
_setcolor(C7);pl=0;
sxl=draw_A5[pl][0];syl=draw_A5[pl][1];pl++;
sx2=draw_A5[pl][0];sy2=draw_A5[pl][1];pl++;
_ellipse(_GBORDER,sxl,syl,sx2,sy2);
sx=draw_A5[pl][0];sy=draw_A5[pl][1];pl++;_moveto(sx,sy);
for (tl=1;tl<=2;tl++){
    sx=draw_A5[pl][0];sy=draw_A5[pl][1];pl++;_lineto(sx,sy);};
sx=draw_A5[pl][0];sy=draw_A5[pl][1];pl++;_moveto(sx,sy);
for (tl=1;tl<=6;tl++){
    sx=draw_A5[pl][0];sy=draw_A5[pl][1];pl++;_lineto(sx,sy);};
sx=draw_A5[pl][0];sy=draw_A5[pl][1];pl++;_moveto(sx,sy);
for (tl=1;tl<=5;tl++){
    sx=draw_A5[pl][0];sy=draw_A5[pl][1];pl++;_lineto(sx,sy);};
A5=(char far *)_fmalloc((unsigned int)
_imagesize(140,50,190,150));    /* calculate memory requirements */
_getimage(140,50,190,150,A5);              /* save array in memory */

_setcolor(Cl);_rectangle(_GFILLINTERIOR,140,50,190,90);
_setcolor(C2);_rectangle(_GFILLINTERIOR,140,91,190,150);
_setcolor(C7);pl=0;
sxl=draw_A6[pl][0];syl=draw_A6[pl][1];pl++;
sx2=draw_A6[pl][0];sy2=draw_A6[pl][1];pl++;
_ellipse(_GBORDER,sxl,syl,sx2,sy2);
sx=draw_A6[pl][0];sy=draw_A6[pl][1];pl++;_moveto(sx,sy);
for (tl=1;tl<=2;tl++){
    sx=draw_A6[pl][0];sy=draw_A6[pl][1];pl++;_lineto(sx,sy);};
sx=draw_A6[pl][0];sy=draw_A6[pl][1];pl++;_moveto(sx,sy);
for (tl=1;tl<=6;tl++){
    sx=draw_A6[pl][0];sy=draw_A6[pl][1];pl++;_lineto(sx,sy);};
sx=draw_A6[pl][0];sy=draw_A6[pl][1];pl++;_moveto(sx,sy);
for (tl=1;tl<=5;tl++){
    sx=draw_A6[pl][0];sy=draw_A6[pl][1];pl++;_lineto(sx,sy);};
A6=(char far *)_fmalloc((unsigned int)
_imagesize(140,50,190,150));    /* calculate memory requirements */
_getimage(140,50,190,150,A6);              /* save array in memory */

_setcolor(Cl);_rectangle(_GFILLINTERIOR,140,50,190,90);
_setcolor(C2);_rectangle(_GFILLINTERIOR,140,91,190,150);
_setcolor(C7);pl=0;
sxl=draw_A7[pl][0];syl=draw_A7[pl][1];pl++;
sx2=draw_A7[pl][0];sy2=draw_A7[pl][1];pl++;
_ellipse(_GBORDER,sxl,syl,sx2,sy2);
sx=draw_A7[pl][0];sy=draw_A7[pl][1];pl++;_moveto(sx,sy);
for (tl=1;tl<=2;tl++){
    sx=draw_A7[pl][0];sy=draw_A7[pl][1];pl++;_lineto(sx,sy);};
sx=draw_A7[pl][0];sy=draw_A7[pl][1];pl++;_moveto(sx,sy);
for (tl=1;tl<=6;tl++){
    sx=draw_A7[pl][0];sy=draw_A7[pl][1];pl++;_lineto(sx,sy);};
sx=draw_A7[pl][0];sy=draw_A7[pl][1];pl++;_moveto(sx,sy);
for (tl=1;tl<=5;tl++){
    sx=draw_A7[pl][0];sy=draw_A7[pl][1];pl++;_lineto(sx,sy);};
A7=(char far *)_fmalloc((unsigned int)
```

```
_imagesize(140,50,190,150));      /* calculate memory requirements */
_getimage(140,50,190,150,A7);              /* save array in memory */

return;}

/*_____


                SUBROUTINE: draw the background                    */

void draw_bg(void){

_setcolor(C1);_rectangle(_GFILLINTERIOR,0,22,319,90);
_setcolor(C2);_rectangle(_GFILLINTERIOR,0,91,319,170);
_setcolor(C7);_rectangle(_GBORDER,0,22,319,170);
notice(5,160);
return;}

/*_____


                SUBROUTINE: press any key to quit                 */

void keyboard(void){
if (_bios_keybrd(_KEYBRD_READY)==0) return; else quit_pgm();}

/*_____


                SUBROUTINE: GRACEFUL EXIT FROM THE PROGRAM          */

void quit_pgm(void){
_clearscreen(_GCLEARSCREEN);_setvideomode(_DEFAULTMODE);exit(0);}

/*_____


                SUBROUTINE: VGA/EGA/CGA compatibility module        */

void graphics_setup(void){goto CGA_mode;

VGA_EGA_mode:
if (_setvideomode(_MRES16COLOR)==0) {goto CGA_mode;}
else {_settextposition(1,5);_settextcolor(C7);
      _outtext("USING C FOR HIGH SPEED ANIMATION");
      _settextposition(23,4);
      _outtext("320x200 4-color VGA and EGA mode");
      _settextposition(25,10);
      _outtext("Press any key to stop");
return;}

CGA_mode:
if (_setvideomode(_MRES4COLOR)==0) {goto abort_message;}
else {C0=0;C1=1;C2=2;C7=3;
```

```
      _settextposition(1,5); _settextcolor(C3);
      _outtext("USING C FOR HIGH SPEED ANIMATION");
      _settextposition(23,9);
      _outtext("320x200 4-color CGA mode");
      _settextposition(25,10);
      _outtext("Press any key to stop");
return;}

abort_message:
printf("\n\nUnable to proceed.\n");
printf("Requires VGA, EGA, or CGA adapter\n");
printf("   with appropriate monitor.\n");
printf("Please refer to the book.\n\n");exit(0);}

/*_____


                  SUBROUTINE: Copyright Notice
      This subroutine displays the standard copyright notice.
      If you are typing in this program from the book you can
      safely omit this subroutine, provided that you also remove
      the instruction "notice()" from the main routine.        */

int copyright[][3]={0x7c00,0x0000,0x0000,0x8231,
0x819c,0x645e,0xba4a,0x4252,0x96d0,0xa231,0x8252,0x955e,0xba4a,
0x43d2,0xf442,0x8231,0x825c,0x945e,0x7c00,0x0000,0x0000};

void notice(float x, float y){
int a,b,c; int tl=0;
for (tl=0;tl<=6;tl++){a=copyright[tl][0];b=copyright[tl][1];
c=copyright[tl][2];_setlinestyle(a);_moveto(x,y);_lineto(x+15,y);
_setlinestyle(b);_moveto(x+16,y);_lineto(x+31,y);_setlinestyle(c);
_moveto(x+32,y);_lineto(x+47,y);y=y+1;};_setlinestyle(0xFFFF);
return;}

/*_____

End of source code                                          */
```

24

Animated Educational Software

Animated computer graphics can be powerful teaching tools, especially at the grade school level. This chapter presents a demonstration program which animates the second sweephand of an analog clock face.

The line drawing in Fig. 24-1 shows the original sketch used to develop the demonstration program. The drawing was useful in determining the positioning of the alphanumeric characters which appear on the clock face and in determining the endpoints of the sweephand as it traverses the circumference of the clock face.

The photograph in Fig. 24-2 shows one frame from the video image generated by the animated demonstration program in Fig. 24-3. The program listing in Fig. 24-3 is the QuickC version. If you are using Turbo C, you should use instead the program listing presented in Fig. E-11 of Appendix E. If you are using the companion disk for this book you can load QC-015.C if you are compiling with QuickC, and you can load TC-015.C if you are using Turbo C.

The demonstration program supports all IBM-compatible graphics adapters. If a VGA, EGA, CGA, or MCGA is present the program uses the 640×200 2-color mode.

This program is noteworthy for its use of large numbers of graphic arrays. Each position of the second sweephand requires an array—60 arrays in all are used during the animation cycle. The database array in the DECLARATIONS section of the source code contains all the endpoints of the second sweephand.

The lengthiest module in the program is the subroutine named **save_array( )**. Here is how it works. For each position of the sweephand, the subroutine draws the hour hand and the minute hand as they appear inside the circle which represents the clock face. Then the subroutine draws the second sweephand in the appropriate position and saves the

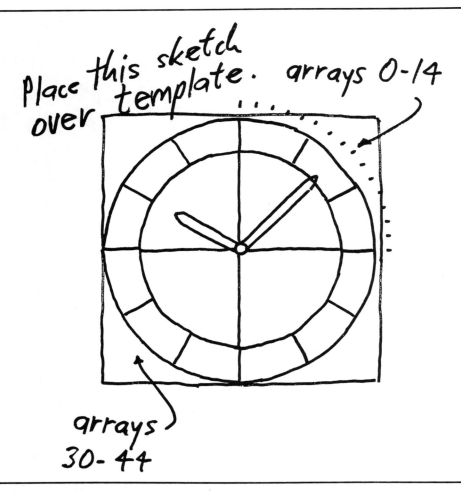

Fig. 24-1. The original template drawing used to obtain the xy coordinates for the animated analog clock face in Fig. 24-3.

appropriate quadrant of the clock fact. Because only four different quadrant-sized array sizes are saved (15 versions of each quadrant), writing the 60 versions of the sweephand back to the screen during the animation cycle is simplified.

After all 60 arrays have been saved, the program clears the screen and draws the complete clock face. Note how the alphanumerics have been saved in tiny arrays, thereby permitting a more precise positioning of each numeric on the face of the clock.

In its present configuration, the program animates only the second sweephand. You can easily modify the routines to animate the minute hand and the hour hand.

The **for/next** delay loop in the animation manager (see the subroutine named **anim( )**) will cause the animation to run at exactly one frame per second on an IBM PC or compatible using an internal 4.77 MHz rate. If you are using at AT or PS/2, you need to make the delay loop pause a bit longer in order to compensate for the faster processing speeds of these computers.

Fig. 24-2. The video display produced by the animated demonstration program in Fig. 24-3.

Fig. 24-3. Program listing for an animated analog clock face. QuickC version. VGA/EGA/CGA/MCGA compatible. For Turbo C version, consult Appendix E.

```
/*_____


                            qc-015.c


        Function:  This program uses the techniques of bitblt
        animation to display a simulated analog clock face.

        Compatibility:  Supports all graphics adapters and monitors.
        The software uses the 640x200 2-color mode.

        Remarks:  The animated clock runs at the correct speed on
        a 4.77 MHz microprocessor.  If your computer runs faster,
        you will be required to add more timing delays by simply
        increasing the size of the variable tn in the declarations
        section of the source code.

        Copyright 1988 Lee Adams and TAB BOOKS Inc.


        _____



                    I N C L U D E    F I L E S                    */

#include <stdio.h>                /* supports the printf function */
```

```
#include <graph.h>          /* supports the graphics functions */
#include <stdlib.h>          /* supports the exit() function */
#include <bios.h>        /* supports read of keyboard buffer */
#include <malloc.h>          /* supports memory allocation */

/*_____

                 D E C L A R A T I O N S                */

struct videoconfig vc;

void keyboard(void);void quit_pgm(void);
void notice(float x,float y);void graphics_setup(void);
void draw_face(void);void draw_sec(void);void anim(void);

int tl=1;
int C0=0,Cl=1,C2=2,C3=3,C4=4,C5=5,C6=6,C7=7,C8=8,C9=9,C10=10,
    Cll=11,Cl2=12,Cl3=13,Cl4=14,Cl5=15,mode_flag=0;
unsigned int t2=1,tn=35408;      /* tn is set for a 4.77 MHz rate */

                /* pointers to graphic arrays */
char far *num_array0;char far *num_arrayl;char far *num_array2;
char far *num_array3;char far *num_array4;char far *num_array5;
char far *num_array6;char far *num_array7;char far *num_array8;
char far *num_array9;
char far *face_array;char far *face_arrayl;char far *face_array2;

char far *face_array3;char far *face_array4;
char far *gr_array0;char far *gr_arrayl;char far *gr_array2;
char far *gr_array3;char far *gr_array4;char far *gr_array5;
char far *gr_array6;char far *gr_array7;char far *gr_array8;
char far *gr_array9;char far *gr_arrayl0;char far *gr_arrayll;
char far *gr_arrayl2;char far *gr_arrayl3;char far *gr_arrayl4;
char far *gr_arrayl5;char far *gr_arrayl6;char far *gr_arrayl7;
char far *gr_arrayl8;char far *gr_arrayl9;char far *gr_array20;
char far *gr_array21;char far *gr_array22;char far *gr_array23;
char far *gr_array24;char far *gr_array25;char far *gr_array26;
char far *gr_array27;char far *gr_array28;char far *gr_array29;
char far *gr_array30;char far *gr_array31;char far *gr_array32;
char far *gr_array33;char far *gr_array34;char far *gr_array35;
char far *gr_array36;char far *gr_array37;char far *gr_array38;
char far *gr_array39;char far *gr_array40;char far *gr_array41;
char far *gr_array42;char far *gr_array43;char far *gr_array44;
char far *gr_array45;char far *gr_array46;char far *gr_array47;
char far *gr_array48;char far *gr_array49;char far *gr_array50;
char far *gr_array51;char far *gr_array52;char far *gr_array53;
char far *gr_array54;char far *gr_array55;char far *gr_array56;
char far *gr_array57;char far *gr_array58;char far *gr_array59;

/*_____

                 M A I N   R O U T I N E                */

main(){
```

```
graphics_setup();                               /* establish graphics mode */
_getvideoconfig(&vc);                           /* initialize video table */
draw_face();                              /* create the generic clock face */
draw_sec();                    /* create 60 versions of the second-hand */
anim();                                     /* animate the clock face */
quit_pgm();}                           /* end the program gracefully */

/*_____


                    SUBROUTINE: animation loop                    '*/

void anim(void){
for (tl=1;tl!=2; ){                                       /* endless loop */
    _putimage(320,58,gr_array0,_GPSET);for (t2=1;t2<=tn;t2++);
    _putimage(320,58,gr_array1,_GPSET);for (t2=1;t2<=tn;t2++);
    _putimage(320,58,gr_array2,_GPSET);for (t2=1;t2<=tn;t2++);
    _putimage(320,58,gr_array3,_GPSET);for (t2=1;t2<=tn;t2++);
    _putimage(320,58,gr_array4,_GPSET);for (t2=1;t2<=tn;t2++);
    keyboard();
    _putimage(320,58,gr_array5,_GPSET);for (t2=1;t2<=tn;t2++);
    _putimage(320,58,gr_array6,_GPSET);for (t2=1;t2<=tn;t2++);
    _putimage(320,58,gr_array7,_GPSET);for (t2=1;t2<=tn;t2++);
    _putimage(320,58,gr_array8,_GPSET);for (t2=1;t2<=tn;t2++);
    _putimage(320,58,gr_array9,_GPSET);for (t2=1;t2<=tn;t2++);
    keyboard();
    _putimage(320,58,gr_array10,_GPSET);for (t2=1;t2<=tn;t2++);
    _putimage(320,58,gr_array11,_GPSET);for (t2=1;t2<=tn;t2++);
    _putimage(320,58,gr_array12,_GPSET);for (t2=1;t2<=tn;t2++);
    _putimage(320,58,gr_array13,_GPSET);for (t2=1;t2<=tn;t2++);
    _putimage(320,58,gr_array14,_GPSET);for (t2=1;t2<=tn;t2++);
    keyboard();_putimage(320,58,face_array1,_GPSET);
    _putimage(320,100,gr_array15,_GPSET);for (t2=1;t2<=tn;t2++);
    _putimage(320,100,gr_array16,_GPSET);for (t2=1;t2<=tn;t2++);
    _putimage(320,100,gr_array17,_GPSET);for (t2=1;t2<=tn;t2++);
    _putimage(320,100,gr_array18,_GPSET);for (t2=1;t2<=tn;t2++);
    _putimage(320,100,gr_array19,_GPSET);for (t2=1;t2<=tn;t2++);
    keyboard();
    _putimage(320,100,gr_array20,_GPSET);for (t2=1;t2<=tn;t2++);
    _putimage(320,100,gr_array21,_GPSET);for (t2=1;t2<=tn;t2++);
    _putimage(320,100,gr_array22,_GPSET);for (t2=1;t2<=tn;t2++);
    _putimage(320,100,gr_array23,_GPSET);for (t2=1;t2<=tn;t2++);
    _putimage(320,100,gr_array24,_GPSET);for (t2=1;t2<=tn;t2++);
    keyboard();
    _putimage(320,100,gr_array25,_GPSET);for (t2=1;t2<=tn;t2++);
    _putimage(320,100,gr_array26,_GPSET);for (t2=1;t2<=tn;t2++);
    _putimage(320,100,gr_array27,_GPSET);for (t2=1;t2<=tn;t2++);
    _putimage(320,100,gr_array28,_GPSET);for (t2=1;t2<=tn;t2++);
    _putimage(320,100,gr_array29,_GPSET);for (t2=1;t2<=tn;t2++);
    keyboard();_putimage(320,100,face_array2,_GPSET);
    _putimage(220,100,gr_array30,_GPSET);for (t2=1;t2<=tn;t2++);
    _putimage(220,100,gr_array31,_GPSET);for (t2=1;t2<=tn;t2++);
    _putimage(220,100,gr_array32,_GPSET);for (t2=1;t2<=tn;t2++);
    _putimage(220,100,gr_array33,_GPSET);for (t2=1;t2<=tn;t2++);
```

```
     _putimage(220,100,gr_array34,_GPSET);for (t2=1;t2<=tn;t2++);
     keyboard();
     _putimage(220,100,gr_array35,_GPSET);for (t2=1;t2<=tn;t2++);
     _putimage(220,100,gr_array36,_GPSET);for (t2=1;t2<=tn;t2++);
     _putimage(220,100,gr_array37,_GPSET);for (t2=1;t2<=tn;t2++);
     _putimage(220,100,gr_array38,_GPSET);for (t2=1;t2<=tn;t2++);
     _putimage(220,100,gr_array39,_GPSET);for (t2=1;t2<=tn;t2++);
     keyboard();
     _putimage(220,100,gr_array40,_GPSET);for (t2=1;t2<=tn;t2++);
     _putimage(220,100,gr_array41,_GPSET);for (t2=1;t2<=tn;t2++);
     _putimage(220,100,gr_array42,_GPSET);for (t2=1;t2<=tn;t2++);
     _putimage(220,100,gr_array43,_GPSET);for (t2=1;t2<=tn;t2++);
     _putimage(220,100,gr_array44,_GPSET);for (t2=1;t2<=tn;t2++);
     keyboard();_putimage(220,100,face_array3,_GPSET);
     _putimage(220,58,gr_array45,_GPSET);for (t2=1;t2<=tn;t2++);
     _putimage(220,58,gr_array46,_GPSET);for (t2=1;t2<=tn;t2++);
     _putimage(220,58,gr_array47,_GPSET);for (t2=1;t2<=tn;t2++);
     _putimage(220,58,gr_array48,_GPSET);for (t2=1;t2<=tn;t2++);
     _putimage(220,58,gr_array49,_GPSET);for (t2=1;t2<=tn;t2++);
     keyboard();
     _putimage(220,58,gr_array50,_GPSET);for (t2=1;t2<=tn;t2++);
     _putimage(220,58,gr_array51,_GPSET);for (t2=1;t2<=tn;t2++);
     _putimage(220,58,gr_array52,_GPSET);for (t2=1;t2<=tn;t2++);
     _putimage(220,58,gr_array53,_GPSET);for (t2=1;t2<=tn;t2++);
     _putimage(220,58,gr_array54,_GPSET);for (t2=1;t2<=tn;t2++);
     keyboard();
     _putimage(220,58,gr_array55,_GPSET);for (t2=1;t2<=tn;t2++);
     _putimage(220,58,gr_array56,_GPSET);for (t2=1;t2<=tn;t2++);
     _putimage(220,58,gr_array57,_GPSET);for (t2=1;t2<=tn;t2++);
     _putimage(220,58,gr_array58,_GPSET);for (t2=1;t2<=tn;t2++);
     _putimage(220,58,gr_array59,_GPSET);for (t2=1;t2<=tn;t2++);
     keyboard();_putimage(220,58,face_array4,_GPSET);
     };
return;}

/*_____



                  SUBROUTINE: create the clock face              */

void draw_face(void){

_settextposition(1,1);_outtext("0123456789");
num_array0=(char far *)_fmalloc((unsigned int)_imagesize(0,0,7,7));
_getimage(0,0,7,7,num_array0);
num_array1=(char far *)_fmalloc((unsigned int)_imagesize(8,0,15,7));
_getimage(8,0,15,7,num_array1);
num_array2=(char far *)_fmalloc((unsigned int)_imagesize(16,0,23,7));
_getimage(16,0,23,7,num_array2);
num_array3=(char far *)_fmalloc((unsigned int)_imagesize(24,0,31,7));
_getimage(24,0,31,7,num_array3);
num_array4=(char far *)_fmalloc((unsigned int)_imagesize(32,0,39,7));
_getimage(32,0,39,7,num_array4);
num_array5=(char far *)_fmalloc((unsigned int)_imagesize(40,0,47,7));
```

```
_getimage(40,0,47,7,num_array5);
num_array6=(char far *)_fmalloc((unsigned int)_imagesize(48,0,55,7));
_getimage(48,0,55,7,num_array6);
num_array7=(char far *)_fmalloc((unsigned int)_imagesize(56,0,63,7));
_getimage(56,0,63,7,num_array7);
num_array8=(char far *)_fmalloc((unsigned int)_imagesize(64,0,71,7));
_getimage(64,0,71,7,num_array8);
num_array9=(char far *)_fmalloc((unsigned int)_imagesize(72,0,79,7));
_getimage(72,0,79,7,num_array9);
_settextposition(1,1);_outtext("          ");


_ellipse(_GBORDER,202,46,438,154);                    /* draw the circle */

                                      /* create hour-hand, minute-hand */
_moveto(264,86);_lineto(272,85);_lineto(322,98);
_lineto(319,102);_lineto(266,88);_lineto(264,86);
_lineto(264,86);_floodfill(300,95,Cl);
_moveto(316,99);_lineto(379,71);_lineto(385,71);
_lineto(384,74);_lineto(320,102);_lineto(316,99);
_lineto(316,99);_floodfill(360,82,Cl);

                                /* install alphanumerics on clock face */
_putimage(370,55,num_array1,_GOR);_putimage(407,73,num_array2,_GOR);
_putimage(420,97,num_array3,_GOR);_putimage(405,120,num_array4,_GOR);
_putimage(370,138,num_array5,_GOR);_putimage(318,144,num_array6,_GOR);
_putimage(266,138,num_array7,_GOR);_putimage(226,120,num_array8,_GOR);
_putimage(210,97,num_array9,_GOR);_putimage(222,73,num_array1,_GOR);
_putimage(230,73,num_array0,_GOR);_putimage(260,56,num_array1,_GOR);
_putimage(268,56,num_array1,_GOR);_putimage(312,49,num_array1,_GOR);
_putimage(320,49,num_array2,_GOR);notice(5,193);

    /* save quarters of clock face for clean-up during animation */
face_array=(char far *)_fmalloc((unsigned int)_imagesize(202,46,438,154));
_getimage(202,46,438,154,face_array);
face_array1=(char far *)_fmalloc((unsigned int)_imagesize(320,58,420,100));
_getimage(320,58,420,100,face_array1);
face_array2=(char far *)_fmalloc((unsigned int)_imagesize(320,100,420,143));
_getimage(320,100,420,143,face_array2);
face_array3=(char far *)_fmalloc((unsigned int)_imagesize(220,100,320,143));
_getimage(220,100,320,143,face_array3);
face_array4=(char far *)_fmalloc((unsigned int)_imagesize(220,58,320,100));
_getimage(220,58,320,100,face_array4);

return;}

/*_____


          SUBROUTINE: create 60 versions of the second-hand        */

void draw_sec(void){

_moveto(320,100);_lineto(320,58);
gr_array0=(char far *)_fmalloc((unsigned int)_imagesize(320,58,420,100));
```

```
_getimage(320,58,420,100,gr_array0);_putimage(202,46,face_array,_GPSET);
_moveto(320,100);_lineto(329,58);
gr_array1=(char far *)_fmalloc((unsigned int)_imagesize(320,58,420,100));
_getimage(320,58,420,100,gr_array1);_putimage(202,46,face_array,_GPSET);
_moveto(320,100);_lineto(340,59);
gr_array2=(char far *)_fmalloc((unsigned int)_imagesize(320,58,420,100));
_getimage(320,58,420,100,gr_array2);_putimage(202,46,face_array,_GPSET);
_moveto(320,100);_lineto(348,60);
gr_array3=(char far *)_fmalloc((unsigned int)_imagesize(320,58,420,100));
_getimage(320,58,420,100,gr_array3);_putimage(202,46,face_array,_GPSET);
_moveto(320,100);_lineto(358,62);
gr_array4=(char far *)_fmalloc((unsigned int)_imagesize(320,58,420,100));
_getimage(320,58,420,100,gr_array4);_putimage(202,46,face_array,_GPSET);
_moveto(320,100);_lineto(367,63);
gr_array5=(char far *)_fmalloc((unsigned int)_imagesize(320,58,420,100));
_getimage(320,58,420,100,gr_array5);_putimage(202,46,face_array,_GPSET);
_moveto(320,100);_lineto(375,66);
gr_array6=(char far *)_fmalloc((unsigned int)_imagesize(320,58,420,100));
_getimage(320,58,420,100,gr_array6);_putimage(202,46,face_array,_GPSET);
_moveto(320,100);_lineto(381,69);
gr_array7=(char far *)_fmalloc((unsigned int)_imagesize(320,58,420,100));
_getimage(320,58,420,100,gr_array7);_putimage(202,46,face_array,_GPSET);
_moveto(320,100);_lineto(388,72);
gr_array8=(char far *)_fmalloc((unsigned int)_imagesize(320,58,420,100));
_getimage(320,58,420,100,gr_array8);_putimage(202,46,face_array,_GPSET);
_moveto(320,100);_lineto(395,75);
gr_array9=(char far *)_fmalloc((unsigned int)_imagesize(320,58,420,100));
_getimage(320,58,420,100,gr_array9);_putimage(202,46,face_array,_GPSET);
_moveto(320,100);_lineto(400,79);
gr_array10=(char far *)_fmalloc((unsigned int)_imagesize(320,58,420,100));
_getimage(320,58,420,100,gr_array10);_putimage(202,46,face_array,_GPSET);
_moveto(320,100);_lineto(405,83);
gr_array11=(char far *)_fmalloc((unsigned int)_imagesize(320,58,420,100));
_getimage(320,58,420,100,gr_array11);_putimage(202,46,face_array,_GPSET);
_moveto(320,100);_lineto(409,87);
gr_array12=(char far *)_fmalloc((unsigned int)_imagesize(320,58,420,100));
_getimage(320,58,420,100,gr_array12);_putimage(202,46,face_array,_GPSET);
_moveto(320,100);_lineto(411,92);
gr_array13=(char far *)_fmalloc((unsigned int)_imagesize(320,58,420,100));
_getimage(320,58,420,100,gr_array13);_putimage(202,46,face_array,_GPSET);
_moveto(320,100);_lineto(412,96);
gr_array14=(char far *)_fmalloc((unsigned int)_imagesize(320,58,420,100));
_getimage(320,58,420,100,gr_array14);_putimage(202,46,face_array,_GPSET);
_moveto(320,100);_lineto(413,100);
gr_array15=(char far *)_fmalloc((unsigned int)_imagesize(320,100,420,143));
_getimage(320,100,420,143,gr_array15);_putimage(202,46,face_array,_GPSET);
_moveto(320,100);_lineto(412,104);
gr_array16=(char far *)_fmalloc((unsigned int)_imagesize(320,100,420,143));
_getimage(320,100,420,143,gr_array16);_putimage(202,46,face_array,_GPSET);
_moveto(320,100);_lineto(411,109);
gr_array17=(char far *)_fmalloc((unsigned int)_imagesize(320,100,420,143));
_getimage(320,100,420,143,gr_array17);_putimage(202,46,face_array,_GPSET);
_moveto(320,100);_lineto(409,114);
gr_array18=(char far *)_fmalloc((unsigned int)_imagesize(320,100,420,143));
```

```
_getimage(320,100,420,143,gr_array18);_putimage(202,46,face_array,_GPSET);
_moveto(320,100);_lineto(405,117);
gr_array19=(char far *)_fmalloc((unsigned int)_imagesize(320,100,420,143));
_getimage(320,100,420,143,gr_array19);_putimage(202,46,face_array,_GPSET);
_moveto(320,100);_lineto(400,121);
gr_array20=(char far *)_fmalloc((unsigned int)_imagesize(320,100,420,143));
_getimage(320,100,420,143,gr_array20);_putimage(202,46,face_array,_GPSET);
_moveto(320,100);_lineto(395,125);
gr_array21=(char far *)_fmalloc((unsigned int)_imagesize(320,100,420,143));
_getimage(320,100,420,143,gr_array21);_putimage(202,46,face_array,_GPSET);
_moveto(320,100);_lineto(388,128);
gr_array22=(char far *)_fmalloc((unsigned int)_imagesize(320,100,420,143));
_getimage(320,100,420,143,gr_array22);_putimage(202,46,face_array,_GPSET);
_moveto(320,100);_lineto(381,132);
gr_array23=(char far *)_fmalloc((unsigned int)_imagesize(320,100,420,143));
_getimage(320,100,420,143,gr_array23);_putimage(202,46,face_array,_GPSET);
_moveto(320,100);_lineto(375,134);
gr_array24=(char far *)_fmalloc((unsigned int)_imagesize(320,100,420,143));
_getimage(320,100,420,143,gr_array24);_putimage(202,46,face_array,_GPSET);
_moveto(320,100);_lineto(367,136);
gr_array25=(char far *)_fmalloc((unsigned int)_imagesize(320,100,420,143));
_getimage(320,100,420,143,gr_array25);_putimage(202,46,face_array,_GPSET);
_moveto(320,100);_lineto(358,138);
gr_array26=(char far *)_fmalloc((unsigned int)_imagesize(320,100,420,143));
_getimage(320,100,420,143,gr_array26);_putimage(202,46,face_array,_GPSET);
_moveto(320,100);_lineto(348,140);
gr_array27=(char far *)_fmalloc((unsigned int)_imagesize(320,100,420,143));
_getimage(320,100,420,143,gr_array27);_putimage(202,46,face_array,_GPSET);
_moveto(320,100);_lineto(340,142);
gr_array28=(char far *)_fmalloc((unsigned int)_imagesize(320,100,420,143));
_getimage(320,100,420,143,gr_array28);_putimage(202,46,face_array,_GPSET);
_moveto(320,100);_lineto(329,143);
gr_array29=(char far *)_fmalloc((unsigned int)_imagesize(320,100,420,143));
_getimage(320,100,420,143,gr_array29);_putimage(202,46,face_array,_GPSET);
_moveto(320,100);_lineto(320,143);
gr_array30=(char far *)_fmalloc((unsigned int)_imagesize(220,100,320,143));
_getimage(220,100,320,143,gr_array30);_putimage(202,46,face_array,_GPSET);
_moveto(320,100);_lineto(310,143);
gr_array31=(char far *)_fmalloc((unsigned int)_imagesize(220,100,320,143));
_getimage(220,100,320,143,gr_array31);_putimage(202,46,face_array,_GPSET);
_moveto(320,100);_lineto(300,142);
gr_array32=(char far *)_fmalloc((unsigned int)_imagesize(220,100,320,143));
_getimage(220,100,320,143,gr_array32);_putimage(202,46,face_array,_GPSET);
_moveto(320,100);_lineto(290,140);
gr_array33=(char far *)_fmalloc((unsigned int)_imagesize(220,100,320,143));
_getimage(220,100,320,143,gr_array33);_putimage(202,46,face_array,_GPSET);
_moveto(320,100);_lineto(281,138);
gr_array34=(char far *)_fmalloc((unsigned int)_imagesize(220,100,320,143));
_getimage(220,100,320,143,gr_array34);_putimage(202,46,face_array,_GPSET);
_moveto(320,100);_lineto(273,136);
gr_array35=(char far *)_fmalloc((unsigned int)_imagesize(220,100,320,143));
_getimage(220,100,320,143,gr_array35);_putimage(202,46,face_array,_GPSET);
_moveto(320,100);_lineto(266,134);
gr_array36=(char far *)_fmalloc((unsigned int)_imagesize(220,100,320,143));
```

```
_getimage(220,100,320,143,gr_array36);_putimage(202,46,face_array,_GPSET);
_moveto(320,100);_lineto(258,132);
gr_array37=(char far *)_fmalloc((unsigned int)_imagesize(220,100,320,143));
_getimage(220,100,320,143,gr_array37);_putimage(202,46,face_array,_GPSET);
_moveto(320,100);_lineto(250,128);
gr_array38=(char far *)_fmalloc((unsigned int)_imagesize(220,100,320,143));
_getimage(220,100,320,143,gr_array38);_putimage(202,46,face_array,_GPSET);
_moveto(320,100);_lineto(245,125);
gr_array39=(char far *)_fmalloc((unsigned int)_imagesize(220,100,320,143));
_getimage(220,100,320,143,gr_array39);_putimage(202,46,face_array,_GPSET);
_moveto(320,100);_lineto(240,121);
gr_array40=(char far *)_fmalloc((unsigned int)_imagesize(220,100,320,143));
_getimage(220,100,320,143,gr_array40);_putimage(202,46,face_array,_GPSET);
_moveto(320,100);_lineto(235,117);
gr_array41=(char far *)_fmalloc((unsigned int)_imagesize(220,100,320,143));
_getimage(220,100,320,143,gr_array41);_putimage(202,46,face_array,_GPSET);
_moveto(320,100);_lineto(231,114);
gr_array42=(char far *)_fmalloc((unsigned int)_imagesize(220,100,320,143));
_getimage(220,100,320,143,gr_array42);_putimage(202,46,face_array,_GPSET);
_moveto(320,100);_lineto(229,110);
gr_array43=(char far *)_fmalloc((unsigned int)_imagesize(220,100,320,143));
_getimage(220,100,320,143,gr_array43);_putimage(202,46,face_array,_GPSET);
_moveto(320,100);_lineto(227,104);
gr_array44=(char far *)_fmalloc((unsigned int)_imagesize(220,100,320,143));
_getimage(220,100,320,143,gr_array44);_putimage(202,46,face_array,_GPSET);
_moveto(320,100);_lineto(226,100);
gr_array45=(char far *)_fmalloc((unsigned int)_imagesize(220,58,320,100));
_getimage(220,58,320,100,gr_array45);_putimage(202,46,face_array,_GPSET);
_moveto(320,100);_lineto(227,96);
gr_array46=(char far *)_fmalloc((unsigned int)_imagesize(220,58,320,100));
_getimage(220,58,320,100,gr_array46);_putimage(202,46,face_array,_GPSET);
_moveto(320,100);_lineto(229,92);
gr_array47=(char far *)_fmalloc((unsigned int)_imagesize(220,58,320,100));
_getimage(220,58,320,100,gr_array47);_putimage(202,46,face_array,_GPSET);
_moveto(320,100);_lineto(231,87);
gr_array48=(char far *)_fmalloc((unsigned int)_imagesize(220,58,320,100));
_getimage(220,58,320,100,gr_array48);_putimage(202,46,face_array,_GPSET);
_moveto(320,100);_lineto(235,83);
gr_array49=(char far *)_fmalloc((unsigned int)_imagesize(220,58,320,100));
_getimage(220,58,320,100,gr_array49);_putimage(202,46,face_array,_GPSET);
_moveto(320,100);_lineto(240,79);
gr_array50=(char far *)_fmalloc((unsigned int)_imagesize(220,58,320,100));
_getimage(220,58,320,100,gr_array50);_putimage(202,46,face_array,_GPSET);
_moveto(320,100);_lineto(245,75);
gr_array51=(char far *)_fmalloc((unsigned int)_imagesize(220,58,320,100));
_getimage(220,58,320,100,gr_array51);_putimage(202,46,face_array,_GPSET);
_moveto(320,100);_lineto(250,72);
gr_array52=(char far *)_fmalloc((unsigned int)_imagesize(220,58,320,100));
_getimage(220,58,320,100,gr_array52);_putimage(202,46,face_array,_GPSET);
_moveto(320,100);_lineto(258,69);
gr_array53=(char far *)_fmalloc((unsigned int)_imagesize(220,58,320,100));
_getimage(220,58,320,100,gr_array53);_putimage(202,46,face_array,_GPSET);
_moveto(320,100);_lineto(266,66);
gr_array54=(char far *)_fmalloc((unsigned int)_imagesize(220,58,320,100));
```

```
_getimage(220,58,320,100,gr_array54);_putimage(202,46,face_array,_GPSET);
_moveto(320,100);_lineto(273,63);
gr_array55=(char far *)_fmalloc((unsigned int)_imagesize(220,58,320,100));
_getimage(220,58,320,100,gr_array55);_putimage(202,46,face_array,_GPSET);
_moveto(320,100);_lineto(281,62);
gr_array56=(char far *)_fmalloc((unsigned int)_imagesize(220,58,320,100));
_getimage(220,58,320,100,gr_array56);_putimage(202,46,face_array,_GPSET);
_moveto(320,100);_lineto(290,60);
gr_array57=(char far *)_fmalloc((unsigned int)_imagesize(220,58,320,100));
_getimage(220,58,320,100,gr_array57);_putimage(202,46,face_array,_GPSET);
_moveto(320,100);_lineto(300,59);
gr_array58=(char far *)_fmalloc((unsigned int)_imagesize(220,58,320,100));
_getimage(220,58,320,100,gr_array58);_putimage(202,46,face_array,_GPSET);
_moveto(320,100);_lineto(310,58);
gr_array59=(char far *)_fmalloc((unsigned int)_imagesize(220,58,320,100));
_getimage(220,58,320,100,gr_array59);_putimage(202,46,face_array,_GPSET);

return;}

/*_____

                 SUBROUTINE: press any key to quit                */

void keyboard(void){
if (_bios_keybrd(_KEYBRD_READY)==0) return; else quit_pgm();}

/*_____

            SUBROUTINE: GRACEFUL EXIT FROM THE PROGRAM            */

void quit_pgm(void){
_clearscreen(_GCLEARSCREEN);_setvideomode(_DEFAULTMODE);exit(0);}

/*_____
            SUBROUTINE: VGA/EGA/CGA compatibility module          */

void graphics_setup(void){

CGA_mode:
if (_setvideomode(_HRESBW)==0) {goto abort_message;}
else {mode_flag=4;
     C0=0,C1=1,C2=1,C3=1,C4=1,C5=1,C6=1,C7=1,C8=1,C9=1,C10=1,
     C11=1,C12=1,C13=1,C14=1,C15=1;
     _settextposition(1,24);
     _outtext("USING C FOR HIGH SPEED ANIMATION");
     _settextposition(25,30);_outtext("Press any key to quit...");
     _settextposition(23,22);
     _outtext("640x200 2-color VGA, EGA and CGA mode");
     _settextposition(3,23);
     _outtext("Bitblt animation of a clock face...");
     return;}
```

```
abort_message:
printf("\n\nUnable to proceed.\n");
printf("Requires VGA, EGA, or CGA adapter\n");
printf("   with appropriate monitor.\n");
printf("Please refer to the book.\n\n");exit(0);}
```

```
/*_____


                    SUBROUTINE: Copyright Notice
    This subroutine displays the standard copyright notice.
    If you are typing in this program from the book you can
    safely omit this subroutine, provided that you also remove
    the instruction "notice()" from the main routine.          */
```

```
int copyright[][3]={0x7c00,0x0000,0x0000,0x8231,
0x819c,0x645e,0xba4a,0x4252,0x96d0,0xa231,0x8252,0x955e,0xba4a,
0x43d2,0xf442,0x8231,0x825c,0x945e,0x7c00,0x0000,0x0000};
```

```
void notice(float x, float y){
int a,b,c; int tl=0;
for (tl=0;tl<=6;tl++){a=copyright[tl][0];b=copyright[tl][1];
c=copyright[tl][2];_setlinestyle(a);_moveto(x,y);_lineto(x+15,y);
_setlinestyle(b);_moveto(x+16,y);_lineto(x+31,y);_setlinestyle(c);
_moveto(x+32,y);_lineto(x+47,y);y=y+1;};_setlinestyle(0xFFFF);
return;}
```

```
/*_____


                        End of source code                    */
```

VI

REAL-TIME ANIMATION

Dynamic Concepts

25

Practical Techniques for Real-time Animation

Real-time animation techniques provide the opportunity for the user to interact with the software while the animation cycle is in progress. Because the microprocessor is often creating the images and animating them simultaneously, keyboard input can be accepted and acted upon in order to change the direction of moving objects. Therein lies the real attraction to real-time animation: the user is a dynamic component of the animation.

True real-time animation is hidden-page animation, as shown in Fig. 25-1. The computer draws a frame on a hidden page. When the frame is finished, the hidden page becomes the display page. The previous display page—which is now the new hidden page—is blanked and the computer begins drawing the next frame on this hidden page. The display page flips back and forth between these two pages in a ping-pong manner in order to hide the drawing process from the viewer during the animation cycle.

VGA/EGA HIDDEN-PAGE ANIMATION

VGA and EGA graphics adapters contain enough display memory to permit multiple graphics pages. In the 640×200 16-color mode, for example, four pages are available on a VGA and an EGA (with 256 display memory—the standard configuration). The 320×200 16-color mode provides eight pages. Although the 640×350 16-color mode provides two pages, the slow drawing time of this mode tends to make it less than the ideal choice for real-time animation. Only one page is available in the 640×480 16-color mode.

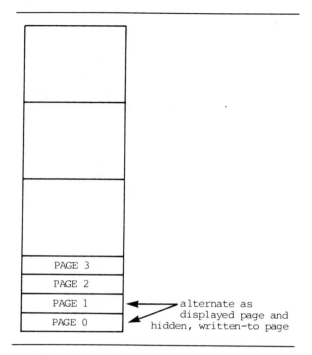

Fig. 25-1. Fundamental concepts of real-time animation using VGA and EGA graphics adapters.

CGA HIDDEN-PAGE ANIMATION

If you are using a CGA, only 16K of display memory is resident on the board. However, you can use C to write to a simulated hidden page in user RAM, as depicted in Fig. 25-2. When each image is finished, a short memory-move instruction can be used to transfer the image up to the CGA's screen buffer at B8000 hex. The CGA assembly language graphics routines in the appendices use this approach. Neither QuickC nor Turbo C can be easily configured to write graphics to a simulated hidden page in user RAM.

TWO FORMS OF REAL-TIME ANIMATION

There are actually two forms of real-time animation: hidden-page animation and arcade-style animation. When using hidden-page animation, the microcomputer draws fresh graphics on a hidden page during each frame of the animation cycle, as described earlier. When using arcade-style animation, the computer users bitblt animation of a previously-created graphic array, but permits the user to control the direction of movement by keyboard input. Examples of both styles of real-time animation are presented in demonstration programs in the next two chapters.

DYNAMIC KEYBOARD INPUT

Special keyboard routines are required by real-time animation programs. These routines must operate quickly, simply checking on-the-fly the keyboard buffer for keystrokes and then returning to the animation loop.

Figure 25-3 illustrates a typical dynamic keyboard routine. Note how program control is returned to the caller if no keystroke is waiting in the keyboard buffer. This keeps

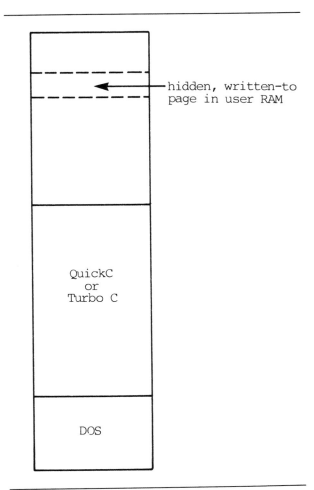

hidden, written-to
page in user RAM

Fig. 25-2. When using a CGA
graphics adapter, output is directed
to a simulated page in RAM. Each
completed image is moved to the
screen buffer at B8000 hex.

QuickC
or
Turbo C

DOS

```
void keyboard(void){
union u_type{int a;char b[3];}keystroke;char inkey=0;

if (_bios_keybrd(_KEYBRD_READY)==0) return; /* if no key, return */
keystroke.a=_bios_keybrd(_KEYBRD_READ);    /* fetch ASCII code... */
inkey=keystroke.b[0];                 /* ...and load code into variable */
switch (inkey){              /* make decision based upon ASCII value */
    case 27:   quit_pgm();                            /* Esc key */
    case 104:  sxmove=3;return;             /* h key move right */
    case 102:  sxmove=-3;return;            /* f key move left */
    case 116:  symove=-1;return;             /* t key move up */
    case 98:   symove=1;return;            /* b key move down */
    default:   return;}              /* make routine bullet-proof */
}
```

Fig. 25-3. Dynamic keyboard input routine suitable for controlling real-time animation programs.

animation speed high when no keystrokes are being entered by the user. C's **switch** instruction is used to rapidly test for specific ASCII keystroke codes. If a designated code is found, the appropriate variable is modified and the program branches back to the animation loop. Note the use of the default label in the switch ladder; this makes the subroutine bulletproof.

RUN-TIME PERFORMANCE

When using hidden-page animation, the speed of the run-time module is limited by the time it takes the computer to draw each new frame. Accordingly, simple images produces faster animation speeds. If your animation project requires detailed, complex images, you are likely to be better off using either frame animation or bitblt animation—both of these options can separate the drawing processes from the animation process.

When using arcade-style animation, the run-time performance is limited by the size of the graphic array, the number of colors used by the screen mode, the resolution of the screen mode, and the number of arrays being simultaneously animated. The fastest mode is the 640×200 2-color mode, as was demonstrated by the utility program in Chapter 21. The next speediest is the 320×200 4-color mode. The third best performer is the 320×200 16-color mode. The 640×200, 640×350, and 640×480 16-color modes are poor performers when bitblt animation is used for arcade-style animation programs.

CASE STUDY: A UTILITY PROGRAM

The utility program in Fig. A-6 of Appendix A demonstrates the fundamental techniques involved in real-time, hidden-page animation. The program listing in Fig. A-6 is for QuickC. If you are using the companion disk for this book you can load the program named FUNC-006.C.

The utility program supports VGA and EGA graphics adapters. If a VGA or EGA is present, the program uses the 640×200 16-color mode.

As you watch the program running, a small rectangle seems to move around inside a large rectangle, bouncing off each wall that it encounters.

Here is how the program works. First, the background graphics have been stored on PAGE 2. For each new frame the program first calls a subroutine which moves the image from PAGE 2 onto PAGE 1. By using this method, drawing time is kept to a minimum; it takes a lot less time to move an image from another page than it does to draw the image from scratch.

Next, the object being animated is drawn at the updated position on PAGE 1. Finally, the program calls another subroutine to move the completed image from PAGE 1 onto the display page (PAGE 0). This cycle continues until you press any key.

The page moves are accomplished by C's **movedata** instruction, introduced in previous chapters. The subroutines that manage the page flips are named **pageflip__1to0( )** and **pageflip__2to1( )**, which accurately describes their respective functions.

The animation loop is contained in the **main( )** routine. The **if/then** instructions which control the ricochet of the entity off the rectangle's walls are the same instructions used in the utility program in Chapter 21. After updating the position of the entity, the animation loop calls upon the **pageflip( )** subroutines to move the finished image to the display page and to install a fresh background on the hidden, written-to page. The **keyboard( )** routine is called on each page through the animation loop, of course.

Note how the **setvisualpage** and **setactivepage** instructions have been used to direct C to write to hidden PAGE 1 while displaying PAGE 0. These instructions are used again by the **quit_pgm** routine when the program is gracefully terminated.

Although the actual code used to control real-time, hidden-page animation seems simple, some extremely complex simulations can be managed by this fundamental animation technique. A real-time arcade-style animation prototype which runs at over 30 frames per second is presented as a demonstration program in the next chapter. A functional real-time flight simulation prototype which is capable of inverted flight and 360-degree rolls and loops is presented as a demonstration program in Chapter 27.

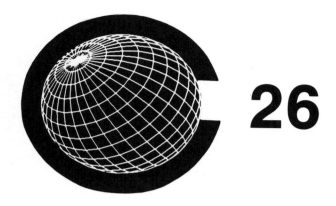

26

Arcade-style Software

The demonstration program in this chapter illustrates high-speed arcade-style animation using C. As the dot-matrix printout in Fig. 26-1 shows, a small ball is permitted to ricochet off a number of surfaces, including a peninsula placed at a random location on the playing field.

The graphic array which contains the image of the ball is depicted in Fig. 26-2. During the animation cycle, you can control the direction of the ball by using the F/T/H/B keys (see Fig. 26-6). Note that your keyboard input is complicated by the ball's ricochets and by the speed of the moving ball.

MANAGING THE RICOCHETS

The xy coordinates of the playing field are illustrated in Fig. 26-3. These locations—especially the tip of the peninsula—are required in order to write a routine which will detect when the ball collides with a boundary. Figure 26-4 shows some of the collision scenarios which must be managed by the ricochet routine. It is important to note that the edges of the graphic array must be monitored, not the edges of the ball, because the PSET logical operator might otherwise overwrite parts of the boundaries of the playing field.

By splitting the playing field into three zones as shown in Fig. 26-5, the complexity of the collision logic can be reduced considerably. Simple **if/then** instructions can be gathered into logical groups which control the action of the ball in these three zones of movement.

The photograph in Fig. 26-7 shows one frame from the video image generated by the animated demonstration program in Fig. 26-8. The program listing in Fig. 26-8 is

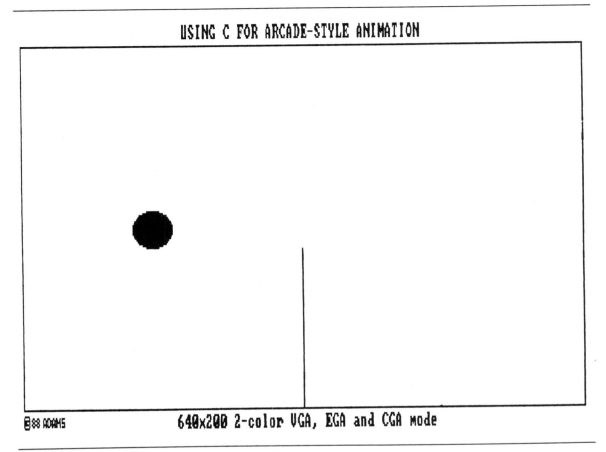

Fig. 26-1. Dot-matrix print-out of the video display produced by the animated demonstration program in Fig. 26-8.

Fig. 26-2. The ricocheting ball that is animated by the demonstration program in Fig. 26-8.

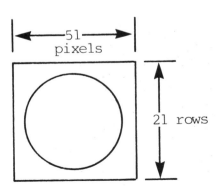

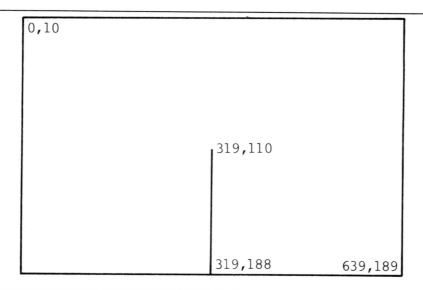

Fig. 26-3. The vertices of the playing field.

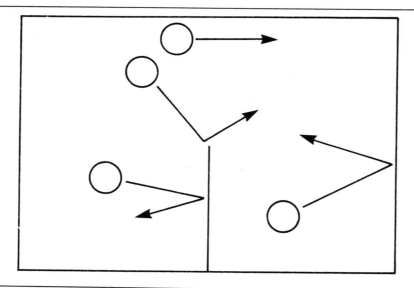

Fig. 26-4. Some of the possible ricochets that must be gracefully handled by the real-time animation loop.

the QuickC version. If you are using Turbo C, you should use instead the program listing presented in Fig. E-12 of Appendix E. If you are using the companion disk for this book, you can load program QC-016.C with QuickC; you can load program TC-016.C with Turbo C.

The program supports all IBM-compatible graphics adapters. If a VGA, EGA, CGA, or MCGA is present, the program runs in the 640×200 2-color mode at over 30 frames

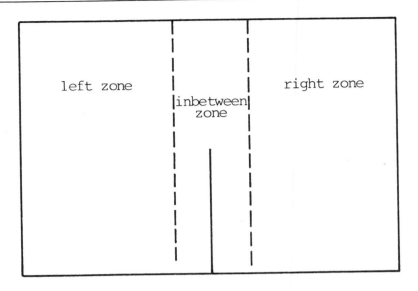

Fig. 26-5. The real-time animation loop manages the ricocheting ball by implementing three travel zones.

Fig. 26-6. Keyboard controls for the animated arcade-style demonstration program in Fig. 26-8.

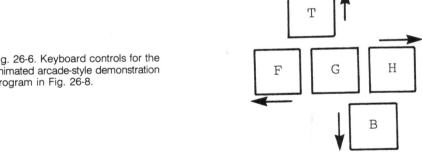

per second. By changing one line in the compatibility module you can configure the program to run in the 640×200 16-color mode on your VGA or EGA.

ANALYSIS OF THE PROGRAM

The most important module in this demonstration program is the animation manager in the **main( )** routine. Note how the beginning of the animation loop has been labelled **ANIMATE**. This provides a handy target for use by each of the three subsets of the animation manager, **LEFT_ARENA**, **RIGHT_ARENA**, and **IN_BETWEEN**. After completing their assigned tasks, each of these three subjects jumps back to the beginning of the animation loop.

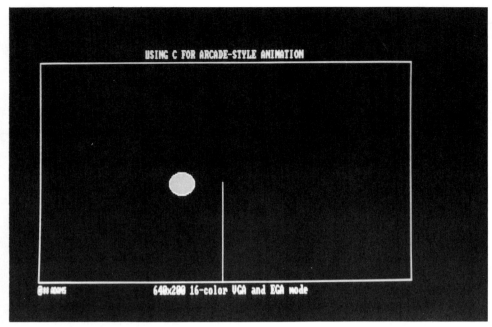

Fig. 26-7. The video display produced by the animated demonstration program in Fig. 26-8.

As illustrated in Fig. 26-5, three movement zones are used by the ricocheting ball. Each subset of the animation manager must monitor a different set of possible collisions. **LEFT_ARENA**, for example, must check for collisions between the moving ball and the left boundary, bottom boundary, and top boundary. A few wrinkles are added to its test for a collision with the peninsula. The instruction: **if (sy1 > =81)** checks to see if the ball is within vertical striking range of the peninsula. If not, the ball is permitted to continue its journey towards the right.

RIGHT_ARENA checks for situations which are a mirror image of those monitored by **LEFT_ARENA**. The routine checks for collisions between the moving ball and the right boundary, bottom boundary, and top boundary. The instruction: (sy1 > =81) tests to see if the ball is low enough to strike the peninsula. If not, the ball is allowed to continue to move towards the left.

IN_BETWEEN is responsible for testing for only two conditions: a collision with the top boundary and a downward collision with the tip of the peninsula. In fact, the tip scenario is the compelling reason for the existence of **IN_BETWEEN** in the first place. There is simply no efficient way for either of the two other routines to test for this unusual condition. As the program runs, you can see how often the ball does in fact strike the tip of the peninsula during its travels about the playing field.

A blip is generated through the sound speaker whenever the ball strikes a surface. The subroutine which controls this sound effect is named **sound( )**; it is located just before the compatibility module in the source code. In the Turbo C version of the demonstration program the subroutine is called **noise( )**, because Turbo C has a built-in function called **sound( )**. You can see how the animation loop calls the sound effect routine whenever a collision is detected.

By reviewing the three subsets of the animation manager, you can easily build an animation engine that manages a pinball-like environment. The most important principle to grasp is that of nested **if/then** instructions, which allow you to test for a wide variety of specialized conditions.

If you are compiling this program with Turbo C, you can safely ignore the warning message from the compiler concerning unreachable code. The three **goto** instructions in the animation loop cause Turbo C to believe that certain portions of the source code are unreachable. QuickC does not generate any warning messages when this code is compiled.

Fig. 26-8. Program listing for arcade-style animation—QuickC version. VGA/EGA/CGA/MCGA compatible. For Turbo C version, consult Appendix E.

```
/*_____


                          qc-016.c


   Function:  This program demonstrates arcade animation
   techniques.  The user can use the keyboard to control the
   high-speed movement of a ricocheting ball on the screen.

   Compatibility:  Supports all graphics adapters and monitors.
   The software uses the 640x200 2-color mode on the VGA, EGA,
   and CGA.  By changing a single line in the configuration
   subroutine you can run this program in the 16-color mode.

   Remarks:  Refer to the book for a description of keyboard
   controls.

   Copyright 1988 Lee Adams and TAB BOOKS Inc.

   _____


                 I N C L U D E     F I L E S            */

#include <stdio.h>           /* supports the printf function */
#include <graph.h>          /* supports the graphics functions */
#include <stdlib.h>          /* supports the exit() function */
#include <bios.h>          /* supports read of keyboard buffer */
#include <malloc.h>           /* supports memory allocation */
#include <conio.h>           /* supports port manipulation */

/*_____


                 D E C L A R A T I O N S            */

struct videoconfig vc;

void keyboard(void);void quit_pgm(void);
void notice(float x,float y);void graphics_setup(void);
void sound(int hertz,int duration);
```

```
int tl=l,t2=l,xl=220,yl=100,x2=270,y2=120,
    sx=220,sy=100,sxmove=3,symove=-1,sxl,syl;
int C0=0,Cl=l,C2=2,C3=3,C4=4,C5=5,C6=6,C7=7,C8=8,C9=9,C10=10,
    Cll=11,C12=12,C13=13,Cl4=14,C15=15,mode_flag=0;
int hz=450;


char far *gr_arrayl;                        /* pointer to graphic array */

/*_____

                      M A I N   R O U T I N E                  */

main(){
graphics_setup();                           /* establish graphics mode */
_getvideoconfig(&vc);                       /* initialize video table */


                          /* create and store the graphic array */
_setcolor(C7);_ellipse(_GBORDER,xl+3,yl+1,x2-3,y2-1);
_setcolor(C4);_floodfill(xl+25,yl+10,C7);
gr_arrayl=(char far*)_fmalloc((unsigned int)_imagesize(xl,yl,x2,y2));
_getimage(xl,yl,x2,y2,gr_arrayl);
_setcolor(C0);_rectangle(_GFILLINTERIOR,xl,yl,x2,y2);


                  /* create background and install graphic array */
_setcolor(C7);
_rectangle(_GBORDER,0,10,639,189);          /* animation boundaries */
_moveto(319,188);_lineto(319,110);          /* central barrier */
_setcolor(C7);notice(0,192);
_putimage(sx,sy,gr_arrayl,_GPSET);          /* install block graphic */


          /*_____bitblt animation manager_____*/

ANIMATE:                                    /* animation loop begins here */
if (sxl<=268) goto LEFT_ARENA;
if (sxl>=320) goto RIGHT_ARENA;
goto IN_BETWEEN;

LEFT_ARENA:
    if (sxl>=266){                                  /* right boundary */
        if (syl>=81){sound(hz,300);sxmove=-3;}}  /* hits barrier */
    if (sxl<=3) {sound(hz,300);sxmove=3;}        /* left boundary */
    if (syl>=168) {sound(hz,300);symove=-1;}  /* bottom boundary */
    if (syl<=11) {sound(hz,300);symove=1;}       /* top boundary */
    sxl=sx+sxmove;syl=sy+symove;          /* calculate new position */
    _putimage(sxl,syl,gr_arrayl,_GPSET);    /* install new array */
    sx=sxl;sy=syl;                          /* update sx,sy variables */
    keyboard();                         /* check for user keyboard input */
goto ANIMATE;                                       /* infinite loop */

RIGHT_ARENA:
    if (sxl>=586) {sound(hz,300);sxmove=-3;}    /* right boundary */
    if (sxl<=322){                                  /* left boundary */
        if (syl>=81){sound(hz,300);sxmove=3;}}   /* hits barrier */
```

```
      if (syl>=168) {sound(hz,300);symove=-1;}   /* bottom boundary */
      if (syl<=11) {sound(hz,300);symove=1;}        /* top boundary */
      sxl=sx+sxmove;syl=sy+symove;        /* calculate new position */
      _putimage(sxl,syl,gr_arrayl,_GPSET);    /* install new array */
      sx=sxl;sy=syl;                      /* update sx,sy variables */
      keyboard();                  /* check for user keyboard input */
      goto ANIMATE;                             /* infinite loop */
IN_BETWEEN:
      if (syl<=11) {sound(hz,300);symove=1;}        /* top boundary */
      if (syl>=89) {sound(hz,300);symove=-1;}   /* hits barrier tip */
      sxl=sx+sxmove;syl=sy+symove;        /* calculate new position */
      _putimage(sxl,syl,gr_arrayl,_GPSET);    /* install new array */
      sx=sxl;sy=syl;                      /* update sx,sy variables */
      keyboard();                  /* check for user keyboard input */
goto ANIMATE;                                  /* infinite loop */


quit_pgm();}                         /* make the code bullet-proof */

/*_____


                SUBROUTINE: dynamic keyboard input
      The subroutine is called by the main routine on each pass
      through the animation loop.  If the Esc key is pressed, the
      arcade game will terminate.  Press <h> to move right; press
      <f> to move left.  Press <t> to move up; press <b> to move
      down.                                                      */

void keyboard(void){
union u_type{int a;char b[3];}keystroke;char inkey=0;

if (_bios_keybrd(_KEYBRD_READY)==0) return; /* if no key, return */
keystroke.a=_bios_keybrd(_KEYBRD_READ);     /* fetch ASCII code... */
inkey=keystroke.b[0];              /* ...and load code into variable */
switch (inkey){            /* make decision based upon ASCII value */
   case 27:  quit_pgm();                                /* Esc key */
   case 104: sxmove=3;return;               /* h key move right */
   case 102: sxmove=-3;return;               /* f key move left */
   case 116: symove=-1;return;                 /* t key move up */
   case 98:  symove=1;return;                 /* b key move down */
   default:  return;}             /* make routine bullet-proof */
}
/*_____


                SUBROUTINE: GRACEFUL EXIT FROM THE PROGRAM        */

void quit_pgm(void){
_clearscreen(_GCLEARSCREEN);_setvideomode(_DEFAULTMODE);exit(0);}

/*_____
```

SUBROUTINE: GENERATE A SOUND

Enter with frequency, expressed as hertz in the range
40 to 4660. A comfortable frequency range for the human
ear is 40 to 2400. Enter with duration, expressed as an
integer to be used in a simple for...next delay loop.   */

```c
void sound(int hertz,int duration){
int tl=1,high_byte=0,low_byte=0;
short count=0;unsigned char old_port=0,new_port=0;

if (hertz<40) return;        /* avoid math overflow for int count */
if (hertz>4660) return;      /* avoid math underflow for low_byte */
count=1193180L/hertz;                   /* determine timer count */
high_byte=count/256;low_byte=count-(high_byte*256);
outp(0x43,0xB6);                     /* prep the timer register */
outp(0x42,low_byte);                      /* send the low byte */
outp(0x42,high_byte);                    /* send the high byte */
old_port=inp(0x61);              /* store the existing port value */
new_port=(old_port | 0x03);   /* use OR to set bits 0 and 1 to on */
outp(0x61,new_port);                    /* turn on the speaker */
for (tl=1;tl<=duration;tl++);                           /* wait */
outp(0x61,old_port);                   /* turn off the speaker */
return;}                               /* return to caller */
```

/*_____

SUBROUTINE: VGA/EGA/CGA compatibility module   */

```c
void graphics_setup(void){

goto CGA_mode;   /* if you have a VGA or EGA, you can delete this
                    line to force the software to use the 640x200
                    16-color mode (which animates slower than the
                    640x200 2-color mode).                         */
VGA_EGA_mode:
if (_setvideomode(_HRES16COLOR)==0) {goto CGA_mode;}
else {mode_flag=3;
     _settextposition(1,24);_settextcolor(C7);
     _outtext("USING C FOR ARCADE-STYLE ANIMATION");
     _settextposition(25,26);
     _outtext("640x200 16-color VGA and EGA mode");
     return;}

CGA_mode:
if (_setvideomode(_HRESBW)==0) {goto abort_message;}
else {mode_flag=4;
     C0=0,C1=1,C2=1,C3=1,C4=1,C5=1,C6=1,C7=1,C8=1,C9=1,C10=1,
     C11=1,C12=1,C13=1,C14=1,C15=1;
     _settextposition(1,24);
     _outtext("USING C FOR ARCADE-STYLE ANIMATION");
     _settextposition(25,23);
     _outtext("640x200 2-color VGA, EGA and CGA mode");
```

```
        return;}

abort_message:
printf("\n\nUnable to proceed.\n");
printf("Requires VGA, EGA, or CGA adapter\n");
printf("   with appropriate monitor.\n");
printf("Please refer to the book.\n\n");exit(0);}
```

```
/*_____


                   SUBROUTINE: Copyright Notice
    This subroutine displays the standard copyright notice.
    If you are typing in this program from the book you can
    safely omit this subroutine, provided that you also remove
    the instruction "notice()" from the main routine.          */

int copyright[][3]={0x7c00,0x0000,0x0000,0x8231,
0x819c,0x645e,0xba4a,0x4252,0x96d0,0xa231,0x8252,0x955e,0xba4a,
0x43d2,0xf442,0x8231,0x825c,0x945e,0x7c00,0x0000,0x0000};

void notice(float x, float y){
int a,b,c; int tl=0;
for (tl=0;tl<=6;tl++){a=copyright[tl][0];b=copyright[tl][1];
c=copyright[tl][2];_setlinestyle(a);_moveto(x,y);_lineto(x+15,y);
_setlinestyle(b);_moveto(x+16,y);_lineto(x+31,y);_setlinestyle(c);
_moveto(x+32,y);_lineto(x+47,y);y=y+1;};_setlinestyle(0xFFFF);
return;}
```

```
/*_____


                   End of source code                   */
```

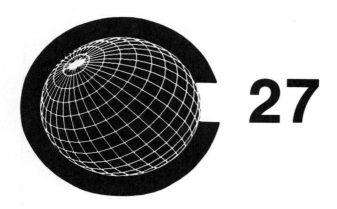

Flight Simulation

Even highly complex undertakings like microcomputer flight simulation can be readily produced using C, provided that the real-time animation techniques of Chapter 25 and the 3D modeling techniques of Chapter 14 have been understood.

This chapter presents a full-function flight simulation prototype capable of climbs, dives, banks, rolls, inverted flight, 360-degree rolls, and 360-degree loops. The aircraft flies over a 16-square grid which is completely clipped in both 3D and 2D.

The start-up position of the aircraft is depicted in Fig. 27-1. The movement of the aircraft is simulated by moving the terrain past the viewpoint—not by moving the viewpoint. The viewpoint, of course, is located at 0,0,0 in 3D space and never moves, as you learned in Chapter 14. By moving the terrain a specified distance past the viewpoint for each frame, an animation cycle is created.

The graphical user interface is illustrated in Fig. 27-2. The reticule (or crosshairs) is helpful for retaining your bearings while performing loops and rollovers. The horizon line provides an indication of your pitch attitude.

The keyboard controls for the flight simulation prototype are similar to those used in the previous chapter: F/T/H/B. If you press B, for example, the aircraft will continue to pull up at a greater rate until you press G to hold it steady at the current pitch attitude. As indicated in Fig. 27-3, you can loop completely over if you press B and then take no further action at the keyboard.

Figure 27-4 illustrates a 360-degree rollover. If you press either F or H and allow the flight simulation to continue unchecked, the heading of the aircraft will change as the rollover begins. Eventually, you will be flying upside-down and, finally, back to your original roll attitude.

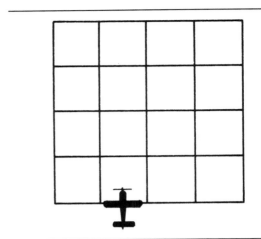

Fig. 27-1. The terrain grid over which the flight simulation prototype will fly and the aircraft's start-up position.

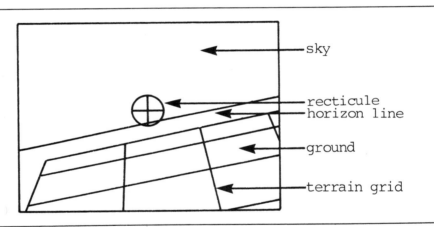

Fig. 27-2. Fundamental graphical elements of the flight simulation prototype in Fig. 27-7.

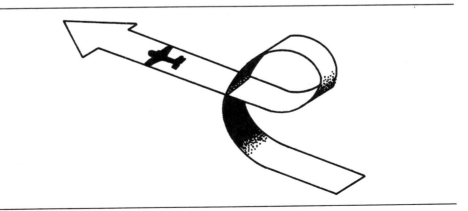

Fig. 27-3. The flight simulation prototype in Fig. 27-7 supports full acrobatic loops.

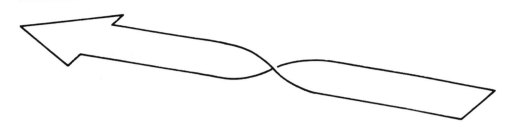

Fig. 27-4. The flight simulation prototype in Fig. 27-7 supports upside-down flight and full 360-degree rolls.

3D LINE CLIPPING

When using 3D computer images, it is important not to attempt to display xyz coordinates that are behind the viewpoint. These lines will be displayed backwards and upside-down by the 3D formulas. Figure 27-5 shows the two types of line clipping which must occur in a flight simulation environment: 2D line clipping and 3D line clipping. The 2D line clipping routine used in the demonstration program in this chapter has been discussed in previous chapters. The 3D line clipping routine simply tests the value of the z coordinate to see if it is greater than one (see Chapter 14). If so, the line is clipped in 3D using trigonometry in a manner similar to the 2D clipping routine (except that it is clipped in two planes).

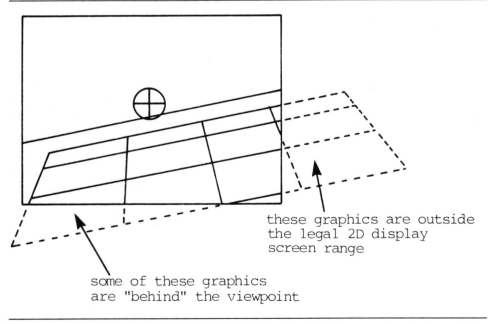

these graphics are outside
the legal 2D display
screen range

some of these graphics
are "behind" the viewpoint

Fig. 27-5. Graphics which lay behind the viewpoint must be clipped in 3D space, otherwise the projection formulas will display them backwards and upside-down. Graphics which are simply outside the range of the 2D screen can be clipped by a standard line-clipping agorithm.

THE DEMONSTRATION PROGRAM

The photograph in Fig. 27-6 shows a typical frame from the animated demonstration program in Fig. 27-7. The program listing in Fig. 27-7 is for QuickC. If you are using Turbo C you should use instead the program listing presented in Fig. E-13 of Appendix E. If you are using the companion disk for this book, you can load program QC-017.C using Quick C; you can load program TC-017.C using Turbo C.

The demonstration program supports VGA and EGA graphics adapters. If a VGA or EGA is present, the program uses the 640×200 16-color mode.

ANALYSIS OF THE PROGRAM

Although a thorough analysis of a flight simulation prototype could easily fill an entire book by itself, the commentary in this chapter will serve to get you started if you have aspirations of writing advanced flying simulations using your C compiler.

Note the variables which have been defined in the DECLARATIONS section of the source code. Each variable has been supported by a comment so that you can see who does what, so to speak. If you want the aircraft to fly at a faster/slower speed, simply adjust the start-up value of the variable name **m**. Making **m** equal to 1.1, for example, will increase the airspeed of your aircraft by 10%. If you want the aircraft to face in a different direction at start-up, modify variable **r1**.

Note the variables named **mx**, **my**, and **mz**. These define the xyz coordinates of the start-up position of the aircraft on the 16-square grid. As Fig. 27-1 illustrates, you could position yourself at the center of the terrain map by changing each of these variables to equal zero at start-up. The grid terrain is 160 units by 160 units. Each square on the grid is sized 40 units by 40 units.

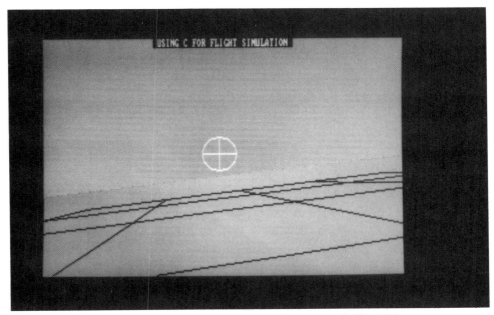

Fig. 27-6. The video display produced by the demonstration program in Fig. 27-7.

The Animation Loop

The foundation of this demonstration program is the animation loop located in the **main( )** routine. The animation manager calls all other subroutines as they are needed and then uses a simple **goto** instruction to maintain an infinite loop.

Notice the final line in the animation loop. The **p=1-p** algorithm is a handy way to flip pages during the hidden page animation process. There is no necessity for you to keep track of the two pages during the animation loop; the **p=1-p** algorithm does it for you, conveniently swapping the value of p from 0 to 1 and from 1 to 0.

Each of the tasks performed by **main( )** is documented by the comments. It is well worth your time to carefully peruse the source code and read the comments placed inside each of the subroutines too.

The Terrain

It is interesting to note that only the four corners of the terrain have been provided as xyz coordinates. Note the subroutine named **corner( )**, which calculates the view coordinates for these four corners.

Another subroutine, named **grid( )**, is responsible for extrapolating from these four corners the vertices required to draw the rest of the grid. The center line of the grid, for example, will lie halfway between the two outside corners in the x plane, no matter what angle is used to display the terrain. Trigonometry tells us that it will also lie halfway between the two outside corners in the y and z planes. You can see how simple division will produce all the xyz coordinates necessary to draw the enter 16-square grid. (In the subroutine, division is not actually used. Instead, multiplication by .5 is used instead of dividing by 2, for example, because this form of math runs much faster on personal computers.)

The Keyboard Routine

The keyboard routine, named **keyboard( )**, modifies the yaw, roll, and pitch angle-change factors based upon which key you have pressed. In addition, as you can see by inspecting this routine, the + key will add .1 to the **m** movement factor; the − key will subtract .1. These two keys allow you to increase or decrease the airspeed of the simulation while you are flying the prototype over the terrain grid.

Using Integers

In its present format, the flight simulation prototype uses floating-point numbers (as required by the sine and cosine functions). Unless you are using a math coprocessor chip, this regime will not produce acceptably fast rates of animation. In order to user faster-running integer math, you would require a look-up table for the sine and cosine values.

FURTHER STUDIES

Any serious attempt to write advanced flight simulation programs using C requires a thorough understanding of 3D algorithms. The next book in the TAB C graphics programming series provides an in-depth discussion of 3D formulas, hidden surface removal, solid modeling algorithms, and computer-controlled shading routines.

Fig. 27-7. Program listing for a real-time flight simulation prototype—QuickC version. VGA/EGA/CGA/MCGA compatible. If you are using a CGA, consult Appendix B and Appendix D. For Turbo C version, consult Appendix E.

```
/*_____

                              qc-017.c

      Function:  This program demonstrates real-time animation
      techniques applied to a flight simulation prototype.

      Compatibility:  Supports VGA and EGA graphics adapters and
      monitors.  The software uses the 640x200 16-color mode.

      Remarks:  Refer to the book for an explanation of the
      process control logic, the 3D formulas, and the line clipping
      routines which are used by this program.

      Copyright 1988 Lee Adams and TAB BOOKS Inc.

      _____


                    I N C L U D E    F I L E S            */

#include <stdio.h>              /* supports the printf function */
#include <graph.h>            /* supports the graphics functions */
#include <stdlib.h>              /* supports the exit( ) function */
#include <bios.h>          /* supports read of keyboard buffer */
#include <math.h>        /* supports the sine and cosine functions */

/*_____


                    D E C L A R A T I O N S               */

struct videoconfig vc;                 /* QuickC's video data table */

void graphics_setup(void);void keyboard(void);void quit_pgm(void);
void notice(float x,float y);void calc_3D(void);void window(void);
void clip_2D(void);void yaw_change(void);void translation(void);
void crash(void);void draw_horizon(void);void horiz3D(void);
void corner(void);void window(void);void grid(void);
void draw_grid(void);void clip_3D(void);void window_terrain(void);
void draw_line(void);

int t1=1,t2=1;                                    /* loop counters */
int p=0;                    /* toggle for active page and visual page */
int C0=0,C1=1,C2=2,C3=3,C4=4,C5=5,C6=6,C7=7,C8=8,C9=9,C10=10,
    C11=11,C12=12,C13=13,C14=14,C15=15,mode_flag=0;    /* colors */
int p1=1;          /* status flag for clipping lines in 3D space */
int p2=1;          /* status flag for clipping lines in 2D space */
int g=7;                                         /* color attribute */

float x=0,y=0,z=0;                         /* xyz world coordinates */
```

```
float x01=0,x2=0,x3=0,x4=0,x5=0,x6=0,x7=0,x8=0,x9=0,x10=0,x11=0,
     x12=0,x13=0,x14=0,x15=0,x16=0;            /* vertices of grid */
float y01=0,y2=0,y3=0,y4=0,y5=0,y6=0,y7=0,y8=0,y9=0,y10=0,y11=0,
     y12=0,y13=0,y14=0,y15=0,y16=0;            /* vertices of grid */
float z01=0,z2=0,z3=0,z4=0,z5=0,z6=0,z7=0,z8=0,z9=0,z10=0,z11=0,
     z12=0,z13=0,z14=0,z15=0,z16=0;            /* vertices of grid */
float L=0;            /* offset used to extrapolate grid vertices */
float sx=0,sy=0;            /* display coords, output of 3D formulas */
float xa=0,ya=0,za=0;  /* used in 3D formulas & 3D line clipping */
float xb=0,yb=0,zb=0;         /* used in 3D line clipping routine */
float xc=0,yc=0,zc=0;   /* temporary values in 3D line clipping */
float sxa=0,sya=0,sxb=0,syb=0;           /* 2D line endpoints */
float sxs=0,sys=0;      /* temp storage of 2D line startpoint */
float temp_swap=0;                /* used for variable swaps */

float d=620;                     /* angular perspective factor */
double r1=6.28319;          /* yaw angle, expressed in radians */
double r2=6.28319;         /* roll angle, expressed in radians */
double r3=6.28319;        /* pitch angle, expressed in radians */
float r1a=0,r2a=0,r3a=0;              /* angle change factors */
double sr1=0,sr2=0,sr3=0;           /* sine rotation factors */
double cr1=0,cr2=0,cr3=0;         /* cosine rotation factors */
float mx=24,my=-7.7,mz=-88;  /* viewpoint position (translation) */
float m=1;                       /* viewpoint change factor */
float ml=0;                      /* lateral movement factor */
float myl=0;                     /* up-down movement change */
float mxl=0;                   /* left-right movement change */
float mzl=0;                    /* forward movement change */
float maxx=639,minx=0,maxy=199,miny=0;   /* 2D clipping viewport */
float c=0;                  /* used in line-clipping routine */
int crash_flag=0;   /* toggle flag to control animation re-start */
float rx=0,ry=0;        /* scaling values used in window mapping */
float screen_x=639,screen_y=199;      /* used in window mapping */

/*_____


              M A I N    R O U T I N E                  */

main(){
graphics_setup();                  /* establish graphics mode */
_getvideoconfig(&vc);              /* initialize video table */

rx=screen_x/799;ry=screen_y/599;      /* define windowing ratio */

RESTART:                  /* re-start here after the crash routine */
_setactivepage(p);_setvisualpage(1-p);p=1-p;  /* set active page */

ANIMATE:                            /* animation loop begins here */
_clearscreen(_GCLEARSCREEN);          /* blank the hidden page */
keyboard();                           /* check the keyboard */

r2=r2+r2a;r3=r3+r3a;         /* new r2 roll & r3 pitch angles */
if (r2>6.28319) r2=r2-6.28319;    /* inhibit range of roll angle */
```

```
if (r2<=0) r2=r2+6.28319;          /* inhibit range of roll angle */
if (r3>6.28319) r3=r3-6.28319;   /* inhibit range of pitch angle */
if (r3<=0) r3=r3+6.28319;          /* inhibit range of pitch angle */
yaw_change(); /* calculate new yaw change, based upon roll angle */
rl=rl+rla;                                            /* new yaw angle */
if (rl>6.28319) rl=rl-6.28319;    /* inhibit range of yaw angle */
if (rl<=0) rl=rl+6.28319;          /* inhibit range of yaw angle */
srl=sin(rl);sr2=sin(r2);sr3=sin(r3);       /* new sine factors */
crl=cos(rl);cr2=cos(r2);cr3=cos(r3);       /* new cosine factors */
translation();                          /* calculate movement factors */
if (my>0) crash();           /* if crash, jump to crash routine */
if (crash_flag==1){
    crash_flag=0;goto RESTART;};    /* reset flag, loop to restart */
g=C2;draw_horizon();           /* set color and draw the horizon line */
corner();     /* calculate view coords for corners of terrain map */
grid();           /* calculate all other vertices for terrain map */
g=C0;draw grid();                  /* set color and draw the terrain */
_setcolor(C7);_ellipse(_GBORDER,289,85,349,113);       /* gunsight */
_moveto(319,86);_lineto(319,112);_moveto(290,99);_lineto(348,99);
_settextposition(1,26);_outtext(" USING C FOR FLIGHT SIMULATION ");
_setactivepage(p);_setvisualpage(1-p);p=1-p;       /* flip pages */
goto ANIMATE;}                                     /* infinite loop */

/*_____



                    SUBROUTINE: yaw change
    This subroutine calculates the new rla yaw change factor,
    based upon the r2 roll angle.                            */

void yaw_change(void){
if (r2>=0){                                /* normal roll right */
    if (r2<=1.57079){
        rla=(r2/.017453)*.00349;return;};
    };
if (r2<=6.28319){                          /* normal roll left */
    if (r2>=4.71239){
        rla=((6.28319-r2)/.017453)*(-.00349);return;};
    };
if (r2>1.57079){                           /* inverted roll right */
    if (r2<=3.14159){
        rla=((3.14159-r2)/.017453)*.00349;return;};
    };
if (r2>3.14159){                           /* inverted roll left */
    if (r2<4.71239){
        rla=((r2-3.14159)/.017453)*(-.00349);return;};
    };
return;}

/*_____



                    SUBROUTINE: movement routine
    This subroutine calculates the translation factors which
```

```
               control the movement of the viewpoint over the landmarks,
               dependent upon r1 yaw and r3 pitch.                        */

void translation(void){
ml=cr3*m;               /* lateral movement factor linked to pitch */
myl=(-1)*sr3*m;                 /* vertical movement linked to pitch */
if (r3>0){                 /* airspeed decreases as pitch increases */
   if (r3<=1.57079) myl=cr3*myl;
   };
if (r3>1.57079){                          /* inverted nose up mode */
   if (r3<3.14159) myl=(-1)*cr3*myl;
   };
mxl=(-1)*srl*ml;mzl=crl*ml;    /* lateral movement linked to yaw */
mx=mx+mxl;my=my+myl;mz=mz+mzl;              /* new movement factors */
return;}


/*_____



                    SUBROUTINE: crash scenario
     This subroutine handles a ground crash.  After a pause, the
     user is placed back into the simulation at start-up.          */

void crash(void){
_setactivepage(0);_clearscreen(_GCLEARSCREEN);_setvisualpage(0);
_settextcolor(C12);_settextposition(10,35);
_outtext("C R A S H !");_settextcolor(C7);             /* message */
for (tl=1;tl<=5;tl++){for (t2=1;t2<=30000;t2++);};         /* pause */
pl=1;g=C7;p=0;                       /* restore start-up values */
rl=6.28319;r2=6.28319;r3=6.28319;    /* restore start-up values */
rla=0;r2a=0;r3a=0;                   /* restore start-up values */
mx=24;my=-7.7;mz=-78;m=1;            /* restore start-up values */
crash_flag=1;         /* set flag for inspection by main routine */
return;}


/*_____



                    SUBROUTINE: draw the horizon line            */

void draw_horizon(void){
if (r3>1.57079){                        /* test if inverted flight */
   if (r3<4.71239) goto INVERTED;
   };
x=-8000;y=0;z=-10000;       /* left world coordinates of horizon */
horiz3D();              /* calculate unclipped display coordinates */
window();           /* map display coordinates to fit 640x200 screen */
sxa=sx;sya=sy;                               /* left end of line */
x=8000;y=0;z=-10000;       /* right world coordinates of horizon */
horiz3D();              /* calculate unclipped display coordinates */
window();           /* map display coordinates to fit 640x200 screen */
sxb=sx;syb=sy;                              /* right end of line */
clip_2D();                    /* clip line to fit display screen */
```

```
_setcolor(g);_moveto(sxa,sya);_lineto(sxb,syb);        /* draw line */
_floodfill(319,199,g);                          /* area fill for ground */
_setcolor(Cl);_floodfill(319,0,g);              /* area fill for sky */
return;

INVERTED:                                      /* same as above but (-1)*z */
x=-8000;y=0;z=10000;horiz3D();window();sxa=sx;sya=sy;
x=8000;y=0;z=10000;horiz3D();window();sxb=sx;syb=sy;clip_2D();
_setcolor(g);_moveto(sxa,sya)_lineto(sxb,syb);        /* draw line */
return;}

/*_____


            SUBROUTINE: 3D formulas for horizon                 */

void horiz3D(void){
x=(-1)*x;za=cr3*z-sr3*y;ya=sr3*z+cr3*y;xa=cr2*x+sr2*ya;
y=cr2*ya-sr2*x;sx=d*xa/za;sy=d*y/za;return;}

/*_____


            SUBROUTINE: 2D LINE-CLIPPING
    Enter with sxa,sya and sxb,syb endpoints of 2D line to be
    clipped.  Returns display coordinates for line clipped to
    fit physical screen viewport defined by minx,miny and
    maxx,maxy.  Sets toggle flag p2 to zero if entire line is
    off the screen.                                            */

void clip_2D(void){
if (sxa>sxb) {temp_swap=sxa;sxa=sxb;sxb=temp_swap;
             temp_swap=sya;sya=syb;syb=temp_swap;};
if (sxa<minx) {if (sxb<minx) {p2=0;return;}}
if (sxa>maxx) {if (sxb>maxx) {p2=0;return;}}
if (sya<miny) {if (syb<miny) {p2=0;return;}}
if (sya>maxy) {if (syb>maxy) {p2=0;return;}}
if (sxa<minx) {{c=(syb-sya)/(sxb-sxa)*(sxb-minx);   /* push right */
              sxa=minx;sya=syb-c;};
              if (sya<miny) if (syb<miny) return;
              if (sya>maxy) if (syb>maxy) return;
              };
if (sxb>maxx) {{c=(syb-sya)/(sxb-sxa)*(maxx-sxa);   /* push left */
              sxb=maxx;syb=sya+c;};
              if (sya<miny) if (syb<miny) return;
              if (sya>maxy) if (syb>maxy) return;
              };
if (sya>syb) {temp_swap=sya;sya=syb;syb=temp_swap;
             temp_swap=sxa;sxa=sxb;sxb=temp_swap;};
if (sya<miny) {c=(sxb-sxa)/(syb-sya)*(syb-miny);    /* push down */
              .sxa=sxb-c;sya=miny;};
if (syb>maxy) {c=(sxb-sxa)/(syb-sya)*(maxy-sya);    /* push up */
              sxb=sxa+c;syb=maxy;};
return;}
```

```
/*_____


              SUBROUTINE: window mapping function for horizon         */

void window(void){
sx=sx+399;sy=sy+299;rx=screen_x/799;ry=screen_y/599;sx=sx*rx;
sy=sy*ry;return;}

/*_____


              SUBROUTINE: view coords for corners of terrain
       This subroutine calculates the rotated and translated view
       coordinates for the four corners of the terrain.  The rest
       of the terrain's vertices can be extrapolated from these
       four vertices.                                                */

void corner(void){
x=-80;y=0;z=-80;calc_3D();x01=x;y01=y;z01=z;
x=80;y=0;z=-80;calc_3D();x2=x;y2=y;z2=z;
x=80;y=0;z=80;calc_3D();x3=x;y3=y;z3=z;
x=-80;y=0;z=80;calc_3D();x4=x;y4=y;z4=z;
return;}

/*_____


              SUBROUTINE: generic 3D translation & rotation formulas
       This subroutine first translates the terrain landmarks in
       order to simulate the movement of the aircraft, then the
       translated coordinates are rotated to simulate the effects
       of yaw, pitch, and roll in 3D airspace.                      */

void calc_3D(void){
x=x-mx;y=y+my;z=z+mz;                          /* translation */
xa=cr1*x-sr1*z;za=sr1*x+cr1*z;                        /* yaw */
z=cr3*za-sr3*y;ya=sr3*za+cr3*y;                     /* pitch */
x=cr2*xa+sr2*ya;y=cr2*ya-sr2*xa;                     /* roll */
return;}

/*_____


              SUBROUTINE: extrapolation of vertices for grid
       This subroutine uses simple geometry to extrapolate 16
       vertices of a grid in 3D space from four known corner
       locations.                                                   */

void grid(void){
L=.25*(x2-x01);x5=x01+L;x6=x5+L;x7=x6+L;
L=.25*(y2-y01);y5=y01+L;y6=y5+L;y7=y6+L;
L=.25*(z2-z01);z5=z01+L;z6=z5+L;z7=z6+L;
L=.25*(x3-x4);x8=x4+L;x9=x8+L;x10=x9+L;
```

```
L=.25*(y3-y4);y8=y4+L;y9=y8+L;y10=y9+L;
L=.25*(z3-z4);z8=z4+L;z9=z8+L;z10=z9+L;
L=.25*(x4-x01);x11=x01+L;x12=x11+L;x13=x12+L;
L=.25*(y4-y01);y11=y01+L;y12=y11+L;y13=y12+L;
L=.25*(z4-z01);z11=z01+L;z12=z11+L;z13=z12+L;
L=.25*(x3-x2);x14=x2+L;x15=x14+L;x16=x15+L;
L=.25*(y3-y2);y14=y2+L;y15=y14+L;y16=y15+L;
L=.25*(z3-z2);z14=z2+L;z15=z14+L;z16=z15+L;
return;}
```

```
/*_____



               SUBROUTINE: draw the grid terrain
     This subroutine draws a sixteen-square grid.  If pl equals
     zero then the line is completely clipped and invisible.      */

void draw_grid(void){
_setcolor(g);
xa=x01;ya=y01;za=z01;xb=x2;yb=y2;zb=z2;pl=1;clip_3D();
if (pl==1) draw_line();
xa=x11;ya=y11;za=z11;xb=x14;yb=y14;zb=z14;pl=1;clip_3D();
if (pl==1) draw_line();
xa=x12;ya=y12;za=z12;xb=x15;yb=y15;zb=z15;pl=1;clip_3D();
if (pl==1) draw_line();
xa=x13;ya=y13;za=z13;xb=x16;yb=y16;zb=z16;pl=1;clip_3D();
if (pl==1) draw_line();
xa=x4;ya=y4;za=z4;xb=x3;yb=y3;zb=z3;pl=1;clip_3D();
if (pl==1) draw_line();
xa=x01;ya=y01;za=z01;xb=x4;yb=y4;zb=z4;pl=1;clip_3D();
if (pl==1) draw_line();
xa=x5;ya=y5;za=z5;xb=x8;yb=y8;zb=z8;pl=1;clip_3D();
if (pl==1) draw_line();
xa=x6;ya=y6;za=z6;xb=x9;yb=y9;zb=z9;pl=1;clip_3D();
if (pl==1) draw_line();
xa=x7;ya=y7;za=z7;xb=x10;yb=y10;zb=z10;pl=1;clip_3D();
if (pl==1) draw_line();
xa=x2;ya=y2;za=z2;xb=x3;yb=y3;zb=z3;pl=1;clip_3D();
if (pl==1) draw_line();
return;}
```

```
/*_____



                SUBROUTINE: draw clipped line on screen          */

void draw_line(void){
p2=1;clip_2D();    /* p2 will be set to zero if line is invisible */
if (p2==1){_moveto(sxa,sya);_lineto(sxb,syb);}
return;}
```

```
/*_____
```

SUBROUTINE: window mapping function for terrain
This subroutine maps a world space window of 800x600 to fit
the 640x200 screen, thereby ensuring the integrity of the
4:3 screen ratio and avoid distortion during 3D rotations.   */

```c
void window_terrain(void){
sxa=sxa+399;sya=sya+299;sxa=sxa*rx;sya=sya*ry;
sxb=sxb+399;syb=syb+299;sxb=sxb*rx;syb=syb*ry;
return;}
```

/*_____

SUBROUTINE: clip lines in 3D space
This subroutine clips portions of lines which fall behind
the viewpoint in 3D space and which would be invisible to
the observer. Enter with xa,ya,za,xb,yb,zb view coordinates
for endpoints of line to be clipped in 3D space.   */

```c
void clip_3D(void){
if (za>=-1) goto LABEL1630;        /* xa,ya,za requires clipping */
goto LABEL1640;                         /* xa,ya,za is ok */

LABEL1630:
if (zb>=-1) {pl=0;return;};           /* both endpoints hidden */
temp_swap=xb;xb=xa;xa=temp_swap;
temp_swap=yb;yb=ya:ya=temp_swap;
temp_swap=zb;zb=za;za=temp_swap;
goto LABEL1660;                /* only xb,yb,zb requires clipping */

LABEL1640:                /* xa,ya,za is ok, now test xb,yb,zb */
if (zb>=-1) goto LABEL1660;    /* only xb,yb,zb requires clipping */

LABEL1650:          /* calculate display coords and map to screen */
sxa=d*xa/za;sya=d*ya/za;sxb=d*xb/zb;syb=d*yb/zb;
window_terrain();return;

LABEL1660:                                    /* clip xb,yb,zb */
c=(xb-xa)/(zb-za)*(zb+1);xc=xb-c;
c=(yb-ya)/(zb-za)*(zb+1);yc=yb-c;zc=-1;
xb=xc;yb=yc;zb=zc;goto LABEL1650;
return;}
```

/*_____

SUBROUTINE: dynamic keyboard input
The subroutine is called on each pass through the animation
loop. If the Esc key is pressed, the flight simulation will
terminate. Press <h> to roll right, <f> to roll left.
Press <t> to push the aircraft's nose down, press <b> to
raise the nose. The aircraft will continue to roll, climb,
or dive unless the <g> key is pressed to hold its current

```
            attitude.  Press <+> to increase throttle, press <-> to
            decrease throttle.                                             */

void keyboard(void){
union u_type{int a;char b[3];}keystroke;char inkey=0;

if (_bios_keybrd(_KEYBRD_READY)==0) return; /* if no key, return */
keystroke.a=_bios_keybrd(_KEYBRD_READ);    /* fetch ASCII code... */
inkey=keystroke.b[0];              /* ...and load code into variable */
switch (inkey){              /* make decision based upon ASCII value */
    case 27:  quit_pgm();                          /* Esc key */
    case 104: r2a=r2a+.017453;return;       /* h key roll right */
    case 102: r2a=r2a-.017453;return;        /* f key roll left */
    case 116: r3a=r3a-.008726;return;            /* t key dive */
    case 98:  r3a=r3a+.008726;return;           /* b key climb */
    case 103: r2a=0;r3a=0;return;                /* g key hold */
    case 61:  m=m+.1;return;            /* + key increase throttle */
    case 45:  m=m-.1;return;            /* - key decrease throttle */
    default:  return;}              /* make routine bullet-proof */
}

/*_____


            SUBROUTINE: GRACEFUL EXIT FROM THE PROGRAM               */

void quit_pgm(void){
_setvisualpage(0);_setactivepage(0);
_clearscreen(_GCLEARSCREEN);_setvideomode(_DEFAULTMODE);exit(0);}

/*_____
            SUBROUTINE: VGA/EGA compatibility module                */

void graphics_setup(void){
VGA_EGA_mode:
if (_setvideomode(_HRES16COLOR)==0) {goto abort_message;}
else {maxx=639;minx=0;maxy=199;miny=0;      /* clipping viewport */
      screen_x=639;screen_y=199;           /* windowing viewport */
      _setcolor(C7);_settextcolor(C7);return;}

abort_message:
printf("\n\nUnable to proceed.\n");
printf("Requires VGA or EGA adapter\n");
printf("   with appropriate monitor.\n");
printf("Please refer to the book.\n\n");exit(0);}

/*_____

            SUBROUTINE: Copyright Notice
    This subroutine displays the standard copyright notice.
    If you are typing in this program from the book you can
    safely omit this subroutine, provided that you also remove
    the instruction "notice()" from the main routine.              */
```

```
int copyright[ ][3]={0x7c00,0x0000,0x0000,0x8231,
0x819c,0x645e,0xba4a,0x4252,0x96d0,0xa231,0x8252,0x955e,0xba4a,
0x43d2,0xf442,0x8231,0x825c,0x945e,0x7c00,0x0000,0x0000};

void notice(float x, float y){
int a,b,c; int tl=0;
for (tl=0;tl<=6;tl++){a=copyright[tl][0];b=copyright[tl][1];
c=copyright[tl][2];_setlinestyle(a);_moveto(x,y);_lineto(x+15,y);
_setlinestyle(b);_moveto(x+16,y);_lineto(x+31,y);_setlinestyle(c);
_moveto(x+32,y);_lineto(x+47,y);y=y+1;};_setlinestyle(0xFFFF);
return;}

/*_____

                        End of source code                    */
```

APPENDICES

Summary of C
Routines for Graphics

This appendix contains seven brief program listings. Each program demonstrates a single algorithm important to C graphics programming. In particular, the program listings teach how to save a screen image to disk, how to retrieve a screen image from disk, how to generate sound effects, how to produce frame animation at 14 frames per second and faster, how to produce bitblt animation at 43 frames pe second and faster.

The program listings in Appendix A are for QuickC version 1.00 and newer. If you are using Turbo C version 1.5 and newer, refer to Appendix E. If you are using Turbo C version 1.0, refer to Appendix B. If you are using another C compiler, refer to Appendix B.

SAVING VGA AND EGA SCREEN IMAGES

The program listing in Fig. A-1 illustrates how to save a VGA or EGA screen image to disk. The algorithm employs direct manipulation of the VGA/EGA registers in order to permit access to each bit plane. The screen image is saved on disk as four separate binary image files with the filename extension BLU, GRN, RED, and INT. This methodology works with multiplane-per-pixel screen modes only. The program in Fig. A-1 will run in either the 640×480 16-color mode, the 640×350 16-color mode, or the 640×200 16-color mode, depending upon the graphics adapter and monitor present. Refer to Chapter 13 for a detailed analysis of how the algorithm works.

SAVING CGA SCREEN IMAGES

Multibit-per-pixel screen modes, which use a single bit plane, require a different screen-saving algorithm. The program listing in Fig. A-4 demonstrates how to save a CGA screen image to disk. The program can be used to save either the 640×200 2-color mode or the 320×200 4-color mode of the CGA, MCGA, EGA, and VGA. The screen image is saved on disk as a single binary image file with the filename extension BIN. Refer to Chapter 13 for further explanation of how the algorithm operates.

GRAPHICS MODE CONFIGURATION MODULE

The demonstration program in Fig. A-2 contains a configuration module which will permit your original C programs to detect and to run on any IBM-compatible graphics adapter. Provided that you have embedded a windowing routine (see Chapter 12) in your source code, your program will be capable of modifying itself at run-time to execute in either the 640×480 16-color mode, or the 640×350 16-color mode, or the 640×200 16-color mode, or the 620×200 2-color mode, or the 320×200 4-color mode. Such a capability increases the portability of your original C graphics programs.

SOUND EFFECTS

A variety of different sound effects can be generated by the program listing in Fig. A-3. The **outp** instruction is used to directly manipulate the speaker hardware. Refer to Chapter 13 for a detailed explanation of the algorithm.

FRAME ANIMATION

The program listing in Fig. A-5 demonstrates the fundamental algorithm used during high-speed frame animation. This algorithm is the driving force behind the animated hovering hummingbird in Chapter 19, the rotating 3D model in Chapter 20, and the animated business chart in Chapter 18. The program will execute in the 640×200 16-color mode if a VGA or EGA is present. It uses the 640×200 2-color mode if a CGA or MCGA is present. On a VGA or EGA, where multiple pages are available in display memory, the program animates at 14 frames per second, although higher animation rates approaching 36 frames per second are readily achieved (refer to the demonstration program in Chapter 19). On a CGA, where only a single page is available in display memory, the **movedata** instruction is used to swap the graphics data in and out of user RAM. Serious program developers will want to employ an assembly language subroutine to accomplish these moves (see the library of assembly language graphics routines in Appendix D). Refer to Chapter 17 for a detailed discussion of frame animation programming techniques.

REAL-TIME ANIMATION

An example of real-time animation is provided by the program listing in Fig. A-6. The fundamental hidden-page algorithm used by this program is the foundation of the flight simulation program in Chapter 27. Refer to Chapter 25 for a detailed discussion of real-time animation programming techniques.

BITBLT ANIMATION

The program listing in Fig. A-7 illustrates the fundamental methodology of bitblt animation. The ball, which richochets off the four walls of its enclosure, is animated at 43 frames per second and faster, although the animation rate is mitigated by the hardware's refresh rate of the screen. The routines employed by the program form the foundation for the arcade-style demonstration program in Chapter 26, the talking caricature in Chapter 22, the walking figure in Chapter 23, and the simulated analog clock face in Chapter 23. Refer to Chapter 21 for a detailed discussion of bitblt animation programming techniques.

Fig. A-1. Program listing which demonstrates how to save a VGA or EGA screen image to disk as a binary image file—QuickC version. VGA/EGA compatible.

```
/*_____


                              func-001.c


      Function:  This program demonstrates how to save a VGA or EGA
      screen image to a disk file.  The program also retrieves a
      previously-saved image from a disk file and displays it on
      the screen.

      Compatibility:  Supports VGA and EGA modes.
      The software uses the 640x480 16-color mode if a VGA is
      present, the 640x350-16 color mode if an EGA and enhanced
      monitor are present, and the 640x200 16-color mode if an EGA
      and standard monitor are present.

      Remarks:  The four individual bit planes are saved on disk as
      separate binary files with the BLU, GRN, RED, and INT
      extensions. In particular, each bit plane is first moved to a
      temporary buffer in the default data segment.  From there, it
      is written to disk.  Refer to the book for further guidance.

      Copyright 1988 Lee Adams and TAB BOOKS Inc.


      _____


                    I N C L U D E    F I L E S              */

#include <dos.h>                        /* supports the BIOS call
                                           and seg register reads */
#include <stdio.h>               /* supports the printf function
                                        and file read/write */
#include <graph.h>          /* supports the graphics functions */
#include <conio.h>            /* supports port manipulation */
#include <memory.h>            /* supports memory moves */

/*_____


                    D E C L A R A T I O N S                 */

struct videoconfig vc;
struct SREGS segregs;

void keyboard(void);void quit_pgm(void);
```

```
void notice(float x,float y);
void coords(void);void graphics_setup(void);
void savescrn(void);void loadscrn(void);

float sx,sy,sxl,syl,sx2,sy2;
float x_res,y_res;
int C0=0,Cl=1,C2=2,C3=3,C4=4,C5=5,C6=6,C7=7,C8=8,C9=9,C10=10,
    Cll=11,C12=12,C13=13,C14=14,C15=15,mode_flag=0;

unsigned int segment;            /* value of data segment register */
unsigned int offset;             /* destination offset for movedata */

FILE *image_file;                          /* data stream */
unsigned int plane_length;          /* length of one bit plane */
char image_buffer[38400];     /* enough for VGA plane if reqd */
/*_____ _____
                 M A I N    R O U T I N E                  */

main(){
graphics_setup();                 /* establish graphics mode */
_getvideoconfig(&vc);             /* initialize video table */

_setcolor(C4);
sx=130;sy=200;coords();sxl=sx;syl=sy;
sx=210;sy=300;coords();sx2=sx;sy2=sy;
_rectangle(_GFILLINTERIOR,sxl,syl,sx2,sy2);
_setcolor(C2);
sx=230;sy=200;coords();sxl=sx;syl=sy;
sx=310;sy=300;coords();sx2=sx;sy2=sy;
_rectangle(_GFILLINTERIOR,sxl,syl,sx2,sy2);
_setcolor(Cl);
sx=330;sy=200;coords();sxl=sx;syl=sy;
sx=410;sy=300;coords();sx2=sx;sy2=sy;
_rectangle(_GFILLINTERIOR,sxl,syl,sx2,sy2);
_setcolor(C7);
sx=430;sy=200;coords();sxl=sx;syl=sy;
sx=510;sy=300;coords();sx2=sx;sy2=sy;
_rectangle(_GFILLINTERIOR,sxl,syl,sx2,sy2);
_setcolor(C7);notice(0,0);

savescrn();                  /* save the screen image to disk */
_clearscreen(_GCLEARSCREEN);           /* clear the screen */
loadscrn();            /* retrieve the image files from disk */

keyboard();                   /* wait for user to press <Esc> */
quit_pgm();                      /* end the program gracefully */
}
/*_____
```

SUBROUTINE: SAVE SCREEN IMAGE TO DISK

This subroutine saves the current screen image to disk as a
set of binary image files. Each bit plane is saved as an

```
                    individual file, with a BLU, GRN, RED, or INT extension.        */

void savescrn(void){
segread(&segregs);segment=segregs.ds; /* determine segment value */
offset=(unsigned int)image_buffer;       /* determine offset value */

image_file=fopen("B:IMAGE1.BLU","wb");              /* open the file */
outp(0x3ce,4);outp(0x3cf,0);        /* set EGA,VGA to read plane 0 */
movedata(0xa000,0x0000,segment,offset,plane_length);
fwrite((char *)image_buffer,1,plane_length,image_file);
fclose(image_file);                            /* close the file */

image_file=fopen("B:IMAGE1.GRN","wb");              /* open the file */
outp(0x3ce,4);outp(0x3cf,1);        /* set EGA,VGA to read plane 1 */
movedata(0xa000,0x0000,segment,offset,plane_length);
fwrite((char *)image_buffer,1,plane_length,image_file);
fclose(image_file);                            /* close the file */

image_file=fopen("B:IMAGE1.RED","wb");              /* open the file */
outp(0x3ce,4);outp(0x3cf,2);        /* set EGA,VGA to read plane 2 */
movedata(0xa000,0x0000,segment,offset,plane_length);
fwrite((char *)image_buffer,1,plane_length,image_file);
fclose(image_file);                            /* close the file */

image_file=fopen("B:IMAGE1.INT","wb");              /* open the file */
outp(0x3ce,4);outp(0x3cf,3);        /* set EGA,VGA to read plane 3 */
movedata(0xa000,0x0000,segment,offset,plane_length);
fwrite((char *)image_buffer,1,plane_length,image_file);
fclose(image_file);                            /* close the file */

outp(0x3ce,4);outp(0x3cf,0);            /* restore EGA,VGA registers */
return;}
/*_____


                    SUBROUTINE: LOAD SCREEN IMAGE FROM DISK

    This subroutine loads previously-saved binary image files
    from disk.  Each binary image file is loaded from disk into
    a temporary buffer in the default data segment, from where
    it is moved to the VGA or EGA display memory.                      */

void loadscrn(void){
segread(&segregs);segment=segregs.ds; /* determine segment value */
offset=(unsigned int)image_buffer;       /* determine offset value */

image_file=fopen("B:IMAGE1.BLU","rb");              /* open the file */
outp(0x3c4,2);outp(0x3c5,1);        /* set EGA,VGA to write plane 0 */
fread((char *)image_buffer,1,plane_length,image_file);
movedata(segment,offset,0xa000,0x0000,plane_length);
fclose(image_file);                            /* close the file */

image_file=fopen("B:IMAGE1.GRN","rb");              /* open the file */
outp(0x3c4,2);outp(0x3c5,2);        /* set EGA,VGA to write plane 1 */
fread((char *)image_buffer,1,plane_length,image_file);
```

```
movedata(segment,offset,0xa000,0x0000,plane_length);
fclose(image_file);                         /* close the file */

image_file=fopen("B:IMAGE1.RED","rb");        /* open the file */
outp(0x3c4,2);outp(0x3c5,4);     /* set EGA,VGA to write plane 2 */
fread((char *)image_buffer,1,plane_length,image_file);
movedata(segment,offset,0xa000,0x0000,plane_length);
fclose(image_file);                         /* close the file */

image_file=fopen("B:IMAGE1.INT","rb");        /* open the file */
outp(0x3c4,2);outp(0x3c5,8);     /* set EGA,VGA to write plane 3 */
fread((char *)image_buffer,1,plane_length,image_file);
movedata(segment,offset,0xa000,0x0000,plane_length);
fclose(image_file);                         /* close the file */

outp(0x3c4,2);outp(0x3c5,0xF);    /* restore EGA,VGA registers */
return;}
/*_____
```

```
            SUBROUTINE: CHECK THE KEYBOARD BUFFER           */

void keyboard(void){
union u_type {int a;char b[3];} keystroke;
int get_keystroke(void);        /* declare a local subroutine */

do keystroke.a=get_keystroke();
while (keystroke.b[0]!=27);      /* return if <Esc> is pressed */
}

/*          LOCAL SUBROUTINE: RETRIEVE ONE KEYSTROKE          */

int get_keystroke(void){
union REGS regs;regs.h.ah=0;return int86(0x16,&regs,&regs);}

/*_____
```

```
            SUBROUTINE: GRACEFUL EXIT FROM THE PROGRAM        */

void quit_pgm(void){
_clearscreen(_GCLEARSCREEN);_setvideomode(_DEFAULTMODE);}

/*_____
```

```
            SUBROUTINE: VGA/EGA compatibility module
```

This subroutine invokes the highest-resolution graphics mode
which is permitted by the hardware. The 640x480 16-color mode
is established if a VGA is present. The 640x350 16-color mode
is established if an EGA is being used with an enhanced color
display monitor or a multiscanning monitor. The 640x200
16-color mode is established if an EGA is being used with a
standard color monitor.   */

```
void graphics_setup(void){

VGA_mode:
if (_setvideomode(_VRES16COLOR)==0) {goto EGA_ECD_mode;}
else {x_res=640;y_res=480;mode_flag=1;
      plane_length=38400;
      _settextcolor(7);_settextposition(30,27);
      _outtext("640x480 16-color VGA mode");
      _settextposition(1,27);
      _outtext("USING C TO SAVE SCREEN IMAGES");
      return;}

EGA_ECD_mode:
if (_setvideomode(_ERESCOLOR)==0) {goto EGA_SCD_mode;}
else {x_res=640;y_res=350;mode_flag=2;
      plane_length=28000;
      _settextcolor(7);_settextposition(25,27);
      _outtext("640x350 16-color EGA mode");
      _settextposition(1,27);
      _outtext("USING C TO SAVE SCREEN IMAGES");
      return;}

EGA_SCD_mode:
if (_setvideomode(_HRES16COLOR)==0) {goto abort_message;}
else {x_res=640;y_res=200;mode_flag=3;
      plane_length=16000;
      _settextcolor(7);_settextposition(25,27);
      _outtext("640x200 16-color EGA mode");
      _settextposition(1,27);
      _outtext("USING C TO SAVE SCREEN IMAGES");
      return;}

abort_message:
printf("\n\nUnable to proceed.\n");
printf("Requires VGA or EGA adapter\n");
printf("  with appropriate monitor.\n");
printf("Please refer to the book.\n\n");
exit(0);
}
/*_____

              SUBROUTINE: coords()

   This subroutine accepts sx,sy device-independent display
   coordinates and returns sx,sy device-dependent screen
   coordinates scaled to fit the 640x480, 640x350, 640x200, or
   320x200 screen, depending upon the graphics mode being used. */

void coords(void){
sx=sx*(x_res/640);sy=sy*(y_res/480);return;}

/*_____

           SUBROUTINE: Copyright Notice

   This subroutine displays the standard copyright notice.
```

```
      If you are typing in this program from the book you can
      safely omit this subroutine, provided that you also remove
      the instruction "notice()" from the main routine.          */

int copyright[][3]={0x7c00,0x0000,0x0000,0x8231,
0x819c,0x645e,0xba4a,0x4252,0x96d0,0xa231,0x8252,0x955e,0xba4a,
0x43d2,0xf442,0x8231,0x825c,0x945e,0x7c00,0x0000,0x0000};

void notice(float x, float y){
int a,b,c; int tl=0;
for (tl=0;tl<=6;tl++){a=copyright[tl][0];b=copyright[tl][1];
c=copyright[tl][2];_setlinestyle(a);_moveto(x,y);_lineto(x+15,y);
_setlinestyle(b);_moveto(x+16,y);_lineto(x+31,y);_setlinestyle(c);
_moveto(x+32,y);_lineto(x+47,y);y=y+1;};_setlinestyle(0xFFFF);
return;}

/*_____



                        End of source code                    */
```

Fig. A-2. Program listing which demonstrates an automatic configuration module. Using this module, and using the window mapping routine, you can write programs that will run in device-dependent modes on all IBM-compatible graphics adapters—QuickC version. VGA/EGA/CGA/MCGA compatible. For Turbo C version, consult Appendix E.

```
/*_____

                              func-002.c

      Function:  This program demonstrates automatic configuration
      of the software to match the graphics hardware.

      Compatibility:  Supports all graphics adapters and monitors.
      The software uses the 640x480 16-color mode if a VGA is
      present, the 640x350 16-color mode if an EGA and enhanced
      monitor are present, the 640x200 16-color mode if an EGA and
      standard monitor are present, and the 320x200 4-color mode
      if a CGA is present.

      Remarks:  This program is intended as a framework upon which
      software can be developed.  Refer to the book for further
      guidance.

      Copyright 1988 Lee Adams and TAB BOOKS Inc.

      _____



                   I N C L U D E   F I L E S               */

#include <dos.h>                      /* supports the BIOS call */
#include <stdio.h>                    /* supports the printf function */
```

```
#include <graph.h>                    /* supports the graphics functions */

/*_____

                        D E C L A R A T I O N S             */

struct videoconfig vc;                          /* video data table */

                    /* declare global variables */
int C0=0,C1=1,C2=2,C3=3,C4=4,C5=5,          /* color code variables */
    C6=6,C7=7,C8=8,C9=9,C10=10,C11=11,
    C12=12,C13=13,C14=14,C15=15,mode_flag=0;
float x_res,y_res;       /* screen resolution for mapping routine */
float sx,sy;             /* device-independent screen coordinates */

                /* declare global subroutines */
void keyboard(void);void quit_pgm(void);void get_coords(void);
void graphics_setup(void);

/*_____

                    M A I N   R O U T I N E                 */

main(){
graphics_setup();                    /* establish graphics mode */
_getvideoconfig(&vc);                /* initialize video table */

keyboard();                      /* wait for user to press <Esc> */
quit_pgm();}                      /* end the program gracefully */

/*_____

            SUBROUTINE: CHECK THE KEYBOARD BUFFER           */

void keyboard(void){
union u_type {int a;char b[3];} keystroke;
int get_keystroke(void);              /* declare a local subroutine */
do keystroke.a=get_keystroke();
while (keystroke.b[0]!=27);           /* return if <Esc> is pressed */
}

/*          LOCAL SUBROUTINE: RETRIEVE ONE KEYSTROKE         */

int get_keystroke(void){
union REGS regs;regs.h.ah=0;return int86(0x16,&regs,&regs);}

/*_____

            SUBROUTINE: GRACEFUL EXIT FROM THE PROGRAM      */

void quit_pgm(void){
```

```
_clearscreen(_GCLEARSCREEN);_setvideomode(_DEFAULTMODE);}
```

```
/*_____


               SUBROUTINE: VGA/EGA/CGA compatibility module

    This subroutine invokes the highest-resolution graphics mode
    which is permitted by the hardware.  The 640x480 16-color mode
    is established if a VGA is present.  The 640x350 16-color mode
    is established if an EGA is being used with an enhanced color
    display monitor or a multiscanning monitor.  The 640x200
    16-color mode is established if an EGA is being used with a
    standard color monitor.  The 320x200 4-color mode is invoked
    if a CGA is present.                                        */

void graphics_setup(void){

VGA_mode:
if (_setvideomode(_VRES16COLOR)==0) {goto EGA_ECD_mode;}
else {x_res=640;y_res=480;mode_flag=1;
     _settextcolor(7);_settextposition(30,30);
     _outtext("640x480 16-color VGA mode");
     return;}

EGA_ECD_mode:
if (_setvideomode(_ERESCOLOR)==0) {goto EGA_SCD_mode;}
else {x_res=640;y_res=350;mode_flag=2;
     _settextcolor(7);_settextposition(25,30);
     _outtext("640x350 16-color EGA mode");
     return;}

EGA_SCD_mode:
if (_setvideomode(_HRES16COLOR)==0) {goto CGA_mode;}
else {x_res=640;y_res=200;mode_flag=3;
     _settextcolor(7);_settextposition(25,30);
     _outtext("640x200 16-color EGA mode");
     return;}

CGA_mode:
if (_setvideomode(_MRES4COLOR)==0) {goto abort_message;}
else {x_res=320;y_res=200;C0=0;C1=3;C2=3;C3=3;C4=3;C5=3;C6=2;C7=3;
     C8=2;C9=1;C10=3;C11=1;C12=3;C13=1;C14=3;C15=3;mode_flag=4;
     _settextcolor(3);_settextposition(25,10);
     _outtext("320x200 4-color CGA mode");
     return;}

abort_message:
printf("\n\nUnable to proceed.\n");
printf("Requires VGA, EGA, or CGA adapter\n");
printf("   with appropriate monitor.\n");
printf("Please refer to the book.\n\n");
exit(0);
}
```

```
/*_____


                    SUBROUTINE: coords()


    This subroutine accepts sx,sy device-independent display
    coordinates and returns sx,sy device-dependent screen
    coordinates scaled to fit the 640x480, 640x350, 640x200, or
    320x200 screen, depending upon the graphics mode being used. */

void coords(void){
sx=sx*(x_res/640);sy=sy*(y_res/480);return;}


    /*_____



                    End of source code                      */
```

Fig. A-3. Program listing which demonstrates how to save a CGA screen image to disk as a binary image file—QuickC version. VGA/EGA/CGA/MCGA compatible. For Turbo C version, consult Appendix E.

```
/*_____

                        func-003.c

    Function:  This program demonstrates how to generate sounds.

    Compatibility:  The software uses the default text mode.

    Remarks:  This program is intended as a framework upon which
    software can be developed.  In its current form, the program
    turns on the speaker, emits a tone, and turns off the speaker
    on each occasion a sound is desired.  Rising or falling tones
    are generated as a stairstepping action.  In order to
    produce a smooth slide (such as a siren, for example), simply
    modify this program so that the speaker is left on while
    you manipulate the sound frequency (hertz).  The current
    timing loops have been tested on an IBM PC.  You may wish ·to
    slow down the loops if you are using a faster computer, such
    as an XT, AT, or PS/2.

    Copyright 1988 Lee Adams and TAB BOOKS Inc.

    _____


                INCLUDE    FILES                            */

#include <conio.h>              /* supports port manipulation */
#include <stdlib.h>                 /* supports exit() routine */

    /*_____
```

```
                    D E C L A R A T I O N S                    */

int hz=100;
void sound(int hertz,int duration);

/*_____


                    M A I N   R O U T I N E                    */

main(){

for (hz=50;hz<=1600;hz+=50)                    /* a rising tone */
    sound(hz,5000);

for (hz=1;hz<=20000;hz++);                           /* pause */

for (hz=2000;hz>=250;hz-=50)                   /* a falling tone */
    sound(hz,5000);

for (hz=1;hz<=6000;hz++);                            /* pause */

sound(40,30000);                              /* a single tone */

exit(0);}                                   /* end the program */

/*_____
```

SUBROUTINE: GENERATE A SOUND

```
    Enter with frequency, expressed as hertz in the range
    40 to 4660.  A comfortable frequency range for the human
    ear is 40 to 2400.  Enter with duration, expressed as an
    integer to be used in a simple for...next delay loop.      */

void sound(int hertz,int duration){
int t1=1,high_byte=0,low_byte=0;
short count=0;unsigned char old_port=0,new_port=0;

if (hertz<40) return;        /* avoid math overflow for int count */
if (hertz>4660) return;      /* avoid math underflow for low_byte */

count=1193180L/hertz;                     /* determine timer count */
high_byte=count/256;low_byte=count-(high_byte*256);

outp(0x43,0xB6);                       /* prep the timer register */
outp(0x42,low_byte);                        /* send the low byte */
outp(0x42,high_byte);                       /* send the high byte */

old_port=inp(0x61);              /* store the existing port value */
new_port=(old_port | 0x03);  /* use OR to set bits 0 and 1 to on */
```

```
outp(0x61,new_port);                        /* turn on the speaker */
for (tl=1;tl<=duration;tl++);                          /* wait */
outp(0x61,old_port);                       /* turn off the speaker */

return;}                                       /* return to caller */

/*_____


                        End of source code                     */
```

Fig. A-4. Program listing which demonstrates how to save a CGA screen image to disk as a binary image file—QuickC version. VGA/EGA/CGA/MCGA compatible.

```
/*_____

                              func-004.c

    Function:  This program demonstrates how to save a CGA
    screen image to a disk file.  The program also retrieves a
    previously-saved image from a disk file and displays it on
    the screen.

    Compatibility:  Supports all graphics adapters.
    The software uses the 320x200 4-color mode if a VGA, EGA,
    CGA is present.

    Remarks:  The screen buffer at address B8000 hex is first
    moved to a temporary buffer in the default data segment.
    From there, it is written to disk.  Although this program uses
    the 320x200 4-color mode, the algorithm works also for the
    640x200 2-color mode because the buffer for both modes is
    16384 bytes in length.  Refer to the book.

    Copyright 1988 Lee Adams and TAB BOOKS Inc.

    _____


                  I N C L U D E    F I L E S               */

#include <dos.h>                         /* supports the BIOS call
                                           and seg register reads */
#include <stdio.h>                    /* supports the printf function
                                             and file read/write */
#include <graph.h>              /* supports the graphics functions */
#include <memory.h>                      /* supports memory moves */

/*_____
```

```
                    D E C L A R A T I O N S                    */

struct videoconfig vc;
struct SREGS segregs;

void keyboard(void);void quit_pgm(void);
void notice(float x,float y);
void coords(void);void graphics_setup(void);
void savescrn(void);void loadscrn(void);

float sx,sy,sxl,syl,sx2,sy2,x_res,y_res;
int C0=0,Cl=1,C2=2,C3=3;                   /* software color codes */
unsigned int segment;              /* value of data segment register */
unsigned int offset;            /* destination offset for movedata */
FILE *image_file;                                   /* data stream */
char image_buffer[16384];             /* size of CGA screen buffer */

 /*_____




                    M A I N   R O U T I N E                    */

main(){
graphics_setup();                      /* establish graphics mode */
_getvideoconfig(&vc);                    /* initialize video table */

_setcolor(C3);sx=130;sy=200;coords();sxl=sx;syl=sy;
sx=210;sy=300;coords();sx2=sx;sy2=sy;
_rectangle(_GBORDER,sxl,syl,sx2,sy2);
_setcolor(Cl);sx=230;sy=200;coords();sxl=sx;syl=sy;
sx=310;sy=300;coords();sx2=sx;sy2=sy;
_rectangle(_GFILLINTERIOR,sxl,syl,sx2,sy2);
_setcolor(C2);sx=330;sy=200;coords();sxl=sx;syl=sy;
sx=410;sy=300;coords();sx2=sx;sy2=sy;
_rectangle(_GFILLINTERIOR,sxl,syl,sx2,sy2);
_setcolor(C3);sx=430;sy=200;coords();sxl=sx;syl=sy;
sx=510;sy=300;coords();sx2=sx;sy2=sy;
_rectangle(_GFILLINTERIOR,sxl,syl,sx2,sy2);;notice(0,193);

savescrn();                         /* save the screen image to disk */
_clearscreen(_GCLEARSCREEN);                    /* clear the screen */
loadscrn();                    /* retrieve the image files from disk */

keyboard();                         /* wait for user to press <Esc> */
quit_pgm();                        /* end the program gracefully */
}
 /*_____
```

```
                SUBROUTINE: SAVE SCREEN IMAGE TO DISK

    This subroutine saves the current CGA screen image to disk
    as a binary image file.                                      */

void savescrn(void){
segread(&segregs);segment=segregs.ds; /* determine segment value */
offset=(unsigned int)image_buffer;     /* determine offset value */

image_file=fopen("B:IMAGE1.BIN","wb");              /* open the file */
movedata(0xb800,0x0000,segment,offset,16384);
fwrite((char *)image_buffer,1,16384,image_file);
fclose(image_file);                                /* close the file */
return;}

/*_____


                SUBROUTINE: LOAD SCREEN IMAGE FROM DISK

    This subroutine loads a previously-saved binary image file
    from disk.                                                   */

void loadscrn(void){
segread(&segregs);segment=segregs.ds; /* determine segment value */
offset=(unsigned int)image_buffer;     /* determine offset value */

image_file=fopen("B:IMAGE1.BIN","rb");              /* open the file */
fread((char *)image_buffer,1,16384,image_file);
movedata(segment,offset,0xB800,0x0000,16384);
fclose(image_file);                                /* close the file */
return;}

/*_____


                SUBROUTINE: CHECK THE KEYBOARD BUFFER           */

void keyboard(void){
union u_type {int a;char b[3];} keystroke;
int get_keystroke(void);            /* declare a local subroutine */

do keystroke.a=get_keystroke();
while (keystroke.b[0]!=27);         /* return if <Esc> is pressed */
}

/*           LOCAL SUBROUTINE: RETRIEVE ONE KEYSTROKE           */

int get_keystroke(void){
union REGS regs;regs.h.ah=0;return int86(0x16,&regs,&regs);}

/*_____
```

```
                    SUBROUTINE: GRACEFUL EXIT FROM THE PROGRAM              */
void quit_pgm(void){
_clearscreen(_GCLEARSCREEN);_setvideomode(_DEFAULTMODE);}

/*_____


                    SUBROUTINE: VGA/EGA/CGA compatibility module

    This subroutine invokes the CGA 320x200 4-color mode if a
    VGA, EGA, or CGA is present.                                            */
void graphics_setup(void){

CGA_mode:
if (_setvideomode(_MRES4COLOR)==0) {goto abort_message;}
else {x_res=320;y_res=200;
      _settextcolor(C3);_settextposition(20,9);
      _outtext("320x200 4-color CGA mode");
      _settextposition(4,7);
      _outtext("USING C TO SAVE SCREEN IMAGES");
      return;}

abort_message:
printf("\n\nUnable to proceed.\n");
printf("Requires VGA, EGA, or CGA adapter\n");
printf("   with appropriate monitor.\n");
printf("Please refer to the book.\n\n");
exit(0);
}
/*_____


                    SUBROUTINE: coords()

    This subroutine accepts sx,sy device-independent display
    coordinates and returns sx,sy device-dependent screen
    coordinates scaled to fit the 640x480, 640x350, 640x200, or
    320x200 screen, depending upon the graphics mode being used. */

void coords(void){
sx=sx*(x_res/640);sy=sy*(y_res/480);return;}

/*_____


                    SUBROUTINE: Copyright Notice

    This subroutine displays the standard copyright notice.
    If you are typing in this program from the book you can
```

```
                safely omit this subroutine, provided that you also remove
                the instruction "notice()" from the main routine.            */

int copyright[][3]={0x7c00,0x0000,0x0000,0x8231,
0x819c,0x645e,0xba4a,0x4252,0x96d0,0xa231,0x8252,0x955e,0xba4a,
0x43d2,0xf442,0x8231,0x825c,0x945e,0x7c00,0x0000,0x0000};

void notice(float x, float y){
int a,b,c; int tl=0;
for (tl=0;tl<=6;tl++){a=copyright[tl][0];b=copyright[tl][1];
c=copyright[tl][2];_setlinestyle(a);_moveto(x,y);_lineto(x+15,y);
_setlinestyle(b);_moveto(x+16,y);_lineto(x+31,y);_setlinestyle(c);
_moveto(x+32,y);_lineto(x+47,y);y=y+1;};_setlinestyle(0xFFFF);
return;}

/*_____


                              End of source code                        */
```

Fig. A-5. Program listing which demonstrates frame animation at 14 fps—QuickC version. VGA/EGA/CGA/MCGA compatible. For Turbo C version, consult Appendix E.

```
/*_____

                                  func-005.c

        Function:  This program demonstrates the fundamental
        algorithms involved in high speed frame animation.

        Compatibility:  Supports all graphics adapters and monitors.
        The software uses the 640x200 16-color mode if a VGA or an
        EGA is present.  The 640x200 2-color mode is used if a
        CGA is present.

        Remarks:  The 640x200 16-color mode is used with the VGA and
        EGA because four graphics pages are required by this animated
        program.  If a CGA is present, the extra pages required by
        the program are stored in user RAM.

        Copyright 1988 Lee Adams and TAB BOOKS Inc.

        _____


                        I N C L U D E    F I L E S                       */

#include <stdio.h>              /* supports the printf function */
#include <graph.h>             /* supports the graphics functions */
```

```
#include <stdlib.h>              /* supports the exit() function */
#include <memory.h>                /* supports memory moves */
#include <bios.h>            /* supports read of keyboard buffer */

/*_____


                    D E C L A R A T I O N S              */

struct videoconfig vc;

void keyboard(void);void quit_pgm(void);
void notice(float x,float y);void coords(void);
void graphics_setup(void);void labels(void);void blocks(void);

void animVGAEGA(void);                        /* EGA and VGA only */
void animCGA(void);                                  /* CGA only */
void pagemove(unsigned source,unsigned target);      /* CGA only */

int frame=0,t1=1,t2=2;
float sx,sy;float x_res,y_res;
int C0=0,C1=1,C2=2,C3=3,C4=4,C5=5,C6=6,C7=7,C8=8,C9=9,C10=10,
    C11=11,C12=12,C13=13,C14=14,C15=15,mode_flag=0;
char fill_50[]={85,170,85,170,85,170,85,170};

/*_____


                    M A I N    R O U T I N E            */

main(){
graphics_setup();                    /* establish graphics mode */
_getvideoconfig(&vc);                 /* initialize video table */
_setcolor(C7);_settextcolor(C7);
if (mode_flag==3) {_setfillmask(NULL);};      /* if VGA or EGA */
if (mode_flag==4) {_setfillmask(fill_50);};        /* if CGA */

if (mode_flag==3) {_setvisualpage(0);_setactivepage(0);};
_clearscreen(_GCLEARSCREEN);
frame=0;                                  /* set the frame flag */
labels();                      /* create the alphanumeric labels */
blocks();                               /* draw the graphics */
if (mode_flag==4) {pagemove(0xB800,0x8800);}       /* if CGA */

if (mode_flag==3) {_setvisualpage(1);_setactivepage(1);};
_clearscreen(_GCLEARSCREEN);
frame=1;                                  /* set the frame flag */
labels();                      /* create the alphanumeric labels */
blocks();                               /* draw the graphics */
if (mode_flag==4) {pagemove(0xB800,0x8C00);}       /* if CGA */

if (mode_flag==3) {_setvisualpage(2);_setactivepage(2);};
```

```
_clearscreen(_GCLEARSCREEN);
frame=2;                                        /* set the frame flag */
labels();                          /* create the alphanumeric labels */
blocks();                                      /* draw the graphics */
if (mode_flag==4) {pagemove(0xB800,0x9000);}         /* if CGA */

if (mode_flag==3) {_setvisualpage(3);_setactivepage(3);};
_clearscreen(_GCLEARSCREEN);
frame=3;                                        /* set the frame flag */
labels();                          /* create the alphanumeric labels */
blocks();                                      /* draw the graphics */
if (mode_flag==4) {pagemove(0xB800,0x9400);};        /* if CGA */

if (mode_flag==3) {_setvisualpage(0);_setactivepage(0);};
if (mode_flag==4) {pagemove(0x8800,0xB800);};

for (t1=1;t1<=30000;t1++);               /* pause before animating */
if (mode_flag==3) animVGAEGA();       /* animation for VGA and EGA */
if (mode_flag==4) animCGA();                /* animation for CGA */

quit_pgm();}                         /* end the program gracefully */

/*_____

          SUBROUTINE: frame animation manager for VGA and EGA      */

void animVGAEGA(void){
for (t1=1;t1!=2; ){                      /* animate for endless loop */
   _setvisualpage(1);for (t2=1;t2<=3000;t2++);
   _setvisualpage(2);for (t2=1;t2<=3000;t2++);
   _setvisualpage(3);for (t2=1;t2<=30000;t2++);keyboard();
   _setvisualpage(2);for (t2=1;t2<=3000;t2++);
   _setvisualpage(1);for (t2=1;t2<=3000;t2++);
   _setvisualpage(0);for (t2=1;t2<=10000;t2++);keyboard();};
return;}

/*_____

          SUBROUTINE: frame animation manager for CGA           */

void animCGA(void){
for (t1=1;t1!=2; ){                      /* animate for endless loop */
   pagemove(0x8C00,0xB800);for (t2=1;t2<=3000;t2++);
   pagemove(0x9000,0xB800);for (t2=1;t2<=3000;t2++);
   pagemove(0x9400,0xB800);for (t2=1;t2<=30000;t2++);keyboard();
   pagemove(0x9000,0xB800);for (t2=1;t2<=3000;t2++);
   pagemove(0x8C00,0xB800);for (t2=1;t2<=3000;t2++);
   pagemove(0x8800,0xB800);for (t2=1;t2<=10000;t2++);keyboard();};
   return;}

/*_____
```

```
                    SUBROUTINE: pagemove for CGA
This subroutine is called during the graphics drawing process
in order to store the frames in user RAM.  This subroutine is
also called during the frame animation process in order to
flip the previously-stored pages onto the CGA display buffer
at B8000 hex.  For serious development work, you would want
to use a short assembly language subroutine instead.          */

void pagemove(unsigned source, unsigned target){
movedata(source,0x0000,target,0x0000,16000);return;}


/*_____ ___ _____



                  SUBROUTINE: alphanumeric labels              */

void labels(void){
_settextcolor(C7);_settextposition(25,23);
if (mode_flag==3) {_outtext("640x200 16-color VGA and EGA mode");}
if (mode_flag==4) {_outtext("640x200 2-color CGA mode");}
_settextposition(1,21);
_outtext("USING C FOR HIGH SPEED FRAME ANIMATION");
_settextposition(4,16);
_outtext("High speed rotation of a simple geometric shape...");
_settextposition(22,29);_outtext("Press any key to quit.");
_settextposition(12,1);_outtext("Animation rate:");
_settextposition(13,1);
if (mode_flag==3) _outtext("14 frames per second");
if (mode_flag==4) _outtext("7 frames per second");
return;}


/*_____



                  SUBROUTINE: draw the graphics               */

void blocks(void){
if (frame==0) {sx=209;sy=139;coords();_moveto(sx,sy);
               sx=389;sy=139;coords();_lineto(sx,sy);
               sx=389;sy=339;coords();_lineto(sx,sy);
               sx=209;sy=339;coords();_lineto(sx,sy);
               sx=209;sy=139;coords();_lineto(sx,sy);};
if (frame==1) {sx=218;sy=141;coords();_moveto(sx,sy);
               sx=387;sy=151;coords();_lineto(sx,sy);
               sx=379;sy=337;coords();_lineto(sx,sy);
               sx=211;sy=327;coords();_lineto(sx,sy);
               sx=218;sy=141;coords();_lineto(sx,sy);};
if (frame==2) {sx=226;sy=149;coords();_moveto(sx,sy);
               sx=382;sy=161;coords();_lineto(sx,sy);
               sx=371;sy=331;coords();_lineto(sx,sy);
               sx=214;sy=318;coords();_lineto(sx,sy);
               sx=226;sy=149;coords();_lineto(sx,sy);};
```

```
if (frame==3) {sx=236;sy=150;coords();_moveto(sx,sy);
               sx=378;sy=170;coords();_lineto(sx,sy);
               sx=359;sy=327;coords();_lineto(sx,sy);
               sx=218;sy=308;coords();_lineto(sx,sy);
               sx=236;sy=150;coords();_lineto(sx,sy);};
_setcolor(C4);sx=299;sy=239;coords();_floodfill(sx,sy,C7);
_setcolor(C7);sx=5;sy=460;coords();notice(sx,sy);       /* notice */
return;}

/*_____

            SUBROUTINE: press any key to quit                 */

void keyboard(void){
if (_bios_keybrd(_KEYBRD_READY)==0) return; else quit_pgm();}

/*_____
            SUBROUTINE: GRACEFUL EXIT FROM THE PROGRAM        */

void quit_pgm(void){
if (mode_flag==3) {_setvisualpage(0);_setactivepage(0);};
_clearscreen(_GCLEARSCREEN);_setvideomode(_DEFAULTMODE);exit(0);}

/*_____


            SUBROUTINE: VGA/EGA/CGA compatibility module      */

void graphics_setup(void){
VGA_EGA_mode:
if (_setvideomode(_HRES16COLOR)==0) {goto CGA_mode;}
else {x_res=640;y_res=200;mode_flag=3;
      return;}

CGA_mode:
if (_setvideomode(_HRESBW)==0) {goto abort_message;}
else {x_res=640;y_res=200;mode_flag=4;
      C0=0,C1=1,C2=1,C3=1,C4=1,C5=1,C6=1,C7=1,C8=1,C9=1,C10=1,
      C11=1,C12=1,C13=1,C14=1,C15=1;
      return;}

abort_message:
printf("\n\nUnable to proceed.\n");
printf("Requires VGA, EGA, or CGA adapter\n");
printf("   with appropriate monitor.\n");
printf("Please refer to the book.\n\n");exit(0);}

/*_____

            SUBROUTINE: coords()
    This subroutine accepts sx,sy device-independent display
```

```
coordinates and returns sx,sy device-dependent screen
coordinates scaled to fit the 640x480, 640x350, 640x200, or
320x200 screen, depending upon the graphics mode being used. */

void coords(void){sx=sx*(x_res/640);sy=sy*(y_res/480);return;}

/*_____


                 SUBROUTINE: Copyright Notice
    This subroutine displays the standard copyright notice.
    If you are typing in this program from the book you can
    safely omit this subroutine, provided that you also remove
    the instruction "notice()" from the main routine.          */
int copyright[][3]={0x7c00,0x0000,0x0000,0x8231,
0x819c,0x645e,0xba4a,0x4252,0x96d0,0xa231,0x8252,0x955e,0xba4a,
0x43d2,0xf442,0x8231,0x825c,0x945e,0x7c00,0x0000,0x0000};

void notice(float x, float y){
int a,b,c; int tl=0;
for (tl=0;tl<=6;tl++){a=copyright[tl][0];b=copyright[tl][1];
c=copyright[tl][2];_setlinestyle(a);_moveto(x,y);_lineto(x+15,y);
_setlinestyle(b);_moveto(x+16,y);_lineto(x+31,y);_setlinestyle(c);
_moveto(x+32,y);_lineto(x+47,y);y=y+1;};_setlinestyle(0xFFFF);
return;}

/*_____


                      End of source code                       */
```

Fig. A-6. Program listing which demonstrates real-time animation on VGA and EGA graphics adapters—QuickC version. VGA/EGA compatible. Refer to Appendix B and Appendix D if you are using a CGA.

```
/*_____


                          func-006.c

    Function:  This program demonstrates the fundamental
    algorithms involved in real-time animation.

    Compatibility:  Supports VGA and EGA graphics adapters and
    monitors.  The software uses the 640x200 16-color mode if
    a VGA or an EGA is present.

    Remarks:  The program draws the graphics on a hidden page.
    When an image has been completed, a movedata routine is
    employed to move the image from the hidden page to the
```

visible display page. The hidden page is then cleared and
work begins on the next frame in the animation sequence.

```
                    I N C L U D E    F I L E S              */

#include <stdio.h>              /* supports the printf function */
#include <graph.h>            /* supports the graphics functions */
#include <stdlib.h>            /* supports the exit() function */
#include <memory.h>              /* supports memory moves */
#include <bios.h>          /* supports read of keyboard buffer */
#include <conio.h>              /* supports port manipulation */

/*_____

                    D E C L A R A T I O N S              */

struct videoconfig vc;

void keyboard(void);void quit_pgm(void);
void notice(float x,float y);void coords(void);
void graphics_setup(void);
void pageflip_1to0(void);void pageflip_2to1(void);

int sx1=220,sy1=100,sxmove=4,symove=-1,t1=1;
int C0=0,C1=1,C2=2,C3=3,C4=4,C5=5,C6=6,C7=7,C8=8,C9=9,C10=10,
    C11=11,C12=12,C13=13,C14=14,C15=15;

/*_____

                    M A I N    R O U T I N E              */


 main(){
 graphics_setup();                        /* establish graphics mode*/
_getvideoconfig(&vc);                     /* initialize video table */
_setcolor(C7);_settextcolor(C7);

_setvisualpage(0);_setactivepage(2);           /* write to page 2 */
_settextposition(1,20);
_outtext("USING C FOR HIGH SPEED REAL-TIME ANIMATION");
_settextposition(23,25);
_outtext("640x200 16-color VGA and EGA mode");
_settextposition(25,30);_outtext("Press any key to quit...");
_rectangle(_GFILLINTERIOR,203,40,439,159);notice(4,191);
_setcolor(C4);_rectangle(_GBORDER,203,40,439,159);
pageflip_2to1();pageflip_1to0(); /* move to page 1 and to page 0 */
_setactivepage(1);                             /* write to page 1 */
_setcolor(C0);
```

```
for (tl=1;tl!=2; ){                        /* animate for endless loop */
   _rectangle(_GBORDER,sxl,syl,sxl+50,syl+20);
   if (sxl>=386) sxmove=-4;
   if (sxl<=204) sxmove=4;
   if (syl>=138) symove=-1;
   if (syl<=41) symove=1;
   sxl=sxl+sxmove;syl=syl+symove;
   pageflip_lto0();pageflip_2tol();keyboard();};

quit_pgm();}                               /* end the program gracefully */
```

```
/*  _____


                      SUBROUTINE: pageflip_lto0
      This subroutine flips the graphic contents from page 1 to
      page 0 on a VGA or EGA.                                     */

void pageflip_lto0(void){
outp(0x03ce,0x08);outp(0x03cf,0xff);outp(0x03c4,0x02);
outp(0x03c5,0x0f);outp(0x03ce,0x05);outp(0x03cf,0x01);
movedata(0xa400,0x0000,0xa000,0x0000,16000);
outp(0x03ce,0x05);outp(0x03cf,0x00);return;}


/*                    SUBROUTINE: pageflip_2tol
      This subroutine flips the graphic contents from page 2 to
      page 1 on a VGA or EGA.                                     */

void pageflip_2tol(void){
outp(0x03ce,0x08);outp(0x03cf,0xff);outp(0x03c4,0x02);
outp(0x03c5,0x0f);outp(0x03ce,0x05);outp(0x03cf,0x01);
movedata(0xa800,0x0000,0xa400,0x0000,16000);
outp(0x03ce,0x05);outp(0x03cf,0x00);return;}

/*_____


                SUBROUTINE: press any key to quit               */

void keyboard(void){
if (_bios_keybrd(_KEYBRD_READY)==0) return; else quit_pgm();}

/*_____


               SUBROUTINE: GRACEFUL EXIT FROM THE PROGRAM        */

void quit_pgm(void){
_setvisualpage(0);_setactivepage(0);
_clearscreen(_GCLEARSCREEN);_setvideomode(_DEFAULTMODE);exit(0);}

/*_____
```

```
                    SUBROUTINE: VGA/EGA compatibility module          */

void graphics_setup(void){

VGA_EGA_mode:
if (_setvideomode(_HRES16COLOR)==0) {goto abort_message;}
   else return;

abort_message:
printf("\n\nUnable to proceed.\n");
printf("Requires VGA, or EGA adapter\n");
printf("   with appropriate monitor.\n");
printf("Please refer to the book.\n\n");exit(0);}

/*_____


                    SUBROUTINE: Copyright Notice
    This subroutine displays the standard copyright notice.
    If you are typing in this program from the book you can
    safely omit this subroutine, provided that you also remove
    the instruction "notice()" from the main routine.          */

int copyright[][3]={0x7c00,0x0000,0x0000,0x8231,
0x819c,0x645e,0xba4a,0x4252,0x96d0,0xa231,0x8252,0x955e,0xba4a,
0x43d2,0xf442,0x8231,0x825c,0x945e,0x7c00,0x0000,0x0000};

void notice(float x, float y){
int a,b,c; int tl=0;

for (tl=0;tl<=6;tl++){a=copyright[tl][0];b=copyright[tl][1];
c=copyright[tl][2];_setlinestyle(a);_moveto(x,y);_lineto(x+15,y);
_setlinestyle(b);_moveto(x+16,y);_lineto(x+31,y);_setlinestyle(c);
_moveto(x+32,y);_lineto(x+47,y);y=y+1;};_setlinestyle(0xFFFF);
return;}

/*_____


                    End of source code                       */
```

Fig. A-7. Program listing which demonstrates bitblt animation at 43 fps—QuickC version. VGA/EGA/CGA/MCGA compatible. For Turbo C version, consult Appendix E.

```
/*_____

                         func-007.c

    Function:  This program demonstrates the fundamental
    algorithms involved in bitblt animation.
```

Compatibility: Supports all graphics adapters and monitors.
By default, the software uses the 640x200 2-color mode in
order to animate at 43 frames per second. However, if you
have a VGA or EGA you can delete one line in the
compatibility subroutine in order to force the program to
use the 640x200 16-color mode (and animate at 11 frames
per second).

Remarks: The run-time speed of bitblt animation is
inversely proportional to the screen resolution. Coarser
resolution with fewer available screen colors will yield
quicker bitblt animation (graphic array animation).
Refer to the book for further guidance.

Copyright 1988 Lee Adams and TAB BOOKS Inc.

```
                    I N C L U D E    F I L E S              */

#include <stdio.h>                /* supports the printf function */
#include <graph.h>              /* supports the graphics functions */
#include <stdlib.h>               /* supports the exit() function */
#include <bios.h>            /* supports read of keyboard buffer */
#include <malloc.h>                /* supports memory allocation */

/*_____


                    D E C L A R A T I O N S              */

struct videoconfig vc;

void keyboard(void);void quit_pgm(void);
void notice(float x,float y);void graphics_setup(void);

int tl=1,xl=220,yl=100,x2=270,y2=120,
    sx=220,sy=100,sxmove=3,symove=-1,sxl,syl;
int C0=0,Cl=1,C2=2,C3=3,C4=4,C5=5,C6=6,C7=7,C8=8,C9=9,C10=10,
    Cll=11,C12=12,C13=13,C14=14,C15=15,mode_flag=0;

char far *gr_arrayl;                    /* pointer to graphic array */


/*_____


                    M A I N    R O U T I N E              */

main(){
graphics_setup();                    /* establish graphics mode */
_getvideoconfig(&vc);                 /* initialize video table */
```

```
/*------------ create and store the graphic array -------------*/

_setcolor(C7);_ellipse(_GBORDER,xl+3,yl+1,x2-3,y2-1);
_setcolor(C4);_floodfill(xl+25,yl+10,C7);
gr_arrayl=(char far*)_fmalloc((unsigned int)_imagesize(xl,yl,x2,y2))
_getimage(xl,yl,x2,y2,gr_arrayl);
_setcolor(C0);_rectangle(_GFILLINTERIOR,xl,yl,x2,y2);

/*              ----------------------------------         */

_setcolor(C7);
_rectangle(_GBORDER,201,40,439,159);      /* animation boundaries */
_setcolor(C7);notice(0,192);
_putimage(sx,sy,gr_arrayl,_GPSET);        /* install block graphic */
_settextposition(12,1);_outtext("Ready to animate...");
for (tl=1;tl<=30000;tl++);                          /* pause */
for (tl=1;tl<=30000;tl++);                          /* pause */
for (tl=1;tl<=30000;tl++);                          /* pause */
for (tl=1;tl<=30000;tl++);                          /* pause */
_settextposition(12,1);_outtext("Animation rate:    ");
_settextposition(13,1);
if (mode_flag==4)
   _outtext("43 frames per second");    /* if 640x200 2-clr mode */
if (mode_flag==3)
   _outtext("11 frames per second");    /* if 640x200 16-clr mode */

/*----------------- bitblt animation manager -----------------*/

for (tl=1;tl!=20; ){              /* animate for endless loop */
    if (sxl>=386) sxmove=-3;            /* test for right boundary */
    if (sxl<=204) sxmove=3;             /* test for left boundary */
    if (syl>=138) symove=-1;           /* test for bottom boundary */
    if (syl<=41) symove=1;              /* test for top boundary */
    sxl=sx+sxmove;syl=sy+symove;       /* calculate new position */
    _putimage(sxl,syl,gr_arrayl,_GPSET);    /* install new array */
    sx=sxl;sy=syl;                      /* update sx,sy variables */
    keyboard();};              /* check for user keyboard input */

/*              ----------------------         */

quit_pgm();}                        /* end the program gracefully */

/*_____




              SUBROUTINE: press any key to quit              */

void keyboard(void){
if (_bios_keybrd(_KEYBRD_READY)==0) return; else quit_pgm();}

/*_____
```

```
                SUBROUTINE: GRACEFUL EXIT FROM THE PROGRAM          */

void quit_pgm(void){
_clearscreen(_GCLEARSCREEN);_setvideomode(_DEFAULTMODE);exit(0);}

/*_____


                SUBROUTINE: VGA/EGA/CGA compatibility module        */

void graphics_setup(void){

goto CGA_mode;   /* if you have a VGA or EGA, you can delete this
                    line to force the software to use the 640x200
                    16-color mode (which runs much slower than the
                    default 640x200 2-color mode).                  */
VGA_EGA_mode:
if (_setvideomode(_HRES16COLOR)==0) {goto CGA_mode;}
else {mode_flag=3;
     _settextposition(1,24);_settextcolor(C7);
     _outtext("USING C FOR HIGH SPEED ANIMATION");
     _settextposition(25,30);_outtext("Press any key to quit...");
     _settextposition(22,25);
     _outtext("640x200 16-color VGA and EGA mode");
     _settextposition(4,16);
     _outtext("High speed bitblt animation of a geometric shape...");
     return;}

CGA_mode:
if (_setvideomode(_HRESBW)==0) {goto abort_message;}
else {mode_flag=4;
     C0=0,C1=1,C2=1,C3=1,C4=1,C5=1,C6=1,C7=1,C8=1,C9=1,C10=1,
     C11=1,C12=1,C13=1,C14=1,C15=1;
     _settextposition(1,24);
     _outtext("USING C FOR HIGH SPEED ANIMATION");
     _settextposition(25,30);_outtext("Press any key to quit...");
     _settextposition(22,22);
     _outtext("640x200 2-color VGA, EGA and CGA mode");
     _settextposition(4,16);
     _outtext("High speed bitblt animation of a geometric shape...")
     return;}

abort_message:
printf("\n\nUnable to proceed.\n");
printf("Requires VGA, EGA, or CGA adapter\n");
printf("   with appropriate monitor.\n");
printf("Please refer to the book.\n\n");exit(0);}

 /*_____
```

```
                    SUBROUTINE: Copyright Notice
      This subroutine displays the standard copyright notice.
      If you are typing in this program from the book you can
      safely omit this subroutine, provided that you also remove
      the instruction "notice()" from the main routine.          */

int copyright[ ][3]={0x7c00,0x0000,0x0000,0x8231,
0x819c,0x645e,0xba4a,0x4252,0x96d0,0xa231,0x8252,0x955e,0xba4a,
0x43d2,0xf442,0x8231,0x825c,0x945e,0x7c00,0x0000,0x0000};

void notice(float x, float y){
int a,b,c; int tl=0;
for (tl=0;tl<=6;tl++){a=copyright[tl][0];b=copyright[tl][1];
c=copyright[tl][2];_setlinestyle(a);_moveto(x,y);_lineto(x+15,y);
_setlinestyle(b);_moveto(x+16,y);_lineto(x+31,y);_setlinestyle(c);
_moveto(x+32,y);_lineto(x+47,y);y=y+1;};_setlinestyle(0xFFFF);
return;}

/*_____


                        End of source code                      */
```

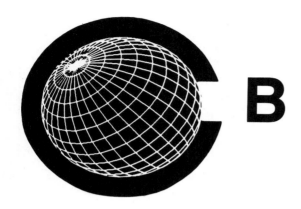 B

How to Use Assembly Language Graphics Routines

Microsoft QuickC and Borland Turbo C (beginning with version 1.5) contain built-in graphics routines. The demonstration programs throughout this book rely upon the graphics capabilities found in these popular C compilers.

However, if you prefer to use a C compiler which lacks built-in graphics routines (such as Turbo C version 1.0, for example), you can incorporate into your programs an assortment of assembly language graphics drivers. The source code for a library of assembly language subroutines for VGA and EGA graphics is provided in Appendix C. The source code for a selection of assembly language subroutines for CGA graphics is provided in Appendix D.

These assembly language modules provide the ability to set a graphics mode (__EGAMODE and __CGAMODE), clear the screen (__EGACLS and __CGACLS), draw a line (__EGADRAW and __CGADRAW), fill a random polygon with color (__EGAFILL and __CGAFILL), and copy a graphics page from one location to another (__EGACOPY and __CGACOPY). By combining these assembly language modules with the C graphics routines contained in Appendix A, you can begin to explore high-performance graphics on your personal computer.

REQUIRED SOFTWARE TOOLS

In addition to your C compiler, you will need an assembler such as IBM Macro Assembler or Microsoft Macro Assembler. You will also require a text editor with which to create your assembly language source code. You can use any word processor which can save text on disk as ASCII files, or you can use the EDLIN editor provided with DOS.

THE INTERFACE TO ASSEMBLY LANGUAGE

Because C is a highly-structured programming language, it is very easy to use it in combination with assembly language subroutines. Simply stated, four steps are involved. First, use your favorite text editor to create the source code for the assembly language subroutine. Second, use an assembler to compile the source code into an OBJ file. Third, tell your C compiler that your C program will be calling the assembly language subroutine and tell your C compiler where to find the OBJ file. Fourth, call the assembly language subroutine from your C program in the same manner you would invoke any built-in C function. Provided that you have written the assembly language subroutines correctly, the interface between C and assembly language will be seamless and smooth-running.

PASSING PARAMETERS TO THE SUBROUTINE

Parameters which the C program wishes to pass to the assembly language subroutine are placed onto the stack when the subroutine is called. The subroutine simply retrieves these parameters from the stack. A slight wrinkle is introduced to this regime by the memory model used by your C program.

C MEMORY MODELS

If you are using a compact memory model, the C compiler limits executable code to a single 64K segment but permits up to 1 MB of data. In this instance, the C program places the IP instruction pointer onto the stack when it calls the assembly language subroutine. The IP is the address of the next C instruction to be executed when the program returns from the assembly language subroutine. Because the executable code resides in a single 64K segment, only the offset portion of the CS:IP duo is required.

If you are using a medium memory model, the C compiler limits normal data to a single 64K segment but permits up to 1 MB of executable code. In this instance, the C program places both the CS code segment and the IP instruction pointer onto the stack when it calls the assembly language subroutine. Because the C program needs to know which segment holds the next executable C instruction, both the segment portion and the offset portion of the CS:IP duo are required.

When a C medium memory model is used, a far call is used to jump to the assembly language subroutine. When a C compact memory model is used, a near call is used to jump to the assembly language subroutine. The source code for the assembly language module must take this into consideration, as illustrated in Fig. B-1, which provides a bulletproof template into which any assembly language routines can be written, depending upon which C memory model you are using.

The integrated programming environment of the QuickC editor is restricted to the medium memory model (up to 1 MB of executable code and up to 64K in the default data segment, although you can also use the far heap for data). Turbo C, on the other hand, can be configured via its pull-down menu system to use different memory models, including tiny, small, compact, medium, large, and huge.

NEAR CALL VS FAR CALL

If your C program passes parameters to the assembly language subroutine, the issue of *near call* versus *far call* becomes doubly important. As Fig. B-2 illustrates, the size

Turbo C 1.0 and C compilers which use near calls	QuickC and C compilers which use far calls
_TEXT SEGMENT BYTE PUBLIC ´CODE´ ASSUME CS:_TEXT PUBLIC _EGADRAW . . . _EGADRAW PROC NEAR . . . RET _EGADRAW ENDP _TEXT ENDS	name_TEXT SEGMENT WORD PUBLIC ´CODE´ ASSUME CS:name_TEXT PUBLIC _EGADRAW . . . _EGADRAW PROC FAR . . . RET _EGADRAW ENDP name_TEXT ENDS
place names of assembly language OBJ files and C source file into the Project File menu.	place the assembly language OBJ module into your QLB file. Declare it as EXTERN name( ) in your C program.

Fig. B-1. Assembly language interface differences between Turbo C and QuickC.

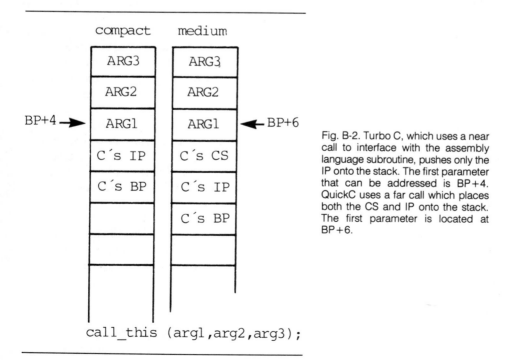

Fig. B-2. Turbo C, which uses a near call to interface with the assembly language subroutine, pushes only the IP onto the stack. The first parameter that can be addressed is BP+4. QuickC uses a far call which places both the CS and IP onto the stack. The first parameter is located at BP+6.

call_this (arg1,arg2,arg3);

of the stack inherited by the assembly language varies according to the C memory model being used.

In order to fetch any parameters it needs, the assembly language routine sets the BP register to point to the top of the stack. It then uses an offset calculation to find the desired parameter. As Fig. B-2 shows, the first parameter is located at **BP+4** is a compact memory model is being used, but it is located at **BP+6** if a medium memory model is being used. Remember, in a compact memory model only the IP is saved on the stack by the C program, but in a medium memory model both the CS and IP are saved on the stack. In either instance, this saving of executable code addresses is performed after the C program has placed the parameters onto the stack.

The assembly language graphics drivers in Appendix C and in Appendix D have been created for C programs which use the compact memory model. In particular, they have been crafted for the compact memory model of Turbo C 1.0. If you prefer to use the medium memory model, then you can adapt the assembly language subroutines by editing the BP+n instructions found throughout the code. Simply add 2 units to each BP+n instruction. **BP+8** would be replaced with **BP+10**, for example.

WHERE TO PUT THE OBJ FILE

After you have used an assembler to compile your assembly language source code into an OBJ file, you tell your C compiler where to find the OBJ file.

If you are using Turbo C 1.0, use DOS to copy the OBJ file onto the same disk where you are keeping your **#include** files. Then, place the name of the assembly language OBJ file and the name of your C source file into the Project File menu. When Turbo C begins to compile a program, it first checks the contents of the PRJ project file to determine which modules to use to create the resulting EXE program. (Refer to Chapter 7 for further guidance on setting up and using the Turbo C programming environment.) To use the assembly language subroutine from your C program, simply call it like you would any other built-in C function. If the name of the subroutine were **EGADRAW**, for example, you would invoke it via **EGADRAW(parameter 1, parameter 2, . . .)**.

If you are using QuickC, place the assembly language OBJ file into your QLB file. QuickBASIC loads the QLB file into high memory when QuickBASIC is first invoked from DOS, so your assembly language subroutine is already available in memory while you are programming. To use an assembly language subroutine called **EGADRAW**, for example, declare it as **EXTERN EGADRAW( );** near the beginning of your C program. You can then call the subroutine with the following syntax: **EGADRAW(parameter 1, parameter 2 . . .)**. Refer to Chapter 6 for further guidance on setting up and using the QuickC programming environment.

LOCAL VARIABLES

Many of the assembly language subroutines in Appendix C and Appendix D are relatively short and simple. However, the area fill routine and the line drawing routine need to create and keep track of local variables. To keep the interface between C and assembly language as straightforward as possible, the assembly language subroutines set up their own stack and use it to store their local variables, rather than using variables from C's data areas.

For a detailed discussion and BASICA source code for area fill algorithms for random polygons, refer to *SUPERCHARGED GRAPHICS: A Programmers Sourcecode Toolbox* (#2959), available through your favorite bookstore or order direct from TAB Books.

USING *BIOS* INTERRUPTS

You can also use the BIOS video routines of your personal computer to enhance the graphics capabilities of a C compiler which lacks a built-in graphics library. These BIOS video routines are especially useful for setting up a graphics mode, for manipulating the color palette of the VGA and EGA, and even for writing pixels.

To call a BIOS video routine from assembly language, place the BIOS function number into the AH register, any other required parameters into the other designated registers, and execute an INT 10 hex instruction. The requirements of the BIOS write pixel function are shown in Fig. B-3. The requirements of the BIOS set mode function are illustrated in Fig. B-4. The requirements of the BIOS set palette function are depicted in Fig. B-5. Listings for other BIOS interrupts can be found in the DOS technical reference and in a variety of DOS-oriented books.

To call a BIOS video function directly from your C program, use the following algorithm, which invokes BIOS function 10 hex after loading register AL with 03 hex in order to establish the 80-column color text mode.

```
union REGS regs;
regs.h.ah=0×10;
```

FUNCTION AH	COLOR AL	X CX	Y DX	PAGE BH	Remarks
12 0C	0-3	0-319	0-199	--	320x299 4-clr CGA
12 0C	0-1	0-639	0-199	--	640x200 2-clr CGA
12 0C	0-15	0-319	0-199	0-7	320x200 16-clr EGA
12 0C	0-15	0-639	0-199	0-3	640x200 16-clr EGA
12 0C	0-15	0-639	0-349	0-1	640x350 16-clr EGA
12 0C	0-15	0-639	0-479	0	640x480 16-clr VGA
12 0C	0-255	0-319	0-199	0-3	320x200 256-clr VGA/MCGA

```
if bit 7 of AL is 1, then the color is XOR´d
with the existing screen pixel color
```

Fig. B-3. Using BIOS interrupt 10H to write a pixel on a VGA, TGA, or CGA.

regs.h.al=0×03;
return int86(0×16,&regs,&regs);

If you are using QuickC, refer to the demonstration program in Chapter 9 for an example of this technique. If you are using Turbo C, refer to the demonstration program in Fig. E-1 of Appendix E.

FUNCTION AH	MODE AL		Remarks
0	3	03	80-column color text
0	4	04	320x200 4-clr CGA
0	6	06	640x200 2-clr CGA
0	13	0D	320x200 16-clr EGA
0	14	0E	640x200 16-clr EGA
0	16	10	640x350 16-clr EGA
0	18	12	640x480 16-clr VGA
0	19	13	320x200 256-clr VGA/MCGA

Fig. B-4. Using BIOS interrupt 10H to set the screen mode.

FUNCTION AH		SOFTWARE COLOR BH	HARDWARE COLOR BL	Remarks
11	0B	0-15	0-15	320x200 16-clr EGA
11	0B	0-15	0-15	640x200 16-clr EGA
11	0B	0-15	0-63	640x350 16-clr EGA
11	0B	0-15	0-15	640x480 16-clr VGA
11	0B	0-255	0-255	320x200 256-clr VGA/MCGA

Fig. B-5. Using BIOS interrupt 10H to set the palette on a VGA or TGA.

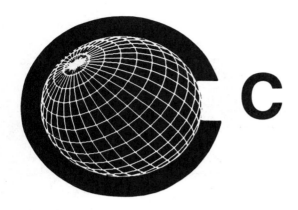 C

Assembly Language Routines for EGA and VGA

The assembly language program listing in Fig. C-1 provides VGA and EGA graphics capabilities for C compilers which lack built-in graphics routines. The source code, entitled GRFX-EGA.ASM, provides six functions: __EGACLS, __EGADRAW, __EGAFILL, __EGACOPY, __EGAVIEW, and __EGAMODE.

__EGAMODE changes the screen mode. To invoke the 640×200 16-color mode from your C program, call the assembly language subroutine with the syntax EGAMODE(14);. To return to the 8-column color text mode, call the assembly language subroutine with the syntax EGAMODE(3);.

__EGACLS clears the 640×200 16-color screen. You can clear any of the four pages available in the 640×200 16-color mode. To clear a screen from your C program, call the assembly language subroutine with the syntax EGACLS(page); where page is 0, 1, 2, or 3.

__EGADRAW draws a line from one point to another in the 640×200 16-color mode. The syntax is EGADRAW(x1,y1,x2,y2,color,page);, where oordinates must be integers within the screen's legal range.

__EGACOPY copies the contents of one graphics page to another. Call this subroutine with the syntax EGACOPY(source,target);, where source and target are page numbers in the range 0 to 3.

__EGAVIEW selects the display page. Call it with the syntax:
EGAVIEW(page); where page is in the range 0 to 3.

__EGAFILL can be used to fill complex random polygons with color. The calling syntax is EGAFILL(x1,y1,color,boundary,page);, where color is the fill color in the range 0 to 15, **boundary** is the polygon's boundary color in the range 0 to 15, and **page** is in the range 0 to 3.

In its current form, GRFX-EGA.ASM is designed for C programs which use the compact memory model and near calls. Refer to Appendix B for further discussion of the interface between C and assembly language.

Fig. C-1. Program listing for a set of assembly language graphics drivers, designed to support the 640×200 16-color mode of the VGA and EGA. Compatible with Turbo C 1.0 and all other C compilers that use near calls to interface with assembly language modules. VGA/EGA compatible.

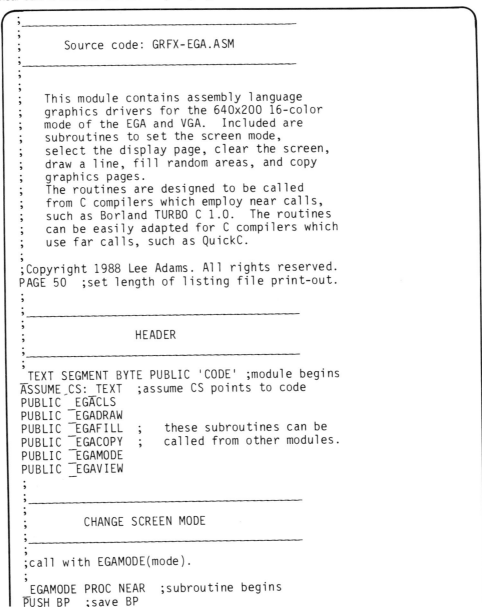

```
;_____
;
;        Source code: GRFX-EGA.ASM
;
;_____
;
;
;    This module contains assembly language
;    graphics drivers for the 640x200 16-color
;    mode of the EGA and VGA.  Included are
;    subroutines to set the screen mode,
;    select the display page, clear the screen,
;    draw a line, fill random areas, and copy
;    graphics pages.
;    The routines are designed to be called
;    from C compilers which employ near calls,
;    such as Borland TURBO C 1.0.  The routines
;    can be easily adapted for C compilers which
;    use far calls, such as QuickC.
;
;Copyright 1988 Lee Adams. All rights reserved.
PAGE 50  ;set length of listing file print-out.
;
;_____
;
;                HEADER
;
;_____
;
_TEXT SEGMENT BYTE PUBLIC 'CODE' ;module begins
ASSUME _CS: _TEXT   ;assume CS points to code
PUBLIC _EGACLS
PUBLIC _EGADRAW
PUBLIC _EGAFILL  ;   these subroutines can be
PUBLIC _EGACOPY  ;   called from other modules.
PUBLIC _EGAMODE
PUBLIC _EGAVIEW
;
;_____
;
;         CHANGE SCREEN MODE
;
;_____
;
;call with EGAMODE(mode).
;
_EGAMODE PROC NEAR   ;subroutine begins
PUSH BP ;save BP
```

```
    MOV  BP,SP  ;use BP in addressing mode
    MOV  AX,[BP+4]  ;get mode number from stack
    SUB  AH,AH  ;set AH to BIOS function 0
    INT  10H    ;call BIOS routine to set mode
    POP  BP     ;restore BP
    RET         ;return to caller
_EGAMODE ENDP   ;subroutine ends
;
;_____
;
;       CLS 640x200 16-color screen
;
;_____
;
;call with EGACLS(page).
;expects 640x200 16-color mode to be in effect.
;
_EGACLS PROC NEAR   ;subroutine begins
PUSH BP   ;save BP
MOV  BP,SP  ;set addressing mode
PUSH SI     ;save for caller
PUSH DI     ;save for caller
PUSH ES     ;save for caller
MOV  AX,00H  ;put page 0 offset into AX
MOV  BX,4000H   ;length of a graphics page
MOV  CX,[BP+4]  ;get page number from stack
JCXZ PAGE_0     ;if page 0 then jump
;
HIGHER_PAGE:
   ADD  AX,BX   ;add length of 1 page to seg
   LOOP HIGHER_PAGE  ;repeat for each page
;
PAGE_0:
   MOV  BX,AX   ;put page offset into BX
   MOV  AX,0A000H
   MOV  ES,AX   ;set ES to A000 hex
;
;set the graphics registers
MOV  AL,08H
MOV  DX,03CEH
OUT  DX,AL  ;bit mask register
MOV  AL,0FFH
MOV  DX,03CFH
OUT  DX,AL  ;set bit mask to 11111111B
MOV  AL,02H
MOV  DX,03C4H
OUT  DX,AL  ;map mask register
MOV  AL,0FFH
MOV  DX,03C5H
OUT  DX,AL  ;set all bit planes to write
MOV  AL,03H
MOV  DX,03CEH
OUT  DX,AL  ;data rotate register
MOV  AL,00H
MOV  DX,03CFH
```

```
OUT  DX,AL  ;set to normal write mode
;
;CLS the appropriate graphics page
MOV  CX,4000H  ;set counter to 16000 bytes
SUB  AL,AL  ;set AL to zero
BLANK_PAGE:
  MOV  ES:[BX],AL  ;set 8 pixels to black
  INC  BX  ;set BX to next address
  LOOP BLANK_PAGE  ;write 16000 bytes
;
POP  ES  ;restore ES
POP  DI  ;restore DI
POP  SI  ;restore SI
POP  BP  ;restore BP
RET      ;return to caller
_EGACLS ENDP  ;subroutine ends
;
;_____
;
;   DRAW LINE in 640x200 16-color mode
;_____
;
;call with EGADRAW(x1,y1,x2,y2,color,page).
;expects 640x200 16-color mode to be in effect.
;
_EGADRAW PROC NEAR  ;subroutine begins
PUSH BP  ;save BP
MOV  BP,SP  ;use BP in addressing mode
PUSH SI      ;save SI for caller
PUSH DI      ;save DI for caller
PUSH ES      ;save for caller
;
;select display memory segment
MOV  AX,0A000H  ;EGA/VGA display memory
MOV  ES,AX  ;ES is A000H seg address
;
;calculate slope of line
MOV  DI,1
MOV  DX,[BP+10]  ;get Y2
MOV  AX,[BP+6]  ;get Y1
SUB  DX,AX
JGE  SAVE_Y
NEG  DI
NEG  DX
SAVE_Y: PUSH DI  ;save DELDY
MOV  CX,[BP+8]  ;get X2
MOV  AX,[BP+4]  ;get X1
MOV  SI,1
SUB  CX,AX
JGE  SAVE_X
NEG  SI
NEG  CX
SAVE_X: PUSH SI  ;save DELDX
CMP  CX,DX
```

```
JGE   DIAG_SET
MOV   SI,0
XCHG  CX,DX
JMP   SAVE_DELSXY
DIAG_SET: MOV DI,0
SAVE_DELSXY:
   PUSH CX  ;save DELS
   PUSH DX  ;save DELP
   PUSH SI  ;save DELSX
   PUSH DI  ;save DELSY
MOV   AX,[BP-14]  ;get DELP
SAL   AX,1
PUSH AX   ;save DELSE
SUB   AX,CX
MOV   BX,AX
SUB   AX,CX
PUSH AX   ;save DELDE
INC   CX  ;initialize loop counter
MOV   DX,[BP+4]  ;get X1
MOV   AX,[BP+6]  ;get Y1
;
;loop to plot pixels along the line
LINE_LOOP:
CALL  WRITE_EGA_PIXEL
CMP   BX,0
JGE   DIAGONAL
STRAIGHT:
   ADD   DX,[BP-16]  ;DELSX
   ADD   AX,[BP-18]  ;DELSY
   ADD   BX,[BP-20]  ;DELSE
   LOOP  LINE_LOOP
   JMP   EXIT
DIAGONAL:
   ADD   DX,[BP-10]  ;DELDX
   ADD   AX,[BP-8]   ;DELDY
   ADD   BX,[BP-22]  ;DELDE
   LOOP  LINE_LOOP
;
EXIT:
SUB   BP,6  ;reposition BP
MOV   SP,BP ;reposition SP
POP   ES        ;restore ES
POP   DI        ;restore DI
POP   SI        ;restore SI
POP   BP        ;restore BP
RET        ;return to caller
_EGADRAW ENDP  ;subroutine ends
;_____
;
WRITE_EGA_PIXEL PROC NEAR  ;local subroutine
PUSH AX
PUSH BX
PUSH CX
PUSH DX
```

```
MOV  CX,DX   ;put x-coord into CX
MOV  DX,AX   ;put y-coord into DX
MOV  AX,[BP+12] ;get color
MOV  BX,[BP+14] ;get page number
PUSH AX   ;save color
MOV  AX,DX   ;put y-coord into AX
PUSH CX   ;save x-coord
PUSH DX
MOV  CX,80
MUL  CX   ;y*80=offset to start of row
POP  DX
POP  CX   ;restore x-coord to CX
PUSH CX   ;save x-coord
SHR  CX,1   ;divide by 2
SHR  CX,1   ;divide by 4
SHR  CX,1   ;divide by 8
ADD  AX,CX   ;offset into the page
SUB  BH,BH   ;make BH zero, BL=page
MOV  CX,BX   ;page #=counter in CX
MOV  BX,4000H ;length of a page
JCXZ PAGE_0   ;if zero then jump
HIGHER_PAGE:
   ADD  AX,BX   ;add length of 1 page
   LOOP HIGHER_PAGE ;add again if required
PAGE_0:
POP  CX   ;get x-coord
MOV  BX,AX   ;put offset into BX
AND  CL,07H   ;shift counter for bit mask
MOV  AL,080H   ;put mask 10000000 into AL
SHR  AL,CL   ;reposition the bit mask
MOV  DH,3
MOV  DL,0CEH   ;select the graphics chip
MOV  AH,08H   ;bit mask register
CALL SET_REGISTER   ;set the bit mask
POP  AX   ;get color
MOV  CH,AL   ;put color into CH
BLANK_DOT:
   MOV  DL,0C4H   ;sequencer register port
   MOV  AH,02H   ;map mask register
   MOV  AL,0FFH   ;enable all 4 bit planes
   CALL SET_REGISTER
   MOV  AL,ES:[BX]   ;latch the byte
   SUB  AL,AL   ;set AL to zero (ie black)
   MOV  ES:[BX],AL   ;blank the pixel
MOV  DL,0C4H   ;sequencer register port
MOV  AH,02H   ;map mask register
MOV  AL,CH   ;put color into AL
AND  AL,0FH   ;force to 0-15 range
CALL SET_REGISTER   ;set bit planes
MOV  AL,ES:[BX]   ;latch the byte
MOV  AL,0FFH   ;set all bits to 1
MOV  ES:[BX],AL   ;color the pixel
;
;restore the graphics registers
```

```
        CALL SET_REGISTER  ;enable all 4 bit planes
        MOV  DL,0CEH  ;select the graphics chip
        MOV  AH,03H  ;select XOR
        SUB  AL,AL  ;set AL to zero
        CALL SET_REGISTER
        MOV  AH,08H  ;bit mask register
        MOV  AL,0FFH  ;all bits on
        CALL SET_REGISTER
        ;
        POP  DX
        POP  CX
        POP  BX
        POP  AX
        RET  ;return to caller
        WRITE_EGA_PIXEL ENDP  ;end of subroutine
        ;_____
        ;
        SET_REGISTER PROC NEAR  ;local subroutine
        ;AH=index, AL=data, DX=port
        XCHG AL,AH  ;put index into AL
        OUT  DX,AL  ;set index register
        INC  DX  ;set DX to data register
        XCHG AL,AH  ;put data into AL
        OUT  DX,AL  ;send data
        DEC  DX  ;restore DX port address
        RET  ;return to caller
        SET_REGISTER ENDP  ;end of subroutine
        ;
        ;_____
        ;
        ;         COPY 640x200 16-color screen
        ;_____
        ;
        ;call with EGACOPY(source,target).
        ;expects 640x200 16-color mode to be in effect.
        ;
        _EGACOPY PROC NEAR  ;subroutine begins
        PUSH BP  ;save BP
        MOV  BP,SP  ;use BP in addressing mode
        PUSH SI     ;save SI for caller
        PUSH DI     ;save DI for caller
        PUSH ES     ;save ES for caller
        PUSH DS     ;save DS for caller
        ;
        ;set the graphics registers
        MOV  AL,08H
        MOV  DX,03CEH
        OUT  DX,AL  ;bit mask register
        MOV  AL,0FFH
        MOV  DX,03CFH
        OUT  DX,AL  ;set bit mask to 11111111B
        MOV  AL,02H
        MOV  DX,03C4H
        OUT  DX,AL  ;map mask register
```

```
        MOV   AL,0FH
        MOV   DX,03C5H
        OUT   DX,AL   ;set all bit planes for write
        MOV   AL,05H
        MOV   DX,03CEH
        OUT   DX,AL   ;mode register
        MOV   AL,01H
        MOV   DX,03CFH
        OUT   DX,AL   ;set to write mode 1
        ;
        ;assign source, target addresses
        MOV   AX,00H   ;put 0 offset into AX
        MOV   BX,4000H   ;length of a graphics page
        MOV   CX,[BP+4]   ;get source page number
        JCXZ  PAGE_0   ;if page 0 then jump
        HIGHER_PAGE:
          ADD  AX,BX   ;add length of page to seg
          LOOP HIGHER_PAGE   ;repeat
        PAGE_0:
        MOV   DX,AX   ;store source offset in DX
        MOV   AX,00H   ;put 0 offset into AX
        MOV   CX,[BP+6]   ;get target page number
        JCXZ  PAGE_ZERO   ;if page 0 then jump
        UPPER_PAGE:
          ADD  AX,BX   ;add length of page to seg
          LOOP UPPER_PAGE   ;repeat
        PAGE_ZERO:
        MOV   DI,AX   ;put target page into DI
        MOV   SI,DX   ;put source page into SI
        ;
        ;execute the page move
        MOV   AX,0A000H   ;display memory segment
        MOV   ES,AX   ;target segment
        MOV   DS,AX   ;source segment
        MOV   CX,3E80H   ;count 16000 bytes
        REP   MOVSB   ;move the page
        ;
        ;restore graphics registers
        MOV   AL,05H
        MOV   DX,03CEH
        OUT   DX,AL   ;mode register
        MOV   AL,00H
        MOV   DX,03CFH
        OUT   DX,AL   ;set to write mode 0
        ;
        POP   DS
        POP   ES
        POP   DI
        POP   SI
        POP   BP
        RET           ;return to caller
        _EGACOPY ENDP  ;subroutine ends
        ;
        ;_____
```

```
;
;               SELECT DISPLAY PAGE
;_____
;
;To display page 0, call EGAVIEW0.
;To display page 1, call EGAVIEW1.
;To display page 2, call EGAVIEW2.
;To display page 3, call EGAVIEW3.
;Expects 640x200 16-color mode to be in effect.
;
_EGAVIEW0 PROC NEAR  ;subroutine begins here
MOV  AX,0CH
MOV  DX,03D4H
OUT  DX,AL     ;set the EGA/VGA start-address register
MOV  AX,0H     ;page 0
MOV  DX,03D5H
OUT  DX,AL     ;change to page 0
RET            ;return to caller
_EGAVIEW0 ENDP  ;subroutine ends here
;_____
;
_EGAVIEW1 PROC NEAR  ;subroutine begins here
MOV  AX,0CH
MOV  DX,03D4H
OUT  DX,AL
MOV  AX,040H  ;page 1
MOV  DX,03D5H
OUT  DX,AL     ;change to page 1
RET
_EGAVIEW1 ENDP  ;subroutine ends here
;_____
;
_EGAVIEW2 PROC NEAR  ;subroutine begins here
MOV  AX,0CH
MOV  DX,03D4H
OUT  DX,AL
MOV  AX,080H  ;page 2
MOV  DX,03D5H
OUT  DX,AL     ;change to page 2
RET
_EGAVIEW2 ENDP   ;subroutine ends here
;_____
;
_EGAVIEW3 PROC NEAR  ;subroutine starts here
MOV  AX,0CH
MOV  DX,03D4H
OUT  DX,AL
MOV  AX,0C0H  ;page 3
MOV  DX,03D5H
OUT  DX,AL     ;change to page 3
RET
_EGAVIEW3 ENDP  ;subroutine ends here
;
;_____
```

```
;
;            AREA FILL ROUTINE
;_____
;
;call with _EGAFILL(X1,Y1,color,boundary,page).
;expects 640x200 16-color mode to be in effect.
;
_EGAFILL PROC NEAR   ;subroutine begins
;_____
;
;MAIN ROUTINE
;_____
;
CLI
PUSH AX
PUSH BP
PUSH ES
MOV  AX,SS
MOV  ES,AX   ;save SS in ES
MOV  BP,SP   ;save SP in BP
MOV  AX,9C00H ;new stack segment address
MOV  SS,AX   ;new stack segment at 9C00 hex
MOV  AX,14BEH ;bottom of new stack
MOV  SP,AX   ;new stack now active
PUSH ES ;save C's SS
PUSH BP ;save C's SP
;_____
;
;transfer passed parameters to new stack
MOV  AX,ES:[BP+16]
PUSH AX  ;store page on subroutine stack
MOV  AX,ES:[BP+8]
PUSH AX  ;store X1 on subroutine stack
MOV  AX,ES:[BP+10]
PUSH AX  ;store Y1 on subroutine stack
MOV  AX,ES:[BP+12]

PUSH AX  ;store color on subroutine stack
MOV  AX,ES:[BP+14]
PUSH AX  ;store boundary on subroutine stack
MOV  BP,SP  ;use BP as offset pointer
;_____
;
;save all registers on new stack
PUSH DS
PUSH BX
PUSH CX
PUSH DX
PUSH SI
PUSH DI
PUSHF
;_____
;
;store local variables on new stack
MOV  AX,13BAH
```

```
PUSH AX  ;store read pointer
MOV  AX,13BEH
PUSH AX  ;store write pointer
MOV  AX,0  ;dummy value
PUSH AX  ;up-flag
PUSH AX  ;write count
PUSH AX  ;down-flag
PUSH AX  ;read count
PUSH AX  ;above/below pixel x-coordinate
PUSH AX  ;above/below pixel y-coordinate
PUSH AX  ;temporary storage of X1
PUSH AX  ;temporary storage of Y1
;_____
;
;RANGE CHECKING
;_____
;
;ensure legal range of X1,Y1 seed point
MOV  AX,[BP+6]  ;get X1
CMP  AX,0
JAE  A1
JMP  ALL_DONE  ;if X1<0 then abort
A1:
CMP  AX,639
JBE  A2
JMP  ALL_DONE  ;if X1>639 then abort
A2:
MOV  AX,[BP+4]  ;get Y1
CMP  AX,0
JAE  A3
JMP  ALL_DONE  ;if Y1<0 then abort
A3:
CMP  AX,199
JBE  A4
JMP  ALL_DONE  ;if Y1>199 then abort
A4:
;_____
;
;FILL ROUTINE
;_____
;
;start filling the polygon
CALL FILL_LINE  ;fill first scan line
MOV  AX,[BP-22]  ;get write count flag
CMP  AX,0  ;check if a seed was stored
JNE  FILL_LOOP  ;if write count set, continue
JMP  ALL_DONE  ;if no seeds stored, exit
;_____
;
FILL_LOOP:
;retrieve seed from FIFO queue
MOV  BX,SP  ;save stack pointer
MOV  SP,[BP-16]  ;activate read pointer
POP  CX  ;get seed x-coordinate
```

```
POP  DX  ;get seed y-coordinate
MOV  AX,SP  ;save read pointer
MOV  SP,BX  ;restore stack pointer
DEC  AX
DEC  AX
DEC  AX
DEC  AX
DEC  AX
DEC  AX
DEC  AX
DEC  AX  ;adjust read pointer
MOV  [BP-16],AX  ;store new read pointer
MOV  [BP+6],CX  ;store new X1
MOV  [BP+4],DX  ;store new Y1
MOV  AX,[BP-26]  ;get read count
INC  AX  ;increment read count
MOV  [BP-26],AX  ;store new read count
;_____
;
;
CALL FILL_LINE  ;fill a scan line
MOV  AX,[BP-22]  ;get write count
MOV  CX,[BP-26]  ;get read count
CMP  AX,CX  ;does read count = write count?
JNE  A5  ;if not, continue fill
JMP  ALL_DONE  ;otherwise, exit
A5:
JMP  FILL_LOOP  ;loop back
;_____
;
;EXIT ROUTINE
;_____
;
ALL_DONE:
MOV  AX,14A2H
MOV  SP,AX  ;reposition stack pointer
POPF
POP  DI
POP  SI
POP  DX
POP  CX
POP  BX
POP  DS
MOV  AX,[BP+10]  ;get C's SP
MOV  SP,AX
MOV  AX,[BP+12]  ;get C's SS
MOV  SS,AX  ;C's stack is restored
POP  ES
POP  BP
POP  AX
STI
RET      ;return to caller
_EGAFILL ENDP  ;subroutine ends
;_____
;
```

```
;fill one scan line
;_____
;
;subroutine to fill one scan line, check
;adjacent pixels, store seed coordinates
PUBLIC FILL_LINE
FILL_LINE PROC NEAR   ;local subroutine
    MOV   CX,[BP+6]  ;get X1
    MOV   DX,[BP+4]  ;get Y1
    MOV   BH,[BP+8]  ;get page
    MOV   AH,13
    INT   10H  ;read current pixel
SUB  AH,AH  ;color is in AL
MOV  CX,[BP+2]  ;get CLR
CMP  AX,CX  ;is seed point already filled?
JNE  A6  ;if not, continue fill
RET  ;else abort this scan line
A6:
MOV  CX,[BP]  ;get BOUNDARY
CMP  AX,CX  ;check for boundary
JNE  A7  ;if not, continue fill
RET  ;else abort this scan line
A7:
MOV  AX,0
MOV  [BP-20],AX  ;set up-flag to write
MOV  [BP-24],AX  ;set down-flag to write
MOV  AX,[BP+6]  ;get X1
MOV  [BP-32],AX  ;save as X3
MOV  BX,[BP+4]  ;get Y1
MOV  [BP-34],BX  ;save as Y3
;_____
;
;fill towards right
RIGHT_LOOP:
CALL WRITE_PIXEL  ;set one pixel
MOV  AX,[BP+6]  ;get X1
INC  AX  ;move one pixel towards right
MOV [BP+6],AX  ;store new X1
CMP  AX,640  ;is X1 > 639?
JNE  A8  ;if not, continue fill
JMP  GO_LEFT  ;else start to fill left
A8:
    MOV   CX,AX  ;put X1 into CX
    MOV   DX,[BP+4]  ;get Y1
    MOV   BH,[BP+8]  ;get page
    MOV   AH,13
    INT   10H  ;check color of pixel
SUB  AH,AH  ;color is in AL
MOV  CX,[BP]  ;get boundary
CMP  AX,CX  ;check for boundary
JNE  A9  ;if not, continue fill
JMP  GO_LEFT  ;else start to fill left
A9:
JMP  RIGHT_LOOP  ;keep filling right
```

```
;_____
;
;
;fill towards left
GO_LEFT:
MOV  AX,[BP-32]  ;retrieve active x-seed
MOV  [BP+6],AX  ;store as X1
MOV  AX,[BP-34]  ;retrieve active y-seed
MOV  [BP+4],AX  ;store as Y1
JMP  A10  ;this pixel already set
LEFT_LOOP:
CALL WRITE_PIXEL  ;set one pixel
A10:
MOV  AX,[BP+6]  ;get X1
DEC  AX  ;move one pixel towards left
MOV  [BP+6],AX  ;store new X1
CMP  AX,-1  ;IS X1 < 0?
JNE  A11  ;if not, continue fill
RET  ;else stop filling this scan line
A11:
    MOV  CX,AX  ;put X1 into CX
    MOV  DX,[BP+4]  ;get Y1
    MOV  BH,[BP+8]  ;get page
    MOV  AH,13
    INT  10H  ;check color of pixel
SUB  AH,AH  ;color is in AL
MOV  CX,[BP]  ;get boundary
CMP  AX,CX  ;check for boundary
JNE  A12  ;if not, continue fill
RET  ;else stop filling this scan line
A12:
JMP  LEFT_LOOP  ;keep filling left
FILL_LINE ENDP  ;end of subroutine
;_____
;
;
;set one pixel
;_____
;
PUBLIC WRITE_PIXEL
WRITE_PIXEL PROC NEAR  ;local subroutine
    MOV  CX,[BP+6]  ;get X1
    MOV  DX,[BP+4]  ;get Y1
    MOV  AX,[BP+2]  ;get CLR
    MOV  AH,12
    MOV  BH,[BP+8]  ;get page
    INT  10H  ;write pixel
CHECK_UP:
MOV  AX,[BP+4]  ;get Y1
CMP  AX,0  ;is this the top line?
JNE  A13  ;if not, continue search
JMP  CHECK_DOWN  ;else start checking down
A13:
MOV  AX,[BP+6]  ;get X1
MOV  [BP-28],AX  ;save as X2
MOV  AX,[BP+4]  ;get Y1
```

```
DEC  AX   ;set y to pixel above
MOV  [BP-30],AX  ;store as Y2
    MOV  CX,[BP-28]  ;get X2
    MOV  DX,AX  ;put Y2 into DX
    MOV  BH,[BP+8]  ;get page
    MOV  AH,13
    INT  10H  ;check color of pixel above
SUB  AH,AH  ;color is in AL
MOV  CX,[BP]  ;get BOUNDARY
CMP  AX,CX  ;check for boundary
JE A14  ;if yes, set flag to write
JMP  A15  ;else continue
A14:
MOV  BX,0
MOV  [BP-20],BX  ;set up-flag to write
JMP  CHECK_DOWN  ;and check down
A15:
MOV  CX,[BP+2]  ;get CLR
CMP  AX,CX  ;is it the fill color?
JNE  A16  ;if not, attempt a seed store
JMP  CHECK_DOWN  ;else begin check down

A16:
MOV  AX,[BP-20]  ;get up-flag
CMP  AX,1  ;is up-flag in non-write state?
JNE  A17  ;if write state, continue
JMP  CHECK_DOWN  ;else begin check down
A17:
;_____
;
;store seed in FIFO queue
MOV  BX,SP  ;save stack pointer
MOV  SP,[BP-18]  ;activate write pointer
MOV  CX,[BP-28]  ;get X2
MOV  DX,[BP-30]  ;get Y2
PUSH DX   ;store seed y-coordinate
PUSH CX   ;store seed x-coordinate
MOV  [BP-18],SP  ;store new write pointer
MOV  SP,BX  ;restore stack pointer
MOV  AX,[BP-22]  ;get write count
INC  AX   ;increment write count
MOV  [BP-22],AX  ;store new write count
MOV  AX,1
MOV  [BP-20],AX  ;set up-flag to non-write
;_____
;
CHECK_DOWN:
MOV  AX,[BP+4]  ;get Y1
CMP  AX,199  ;is this the bottom line?
JNE  A18  ;if not, continue search
RET  ;else stop search
A18:
MOV  AX,[BP+6]  ;get X1
MOV  [BP-28],AX  ;save as X2
MOV  AX,[BP+4]  ;get Y1
```

```
INC  AX   ;move one pixel down
MOV  [BP-30],AX  ;save as Y2
   MOV  CX,[BP-28]  ;get X2
   MOV  DX,AX  ;put Y2 into DX
   MOV  BH,[BP+8]  ;get page
   MOV  AH,13
   INT  10H  ;check color of pixel below
SUB  AH,AH  ;color is in AL
MOV  CX,[BP]  ;get BOUNDARY
CMP  AX,CX  ;check for boundary
JE   A19  ;if yes, set flag for write
JMP  A20  ;else continue
A19:
MOV  BX,0
MOV  [BP-24],BX  ;set down-flag to write
RET  ;and end the search
A20:
MOV  CX,[BP+2]  ;get CLR
CMP  AX,CX  ;is the pixel already filled?
JNE  A21  ;if not, attempt a seed store
RET  ;else end search
A21:
MOV  AX,[BP-24]  ;get down-flag
CMP  AX,1  ;is down-flag in non-write state?
JNE  A22  ;if flag is write, continue
RET  ;else stop
A22:
;_____
;
;store seed in FIFO queue
MOV  BX,SP  ;save stack pointer
MOV  SP,[BP-18]  ;activate write pointer
MOV  CX,[BP-28]  ;get X2
MOV  DX,[BP-30]  ;get Y2
PUSH DX   ;store seed y-coordinate
PUSH CX   ;store seed x-coordinate
MOV  [BP-18],SP  ;store new write pointer
MOV  SP,BX  ;restore stack pointer
MOV  AX,[BP-22]  ;get write count
INC  AX   ;increment write count
MOV  [BP-22],AX  ;store new write count
MOV  AX,1
MOV  [BP-24],AX  ;set down-flag to non-write
RET
WRITE_PIXEL ENDP  ;end of subroutine
;
;_____
;
;               CLOSING
;_____
;
_TEXT ENDS  ;module ends
END          ;tell MASM to stop compiling
```

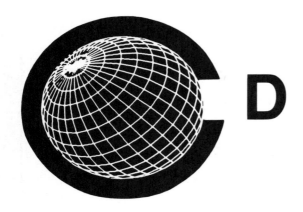
D

Assembly Language Routines for CGA

The assembly language program listing in Fig. D-1 provides CGA graphics capabilities for C compilers which lack built-in graphics routines. The source code, entitled GRFX-CGA.ASM, provides five functions: **__CGACLS**, **__CGADRAW**, **__CGAFILL**, **__CGACOPY**, and **__CGAMODE**.

In order to facilitate animation programming, the subroutines perform their graphics output on a simulated hidden page located at 3C000 hex in user RAM. You can easily modify the subroutines to write directly to the CGA screen buffer. The source code has been seeded with numerous comments to assist any modifications you may wish to make.

__CGAMODE changes the screen mode. To invoke the 320×200 4-color mode from your C program, call the assembly language subroutine with the syntax **CGAMODE(4);**. To return to the 80-column color text mode, call the assembly language subroutine with the syntax **CGAMODE(3);**.

__CGACLS clears the 320×200 4-color screen. Call this subroutine with the syntax **CGACLS( );**. The subroutine blanks the hidden page located at 3C000 hex in user RAM. Change the appropriate line in the source code to B8000 hex if you prefer to clear the CGA screen buffer directly. **__CGADRAW** draws a line from one point to another in the 320×200 4-color mode. The syntax is **CGADRAW(x1,y1,x2,y2,color);**, where **color** is from 0 to 3. The **x1,y1,x2,y2** coordinates must be integers within the screen's legal range. The subroutine draws graphics on a hidden page located at 3C000 hex in user RAM. Change the appropriate line in the source code to B8000 hex if you prefer to draw directly to the CGA screen buffer.

__CGACOPY copies the contents of the hidden graphics page to the CGA screen buffer. Call this subroutine with the syntax **CGACOPY( );**.

__**CGAFILL** can be used to fill complex random polygons with color. The calling syntax is **CGAFILL(x1,y1,color,boundary,page);**, where **color** is the fill color in the range 0 to 3, **boundary** is the polygon's boundary color in the range 0 to 3, and **page** is 0. This subroutine operates directly on the CGA screen buffer at B8000 hex.

In its current form, GRFX-CGA.ASM is designed for C programs which use the compact memory model and near calls. Refer to Appendix B for further discussion of the interface between C and assembly language.

Fig. D-1. Program listing for a set of assembly language graphics drivers, designed to support the 320×200 4-color mode of the CGA. Compatible with Turbo C 1.0 and all other C compilers which use near calls to interface with assembly language modules. VGA/EGA/CGA/MCGA compatible.

```
;_____
;
;        Source code: GRFX-CGA.ASM
;
;_____
;
;
;
;   This module contains assembly language
;   graphics drivers for the 320x200 4-color
;   mode of the CGA and MCGA.  Included are
;   subroutines to set the screen mode,
;   clear the screen, draw a line, fill random
;   areas, and copy graphics pages.
;   The routines are designed to be called
;   from C compilers which employ near calls,
;   such as Borland TURBO C 1.0.  The routines
;   can be easily adapted for C compilers which
;   use far calls, such as QuickC.
;
;   Most routines are set up to write graphics
;   to a hidden page located at address
;   3C000 hex in RAM.  The page copy routine
;   will move the graphics up to the CGA's
;   display buffer at B8000 hex, thereby
;   enabling real-time animation using
;   a written-to, hidden page.  You can, however,
;   easily change the address to make the routines
;   write directly to the display buffer.
;
;Copyright 1988 Lee Adams. All rights reserved.
;
PAGE 50  ;set length of listing file print-out.
;
;_____
;
;                 HEADER
;
;_____
;
_TEXT SEGMENT BYTE PUBLIC 'CODE' ;module begins
ASSUME CS:_TEXT  ;assume CS points to code
PUBLIC _CGAMODE
PUBLIC _CGACOPY
```

```
PUBLIC _CGAFILL    ;   these subroutines can be
PUBLIC _CGACLS     ;   called from other modules.
PUBLIC _CGADRAW
;
;_____
;
;           CHANGE SCREEN MODE
;_____
;
;call with CGAMODE(mode).
;Note: mode 4 is the 320x200 4-color mode.
;      mode 3 is the 80-col. color text mode.
;
_CGAMODE PROC NEAR  ;subroutine begins
PUSH BP   ;save BP
MOV  BP,SP  ;use BP in addressing mode
MOV  AX,[BP+4]  ;get mode number from stack
SUB  AH,AH  ;set AH to BIOS function 0
INT  10H    ;call BIOS routine to set mode
POP  BP     ;restore BP
RET         ;return to caller
_CGAMODE ENDP   ;subroutine ends
;
;_____
;
;           CLS 320x200 4-color mode
;_____
;
;call with CGACLS.
;Expects 320x200 4-color mode to be in effect.
;Blanks the hidden active page at 3C000 hex.
;
_CGACLS PROC NEAR   ;subroutine begins
;
PUSH AX
PUSH CX
PUSH DI
PUSH ES
;
;fill entire screen with color 0
MOV  AX,3C00H    ;page location, use B800H if you prefer
MOV  ES,AX       ;ES=hidden page
MOV  AX,00H      ;color black
MOV  DI,00H      ;offset into buffer
MOV  CX,1024     ;loop counter
START: MOV ES:[DI],AL  ;in-line code is very fast
       INC  DI          ;inc address
       MOV ES:[DI],AL
       INC  DI
       MOV ES:[DI],AL
       INC  DI
       MOV ES:[DI],AL
       INC  DI
       MOV ES:[DI],AL
```

```
        INC  DI
        MOV ES:[DI],AL
        INC  DI
        MOV ES:[DI],AL
        INC  DI
        MOV ES:[DI],AL
        INC  DI
        MOV ES:[DI],AL
        INC  DI
        MOV ES:[DI],AL
        INC  DI
        MOV ES:[DI],AL
        INC  DI
        MOV ES:[DI],AL
        INC  DI
        MOV ES:[DI],AL
        INC  DI
        MOV ES:[DI],AL
        INC  DI
        MOV ES:[DI],AL
        INC  DI
        MOV ES:[DI],AL
        INC  DI
        MOV ES:[DI],AL
        INC  DI
        LOOP START       ;16*1024=16384
JMP   EXIT
;
EXIT: POP  ES
      POP  DI
      POP  CX
      POP  AX   ;restore registers
      RET        ;return to caller
 _CGACLS ENDP    ;subroutine ends
;
;_____
;
;    DRAW LINE in 320x200 4-color mode
;
;_____
;
;call with CGADRAW(x1,y1,x2,y2,color).
;This subroutine draws lines on a hidden page
;located at address 3C000 hex in RAM.  Simply
;change one line of code if you wish to
;draw directly on the CGA's display buffer
;located at B8000 hex.  When you call this
;subroutine, be sure to use hex values for
;the color parameter...   black=00 hex,
;cyan=55 hex, magenta=AA hex, white=FF hex.
;
 _CGADRAW PROC NEAR  ;subroutine begins
PUSH BP
MOV  BP,SP ;use BP in addressing mode
PUSH SI
PUSH DI
PUSH ES
```

```
;
;select location of written-to page
MOV  AX,3C00H  ;page location, set to B800H if you prefer
MOV  ES,AX     ;ES holds segment address
;
;calculate slope of line
MOV  DI,1
MOV  DS,[BP+10]      ;get Y2
MOV  AX,[BP+6]       ;get Y1
SUB  DX,AX
JGE  SAVE_Y
NEG  DI
NEG  DX
SAVE_Y: PUSH DI  ;save DELDY
MOV  CX,[BP+8]     ;get X2
MOV  AX,[BP+4]     ;get X1
MOV  SI,1
SUB  CX,AX
JGE  SAVE_X
NEG  SI
NEG  CX
SAVE_X: PUSH SI  ;save DELDX
        CMP  CX,DX
        JGE  DIAG_SET
        MOV  SI,0
        XCHG CX,DX
        JMP  SAVE_DELSXY
DIAG_SET: MOV  DI,0
SAVE_DELSXY:
   PUSH CX  ;save DELS
   PUSH DX  ;save DELP
   PUSH SI  ;save DELSX
   PUSH DI  ;save DELSY
MOV  AX,[BP-14]    ;get DELP
SAL  AX,1
PUSH AX             ;save DELSE
SUB  AX,CX
MOV  BX,AX
SUB  AX,CX
PUSH AX             ;save DELDE
INC  CX             ;initialize counter
MOV  DX,[BP+4]     ;get X1
MOV  AX,00000011B  ;store masks at BP-24 and offset
PUSH AX
MOV  AX,00001100B
PUSH AX
MOV  AX,00110000B
PUSH AX
MOV  AX,11000000B
PUSH AX
MOV  AX,[BP+6]     ;get Y1
;_____
;
;loop to plot points along line
LINELOOP:
```

```
          CALL DRAW
          CMP  BX,0
          JGE  DIAGONAL
          STRAIGHT:
            ADD DX,[BP-16] ;DELSX
            ADD AX,[BP-18] ;DELSY
            ADD BX,[BP-20] ;DELSE
            LOOP LINELOOP
            JMP  LINEEXIT
          DIAGONAL:
            ADD DX,[BP-10] ;DELDX
            ADD AX,[BP-8]  ;DELDY
            ADD BX,[BP-22] ;DELDE
            LOOP LINELOOP
          LINEEXIT:
            MOV  AX,BP
            MOV  SP,AX
            POP  BP
            RET          ;return to C pgm
          _CGADRAW ENDP      ;subroutine ends
          ;_____
          ;
          DRAW PROC NEAR
            PUSH AX ;save Y coord
            PUSH DX ;save X coord
            PUSH CX ;save loop counter
          SHR  AL,1
          JC   ODD
          MOV  DI,0
          JMP  SHORT COMMON
          ODD: MOV DI,2000H
          COMMON: MOV  CX,80
                  PUSH DX
                      MUL  CX
                      ADD  DI,AX
                  POP  DX
                      MOV  SI,DX
                      SHR  DX,1
                      SHR  DX,1
                      ADD  DI,DX
                      AND  SI,03H
                      SHL  SI,1 ;make 0 to 6 range
                      MOV  AX,[BP-24+SI] ;mask
                      MOV  DH,[BP+12]    ;get color (hex)
                      AND  DH,AL
                      NOT  AL
                      MOV  AH,ES:[DI]
                      AND  AH,AL
                      OR   AH,DH
                      MOV  ES:[DI],AH
          POP  CX   ;restore loop counter
          POP  DX   ;restore X coord
          POP  AX   ;restore Y coord
          RET       ;return to caller
```

```
DRAW ENDP
;
;_____
;
;        COPY 320x200 4-color screen
;_____
;
;call with CGACOPY.
;    This subroutine copies a hidden page
;    located at address 3C000 hex to the
;    CGA's display buffer at address B8000 hex.
;    You can alter the addresses of the source
;    page and target page if you wish.
;    This subroutine works equally well for
;    the 640x200 2-color mode.
;
 _CGACOPY PROC NEAR   ;subroutine begins
PUSH CX
PUSH DS
PUSH ES
PUSH SI
PUSH DI
PUSHF
MOV CX,03C00H ;source address, alter if you prefer.
MOV DS,CX ;load DS with page 0 address
MOV CX,0B800H ;target address, alter if you prefer.
MOV ES,CX ;load ES with page 1 address
CLD ;set flag to incremental count
MOV SI,0 ;load SI with offset 0
MOV DI,0 ;load DI with offset 0
MOV CX,16384 ;count 16384
REP MOVSB ;transfer 16384 bytes of data
POPF
POP DI
POP SI
POP ES
POP DS
POP CX
RET          ;return to C program
_CGACOPY ENDP   ;subroutine ends
;
;_____
;
;              AREA FILL ROUTINE
;_____
;
;call with  CGAFILL(X1,Y1,color,boundary,page).
;Expects 320x200 4-color mode to be in effect.
;This subroutine writes to the CGA's display
;buffer at B8000 hex.  It fills a random polygon
;which can include islands, peninsulas, etc.
;Note: set the page parameter to zero when
;using the CGA's 320x200 4-color mode.
;
```

```
_CGAFILL PROC NEAR   ;subroutine begins
;_____
;
;MAIN ROUTINE
;_____
;
CLI
PUSH AX
PUSH BP
PUSH ES
MOV   AX,SS
MOV   ES,AX  ;save SS in ES
MOV   BP,SP  ;save SP in BP
MOV   AX,9C00H ;new stack segment address
MOV   SS,AX  ;new stack segment at 9C00 hex
MOV   AX,14BEH  ;bottom of new stack
MOV   SP,AX  ;new stack now active
PUSH ES  ;save C's SS
PUSH BP  ;save C's SP
;_____
;
;transfer passed parameters to new stack
MOV   AX,ES:[BP+16]
PUSH AX   ;store page on subroutine stack
MOV   AX,ES:[BP+8]
PUSH AX   ;store X1 on subroutine stack
MOV   AX,ES:[BP+10]
PUSH AX   ;store Y1 on subroutine stack
MOV   AX,ES:[BP+12]
PUSH AX   ;store color on subroutine stack
MOV   AX,ES:[BP+14]
PUSH AX   ;store boundary on subroutine stack
MOV   BP,SP  ;use BP as offset pointer
;_____
;
;save all registers on new stack
PUSH DS
PUSH BX
PUSH CX
PUSH DX
PUSH SI
PUSH DI
PUSHF
;_____
;
;store local variables on new stack
MOV   AX,13BAH
PUSH AX   ;store read pointer
MOV   AX,13BEH
PUSH AX   ;store write pointer
MOV   AX,0  ;dummy value
PUSH AX   ;up-flag
PUSH AX   ;write count
PUSH AX   ;down-flag
```

```
PUSH AX   ;read count
PUSH AX   ;above/below pixel x-coordinate
PUSH AX   ;above/below pixel y-coordinate
PUSH AX   ;temporary storage of X1
PUSH AX   ;temporary storage of Y1
;_____
;
;RANGE CHECKING
;_____
;
;ensure legal range of X1,Y1 seed point
MOV  AX,[BP+6]  ;get X1
CMP  AX,0
JAE  A1
JMP  ALL_DONE   ;if X1<0 then abort
A1:
CMP  AX,319
JBE  A2
JMP  ALL_DONE   ;if X1>319 then abort
A2:
MOV  AX,[BP+4]  ;get Y1
CMP  AX,0
JAE  A3
JMP  ALL_DONE   ;if Y1<0 then abort
A3:
CMP  AX,199
JBE  A4
JMP  ALL_DONE   ;if Y1>199 then abort
A4:
;_____
;
;FILL ROUTINE
;_____
;
;start filling the polygon
CALL FILL_LINE  ;fill first scan line
MOV  AX,[BP-22]  ;get write count flag
CMP  AX,0   ;check if a seed was stored
JNE  FILL_LOOP  ;if write count set, continue
JMP  ALL_DONE   ;if no seeds stored, exit
;_____
;
FILL_LOOP:
;retrieve seed from FIFO queue
MOV  BX,SP   ;save stack pointer
MOV  SP,[BP-16]  ;activate read pointer
POP  CX   ;get seed x-coordinate
POP  DX   ;get seed y-coordinate
MOV  AX,SP   ;save read pointer
MOV  SP,BX   ;restore stack pointer
DEC  AX
DEC  AX
DEC  AX
DEC  AX
```

```
        DEC   AX
        DEC   AX
        DEC   AX
        DEC   AX   ;adjust read pointer
        MOV   [BP-16],AX  ;store new read pointer
        MOV   [BP+6],CX   ;store new X1
        MOV   [BP+4],DX   ;store new Y1
        MOV   AX,[BP-26]  ;get read count
        INC   AX   ;increment read count
        MOV   [BP-26],AX  ;store new read count
        ;_____
        ;
        CALL FILL_LINE   ;fill a scan line
        MOV   AX,[BP-22]  ;get write count
        MOV   CX,[BP-26]  ;get read count
        CMP   AX,CX  ;does read count = write count?
        JNE   A5   ;if not, continue fill
        JMP   ALL_DONE   ;otherwise, exit
        A5:
        JMP   FILL_LOOP   ;loop back
        ;_____
        ;
        ;EXIT ROUTINE
        ;
        ;_____
        ;
        ALL_DONE:
        MOV   AX,14A2H
        MOV   SP,AX   ;reposition stack pointer
        POPF
        POP   DI
        POP   SI
        POP   DX
        POP   CX
        POP   BX
        POP   DS
        MOV   AX,[BP+10]  ;get C's SP
        MOV   SP,AX
        MOV   AX,[BP+12]  ;get C's SS
        MOV   SS,AX   ;C's stack is restored
        POP   ES
        POP   BP
        POP   AX
        STI
        RET        ;return to caller
        _CGAFILL ENDP   ;subroutine ends
        ;_____
        ;
        ;fill one scan line
        ;
        ;_____
        ;
        ;subroutine to fill one scan line, check
        ;adjacent pixels, store seed coordinates
        PUBLIC FILL_LINE
        FILL_LINE PROC NEAR   ;local subroutine
```

```
        MOV   CX,[BP+6]  ;get X1
        MOV   DX,[BP+4]  ;get Y1
        MOV   BH,[BP+8]  ;get page
        MOV   AH,13
        INT   10H  ;read current pixel
SUB  AH,AH  ;color is in AL
MOV  CX,[BP+2]  ;get CLR
CMP  AX,CX  ;is seed point already filled?
JNE  A6  ;if not, continue fill
RET  ;else abort this scan line
A6:
MOV  CX,[BP]  ;get BOUNDARY
CMP  AX,CX  ;check for boundary
JNE  A7  ;if not, continue fill
RET  ;else abort this scan line
A7:
MOV  AX,0
MOV  [BP-20],AX  ;set up-flag to write
MOV  [BP-24],AX  ;set down-flag to write
MOV  AX,[BP+6]  ;get X1
MOV  [BP-32],AX  ;save as X3
MOV  BX,[BP+4]  ;get Y1
MOV  [BP-34],BX  ;save as Y3
;_____
;
;fill towards right
RIGHT_LOOP:
CALL WRITE_PIXEL  ;set one pixel
MOV  AX,[BP+6]  ;get X1
INC  AX  ;move one pixel towards right
MOV [BP+6],AX  ;store new X1
CMP  AX,320  ;is X1 > 319?
JNE  A8  ;if not, continue fill
JMP  GO_LEFT  ;else start to fill left
A8:
        MOV   CX,AX  ;put X1 into CX
        MOV   DX,[BP+4]  ;get Y1
        MOV   BH,[BP+8]  ;get page
        MOV   AH,13
        INT   10H  ;check color of pixel
SUB  AH,AH  ;color is in AL
MOV  CX,[BP]  ;get boundary
CMP  AX,CX  ;check for boundary
JNE  A9  ;if not, continue fill
JMP  GO_LEFT  ;else start to fill left
A9:
JMP  RIGHT_LOOP  ;keep filling right
;_____
;
;fill towards left
GO_LEFT:
MOV  AX,[BP-32]  ;retrieve active x-seed
MOV  [BP+6],AX  ;store as X1
MOV  AX,[BP-34]  ;retrieve active y-seed
```

```
MOV  [BP+4],AX  ;store as Y1
JMP  A10  ;this pixel already set
LEFT_LOOP:
CALL WRITE_PIXEL  ;set one pixel
A10:
MOV  AX,[BP+6]  ;get X1
DEC  AX  ;move one pixel towards left
MOV  [BP+6],AX  ;store new X1
CMP  AX,-1  ;IS X1 < 0?
JNE  A11  ;if not, continue fill
RET  ;else stop filling this scan line
A11:
    MOV  CX,AX  ;put X1 into CX
    MOV  DX,[BP+4]  ;get Y1
    MOV  BH,[BP+8]  ;get page
    MOV  AH,13
    INT  10H  ;check color of pixel
SUB  AH,AH  ;color is in AL
MOV  CX,[BP]  ;get boundary
CMP  AX,CX  ;check for boundary
JNE  A12  ;if not, continue fill
RET  ;else stop filling this scan line
A12:
JMP  LEFT_LOOP  ;keep filling left
FILL_LINE ENDP  ;end of subroutine
;_____
;
;set one pixel
;
;_____
;
PUBLIC WRITE_PIXEL
WRITE_PIXEL PROC NEAR  ;local subroutine
    MOV  CX,[BP+6]  ;get X1

    MOV  DX,[BP+4]  ;get Y1
    MOV  AX,[BP+2]  ;get CLR
    MOV  AH,12
    MOV  BH,[BP+8]  ;get page
    INT  10H  ;write pixel
CHECK_UP:
MOV  AX,[BP+4]  ;get Y1
CMP  AX,0  ;is this the top line?
JNE  A13  ;if not, continue search
JMP  CHECK_DOWN  ;else start checking down
A13:
MOV  AX,[BP+6]  ;get X1
MOV  [BP-28],AX  ;save as X2
MOV  AX,[BP+4]  ;get Y1
DEC  AX  ;set y to pixel above
MOV  [BP-30],AX  ;store as Y2
    MOV  CX,[BP-28]  ;get X2
    MOV  DX,AX  ;put Y2 into DX
    MOV  BH,[BP+8]  ;get page
    MOV  AH,13
    INT  10H  ;check color of pixel above
```

```
SUB  AH,AH  ;color is in AL
MOV  CX,[BP]  ;get BOUNDARY
CMP  AX,CX  ;check for boundary
JE   A14  ;if yes, set flag to write
JMP  A15  ;else continue
A14:
MOV  BX,0
MOV  [BP-20],BX  ;set up-flag to write
JMP  CHECK_DOWN  ;and check down
A15:
MOV  CX,[BP+2]  ;get CLR
CMP  AX,CX  ;is it the fill color?
JNE  A16  ;if not, attempt a seed store
JMP  CHECK_DOWN  ;else begin check down
A16:
MOV  AX,[BP-20]  ;get up-flag
CMP  AX,1  ;is up-flag in non-write state?
JNE  A17  ;if write state, continue
JMP  CHECK_DOWN  ;else begin check down
A17:
;_____
;
;store seed in FIFO queue
MOV  BX,SP  ;save stack pointer
MOV  SP,[BP-18]  ;activate write pointer
MOV  CX,[BP-28]  ;get X2
MOV  DX,[BP-30]  ;get Y2
PUSH DX  ;store seed y-coordinate
PUSH CX  ;store seed x-coordinate
MOV  [BP-18],SP  ;store new write pointer
MOV  SP,BX  ;restore stack pointer
MOV  AX,[BP-22]  ;get write count
INC  AX  ;increment write count
MOV  [BP-22],AX  ;store new write count
MOV  AX,1
MOV  [BP-20],AX  ;set up-flag to non-write
;_____
;
CHECK_DOWN:
MOV  AX,[BP+4]  ;get Y1
CMP  AX,199  ;is this the bottom line?
JNE  A18  ;if not, continue search
RET  ;else stop search
A18:
MOV  AX,[BP+6]  ;get X1
MOV  [BP-28],AX  ;save as X2
MOV  AX,[BP+4]  ;get Y1
INC  AX  ;move one pixel down
MOV  [BP-30],AX  ;save as Y2
    MOV  CX,[BP-28]  ;get X2
    MOV  DX,AX  ;put Y2 into DX
    MOV  BH,[BP+8]  ;get page
    MOV  AH,13
    INT  10H  ;check color of pixel below
```

```
SUB  AH,AH  ;color is in AL
MOV  CX,[BP]  ;get BOUNDARY
CMP  AX,CX  ;check for boundary
JE   A19  ;if yes, set flag for write
JMP  A20  ;else continue
A19:
MOV  BX,0
MOV  [BP-24],BX  ;set down-flag to write
RET  ;and end the search
A20:
MOV  CX,[BP+2]  ;get CLR
CMP  AX,CX  ;is the pixel already filled?
JNE  A21  ;if not, attempt a seed store
RET  ;else end search
A21:
MOV  AX,[BP-24]  ;get down-flag
CMP  AX,1  ;is down-flag in non-write state?
JNE  A22  ;if flag is write, continue
RET  ;else stop
A22:
;_____
;
;store seed in FIFO queue
MOV  BX,SP  ;save stack pointer
MOV  SP,[BP-18]  ;activate write pointer
MOV  CX,[BP-28]  ;get X2
MOV  DX,[BP-30]  ;get Y2
PUSH DX  ;store seed y-coordinate
PUSH CX  ;store seed x-coordinate
MOV  [BP-18],SP  ;store new write pointer
MOV  SP,BX  ;restore stack pointer
MOV  AX,[BP-22]  ;get write count
INC  AX  ;increment write count
MOV  [BP-22],AX  ;store new write count
MOV  AX,1
MOV  [BP-24],AX  ;set down-flag to non-write
RET
WRITE_PIXEL ENDP  ;end of subroutine
;
;_____
;
;                  CLOSING
;
;_____
;
_TEXT ENDS  ;module ends
END           ;tell MASM to stop compiling
```

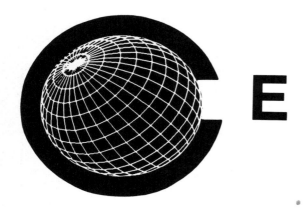

E

Demonstration Programs for Turbo C

This appendix contains 17 program listings for use in the integrated programming environment of Borland Turbo C. The programs in Figs. E-1 through E-13 have been adapted from demonstration programs in the main body of the book. The listings in Figs. E-14 through E-17 have been adapted from the utility programs in Appendix A.

These program listings are ready to compile and run with Borland Turbo C version 1.5 and newer using the medium memory model. (If you are using Turbo C 1.0, refer to Appendix B.)

THE PROJECT FILE

Because the programs use the built-in graphics routines of Turbo C's graphics library, GRAPHICS.LIB, you must create a PRJ project file for each program. If you wished to run TC-011.C, for example, you would first create a project file named TC-011.PRJ. The project file merely contains the names of the files to be used by the compiler during creation of the EXE run-time file. In this case, the PRJ file would consist of the names of the required files: TC-011.C and GRAPHICS.LIB. After the PRJ file has been created, simply load TC-011.C from disk and run it. Refer to Chapter 7 for further guidance on setting up and using the Turbo C integrated programming environment.

HOW THE PROGRAMS WERE ADAPTED

Despite claims by both Turbo C and QuickC concerning the spirit of ANSI compatibility, differences between process control instructions made it necessary to perform the following modifications during adaptation of the programs for Turbo C.

1. If the program employed the **exit(0)** function, then the **#include < process.h >** directive was used instead of the **#include < stdlib.h >** directive used by QuickC.

2. If keyboard polling was required, then the **bioskey( )** function was used instead of the **__bios__keybrd( )** function used by QuickC. If the program wanted to determine if a keystroke was waiting in the keyboard buffer, then **bioskey(1)** was used instead of the **__bios__keybrd(__KEYBRD__READY)** function required by QuickC. If the program needed to fetch a keystroke from the keyboard buffer, then the function **bioskey(0)** was used instead of the **__bios__keybrd(__KEYBRD__READ)** function used by QuickC.

3. If the program manipulated hardware ports, the functions **outportb( )** and **inportb( )** were substituted for the QuickC functions **outp( )** and **inp( )**. In addition, the directive **#include < dos.h >** was used instead of the directive **#include < bios.h >** used by QuickC.

4. If the **movedata( )** function was used by the program, then the directive **#include < mem.h >** was used instead of QuickC's directive **#include < memory.h >**.

5. If graphic arrays were used by the program, then the directive **#include < malloc.h >** was used instead of QuickC's directive **#include < alloc.h >**, and the **farmalloc( )** function was used instead of QuickC's **__fmalloc( )** function.

By simply reversing this methodology you could easily adapt your original Turbo C programs to run under QuickC, of course. Refer to Chapter 4 for further discussion of process control differences between Turbo C and QuickC.

GRAPHICS SYNTAX

The graphics syntax used by Turbo C and QuickC is noteworthy more for its differences than its similarities. Of the 25 graphics instructions used throughout this book, 11 were completely different syntactically. For example, while Turbo C uses the **cleardevice( )** function to clear the screen, QuickC uses the **__clearscreen(__GCLEARSCREEN)** function.

Of the remaining 14 graphics instructions, trivial differences make adaptation an exercises fraught with pitfalls. For example, Turbo C uses the **setcolor** instruction to define the active color, while QuickC uses **__setcolor** to perform the same function. As the saying goes, so close yet so far. Refer to Chapter 5 for a detailed discussion of the syntax differences between Turbo C and QuickC as they relate to graphics instructions.

NOTES ON THE PROGRAM LISTINGS

The program in Fig. E-1, Hues and Halftones, performs essentially the same in both Turbo C and QuickC versions.

The airbrushed effect in Fig. E-2, however, is markedly different between the Turbo C and QuickC versions. Because Turbo C uses an overwrite algorithm to lay fill patterns onto the screen, any previously-existing screen color is obliterated. The Turbo C version of the program displays an airbrushed effect ranging from black to dark blue. Because QuickC only sets pixels as required, the existing background is preserved. The airbrushed effect in the QuickC version ranges from light blue to dark blue.

The program in Fig. E-3, Sculptured Background Effect, produces the same graphics in both Turbo C and QuickC versions.

The listing in Fig. E-4, Airbrushed Background Effect, displays an airbrushed background which ranges from black to dark blue in the Turbo C version, and which ranges from light blue to dark blue in the QuickC version. Turbo C overwrites previously-existing graphics. QuickC is able to mix the new fill pattern with previously-existing graphics.

How To Generate A 3D Image, shown in Fig. E-5, performs the same in both Turbo C and QuickC versions.

The program in Fig. E-6, Business Chart In 2D, iterates the airbrush differences between Turbo C and QuickC. In addition, Turbo C's use of graphics coordinates to position text output made adaptation a bit tricky, although the graphics coordinate approach makes text output much more versatile. QuickC uses alpha coordinates for text output.

The listing in Fig. E-7, Animated Business Chart, generates similar animation and graphics in both the Turbo C version and the QuickC version.

The animated hummingbird shown in Fig. E-8 animates similarly in both Turbo C and QuickC versions, but Turbo C's **floodfill( )** function was unable to paint the hummingbird's torso. The Turbo C version uses an outline drawing of the hummingbird; the QuickC version uses a solid drawing.

The program in Fig. E-9, Animated Rotation of 3D Model, generates identical animation and graphics in both the Turbo C and QuickC versions.

The walking figure of Fig. E-10 runs the same in both Turbo C and QuickC versions if the 320×200 4-color mode is used. Although the QuickC version of the program permits the user to use the 320×200 16-color mode if desired, Turbo C provides no support for the 320×200 16-color mode.

The listing in Fig. E-11, Animated Clock Face Simulation, produces the same animation in both Turbo C and QuickC versions. The **circle( )** function of Turbo C produced an ellipse of a slightly different aspect ratio than the ellipse generated by QuickC's **_ellipse( )** function.

The arcade-style animation program in Fig. E-12 produces similar output in both Turbo C and QuickC versions.

The flight simulation prototype listed in Fig. E-13 generates identical animation and graphics in both Turbo C and QuickC versions.

The configuration module, shown in Fig. E-14, is substantively different from the algorithm employed by QuickC, although the end result is the same: the ability of your C program to modify itself at run-time to execute on any IBM-compatible graphics adapter. Refer to Chapter 7 for a detailed discussion of this important algorithm. The Turbo C functions are better at determining which graphics adapter is present, while the QuickC functions are better at determining which graphics adapters are missing.

How To Produce Sounds, listed in Fig. E-15, performs identically in both Turbo C and QuickC versions. Note that Turbo C contains a built-in sound routine called, appropriately enough, **sound( )**.

The frame animation utility program in Fig. E-16, performs similarly in both Turbo C and QuickC versions.

The bitblt animation utility program in Fig. E-17 generates similar output in both Turbo C and QuickC versions.

SPURIOUS ERROR MESSAGES

Some of the demonstration programs use a **GOTO** instruction to force the graphics adapter into a particular mode, rather than allowing the configuration module to invoke the highest mode available on the installed hardware. In this instance Turbo C always issues an UNREACHABLE CODE warning during compilation. Under these circumstances the warning message can be safely ignored.

A few demonstration programs use a **GOTO** instruction in the animation loop because it executes quicker than a **for** . . . **next** loop. Again, the unreachable code warning issued by Turbo C can be safely ignored during compilation.

Some of the demonstration programs use a line-clipping subroutine which, although complex and convoluted, has been rigorously tested, debugged, and found to perform without flaw in IBM BASICA, GW-BASIC, QuickBASIC, Turbo BASIC, and QuickC. However, Turbo C issues an UNREACHABLE CODE warning during compilation.

Fig. E-1. Hues and halftones—Turbo C version, VGA/EGA/CGA/MCGA compatible. Refer to the main body of the book for discussion.

```
/*_____


tc-002.c

Function:  This program displays the versatile range of
colors available on VGA, EGA, and CGA graphics adapters.

Compatibility:  Supports all graphics adapters and monitors.
The software uses the 640x480 16-color mode if a VGA is
present, the 640x350 16-color mode if an EGA and enhanced
monitor are present, the 640x200 16-color mode if an EGA and
standard monitor are present, and the 320x200 4-color mode
if a CGA or MCGA is present.

Copyright 1988 Lee Adams and TAB BOOKS Inc.


_____


INCLUDE   FILES                                      */

#include <dos.h>                    /* supports the BIOS call */
#include <stdio.h>                /* supports the printf function */
#include <graphics.h>          /* supports the graphics functions */
#include <process.h>              /* supports the exit function */


/*_____


DECLARATIONS                                         */

char fill_3[ ]={0,32,0,0,0,2,0,0};            /*    3% fill */
char fill_6[ ]={32,0,2,0,128,0,8,0};          /* 6.25% fill */
char fill_12[ ]={32,2,128,8,32,2,128,8};      /* 12.5% fill */
char fill_25[ ]={68,17,68,17,68,17,68,17};    /*   25% fill */
```

```
char fill_37[ ]={146,41,148,73,164,73,146,73};      /* 37.5% fill */
char fill_50[ ]={85,170,85,170,85,170,85,170};      /*   50% fill */
char fill_62[ ]={109,214,107,182,91,182,109,182};   /* 62.5% fill */
char fill_75[ ]={187,238,187,238,187,238,187,238};  /*   75% fill */
char fill_87[ ]={223,253,127,247,223,253,127,247};  /* 87.5% fill */

/*                                      declare global subroutines */
void keyboard(void);void quit_pgm(void);void halftone_swatch(void);
void notice(float x,float y);void graphics_setup(void);

/*                                       declare global variables */
float x,y,h,v,xl,vl;float sxl,syl,sx2,sy2;
int C0=0,Cl=1,C2=2,C3=3,C4=4,C5=5,C6=6,C7=7,C8=8,C9=9,C10=10,
    Cll=11,Cl2=12,Cl3=13,Cl4=14,Cl5=15,CLR,mode_flag=0;
float x_res,y_res;

/*_____


M A I N    R O U T I N E                                      */

main(){
graphics_setup();                       /* establish graphics mode */

CLR=C8;halftone_swatch();
x=xl;y=y+vl;CLR=C7;halftone_swatch();
x=xl;y=y+vl;CLR=Cl5;halftone_swatch();
x=xl;y=y+vl;CLR=Cl;halftone_swatch();
x=xl;y=y+vl;CLR=C9;halftone_swatch();
x=xl;y=y+vl;CLR=C6;halftone_swatch();
x=xl;y=y+vl;CLR=Cl4;halftone_swatch();
x=xl;y=y+vl;CLR=C4;halftone_swatch();
x=xl;y=y+vl;CLR=Cl2;halftone_swatch();
x=xl;y=y+vl;CLR=C5;halftone_swatch();
x=xl;y=y+vl;CLR=Cl3;halftone_swatch();
x=xl;y=y+vl;CLR=C3;halftone_swatch();
x=xl;y=y+vl;CLR=Cll;halftone_swatch();
x=xl;y=y+vl;CLR=C2;halftone_swatch();
x=xl;y=y+vl;CLR=Cl0;halftone_swatch();
setcolor(C7);rectangle(sxl,syl,sx2,sy2);

notice(sxl+1,sy2+2);                                    /* notice */

keyboard();                      /* wait for user to press <Esc> */
quit_pgm();                       /* end the program gracefully */
}
/*_____


SUBROUTINE: DRAW HALFTONE SWATCHES                              */

void halftone_swatch(void){
```

```
setfillpattern(fill_3,CLR);bar(x,y,x+h,y+v);
x=x+h;setfillpattern(fill_6,CLR);bar(x,y,x+h,y+v);
x=x+h;setfillpattern(fill_12,CLR);bar(x,y,x+h,y+v);
x=x+h;setfillpattern(fill_25,CLR);bar(x,y,x+h,y+v);
x=x+h;setfillpattern(fill_37,CLR);bar(x,y,x+h,y+v);
x=x+h;setfillpattern(fill_50,CLR);bar(x,y,x+h,y+v);
x=x+h;setfillpattern(fill_62,CLR);bar(x,y,x+h,y+v);
x=x+h;setfillpattern(fill_75,CLR);bar(x,y,x+h,y+v);
x=x+h;setfillpattern(fill_87,CLR);bar(x,y,x+h,y+v);
x=x+h;setfillstyle(SOLID_FILL,CLR);bar(x,y,x+h,y+v);
return;}

/*_____


SUBROUTINE: CHECK THE KEYBOARD BUFFER                          */

void keyboard(void){
union u_type {int a;char b[3];} keystroke;
int get_keystroke(void);            /* declare a local subroutine */

do keystroke.a=get_keystroke();
while (keystroke.b[0]!=27);          /* return if <Esc> is pressed */
}

/* LOCAL SUBROUTINE: RETRIEVE ONE KEYSTROKE                     */

int get_keystroke(void){
union REGS regs;regs.h.ah=0;return int86(0x16,&regs,&regs);}

/*_____


SUBROUTINE: GRACEFUL EXIT FROM THE PROGRAM                     */

void quit_pgm(void){
cleardevice();restorecrtmode();exit(0);}


/*_____


SUBROUTINE: VGA/EGA/CGA/MCGA compatibility module
```

This subroutine invokes the highest-resolution graphics mode
which is permitted by the hardware. The 640x480 16-color mode
is established if a VGA is present. The 640x350 16-color mode
is established if an EGA is being used with an enhanced color
display monitor or a multiscanning monitor. The 640x200
16-color mode is established if an EGA is being used with a
standard color monitor. The 320x200 4-color mode is invoked
if a CGA or MCGA is present.   */

```
void graphics_setup(void){
int graphics_adapter,graphics_mode;
detectgraph(&graphics_adapter,&graphics_mode);
if (graphics_adapter==VGA) goto VGA_mode;              /* if VGA */
if (graphics_mode==EGAHI) goto EGA_ECD_mode;    /* if EGA and ECD */
if (graphics_mode==EGALO) goto EGA_SCD_mode;    /* if EGA and SCD */
if (graphics_adapter==CGA) goto CGA_mode;             /* if CGA */
if (graphics_adapter==MCGA) goto MCGA_mode;          /* if MCGA */
goto abort_message;              /* if no VGA, EGA, CGA, or MCGA */

VGA_mode:                        /* establish 640x480 16-color mode */
graphics_adapter=VGA;graphics_mode=VGAHI;
initgraph(&graphics_adapter,&graphics_mode,"");
x_res=640;y_res=480;mode_flag=1;x=19;y=39;h=60;v=24;x1=19;
v1=25;sx1=18;sy1=38;sx2=620;sy2=414;
setcolor(C7);outtextxy(216,472,"640x480 16-color VGA mode");
outtextxy(128,0,"U S I N G    C    T O    D I S P L A Y    H U E S");
return;

EGA_ECD_mode:                    /* establish 640x350 16-color mode */
graphics_adapter=EGA;graphics_mode=EGAHI;
initgraph(&graphics_adapter,&graphics_mode,"");
x_res=640;y_res=350;mode_flag=2;x=19;y=28;h=60;v=18;x1=19;
v1=19;sx1=18;sy1=27;sx2=620;sy2=313;
setcolor(C7);outtextxy(216,342,"640x350 16-color EGA mode");
outtextxy(128,0,"U S I N G    C    T O    D I S P L A Y    H U E S");
return;

EGA_SCD_mode:                    /* establish 640x200 16-color mode */
graphics_adapter=EGA;graphics_mode=EGALO;
initgraph(&graphics_adapter,&graphics_mode,"");
x_res=640;y_res=200;C0=0;mode_flag=3;x=19;y=16;h=60;v=10;x1=19;
v1=11;sx1=18;sy1=15;sx2=620;sy2=181;
setcolor(C7);outtextxy(216,192,"640x200 16-color EGA mode");
outtextxy(128,0,"U S I N G    C    T O    D I S P L A Y    H U E S");
return;

CGA_mode:                        /* establish 320x200 4-color mode */
graphics_adapter=CGA;graphics_mode=CGAC3;
initgraph(&graphics_adapter,&graphics_mode,"");
x_res=320;y_res=200;C0=0;C1=3;C2=1;C3=2;C4=1;C5=3;C6=2;C7=1;
C8=3;C9=1;C10=2;C11=3;C12=2;C13=1;C14=3;C15=2;
mode_flag=4;x=10;y=16;h=30;v=10;x1=10;
v1=11;sx1=9;sy1=15;sx2=310;sy2=181;
setcolor(C7);outtextxy(64,342,"320x200 4-color CGA mode");
outtextxy(64,0,"USING C TO DISPLAY HUES");
return;

MCGA_mode:                       /* establish 320x200 4-color mode */
graphics_adapter=MCGA;graphics_mode=MCGAC3;
initgraph(&graphics_adapter,&graphics_mode,"");
```

```
x_res=320;y_res=200;C0=0;Cl=3;C2=1;C3=2;C4=1;C5=3;C6=2;C7=1;
C8=3;C9=1;C10=2;C11=3;C12=2;C13=1;C14=3;C15=2;
mode_flag=4;x=10;y=16;h=30;v=10;xl=10;
vl=11;sxl=9;syl=15;sx2=310;sy2=181;
setcolor(C7);outtextxy(64,342,"320x200 4-color MCGA mode");
return;


abort_message:
printf("\n\nUnable to proceed.\n");
printf("Requires VGA, EGA, MCGA, or CGA adapter\n");
printf("    with appropriate monitor.\n");
printf("Please refer to the book.\n\n");
exit(0);
}
```

```
/*_____



SUBROUTINE: Copyright Notice

This subroutine displays the standard copyright notice.
If you are typing in this program from the book you can
safely omit this subroutine, provided that you also remove
the instruction "notice()" from the main routine.                    */


int copyright[][3]={0x7c00,0x0000,0x0000,0x8231,
0x819c,0x645e,0xba4a,0x4252,0x96d0,0xa231,0x8252,0x955e,0xba4a,
0x43d2,0xf442,0x8231,0x825c,0x945e,0x7c00,0x0000,0x0000};


void notice(float x, float y){
int a,b,c; int tl=0;
for (tl=0;tl<=6;tl++){a=copyright[tl][0];b=copyright[tl][1];
c=copyright[tl][2];
setlinestyle(USERBIT_LINE,a,NORM_WIDTH);
moveto(x,y);lineto(x+15,y);
setlinestyle(USERBIT_LINE,b,NORM_WIDTH);
moveto(x+16,y);lineto(x+31,y);
setlinestyle(USERBIT_LINE,c,NORM_WIDTH);
moveto(x+32,y);lineto(x+47,y);y=y+1;};
setlinestyle(USERBIT_LINE,0xFFFF,NORM_WIDTH);
return;}


/*_____


End of source code                                    */
```

Fig. E-2. Illustrating with dynamic coordinates—Turbo C version, VGA/EGA/CGA/MCGA compatible. Refer to the main body of the book for discussion.

```
/*_____

tc-003.c

Function:  This program demonstrates how to draw on the
screen using dynamic coordinates.

Compatibility:  Supports all graphics adapters and monitors.
The software uses the 640x480 16-color mode if a VGA is
present, the 640x350 16-color mode if an EGA and enhanced
monitor are present, the 640x200 16-color mode if an EGA and
standard monitor are present, and the 320x200 4-color mode
if a CGA or MCGA is present.

Remarks:  Refer to the book for guidance in preparing a
template and for instruction in design techniques.

Copyright 1988 Lee Adams and TAB BOOKS Inc.

        _____


I N C L U D E    F I L E S                              */

#include <dos.h>                     /* supports the BIOS call */
#include <stdio.h>                /* supports the printf function */
#include <graphics.h>          /* supports the graphics functions */
#include <process.h>              /* supports the exit function */

/*_____


D E C L A R A T I O N S                                 */

char fill_3[ ]={0,32,0,0,0,2,0,0};                 /*     3% fill */
char fill_6[ ]={32,0,2,0,128,0,8,0};               /* 6.25% fill */
char fill_12[ ]={32,2,128,8,32,2,128,8};           /* 12.5% fill */
char fill_25[ ]={68,17,68,17,68,17,68,17};         /*    25% fill */
char fill_37[ ]={146,41,148,73,164,73,146,73};     /* 37.5% fill */
char fill_50[ ]={85,170,85,170,85,170,85,170};     /*    50% fill */
char fill_62[ ]={109,214,107,182,91,182,109,182};  /* 62.5% fill */
char fill_75[ ]={187,238,187,238,187,238,187,238}; /*    75% fill */
char fill_87[ ]={223,253,127,247,223,253,127,247}; /* 87.5% fill */

void keyboard(void);void quit_pgm(void);    /* global subroutines */
void notice(float x, float y);
void graphics_setup(void);void coords(void);

float sx=0,sy=0;                     /* screen display coordinates */
float x_res=0,y_res=0;                   /* dimensions of screen */
int C0=0,Cl=1,C2=2,C3=3,C4=4,C5=5,C6=6,C7=7,C8=8,C9=9,Cl0=10,
```

```
Cll=11,Cl2=12,Cl3=13,Cl4=14,Cl5=15,mode_flag=0;
float sxl=0,syl=0,sx2=0,sy2=0;

/*_____


MAIN    ROUTINE                                              */

main(){
graphics_setup();                          /* establish graphics mode */

setfillpattern(fill_25,C7);
sx=0;sy=24;coords();sxl=sx;syl=sy;
sx=639;sy=454;coords();sx2=sx;sy2=sy;
bar(sxl,syl,sx2,sy2);                          /* draw background */
setfillstyle(SOLID_FILL,C0);
sx=200;sy=108;coords();sxl=sx;syl=sy;
sx=500;sy=420;coords();sx2=sx;sy2=sy;
bar(sxl,syl,sx2,sy2);                            /* dropshadow */
setfillstyle(SOLID_FILL,C9);
sx=170;sy=72;coords();sxl=sx;syl=sy;
sx=470;sy=384;coords();sx2=sx;sy2=sy;
bar(sxl,syl,sx2,sy2);                        /* the block graphic */

/*                         add halftoning to the block graphic */
sx=170;sy=72;coords();sxl=sx;syl=sy;
sx=470;sy=98;coords();sx2=sx;sy2=sy;
setfillpattern(fill_6,Cl);bar(sxl,syl,sx2,sy2);
sx=170;sy=98;coords();sxl=sx;syl=sy;
sx=470;sy=132;coords();sx2=sx;sy2=sy;
setfillpattern(fill_12,Cl);bar(sxl,syl,sx2,sy2);
sx=170;sy=132;coords();sxl=sx;syl=sy;
sx=470;sy=168;coords();sx2=sx;sy2=sy;
setfillpattern(fill_25,Cl);bar(sxl,syl,sx2,sy2);
sx=170;sy=168;coords();sxl=sx;syl=sy;
sx=470;sy=204;coords();sx2=sx;sy2=sy;
setfillpattern(fill_37,Cl);bar(sxl,syl,sx2,sy2);
sx=170;sy=204;coords();sxl=sx;syl=sy;
sx=470;sy=240;coords();sx2=sx;sy2=sy;
setfillpattern(fill_50,Cl);bar(sxl,syl,sx2,sy2);
sx=170;sy=240;coords();sxl=sx;syl=sy;
sx=470;sy=276;coords();sx2=sx;sy2=sy;
setfillpattern(fill_62,Cl);bar(sxl,syl,sx2,sy2);
sx=170;sy=276;coords();sxl=sx;syl=sy;
sx=470;sy=312;coords();sx2=sx;sy2=sy;
setfillpattern(fill_75,Cl);bar(sxl,syl,sx2,sy2);
sx=170;sy=312;coords();sxl=sx;syl=sy;
sx=470;sy=348;coords();sx2=sx;sy2=sy;
setfillpattern(fill_87,Cl);bar(sxl,syl,sx2,sy2);
sx=170;sy=348;coords();sxl=sx;syl=sy;
sx=470;sy=384;coords();sx2=sx;sy2=sy;

setfillstyle(SOLID_FILL,Cl);bar(sxl,syl,sx2,sy2);

setcolor(C7);                                  /* draw the star */
```

```
sx=319;sy=96;coords();moveto(sx,sy);
sx=350;sy=192;coords();lineto(sx,sy);
sx=445;sy=192;coords();lineto(sx,sy);
sx=370;sy=254;coords();lineto(sx,sy);
sx=398;sy=350;coords();lineto(sx,sy);
sx=319;sy=293;coords();lineto(sx,sy);
sx=240;sy=350;coords();lineto(sx,sy);
sx=270;sy=254;coords();lineto(sx,sy);
sx=192;sy=192;coords();lineto(sx,sy);
sx=290;sy=192;coords();lineto(sx,sy);
sx=319;sy=96;coords();lineto(sx,sy);
sx=319;sy=238;coords();setfillstyle(SOLID_FILL,C7);
floodfill(sx,sy,C7);

sx=0;sy=0;coords();notice(sx,sy);                      /* notice */

keyboard();                           /* wait for user to press <Esc> */
quit_pgm();                           /* end the program gracefully */
}
/*__ _____


SUBROUTINE: CHECK THE KEYBOARD BUFFER                              */

void keyboard(void){
union u_type {int a;char b[3];} keystroke;
int get_keystroke(void);            /* declare a local subroutine */

do keystroke.a=get_keystroke();
while (keystroke.b[0]!=27);          /* return if <Esc> is pressed */
}

/* LOCAL SUBROUTINE: RETRIEVE ONE KEYSTROKE                        */

int get_keystroke(void){
union REGS regs;regs.h.ah=0;return int86(0x16,&regs,&regs);}

/*_____


SUBROUTINE: GRACEFUL EXIT FROM THE PROGRAM                        */

void quit_pgm(void){
cleardevice();restorecrtmode();exit(0);}

/*_____


SUBROUTINE: VGA/EGA/CGA/MCGA compatibility module
```

This subroutine invokes the highest-resolution graphics mode
which is permitted by the hardware. The 640x480 16-color mode
is established if a VGA is present. The 640x350 16-color mode
is established if an EGA is being used with an enhanced color
display monitor or a multiscanning monitor. The 640x200

```
16-color mode is established if an EGA is being used with a
standard color monitor.  The 320x200 4-color mode is invoked
if a CGA or MCGA is present.                                 */

void graphics_setup(void){
int graphics_adapter,graphics_mode;
detectgraph(&graphics_adapter,&graphics_mode);
if (graphics_adapter==VGA) goto VGA_mode;               /* if VGA */
if (graphics_mode==EGAHI) goto EGA_ECD_mode;    /* if EGA and ECD */
if (graphics_mode==EGALO) goto EGA_SCD_mode;    /* if EGA and SCD */
if (graphics_adapter==CGA) goto CGA_mode;               /* if CGA */
if (graphics_adapter==MCGA) goto MCGA_mode;            /* if MCGA */
goto abort_message;                 /* if no VGA, EGA, CGA, or MCGA */

VGA_mode:                       /* establish 640x480 16-color mode */
graphics_adapter=VGA;graphics_mode=VGAHI;
initgraph(&graphics_adapter,&graphics_mode,"");
x_res=640;y_res=480;C0=0;C1=1;C2=2;C3=3;C4=4;C5=5,C6=6;C7=7;
C8=8;C9=9;C10=10;C11=11;C12=12;C13=13;C14=14;C15=15;
mode_flag=1;
setcolor(C7);outtextxy(0,472,"640x480 16-color VGA mode.");
return;

EGA_ECD_mode:                   /* establish 640x350 16-color mode */
graphics_adapter=EGA;graphics_mode=EGAHI;
initgraph(&graphics_adapter,&graphics_mode,"");
x_res=640;y_res=350;C0=0;C1=1;C2=2;C3=3;C4=4;C5=5,C6=6;C7=7;
C8=8;C9=9;C10=10;C11=11;C12=12;C13=13;C14=14;C15=15;
mode_flag=2;
setcolor(C7);outtextxy(0,342,"640x350 16-color EGA mode.");
return;

EGA_SCD_mode:                   /* establish 640x200 16-color mode */
graphics_adapter=EGA;graphics_mode=EGALO;
initgraph(&graphics_adapter,&graphics_mode,"");
x_res=640;y_res=200;C0=0;C1=1;C2=2;C3=3;C4=4;C5=5,C6=6;C7=7;
C8=8;C9=9;C10=10;C11=11;C12=12;C13=13;C14=14;C15=15;
mode_flag=3;
setcolor(C7);outtextxy(0,192,"640x200 16-color EGA mode.");
return;

CGA_mode:                       /* establish 320x200 4-color mode */
graphics_adapter=CGA;graphics_mode=CGAC3;
initgraph(&graphics_adapter,&graphics_mode,"");
x_res=320;y_res=200;C0=0;C1=1;C2=1;C3=1;C4=1;C5=1,C6=1;C7=3;
C8=1;C9=0;C10=1;C11=1;C12=1;C13=2;C14=1;C15=3;
mode_flag=4;
setcolor(C7);outtextxy(0,192,"320x200 4-color CGA mode.");
return;

MCGA_mode:                      /* establish 320x200 4-color mode */
graphics_adapter=MCGA;graphics_mode=MCGAC3;
initgraph(&graphics_adapter,&graphics_mode,"");
x_res=320;y_res=200;C0=0;C1=1;C2=1;C3=1;C4=1;C5=1;C6=1;C7=3;
```

```
C8=1;C9=0;C10=1;C11=1;C12=1;C13=2;C14=1;C15=3;
mode_flag=4;
setcolor(C7);outtextxy(0,192,"320x200 4-color MCGA mode.");
return;

abort_message:
printf("\n\nUnable to proceed.\n");
printf("Requires VGA, EGA, MCGA, or CGA adapter\n");
printf("   with appropriate monitor.\n");
printf("Please refer to the book.\n\n");
exit(0);
}
/*_____
```

SUBROUTINE: coords()

This subroutine accepts sx,sy device-independent display
coordinates and returns sx,sy device-dependent screen
coordinates scaled to fit the 640x480, 640x350, 640x200, or
320x200 screen, depending upon the graphics mode being used.   */

```
void coords(void){
sx=sx*(x_res/640);sy=sy*(y_res/480);return;}

/*_____
```

SUBROUTINE: Copyright Notice

This subroutine displays the standard copyright notice.
If you are typing in this program from the book you can
safely omit this subroutine, provided that you also remove
the instruction "notice()" from the main routine.   */

```
int copyright[][3]={0x7c00,0x0000,0x0000,0x8231,
0x819c,0x645e,0xba4a,0x4252,0x96d0,0xa231,0x8252,0x955e,0xba4a,
0x43d2,0xf442,0x8231,0x825c,0x945e,0x7c00,0x0000,0x0000};
for (tl=0;tl<=6;tl++){a=copyright[tl][0];b=copyright[tl][1];
c=copyright[tl][2];
setlinestyle(USERBIT_LINE,a,NORM_WIDTH);
moveto(x,y);lineto(x+15,y);
setlinestyle(USERBIT_LINE,b,NORM_WIDTH);
moveto(x+16,y);lineto(x+31,y);
setlinestyle(USERBIT_LINE,c,NORM_WIDTH);
moveto(x+32,y);lineto(x+47,y);y=y+1;};
setlinestyle(USERBIT_LINE,0xFFFF,NORM_WIDTH);
return;}

/*_____

End of source code                                               */
```

Fig. E-3. Sculpted background effect—Turbo C version, VGA/EGA/CGA/MCGA compatible. Refer to the main body of the book for discussion.

```
/*_____

tc-004.c

Function:  This program demonstrates how to simulate a
sculptured background graphic.

Compatibility:  Supports all graphics adapters and monitors.
The software uses the 640x480 16-color mode if a VGA is
present, the 640x350 16-color mode if an EGA and enhanced
monitor are present, the 640x200 16-color mode if an EGA and
standard monitor are present, and the 320x200 4-color mode
if a CGA or MCGA is present.

Remarks:  By altering two variables in the declarations
module you can try out different color combinations.
The brightness control and the contrast control on your
monitor have a strong effect on the image's appearance.

Copyright 1988 Lee Adams and TAB BOOKS Inc.

_____


I N C L U D E    F I L E S                              */

#include <dos.h>                    /* supports the DOS call */
#include <stdio.h>              /* supports the printf function */
#include <graphics.h>      /* supports the graphics functions */

/*_____


D E C L A R A T I O N S                                 */

void keyboard(void);              /* declare global subroutines */
void quit_pgm(void);
void graphics_setup(void);void coords(void);
void notice (float x, float y);

/*                            declare global variables */
float sx=0,sy=0,x_res=0,y_res=0,sx1=0,sy1=0,sx2=0,sy2=0;
int C0=0,C1=1,C2=2,C3=3,C4=4,C5=5,C6=6,C7=7,C8=8,C9=9,C10=10,
C11=11,C12=12,C13=13,C14=14,C15=15,mode_flag=0;
int t=1,t1=1;                        /* counters for loops */
float x=52,y=32,x1=52,h1=80,v1=30,h2=81,v2=31,h3=90,v3=35;
int bg=2,shadow=0,hilite=10;

/*_____
```

```
M A I N     R O U T I N E                                      */
main(){
graphics_setup();                    /* establish graphics mode */

bg=C2;shadow=C0;hilite=Cl0;
setfillstyle(SOLID_FILL,bg);
sx=0;sy=24;coords();sxl=sx;syl=sy;
sx=639;sy=454;coords();sx2=sx;sy2=sy;
bar(sxl,syl,sx2,sy2);                                /* bg */
sx=619;sy=41;coords();moveto(sx,sy);setcolor(hilite);
sx=619;sy=437;coords();lineto(sx,sy);
sx=620;sy=41;coords();moveto(sx,sy);
sx=620;sy=437;coords();lineto(sx,sy);
sx=19;sy=437;coords();lineto(sx,sy);
setcolor(shadow);sx=19;sy=41;coords();lineto(sx,sy);
sx=20;sy=437;coords();moveto(sx,sy);
sx=20;sy=41;coords();lineto(sx,sy);
sx=620;sy=41;coords();lineto(sx,sy);

for (tl=1;tl<=4;tl++){            /* loop for 4 rows of pedestals */
for (t=1;t<=6;t++){           /* nested loop for 6 pedestals per row */
moveto(x,y);setcolor(hilite);lineto(x+hl,y);
setcolor(shadow);moveto(x+hl,y+1);lineto(x+hl,y+vl);
moveto(x+h2,y+1);lineto(x+h2,y+vl);lineto(x,y+vl);
setcolor(hilite);lineto(x,y);moveto(x+1,y+vl);
lineto(x+1,y);x=x+h3;};          /* reposition x for next pedestal */
x=xl;y=y+v3;};                   /* reposition x,y for next row */

setcolor(C7);notice(0,0);                             /* notice */
keyboard();                        /* wait for user to press <Esc> */
quit_pgm();                        /* end the program gracefully */
}
/*_____


SUBROUTINE: CHECK THE KEYBOARD BUFFER                          */

void keyboard(void){
union u_type {int a;char b[3];} keystroke;
int get_keystroke(void);           /* declare a local subroutine */

do keystroke.a=get_keystroke();
while (keystroke.b[0]!=27);         /* return if <Esc> is pressed */
}

/* LOCAL SUBROUTINE: RETRIEVE ONE KEYSTROKE                     */

int get_keystroke(void){
union REGS regs;regs.h.ah=0;return int86(0x16,&regs,&regs);}

/*_____
```

```
SUBROUTINE: GRACEFUL EXIT FROM THE PROGRAM                              */

void quit_pgm(void){
cleardevice();restorecrtmode();exit(0);}

/*_____


SUBROUTINE: VGA/EGA/CGA/MCGA compatibility module
```

This subroutine invokes the highest-resolution graphics mode
which is permitted by the hardware. The 640x480 16-color mode
is established if a VGA is present. The 640x350 16-color mode
is established if an EGA is being used with an enhanced color
display monitor or a multiscanning monitor. The 640x200
16-color mode is established if an EGA is being used with a
standard color monitor. The 320x200 4-color mode is invoked
if a CGA or MCGA is present.   */

```
void graphics_setup(void){
int graphics_adapter,graphics_mode;
detectgraph(&graphics_adapter,&graphics_mode);
if (graphics_adapter==VGA) goto VGA_mode;                    /* if VGA */
if (graphics_mode==EGAHI) goto EGA_ECD_mode;      /* if EGA and ECD */
if (graphics_mode==EGALO) goto EGA_SCD_mode;      /* if EGA and SCD */
if (graphics_adapter==CGA) goto CGA_mode;                    /* if CGA */
if (graphics_adapter==MCGA) goto MCGA_mode;                 /* if MCGA */
goto abort_message;                     /* if no VGA, EGA, CGA, or MCGA */

VGA_mode:                        /* establish 640x480 16-color mode */
graphics_adapter=VGA;graphics_mode=VGAHI;
initgraph(&graphics_adapter,&graphics_mode,"");
x_res=640;y_res=480;mode_flag=1;setcolor(C7);
x=52;y=77;x1=52;h1=80;v1=72;h2=81;v2=73;h3=90;v3=84;
outtextxy(0,472,"640x480 16-color VGA mode.");
outtextxy(160,0,"USING C TO CREATE A SCULPTURED BACKGROUND");
return;

EGA_ECD_mode:                    /* establish 640x350 16-color mode */
graphics_adapter=EGA;graphics_mode=EGAHI;
initgraph(&graphics_adapter,&graphics_mode,"");
x_res=640;y_res=350;mode_flag=2;setcolor(C7);
x=52;y=56;x1=52;h1=80;v1=53;h2=81;v2=54;h3=90;v3=61;
outtextxy(0,342,"640x350 16-color EGA mode.");
outtextxy(160,0,"USING C TO CREATE A SCULPTURED BACKGROUND");
return;

EGA_SCD_mode:                    /* establish 640x200 16-color mode */
graphics_adapter=EGA;graphics_mode=EGALO;
initgraph(&graphics_adapter,&graphics_mode,"");
x_res=640;y_res=200;mode_flag=3;setcolor(C7);
x=52;y=32;x1=52;h1=80;v1=30;h2=81;v2=31;h3=90;v3=35;
outtextxy(0,192,"640x200 16-color EGA mode.");
```

```
outtextxy(160,0,"USING C TO CREATE A SCULPTURED BACKGROUND");
return;

CGA_mode:                              /* establish 320x200 4-color mode */
graphics_adapter=CGA;graphics_mode=CGAC3;
initgraph(&graphics_adapter,&graphics_mode,"");
x_res=320;y_res=200;C0=0;C2=2;C7=3;C10=3;mode_flag=4;setcolor(C7);
x=26;y=32;x1=26;h1=40;v1=30;h2=41;v2=31;h3=45;v3=35;
outtextxy(0,192,"320x200 4-color CGA mode.");
outtextxy(88,0,"SCULPTURED BACKGROUND");
return;

MCGA_mode:                             /* establish 320x200 4-color mode */
graphics_adapter=MCGA;graphics_mode=MCGAC3;
initgraph(&graphics_adapter,&graphics_mode,"");
x_res=320;y_res=200;C0=0;C2=2;C7=3;C10=3;mode_flag=4;setcolor(C7);
x=26;y=32;x1=26;h1=40;v1=30;h2=41;v2=31;h3=45;v3=35;
outtextxy(0,192,"320x200 4-color MCGA mode.");
outtextxy(88,0,"SCULPTURED BACKGROUND");
return;

abort_message:
printf("\n\nUnable to proceed.\n");
printf("Requires VGA, EGA, MCGA, or CGA adapter\n");
printf("   with appropriate monitor.\n");
printf("Please refer to the book.\n\n");
exit(0);
}
/*_____


SUBROUTINE: coords()
```

This subroutine accepts sx,sy device-independent display
coordinates and returns sx,sy device-dependent screen
coordinates scaled to fit the 640x480, 640x350, 640x200, or
320x200 screen, depending upon the graphics mode being used.   */

```
void coords(void){
sx=sx*(x_res/640);sy=sy*(y_res/480);return;}

/*_____


SUBROUTINE: Copyright Notice
```

This subroutine displays the standard copyright notice.
If you are typing in this program from the book you can
safely omit this subroutine, provided that you also remove
the instruction "notice()" from the main routine.   */

```
int copyright[][3]={0x7c00,0x0000,0x0000,0x8231,
0x819c,0x645e,0xba4a,0x4252,0x96d0,0xa231,0x8252,0x955e,0xba4a,
0x43d2,0xf442,0x8231,0x825c,0x945e,0x7c00,0x0000,0x0000};
```

```
void notice(float x, float y){
int a,b,c; int tl=0;
for (tl=0;tl<=6;tl++){a=copyright[tl][0];b=copyright[tl][1];
c=copyright[tl][2];
setlinestyle(USERBIT_LINE,a,NORM_WIDTH);
moveto(x,y);lineto(x+15,y);
setlinestyle(USERBIT_LINE,b,NORM_WIDTH);
moveto(x+16,y);lineto(x+31,y);
setlinestyle(USERBIT_LINE,c,NORM_WIDTH);
moveto(x+32,y);lineto(x+47,y);y=y+1;};
setlinestyle(USERBIT_LINE,0xFFFF,NORM_WIDTH);
return;}

/*_____

End of source code                                      */
```

Fig. E-4. Airbrushed background effect—Turbo C version, VGA/EGA/CGA/MCGA compatible. Refer to the main body of the book for discussion.

```
/*_____

tc-005.c

Function:  This program demonstrates how to simulate an
airbrushed background.

Compatibility:  Supports all graphics adapters and monitors.
The software uses the 640x480 16-color mode is a VGA is
present, the 640x350 16-color mode if an EGA and enhanced
monitor are present, the 640x200 16-color mode if an EGA and
standard monitor are present, and the 320x200 4-color mode
if a CGA or MCGA is present.

Remarks:  By altering a variable in the declarations
module you can try out different foreground colors.

Copyright 1988 Lee Adams and TAB BOOKS Inc.

_____


I N C L U D E    F I L E S                              */

#include <dos.h>                       /* supports the BIOS call */
#include <stdio.h>                 /* supports the printf function */
#include <graphics.h>           /* supports the graphics functions */

/*_____


D E C L A R A T I O N S                                 */

char fill_3[]={0,32,0,0,0,2,0,0};                  /*    3% fill */
```

```
char fill_6[ ]={32,0,2,0,128,0,8,0};                /* 6.25% fill */
char fill_12[ ]={32,2,128,8,32,2,128,8};            /* 12.5% fill */
char fill_25[ ]={68,17,68,17,68,17,68,17};          /*   25% fill */
char fill_37[ ]={146,41,148,73,164,73,146,73};      /* 37.5% fill */
char fill_50[ ]={85,170,85,170,85,170,85,170};      /*   50% fill */
char fill_62[ ]={109,214,107,182,91,182,109,182};   /* 62.5% fill */
char fill_75[ ]={187,238,187,238,187,238,187,238};  /*   75% fill */
char fill_87[ ]={223,253,127,247,223,253,127,247};  /* 87.5% fill */


void keyboard(void);void quit_pgm(void);void graphics_setup(void);
void coords(void);void notice(float x,float y);


float sx=0,sy=0,sx1=0,sy1=0,sx2=0,sy2=0,x_res=0,y_res=0;
int C0=0,C1=1,C2=2,C3=3,C4=4,C5=5,C6=6,C7=7,C8=8,C9=9,C10=10,
C11=11,C12=12,C13=13,C14=14,C15=15,mode_flag=0;
int fg,bg;                       /* foreground & background colors */

/*_____



M A I N   R O U T I N E                                      */
main(){
graphics_setup();                       /* establish graphics mode */

fg=C1;                                     /* set foreground hue */

setfillpattern(fill_6,fg);sx=0;sy=48;coords();sx1=sx;sy1=sy;
sx=639;sy=96;coords();sx2=sx;sy2=sy;bar(sx1,sy1,sx2,sy2);
setfillpattern(fill_12,fg);sx=0;coords();sx1=sx;sy1=sy2+1;
sx=639;sy=144;coords();sx2=sx;sy2=sy;bar(sx1,sy1,sx2,sy2);
setfillpattern(fill_25,fg);sx=0;coords();sx1=sx;sy1=sy2+1;
sx=639;sy=192;coords();sx2=sx;sy2=sy;bar(sx1,sy1,sx2,sy2);
setfillpattern(fill_37,fg);sx=0;coords();sx1=sx;sy1=sy2+1;
sx=639;sy=240;coords();sx2=sx;sy2=sy;bar(sx1,sy1,sx2,sy2);
setfillpattern(fill_50,fg);sx=0;coords();sx1=sx;sy1=sy2+1;
sx=639;sy=288;coords();sx2=sx;sy2=sy;bar(sx1,sy1,sx2,sy2);
setfillpattern(fill_62,fg);sx=0;coords();sx1=sx;sy1=sy2+1;
sx=639;sy=336;coords();sx2=sx;sy2=sy;bar(sx1,sy1,sx2,sy2);
setfillpattern(fill_75,fg);sx=0;coords();sx1=sx;sy1=sy2+1;
sx=639;sy=384;coords();sx2=sx;sy2=sy;bar(sx1,sy1,sx2,sy2);
setfillpattern(fill_87,fg);sx=0;coords();sx1=sx;sy1=sy2+1;
sx=639;sy=432;coords();sx2=sx;sy2=sy;bar(sx1,sy1,sx2,sy2);
setfillstyle(SOLID_FILL,fg);sx=0;coords();sx1=sx;sy1=sy2+1;
sx=639;sy=454;coords();sx2=sx;sy2=sy;bar(sx1,sy1,sx2,sy2);

setcolor(C7);notice(0,0);                              /* notice */
keyboard();                      /* wait for user to press <Esc> */
quit_pgm();                      /* end the program gracefully */
}
/*_____
```

```
SUBROUTINE: CHECK THE KEYBOARD BUFFER                                  */

void keyboard(void){
union u_type {int a;char b[3];} keystroke;
int get_keystroke(void);            /* declare a local subroutine */

do keystroke.a=get_keystroke();
while (keystroke.b[0]!=27);          /* return if <Esc> is pressed */
}

/* LOCAL SUBROUTINE: RETRIEVE ONE KEYSTROKE                           */

int get_keystroke(void){
union REGS regs;regs.h.ah=0;return int86(0x16,&regs,&regs);}

/*_____


SUBROUTINE: GRACEFUL EXIT FROM THE PROGRAM                          */

void quit_pgm(void){
cleardevice();restorecrtmode();exit(0);}

/*_____


SUBROUTINE: VGA/EGA/CGA/MCGA compatibility module

This subroutine invokes the highest-resolution graphics mode
which is permitted by the hardware.  The 640x480 16-color mode
is established if a VGA is present.  The 640x350 16-color mode
is established if an EGA is being used with an enhanced color
display monitor or a multiscanning monitor.  The 640x200
16-color mode is established if an EGA is being used with a
standard color monitor.  The 320x200 4-color mode is invoked
if a CGA or MCGA is present.                                        */

void graphics_setup(void){
int graphics_adapter,graphics_mode;
detectgraph(&graphics_adapter,&graphics_mode);
if (graphics_adapter==VGA) goto VGA_mode;                  /* if VGA */
if (graphics_mode==EGAHI) goto EGA_ECD_mode;   /* if EGA and ECD */
if (graphics_mode==EGALO) goto EGA_SCD_mode;   /* if EGA and SCD */
if (graphics_adapter==CGA) goto CGA_mode;                  /* if CGA */
if (graphics_adapter==MCGA) goto MCGA_mode;             /* if MCGA */
goto abort_message;                  /* if no VGA, EGA, CGA, or MCGA */

VGA_mode:                          /* establish 640x480 16-color mode */
graphics_adapter=VGA;graphics_mode=VGAHI;
initgraph(&graphics_adapter,&graphics_mode,"");
x_res=640;y_res=480;mode_flag=1;setcolor(C7);
outtextxy(216,472,"640x480 16-color VGA mode.");
outtextxy(160,0,"USING C TO SIMULATE AN AIRBRUSHED BACKGROUND");
return;
```

```
EGA_ECD_mode:                    /* establish 640x350 16-color mode */
graphics_adapter=EGA;graphics_mode=EGAHI;
initgraph(&graphics_adapter,&graphics_mode,"");
x_res=640;y_res=350;mode_flag=2;setcolor(C7);
outtextxy(216,342,"640x350 16-color EGA mode.");
outtextxy(160,0,"USING C TO SIMULATE AN AIRBRUSHED BACKGROUND");
return;

EGA_SCD_mode:                    /* establish 640x200 16-color mode */
graphics_adapter=EGA;graphics_mode=EGALO;
initgraph(&graphics_adapter,&graphics_mode,"");

x_res=640;y_res=200;mode_flag=3;setcolor(C7);
outtextxy(216,192,"640x200 16-color EGA mode.");
outtextxy(160,0,"USING C TO SIMULATE AN AIRBRUSHED BACKGROUND");
return;

CGA_mode:                        /* establish 320x200 4-color mode */
graphics_adapter=CGA;graphics_mode=CGAC3;
initgraph(&graphics_adapter,&graphics_mode,"");
x_res=320;y_res=200;C0=0;Cl=1;C7=3;C9=3;mode_flag=4;setcolor(C7);
outtextxy(72,192,"320x200 4-color CGA mode.");
outtextxy(88,0,"AIRBRUSHED BACKGROUND");
return;

MCGA_mode:                       /* establish 320x200 4-color mode */
graphics_adapter=MCGA;graphics_mode=MCGAC3;
initgraph(&graphics_adapter,&graphics_mode,"");
x_res=320;y_res=200;C0=0;Cl=1;C7=3;C9=3;mode_flag=4;setcolor(C7);
outtextxy(72,192,"320x200 4-color MCGA mode.");
outtextxy(88,0,"AIRBRUSHED BACKGROUND");
return;

abort_message:
printf("\n\nUnable to proceed.\n");
printf("Requires VGA, EGA, MCGA, or CGA adapter\n");
printf("   with appropriate monitor.\n");
printf("Please refer to the book.\n\n");
exit(0);
}
/*_____


SUBROUTINE: coords()

This subroutine accepts sx,sy device-independent display
coordinates and returns sx,sy device-dependent screen
coordinates scaled to fit the 640x480, 640x350, 640x200, or
320x200 screen, depending upon the graphics mode being used.    */

void coords(void){
sx=sx*(x_res/640);sy=sy*(y_res/480);return;}

/*_____
```

```
SUBROUTINE: Copyright Notice

This subroutine displays the standard copyright notice.
If you are typing in this program from the book you can
safely omit this subroutine, provided that you also remove
the instruction "notice()" from the main routine.                    */


int copyright[][3]={0x7c00,0x0000,0x0000,0x8231,
0x819c,0x645e,0xba4a,0x4252,0x96d0,0xa231,0x8252,0x955e,0xba4a,
0x43d2,0xf442,0x8231,0x825c,0x945e,0x7c00,0x0000,0x0000};

void notice(float x, float y){
int a,b,c; int tl=0;
for (tl=0;tl<=6;tl++){a=copyright[tl][0];b=copyright[tl][1];
c=copyright[tl][2];
setlinestyle(USERBIT_LINE,a,NORM_WIDTH);
moveto(x,y);lineto(x+15,y);
setlinestyle(USERBIT_LINE,b,NORM_WIDTH);
moveto(x+16,y);lineto(x+31,y);
setlinestyle(USERBIT_LINE,c,NORM_WIDTH);
moveto(x+32,y);lineto(x+47,y);y=y+1;};
setlinestyle(USERBIT_LINE,0xFFFF,NORM_WIDTH);
return;}

/*_____

End of source code                                                  */
```

Fig. E-5. How to generate a 3D image—Turbo C version, VGA/EGA/CGA/MCGA compatible. Refer to the main body of the book for discussion.

```
/*_____

tc-006.c

Function:  This program demonstrates how to create accurate
3D images on the display screen.

Compatibility:  Supports all graphics adapters and monitors.
The software uses the 640x480 16-color mode if a VGA is
present, the 640x350 16-color mode if an EGA and enhanced
monitor are present, the 640x200 16-color mode if an EGA and
standard monitor are present, and the 320x200 4-color mode
if a CGA or MCGA is present.

Remarks:  In addition to the standard 3D perspective formulas,
versatile viewport and line-clipping routines are provided.

Copyright 1988 Lee Adams and TAB BOOKS Inc.

_____
```

```
I N C L U D E    F I L E S                                        */

#include <dos.h>                    /* supports the BIOS call */
#include <stdio.h>                  /* supports the printf function */
#include <graphics.h>              /* supports the graphics functions */
#include <math.h>               /* supports sine and cosine functions */

/*_____


D E C L A R A T I O N S                                          */

/*                                        declare global variables */
float x=0.0,y=0.0,z=0.0;                      /* world coordinates */
float sx=0.0,sy=0.0;          /* output of 3D perspective formulas */
float xa=0.0,ya=0.0,za=0.0;    /* temporary values in 3D formulas */
float sxa=0.0,sya=0.0,sxb=0.0,syb=0.0;        /* 2D line endpoints */
float sxs=0.0,sys=0.0;     /* temp storage of 2D line startpoint */
float temp_swap=0.0;                 /* used for variable swaps */
float d=1200.0;                   /* angular perspective factor */
double r1=5.68319;                    /* yaw angle in radians */
double r2=6.28319;                    /* roll angle in radians */
double r3=5.79778;                   /* pitch angle in radians */
double sr1=0.0,sr2=0.0,sr3=0.0;       /* sine rotation factors */
double cr1=0.0,cr2=0.0,cr3=0.0;      /* cosine rotation factors */
float mx=0.0,my=0.0,mz=-350.0;          /* viewpoint position */
int maxx=638,minx=1,maxy=198,miny=1;       /* clipping viewport */
float screen_x=639,screen_y=199;     /* dimensions of screen mode */
float c=0.0;                      /* used in line-clipping routine */
float rx=0.0,ry=0.0;   /* scaling values used in mapping routine */
int t1=0,t2=0;                               /* loop counters */
int pl=0;                                    /* array indexer */

/*        database of xyz cartesian world coordinates for 3D cube */
int array1[][3]={
30,-30,30, 30,-30,-30, -30,-30,-30, -30,-30,30, 30,-30,30,
30,30,-30, -30,30,-30, -30,-30,-30, 30,-30,-30, 30,30,-30,
-30,30,-30, -30,30,30, -30,-30,30, -30,-30,-30, -30,30,-30,
-30,30,30, 30,30,30, 30,-30,30, -30,-30,30, -30,30,30,
30,30,30, 30,30,-30, 30,-30,-30, 30,-30,30, 30,30,30,
-30,30,-30, 30,30,-30, 30,30,30, -30,30,30, -30,30,-30};

int C0=0,C1=1,C2=2,C3=3,C4=4,C5=5,C6=7,C7=7,C8=8,C9=9,C10=10,
C11=11,C12=12,C13=13,C14=14,C15=15,mode_flag=0;
float sx1,sy1,sx2,sy2;
float x_res,y_res;

/*                                  declare global subroutines */
void keyboard(void);void quit_pgm(void);void calc_3d(void);
void rotation(void);void window(void);void viewport(void);
void graphics_setup(void);void coords(void);
void notice(float x,float y);
```

```
/*_____


M A I N    R O U T I N E                                      */

main(){
graphics_setup();                        /* establish graphics mode */

setcolor(C7);sx=0;sy=24;coords();sxl=sx;syl=sy;
sx=638;sy=455;coords();sx2=sx;sy2=sy;
rectangle(sxl,syl,sx2,sy2);

rotation();        /* calculate yaw, roll, pitch rotation factors */
for (t2=1;t2<=6;t2++)                      /* draw 6 sides of the cube */
{if (t2<4) setlinestyle(USERBIT_LINE,0x8888,NORM_WIDTH);
else setlinestyle(USERBIT_LINE,0xffff,NORM_WIDTH);
x=arrayl[pl][0];y=arrayl[pl][1];z=arrayl[pl][2];
calc_3d();window();sxa=sx;sya=sy;
for (tl=1;tl<=4;tl++)
{pl++;x=arrayl[pl][0];y=arrayl[pl][1];z=arrayl[pl][2];
calc_3d();window();sxs=sx;sys=sy;sxb=sx;syb=sy;viewport();
moveto(sxa,sya);lineto(sxb,syb);sxa=sxs;sya=sys;};
pl++;};

notice(0,0);
keyboard();                              /* wait for user to press <Esc> */
quit_pgm();}                             /* end the program gracefully */

/*_____


SUBROUTINE: CALCULATE SIN, COS FACTORS

Enter with rl,r2,r3 viewing angles for yaw, roll, pitch
expressed in radians (0.0 through 6.28319).  Returns sine
and cosine factors.                                          */

void rotation(void){
srl=sin(rl);sr2=sin(r2);sr3=sin(r3);crl=cos(rl);cr2=cos(r2);
cr3=cos(r3);return;}

/*_____


SUBROUTINE: STANDARD 3D FORMULAS

Enter with x,y,z cartesian world coordinates.  Returns sx,sy
cartesian display coordinates.  Returns x,y,z cartesian view
coordinates.                                                */

void calc_3d(void){
x=(-1)*x;xa=crl*x-srl*z;za=srl*x+crl*z;x=cr2*xa+sr2*y;
ya=cr2*y-sr2*xa;z=cr3*za-sr3*ya;y=sr3*za+cr3*ya;x=x+mx;y=y+my;
z=z+mz;sx=d*x/z;sy=d*y/z;return;}
```

```
/*_____


SUBROUTINE: MAP CARTESIAN COORDS TO PHYSICAL SCREEN COORDS

Enter with sx,sy cartesian display coordinates.  Returns sx,sy
unclipped physical display coordinates.                        */

void window(void){
sx=sx+399;sy=sy+299;rx=screen_x/799;ry=screen_y/599;sx=sx*rx;
sy=sy*ry;return;}


/*_____


SUBROUTINE: 2D LINE-CLIPPING

Enter with sxa,sya and sxb,syb endpoints of line to be
clipped.  Returns display coordinates for line clipped to
fit physical screen viewport defined by minx,miny and
maxx,maxy.                                                     */

void viewport(void){
if (sxa>sxb) {temp_swap=sxa;sxa=sxb;sxb=temp_swap;
temp_swap=sya;sya=syb;syb=temp_swap;};
if (sxa<minx) if (sxb<minx) return;
if (sxa>maxx) if (sxb>maxx) return;
if (sya<miny) if (syb<miny) return;
if (sya>maxy) if (syb>maxy) return;

if (sxa<minx) {{c=(syb-sya)/(sxb-sxa)*(sxb-minx);  /* push right */
sxa=minx;sya=syb-c;};
if (sya<miny) if (syb<miny) return;
if (sya>maxy) if (syb>maxy) return;
};

if (sxb>maxx) {{c=(syb-sya)/(sxb-sxa)*(maxx-sxa);   /* push left */
sxb=maxx;syb=sya+c;};
if (sya<miny) if (syb<miny) return;
if (sya>maxy) if (syb>maxy) return;
};

if (sya>syb) {temp_swap=sya;sya=syb;syb=temp_swap;
temp_swap=sxa;sxa=sxb;sxb=temp_swap;};

if (sya<miny) {c=(sxb-sxa)/(syb-sya)*(syb-miny);    /* push down */
sxa=sxb-c;sya=miny;};

if (syb>maxy) {c=(sxb-sxa)/(syb-sya)*(maxy-sya);     /* push up */
sxb=sxa+c;syb=maxy;};
return;}

/*_____
```

```
SUBROUTINE: CHECK THE KEYBOARD BUFFER                          */

void keyboard(void){
union u_type {int a;char b[3];} keystroke;
int get_keystroke(void);           /* declare a local subroutine */

do keystroke.a=get_keystroke();
while (keystroke.b[0]!=27);         /* return if <Esc> is pressed */
}

/* LOCAL SUBROUTINE: RETRIEVE ONE KEYSTROKE                     */

int get_keystroke(void){
union REGS regs;regs.h.ah=0;return int86(0x16,&regs,&regs);}

/*_____


SUBROUTINE: GRACEFUL EXIT FROM THE PROGRAM                    */

void quit_pgm(void){
cleardevice();restorecrtmode();exit(0);}

/*_____


SUBROUTINE: VGA/EGA/CGA/MCGA compatibility module

This subroutine invokes the highest-resolution graphics mode
which is permitted by the hardware.  The 640x480 16-color mode
is established if a VGA is present.  The 640x350 16-color mode
is established if an EGA is being used with an enhanced color
display monitor or a multiscanning monitor.  The 640x200
16-color mode is established if an EGA is being used with a
standard color monitor.  The 320x200 4-color mode is invoked
if a CGA or MCGA is present.                                  */

void graphics_setup(void){
int graphics_adapter,graphics_mode;
detectgraph(&graphics_adapter,&graphics_mode);
if (graphics_adapter==VGA) goto VGA_mode;              /* if VGA */
if (graphics_mode==EGAHI) goto EGA_ECD_mode;   /* if EGA and ECD */
if (graphics_mode==EGALO) goto EGA_SCD_mode;   /* if EGA and SCD */
if (graphics_adapter==CGA) goto CGA_mode;             /* if CGA */
if (graphics_adapter==MCGA) goto MCGA_mode;           /* if MCGA */
goto abort_message;               /* if no VGA, EGA, CGA, or MCGA */

VGA_mode:                     /* establish 640x480 16-color mode */
graphics_adapter=VGA;graphics_mode=VGAHI;
initgraph(&graphics_adapter,&graphics_mode,"");
x_res=640;y_res=480;mode_flag=1;
maxx=638;minx=1;maxy=478;miny=1;screen_x=639;screen_y=479;
setcolor(C7);outtextxy(0,472,"640x480 16-color VGA mode.");
```

```
outtextxy(200,0,"USING C TO GENERATE 3D IMAGES");
return;

EGA_ECD_mode:                    /* establish 640x350 16-color mode */
graphics_adapter=EGA;graphics_mode=EGAHI;
initgraph(&graphics_adapter,&graphics_mode,"");
x_res=640;y_res=350;mode_flag=2;
maxx=638;minx=1;maxy=348;miny=1;screen_x=639;screen_y=349;
setcolor(C7);outtextxy(0,342,"640x350 16-color EGA mode.");
outtextxy(200,0,"USING C TO GENERATE 3D IMAGES");
return;

EGA_SCD_mode:                    /* establish 640x200 16-color mode */
graphics_adapter=EGA;graphics_mode=EGALO;
initgraph(&graphics_adapter,&graphics_mode,"");
x_res=640;y_res=200;mode_flag=3;
maxx=638;minx=1;maxy=198;miny=1;screen_x=639;screen_y=199;

setcolor(C7);outtextxy(0,192,"640x200 16-color EGA mode.");
outtextxy(200,0,"USING C TO GENERATE 3D IMAGES");
return;

CGA_mode:                        /* establish 320x200 4-color mode */
graphics_adapter=CGA;graphics_mode=CGAC3;
initgraph(&graphics_adapter,&graphics_mode,"");
x_res=320;y_res=200;C7=3;mode_flag=4;
maxx=318;minx=1;maxy=198;miny=1;screen_x=319;screen_y=199;
setcolor(C7);outtextxy(0,192,"320x200 4-color CGA mode.");
outtextxy(128,0,"3D IMAGES");
return;

MCGA_mode:                       /* establish 320x200 4-color mode */
graphics_adapter=MCGA;graphics_mode=MCGAC3;
initgraph(&graphics_adapter,&graphics_mode,"");
x_res=320;y_res=200;C7=3;mode_flag=4;
maxx=318;minx=1;maxy=198;miny=1;screen_x=319;screen_y=199;
setcolor(C7);outtextxy(0,192,"320x200 4-color MCGA mode.");
outtextxy(128,0,"3D IMAGES");
return;

abort_message:
printf("\n\nUnable to proceed.\n");
printf("Requires VGA, EGA, MCGA, or CGA adapter\n");
printf("   with appropriate monitor.\n");
printf("Please refer to the book.\n\n");
exit(0);
}
/*_____
```

SUBROUTINE: coords()

This subroutine accepts sx,sy device-independent display
coordinates and returns sx,sy device-dependent screen

```
coordinates scaled to fit the 640x480, 640x350, 640x200, or
320x200 screen, depending upon the graphics mode being used.      */

void coords(void){
sx=sx*(x_res/640);sy=sy*(y_res/480);return;}

/*_____


SUBROUTINE: Copyright Notice

This subroutine displays the standard copyright notice.
If you are typing in this program from the book you can
safely omit this subroutine, provided that you also remove
the instruction "notice()" from the main routine.               */

int copyright[][3]={0x7c00,0x0000,0x0000,0x8231,
0x819c,0x645e,0xba4a,0x4252,0x96d0,0xa231,0x8252,0x955e,0xba4a,
0x43d2,0xf442,0x8231,0x825c,0x945e,0x7c00,0x0000,0x0000};

void notice(float x, float y){
int a,b,c; int tl=0;
for (tl=0;tl<=6;tl++){a=copyright[tl][0];b=copyright[tl][1];
c=copyright[tl][2];
setlinestyle(USERBIT_LINE,a,NORM_WIDTH);
moveto(x,y);lineto(x+15,y);
setlinestyle(USERBIT_LINE,b,NORM_WIDTH);
moveto(x+16,y);lineto(x+31,y);
setlinestyle(USERBIT_LINE,c,NORM_WIDTH);
moveto(x+32,y);lineto(x+47,y);y=y+1;};
setlinestyle(USERBIT_LINE,0xFFFF,NORM_WIDTH);
return;}

/*_____

End of source code                                               */
```

Fig. E-6. Business chart in 2D—Turbo C version, VGA/EGA/CGA/MCGA compatible. Refer to the main body of the book for discussion.

```
/*_____

tc-007.c

Function:  This program demonstrates how to produce high-impact
business graphics.

Compatibility:  Supports all graphics adapters and monitors.
The software uses the 640x200 16-color mode if a VGA or EGA is
present; the 640x200 2-color mode if a CGA or MCGA is present.

Remarks:  Refer to the book.
```

```
I N C L U D E   F I L E S                                        */

#include <dos.h>                        /* supports the BIOS call */
#include <stdio.h>                    /* supports the printf function */
#include <graphics.h>              /* supports the graphics functions */

/*_____


D E C L A R A T I O N S                                         */

char fill_3[]={0,32,0,0,0,2,0,0};                 /*    3% fill */
char fill_6[]={32,0,2,0,128,0,8,0};               /* 6.25% fill */
char fill_12[]={32,2,128,8,32,2,128,8};           /* 12.5% fill */
char fill_25[]={68,17,68,17,68,17,68,17};         /*   25% fill */
char fill_37[]={146,41,148,73,164,73,146,73};     /* 37.5% fill */
char fill_50[]={85,170,85,170,85,170,85,170};     /*   50% fill */
char fill_62[]={109,214,107,182,91,182,109,182};  /* 62.5% fill */
char fill_75[]={187,238,187,238,187,238,187,238}; /*   75% fill */
char fill_87[]={223,253,127,247,223,253,127,247}; /* 87.5% fill */

void keyboard(void);void quit_pgm(void);
void notice(float x,float y);
void coords(void);void graphics_setup(void);

int fg=1;                                      /* foreground color */

float sx,sy,sx1,sy1,sx2,sy2;
float sybase;
float x_res,y_res;
int C0=0,C1=1,C2=2,C3=3,C4=4,C5=5,C6=6,C7=7,C8=8,C9=9,C10=10,
C11=11,C12=12,C13=13,C14=14,C15=15,mode_flag=0;

/*_____


M A I N   R O U T I N E                                         */

main(){
graphics_setup();                       /* establish graphics mode */

fg=C1;

/*                                           draw the background */
setfillpattern(fill_6,fg);
sx=70;sy=38;coords();sx1=sx;sy1=sy;
sx=639;sy=72;coords();sx2=sx;sy2=sy;
bar(sx1,sy1,sx2,sy2);
setfillpattern(fill_12,fg);
```

```
sx=70;coords();sxl=sx;syl=sy2+1;
sx=639;sy=108;coords();sx2=sx;sy2=sy;
bar(sxl,syl,sx2,sy2);
setfillpattern(fill_25,fg);
sx=70;coords();sxl=sx;syl=sy2+1;
sx=639;sy=144;coords();sx2=sx;sy2=sy;
bar(sxl,syl,sx2,sy2);
setfillpattern(fill_37,fg);
sx=70;coords();sxl=sx;syl=sy2+1;
sx=639;sy=180;coords();sx2=sx;sy2=sy;
bar(sxl,syl,sx2,sy2);
setfillpattern(fill_50,fg);
sx=70;coords();sxl=sx;syl=sy2+1;
sx=639;sy=216;coords();sx2=sx;sy2=sy;
bar(sxl,syl,sx2,sy2);
setfillpattern(fill_62,fg);
sx=70;coords();sxl=sx;syl=sy2+1;
sx=639;sy=252;coords();sx2=sx;sy2=sy;
bar(sxl,syl,sx2,sy2);
setfillpattern(fill_75,fg);
sx=70;coords();sxl=sx;syl=sy2+1;
sx=639;sy=288;coords();sx2=sx;sy2=sy;
bar(sxl,syl,sx2,sy2);
setfillpattern(fill_87,fg);
sx=70;coords();sxl=sx;syl=sy2+1;
sx=639;sy=324;coords();sx2=sx;sy2=sy;
bar(sxl,syl,sx2,sy2);
setfillstyle(SOLID_FILL,fg);
sx=70;coords();sxl=sx;syl=sy2+1;
sx=639;sy=396;coords();sx2=sx;sy2=sy;
bar(sxl,syl,sx2,sy2);

/*                                      draw the axis display */
if (mode_flag==4) C7=0;
setfillstyle(SOLID_FILL,C7);

sx=80;sy=60;coords();sxl=sx;syl=sy;
sx=85;sy=384;coords();sx2=sx;sy2=sy;
bar(sxl,syl,sx2,sy2);
sx=80;sy=380;coords();sxl=sx;syl=sy;sybase=sy-1;
sx=600;sy=384;coords();sx2=sx;sy2=sy;
bar(sxl,syl,sx2,sy2);

/*                                      display the text labels */
if (mode_flag==4) C7=1;
setcolor(C7);moveto(112,168);
outtext("Jan Feb Mar Apr May Jun Jul Aug Sep Oct Nov Dec");
setcolor(Cl2);moveto(184,176);
outtext("M O N T H L Y    S A L E S    T O    D A T E");
setcolor(C7);moveto(24,24);outtext("SALES");
moveto(0,40);outtext("$100,000");
moveto(0,64);outtext("$ 80,000");
moveto(0,88);outtext("$ 60,000");
moveto(0,112);outtext("$ 40,000");
moveto(0,136);outtext("$ 20,000");
```

```
/*                                       draw the monthly levels */
setfillstyle(SOLID_FILL,Cl4);
sx=108;sy=204;coords();sxl=sx;syl=sy;
sx=138;coords();sx2=sx;sy2=sybase;
bar(sxl,syl,sx2,sy2);
setfillstyle(SOLID_FILL,Cl0);
sx=148;sy=178;coords();sxl=sx;syl=sy;
sx=178;coords();sx2=sx;sy2=sybase;
bar(sxl,syl,sx2,sy2);
setfillstyle(SOLID_FILL,Cl1);
sx=188;sy=240;coords();sxl=sx;syl=sy;
sx=218;coords();sx2=sx;sy2=sybase;
bar(sxl,syl,sx2,sy2);
setfillstyle(SOLID_FILL,Cl3);
sx=228;sy=264;coords();sxl=sx;syl=sy;
sx=258;coords();sx2=sx;sy2=sybase;
bar(sxl,syl,sx2,sy2);
setfillstyle(SOLID_FILL,Cl4);
sx=268;sy=175;coords();sxl=sx;syl=sy;
sx=298;coords();sx2=sx;sy2=sybase;
bar(sxl,syl,sx2,sy2);
setfillstyle(SOLID_FILL,Cl0);
sx=308;sy=144;coords();sxl=sx;syl=sy;
sx=338;coords();sx2=sx;sy2=sybase;
bar(sxl,syl,sx2,sy2);
setfillstyle(SOLID_FILL,Cl1);
sx=348;sy=134;coords();sxl=sx;syl=sy;
sx=378;coords();sx2=sx;sy2=sybase;
bar(sxl,syl,sx2,sy2);
setfillstyle(SOLID_FILL,C7);
sx=388;sy=139;coords();sxl=sx;syl=sy;
sx=418;coords();sx2=sx;sy2=sybase;
bar(sxl,syl,sx2,sy2);
setcolor(C7);
sx=428;sy=115;coords();sxl=sx;syl=sy;
sx=458;coords();sx2=sx;sy2=sybase+1;
rectangle(sxl,syl,sx2,sy2);
sx=468;sy=110;coords();sxl=sx;syl=sy;
sx=498;coords();sx2=sx;sy2=sybase+1;
rectangle(sxl,syl,sx2,sy2);
sx=508;sy=106;coords();sxl=sx;syl=sy;
sx=538;coords();sx2=sx;sy2=sybase+1;
rectangle(sxl,syl,sx2,sy2);
sx=548;sy=101;coords();sxl=sx;syl=sy;
sx=578;coords();sx2=sx;sy2=sybase+1;
rectangle(sxl,syl,sx2,sy2);

if (mode_flag==4) C7=1;
setcolor(C7);notice(0,0);
keyboard();                    /* wait for user to press <Esc> */
quit_pgm();                    /* end the program gracefully */
}
/*_____
```

```
SUBROUTINE: CHECK THE KEYBOARD BUFFER                                */

void keyboard(void){
union u_type {int a;char b[3];} keystroke;
int get_keystroke(void);           /* declare a local subroutine */

do keystroke.a=get_keystroke();
while (keystroke.b[0]!=27);         /* return if <Esc> is pressed */
}

/* LOCAL SUBROUTINE: RETRIEVE ONE KEYSTROKE                          */

int get_keystroke(void){
union REGS regs;regs.h.ah=0;return int86(0x16,&regs,&regs);}

/*_____


SUBROUTINE: GRACEFUL EXIT FROM THE PROGRAM                          */

void quit_pgm(void){
cleardevice();restorecrtmode();exit(0);}

/*_____


SUBROUTINE: VGA/EGA/CGA/MCGA compatibility module

The 640x200 16-color mode is established if a VGA or EGA is
present.  The 640x200 2-color mode is invoked if a CGA or MCGA
is present.                                                         */

void graphics_setup(void){
int graphics_adapter,graphics_mode;
detectgraph(&graphics_adapter,&graphics_mode);
if (graphics_adapter==VGA) goto VGA_EGA_mode;           /* if VGA */
if (graphics_mode==EGAHI) goto VGA_EGA_mode;   /* if EGA and ECD */
if (graphics_mode==EGALO) goto VGA_EGA_mode;   /* if EGA and SCD */
if (graphics_adapter==CGA) goto CGA_mode;               /* if CGA */
if (graphics_adapter==MCGA) goto MCGA_mode;            /* if MCGA */
goto abort_message;              /* if no VGA, EGA, CGA, or MCGA */

VGA_EGA_mode:              /* establish 640x200 16-color mode */
graphics_adapter=EGA;graphics_mode=EGALO;
initgraph(&graphics_adapter,&graphics_mode,"");
x_res=640;y_res=200;mode_flag=3;setcolor(C7);
outtextxy(216,192,"640x200 16-color VGA and EGA mode.");
outtextxy(200,0,"USING C TO PRODUCE BUSINESS GRAPHICS");
return;

CGA_mode:                  /* establish 640x200 2-color mode */
graphics_adapter=CGA;graphics_mode=CGAHI;
initgraph(&graphics_adapter,&graphics_mode,"");
x_res=640;y_res=200;C0=0;C1=1;C2=1;C3=1;C4=1;C5=1;C6=1;C7=1;
```

```
C8=1;C9=1;C10=1;C11=1;C12=1;C13=1;C14=1;C15=1;
mode_flag=4;setcolor(C7);
outtextxy(240,192,"640x200 2-color CGA mode.");
outtextxy(200,0,"USING C TO PRODUCE BUSINESS GRAPHICS");
return;

MCGA_mode:                          /* establish 640x200 2-color mode */
graphics_adapter=MCGA;graphics_mode=MCGAHI;
initgraph(&graphics_adapter,&graphics_mode,"");
x_res=640;y_res=200;C0=0;C1=1;C2=1;C3=1;C4=1;C5=1;C6=1;C7=1;
C8=1;C9=1;C10=1;C11=1;C12=1;C13=1;C14=1;C15=1;
mode_flag=4;setcolor(C7);
outtextxy(240,192,"640x200 2-color MCGA mode.");
outtextxy(200,0,"USING C TO PRODUCE BUSINESS GRAPHICS");
return;

abort_message:
printf("\n\nUnable to proceed.\n");
printf("Requires VGA, EGA, MCGA, or CGA adapter\n");
printf("   with appropriate monitor.\n");
printf("Please refer to the book.\n\n");
exit(0);
}
/*_____


SUBROUTINE: coords()

This subroutine accepts sx,sy device-independent display
coordinates and returns sx,sy device-dependent screen
coordinates scaled to fit the 640x480, 640x350, 640x200, or
320x200 screen, depending upon the graphics mode being used.     */

void coords(void){
sx=sx*(x_res/640);sy=sy*(y_res/480);return;}

/*_____


SUBROUTINE: Copyright Notice

This subroutine displays the standard copyright notice.
If you are typing in this program from the book you can
safely omit this subroutine, provided that you also remove
the instruction "notice()" from the main routine.            */

int copyright[][3]={0x7c00,0x0000,0x0000,0x8231,
0x819c,0x645e,0xba4a,0x4252,0x96d0,0xa231,0x8252,0x955e,0xba4a,
0x43d2,0xf442,0x8231,0x825c,0x945e,0x7c00,0x0000,0x0000};

void notice(float x, float y){
int a,b,c; int tl=0;
for (tl=0;tl<=6;tl++){a=copyright[tl][0];b=copyright[tl][1];
c=copyright[tl][2];
setlinestyle(USERBIT_LINE,a,NORM_WIDTH);
```

```
moveto(x,y);lineto(x+15,y);
setlinestyle(USERBIT_LINE,b,NORM_WIDTH);
moveto(x+16,y);lineto(x+31,y);
setlinestyle(USERBIT_LINE,c,NORM_WIDTH);
moveto(x+32,y);lineto(x+47,y);y=y+1;};
setlinestyle(USERBIT_LINE,0xFFFF,NORM_WIDTH);
return;}

/*_____

End of source code                                            */
```

Fig. E-7. Animated business chart—Turbo C version, VGA/EGA/CGA/MCGA compatible. Refer to the main body of the book for discussion.

```
/*_____

tc-010.c

Function:  This program demonstrates how to animate business
charts by using the high speed techniques of frame animation.

Compatibility:  Supports all graphics adapters and monitors.
The software uses the 640x200 16-color mode if a VGA or an
EGA is present.  The 640x200 2-color mode is used if a
CGA is present.

Remarks:  The 640x200 16-color mode is used with the VGA and
EGA because four graphics pages are required by this animated
program.  Only one page is available in the VGA's 640x480
16-color mode.  Only two pages are available in the EGA's
640x350 16-color mode.  Eight pages are available in the
320x200 16-color mode, but Turbo C 1.5 does not provide graphics
support for that mode.

If a CGA or MCGA is present, the extra graphics pages required by
this program are stored in user RAM, where care must be taken
in order to avoid overwriting the C compiler, the user's
source code, or the operating system.

Copyright 1988 Lee Adams and TAB BOOKS Inc.

_____


INCLUDE    FILES                                              */

#include <stdio.h>                /* supports the printf function */
#include <graphics.h>          /* supports the graphics functions */
#include <process.h>              /* supports the exit() function */
#include <mem.h>                        /* supports memory moves */
```

```
/*_____


DECLARATIONS                                             */

void keyboard(void);void quit_pgm(void);
void notice(float x,float y);
void coords(void);void graphics_setup(void);
void scales(void);void labels(void);void blocks(void);

void animVGAEGA(void);                        /* EGA and VGA only */
void animCGA(void);                              /* CGA only */
void pagemove(unsigned source,unsigned target);  /* CGA only */


float sx,sy,sx1,sy1,sx2,sy2;float x_res,y_res;
int C0=0,C1=1,C2=2,C3=3,C4=4,C5=5,C6=6,C7=7,C8=8,C9=9,C10=10,
C11=11,C12=12,C13=13,C14=14,C15=15,mode_flag=0;
int t1=1,t2=2;

/*                          coordinates for analytic graphics */
float x1=151,x2=262,x3=194,x4=219,x5=245,x6=462;
float y1=105,y2=140,y3=145,y4=180,y5=185,y6=220,
y7=225,y8=259,y9=264,y10=298,y11=303,y12=335,
y13=339,y14=373,y15=377,y16=410;

/*_____


MAIN    ROUTINE                                          */

main(){
graphics_setup();                        /* establish graphics mode */

if (mode_flag==3)                              /* if VGA or EGA */
{setvisualpage(0);setactivepage(0);};
cleardevice();
scales();                        /* create the scale for the chart */
labels();                        /* create the alphanumeric labels */
setcolor(C3);sx=5;sy=460;coords();notice(sx,sy);      /* notice */
blocks();                             /* draw the analytic graphics */
if (mode_flag==4) {pagemove(0xB800,0x8800);}          /* if CGA */


if (mode_flag==3)                              /* if VGA or EGA */
{setvisualpage(1);setactivepage(1);};
cleardevice();
x6=479;x2=265;x3=192;x4=218;
scales();                        /* create the scale for the chart */
labels();                        /* create the alphanumeric labels */
setcolor(C3);sx=5;sy=460;coords();notice(sx,sy);      /* notice */
blocks();                             /* draw the analytic graphics */
if (mode_flag==4) {pagemove(0xB800,0x8C00);}          /* if CGA */
```

```
if (mode_flag==3)                                        /* if VGA or EGA */
{setvisualpage(2);setactivepage(2);};
cleardevice();
x6=492;x2=268;x3=190;x4=217;
scales();                             /* create the scale for the chart */
labels();                             /* create the alphanumeric labels */
setcolor(C3);sx=5;sy=460;coords();notice(sx,sy);          /* notice */
blocks();                                  /* draw the analytic graphics */
if (mode_flag==4) {pagemove(0xB800,0x9000);}              /* if CGA */


if (mode_flag==3)                                        /* if VGA or EGA */
{setvisualpage(3);setactivepage(3);};
cleardevice();
x6=502;x2=271;x3=188;x4=216;
scales();                             /* create the scale for the chart */
labels();                             /* create the alphanumeric labels */
setcolor(C3);sx=5;sy=460;coords();notice(sx,sy);          /* notice */
blocks();                                  /* draw the analytic graphics */
if (mode_flag==4) {pagemove(0xB800,0x9400);}              /* if CGA */
if (mode_flag==3) {setvisualpage(0);setactivepage(0);};


for (tl=1;tl<=30000;tl++);                   /* pause before animating */
if (mode_flag==3) animVGAEGA();        /* animation for VGA and EGA */
if (mode_flag==4) animCGA();           /* animation for CGA and MCGA */

quit_pgm();}                            /* end the program gracefully */

/*_____


SUBROUTINE: frame animation manager for VGA and EGA              */

void animVGAEGA(void){
for (tl=1;tl<=20;tl++){     /* animate 20 cycles of 6 frames each */
setvisualpage(1);for (t2=1;t2<=6000;t2++);
setvisualpage(2);for (t2=1;t2<=6000;t2++);
setvisualpage(3);for (t2=1;t2<=30000;t2++);
setvisualpage(2);for (t2=1;t2<=6000;t2++);
setvisualpage(1);for (t2=1;t2<=6000;t2++);
setvisualpage(0);for (t2=1;t2<=30000;t2++);};
setactivepage(0);setvisualpage(0);
return;}

/*_____


SUBROUTINE: frame animation manager for CGA                     */

void animCGA(void){
for (tl=1;tl<=20;tl++){     /* animate 20 cycles of 6 frames each */
pagemove(0x8C00,0xB800);for (t2=1;t2<=6000;t2++);
pagemove(0x9000,0xB800);for (t2=1;t2<=6000;t2++);
```

```
pagemove(0x9400,0xB800);for (t2=1;t2<=30000;t2++);
pagemove(0x9000,0xB800);for (t2=1;t2<=6000;t2++);
pagemove(0x8C00,0xB800);for (t2=1;t2<=6000;t2++);
pagemove(0x8800,0xB800);for (t2=1;t2<=30000;t2++);};
return;}
```

/*_____

SUBROUTINE: pagemove for CGA

This subroutine is called during the graphics drawing process
in order to store the frames in user RAM. This subroutine is
also called during the frame animation process in order to
flip the previously-stored pages onto the CGA display buffer
at B8000 hex.   */

```
void pagemove(unsigned source, unsigned target){
movedata(source,0x0000,target,0x0000,16000);
return;}
```

/*_____

SUBROUTINE: draw the scales   */

```
void scales(void){
setcolor(C7);
sx=150;sy=420;coords();moveto(sx,sy);
sx=150;sy=82;coords();lineto(sx,sy);
sx=620;sy=82;coords();lineto(sx,sy);

sx=150;sy=82;coords();moveto(sx,sy);
sx=150;sy=78;coords();lineto(sx,sy);
sx=262;sy=82;coords();moveto(sx,sy);
sx=262;sy=78;coords();lineto(sx,sy);
sx=375;sy=82;coords();moveto(sx,sy);
sx=375;sy=78;coords();lineto(sx,sy);
sx=482;sy=82;coords();moveto(sx,sy);
sx=482;sy=78;coords();lineto(sx,sy);
sx=599;sy=82;coords();moveto(sx,sy);
sx=599;sy=78;coords();lineto(sx,sy);
return;}
```

/*_____

SUBROUTINE: alphanumeric labels   */

```
void labels(void){

setcolor(C3);moveto(264,192);
if (mode_flag==3) {outtext("640x200 16-color VGA and EGA mode");}
if (mode_flag==4) {outtext("640x200 2-color CGA and MCGA mode");}
moveto(248,0);
```

```
outtext("USING C TO ANIMATE BUSINESS GRAPHICS");
setcolor(C7);
moveto(24,24);outtext("$ in millions");
moveto(96,48);outtext("Sales");
moveto(32,64);outtext("Cost of Sales");
moveto(88,80);outtext("Profit");
moveto(8,96);outtext("Selling Expenses");
moveto(8,112);outtext("Operating Income");
moveto(32,128);outtext("Interest Paid");
moveto(40,144);outtext("Income Taxes");
moveto(56,160);outtext("Net Profit");
moveto(152,24);outtext("0");
moveto(240,24);outtext("5000");
moveto(360,24);outtext("10000");
moveto(464,24);outtext("15000");
moveto(568,24);outtext("20000");
moveto(360,120);outtext("GRAPHIC INCOME STATEMENT");
moveto(424,128);outtext("FOR 1988");
return;}

/*_____


SUBROUTINE: draw the analytic graphics                        */

void blocks(void){

setfillstyle(SOLID_FILL,C4);
sx=x1;sy=y1;coords();sx1=sx;sy1=sy;
sx=x6;sy=y2;coords();sx2=sx;sy2=sy;
bar(sx1,sy1,sx2,sy2);                            /* sales */

setfillstyle(SOLID_FILL,C7);
sx=x2;sy=y3;coords();sx1=sx;sy1=sy;
sx=x6;sy=y4;coords();sx2=sx;sy2=sy;
bar(sx1,sy1,sx2,sy2);                      /* cost of sales */

setfillstyle(SOLID_FILL,C7);
sx=x1;sy=y5;coords();sx1=sx;sy1=sy;
sx=x2;sy=y6;coords();sx2=sx;sy2=sy;
bar(sx1,sy1,sx2,sy2);                            /* profit */

setfillstyle(SOLID_FILL,C1);
sx=x3;sy=y7;coords();sx1=sx;sy1=sy;
sx=x2;sy=y8;coords();sx2=sx;sy2=sy;
bar(sx1,sy1,sx2,sy2);                   /* selling expenses */

setfillstyle(SOLID_FILL,C1);
sx=x1;sy=y9;coords();sx1=sx;sy1=sy;
sx=x3;sy=y10;coords();sx2=sx;sy2=sy;
bar(sx1,sy1,sx2,sy2);                   /* operating income */

setfillstyle(SOLID_FILL,C2);
sx=x3;sy=y11;coords();sx1=sx;sy1=sy;
```

```
sx=x4;sy=y12;coords();sx2=sx;sy2=sy;
bar(sxl,syl,sx2,sy2);                               /* interest paid */

setfillstyle(SOLID_FILL,C2);
sx=x4;sy=y13;coords();sxl=sx;syl=sy;
sx=x5;sy=y14;coords();sx2=sx;sy2=sy;
bar(sxl,syl,sx2,sy2);                               /* income taxes */

setfillstyle(SOLID_FILL,C2);
sx=x5;sy=y15;coords();sxl=sx;syl=sy;
sx=x2;sy=y16;coords();sx2=sx;sy2=sy;
bar(sxl,syl,sx2,sy2);                               /* net profit */

return;}

/*_____


SUBROUTINE: GRACEFUL EXIT FROM THE PROGRAM                          */

void quit_pgm(void){
cleardevice();restorecrtmode();exit(0);}

/*_____


SUBROUTINE: VGA/EGA/CGA/MCGA compatibility module                   */

void graphics_setup(void){
int graphics_adapter,graphics_mode;
detectgraph(&graphics_adapter,&graphics_mode);
if (graphics_adapter==VGA) goto VGA_EGA_mode;          /* if VGA */
if (graphics_mode==EGAHI) goto VGA_EGA_mode;     /* if EGA and ECD */
if (graphics_mode==EGALO) goto VGA_EGA_mode;     /* if EGA and SCD */
if (graphics_adapter==CGA) goto CGA_mode;             /* if CGA */
if (graphics_adapter==MCGA) goto CGA_mode;            /* if MCGA */
goto abort_message;               /* if no VGA, EGA, CGA, or MCGA */

VGA_EGA_mode:                    /* establish 640x480 16-color mode */
graphics_adapter=EGA;graphics_mode=EGALO;
initgraph(&graphics_adapter,&graphics_mode,"");
x_res=640;y_res=200;mode_flag=3;
return;

CGA_mode:                         /* establish 640x200 2-color mode */
graphics_adapter=CGA;graphics_mode=CGAHI;
initgraph(&graphics_adapter,&graphics_mode,"");
x_res=640;y_res=200;C0=0;Cl=1;C2=1;C3=1;C4=1;C5=1;C6=1;C7=1;
C8=1;C9=1;C10=1;C11=1;C12=1;C13=1;C14=1;C15=1;
mode_flag=4;
return;
```

```
abort_message:
printf("\n\nUnable to proceed.\n");
printf("Requires VGA, EGA, MCGA, or CGA adapter\n");
printf("   with appropriate monitor.\n");
printf("Please refer to the book.\n\n");
exit(0);
}
/*_____



SUBROUTINE: coords()

This subroutine accepts sx,sy device-independent display
coordinates and returns sx,sy device-dependent screen
coordinates scaled to fit the 640x480, 640x350, 640x200, or
320x200 screen, depending upon the graphics mode being used.     */

void coords(void){
sx=sx*(x_res/640);sy=sy*(y_res/480);return;}

/*_____



SUBROUTINE: Copyright Notice

This subroutine displays the standard copyright notice.
If you are typing in this program from the book you can
safely omit this subroutine, provided that you also remove
the instruction "notice()" from the main routine.     */

int copyright[][3]={0x7c00,0x0000,0x0000,0x8231,
0x819c,0x645e,0xba4a,0x4252,0x96d0,0xa231,0x8252,0x955e,0xba4a,
0x43d2,0xf442,0x8231,0x825c,0x945e,0x7c00,0x0000,0x0000};

void notice(float x, float y){
int a,b,c; int tl=0;
for (tl=0;tl<=6;tl++){a=copyright[tl][0];b=copyright[tl][1];
c=copyright[tl][2];
setlinestyle(USERBIT_LINE,a,NORM_WIDTH);
moveto(x,y);lineto(x+15,y);
setlinestyle(USERBIT_LINE,b,NORM_WIDTH);
moveto(x+16,y);lineto(x+31,y);
setlinestyle(USERBIT_LINE,c,NORM_WIDTH);
moveto(x+32,y);lineto(x+47,y);y=y+1;};
setlinestyle(USERBIT_LINE,0xFFFF,NORM_WIDTH);
return;}

/*_____

End of source code                                              */
```

Fig. E-8. Animated hummingbird—Turbo C version, VGA/EGA/CGA/MCGA compatible. Refer to the main body of the book for discussion.

```
/*_____

tc-011.c

Function:  This program demonstrates high speed frame
animation of a hovering hummingbird.  The software takes
the format of a scientific presentation graphic.

Compatibility:  Supports all graphics adapters and monitors.
The software uses the 640x200 16-color mode if a VGA or an
EGA is present.  The 640x200 2-color mode is used if a
CGA is present.

Remarks:  The speed of the microprocessor has a dramatic
effect upon the required animation speed.  The current
delay loops in the animation routines are suited for a
standard 8088 CPU running at 4.77 MHz as found on an IBM PC.
If your personal computer runs faster, you may wish to add
longer delays in the animation routines.  Refer to the book.

Copyright 1988 Lee Adams and TAB BOOKS Inc.

_____


INCLUDE    FILES                                        */

#include <stdio.h>            /* supports the printf function */
#include <graphics.h>      /* supports the graphics functions */
#include <process.h>         /* supports the exit() function */
#include <mem.h>                    /* supports memory moves */
#include <bios.h>       /* supports read of keyboard buffer */

/*_____


DECLARATIONS                                            */

void keyboard(void);void quit_pgm(void);
void notice(float x,float y);void coords(void);
void graphics_setup(void);void labels(void);void draw_bird(void);

void animVGAEGA(void);                     /* EGA and VGA only */
void animCGA(void);                              /* CGA only */
void pagemove(unsigned source,unsigned target);  /* CGA only */

int frame=0,t1=1,t2=2;
float sx,sy,sx1,sy1,sx2,sy2;float x_res,y_res;
int C0=0,C1=1,C2=2,C3=3,C4=4,C5=5,C6=6,C7=7,C8=8,C9=9,C10=10,
C11=11,C12=12,C13=13,C14=14,C15=15,mode_flag=0;
```

```
char fill_75[ ]={187,238,187,238,187,238,187,238};

int pl=0;                               /* pointer into arrays */
int array1[ ][2]={                      /* xy coordinates for body */
205,219, 208,218, 212,214, 218,212, 221,208, 229,197,
232,192, 241,187, 250,183, 258,183, 265,185, 273,189,
282,198, 377,180, 376,182, 310,200, 297,207, 289,211,
286,217, 282,221, 278,230, 269,238, 256,248, 249,253,
240,261, 235,269, 231,278, 228,280, 214,294, 199,304,
188,310, 181,317, 177,324, 176,321, 169,328, 168,325,
162,330, 162,326, 135,340, 126,345, 120,345, 111,346,
106,349,  58,390,  49,399,  42,405,  42,402,  51,391,
74,364,  87,353,  99,339, 107,324, 114,309, 127,289,
138,274, 146,259};

int array2[ ][2]={         /* xy coordinates for near wing, frame 0 */
146,259, 143,246, 136,234, 128,221, 110,199,  98,184,
88,169,  79,144,  76,136,  74,118,  73, 98,  69, 72,
74, 69,  80, 71,  86, 74, 107,101, 119,112, 124,118,
143,139, 154,154, 161,166, 166,171, 181,188, 187,195,
193,200, 197,209, 205,219, 179,259};

int array3[ ][2]={         /* xy coordinates for far wing, frame 0 */
119,112, 118, 99, 118, 87, 121, 59, 121, 52, 126, 49,
134, 47, 139, 62, 146, 73, 154, 88, 174,129, 187,170,
194,184, 199,197, 207,209, 212,214, 139, 99};

int array4[ ][2]={                      /* xy coordinates for eye */
248,199, 250,196, 258,195, 261,197, 263,200, 261,204,
258,207, 252,205, 250,203, 248,199, 257,200};

int array5[ ][2]={         /* xy coordinates for throat markings */
212,214, 218,212, 224,212, 222,217, 239,217, 237,219,
245,222, 259,219, 258,222, 269,220, 268,224, 278,220,
278,224, 282,221, 278,230, 269,238, 256,248, 249,253,
240,261, 240,258, 234,261, 234,257, 232,258, 232,253,
226,252, 227,249, 219,248, 222,244, 219,242, 220,240,
211,238, 214,230, 211,228, 212,214, 239,239};

int array6[ ][2]={         /* xy coordinates for near wing, frame 1 */
146,259, 140,250, 129,245, 109,234,  92,219,  82,209,
77,193,  73,179,  74,159,  78,146,  84,136,  96,138,
119,147, 129,157, 140,165, 152,178, 159,184, 175,199,
189,210, 194,213, 205,219,  85,179};

int array7[ ][2]={         /* xy coordinates for far wing, frame 1 */
152,178, 151,156, 151,137, 154,121, 156,113, 164, 98,
166, 89, 170, 84, 178, 93, 180,100, 185,107, 188,127,
191,148, 193,169, 197,179, 202,199, 212,214, 177,119};

int array8[ ][2]={         /* xy coordinates for near wing, frame 2 */
146,259, 119,258, 104,253,  98,249,  93,241,  90,237,

90,228,  94,204,  97,198, 106,193, 124,190, 137,189,
```

```
151,195, 163,199, 175,208, 205,219, 109,242};

int array9[][2]={          /* xy coordinates for far wing, frame 2 */
163,199, 163,184, 169,171, 169,152, 173,144, 178,138,
187,127, 194,119, 199,118, 202,125, 203,134, 204,162,
207,179, 209,195, 210,207, 212,214, 199,139};

int array10[][2]={        /* xy coordinates for near wing, frame 3 */
146,259, 137,270, 124,277, 118,277, 114,276, 111,269,
112,260, 114,258, 125,246, 127,237, 139,228, 163,219,
174,218, 179,218, 191,219, 205,219, 119,269};

int array11[][2]={        /* xy coordinates for far wing, frame 3 */
174,218, 178,203, 185,185, 192,177, 199,169, 211,160,
224,157, 227,161, 227,169, 226,177, 224,188, 217,205,
212,214, 219,179};

/*_____


M A I N   R O U T I N E                                        */

main(){
graphics_setup();                        /* establish graphics mode */
setcolor(C7);

if (mode_flag==3) {setvisualpage(0);setactivepage(0);};
cleardevice();
frame=0;                                        /* set the frame flag */
labels();                         /* create the alphanumeric labels */
draw_bird();                                   /* draw the graphics */
if (mode_flag==4) {pagemove(0xB800,0x8800);}        /* if CGA */

if (mode_flag==3) {setvisualpage(1);setactivepage(1);};
cleardevice();
frame=1;                                        /* set the frame flag */
labels();                         /* create the alphanumeric labels */
draw_bird();                                   /* draw the graphics */
if (mode_flag==4) {pagemove(0xB800,0x8C00);}        /* if CGA */

if (mode_flag==3) {setvisualpage(2);setactivepage(2);};
cleardevice();
frame=2;                                        /* set the frame flag */
labels();                         /* create the alphanumeric labels */
draw_bird();                                   /* draw the graphics */
if (mode_flag==4) {pagemove(0xB800,0x9000);}        /* if CGA */

if (mode_flag==3) {setvisualpage(3);setactivepage(3);};
cleardevice();
frame=3;                                        /* set the frame flag */
labels();                         /* create the alphanumeric labels */
draw_bird();                                   /* draw the graphics */
if (mode_flag==4) {pagemove(0xB800,0x9400);};        /* if CGA */
```

```
if (mode_flag==3) {setvisualpage(0);setactivepage(0);};
if (mode_flag==4) {pagemove(0x8800,0xB800);};

for (t1=1;t1<=30000;t1++);              /* pause before animating */
if (mode_flag==3) animVGAEGA();     /* animation for VGA and EGA */
if (mode_flag==4) animCGA();                /* animation for CGA */

quit_pgm();}                          /* end the program gracefully */
```

```
/*_____
```

```
SUBROUTINE: frame animation manager for VGA and EGA           */
```

```
void animVGAEGA(void){
for (t1=1;t1!=2; ){                      /* animate for endless loop */
setvisualpage(1);for (t2=1;t2<=1000;t2++);
setvisualpage(2);for (t2=1;t2<=1000;t2++);
setvisualpage(3);for (t2=1;t2<=1000;t2++);keyboard();
setvisualpage(2);for (t2=1;t2<=1000;t2++);
setvisualpage(1);for (t2=1;t2<=1000;t2++);
setvisualpage(0);for (t2=1;t2<=1000;t2++);keyboard();};
return;}
```

```
/*_____
```

```
SUBROUTINE: frame animation manager for CGA                   */
```

```
void animCGA(void){
for (t1=1;t1!=2; ){                      /* animate for endless loop */
pagemove(0x8C00,0xB800);for (t2=1;t2<=1000;t2++);
pagemove(0x9000,0xB800);for (t2=1;t2<=1000;t2++);
pagemove(0x9400,0xB800);for (t2=1;t2<=1000;t2++);keyboard();
pagemove(0x9000,0xB800);for (t2=1;t2<=1000;t2++);
pagemove(0x8C00,0xB800);for (t2=1;t2<=1000;t2++);
pagemove(0x8800,0xB800);for (t2=1;t2<=1000;t2++);keyboard();};
return;}
```

```
/*_____
```

```
SUBROUTINE: pagemove for CGA

This subroutine flips a graphics page from the screen buffer
into RAM or from RAM to the screen buffer.                     */

void pagemove(unsigned source, unsigned target){
movedata(source,0x0000,target,0x0000,16000);return;}
```

```
/*_____
```

```
SUBROUTINE: display the alphanumeric labels                        */

void labels(void){
setcolor(C7);moveto(0,192);
if (mode_flag==3) {outtext("640x200 16-color VGA and EGA mode");}
if (mode_flag==4) {outtext("640x200 2-color CGA mode");}
moveto(168,0);
outtext("USING C FOR HIGH SPEED FRAME ANIMATION");
moveto(408,192);outtext("Press any key to quit.");
setcolor(C14);moveto(424,40);
outtext("Ruby-throated Hummingbird");
setcolor(C7);
moveto(440,56);
outtext("(Archilochus colubris)");
moveto(408,88);
outtext("Range: Central & eastern U.S.");
moveto(408,104);outtext("Breeds from southern");
moveto(408,112);outtext("Canada to the Gulf Coast.");
moveto(408,128);outtext("Depicted here in its");
moveto(408,136);outtext("characteristic hovering");
moveto(408,144);outtext("flight pattern.");
setcolor(C12);
moveto(408,160);outtext("Animation rate:");
setcolor(C7);
moveto(408,168);
if (mode_flag==3) {outtext("    36 frames per second.");}
if (mode_flag==4) {outtext("    10 frames per second.");}
return;}

/*_____


SUBROUTINE: draw the graphics                                     */

void draw_bird(void){

setcolor(C7);setfillstyle(SOLID_FILL,C7);
sx=0;sy=30;coords();sx1=sx;sy1=sy;
sx=385;sy=458;coords();sx2=sx;sy2=sy;
bar(sx1,sy1,sx2,sy2);
setcolor(C0);

pl=0;                              /* draw the hummingbird's body */
sx=array1[pl][0];sy=array1[pl][1];pl++;coords();moveto(sx,sy);
for (tl=1;tl<=55;tl++){
sx=array1[pl][0];sy=array1[pl][1];pl++;
coords();lineto(sx,sy);};

if (frame==0) {
pl=0;                              /* draw near wings for frame 0 */
sx=array2[pl][0];sy=array2[pl][1];pl++;coords();moveto(sx,sy);
for (tl=1;tl<=26;tl++){
sx=array2[pl][0];sy=array2[pl][1];pl++;
coords();lineto(sx,sy);};
```

```
sx=array2[pl][0];sy=array2[pl][1];coords();
pl=0;
sx=array3[pl][0];sy=array3[pl][1];pl++;coords();moveto(sx,sy);
for (tl=1;tl<=15;tl++){
sx=array3[pl][0];sy=array3[pl][1];pl++;
coords();lineto(sx,sy);};
sx=array3[pl][0];sy=array3[pl][1];coords();
}

if (frame==1) {
pl=0;                              /* draw near wings for frame 1 */
sx=array6[pl][0];sy=array6[pl][1];pl++;coords();moveto(sx,sy);
for (tl=1;tl<=20;tl++){
sx=array6[pl][0];sy=array6[pl][1];pl++;
coords();lineto(sx,sy);};
sx=array6[pl][0];sy=array6[pl][1];coords();
pl=0;
sx=array7[pl][0];sy=array7[pl][1];pl++;coords();moveto(sx,sy);
for (tl=1;tl<=16;tl++){
sx=array7[pl][0];sy=array7[pl][1];pl++;
coords();lineto(sx,sy);};
sx=array7[pl][0];sy=array7[pl][1];coords();
}

if (frame==2) {
pl=0;                              /* draw near wings for frame 2 */
sx=array8[pl][0];sy=array8[pl][1];pl++;coords();moveto(sx,sy);
for (tl=1;tl<=15;tl++){
sx=array8[pl][0];sy=array8[pl][1];pl++;
coords();lineto(sx,sy);};
sx=array8[pl][0];sy=array8[pl][1];coords();
pl=0;
sx=array9[pl][0];sy=array9[pl][1];pl++;coords();moveto(sx,sy);
for (tl=1;tl<=15;tl++){
sx=array9[pl][0];sy=array9[pl][1];pl++;
coords();lineto(sx,sy);};
sx=array9[pl][0];sy=array9[pl][1];coords();
}

if (frame==3) {
pl=0;                              /* draw near wings for frame 3 */
sx=array10[pl][0];sy=array10[pl][1];pl++;coords();moveto(sx,sy);
for (tl=1;tl<=15;tl++){
sx=array10[pl][0];sy=array10[pl][1];pl++;
coords();lineto(sx,sy);};
sx=array10[pl][0];sy=array10[pl][1];coords();
pl=0;
sx=array11[pl][0];sy=array11[pl][1];pl++;coords();moveto(sx,sy);
for (tl=1;tl<=12;tl++){
sx=array11[pl][0];sy=array11[pl][1];pl++;
coords();lineto(sx,sy);};
sx=array11[pl][0];sy=array11[pl][1];coords();
}
```

```
setcolor(C0);
pl=0;                                /* draw the hummingbird's eye */
sx=array4[pl][0];sy=array4[pl][1];pl++;coords();moveto(sx,sy);
for (tl=1;tl<=9;tl++){
sx=array4[pl][0];sy=array4[pl][1];pl++;
coords();lineto(sx,sy);};
sx=array4[pl][0];sy=array4[pl][1];coords();
setfillstyle(SOLID_FILL,C0);floodfill(sx,sy,C0);

setcolor(C4);setfillstyle(SOLID_FILL,C4);
pl=0;                                /* draw the throat markings */
sx=array5[pl][0];sy=array5[pl][1];pl++;coords();moveto(sx,sy);
for (tl=1;tl<=33;tl++){
sx=array5[pl][0];sy=array5[pl][1];pl++;
coords();lineto(sx,sy);};
sx=array5[pl][0];sy=array5[pl][1];coords();floodfill(sx,sy,C4);

setcolor(C0);sx=5;sy=436;coords();notice(sx,sy);       /* notice */
setcolor(C7);return;}

/*_____


SUBROUTINE: press any key to quit                            */

void keyboard(void){
if (bioskey(1)==0) return; else quit_pgm();}

/*_____


SUBROUTINE: GRACEFUL EXIT FROM THE PROGRAM                   */

void quit_pgm(void){
if (mode_flag==3) {setvisualpage(0);setactivepage(0);};
cleardevice();restorecrtmode();exit(0);}

/*_____

SUBROUTINE: VGA/EGA/CGA/MCGA compatibility module            */

void graphics_setup(void){
int graphics_adapter,graphics_mode;
detectgraph(&graphics_adapter,&graphics_mode);
if (graphics_adapter==VGA) goto VGA_EGA_mode;         /* if VGA */
if (graphics_mode==EGAHI) goto VGA_EGA_mode;    /* if EGA and ECD */
if (graphics_mode==EGALO) goto VGA_EGA_mode;    /* if EGA and SCD */
if (graphics_adapter==CGA) goto CGA_mode;             /* if CGA */
if (graphics_adapter==MCGA) goto CGA_mode;            /* if MCGA */
goto abort_message;                 /* if no VGA, EGA, CGA, or MCGA */

VGA_EGA_mode:                 /* establish 640x200 16-color mode */
graphics_adapter=EGA;graphics_mode=EGALO;
initgraph(&graphics_adapter,&graphics_mode,"");
```

```
x_res=640;y_res=200;mode_flag=3;
return;

CGA_mode:                           /* establish 640x200 2-color mode */
graphics_adapter=CGA;graphics_mode=CGAHI;
initgraph(&graphics_adapter,&graphics_mode,"");
x_res=640;y_res=200;mode_flag=4;
C0=0;C1=1;C2=1;C3=1;C4=0;C5=1,C6=1;C7=1;
C8=1;C9=1;C10=1;C11=1;C12=1;C13=1;C14=1;C15=1;
return;

abort_message:
printf("\n\nUnable to proceed.\n");
printf("Requires VGA, EGA, MCGA, or CGA adapter\n");
printf("    with appropriate monitor.\n");
printf("Please refer to the book.\n\n");
exit(0);
}
/*_____


SUBROUTINE: coords()

This subroutine accepts sx,sy device-independent display
coordinates and returns sx,sy device-dependent screen
coordinates scaled to fit the 640x480, 640x350, 640x200, or
320x200 screen, depending upon the graphics mode being used.      */

void coords(void){
sx=sx*(x_res/640);sy=sy*(y_res/480);return;}

    /*_____


SUBROUTINE: Copyright Notice

This subroutine displays the standard copyright notice.
If you are typing in this program from the book you can
safely omit this subroutine, provided that you also remove
the instruction "notice()" from the main routine.                */

int copyright[][3]={0x7c00,0x0000,0x0000,0x8231,
0x819c,0x645e,0xba4a,0x4252,0x96d0,0xa231,0x8252,0x955e,0xba4a,
0x43d2,0xf442,0x8231,0x825c,0x945e,0x7c00,0x0000,0x0000};

void notice(float x, float y){
int a,b,c; int tl=0;
for (tl=0;tl<=6;tl++){a=copyright[tl][0];b=copyright[tl][1];
c=copyright[tl][2];
setlinestyle(USERBIT_LINE,a,NORM_WIDTH);
moveto(x,y);lineto(x+15,y);
setlinestyle(USERBIT_LINE,b,NORM_WIDTH);
moveto(x+16,y);lineto(x+31,y);
setlinestyle(USERBIT_LINE,c,NORM_WIDTH);
```

```
moveto(x+32,y);lineto(x+47,y);y=y+1;};
setlinestyle(USERBIT_LINE,0xFFFF,NORM_WIDTH);
return;}

/*_____

End of source code                                    */
```

Fig. E-9. Animated rotation of 3D model—Turbo C version, VGA/EGA compatible. Refer to the main body of the book for discussion.

```
/*_____

tc-012.c

Function:  This program demonstrates high speed frame
animation of a 3D shaded object.  Visual perception of the
model is improved by the rotation of the model, which
enhances the three dimensional effect.

Compatibility:  Supports VGA and EGA graphics adapters and
monitors.  The software uses the 640x200 16-color mode.

Remarks:  The speed of the microprocessor has a dramatic
effect upon the required animation speed.  Refer to the book.

Copyright 1988 Lee Adams and TAB BOOKS Inc.

_____


INCLUDE    FILES                                      */

#include <stdio.h>              /* supports the printf function */
#include <graphics.h>          /* supports the graphics functions */
#include <process.h>            /* supports the exit() function */
#include <bios.h>             /* supports read of keyboard buffer */
#include <math.h>         /* supports the sine and cosine functions */

/*_____


DECLARATIONS                                          */

void keyboard(void);void quit_pgm(void);
void notice(float x,float y);void coords(void);
void graphics_setup(void);void labels(void);void draw_object(void);
void calc_3d(void);void rotation(void);void window(void);
void line_clip(void);void get_coords(void);void draw_poly(void);
void animVGAEGA(void);
```

```
int t1=1,t2=2,t3=1;                              /* loop counters */
float x_res,y_res;          /* used by compatibility mapping routine */
int C0=0,C1=1,C2=2,C3=3,C4=4,C5=5,C6=6,C7=7,C8=8,C9=9,C10=10,
C11=11,C12=12,C13=13,C14=14,C15=15,mode_flag=0;        /* colors */
int CLR,CLR1,CLR2,CLR3,EDGE;

int p1=0,p2=0;                                /* pointer into arrays */
float x=0.0,y=0.0,z=0.0;                       /* world coordinates */
float sx=0.0,sy=0.0;          /* output of 3D perspective formulas */
float xa=0.0,ya=0.0,za=0.0;    /* temporary values in 3D formulas */
float sxa=0.0,sya=0.0,sxb=0.0,syb=0.0;         /* 2D line endpoints */
float sxs=0.0,sys=0.0;       /* temp storage of 2D line startpoint */
float temp_swap=0.0;                       /* used for variable swaps */
float d=1200.0;                          /* angular perspective factor */
double r1=.48539;                          /* yaw angle in radians */
double r2=6.28319;                         /* roll angle in radians */
double r3=5.79778;                         /* pitch angle in radians */
double sr1=0.0,sr2=0.0,sr3=0.0;            /* sine rotation factors */
double cr1=0.0,cr2=0.0,cr3=0.0;          /* cosine rotation factors */
float mx=0.0,my=-5.0,mz=-250.0;              /* viewpoint position */
int maxx=638,minx=1,maxy=198,miny=1;         /* clipping viewport */
float c=0.0;                          /* used in line-clipping routine */
float screen_x=639,screen_y=199;     /* dimensions of screen mode */
float rx=0.0,ry=0.0;    /* scaling values used in mapping routine */

                 /* database of xyz world coordinates */
int array_xyz[][3]={
20,-20,-30, 20,20,-30, 20,20,-20, 20,-20,-20, 20,-20,-30, 20,0,-25,
20,-20,-30, -20,-20,-30, -20,-20,-20, 20,-20,-20, 20,-20,-30, 0,-20,-25

-30,30,-30, 30,30,-30, 30,30,-20, -30,30,-20, -30,30,-30, 0,30,-25,
-30,30,-30, -30,30,-20, -30,-30,-20, -30,-30,-30, -30,30,-30, -30,0,-25
-30,30,-20, 30,30,-20, 30,20,-20, -30,20,-20, -30,30,-20, 0,25,-20,
30,30,-20, 30,-30,-20, 20,-30,-20, 20,30,-20, 30,30,-20, 25,0,-20,
30,-30,-20, -30,-30,-20, -30,-20,-20, 30,-20,-20, 30,-30,-20, 0,-25,-20
-30,-30,-20, -30,30,-20, -20,30,-20, -20,-30,-20, -30,-30,-20, -25,0,-2

20,-30,-20, 20,-20,-20, 20,-20,20, 20,-30,20, 20,-30,-20, 20,-25,0,

-30,-30,30, -30,-20,30, 30,-20,30, 30,-30,30, -30,-30,30, 0,-25,30,
-30,-30,-30, -30,-20,-30, -30,-20,30, -30,-30,30, -30,-30,-30, -30,-25,
-30,-20,-20, -20,-20,-20, -20,-20,30, -30,-20,30, -30,-20,-20, -25,-20,
30,-20,-20, 30,-20,30, 20,-20,30, 20,-20,-20, 30,-20,-20, 25,-20,0,
-30,-20,30, -30,-20,20, 30,-20,20, 30,-20,30, -30,-20,30, 0,-20,25,

20,30,-20, 20,30,30, 20,20,30, 20,20,-20, 20,30,-20, 20,25,0,
20,30,30, 20,-20,30, 20,-20,20, 20,30,20, 20,30,30, 20,0,25,

-30,30,-30, -20,30,-30, -20,30,30, -30,30,30, -30,30,-30, -25,30,0,
20,30,-30, 30,30,-30, 30,30,30, 20,30,30, 20,30,-30, 25,30,0,
-30,30,30, -30,30,20, 30,30,20, 30,30,30, -30,30,30, 0,30,25,

-30,-30,30, -30,30,30, -20,30,30, -20,-30,30, -30,-30,30, -25,0,30,
20,-30,30, 20,30,30, 30,30,30, 30,-30,30, 20,-30,30, 25,0,30,
```

```
-30,30,30, 30,30,30, 30,20,30, -30,20,30, -30,30,30, 0,25,30,
-30,20,-30, -30,30,-30, -30,30,30, -30,20,30, -30,20,-30, -30,25,0,
-30,-30,20, -30,30,20, -30,30,30, -30,-30,30, -30,-30,20, -30,0,25};
```

```
/*_____
```

```
M A I N    R O U T I N E                                    */
```

```
main(){
graphics_setup();                          /* establish graphics mode */

CLR1=C7;CLR2=C9;CLR3=C1;EDGE=C1;    /* color scheme for rendering */

setvisualpage(0);setactivepage(0);cleardevice();
r1=.58539;r2=6.28319;r3=5.79778;labels();draw_object();

setvisualpage(1);setactivepage(1);cleardevice();
r1=r1+.08727;r2=6.28319;r3=r3+.04363;labels();draw_object();

setvisualpage(2);setactivepage(2);cleardevice();
r1=r1+.08727;r2=6.28319;r3=r3+.04363;labels();draw_object();

setvisualpage(3);setactivepage(3);cleardevice();
r1=r1+.08727;r2=6.28319;r3=r3+.04363;labels();draw_object();

setvisualpage(0);setactivepage(0);           /* reset to frame 0 */
for (t1=1;t1<=30000;t1++);                             /* pause */
animVGAEGA();                            /* animation for VGA and EGA */
quit_pgm();}                          /* end the program gracefully */
```

```
/*_____
```

```
SUBROUTINE: display the alphanumeric labels                    */
```

```
void labels(void){
setcolor(C7);moveto(0,192);
outtext("640x200 16-color VGA and EGA mode");
moveto(168,0);
outtext("USING C FOR HIGH SPEED FRAME ANIMATION");
moveto(464,192);outtext("Press any key to stop.");
setcolor(C12);moveto(176,24);
outtext("Animated rotation of solid 3D object");
setcolor(C7);moveto(0,40);outtext("Animation rate:");
moveto(0,48);outtext("36 frames per second.");
return;}
```

```
/*_____
```

```
SUBROUTINE: draw the graphics                                  */
```

```
void draw_object(void){
```

```
rotation();        /* recalculate sine and cosine rotation factors */
pl=0;                                   /* reset array index pointer */

CLR=CLR3;EDGE=CLR3;draw_poly();                             /* step one */
CLR=CLR1;EDGE=CLR1;draw_poly();

draw_poly();                                               /* step two */
CLR=CLR3;EDGE=CLR3;draw_poly();
CLR=CLR2;EDGE=CLR2;for (t3=1;t3<=4;t3++){draw_poly();}

CLR=CLR3;EDGE=CLR3;draw_poly();                          /* step three */

CLR=CLR2;EDGE=CLR2;draw_poly();                           /* step four */
CLR=CLR3;EDGE=CLR3;draw_poly();
CLR=CLR1;EDGE=CLR1;for (t3=1;t3<=3;t3++){draw_poly();}

CLR=CLR3;EDGE=CLR3;for (t3=1;t3<=2;t3++)                  /* step five */
{draw_poly();}

CLR=CLR1;EDGE=CLR1;for (t3=1;t3<=3;t3++)                   /* step six */
{draw_poly();}
CLR=CLR2;EDGE=CLR2;for (t3=1;t3<=3;t3++){draw_poly();}
CLR=CLR3;EDGE=CLR3;for (t3=1;t3<=2;t3++){draw_poly();}

setcolor(C7);sx=5;sy=400;coords();notice(sx,sy);return;}

/*_____


SUBROUTINE: draw and fill polygon in 3D space                      */

void draw_poly(void){

setcolor(Cl3);                    /* set the key matte drawing color */
setfillstyle(SOLID_FILL,Cl3);        /* set the key matte fill color */
get_coords();          /* retrieve xyz vertex coords from database */
calc_3d();                /* 3D rotation, translation, projection */
window();                /* map display coords to fit 4:3 screen */
sxa=sx;sya=sy;                                  /* line start point */

for (tl=1;tl<=4;tl++){                          /* draw 4 lines in 3D */
get_coords();          /* retrieve xyz vertex coords from database */
calc_3d();                /* 3D rotation, translation, projection */
window();                /* map display coords to fit 4:3 screen */
sxs=sx;sys=sy;sxb=sx;syb=sy;        /* line is sxa,sya to sxb,syb */
line_clip();                          /* clip line to screen edges */
moveto(sxa,sya);lineto(sxb,syb);           /* draw the line in 3D */
sxa=sxs;sya=sys;                        /* define next start point */
}                                          /* repeat until done */

get_coords();      /* retrieve xyz area fill coords from database */
calc_3d();window();floodfill(sx,sy,Cl3);              /* area fill */
```

```
  setcolor(CLR);                                    /* set the drawing color */
  setfillstyle(SOLID_FILL,CLR);                       /* set the fill color */

  EDGE=CLR;
  pl=pl-6;                                          /* reset index pointer */
  get_coords();calc_3d();window();sxa=sx;sya=sy;
  for (tl=1;tl<=4;tl++){
  get_coords();calc_3d();window();sxs=sx;sys=sy;sxb=sx;syb=sy;
  line_clip();moveto(sxa,sya);lineto(sxb,syb);
  sxa=sxs;sya=sys;}
  get_coords();calc_3d();window();floodfill(sx,sy,EDGE);

  return;}                                           /* return to caller */

/*_____


SUBROUTINE: frame animation manager for VGA and EGA                 */

void animVGAEGA(void){
  for (tl=1;tl!=2; ){                      /* animate for endless loop */
  setvisualpage(1);for (t2=1;t2<=1500;t2++);
  setvisualpage(2);for (t2=1;t2<=1500;t2++);
  setvisualpage(3);for (t2=1;t2<=30000;t2++);keyboard();
  setvisualpage(2);for (t2=1;t2<=1500;t2++);
  setvisualpage(1);for (t2=1;t2<=1500;t2++);
  setvisualpage(0);for (t2=1;t2<=30000;t2++);keyboard();
  setvisualpage(1);for (t2=1;t2<=2500;t2++);
  setvisualpage(2);for (t2=1;t2<=2500;t2++);
  setvisualpage(3);for (t2=1;t2<=30000;t2++);keyboard();
  setvisualpage(2);for (t2=1;t2<=2500;t2++);
  setvisualpage(1);for (t2=1;t2<=2500;t2++);
  setvisualpage(0);for (t2=1;t2<=30000;t2++);keyboard();};
  return;}

/*_____


SUBROUTINE: RETRIEVE xyz WORLD COORDINATES FROM DATABASE

This subroutine retrieves a set of xyz cartresian world
coordinates from the database.  The index pointer is
automatically incremented.                                        */

void get_coords(void){
x=array_xyz[pl][0];y=array_xyz[pl][1];z=array_xyz[pl][2];
pl++;return;}

/*_____


SUBROUTINE: CALCULATE SIN, COS FACTORS

Enter with r1,r2,r3 viewing angles for yaw, roll, pitch
```

expressed in radians 0.0 through 6.28319. Returns sine
and cosine factors.   */

```
void rotation(void){
sr1=sin(r1);sr2=sin(r2);sr3=sin(r3);cr1=cos(r1);cr2=cos(r2);
cr3=cos(r3);return;}
```

/*_____

SUBROUTINE: STANDARD 3D FORMULAS

Enter with x,y,z cartesian world coordinates. Returns sx,sy
cartesian display coordinates. Returns x,y,z cartesian view
coordinates.   */

```
void calc_3d(void){
x=(-1)*x;xa=cr1*x-sr1*z;za=sr1*x+cr1*z;x=cr2*xa+sr2*y;
ya=cr2*y-sr2*xa;z=cr3*za-sr3*ya;y=sr3*za+cr3*ya;x=x+mx;y=y+my;
z=z+mz;sx=d*x/z;sy=d*y/z;return;}
```

/*_____

SUBROUTINE: MAP CARTESIAN COORDS TO PHYSICAL SCREEN COORDS

Enter with sx,sy cartesian display coordinates derived from
world coordinate space -399,-299 to 400,300. Returns sx,sy
unclipped physical display coordinates.   */

```
void window(void){
sx=sx+399;sy=sy+299;rx=screen_x/799;ry=screen_y/599;sx=sx*rx;
sy=sy*ry;return;}
```

/*_____

SUBROUTINE: 2D LINE-CLIPPING

Enter with sxa,sya and sxb,syb endpoints of line to be
clipped. Returns display coordinates for line clipped to
fit physical screen viewport defined by minx,miny and
maxx,maxy.   */

```
void line_clip(void){
if (sxa>sxb) {temp_swap=sxa;sxa=sxb;sxb=temp_swap;
temp_swap=sya;sya=syb;syb=temp_swap;};

if (sxa<minx) if (sxb<minx) return;
if (sxa>maxx) if (sxb>maxx) return;
if (sya<miny) if (syb<miny) return;
if (sya>maxy) if (syb>maxy) return;
```

```
if (sxa<minx) {{c=(syb-sya)/(sxb-sxa)*(sxb-minx);  /* push right */
sxa=minx;sya=syb-c;};
if (sya<miny) if (syb<miny) return;
if (sya>maxy) if (syb>maxy) return;
};

if (sxb>maxx) {{c=(syb-sya)/(sxb-sxa)*(maxx-sxa);  /* push left */
sxb=maxx;syb=sya+c;};
if (sya<miny) if (syb<miny) return;
if (sya>maxy) if (syb>maxy) return;
};

if (sya>syb) {temp_swap=sya;sya=syb;syb=temp_swap;
temp_swap=sxa;sxa=sxb;sxb=temp_swap;};

if (sya<miny) {c=(sxb-sxa)/(syb-sya)*(syb-miny);   /* push down */
sxa=sxb-c;sya=miny;};

if (syb>maxy) {c=(sxb-sxa)/(syb-sya)*(maxy-sya);    /* push up */
sxb=sxa+c;syb=maxy;};

return;}

/*_____


SUBROUTINE: press any key to quit                          */

void keyboard(void){
if (bioskey(1)==0) return; else quit_pgm();}

/*_____


SUBROUTINE: GRACEFUL EXIT FROM THE PROGRAM                 */

void quit_pgm(void){
if (mode_flag==3) {setvisualpage(0);setactivepage(0);};
cleardevice();restorecrtmode();exit(0);}

/*_____


SUBROUTINE: VGA/EGA/CGA/MCGA compatibility module          */

void graphics_setup(void){
int graphics_adapter,graphics_mode;
detectgraph(&graphics_adapter,&graphics_mode);
if (graphics_adapter==VGA) goto VGA_EGA_mode;          /* if VGA */
if (graphics_mode==EGAHI) goto VGA_EGA_mode;   /* if EGA and ECD */
if (graphics_mode==EGALO) goto VGA_EGA_mode;   /* if EGA and SCD */
if (graphics_adapter==CGA) goto abort_message;         /* if CGA */
if (graphics_adapter==MCGA) goto abort_message;       /* if MCGA */
goto abort_message;             /* if no VGA, EGA, CGA, or MCGA */
```

```
VGA_EGA_mode:                      /* establish 640x200 16-color mode */
graphics_adapter=EGA;graphics_mode=EGALO;
initgraph(&graphics_adapter,&graphics_mode,"");
x_res=640;y_res=200;mode_flag=3;
maxx=638;minx=1;maxy=198;miny=1;              /* clipping viewport */
screen_x=639;screen_y=199;                 /* dimensions of screen */
x_res=640;y_res=200;                       /* resolution of screen */
return;

abort_message:
printf("\n\nUnable to proceed.\n");
printf("Requires VGA or EGA adapter\n");
printf("   with appropriate monitor.\n");
printf("Please refer to the book.\n\n");
exit(0);
}
/*_____


SUBROUTINE: coords()

This subroutine accepts sx,sy device-independent display
coordinates and returns sx,sy device-dependent screen
coordinates scaled to fit the 640x480, 640x350, 640x200, or
320x200 screen, depending upon the graphics mode being used.      */

void coords(void){
sx=sx*(x_res/640);sy=sy*(y_res/480);return;}

/*_____


SUBROUTINE: Copyright Notice

This subroutine displays the standard copyright notice.
If you are typing in this program from the book you can
safely omit this subroutine, provided that you also remove
the instruction "notice()" from the main routine.              */

int copyright[][3]={0x7c00,0x0000,0x0000,0x8231,
0x819c,0x645e,0xba4a,0x4252,0x96d0,0xa231,0x8252,0x955e,0xba4a,
0x43d2,0xf442,0x8231,0x825c,0x945e,0x7c00,0x0000,0x0000};

void notice(float x, float y){
int a,b,c; int tl=0;

for (tl=0;tl<=6;tl++){a=copyright[tl][0];b=copyright[tl][1];
c=copyright[tl][2];
setlinestyle(USERBIT_LINE,a,NORM_WIDTH);
moveto(x,y);lineto(x+15,y);
setlinestyle(USERBIT_LINE,b,NORM_WIDTH);
moveto(x+16,y);lineto(x+31,y);
setlinestyle(USERBIT_LINE,c,NORM_WIDTH);
```

```
moveto(x+32,y);lineto(x+47,y);y=y+1;};
setlinestyle(USERBIT_LINE,0xFFFF,NORM_WIDTH);
return;}

/*_____

End of source code                                      */
```

Fig. E-10. Animated walking figure—Turbo C version, VGA/EGA/CGA/MCGA compatible. Refer to the main body of the book for discussion.

```
/*_____

tc-014.c

Function:  This program demonstrates high speed animation of
a walking human figure using bitblt animation techniques.

Compatibility:  Supports all graphics adapters and monitors.
If a VGA, EGA, CGA, or MCGA is present, the 320x200 4-color
mode is used.

Remarks:  Refer to the book.

Copyright 1988 Lee Adams and TAB BOOKS Inc.

_____


I N C L U D E    F I L E S                               */

#include <stdio.h>            /* supports the printf function */
#include <graphics.h>       /* supports the graphics functions */
#include <process.h>          /* supports the exit() function */
#include <bios.h>          /* supports read of keyboard buffer */
#include <alloc.h>               /* supports memory allocation */

/*_____


D E C L A R A T I O N S                                  */

void keyboard(void);void quit_pgm(void);
void notice(float x,float y);void graphics_setup(void);
void save_arrays(void);void draw_bg(void);

int t1=1,t2=2;                              /* loop counters */
int C0=0,C1=1,C2=2,C3=3,C4=4,C5=5,C6=6,C7=7,C8=8,C9=9,C10=10,
C11=11,C12=12,C13=13,C14=14,C15=15;
float sx=0,sy=0,sx1=0,sy1=0,sx2=0,sy2=0;
int x=252,x1=-2;
```

```
/*                        graphic arrays will be stored in far heap */
char far *A1;char far *A2;char far *A3;char far *A4;
char far *A5;char far *A6;char far *A7;

int pl=0;                          /* pointer into database arrays */

int draw_A1[][2]={                      /* xy coordinates for frame 1 */
155,53,  171,65,  165,66,  167,72,  170,100, 144,143,
159,146, 162,122, 170,100, 173,125, 183,147, 173,150,
170,150, 157,108, 163,92,  164,72,  168,71,  173,90,
175,106};

int draw_A2[][2]={                      /* xy coordinates for frame 2 */
155,53,  171,65,  165,66,  167,72,  170,100, 141,144,
154,146, 161,122, 170,100, 176,125, 186,146, 177,150,
172,150, 153,107, 162,93,  164,72,  168,71,  175,90,
178,107};

int draw_A3[][2]={                      /* xy coordinates for frame 3 */
155,53,  171,65,  165,66,  167,72,  170,100, 145,146,
159,148, 164,125, 170,100, 175,124, 183,146, 176,150,
172,150, 158,107, 163,93,  164,72,  168,71,  173,89,
174,105};

int draw_A4[][2]={                      /* xy coordinates for frame 4 */
155,53,  171,65,  165,66,  167,72,  170,100, 153,149,
168,150, 168,123, 170,100, 173,123, 183,144, 170,147,
162,109, 165,91,  164,72,  168,71,  172,89,  175,106};

int draw_A5[][2]={                      /* xy coordinates for frame 5 */
155,53,  171,65,  165,66,  167,72,  170,100, 155,150,
170,150, 168,122, 170,100, 169,122, 176,143, 160,146,
166,108, 167,90,  164,72,  168,71,  170,90,  171,108};

int draw_A6[][2]={                      /* xy coordinates for frame 6 */
155,53,  171,65,  165,66,  167,72,  170,100, 158,144,
172,142, 165,122, 170,100, 170,122, 175,150, 162,150,
162,108, 167,91,  164,72,  168,71,  171,89,  174,106};

int draw_A7[][2]={                      /* xy coordinates for frame 7 */
155,53,  171,65,  165,66,  167,72,  170,100, 148,143,
161,145, 163,122, 170,100, 172,124, 178,148, 163,150,
158,110, 164,92,  164,72,  168,71,  172,89,  175,107};

/*_____


M A I N   R O U T I N E                                           */

main(){
graphics_setup();                      /* establish graphics mode */

save_arrays();                     /* create and save graphic arrays */
draw_bg();                                /* draw the background */
```

```
moveto(56,80);outtext("Ready to begin animation...");
for (t1=1;t1<=30000;t1++);                              /* pause */
for (t1=1;t1<=30000;t1++);                              /* pause */
draw_bg();

animation_loop:
for (t1=1;t1<=18;t1++){
putimage(x,50,A1,COPY_PUT);x=x+x1;
for (t2=1;t2<=1000;t2++);keyboard();
putimage(x,50,A2,COPY_PUT);x=x+x1;
for (t2=1;t2<=1000;t2++);keyboard();
putimage(x,50,A3,COPY_PUT);x=x+x1;
for (t2=1;t2<=1000;t2++);keyboard();
putimage(x,50,A4,COPY_PUT);x=x+x1;
for (t2=1;t2<=1000;t2++);keyboard();
putimage(x,50,A5,COPY_PUT);x=x+x1;
for (t2=1;t2<=1000;t2++);keyboard();
putimage(x,50,A6,COPY_PUT);x=x+x1;
for (t2=1;t2<=1000;t2++);keyboard();
putimage(x,50,A7,COPY_PUT);x=x+x1;
for (t2=1;t2<=1000;t2++);};

x=252;
for (t2=1;t2<=30000;t2++);keyboard();
for (t2=1;t2<=30000;t2++);keyboard();
draw_bg();
goto animation_loop;                                   /* infinite loop */

quit_pgm();}                          /* end the program gracefully */

/*_____

SUBROUTINE: create & save graphic arrays                        */

void save_arrays(void){

setfillstyle(SOLID_FILL,C1);bar(140,50,190,90);
setfillstyle(SOLID_FILL,C2);bar(140,91,190,150);
setcolor(C7);pl=0;
sx1=draw_A1[pl][0];sy1=draw_A1[pl][1];pl++;
sx2=draw_A1[pl][0];sy2=draw_A1[pl][1];pl++;
circle(163,59,8);
sx=draw_A1[pl][0];sy=draw_A1[pl][1];pl++;moveto(sx,sy);
for (t1=1;t1<=2;t1++){
sx=draw_A1[pl][0];sy=draw_A1[pl][1];pl++;lineto(sx,sy);};
sx=draw_A1[pl][0];sy=draw_A1[pl][1];pl++;moveto(sx,sy);
for (t1=1;t1<=7;t1++){
sx=draw_A1[pl][0];sy=draw_A1[pl][1];pl++;lineto(sx,sy);};
sx=draw_A1[pl][0];sy=draw_A1[pl][1];pl++;moveto(sx,sy);
for (t1=1;t1<=5;t1++){
sx=draw_A1[pl][0];sy=draw_A1[pl][1];pl++;lineto(sx,sy);};
A1=(char far *)farmalloc((unsigned long)
```

```
imagesize(140,50,190,150));      /* calculate memory requirements */
getimage(140,50,190,150,Al);               /* save array in memory */

setfillstyle(SOLID_FILL,Cl);bar(140,50,190,90);
setfillstyle(SOLID_FILL,C2);bar(140,91,190,150);
pl=0;
sxl=draw_A2[pl][0];syl=draw_A2[pl][l];pl++;
sx2=draw_A2[pl][0];sy2=draw_A2[pl][l];pl++;
circle(163,59,8);
sx=draw_A2[pl][0];sy=draw_A2[pl][l];pl++;moveto(sx,sy);
for (tl=l;tl<=2;tl++){
sx=draw_A2[pl][0];sy=draw_A2[pl][l];pl++;lineto(sx,sy);};
sx=draw_A2[pl][0];sy=draw_A2[pl][l];pl++;moveto(sx,sy);
for (tl=l;tl<=7;tl++){
sx=draw_A2[pl][0];sy=draw_A2[pl][l];pl++;lineto(sx,sy);};
sx=draw_A2[pl][0];sy=draw_A2[pl][l];pl++;moveto(sx,sy);
for (tl=l;tl<=5;tl++){
sx=draw_A2[pl][0];sy=draw_A2[pl][l];pl++;lineto(sx,sy);};
A2=(char far *)farmalloc((unsigned long)
imagesize(140,50,190,150));      /* calculate memory requirements */
getimage(140,50,190,150,A2);               /* save array in memory */

setfillstyle(SOLID_FILL,Cl);bar(140,50,190,90);
setfillstyle(SOLID_FILL,C2);bar(140,91,190,150);
pl=0;
sxl=draw_A3[pl][0];syl=draw_A3[pl][l];pl++;
sx2=draw_A3[pl][0];sy2=draw_A3[pl][l];pl++;
circle(163,59,8);
sx=draw_A3[pl][0];sy=draw_A3[pl][l];pl++;moveto(sx,sy);
for (tl=l;tl<=2;tl++){
sx=draw_A3[pl][0];sy=draw_A3[pl][l];pl++;lineto(sx,sy);};
sx=draw_A3[pl][0];sy=draw_A3[pl][l];pl++;moveto(sx,sy);
for (tl=l;tl<=7;tl++){
sx=draw_A3[pl][0];sy=draw_A3[pl][l];pl++;lineto(sx,sy);};
sx=draw_A3[pl][0];sy=draw_A3[pl][l];pl++;moveto(sx,sy);
for (tl=l;tl<=5;tl++){
sx=draw_A3[pl][0];sy=draw_A3[pl][l];pl++;lineto(sx,sy);};
A3=(char far *)farmalloc((unsigned long)
imagesize(140,50,190,150));      /* calculate memory requirements */
getimage(140,50,190,150,A3);               /* save array in memory */

setfillstyle(SOLID_FILL,Cl);bar(140,50,190,90);
setfillstyle(SOLID_FILL,C2);bar(140,91,190,150);
pl=0;
sxl=draw_A4[pl][0];syl=draw_A4[pl][l];pl++;
sx2=draw_A4[pl][0];sy2=draw_A4[pl][l];pl++;
circle(163,59,8);
sx=draw_A4[pl][0];sy=draw_A4[pl][l];pl++;moveto(sx,sy);
for (tl=l;tl<=2;tl++){
sx=draw_A4[pl][0];sy=draw_A4[pl][l];pl++;lineto(sx,sy);};
sx=draw_A4[pl][0];sy=draw_A4[pl][l];pl++;moveto(sx,sy);
for (tl=l;tl<=6;tl++){
sx=draw_A4[pl][0];sy=draw_A4[pl][l];pl++;lineto(sx,sy);};
```

```
sx=draw_A4[pl][0];sy=draw_A4[pl][1];pl++;moveto(sx,sy);
 for (tl=l;tl<=5;tl++){
 sx=draw_A4[pl][0];sy=draw_A4[pl][1];pl++;lineto(sx,sy);};
A4=(char far *)farmalloc((unsigned long)
imagesize(140,50,190,150));       /* calculate memory requirements */
getimage(140,50,190,150,A4);             /* save array in memory */

setfillstyle(SOLID_FILL,Cl);bar(140,50,190,90);
setfillstyle(SOLID_FILL,C2);bar(140,91,190,150);
pl=0;
sxl=draw_A5[pl][0];syl=draw_A5[pl][1];pl++;
sx2=draw_A5[pl][0];sy2=draw_A5[pl][1];pl++;
circle(163,59,8);
sx=draw_A5[pl][0];sy=draw_A5[pl][1];pl++;moveto(sx,sy);
for (tl=l;tl<=2;tl++){
sx=draw_A5[pl][0];sy=draw_A5[pl][1];pl++;lineto(sx,sy);};
sx=draw_A5[pl][0];sy=draw_A5[pl][1];pl++;moveto(sx,sy);
for (tl=l;tl<=6;tl++){
sx=draw_A5[pl][0];sy=draw_A5[pl][1];pl++;lineto(sx,sy);};
sx=draw_A5[pl][0];sy=draw_A5[pl][1];pl++;moveto(sx,sy);
for (tl=l;tl<=5;tl++){
sx=draw_A5[pl][0];sy=draw_A5[pl][1];pl++;lineto(sx,sy);};
A5=(char far *)farmalloc((unsigned long)
imagesize(140,50,190,150));      /* calculate memory requirements */
getimage(140,50,190,150,A5);             /* save array in memory */

setfillstyle(SOLID_FILL,Cl);bar(140,50,190,90);
setfillstyle(SOLID_FILL,C2);bar(140,91,190,150);
pl=0;
sxl=draw_A6[pl][0];syl=draw_A6[pl][1];pl++;
sx2=draw_A6[pl][0];sy2=draw_A6[pl][1];pl++;
circle(163,59,8);
sx=draw_A6[pl][0];sy=draw_A6[pl][1];pl++;moveto(sx,sy);
for (tl=l;tl<=2;tl++){
sx=draw_A6[pl][0];sy=draw_A6[pl][1];pl++;lineto(sx,sy);};
sx=draw_A6[pl][0];sy=draw_A6[pl][1];pl++;moveto(sx,sy);
for (tl=l;tl<=6;tl++){
sx=draw_A6[pl][0];sy=draw_A6[pl][1];pl++;lineto(sx,sy);};
sx=draw_A6[pl][0];sy=draw_A6[pl][1];pl++;moveto(sx,sy);
for (tl=l;tl<=5;tl++){
sx=draw_A6[pl][0];sy=draw_A6[pl][1];pl++;lineto(sx,sy);};
A6=(char far *)farmalloc((unsigned long)
imagesize(140,50,190,150));      /* calculate memory requirements */
getimage(140,50,190,150,A6);             /* save array in memory */

setfillstyle(SOLID_FILL,Cl);bar(140,50,190,90);
setfillstyle(SOLID_FILL,C2);bar(140,91,190,150);
pl=0;
sxl=draw_A7[pl][0];syl=draw_A7[pl][1];pl++;
sx2=draw_A7[pl][0];sy2=draw_A7[pl][1];pl++;
circle(163,59,8);
sx=draw_A7[pl][0];sy=draw_A7[pl][1];pl++;moveto(sx,sy);
for (tl=l;tl<=2;tl++){
sx=draw_A7[pl][0];sy=draw_A7[pl][1];pl++;lineto(sx,sy);};
```

```
sx=draw_A7[pl][0];sy=draw_A7[pl][1];pl++;moveto(sx,sy);
for (tl=1;tl<=6;tl++){
sx=draw_A7[pl][0];sy=draw_A7[pl][1];pl++;lineto(sx,sy);};
sx=draw_A7[pl][0];sy=draw_A7[pl][1];pl++;moveto(sx,sy);
for (tl=1;tl<=5;tl++){
sx=draw_A7[pl][0];sy=draw_A7[pl][1];pl++;lineto(sx,sy);};
A7=(char far *)farmalloc((unsigned long)
imagesize(140,50,190,150));    /* calculate memory requirements */
getimage(140,50,190,150,A7);              /* save array in memory */

return;}

/*_____


SUBROUTINE: draw the background                              */

void draw_bg(void){

setfillstyle(SOLID_FILL,C1);bar(0,22,319,90);
setfillstyle(SOLID_FILL,C2);bar(0,91,319,170);
setcolor(C7);rectangle(0,22,319,170);notice(5,160);return;}

/*_____


SUBROUTINE: press any key to quit                           */

void keyboard(void){if (bioskey(1)==0) return; else quit_pgm();}

/*_____


SUBROUTINE: GRACEFUL EXIT FROM THE PROGRAM                   */

void quit_pgm(void){cleardevice();restorecrtmode();exit(0);}

/*_____


SUBROUTINE: VGA/EGA/CGA/MCGA compatibility module           */

void graphics_setup(void){
int graphics_adapter,graphics_mode;
detectgraph(&graphics_adapter,&graphics_mode);
if (graphics_adapter==VGA) goto CGA_mode;           /* if VGA */
if (graphics_mode==EGAHI) goto CGA_mode;      /* if EGA and ECD */
if (graphics_mode==EGALO) goto CGA_mode;      /* if EGA and SCD */
if (graphics_adapter==CGA) goto CGA_mode;           /* if CGA */
if (graphics_adapter==MCGA) goto CGA_mode;          /* if MCGA */
goto abort_message;              /* if no VGA, EGA, CGA, or MCGA */
CGA_mode:                    /* establish 320x200 4-color mode */
graphics_adapter=CGA;graphics_mode=CGAC3;
initgraph(&graphics_adapter,&graphics_mode,"");
```

```
C0=0;Cl=l;C2=2;C7=3;setcolor(C7);
outtextxy(40,0,"USING C FOR HIGH SPEED ANIMATION");
outtextxy(72,184,"320x200 4-color CGA mode");
outtextxy(80,192,"Press any key to stop...");
return;

abort_message:
printf("\n\nUnable to proceed.\n");
printf("Requires VGA, EGA, MCGA, or CGA adapter\n");
printf("    with appropriate monitor.\n");
printf("Please refer to the book.\n\n");
exit(0);
}
/*_____


SUBROUTINE: Copyright Notice

This subroutine displays the standard copyright notice.
If you are typing in this program from the book you can
safely omit this subroutine, provided that you also remove
the instruction "notice()" from the main routine.          */

int copyright[][3]={0x7c00,0x0000,0x0000,0x8231,
0x819c,0x645e,0xba4a,0x4252,0x96d0,0xa231,0x8252,0x955e,0xba4a,
0x43d2,0xf442,0x8231,0x825c,0x945e,0x7c00,0x0000,0x0000};

void notice(float x, float y){
int a,b,c; int tl=0;
for (tl=0;tl<=6;tl++){a=copyright[tl][0];b=copyright[tl][1];
c=copyright[tl][2];
setlinestyle(USERBIT_LINE,a,NORM_WIDTH);
moveto(x,y);lineto(x+15,y);
setlinestyle(USERBIT_LINE,b,NORM_WIDTH);
moveto(x+16,y);lineto(x+31,y);
setlinestyle(USERBIT_LINE,c,NORM_WIDTH);
moveto(x+32,y);lineto(x+47,y);y=y+1;};
setlinestyle(USERBIT_LINE,0xFFFF,NORM_WIDTH);
return;}

/*_____

End of source code                                         */
```

Fig. E-11. Animated clock face—Turbo C version, VGA/EGA/CGA/MCGA compatible. Refer to the main body of the book for discussion.

```
/*_____

tc-015.c

Function:  This program uses the techniques of bitblt
animation to display a simulated analog clock face.
```

Compatibility: Supports all graphics adapters and monitors.
The software uses the 640x200 2-color mode.

Remarks: The animated clock runs at the correct speed on
a 4.77 MHz microprocessor. If your computer runs faster,
you will be required to add more timing delays by simply
increasing the size of the variable tn in the declarations
section of the source code.

Copyright 1988 Lee Adams and TAB BOOKS Inc.

_____

```
I N C L U D E    F I L E S                              */

#include <stdio.h>                /* supports the printf function */
#include <graphics.h>         /* supports the graphics functions */
#include <process.h>            /* supports the exit() function */
#include <bios.h>           /* supports read of keyboard buffer */
#include <alloc.h>                /* supports memory allocation */

/*_____


D E C L A R A T I O N S                                 */

void keyboard(void);void quit_pgm(void);
void notice(float x,float y);void graphics_setup(void);
void draw_face(void);void draw_sec(void);void anim(void);

int tl=1;
int C0=0,C1=1,C2=2,C3=3,C4=4,C5=5,C6=6,C7=7,C8=8,C9=9,C10=10,
C11=11,C12=12,C13=13,C14=14,C15=15,mode_flag=0;
unsigned int t2=1,tn=35408;      /* tn is set for a 4.77 MHz rate */

/*                              pointers to graphic arrays */
char far *num_array0;char far *num_array1;char far *num_array2;
char far *num_array3;char far *num_array4;char far *num_array5;
char far *num_array6;char far *num_array7;char far *num_array8;
char far *num_array9;
char far *face_array;char far *face_array1;char far *face_array2;
char far *face_array3;char far *face_array4;
char far *gr_array0;char far *gr_array1;char far *gr_array2;
char far *gr_array3;char far *gr_array4;char far *gr_array5;
char far *gr_array6;char far *gr_array7;char far *gr_array8;
char far *gr_array9;char far *gr_array10;char far *gr_array11;
char far *gr_array12;char far *gr_array13;char far *gr_array14;
char far *gr_array15;char far *gr_array16;char far *gr_array17;
char far *gr_array18;char far *gr_array19;char far *gr_array20;
char far *gr_array21;char far *gr_array22;char far *gr_array23;
char far *gr_array24;char far *gr_array25;char far *gr_array26;
char far *gr_array27;char far *gr_array28;char far *gr_array29;
char far *gr_array30;char far *gr_array31;char far *gr_array32;
```

```
char far *gr_array33;char far *gr_array34;char far *gr_array35;
char far *gr_array36;char far *gr_array37;char far *gr_array38;
char far *gr_array39;char far *gr_array40;char far *gr_array41;
char far *gr_array42;char far *gr_array43;char far *gr_array44;
char far *gr_array45;char far *gr_array46;char far *gr_array47;
char far *gr_array48;char far *gr_array49;char far *gr_array50;
char far *gr_array51;char far *gr_array52;char far *gr_array53;
char far *gr_array54;char far *gr_array55;char far *gr_array56;
char far *gr_array57;char far *gr_array58;char far *gr_array59;

/*_____


M A I N    R O U T I N E                                    */

main(){
graphics_setup();                      /* establish graphics mode */
draw_face();                        /* create the generic clock face */
draw_sec();                     /* create 60 versions of the second-hand */
anim();                                /* animate the clock face */
quit_pgm();}                        /* end the program gracefully */

/*_____


SUBROUTINE: animation loop                                  */

void anim(void){
for (tl=1;tl!=2; ){                                      /* endless loop */
putimage(320,58,gr_array0,COPY_PUT);for (t2=1;t2<=tn;t2++);
putimage(320,58,gr_array1,COPY_PUT);for (t2=1;t2<=tn;t2++);
putimage(320,58,gr_array2,COPY_PUT);for (t2=1;t2<=tn;t2++);
putimage(320,58,gr_array3,COPY_PUT);for (t2=1;t2<=tn;t2++);
putimage(320,58,gr_array4,COPY_PUT);for (t2=1;t2<=tn;t2++);
keyboard();
putimage(320,58,gr_array5,COPY_PUT);for (t2=1;t2<=tn;t2++);
putimage(320,58,gr_array6,COPY_PUT);for (t2=1;t2<=tn;t2++);
putimage(320,58,gr_array7,COPY_PUT);for (t2=1;t2<=tn;t2++);
putimage(320,58,gr_array8,COPY_PUT);for (t2=1;t2<=tn;t2++);
putimage(320,58,gr_array9,COPY_PUT);for (t2=1;t2<=tn;t2++);
keyboard();

putimage(320,58,gr_array10,COPY_PUT);for (t2=1;t2<=tn;t2++);
putimage(320,58,gr_array11,COPY_PUT);for (t2=1;t2<=tn;t2++);
putimage(320,58,gr_array12,COPY_PUT);for (t2=1;t2<=tn;t2++);
putimage(320,58,gr_array13,COPY_PUT);for (t2=1;t2<=tn;t2++);
putimage(320,58,gr_array14,COPY_PUT);for (t2=1;t2<=tn;t2++);
keyboard();putimage(320,58,face_array1,COPY_PUT);
putimage(320,100,gr_array15,COPY_PUT);for (t2=1;t2<=tn;t2++);
putimage(320,100,gr_array16,COPY_PUT);for (t2=1;t2<=tn;t2++);
putimage(320,100,gr_array17,COPY_PUT);for (t2=1;t2<=tn;t2++);
putimage(320,100,gr_array18,COPY_PUT);for (t2=1;t2<=tn;t2++);
putimage(320,100,gr_array19,COPY_PUT);for (t2=1;t2<=tn;t2++);
keyboard();
```

```
putimage(320,100,gr_array20,COPY_PUT);for (t2=1;t2<=tn;t2++);

putimage(320,100,gr_array21,COPY_PUT);for (t2=1;t2<=tn;t2++);
putimage(320,100,gr_array22,COPY_PUT);for (t2=1;t2<=tn;t2++);
putimage(320,100,gr_array23,COPY_PUT);for (t2=1;t2<=tn;t2++);
putimage(320,100,gr_array24,COPY_PUT);for (t2=1;t2<=tn;t2++);
keyboard();
putimage(320,100,gr_array25,COPY_PUT);for (t2=1;t2<=tn;t2++);
putimage(320,100,gr_array26,COPY_PUT);for (t2=1;t2<=tn;t2++);
putimage(320,100,gr_array27,COPY_PUT);for (t2=1;t2<=tn;t2++);
putimage(320,100,gr_array28,COPY_PUT);for (t2=1;t2<=tn;t2++);
putimage(320,100,gr_array29,COPY_PUT);for (t2=1;t2<=tn;t2++);
keyboard();putimage(320,100,face_array2,COPY_PUT);
putimage(220,100,gr_array30,COPY_PUT);for (t2=1;t2<=tn;t2++);
putimage(220,100,gr_array31,COPY_PUT);for (t2=1;t2<=tn;t2++);
putimage(220,100,gr_array32,COPY_PUT);for (t2=1;t2<=tn;t2++);
putimage(220,100,gr_array33,COPY_PUT);for (t2=1;t2<=tn;t2++);
putimage(220,100,gr_array34,COPY_PUT);for (t2=1;t2<=tn;t2++);
keyboard();
putimage(220,100,gr_array35,COPY_PUT);for (t2=1;t2<=tn;t2++);
putimage(220,100,gr_array36,COPY_PUT);for (t2=1;t2<=tn;t2++);
putimage(220,100,gr_array37,COPY_PUT);for (t2=1;t2<=tn;t2++);
putimage(220,100,gr_array38,COPY_PUT);for (t2=1;t2<=tn;t2++);
putimage(220,100,gr_array39,COPY_PUT);for (t2=1;t2<=tn;t2++);
keyboard();
putimage(220,100,gr_array40,COPY_PUT);for (t2=1;t2<=tn;t2++);
putimage(220,100,gr_array41,COPY_PUT);for (t2=1;t2<=tn;t2++);
putimage(220,100,gr_array42,COPY_PUT);for (t2=1;t2<=tn;t2++);
putimage(220,100,gr_array43,COPY_PUT);for (t2=1;t2<=tn;t2++);
putimage(220,100,gr_array44,COPY_PUT);for (t2=1;t2<=tn;t2++);
keyboard();putimage(220,100,face_array3,COPY_PUT);
putimage(220,58,gr_array45,COPY_PUT);for (t2=1;t2<=tn;t2++);
putimage(220,58,gr_array46,COPY_PUT);for (t2=1;t2<=tn;t2++);
putimage(220,58,gr_array47,COPY_PUT);for (t2=1;t2<=tn;t2++);
putimage(220,58,gr_array48,COPY_PUT);for (t2=1;t2<=tn;t2++);
putimage(220,58,gr_array49,COPY_PUT);for (t2=1;t2<=tn;t2++);
keyboard();
putimage(220,58,gr_array50,COPY_PUT);for (t2=1;t2<=tn;t2++);
putimage(220,58,gr_array51,COPY_PUT);for (t2=1;t2<=tn;t2++);
putimage(220,58,gr_array52,COPY_PUT);for (t2=1;t2<=tn;t2++);

putimage(220,58,gr_array53,COPY_PUT);for (t2=1;t2<=tn;t2++);
putimage(220,58,gr_array54,COPY_PUT);for (t2=1;t2<=tn;t2++);
keyboard();
putimage(220,58,gr_array55,COPY_PUT);for (t2=1;t2<=tn;t2++);
putimage(220,58,gr_array56,COPY_PUT);for (t2=1;t2<=tn;t2++);
putimage(220,58,gr_array57,COPY_PUT);for (t2=1;t2<=tn;t2++);
putimage(220,58,gr_array58,COPY_PUT);for (t2=1;t2<=tn;t2++);
putimage(220,58,gr_array59,COPY_PUT);for (t2=1;t2<=tn;t2++);
keyboard();putimage(220,58,face_array4,COPY_PUT);
};
return;}

/*_____
```

```
SUBROUTINE: create the clock face                               */

void draw_face(void){

setcolor(C7);moveto(0,0);outtext("0123456789");
num_array0=(char far *)farmalloc((unsigned long)imagesize(0,0,7,7));
getimage(0,0,7,7,num_array0);
num_array1=(char far *)farmalloc((unsigned long)imagesize(8,0,15,7));
getimage(8,0,15,7,num_array1);
num_array2=(char far *)farmalloc((unsigned long)imagesize(16,0,23,7));
getimage(16,0,23,7,num_array2);
num_array3=(char far *)farmalloc((unsigned long)imagesize(24,0,31,7));
getimage(24,0,31,7,num_array3);
num_array4=(char far *)farmalloc((unsigned long)imagesize(32,0,39,7));
getimage(32,0,39,7,num_array4);
num_array5=(char far *)farmalloc((unsigned long)imagesize(40,0,47,7));
getimage(40,0,47,7,num_array5);
num_array6=(char far *)farmalloc((unsigned long)imagesize(48,0,55,7));
getimage(48,0,55,7,num_array6);
num_array7=(char far *)farmalloc((unsigned long)imagesize(56,0,63,7));
getimage(56,0,63,7,num_array7);
num_array8=(char far *)farmalloc((unsigned long)imagesize(64,0,71,7));
getimage(64,0,71,7,num_array8);
num_array9=(char far *)farmalloc((unsigned long)imagesize(72,0,79,7));
getimage(72,0,79,7,num_array9);
setfillstyle(SOLID_FILL,C0);bar(0,0,88,8);

circle(320,100,132);                             /* draw the circle */

/*                              create hour-hand, minute-hand */
setfillstyle(SOLID_FILL,C7);
moveto(264,86);lineto(272,85);lineto(322,98);
lineto(319,102);lineto(266,88);lineto(264,86);
lineto(264,86);floodfill(300,95,C1);
moveto(316,99);lineto(379,71);lineto(385,71);
lineto(384,74);lineto(320,102);lineto(316,99);
lineto(316,99);floodfill(360,82,C1);

/*                          install alphanumerics on clock face */
putimage(370,55,num_array1,OR_PUT);putimage(407,73,num_array2,OR_PUT);
putimage(420,97,num_array3,OR_PUT);putimage(405,120,num_array4,OR_PUT);
putimage(370,138,num_array5,OR_PUT);putimage(318,144,num_array6,OR_PUT);
putimage(266,138,num_array7,OR_PUT);putimage(226,120,num_array8,OR_PUT);
putimage(210,97,num_array9,OR_PUT);putimage(222,73,num_array1,OR_PUT);
putimage(230,73,num_array0,OR_PUT);putimage(260,56,num_array1,OR_PUT);
putimage(268,56,num_array1,OR_PUT);putimage(312,49,num_array1,OR_PUT);
putimage(320,49,num_array2,OR_PUT);notice(5,193);

/*      save quarters of clock face for clean-up during animation */
face_array=(char far *)farmalloc((unsigned long)imagesize(202,46,438,154));
getimage(202,46,438,154,face_array);
face_array1=(char far *)farmalloc((unsigned long)imagesize(320,58,420,100));
getimage(320,58,420,100,face_array1);
face_array2=(char far *)farmalloc((unsigned long)imagesize(320,100,420,143));
```

```
getimage(320,100,420,143,face_array2);
face_array3=(char far *)farmalloc((unsigned long)imagesize(220,100,320,143));
getimage(220,100,320,143,face_array3);
face_array4=(char far *)farmalloc((unsigned long)imagesize(220,58,320,100));
getimage(220,58,320,100,face_array4);

return; }

/*_____


SUBROUTINE: create 60 versions of the second-hand              */

void draw_sec(void){

moveto(320,100);lineto(320,58);
gr_array0=(char far *)farmalloc((unsigned long)imagesize(320,58,420,100));
getimage(320,58,420,100,gr_array0);putimage(202,46,face_array,COPY_PUT);
moveto(320,100);lineto(329,58);
gr_array1=(char far *)farmalloc((unsigned long)imagesize(320,58,420,100));
getimage(320,58,420,100,gr_array1);putimage(202,46,face_array,COPY_PUT);
moveto(320,100);lineto(340,59);
gr_array2=(char far *)farmalloc((unsigned long)imagesize(320,58,420,100));
getimage(320,58,420,100,gr_array2);putimage(202,46,face_array,COPY_PUT);
moveto(320,100);lineto(348,60);
gr_array3=(char far *)farmalloc((unsigned long)imagesize(320,58,420,100));
getimage(320,58,420,100,gr_array3);putimage(202,46,face_array,COPY_PUT);
moveto(320,100);lineto(358,62);
gr_array4=(char far *)farmalloc((unsigned long)imagesize(320,58,420,100));
getimage(320,58,420,100,gr_array4);putimage(202,46,face_array,COPY_PUT);
moveto(320,100);lineto(367,63);
gr_array5=(char far *)farmalloc((unsigned long)imagesize(320,58,420,100));
getimage(320,58,420,100,gr_array5);putimage(202,46,face_array,COPY_PUT);

moveto(320,100);lineto(375,66);
gr_array6=(char far *)farmalloc((unsigned long)imagesize(320,58,420,100));
getimage(320,58,420,100,gr_array6);putimage(202,46,face_array,COPY_PUT);
moveto(320,100);lineto(381,69);
gr_array7=(char far *)farmalloc((unsigned long)imagesize(320,58,420,100));
getimage(320,58,420,100,gr_array7);putimage(202,46,face_array,COPY_PUT);
moveto(320,100);lineto(388,72);
gr_array8=(char far *)farmalloc((unsigned long)imagesize(320,58,420,100));
getimage(320,58,420,100,gr_array8);putimage(202,46,face_array,COPY_PUT);
moveto(320,100);lineto(395,75);
gr_array9=(char far *)farmalloc((unsigned long)imagesize(320,58,420,100));
getimage(320,58,420,100,gr_array9);putimage(202,46,face_array,COPY_PUT);
moveto(320,100);lineto(400,79);
gr_array10=(char far *)farmalloc((unsigned long)imagesize(320,58,420,100))
getimage(320,58,420,100,gr_array10);putimage(202,46,face_array,COPY_PUT);
moveto(320,100);lineto(405,83);
gr_array11=(char far *)farmalloc((unsigned long)imagesize(320,58,420,100))
getimage(320,58,420,100,gr_array11);putimage(202,46,face_array,COPY_PUT);
moveto(320,100);lineto(409,87);
gr_array12=(char far *)farmalloc((unsigned long)imagesize(320,58,420,100))
getimage(320,58,420,100,gr_array12);putimage(202,46,face_array,COPY_PUT);
```

```
moveto(320,100);lineto(411,92);
gr_array13=(char far *)farmalloc((unsigned long)imagesize(320,58,420,100));
getimage(320,58,420,100,gr_array13);putimage(202,46,face_array,COPY_PUT);
moveto(320,100);lineto(412,96);
gr_array14=(char far *)farmalloc((unsigned long)imagesize(320,58,420,100));
getimage(320,58,420,100,gr_array14);putimage(202,46,face_array,COPY_PUT);
moveto(320,100);lineto(413,100);
gr_array15=(char far *)farmalloc((unsigned long)imagesize(320,100,420,143));
getimage(320,100,420,143,gr_array15);putimage(202,46,face_array,COPY_PUT);
moveto(320,100);lineto(412,104);
gr_array16=(char far *)farmalloc((unsigned long)imagesize(320,100,420,143));
getimage(320,100,420,143,gr_array16);putimage(202,46,face_array,COPY_PUT);
moveto(320,100);lineto(411,109);
gr_array17=(char far *)farmalloc((unsigned long)imagesize(320,100,420,143));
getimage(320,100,420,143,gr_array17);putimage(202,46,face_array,COPY_PUT);
moveto(320,100);lineto(409,114);
gr_array18=(char far *)farmalloc((unsigned long)imagesize(320,100,420,143));
getimage(320,100,420,143,gr_array18);putimage(202,46,face_array,COPY_PUT);
moveto(320,100);lineto(405,117);
gr_array19=(char far *)farmalloc((unsigned long)imagesize(320,100,420,143));
getimage(320,100,420,143,gr_array19);putimage(202,46,face_array,COPY_PUT);
moveto(320,100);lineto(400,121);
gr_array20=(char far *)farmalloc((unsigned long)imagesize(320,100,420,143));
getimage(320,100,420,143,gr_array20);putimage(202,46,face_array,COPY_PUT);
moveto(320,100);lineto(395,125);
gr_array21=(char far *)farmalloc((unsigned long)imagesize(320,100,420,143));
getimage(320,100,420,143,gr_array21);putimage(202,46,face_array,COPY_PUT);
moveto(320,100);lineto(388,128);
gr_array22=(char far *)farmalloc((unsigned long)imagesize(320,100,420,143));
getimage(320,100,420,143,gr_array22);putimage(202,46,face_array,COPY_PUT);
moveto(320,100);lineto(381,132);
gr_array23=(char far *)farmalloc((unsigned long)imagesize(320,100,420,143));
getimage(320,100,420,143,gr_array23);putimage(202,46,face_array,COPY_PUT);
moveto(320,100);lineto(375,134);
gr_array24=(char far *)farmalloc((unsigned long)imagesize(320,100,420,143));
getimage(320,100,420,143,gr_array24);putimage(202,46,face_array,COPY_PUT);
moveto(320,100);lineto(367,136);
gr_array25=(char far *)farmalloc((unsigned long)imagesize(320,100,420,143));
getimage(320,100,420,143,gr_array25);putimage(202,46,face_array,COPY_PUT);
moveto(320,100);lineto(358,138);
gr_array26=(char far *)farmalloc((unsigned long)imagesize(320,100,420,143));
getimage(320,100,420,143,gr_array26);putimage(202,46,face_array,COPY_PUT);
moveto(320,100);lineto(348,140);
gr_array27=(char far *)farmalloc((unsigned long)imagesize(320,100,420,143));
getimage(320,100,420,143,gr_array27);putimage(202,46,face_array,COPY_PUT);
moveto(320,100);lineto(340,142);
gr_array28=(char far *)farmalloc((unsigned long)imagesize(320,100,420,143));
getimage(320,100,420,143,gr_array28);putimage(202,46,face_array,COPY_PUT);
moveto(320,100);lineto(329,143);
gr_array29=(char far *)farmalloc((unsigned long)imagesize(320,100,420,143));
getimage(320,100,420,143,gr_array29);putimage(202,46,face_array,COPY_PUT);
moveto(320,100);lineto(320,143);
gr_array30=(char far *)farmalloc((unsigned long)imagesize(220,100,320,143));
getimage(220,100,320,143,gr_array30);putimage(202,46,face_array,COPY_PUT);
```

```
moveto(320,100);lineto(310,143);
gr_array31=(char far *)farmalloc((unsigned long)imagesize(220,100,320,143));
getimage(220,100,320,143,gr_array31);putimage(202,46,face_array,COPY_PUT);
moveto(320,100);lineto(300,142);
gr_array32=(char far *)farmalloc((unsigned long)imagesize(220,100,320,143));
getimage(220,100,320,143,gr_array32);putimage(202,46,face_array,COPY_PUT);
moveto(320,100);lineto(290,140);
gr_array33=(char far *)farmalloc((unsigned long)imagesize(220,100,320,143));
getimage(220,100,320,143,gr_array33);putimage(202,46,face_array,COPY_PUT);
moveto(320,100);lineto(281,138);
gr_array34=(char far *)farmalloc((unsigned long)imagesize(220,100,320,143));
getimage(220,100,320,143,gr_array34);putimage(202,46,face_array,COPY_PUT);
moveto(320,100);lineto(273,136);
gr_array35=(char far *)farmalloc((unsigned long)imagesize(220,100,320,143));
getimage(220,100,320,143,gr_array35);putimage(202,46,face_array,COPY_PUT);
moveto(320,100);lineto(266,134);
gr_array36=(char far *)farmalloc((unsigned long)imagesize(220,100,320,143));
getimage(220,100,320,143,gr_array36);putimage(202,46,face_array,COPY_PUT);
moveto(320,100);lineto(258,132);
gr_array37=(char far *)farmalloc((unsigned long)imagesize(220,100,320,143));
getimage(220,100,320,143,gr_array37);putimage(202,46,face_array,COPY_PUT);
moveto(320,100);lineto(250,128);
gr_array38=(char far *)farmalloc((unsigned long)imagesize(220,100,320,143));
getimage(220,100,320,143,gr_array38);putimage(202,46,face_array,COPY_PUT);
moveto(320,100);lineto(245,125);
gr_array39=(char far *)farmalloc((unsigned long)imagesize(220,100,320,143));
getimage(220,100,320,143,gr_array39);putimage(202,46,face_array,COPY_PUT);

moveto(320,100);lineto(240,121);
gr_array40=(char far *)farmalloc((unsigned long)imagesize(220,100,320,143));
getimage(220,100,320,143,gr_array40);putimage(202,46,face_array,COPY_PUT);
moveto(320,100);lineto(235,117);
gr_array41=(char far *)farmalloc((unsigned long)imagesize(220,100,320,143));
getimage(220,100,320,143,gr_array41);putimage(202,46,face_array,COPY_PUT);
moveto(320,100);lineto(231,114);
gr_array42=(char far *)farmalloc((unsigned long)imagesize(220,100,320,143));
getimage(220,100,320,143,gr_array42);putimage(202,46,face_array,COPY_PUT);
moveto(320,100);lineto(229,110);
gr_array43=(char far *)farmalloc((unsigned long)imagesize(220,100,320,143));
getimage(220,100,320,143,gr_array43);putimage(202,46,face_array,COPY_PUT);
moveto(320,100);lineto(227,104);
gr_array44=(char far *)farmalloc((unsigned long)imagesize(220,100,320,143));
getimage(220,100,320,143,gr_array44);putimage(202,46,face_array,COPY_PUT);
moveto(320,100);lineto(226,100);
gr_array45=(char far *)farmalloc((unsigned long)imagesize(220,58,320,100));
getimage(220,58,320,100,gr_array45);putimage(202,46,face_array,COPY_PUT);
moveto(320,100);lineto(227,96);
gr_array46=(char far *)farmalloc((unsigned long)imagesize(220,58,320,100));
getimage(220,58,320,100,gr_array46);putimage(202,46,face_array,COPY_PUT);
moveto(320,100);lineto(229,92);
gr_array47=(char far *)farmalloc((unsigned long)imagesize(220,58,320,100));
getimage(220,58,320,100,gr_array47);putimage(202,46,face_array,COPY_PUT);
moveto(320,100);lineto(231,87);
gr_array48=(char far *)farmalloc((unsigned long)imagesize(220,58,320,100));
getimage(220,58,320,100,gr_array48);putimage(202,46,face_array,COPY_PUT);
```

```
moveto(320,100);lineto(235,83);
gr_array49=(char far *)farmalloc((unsigned long)imagesize(220,58,320,100));
getimage(220,58,320,100,gr_array49);putimage(202,46,face_array,COPY_PUT);
moveto(320,100);lineto(240,79);
gr_array50=(char far *)farmalloc((unsigned long)imagesize(220,58,320,100));
getimage(220,58,320,100,gr_array50);putimage(202,46,face_array,COPY_PUT);
moveto(320,100);lineto(245,75);
gr_array51=(char far *)farmalloc((unsigned long)imagesize(220,58,320,100));
getimage(220,58,320,100,gr_array51);putimage(202,46,face_array,COPY_PUT);
moveto(320,100);lineto(250,72);
gr_array52=(char far *)farmalloc((unsigned long)imagesize(220,58,320,100));
getimage(220,58,320,100,gr_array52);putimage(202,46,face_array,COPY_PUT);
moveto(320,100);lineto(258,69);
gr_array53=(char far *)farmalloc((unsigned long)imagesize(220,58,320,100));
getimage(220,58,320,100,gr_array53);putimage(202,46,face_array,COPY_PUT);
moveto(320,100);lineto(266,66);
gr_array54=(char far *)farmalloc((unsigned long)imagesize(220,58,320,100));
getimage(220,58,320,100,gr_array54);putimage(202,46,face_array,COPY_PUT);
moveto(320,100);lineto(273,63);
gr_array55=(char far *)farmalloc((unsigned long)imagesize(220,58,320,100));
getimage(220,58,320,100,gr_array55);putimage(202,46,face_array,COPY_PUT);
moveto(320,100);lineto(281,62);
gr_array56=(char far *)farmalloc((unsigned long)imagesize(220,58,320,100));
getimage(220,58,320,100,gr_array56);putimage(202,46,face_array,COPY_PUT);
moveto(320,100);lineto(290,60);
gr_array57=(char far *)farmalloc((unsigned long)imagesize(220,58,320,100));
getimage(220,58,320,100,gr_array57);putimage(202,46,face_array,COPY_PUT);
moveto(320,100);lineto(300,59);
gr_array58=(char far *)farmalloc((unsigned long)imagesize(220,58,320,100));
getimage(220,58,320,100,gr_array58);putimage(202,46,face_array,COPY_PUT);
moveto(320,100);lineto(310,58);
gr_array59=(char far *)farmalloc((unsigned long)imagesize(220,58,320,100));
getimage(220,58,320,100,gr_array59);putimage(202,46,face_array,COPY_PUT);

return;}

/*_____


SUBROUTINE: press any key to quit                                    */

void keyboard(void){
if (bioskey(1)==0) return; else quit_pgm();}

/*_____


SUBROUTINE: GRACEFUL EXIT FROM THE PROGRAM                           */

void quit_pgm(void){
cleardevice();restorecrtmode();exit(0);}

/*_____
```

```
SUBROUTINE: VGA/EGA/CGA/MCGA compatibility module                        */

void graphics_setup(void){
int graphics_adapter,graphics_mode;
detectgraph(&graphics_adapter,&graphics_mode);
if (graphics_adapter==VGA) goto CGA_mode;              /* if VGA */
if (graphics_mode==EGAHI) goto CGA_mode;          /* if EGA and ECD */
if (graphics_mode==EGALO) goto CGA_mode;          /* if EGA and SCD */
if (graphics_adapter==CGA) goto CGA_mode;             /* if CGA */
if (graphics_adapter==MCGA) goto CGA_mode;            /* if MCGA */
goto abort_message;                        /* if no VGA, EGA, CGA, or MCGA */

CGA_mode:                          /* establish 640x200 2-color mode */
graphics_adapter=CGA;graphics_mode=CGAHI;
initgraph(&graphics_adapter,&graphics_mode,"");
C0=0;C1=1;C2=1;C3=1;C4=1;C5=1,C6=1;C7=1;
C8=1;C9=1;C10=1;C11=1;C12=1;C13=1;C14=1;C15=1;
mode_flag=4;setcolor(C7);
outtextxy(184,0,"USING C FOR HIGH SPEED ANIMATION");
outtextxy(232,192,"Press any key to quit...");
outtextxy(168,176,"640x200 2-color VGA, EGA, CGA, and MCGA mode");
outtextxy(176,16,"Bitblt animation of a clock face...");
return;

abort_message:
printf("\n\nUnable to proceed.\n");
printf("Requires VGA, EGA, MCGA, or CGA adapter\n");
printf("   with appropriate monitor.\n");
printf("Please refer to the book.\n\n");
exit(0);
}
/*_____


SUBROUTINE: Copyright Notice

This subroutine displays the standard copyright notice.
If you are typing in this program from the book you can
safely omit this subroutine, provided that you also remove
the instruction "notice()" from the main routine.                        */

int copyright[ ][3]={0x7c00,0x0000,0x0000,0x8231,
0x819c,0x645e,0xba4a,0x4252,0x96d0,0xa231,0x8252,0x955e,0xba4a,
0x43d2,0xf442,0x8231,0x825c,0x945e,0x7c00,0x0000,0x0000};

void notice(float x, float y){
int a,b,c; int tl=0;
for (tl=0;tl<=6;tl++){a=copyright[tl][0];b=copyright[tl][1];
c=copyright[tl][2];
setlinestyle(USERBIT_LINE,a,NORM_WIDTH);
moveto(x,y);lineto(x+15,y);
setlinestyle(USERBIT_LINE,b,NORM_WIDTH);
moveto(x+16,y);lineto(x+31,y);
```

```
setlinestyle(USERBIT_LINE,c,NORM_WIDTH);
moveto(x+32,y);lineto(x+47,y);y=y+1;};
setlinestyle(USERBIT_LINE,0xFFFF,NORM_WIDTH);
return;}

/*_____

End of source code                                    */
```

Fig. E-12. Animated arcade-style prototype—Turbo C version, VGA/EGA/CGA/MCGA compatible. Refer to the main body of the book for discussion.

```
/*_____

tc-016.c

Function:  This program demonstrates arcade animation
techniques.  The user can use the keyboard to control the
high-speed movement of a ricocheting ball on the screen.

Compatibility:  Supports all graphics adapters and monitors.
The software uses the 640x200 2-color mode on the VGA, EGA,
and CGA.  By changing a single line in the configuration
subroutine you can run this program in the 16-color mode.

Remarks:  Refer to the book for a description of keyboard
controls.

Copyright 1988 Lee Adams and TAB BOOKS Inc.

_____


I N C L U D E    F I L E S                             */

#include <stdio.h>            /* supports the printf function */
#include <graphics.h>      /* supports the graphics functions */
#include <process.h>          /* supports the exit() function */
#include <bios.h>        /* supports read of keyboard buffer */
#include <alloc.h>           /* supports memory allocation */
#include <dos.h>             /* supports port manipulation */

/*_____


D E C L A R A T I O N S                                */

void keyboard(void);void quit_pgm(void);
void notice(float x,float y);void graphics_setup(void);
void noise(int hertz,int duration);

int tl=1,t2=1,x1=220,y1=100,x2=270,y2=120,
```

```
sx=220,sy=100,sxmove=3,symove=-1,sxl,syl;
int C0=0,Cl=1,C2=2,C3=3,C4=4,C5=5,C6=6,C7=7,C8=8,C9=9,Cl0=10,
Cll=11,Cl2=12,Cl3=13,Cl4=14,Cl5=15,mode_flag=0;
int hz=450;

char far *gr_array1;                      /* pointer to graphic array */

/*_____

MAIN    ROUTINE                                              */

main(){
graphics_setup();                           /* establish graphics mode */

/*                          create and store the graphic array */
setcolor(C7);circle(xl+25,yl+10,22);
setfillstyle(SOLID_FILL,C4);floodfill(xl+25,yl+10,C7);
gr_array1=(char far*)farmalloc((unsigned long)imagesize(xl,yl,x2,y2));
getimage(xl,yl,x2,y2,gr_array1);
setfillstyle(SOLID_FILL,C0);bar(xl,yl,x2,y2);

/*                    create background and install graphic array */
setcolor(C7);
rectangle(0,10,639,189);                    /* animation boundaries */
moveto(319,188);lineto(319,110);              /* central barrier */
notice(0,192);
putimage(sx,sy,gr_array1,COPY_PUT);      /* install block graphic */

/*_____bitblt animation manager_____*/

ANIMATE:                                  /* animation loop begins here */
if (sxl<=268) goto LEFT_ARENA;
if (sxl>=320) goto RIGHT_ARENA;
goto IN_BETWEEN;

LEFT_ARENA:
if (sxl>=266){                                    /* right boundary */
if (syl>=81){noise(hz,300);sxmove=-3;}}            /* hits barrier */
if (sxl<=3) {noise(hz,300);sxmove=3;}             /* left boundary */
if (syl>=168) {noise(hz,300);symove=-1;}        /* bottom boundary */
if (syl<=11) {noise(hz,300);symove=1;}            /* top boundary */
sxl=sx+sxmove;syl=sy+symove;              /* calculate new position */
putimage(sxl,syl,gr_array1,COPY_PUT);        /* install new array */
sx=sxl;sy=syl;                           /* update sx,sy variables */
keyboard();                          /* check for user keyboard input */
goto ANIMATE;                                    /* infinite loop */

RIGHT_ARENA:
if (sxl>=586) {noise(hz,300);sxmove=-3;}          /* right boundary */
if (sxl<=322){                                    /* left boundary */
if (syl>=81){noise(hz,300);sxmove=3;}}            /* hits barrier */
if (syl>=168) {noise(hz,300);symove=-1;}        /* bottom boundary */
if (syl<=11) {noise(hz,300);symove=1;}            /* top boundary */
```

```
sx1=sx+sxmove;sy1=sy+symove;              /* calculate new position */
putimage(sx1,sy1,gr_array1,COPY_PUT);         /* install new array */
sx=sx1;sy=sy1;                             /* update sx,sy variables */
keyboard();                         /* check for user keyboard input */
goto ANIMATE;                                     /* infinite loop */

IN_BETWEEN:
if (sy1<=11) {noise(hz,300);symove=1;}              /* top boundary */

if (sy1>=89) {noise(hz,300);symove=-1;}          /* hits barrier tip */
sx1=sx+sxmove;sy1=sy+symove;              /* calculate new position */
putimage(sx1,sy1,gr_array1,COPY_PUT);         /* install new array */
sx=sx1;sy=sy1;                             /* update sx,sy variables */
keyboard();                         /* check for user keyboard input */
goto ANIMATE;                                     /* infinite loop */

quit_pgm();}                        /* make the code bullet-proof */
```

```
/*_____
```

SUBROUTINE: dynamic keyboard input

The subroutine is called by the main routine on each pass
through the animation loop. If the Esc key is pressed, the
arcade game will terminate. Press <h> to move right; press
<f> to move left. Press <t> to move up; press <b> to move
down.   */

```
void keyboard(void){
union u_type{int a;char b[3];}keystroke;char inkey=0;

if (bioskey(1)==0) return;                  /* if no key, return */
keystroke.a=bioskey(0);                   /* fetch ASCII code... */
inkey=keystroke.b[0];              /* ...and load code into variable */
switch (inkey){             /* make decision based upon ASCII value */
case 27:  quit_pgm();                               /* Esc key */
case 104: sxmove=3;return;                   /* h key move right */
case 102: sxmove=-3;return;                   /* f key move left */
case 116: symove=-1;return;                     /* t key move up */
case 98:  symove=1;return;                    /* b key move down */
default:  return;}             /* make routine bullet-proof */
}
/*_____
```

SUBROUTINE: GRACEFUL EXIT FROM THE PROGRAM   */

```
void quit_pgm(void){
cleardevice();restorecrtmode();exit(0);}
```

```
/*_____
```

SUBROUTINE: GENERATE A SOUND

Enter with frequency, expressed as hertz in the range
40 to 4660. A comfortable frequency range for the human
ear is 40 to 2400. Enter with duration, expressed as an
integer to be used in a simple for...next delay loop.   */

```c
void noise(int hertz,int duration){
int tl=1,high_byte=0,low_byte=0;
short count=0;unsigned char old_port=0,new_port=0;

if (hertz<40) return;        /* avoid math overflow for int count */
if (hertz>4660) return;      /* avoid math underflow for low_byte */
count=1193180L/hertz;                    /* determine timer count */
high_byte=count/256;low_byte=count-(high_byte*256);
outportb(0x43,0xB6);                     /* prep the timer register */
outportb(0x42,low_byte);                    /* send the low byte */
outportb(0x42,high_byte);                   /* send the high byte */
old_port=inportb(0x61);          /* store the existing port value */
new_port=(old_port | 0x03);   /* use OR to set bits 0 and 1 to on */
outportb(0x61,new_port);                   /* turn on the speaker */
for (tl=1;tl<=duration;tl++);                            /* wait */
outportb(0x61,old_port);               /* turn off the speaker */
return;}                                /* return to caller */

/*_____

SUBROUTINE: VGA/EGA/CGA/MCGA compatibility module                    */

void graphics_setup(void){
int graphics_adapter,graphics_mode;
detectgraph(&graphics_adapter,&graphics_mode);goto CGA_mode;
if (graphics_adapter==VGA) goto VGA_EGA_mode;         /* if VGA */
if (graphics_mode==EGAHI) goto VGA_EGA_mode;   /* if EGA and ECD */
if (graphics_mode==EGALO) goto VGA_EGA_mode;   /* if EGA and SCD */
if (graphics_adapter==CGA) goto CGA_mode;            /* if CGA */
if (graphics_adapter==MCGA) goto CGA_mode;           /* if MCGA */
goto abort_message;                /* if no VGA, EGA, CGA, or MCGA */

VGA_EGA_mode:                   /* establish 640x200 16-color mode */
graphics_adapter=EGA;graphics_mode=EGALO;
initgraph(&graphics_adapter,&graphics_mode,"");
mode_flag=3;setcolor(C7);
outtextxy(176,192,"640x480 16-color VGA and EGA mode.");
outtextxy(192,0,"USING C FOR ARCADE-STYLE ANIMATION");
return;


CGA_mode:                      /* establish 640x200 2-color mode */
graphics_adapter=CGA;graphics_mode=CGAHI;
initgraph(&graphics_adapter,&graphics_mode,"");
C0=0;C1=1;C2=1;C3=1;C4=1;C5=1;C6=1;C7=1;C8=1;C9=1;C10=1;
C11=1;C12=1;C13=1;C14=1;C15=1;
mode_flag=4;setcolor(C7);
```

```
outtextxy(184,192,"640x200 2-color VGA, EGA, and CGA mode.");
outtextxy(192,0,"USING C FOR ARCADE-STYLE ANIMATION");
return;

abort_message:
printf("\n\nUnable to proceed.\n");
printf("Requires VGA, EGA, MCGA, or CGA adapter\n");
printf("   with appropriate monitor.\n");
printf("Please refer to the book.\n\n");
exit(0);
}
/*_____


SUBROUTINE: Copyright Notice

This subroutine displays the standard copyright notice.
If you are typing in this program from the book you can
safely omit this subroutine, provided that you also remove
the instruction "notice()" from the main routine.            */

int copyright[][3]={0x7c00,0x0000,0x0000,0x8231,
0x819c,0x645e,0xba4a,0x4252,0x96d0,0xa231,0x8252,0x955e,0xba4a,
0x43d2,0xf442,0x8231,0x825c,0x945e,0x7c00,0x0000,0x0000};

void notice(float x, float y){
int a,b,c; int tl=0;
for (tl=0;tl<=6;tl++){a=copyright[tl][0];b=copyright[tl][1];
c=copyright[tl][2];
setlinestyle(USERBIT_LINE,a,NORM_WIDTH);
moveto(x,y);lineto(x+15,y);
setlinestyle(USERBIT_LINE,b,NORM_WIDTH);
moveto(x+16,y);lineto(x+31,y);
setlinestyle(USERBIT_LINE,c,NORM_WIDTH);
moveto(x+32,y);lineto(x+47,y);y=y+1;};
setlinestyle(USERBIT_LINE,0xFFFF,NORM_WIDTH);
return;}

/*_____

End of source code                                           */
```

Fig. E-13. Animated flight simulation prototype—Turbo C version, VGA/EGA compatible. Refer to the main body of the book for discussion.

```
/*_____

tc-017.c

Function:  This program demonstrates real-time animation
techniques applied to a flight simulation prototype.
```

Compatibility: Supports VGA and EGA graphics adapters and
monitors. The software uses the 640x200 16-color mode.

Remarks: Refer to the book for an explanation of the
process control logic, the 3D formulas, and the line clipping
routines which are used by this program.

```
I N C L U D E    F I L E S                                    */

#include <stdio.h>              /* supports the printf function */
#include <graphics.h>         /* supports the graphics functions */
#include <process.h>            /* supports the exit() function */
#include <bios.h>            /* supports read of keyboard buffer */
#include <math.h>          /* supports the sine and cosine functions */

/*_____


D E C L A R A T I O N S                                       */

void graphics_setup(void);void keyboard(void);void quit_pgm(void);
void notice(float x,float y);void calc_3D(void);void window(void);
void clip_2D(void);void yaw_change(void);void translation(void);
void crash(void);void draw_horizon(void);void horiz3D(void);
void corner(void);void window(void);void grid(void);
void draw_grid(void);void clip_3D(void);void window_terrain(void);
void draw_line(void);

int t1=1,t2=1;                              /* loop counters */
int p=0;              /* toggle for active page and visual page */
int C0=0,C1=1,C2=2,C3=3,C4=4,C5=5,C6=6,C7=7,C8=8,C9=9,C10=10,
C11=11,C12=12,C13=13,C14=14,C15=15,mode_flag=0;      /* colors */
int p1=1;           /* status flag for clipping lines in 3D space */
int p2=1;           /* status flag for clipping lines in 2D space */
int g=7;                                    /* color attribute */

float x=0,y=0,z=0;                     /* xyz world coordinates */
float x01=0,x2=0,x3=0,x4=0,x5=0,x6=0,x7=0,x8=0,x9=0,x10=0,x11=0,
x12=0,x13=0,x14=0,x15=0,x16=0;              /* vertices of grid */
float y01=0,y2=0,y3=0,y4=0,y5=0,y6=0,y7=0,y8=0,y9=0,y10=0,y11=0,
y12=0,y13=0,y14=0,y15=0,y16=0;              /* vertices of grid */
float z01=0,z2=0,z3=0,z4=0,z5=0,z6=0,z7=0,z8=0,z9=0,z10=0,z11=0,
z12=0,z13=0,z14=0,z15=0,z16=0;              /* vertices of grid */
float L=0;              /* offset used to extrapolate grid vertices */
float sx=0,sy=0;          /* display coords, output of 3D formulas */
float xa=0,ya=0,za=0;   /* used in 3D formulas & 3D line clipping */
float xb=0,yb=0,zb=0;        /* used in 3D line clipping routine */
float xc=0,yc=0,zc=0;    /* temporary values in 3D line clipping */
float sxa=0,sya=0,sxb=0,syb=0;           /* 2D line endpoints */
```

```
float sxs=0,sys=0;              /* temp storage of 2D line startpoint */
float temp_swap=0;                      /* used for variable swaps */

float d=620;                            /* angular perspective factor */
double r1=6.28319;              /* yaw angle, expressed in radians */
double r2=6.28319;              /* roll angle, expressed in radians */
double r3=6.28319;              /* pitch angle, expressed in radians */
float rla=0,r2a=0,r3a=0;                /* angle change factors */
double srl=0,sr2=0,sr3=0;               /* sine rotation factors */
double crl=0,cr2=0,cr3=0;               /* cosine rotation factors */
float mx=24,my=-7.7,mz=-88;  /* viewpoint position (translation) */
float m=1;                              /* viewpoint change factor */
float ml=0;                             /* lateral movement factor */
float myl=0;                            /* up-down movement change */
float mxl=0;                            /* left-right movement change */
float mzl=0;                            /* forward movement change */
float maxx=639,minx=0,maxy=199,miny=0;  /* 2D clipping viewport */
float c=0;                              /* used in line-clipping routine */
int crash_flag=0;       /* toggle flag to control animation re-start */
float rx=0,ry=0;            /* scaling values used in window mapping */
float screen_x=639,screen_y=199;        /* used in window mapping */

/*_____


M A I N    R O U T I N E                                     */

main(){
graphics_setup();                       /* establish graphics mode */

rx=screen_x/799;ry=screen_y/599;        /* define windowing ratio */

RESTART:                    /* re-start here after the crash routine */
setactivepage(p);setvisualpage(1-p);p=1-p;     /* set active page */

ANIMATE:                                /* animation loop begins here */
cleardevice();                          /* blank the hidden page */
keyboard();                             /* check the keyboard */
r2=r2+r2a;r3=r3+r3a;            /* new r2 roll & r3 pitch angles */
if (r2>6.28319) r2=r2-6.28319;  /* inhibit range of roll angle */
if (r2<=0) r2=r2+6.28319;       /* inhibit range of roll angle */
if (r3>6.28319) r3=r3-6.28319;  /* inhibit range of pitch angle */
if (r3<=0) r3=r3+6.28319;       /* inhibit range of pitch angle */
yaw_change(); /* calculate new yaw change, based upon roll angle */
rl=rl+rla;                              /* new yaw angle */
if (rl>6.28319) rl=rl-6.28319;  /* inhibit range of yaw angle */
if (rl<=0) rl=rl+6.28319;       /* inhibit range of yaw angle */
srl=sin(rl);sr2=sin(r2);sr3=sin(r3);        /* new sine factors */
crl=cos(rl);cr2=cos(r2);cr3=cos(r3);        /* new cosine factors */
translation();                      /* calculate movement factors */
if (my>0) crash();              /* if crash, jump to crash routine */
if (crash_flag==1){
crash_flag=0;goto RESTART;};    /* reset flag, loop to restart */
g=C1;draw_horizon();        /* set color and draw the horizon line */
```

```
corner();     /* calculate view coords for corners of terrain map */
grid();              /* calculate all other vertices for terrain map */
g=C2;draw_grid();                    /* set color and draw the terrain */
setcolor(C7);circle(319,99,30);                        /* gunsight */
moveto(319,86);lineto(319,112);moveto(290,99);lineto(348,99);
outtextxy(208,0," USING C FOR FLIGHT SIMULATION ");
setactivepage(p);setvisualpage(1-p);p=1-p;        /* flip pages */
goto ANIMATE;}                                    /* infinite loop */
```

/*_____

SUBROUTINE: yaw change

This subroutine calculates the new rla yaw change factor,   */
based upon the r2 roll angle.

```
void yaw_change(void){
if (r2>=0){                                    /* normal roll right */
if (r2<=1.57079){
rla=(r2/.017453)*.00349;return;};
};

if (r2<=6.28319){                              /* normal roll left */
if (r2>=4.71239){
rla=((6.28319-r2)/.017453)*(-.00349);return;};
};

if (r2>1.57079){                              /* inverted roll right */
if (r2<=3.14159){
rla=((3.14159-r2)/.017453)*.00349;return;};
};

if (r2>3.14159){                              /* inverted roll left */
if (r2<4.71239){
rla=((r2-3.14159)/.017453)*(-.00349);return;};
};

return;}
```

/*_____

SUBROUTINE: movement routine

This subroutine calculates the translation factors which
control the movement of the viewpoint over the landmarks,   */
dependent upon rl yaw and r3 pitch.

```
void translation(void){
ml=cr3*m;               /* lateral movement factor linked to pitch */
myl=(-1)*sr3*m;              /* vertical movement linked to pitch */
if (r3>0){                  /* airspeed decreases as pitch increases */
if (r3<=1.57079) myl=cr3*myl;
};
```

```
if (r3>1.57079){                         /* inverted nose up mode */
if (r3<3.14159) my1=(-1)*cr3*my1;
};

mx1=(-1)*srl*ml;mz1=crl*ml;    /* lateral movement linked to yaw */
mx=mx+mx1;my=my+my1;mz=mz+mz1;            /* new movement factors */
return;}
```

```
/*_____
```

SUBROUTINE: crash scenario

This subroutine handles a ground crash. After a pause, the
user is placed back into the simulation at start-up.   */

```
void crash(void){
setactivepage(0);cleardevice();setvisualpage(0);
setcolor(C12);moveto(280,80);
outtext("C R A S H !");setcolor(C7);                    /* message */
for (t1=1;t1<=5;t1++){for (t2=1;t2<=30000;t2++);};       /* pause */
p1=1;g=C7;p=0;                          /* restore start-up values */
r1=6.28319;r2=6.28319;r3=6.28319;       /* restore start-up values */
r1a=0;r2a=0;r3a=0;                      /* restore start-up values */
mx=24;my=-7.7;mz=-78;m=1;               /* restore start-up values */
crash_flag=1;          /* set flag for inspection by main routine */
return;}
```

```
/*_____
```

SUBROUTINE: draw the horizon line   */
```
void draw_horizon(void){
if (r3>1.57079){                        /* test if inverted flight */
if (r3<4.71239) goto INVERTED;
};

x=-8000;y=0;z=-10000;        /* left world coordinates of horizon */
horiz3D();              /* calculate unclipped display coordinates */
window();        /* map display coordinates to fit 640x200 screen */
sxa=sx;sya=sy;                                   /* left end of line */
x=8000;y=0;z=-10000;        /* right world coordinates of horizon */
horiz3D();              /* calculate unclipped display coordinates */
window();        /* map display coordinates to fit 640x200 screen */
sxb=sx;syb=sy;                                  /* right end of line */
clip_2D();                      /* clip line to fit display screen */
setcolor(g);moveto(sxa,sya);lineto(sxb,syb);        /* draw line */
return;

INVERTED:                            /* same as above but (-1)*z */
x=-8000;y=0;z=10000;horiz3D();window();sxa=sx;sya=sy;
x=8000;y=0;z=10000;horiz3D();window();sxb=sx;syb=sy;clip_2D();
setcolor(g);moveto(sxa,sya);lineto(sxb,syb);        /* draw line */
return;}
```

```
/*_____


SUBROUTINE: 3D formulas for horizon                           */

void horiz3D(void){
x=(-1)*x;za=cr3*z-sr3*y;ya=sr3*z+cr3*y;xa=cr2*x+sr2*ya;
y=cr2*ya-sr2*x;sx=d*xa/za;sy=d*y/za;return;}

/*_____


SUBROUTINE: 2D LINE-CLIPPING

Enter with sxa,sya and sxb,syb endpoints of 2D line to be
clipped.  Returns display coordinates for line clipped to
fit physical screen viewport defined by minx,miny and
maxx,maxy.  Sets toggle flag p2 to zero if entire line is
off the screen.                                               */


void clip_2D(void){
if (sxa>sxb) {temp_swap=sxa;sxa=sxb;sxb=temp_swap;
temp_swap=sya;sya=syb;syb=temp_swap;};

if (sxa<minx) {if (sxb<minx) {p2=0;return;}}
if (sxa>maxx) {if (sxb>maxx) {p2=0;return;}}
if (sya<miny) {if (syb<miny) {p2=0;return;}}
if (sya>maxy) {if (syb>maxy) {p2=0;return;}}

if (sxa<minx) {{c=(syb-sya)/(sxb-sxa)*(sxb-minx);  /* push right */
sxa=minx;sya=syb-c;};
if (sya<miny) if (syb<miny) return;
if (sya>maxy) if (syb>maxy) return;
};

if (sxb>maxx) {{c=(syb-sya)/(sxb-sxa)*(maxx-sxa);   /* push left */
sxb=maxx;syb=sya+c;};
if (sya<miny) if (syb<miny) return;
if (sya>maxy) if (syb>maxy) return;
};

if (sya>syb) {temp_swap=sya;sya=syb;syb=temp_swap;
temp_swap=sxa;sxa=sxb;sxb=temp_swap;};

if (sya<miny) {c=(sxb-sxa)/(syb-sya)*(syb-miny);     /* push down */
sxa=sxb-c;sya=miny;};

if (syb>maxy) {c=(sxb-sxa)/(syb-sya)*(maxy-sya);      /* push up */
sxb=sxa+c;syb=maxy;};

return;}

/*_____
```

```
SUBROUTINE: window mapping function for horizon                    */

void window(void){
sx=sx+399;sy=sy+299;rx=screen_x/799;ry=screen_y/599;sx=sx*rx;
sy=sy*ry;return;}
```

```
/*_____
```

```
SUBROUTINE: view coords for corners of terrain
```

This subroutine calculates the rotated and translated view
coordinates for the four corners of the terrain. The rest
of the terrain's vertices can be extrapolated from these
four vertices.   */

```
void corner(void){
x=-80;y=0;z=-80;calc_3D();x01=x;y01=y;z01=z;
x=80;y=0;z=-80;calc_3D();x2=x;y2=y;z2=z;
x=80;y=0;z=80;calc_3D();x3=x;y3=y;z3=z;
x=-80;y=0;z=80;calc_3D();x4=x;y4=y;z4=z;
return;}
```

```
/*_____
```

```
SUBROUTINE: generic 3D translation & rotation formulas
```

This subroutine first translates the terrain landmarks in
order to simulate the movement of the aircraft, then the
translated coordinates are rotated to simulate the effects
of yaw, pitch, and roll in 3D airspace.   */

```
void calc_3D(void){
x=x-mx;y=y+my;z=z+mz;                              /* translation */
xa=cr1*x-sr1*z;za=sr1*x+cr1*z;                            /* yaw */
z=cr3*za-sr3*y;ya=sr3*za+cr3*y;                        /* pitch */
x=cr2*xa+sr2*ya;y=cr2*ya-sr2*xa;                        /* roll */
return;}
```

```
/*_____
```

```
SUBROUTINE: extrapolation of vertices for grid
```

This subroutine uses simple geometry to extrapolate 16
vertices of a grid in 3D space from four known corner
locations.   */

```
void grid(void){
L=.25*(x2-x01);x5=x01+L;x6=x5+L;x7=x6+L;
L=.25*(y2-y01);y5=y01+L;y6=y5+L;y7=y6+L;
L=.25*(z2-z01);z5=z01+L;z6=z5+L;z7=z6+L;
L=.25*(x3-x4);x8=x4+L;x9=x8+L;x10=x9+L;
L=.25*(y3-y4);y8=y4+L;y9=y8+L;y10=y9+L;
```

```
L=.25*(z3-z4);z8=z4+L;z9=z8+L;z10=z9+L;
L=.25*(x4-x01);x11=x01+L;x12=x11+L;x13=x12+L;
L=.25*(y4-y01);y11=y01+L;y12=y11+L;y13=y12+L;
L=.25*(z4-z01);z11=z01+L;z12=z11+L;z13=z12+L;
L=.25*(x3-x2);x14=x2+L;x15=x14+L;x16=x15+L;
L=.25*(y3-y2);y14=y2+L;y15=y14+L;y16=y15+L;
L=.25*(z3-z2);z14=z2+L;z15=z14+L;z16=z15+L;
return;}
```

```
/*_____
```

SUBROUTINE: draw the grid terrain

This subroutine draws a sixteen-square grid. If pl equals
zero then the line is completely clipped and invisible.   */

```
void draw_grid(void){
setcolor(g);
xa=x01;ya=y01;za=z01;xb=x2;yb=y2;zb=z2;pl=1;clip_3D();
if (pl==1) draw_line();
xa=x11;ya=y11;za=z11;xb=x14;yb=y14;zb=z14;pl=1;clip_3D();
if (pl==1) draw_line();
xa=x12;ya=y12;za=z12;xb=x15;yb=y15;zb=z15;pl=1;clip_3D();
if (pl==1) draw_line();
xa=x13;ya=y13;za=z13;xb=x16;yb=y16;zb=z16;pl=1;clip_3D();
if (pl==1) draw_line();
xa=x4;ya=y4;za=z4;xb=x3;yb=y3;zb=z3;pl=1;clip_3D();
if (pl==1) draw_line();
xa=x01;ya=y01;za=z01;xb=x4;yb=y4;zb=z4;pl=1;clip_3D();
if (pl==1) draw_line();
xa=x5;ya=y5;za=z5;xb=x8;yb=y8;zb=z8;pl=1;clip_3D();
if (pl==1) draw_line();
xa=x6;ya=y6;za=z6;xb=x9;yb=y9;zb=z9;pl=1;clip_3D();
if (pl==1) draw_line();
xa=x7;ya=y7;za=z7;xb=x10;yb=y10;zb=z10;pl=1;clip_3D();
if (pl==1) draw_line();
xa=x2;ya=y2;za=z2;xb=x3;yb=y3;zb=z3;pl=1;clip_3D();
if (pl==1) draw_line();
return;}
```

```
/*_____
```

SUBROUTINE: draw clipped line on screen   */

```
void draw_line(void){
p2=1;clip_2D();   /* p2 will be set to zero if line is invisible */
if (p2==1){moveto(sxa,sya);lineto(sxb,syb);}
return;}
```

```
/*_____
```

SUBROUTINE: window mapping function for terrain

This subroutine maps a world space window of 800x600 to fit
the 640x200 screen, thereby ensuring the integrity of the
4:3 screen ratio and avoid distortion during 3D rotations.   */

```
void window_terrain(void){
sxa=sxa+399;sya=sya+299;sxa=sxa*rx;sya=sya*ry;
sxb=sxb+399;syb=syb+299;sxb=sxb*rx;syb=syb*ry;
return;}
```

```
/*_____
```

SUBROUTINE: clip lines in 3D space

This subroutine clips portions of lines which fall behind
the viewpoint in 3D space and which would be invisible to
the observer. Enter with xa,ya,za,xb,yb,zb view coordinates
for endpoints of line to be clipped in 3D space.   */

```
void clip_3D(void){
if (za>=-1) goto LABEL1630;              /* xa,ya,za requires clipping */
goto LABEL1640;                                  /* xa,ya,za is ok */

LABEL1630:
if (zb>=-1) {pl=0;return;};                /* both endpoints hidden */
temp_swap=xb;xb=xa;xa=temp_swap;
temp_swap=yb;yb=ya;ya=temp_swap;
temp_swap=zb;zb=za;za=temp_swap;
goto LABEL1660;                  /* only xb,yb,zb requires clipping */

LABEL1640:                       /* xa,ya,za is ok, now test xb,yb,zb */
if (zb>=-1) goto LABEL1660;    /* only xb,yb,zb requires clipping */

LABEL1650:            /* calculate display coords and map to screen */
sxa=d*xa/za;sya=d*ya/za;sxb=d*xb/zb;syb=d*yb/zb;
window_terrain();return;

LABEL1660:                                      /* clip xb,yb,zb */
c=(xb-xa)/(zb-za)*(zb+1);xc=xb-c;
c=(yb-ya)/(zb-za)*(zb+1);yc=yb-c;zc=-1;
xb=xc;yb=yc;zb=zc;goto LABEL1650;
return;}
```

```
/*_____
```

SUBROUTINE: dynamic keyboard input

The subroutine is called on each pass through the animation
loop. If the Esc key is pressed, the flight simulation will
terminate. Press <h> to roll right, <f> to roll left.
Press <t> to push the aircraft's nose down, press <b> to

raise the nose. The aircraft will continue to roll, climb,
or dive unless the <g> key is pressed to hold its current
attitude. Press <+> to increase throttle, press <-> to
decrease throttle.   */

```
void keyboard(void){
union u_type{int a;char b[3];}keystroke;char inkey=0;

if (bioskey(1)==0) return;                      /* if no key, return */
keystroke.a=bioskey(0);                         /* fetch ASCII code... */
inkey=keystroke.b[0];               /* ...and load code into variable */
switch (inkey){             /* make decision based upon ASCII value */
case 27:  quit_pgm();                                   /* Esc key */
case 104: r2a=r2a+.017453;return;              /* h key roll right */
case 102: r2a=r2a-.017453;return;               /* f key roll left */
case 116: r3a=r3a-.008726;return;                    /* t key dive */
case 98:  r3a=r3a+.008726;return;                   /* b key climb */
case 103: r2a=0;r3a=0;return;                        /* g key hold */
case 61:  m=m+.1;return;                /* + key increase throttle */
case 45:  m=m-.1;return;                /* - key decrease throttle */
default:  return;}               /* make routine bullet-proof */
}
```

/*_____

SUBROUTINE: GRACEFUL EXIT FROM THE PROGRAM   */

```
void quit_pgm(void){
setvisualpage(0);setactivepage(0);
cleardevice();restorecrtmode();exit(0);}
```

/*_____

SUBROUTINE: VGA/EGA/CGA/MCGA compatibility module   */

```
void graphics_setup(void){
int graphics_adapter,graphics_mode;
detectgraph(&graphics_adapter,&graphics_mode);
if (graphics_adapter==VGA) goto VGA_EGA_mode;              /* if VGA */
if (graphics_mode==EGAHI) goto VGA_EGA_mode;       /* if EGA and ECD */
if (graphics_mode==EGALO) goto VGA_EGA_mode;       /* if EGA and SCD */
if (graphics_adapter==CGA) goto abort_message;            /* if CGA */
if (graphics_adapter==MCGA) goto abort_message;          /* if MCGA */
goto abort_message;                /* if no VGA, EGA, CGA, or MCGA */

VGA_EGA_mode:                   /* establish 640x200 16-color mode */
graphics_adapter=EGA;graphics_mode=EGALO;
initgraph(&graphics_adapter,&graphics_mode,"");
maxx=639;minx=0;maxy=199;miny=0;            /* clipping viewport */
screen_x=639;screen_y=199;                  /* windowing viewport */
setcolor(C7);
return;
```

```
abort_message:
printf("\n\nUnable to proceed.\n");
printf("Requires VGA or EGA adapter\n");
printf("   with appropriate monitor.\n");
printf("Please refer to the book.\n\n");
exit(0);
}
/*_____


SUBROUTINE: Copyright Notice

This subroutine displays the standard copyright notice.
If you are typing in this program from the book you can
safely omit this subroutine, provided that you also remove
the instruction "notice()" from the main routine.              */

int copyright[ ][3]={0x7c00,0x0000,0x0000,0x8231,
0x819c,0x645e,0xba4a,0x4252,0x96d0,0xa231,0x8252,0x955e,0xba4a,
0x43d2,0xf442,0x8231,0x825c,0x945e,0x7c00,0x0000,0x0000};

void notice(float x, float y){
int a,b,c; int tl=0;
for (tl=0;tl<=6;tl++){a=copyright[tl][0];b=copyright[tl][1];
c=copyright[tl][2];
setlinestyle(USERBIT_LINE,a,NORM_WIDTH);
moveto(x,y);lineto(x+15,y);
setlinestyle(USERBIT_LINE,b,NORM_WIDTH);
moveto(x+16,y);lineto(x+31,y);
setlinestyle(USERBIT_LINE,c,NORM_WIDTH);
moveto(x+32,y);lineto(x+47,y);y=y+1;};
setlinestyle(USERBIT_LINE,0xFFFF,NORM_WIDTH);
return;}


/*_____

End of source code                                             */
```

Fig. E-14. Utility program: how to configure your Turbo C graphics programs to run on all IBM-compatible graphics adapters—
VGA/EGA/CGA/CGA compatible. Refer to the main body of the book for discussion.

```
/*_____

func-002.c

Function:  This program demonstrates automatic configuration
of the software to match the graphics hardware.

Compatibility:  Supports all graphics adapters and monitors.
The software uses the 640x480 16-color mode if a VGA is
present, the 640x350 16-color mode if an EGA and enhanced
```

monitor are present, the 640x200 16-color mode if an EGA and
standard monitor are present, and the 320x200 4-color mode
if a CGA or MCGA is present.

Remarks: This program is intended as a framework upon which
software can be developed. Refer to the book for further
guidance.

Copyright 1988 Lee Adams and TAB BOOKS Inc.

_____

```
I N C L U D E    F I L E S                              */

#include <dos.h>                    /* supports the BIOS call */
#include <stdio.h>                 /* supports the printf function */
#include <graphics.h>              /* supports the graphics functions */
#include <process.h>                /* support for exit function */

    /*_____


D E C L A R A T I O N S                                 */

    /*                            declare global variables */
int C0=0,C1=1,C2=2,C3=3,C4=4,C5=5,          /* color code variables */
C6=6,C7=7,C8=8,C9=9,C10=10,C11=11,
C12=12,C13=13,C14=14,C15=15,mode_flag=0;
float x_res,y_res;      /* screen resolution for mapping routine */
float sx,sy;            /* device-independent screen coordinates */

    /*                            declare global subroutines */
void keyboard(void);void quit_pgm(void);void get_coords(void);
void graphics_setup(void);

    /*_____


M A I N    R O U T I N E                                */

main(){
graphics_setup();                    /* establish graphics mode */

keyboard();                          /* wait for user to press <Esc> */
quit_pgm();}                         /* end the program gracefully */

    /*_____


SUBROUTINE: CHECK THE KEYBOARD BUFFER                    */

void keyboard(void){
union u_type {int a;char b[3];} keystroke;
```

```
int get_keystroke(void);            /* declare a local subroutine */
do keystroke.a=get_keystroke();
while (keystroke.b[0]!=27);         /* return if <Esc> is pressed */
}

/* LOCAL SUBROUTINE: RETRIEVE ONE KEYSTROKE                       */

int get_keystroke(void){
union REGS regs;regs.h.ah=0;return int86(0x16,&regs,&regs);}

/*_____


SUBROUTINE: GRACEFUL EXIT FROM THE PROGRAM                       */

void quit_pgm(void){
cleardevice();restorecrtmode();exit(0);}

/*_____


SUBROUTINE: VGA/EGA/CGA/MCGA compatibility module
```

This subroutine invokes the highest-resolution graphics mode
which is permitted by the hardware. The 640x480 16-color mode
is established if a VGA is present. The 640x350 16-color mode
is established if an EGA is being used with an enhanced color
display monitor or a multiscanning monitor. The 640x200
16-color mode is established if an EGA is being used with a
standard color monitor. The 320x200 4-color mode is invoked
if a CGA or MCGA is present.   */

```
void graphics_setup(void){
int graphics_adapter,graphics_mode;
detectgraph(&graphics_adapter,&graphics_mode);
if (graphics_adapter==VGA) goto VGA_mode;            /* if VGA */
if (graphics_mode==EGAHI) goto EGA_ECD_mode;   /* if EGA and ECD */
if (graphics_mode==EGALO) goto EGA_SCD_mode;   /* if EGA and SCD */
if (graphics_adapter==CGA) goto CGA_mode;            /* if CGA */
if (graphics_adapter==MCGA) goto MCGA_mode;          /* if MCGA */
goto abort_message;              /* if no VGA, EGA, CGA, or MCGA */

VGA_mode:                   /* establish 640x480 16-color mode */
graphics_adapter=VGA;graphics_mode=VGAHI;
initgraph(&graphics_adapter,&graphics_mode,"");
x_res=640;y_res=480;C0=0;C1=1;C2=2;C3=3;C4=4;C5=5,C6=6;C7=7;
C8=8;C9=9;C10=10;C11=11;C12=12;C13=13;C14=14;C15=15;
mode_flag=1;
setcolor(C7);outtextxy(216,472,"640x480 16-color VGA mode.");
return;

EGA_ECD_mode:               /* establish 640x350 16-color mode */
graphics_adapter=EGA;graphics_mode=EGAHI;
initgraph(&graphics_adapter,&graphics_mode,"");
```

```
x_res=640;y_res=350;C0=0;Cl=1;C2=2;C3=3;C4=4;C5=5,C6=6;C7=7;
C8=8;C9=9;C10=10;C11=11;C12=12;C13=13;C14=14;C15=15;
mode_flag=2;
setcolor(C7);outtextxy(216,342,"640x350 16-color EGA mode.");
return;

EGA_SCD_mode:                    /* establish 640x200 16-color mode */
graphics_adapter=EGA;graphics_mode=EGALO;
initgraph(&graphics_adapter,&graphics_mode,"");
x_res=640;y_res=200;C0=0;Cl=1;C2=2;C3=3;C4=4;C5=5,C6=6;C7=7;
C8=8;C9=9;C10=10;C11=11;C12=12;C13=13;C14=14;C15=15;
mode_flag=3;
setcolor(C7);outtextxy(216,192,"640x200 16-color EGA mode.");
return;

CGA_mode:                        /* establish 320x200 4-color mode */
graphics_adapter=CGA;graphics_mode=CGAC3;
initgraph(&graphics_adapter,&graphics_mode,"");
x_res=320;y_res=200;C0=0;Cl=1;C2=1;C3=1;C4=1;C5=1,C6=1;C7=3;
C8=1;C9=0;C10=1;C11=1;C12=1;C13=2;C14=1;C15=3;
mode_flag=4;
setcolor(C7);outtextxy(64,192,"320x200 4-color CGA mode.");
return;
MCGA_mode:                       /* establish 320x200 4-color mode */
graphics_adapter=MCGA;graphics_mode=MCGAC3;
initgraph(&graphics_adapter,&graphics_mode,"");
x_res=320;y_res=200;C0=0;Cl=1;C2=1;C3=1;C4=1;C5=1;C6=1;C7=3;
C8=1;C9=0;C10=1;C11=1;C12=1;C13=2;C14=1;C15=3;
mode_flag=4;
setcolor(C7);outtextxy(64,192,"320x200 4-color MCGA mode.");
return;

abort_message:
printf("\n\nUnable to proceed.\n");
printf("Requires VGA, EGA, MCGA, or CGA adapter\n");
printf("   with appropriate monitor.\n");
printf("Please refer to the book.\n\n");
exit(0);
}
/*_____

SUBROUTINE: coords()

This subroutine accepts sx,sy device-independent display
coordinates and returns sx,sy device-dependent screen
coordinates scaled to fit the 640x480, 640x350, 640x200, or
320x200 screen, depending upon the graphics mode being used.    */

void coords(void){
sx=sx*(x_res/640);sy=sy*(y_res/480);return;}

/*_____

End of source code                                      */
```

Fig. E-15. Utility program: how to produce sounds—VGA/EGA/CGA/CGA compatible. Refer to the main body of the book for discussion.

```
/*_____

func-003.c

Function:  This program demonstrates how to generate sounds.

Compatibility:  The software uses the default text mode.

Remarks:  This program is intended as a framework upon which
software can be developed.  In its current form, the program
turns on the speaker, emits a tone, and turns off the speaker
on each occasion a sound is desired.  Rising or falling tones
are generated as a stairstepping action.  In order to
produce a smooth slide (such as a siren, for example), simply
modify this program so that the speaker is left on while
you manipulate the sound frequency (hertz).  The current
timing loops have been tested on an IBM PC.  You may wish to
slow down the loops if you are using a faster computer, such
as an XT, AT, or PS/2.

Copyright 1988 Lee Adams and TAB BOOKS Inc.

_____


I N C L U D E    F I L E S                              */

#include <dos.h>                    /* supports port manipulation */
#include <process.h>                   /* supports exit() routine */

/*_____


D E C L A R A T I O N S                                 */

int hz=100;
void noise(int hertz,int duration);

/*_____


M A I N    R O U T I N E                                */

main(){

for (hz=50;hz<=1600;hz+=50)                    /* a rising tone */
noise(hz,5000);

for (hz=1;hz<=20000;hz++);                           /* pause */

for (hz=2000;hz>=250;hz-=50)                  /* a falling tone */
```

```
noise(hz,5000);

for (hz=1;hz<=6000;hz++);                              /* pause */

noise(40,30000);                                /* a single tone */

exit(0);}                                      /* end the program */
```

```
/*_____
```

SUBROUTINE: GENERATE A SOUND

Enter with frequency, expressed as hertz in the range
40 to 4660. A comfortable frequency range for the human
ear is 40 to 2400. Enter with duration, expressed as an
integer to be used in a simple for...next delay loop.   */

```
void noise(int hertz,int duration){
int tl=1,high_byte=0,low_byte=0;
short count=0;unsigned char old_port=0,new_port=0;

if (hertz<40) return;        /* avoid math overflow for int count */
if (hertz>4660) return;      /* avoid math underflow for low_byte */

count=1193180L/hertz;                     /* determine timer count */
high_byte=count/256;low_byte=count-(high_byte*256);

outportb(0x43,0xB6);                    /* prep the timer register */
outportb(0x42,low_byte);                     /* send the low byte */
outportb(0x42,high_byte);                    /* send the high byte */

old_port=inportb(0x61);        /* store the existing port value */
new_port=(old_port | 0x03);  /* use OR to set bits 0 and 1 to on */
outportb(0x61,new_port);                    /* turn on the speaker */
for (tl=1;tl<=duration;tl++);                          /* wait */
outportb(0x61,old_port);                   /* turn off the speaker */

return;}                                    /* return to caller */
```

```
/*_____

End of source code                                             */
```

Fig. E-16. Utility program: how to produce frame animation at 14 frames per second—Turbo C version, VGA/EGA/CGA/CGA compatible. Refer to the main body of the book for discussion.

```
/*_____

func-005.c

Function:  This program demonstrates the fundamental
algorithms involved in high speed frame animation.
```

Compatibility: Supports all graphics adapters and monitors.
The software uses the 640x200 16-color mode if a VGA or an
EGA is present. The 640x200 2-color mode is used if a
CGA is present.

Remarks: The 640x200 16-color mode is used with the VGA and
EGA because four graphics pages are required by this animated
program. If a CGA is present, the extra pages required by
the program are stored in user RAM.

Copyright 1988 Lee Adams and TAB BOOKS Inc.

_____

INCLUDE   FILES   */

```
#include <stdio.h>              /* supports the printf function */
#include <graphics.h>          /* supports the graphics functions */
#include <process.h>            /* supports the exit() function */
#include <mem.h>                    /* supports memory moves */
#include <bios.h>          /* supports read of keyboard buffer */
```

/*_____

DECLARATIONS   */

```
void keyboard(void);void quit_pgm(void);
void notice(float x,float y);void coords(void);
void graphics_setup(void);void labels(void);void blocks(void);

void animVGAEGA(void);                        /* EGA and VGA only */
void animCGA(void);                                /* CGA only */
void pagemove(unsigned source,unsigned target);    /* CGA only */

int frame=0,t1=1,t2=2;
float sx,sy;float x_res,y_res;
int C0=0,Cl=1,C2=2,C3=3,C4=4,C5=5,C6=6,C7=7,C8=8,C9=9,C10=10,
Cl1=11,C12=12,Cl3=13,Cl4=14,Cl5=15,mode_flag=0;
char fill_50[]={85,170,85,170,85,170,85,170};
```

/*_____

MAIN   ROUTINE   */

```
main(){
graphics_setup();                     /* establish graphics mode */
setcolor(C7);


if (mode_flag==3) {setvisualpage(0);setactivepage(0);};
cleardevice();
frame=0;                                   /* set the frame flag */
```

```
labels();                             /* create the alphanumeric labels */
blocks();                                      /* draw the graphics */
if (mode_flag==4) {pagemove(0xB800,0x8800);}              /* if CGA */

if (mode_flag==3) {setvisualpage(1);setactivepage(1);};
cleardevice();
frame=1;                                      /* set the frame flag */
labels();                             /* create the alphanumeric labels */
blocks();                                      /* draw the graphics */
if (mode_flag==4) {pagemove(0xB800,0x8C00);}              /* if CGA */

if (mode_flag==3) {setvisualpage(2);setactivepage(2);};
cleardevice();
frame=2;                                      /* set the frame flag */
labels();                             /* create the alphanumeric labels */
blocks();                                      /* draw the graphics */
if (mode_flag==4) {pagemove(0xB800,0x9000);}              /* if CGA */

if (mode_flag==3) {setvisualpage(3);setactivepage(3);};
cleardevice();
frame=3;                                      /* set the frame flag */
labels();                             /* create the alphanumeric labels */
blocks();                                      /* draw the graphics */
if (mode_flag==4) {pagemove(0xB800,0x9400);};             /* if CGA */

if (mode_flag==3) {setvisualpage(0);setactivepage(0);};
if (mode_flag==4) {pagemove(0x8800,0xB800);};

for (tl=1;tl<=30000;tl++);                /* pause before animating */
if (mode_flag==3) animVGAEGA();      /* animation for VGA and EGA */
if (mode_flag==4) animCGA();                /* animation for CGA */

quit_pgm();}                         /* end the program gracefully */

/*_____


SUBROUTINE: frame animation manager for VGA and EGA              */

void animVGAEGA(void){
for (tl=1;tl!=2; ){                    /* animate for endless loop */
setvisualpage(1);for (t2=1;t2<=3000;t2++);
setvisualpage(2);for (t2=1;t2<=3000;t2++);
setvisualpage(3);for (t2=1;t2<=30000;t2++);keyboard();
setvisualpage(2);for (t2=1;t2<=3000;t2++);
setvisualpage(1);for (t2=1;t2<=3000;t2++);
setvisualpage(0);for (t2=1;t2<=10000;t2++);keyboard();};
return;}

/*_____


SUBROUTINE: frame animation manager for CGA                     */

void animCGA(void){
```

```
for (t1=1;t1!=2; ){                    /* animate for endless loop */
pagemove(0x8C00,0xB800);for (t2=1;t2<=3000;t2++);
pagemove(0x9000,0xB800);for (t2=1;t2<=3000;t2++);
pagemove(0x9400,0xB800);for (t2=1;t2<=30000;t2++);keyboard();
pagemove(0x9000,0xB800);for (t2=1;t2<=3000;t2++);
pagemove(0x8C00,0xB800);for (t2=1;t2<=3000;t2++);
pagemove(0x8800,0xB800);for (t2=1;t2<=10000;t2++);keyboard();};
return;}
```

```
/*_____ _____
```

SUBROUTINE: pagemove for CGA

This subroutine is called during the graphics drawing process
in order to store the frames in user RAM. This subroutine is
also called during the frame animation process in order to
flip the previously-stored pages onto the CGA display buffer
at B8000 hex. For serious development work, you would want
to use a short assembly language subroutine instead.   */

```
void pagemove(unsigned source, unsigned target){
movedata(source,0x0000,target,0x0000,16000);return;}
```

```
/*_____
```

SUBROUTINE: alphanumeric labels   */

```
void labels(void){
setcolor(C7);moveto(184,192);
if (mode_flag==3) {outtext("640x200 16-color VGA and EGA mode");}
if (mode_flag==4) {outtext("640x200 2-color CGA mode");}
moveto(168,0);
outtext("USING C FOR HIGH SPEED FRAME ANIMATION");
moveto(128,32);
outtext("High speed rotation of a simple geometric shape...");
moveto(232,176);outtext("Press any key to quit.");
moveto(0,96);outtext("Animation rate:");
moveto(0,104);
if (mode_flag==3) outtext("14 frames per second");
if (mode_flag==4) outtext("7 frames per second");
return;}
```

```
/*_____
```

SUBROUTINE: draw the graphics   */

```
void blocks(void){
if (frame==0) {sx=209;sy=139;coords();moveto(sx,sy);
sx=389;sy=139;coords();lineto(sx,sy);
sx=389;sy=339;coords();lineto(sx,sy);
sx=209;sy=339;coords();lineto(sx,sy);
```

```
sx=209;sy=139;coords();lineto(sx,sy);};
if (frame==1) {sx=218;sy=141;coords();moveto(sx,sy);
sx=387;sy=151;coords();lineto(sx,sy);
sx=379;sy=337;coords();lineto(sx,sy);
sx=211;sy=327;coords();lineto(sx,sy);
sx=218;sy=141;coords();lineto(sx,sy);};
if (frame==2) {sx=226;sy=149;coords();moveto(sx,sy);
sx=382;sy=161;coords();lineto(sx,sy);
sx=371;sy=331;coords();lineto(sx,sy);
sx=214;sy=318;coords();lineto(sx,sy);
sx=226;sy=149;coords();lineto(sx,sy);};
if (frame==3) {sx=236;sy=150;coords();moveto(sx,sy);
sx=378;sy=170;coords();lineto(sx,sy);
sx=359;sy=327;coords();lineto(sx,sy);
sx=218;sy=308;coords();lineto(sx,sy);
sx=236;sy=150;coords();lineto(sx,sy);};
if (mode_flag==3) {setfillstyle(SOLID_FILL,C4);};   /* VGA or EGA */
if (mode_flag==4) {setfillpattern(fill_50,C7);};        /* if CGA */
sx=299;sy=239;coords();floodfill(sx,sy,C7);
setcolor(C7);sx=5;sy=460;coords();notice(sx,sy);        /* notice */
return;}

/*_____


SUBROUTINE: press any key to quit                               */

void keyboard(void){
if (bioskey(1)==0) return; else quit_pgm();}

/*_____


SUBROUTINE: GRACEFUL EXIT FROM THE PROGRAM                      */

void quit_pgm(void){
if(mode_flag==3) {setvisualpage(0);setactivepage(0);};
cleardevice();restorecrtmode();exit(0);}

/*_____


SUBROUTINE: VGA/EGA/CGA/MCGA compatibility module              */

void graphics_setup(void){
int graphics_adapter,graphics_mode;
detectgraph(&graphics_adapter,&graphics_mode);
if (graphics_adapter==VGA) goto VGA_EGA_mode;            /* if VGA */
if (graphics_mode==EGAHI) goto VGA_EGA_mode;     /* if EGA and ECD */
if (graphics_mode==EGALO) goto VGA_EGA_mode;     /* if EGA and SCD */
if (graphics_adapter==CGA) goto CGA_mode;               /* if CGA */
if (graphics_adapter==MCGA) goto CGA_mode;             /* if MCGA */
goto abort_message;              /* if no VGA, EGA, CGA, or MCGA */

VGA_EGA_mode:                    /* establish 640x200 16-color mode */
```

```
graphics_adapter=EGA;graphics_mode=EGALO;
initgraph(&graphics_adapter,&graphics_mode,"");
x_res=640;y_res=200;mode_flag=3;
return;

CGA_mode:                           /* establish 640x200 2-color mode */
graphics_adapter=CGA;graphics_mode=CGAHI;
initgraph(&graphics_adapter,&graphics_mode,"");
x_res=640;y_res=200;mode_flag=4;
C0=0;C1=1;C2=1;C3=1;C4=1;C5=1;C6=1;C7=1;C8=1;C9=1;C10=1;C11=1;
C12=1;C13=1;C14=1;C15=1;return;

abort_message:
printf("\n\nUnable to proceed.\n");
printf("Requires VGA, EGA, MCGA, or CGA adapter\n");
printf("   with appropriate monitor.\n");
printf("Please refer to the book.\n\n");
exit(0);
}
/*_____


SUBROUTINE: coords()

This subroutine accepts sx,sy device-independent display
coordinates and returns sx,sy device-dependent screen
coordinates scaled to fit the 640x480, 640x350, 640x200, or
320x200 screen, depending upon the graphics mode being used.     */
void coords(void){
sx=sx*(x_res/640);sy=sy*(y_res/480);return;}

/*_____


SUBROUTINE: Copyright Notice

This subroutine displays the standard copyright notice.
If you are typing in this program from the book you can
safely omit this subroutine, provided that you also remove
the instruction "notice()" from the main routine.             */

int copyright[][3]={0x7c00,0x0000,0x0000,0x8231,
0x819c,0x645e,0xba4a,0x4252,0x96d0,0xa231,0x8252,0x955e,0xba4a,
0x43d2,0xf442,0x8231,0x825c,0x945e,0x7c00,0x0000,0x0000};

void notice(float x, float y){
int a,b,c; int tl=0;
for (tl=0;tl<=6;tl++){a=copyright[tl][0];b=copyright[tl][1];
c=copyright[tl][2];
setlinestyle(USERBIT_LINE,a,NORM_WIDTH);
moveto(x,y);lineto(x+15,y);
setlinestyle(USERBIT_LINE,b,NORM_WIDTH);
moveto(x+16,y);lineto(x+31,y);
setlinestyle(USERBIT_LINE,c,NORM_WIDTH);
```

```
moveto(x+32,y);lineto(x+47,y);y=y+1;};
setlinestyle(USERBIT_LINE,0xFFFF,NORM_WIDTH);
return;}
```

```
/*_____

End of source code                                          */
```

Fig. E-17. Utility program: how to produce bitblt animation at 43 frames per second—Turbo C version, VGA/EGA/CGA/CGA compatible. Refer to the main body of the book for discussion.

```
/*_____

func-007.c

Function:  This program demonstrates the fundamental
algorithms involved in bitblt animation.

Compatibility:  Supports all graphics adapters and monitors.
By default, the software uses the 640x200 2-color mode in
order to animate at 43 frames per second.  However, if you
have a VGA or EGA you can delete one line in the
compatibility subroutine in order to force the program to
use the 640x200 16-color mode (and animate at 11 frames
per second).

Remarks:  The run-time speed of bitblt animation is
inversely proportional to the screen resolution.  Coarser
resolution with fewer available screen colors will yield
quicker bitblt animation (graphic array animation).
Refer to the book for further guidance.

Copyright 1988 Lee Adams and TAB BOOKS Inc.

_____


I N C L U D E   F I L E S                                   */

#include <stdio.h>            /* supports the printf function */
#include <graphics.h>       /* supports the graphics functions */
#include <process.h>          /* supports the exit() function */
#include <bios.h>        /* supports read of keyboard buffer */
#include <alloc.h>          /* supports memory allocation */

/*_____


D E C L A R A T I O N S                                     */

void keyboard(void);void quit_pgm(void);
void notice(float x,float y);void graphics_setup(void);
```

```
int tl=1,xl=220,yl=100,x2=270,y2=120,
sx=220,sy=100,sxmove=3,symove=-1,sxl,syl;
int C0=0,Cl=1,C2=2,C3=3,C4=4,C5=5,C6=6,C7=7,C8=8,C9=9,Cl0=10,
Cll=11,Cl2=12,Cl3=13,Cl4=14,Cl5=15,mode_flag=0;

char far *gr_arrayl;                    /* pointer to graphic array */

/*_____


M A I N    R O U T I N E                                      */

main(){
graphics_setup();                       /* establish graphics mode */


/*-------------- create and store the graphic array --------------*/

setcolor(C7);circle(xl+25,yl+10,22);
setfillstyle(SOLID_FILL,C4);floodfill(xl+25,yl+10,C7);
gr_arrayl=(char far*)farmalloc((unsigned long)imagesize(xl,yl,x2,y2));
getimage(xl,yl,x2,y2,gr_arrayl);
setfillstyle(SOLID_FILL,C0);bar(xl,yl,x2,y2);

/*              ----------------------------------              */

setcolor(C7);rectangle(201,40,439,159);  /* animation boundaries */
notice(0,192);                                       /* notice */
putimage(sx,sy,gr_arrayl,COPY_PUT);     /* install block graphic */
outtextxy(0,96,"Animation rate:    ");
moveto(0,104);
if (mode_flag==4)
outtext("43 frames per second");       /* if 640x200 2-clr mode */
if (mode_flag==3)
outtext("ll frames per second");       /* if 640x200 16-clr mode */

/*----------------- bitblt animation manager -------------------*/

for (tl=1;tl!=20; ){               /* animate for endless loop */
if (sxl>=386) sxmove=-3;               /* test for right boundary */
if (sxl<=204) sxmove=3;                /* test for left boundary */
if (syl>=138) symove=-1;             /* test for bottom boundary */
if (syl<=41) symove=1;                  /* test for top boundary */
sxl=sx+sxmove;syl=sy+symove;          /* calculate new position */
putimage(sxl,syl,gr_arrayl,COPY_PUT);     /* install new array */
sx=sxl;sy=syl;                        /* update sx,sy variables */
keyboard();};                   /* check for user keyboard input */

/*              ------------------------              */

quit_pgm();}                      /* end the program gracefully */

/*_____
```

```
SUBROUTINE: press any key to quit                                    */

void keyboard(void){
if (bioskey(1)==0) return; else quit_pgm();}

 /*_____


SUBROUTINE: GRACEFUL EXIT FROM THE PROGRAM                           */

void quit_pgm(void){
cleardevice();restorecrtmode();exit(0);}

 /*_____


SUBROUTINE: VGA/EGA/CGA/MCGA compatibility module                    */

void graphics_setup(void){
int graphics_adapter,graphics_mode;
detectgraph(&graphics_adapter,&graphics_mode);

goto CGA_mode; /* If you have a VGA or EGA, you can delete this
line to force the software to use the 640x200 16-color mode
(which runs much slower than the default 640x200 2-color mode).  */

if (graphics_adapter==VGA) goto EGA_SCD_mode;              /* if VGA */
if (graphics_mode==EGAHI) goto EGA_SCD_mode;      /* if EGA and ECD */
if (graphics_mode==EGALO) goto EGA_SCD_mode;      /* if EGA and SCD */
if (graphics_adapter==CGA) goto CGA_mode;                  /* if CGA */
if (graphics_adapter==MCGA) goto CGA_mode;                /* if MCGA */
goto abort_message;                    /* if no VGA, EGA, CGA, or MCGA */


EGA_SCD_mode:                  /* establish 640x200 16-color mode */
graphics_adapter=EGA;graphics_mode=EGALO;
initgraph(&graphics_adapter,&graphics_mode,"");
mode_flag=3;setcolor(C7);
outtextxy(240,192,"Press any key to quit...");
outtextxy(192,0,"USING C FOR HIGH SPEED ANIMATION");
outtextxy(192,176,"640x200 16-color VGA and EGA mode.");
return;

CGA_mode:                       /* establish 640x200 2-color mode */
graphics_adapter=CGA;graphics_mode=CGAHI;
initgraph(&graphics_adapter,&graphics_mode,"");
mode_flag=4;C0=0;C1=1;C2=1;C3=1;C4=1;C5=1,C6=1;C7=1;
C8=1;C9=1;C10=1;C11=1;C12=1;C13=1;C14=1;C15=1;
setcolor(C7);
outtextxy(240,192,"Press any key to quit...");
outtextxy(192,0,"USING C FOR HIGH SPEED ANIMATION");
outtextxy(176,176,"640x200 2-color VGA, EGA, and CGA mode.");
return;
```

```
abort_message:
printf("\n\nUnable to proceed.\n");

printf("Requires VGA, EGA, MCGA, or CGA adapter\n");
printf("   with appropriate monitor.\n");
printf("Please refer to the book.\n\n");
exit(0);
}
/*_____


SUBROUTINE: Copyright Notice

This subroutine displays the standard copyright notice.
If you are typing in this program from the book you can
safely omit this subroutine, provided that you also remove
the instruction "notice()" from the main routine.          */

int copyright[][3]={0x7c00,0x0000,0x0000,0x8231,
0x819c,0x645e,0xba4a,0x4252,0x96d0,0xa231,0x8252,0x955e,0xba4a,
0x43d2,0xf442,0x8231,0x825c,0x945e,0x7c00,0x0000,0x0000};

void notice(float x, float y){
int a,b,c; int tl=0;
for (tl=0;tl<=6;tl++){a=copyright[tl][0];b=copyright[tl][1];
c=copyright[tl][2];
setlinestyle(USERBIT_LINE,a,NORM_WIDTH);
moveto(x,y);lineto(x+15,y);
setlinestyle(USERBIT_LINE,b,NORM_WIDTH);
moveto(x+16,y);lineto(x+31,y);
setlinestyle(USERBIT_LINE,c,NORM_WIDTH);
moveto(x+32,y);lineto(x+47,y);y=y+1;};
setlinestyle(USERBIT_LINE,0xFFFF,NORM_WIDTH);
return;}

/*_____

End of source code                                         */
```

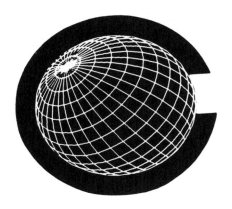

Glossary

acronym—an abbreviation for a group of words.

active page—the graphics page to which the microprocessor is currently writing, also called the written-to page. The active page is not necessarily the same as the page being displayed.

ADA—a compiled, high level, real-time language used by the U.S. military. The term ADA is a registered trademark of the U. S. Government.

additive operators—the + and the − operator, which are addition and subtraction.

addressable—the ability to be addressed directly by a command from the keyboard or by an instruction in a program.

aggregate type—a C array, structure, or union.

ALGOL—a compiled, high level language used for general numeric analysis in scientific computing.

algorithm—a method for solving a problem. See heuristic.

alias—one of several names which refer to the same memory location. See also union.

all-points-addressable—the ability of the microprocessor to read and write each separate pixel on the display monitor. Also called APA.

alphanumeric—a set of characters containing both letters and numbers.

analog—as used in this book, a signal or readout that varies continuously. A digital signal is either fully on or fully off.

analog monitor—a computer monitor which is capable of displaying colors based upon the infinitely varying intensity of the red, green, and blue guns of the cathode ray tube. A digital monitor, on the other hand, typically offers only three intensities: off, normal intensity, and high intensity.

animation—the quick display of separate graphic images in order to deceive the human eye into perceiving motion.

ANSI—an acronym for the American National Standards Institute, which is responsible for defining C language standards in order to assist in program portability between different computer systems.

APA—an acronym for all-points-addressable, which refers to the ability of every pixel on the display monitor to be written to or read by the microprocessor.

APL—an interpreted, high level language used for data processing.

application—another way of saying software or program.

area fill—to fill a specified region of the display screen with a specified color or pattern. The attribute surrounding the region to be filled is generally called the boundary. Efficient area fill routines employ a double-ended queue methodology.

argument—a value passed to a subroutine (function) by the caller.

argument-type list—the listing of arguments found in a function prototype.

arithmetic operator—a mathematical operator such as addition ($+$), multiplication ($*$), et cetera.

array—a set of data elements of similar type grouped together under a single name, usually arranged in rows and columns. Similar in concept to a collection of smaller groups. An array can be scalar (consisting of numeric or string data) or it can be graphic (consisting of pixel attributes).

assembler—a program that converts assembly language source code into native machine code. Sometimes called MASM. An assembler that works with syntax other than assembly language is usually called a compiler.

assembly language—a low level language whose mnemonics and syntax closely reflect the internal workings of the microprocessor's registers.

assignment—to assign a value to a variable. The C assignment operator is $=$. Avoid confusing this with the C equality operator $==$. In C, an arithmetic operation can be performed during the assignment process using the $+=$ addition assignment operator, the $-=$ subtraction assignment operator, the $*=$ multiplication assignment operator, the $/=$ division assignment operator, and the $\%=$ remainder assignment operator. Other assignment variations include the $<<=$ left-shift assignment operator, the $>>=$ right-shift assignment operator, the $\&=$ bitwise-AND assignment operator, and the $\wedge=$ bitwise-XOR assignment operator.

background color—the screen color upon which all graphics are drawn. The background is usually black.

back-up—a duplicate copy of software intended to protect the user form inadvertent damage to the original or to protect the user from loss of the original.

BASIC—a high level, general purpose programming language, often used as a prototype development tool, available in both interpreter and compiler versions. Common versions include IBM BASICA, GW-BASIC, Compaq BASIC, Microsoft QuickBASIC, Borland TURBO BASIC, True BASIC, Better basic, ZBASIC, and the IBM BASIC Compiler. (Each are trademarks of their respective owners.)

binary file—a file stored in binary format, as opposed to ASCII character (text) format. See image file.

binary operator—a C operator used in binary expressions. Binary operators include multiplicative operator ($*,/$), additive operators ($+,-$), shift operators ($<<,>>$), relational operators ($<,>,<=,>=,=,!=,$), bitwise operators ($\&,\,|,\wedge$), logical operators ($\&\&,||$), and the sequential-evaluation operator ($,$).

BIOS—assembly language subroutines stored as native machine code in ROM which provide basic input/output services for DOS and for applications programs. Also called ROM BIOS.

bit array—a graphic array.

bitblt—an acronym for bit boundary block transfer. Also called block graphics and graphic array.

bitblt animation—same as graphic array animation.

bit boundary block transfer—see bitblt.

bit map—an arrangement of bytes in display memory whose bits correspond to the pixels on the display screen. Sometimes used to mean memory-mapped video. The bit map of the VGA and EGA is organized in a linear format distributed over four bit-planes. The bit map of the

Color/Graphics Adapter is organized into two banks, one comprised of even-numbered rows, the other containing odd-numbered rows.

bit plane—one of four separate buffers which are sandwiched together by the VGA and EGA hardware in order to drive the video output. Also called a color plane. On the EGA, plane 0 affects the blue attribute; plane 1 affects the green attribute; plane 2 affects the red attribute; and plane 3 affects the intensity attribute.

bit tiling—mixing pixels of different colors to create patterns or shades. Also called halftone, halftoning, patterns, and patterning.

bitwise operators—**&**, ¦, and ∧, which compare bits to check for true and false conditions. In C these operators are AND (**&**), OR (¦), and XOR (∧).

block—a cohesive sequence of statements, instructions, declarations, or definitions which are enclosed within braces { }.

block graphics—same as graphic array. See bitblt.

braces—the { } tokens which enclose a block in a C program.

buffer—an area of memory used for temporary storage.

bug—a programming oversight in the source code, usually an error in process control logic.

byte—a group of eight adjacent bits.

C—a compiled, high level programming language originally developed for systems programming (writing compilers, operating systems, text editors). C is useful for high-performance graphics because of its low level functions. Also available in interpreter versions. The most popular versions of the language are Microsoft QuickC and Borland Turbo C.

CAD—an acronym for computer aided design and computer assisted design. CAD is to images what word processing is to words and what electronic spreadsheets are to numbers.

CADD—an acronym for computer aided and drafting.

CAE—an acronym for computer aided engineering.

CAL—an acronym for computer aided learning.

call—a program instruction which transfers control to a routine, subroutine (in BASIC), function (in C), procedure (in MASM), subprogram (in QuickBASIC and Turbo BASIC), or to another program.

CAM—an acronym for computer aided manufacturing.

CAP—an acronym for computer aided publishing, sometimes called desktop publishing (but more accurately called page composition).

CAS—an acronym for computer aided styling.

CDF file—comma delimited file. In graphics applications, used for storage of graphics primitives attributes. See data file.

char—a C variable stored in one byte of memory, capable of representing values from −128 to +127. An unsigned char can represent values from 0 to 255. By default, char is signed. A char type is often used to store the integer value of a member of the ASCII alphanumeric character set.

CGA—an acronym for Color/Graphics Adapter. A CGA which conforms to the IBM standard can display a 320×200 4-color graphics mode and a 640×200 2-color graphics mode. Also called a C/GA, a Color/Graphics Card, a color graphics board, and a color card.

COBOL—a compiled, high level language used for business applications.

clipping—see line clipping.

Color/Graphics Adapter—see CGA.

color cycling—producing animation by swapping palette values.

command menu—a set of on-screen icons which represent the commands available to the user of a CAD program.

compact memory model—the allocation of RAM for a C program whereby the size of executable code is limited to 64K but data is limited only by available memory.

compatible—usually intended to mean a personal computer which adheres closely to the hardware standards established by IBM. Compatibility can occur at the hardware level, at the BIOS level, at the operating system level (DOS or OS/2), and at the software level.

compiler—a program that translates an entire file of source code into native machine code prior to execution. The C programming language is usually provided as a compiler such as QuickC, Turbo C, Microsoft C 5.0, Let's ©, Aztec ©, et cetera. See also interpreter.

configure—to determine how the various parts of a personal computer system are to be arranged, or to determine at run-time how the operating system and memory of a personal computer are to be arranged.

constant—a value in a program which does not change during execution. For example, 23 is a constant, but X and Y are variables.

contour drawing—a wire-frame drawing that represents the surface of an object.

copyright—the right to copy an intellectual property such as a book, manuscript, software program, painting, photograph, et cetera.

coordinate system—as used in this book the arrangement of x,y axes in a 2D display or the arrangement of x,y,z axes in a 3D display. A number of incompatible coordinate systems are in use.

core library—the functions (subroutines) that are built into an interactive C compiler (such as QuickC and Turbo C) and that are resident in RAM while the user is working with the compiler.

cosine—the cosine of an angle in a right-angle triangle defines the relationship between the hypotenuse and the adjacent side.

CPU—an acronym for central processing unit, the part of a microcomputer that actually does the computing. Also called the microprocessor.

crash—as used in this book a program failure that causes control to return to the operating system or to the interactive C compiler. See also hang and lock-up.

crosshatch—see hatch.

CRT—cathode ray tube: the displaying hardware of computer monitors and of television sets.

cubic parametric curve—a formula-generated smooth curve created by providing two end points and two control points as parameters for the formula. Also called a fitted curve.

cursor—the user-controlled symbol (icon) that identifies the active location on the display screen.

data file—in graphics programming, a CDF (comma delimited) file used to store attributes of graphics primitives.

debug—the detection and corrections of errors in a program.

declaration—the statements that define the name and attributes of a C variable, function, or type.

decrement—to decrease by a specified amount.

definition—the actual instructions which comprise a function (subroutine). See also prototype.

delete—to remove.

digital—a method of representing data whereby the individual components are either fully on or fully off. See analog.

dimension—the alphanumeric description of the size of an entity in a CAD drafting program.

dimension line—the line and arrows which describe the entity to which a dimension refers in a CAD drafting program.

display coordinates—refers primarily to the converted view coordinates of a 3D modeling program. Display coordinates consist of x and y screen coordinate values. See also view coordinates and world coordinates in this glossary. (Also refer to the Author's books concerning BASIC programming: *High Performance Interactive Graphics,* TAB book 2879; and *Supercharged Graphics,* TAB book 2959.)

distribution disk—the finished program disk which is distributed through marketing channels as commercial software, shareware, or freeware.

dither—used in computer rendering. To dither a line is a modify a line (line styling) to match the adjacent shading pattern. (Also refer to the Author's books concerning BASIC programming: *High Performance Interactive Graphics*, TAB book 2879; and *Supercharged Graphics*, TAB book 2959.)

do-nothing routine—a subroutine which merely returns control to the caller. Do-nothing routines are used during preliminary program development and debugging. Also called a *stub*.

DOS—disk operating system. IBM DOS is often called PC-DOS. Microsoft DOS is often called MS-DOS. Both operating systems are almost but not exactly identical.

double-buffer animation—another name for real-time animation, dynamic page flipping animation, and ping-pong animation. (Also refer to the Author's book concerning BASIC programming: *High-Speed Animation & Simulation For Microcomputers*, TAB book 2859.)

drafting program—an interactive graphics program which performs many of the drawing functions a draftsperson would perform while creating a technical drawing.

dynamic page flipping animation—also called real-time animation: a technique involving display of a completed image while the microprocessor is drawing the next image on a hidden page. When the next image is complete, the graphics pages are flipped and the procedure is continued. (Also refer to the Author's book concerning BASIC programming: *High-Speed Animation & Simulation For Microcomputers*, TAB book 2859.)

ECD—an acronym for enhanced color display. An ECD is a digital display capable of displaying the EGA's 640×350 16-color graphics mode, in addition to all lesser modes.

editor—generally refers to the interface which allows the user to create and modify text data. A graphics editor is the interface which permits the user to create and modify graphics.

EGA—an acronym for enhanced graphics adapter. An EGA which adheres to the IBM standard can display the following graphics modes: 640×350 16-color (out of 64 possible colors), 640×350 2-color, 640×200 16-color, 320×200 16-color, 640×200 2-color, and 320×200 4-color.

elegant—see optimize.

emulation—simulation of unavailable hardware by available hardware/software. The mathematical routines in QuickC and in Turbo C provide emulation of a math coprocessor even when the coprocessor is not present in the microcomputer. (Note: The exe files created by QuickC can use a math chip, however. The QuickC interactive programming environment uses only the emulation mode.)

enhanced graphics adapter—same as EGA.

entity—in computer graphics, a cohesive graphical shape such as a rectangle, circle, or subassembly (as found in a technical drawing).

ergonomics—refers to machine compatibility with human psychology and physiology.

error trapping—using a programmer-defined subroutine to respond to program flow errors caught by the interpreter or by the operating system during run-time.

expression—a combination of operators acting upon variables in order to yield a single value.

extrusion—the act of converting a 2D graphic into a 3D model.

file pointer—a variable that indicates the current position of read and write operations on a file. See stream.

fillet—the round corner function in CAD drafting programs.

firmware—software which is stored in ROM. See BIOS.

fitted curve—see cubic parametric curve.

floating point number—generally, a number which contains a decimal point; specifically, a number expressed in scientific notation (which allows the decimal point to float). A floating point number in C (of type float) is stored in four bytes of memory and can range from as small as 3.4E-38 to as large as 3.4E+38 (which is 340,000,000,000,000,000,000,000,000,000,000,000,000—large enough for most applications!). A *type* float value is accurate to six digits. A floating point value defined as type double occupies eight bytes of memory and can express values ranging from 1.7E-308 to 1.7E+308.

FORTH—a high level/low level, compiler/interpreter, general-purpose language used mainly for robotics and graphics.

formatting—the general layout of a program listing, including tabs, spaces, indentations, and margins.

FORTRAN—a compiled, high level programming language used for scientific and engineering applications. FORTRAN is an acronym for formula translator.

fps—an acronym for frames per second, used to measure the display rate of animation programs. (Also refer to the Author's book concerning BASIC programming: *High-Speed Animation & Simulation For Microcomputers,* Tab book 2859.)

frame—a single image in an animation sequence, usually intended to mean a full screen image.

frame grab—the act of capturing a graphic image and storing it in a buffer or on disk. The graphic image can be one which has been generated by the microcomputer itself or it can be a signal from a video camera, video cassette player, or television set.

frames per second—the rate of animation, expressed as new images per second. Also called fps.

function declaration—statements which define the name, return type, storage class, and parameter list of a function (subroutine). See declaration.

function definition—statements which define the name, return type, storage class, parameter list, and the executable instructions of a function (subroutine). See definition.

geometry—in this book, a branch of mathematics concerned with the relationship between two triangles possessing similar angles.

global variable—a variable in a program which is available to all portions and subroutines of the program. A local variable (also called a static variable) is available only to the subroutine (function) in which it occurs.

gnomon—a visual representation of the x,y,z axis system in a 3D CAD program.

graphic array—a rectangular portion of the display buffer which has been saved in RAM as a bit array for later retrieval.

graphic array animation—placing one or more graphic arrays on the display screen (i.e. into the display buffer) in order to produce animation. Also called *software sprite* animation, *bitblt* animation, and *block* animation. (Also refer to the Author's books concerning BASIC programming: *High-Speed Animation & Simulation For Microcomputers,* TAB book 2859; *High Performance Interactive Graphics,* TAB book 2879; and *Supercharged Graphics,* TAB book 2959.)

graphics driver—a module (usually written in assembly language) designed to create graphics in a particular screen mode.

graphics editor—the interface that allows the user to create and modify computer graphics. CAD programs can be considered to be graphics editors.

graphics programmer—an individual capable of creating, testing, debugging, maintaining, improving, and running graphics programs.

graphics page—an area of RAM containing the data to fill the display screen with graphics. The graphics page may or may not be the same as the screen buffer, which is the currently displayed page.

GW-BASIC—a BASIC interpreter, often used to create prototype programs, manufactured by Microsoft Corporation. GW-BASIC is licensed to various microcomputer manufacturers, most notably Tandy. According to programmers' folklore GW is an acronym for "gee whiz."

hacker—a person who is dedicated to high quality programming, especially programming performed for its own sake. By definition, good hackers are good programmers. In recent years the term has occasionally come to be associated with persons who attempt to unlawfully penetrate computer security systems.

halftoning—mixing pixels of different colors to simulate varying shades of a color. Also called bit tiling. (Also refer to the Author's books concerning BASIC programming: *High Performance Interactive Graphics*, TAB book 2879; and *Supercharged Graphics*, TAB book 2959.)

hang—a program failure resulting in an unwanted endless loop or execution of garbage code. The user can regain control with Ctrl-Break. See also *lock-up* and *crash*.

hardware—the physical and mechanical parts of a microcomputer system.

hatch—the area fill pattern used by CAD software to simulate the ink shading techniques used by many draftspersons.

heap—an area in RAM where data is stored. Also called the default data segment. The far heap is free high memory unused by the program.

hertz—one cycle per second.

heuristic—the use of trial and error to solve a programming problem.

hexadecimal—the base 16 numbering system. The decimal system uses base 10. The base is also called the *radix*.

hex—same as hexadecimal. A hexadecimal value is prefixed by the Ox symbol in C, by the &H symbol in BASIC, and is followed by the H symbol in assembly language.

hidden line—in graphics programming, a line which should be hidden by another graphic. (Also refer to the Author's book concerning BASIC programming: *High Performance Interactive Graphics*, TAB book 2879.)

hidden page—a graphics page which is not currently being displayed.

hidden surface—in graphics modeling, a polygonal plane surface which is hidden by other surfaces.

hidden surface removal—the algorithmic process of removing from the 3D model all surfaces which should be hidden from view. The formulas are usually based upon vector math. (Also refer to the Author's book concerning BASIC programming: *High Performance Interactive Graphics*, TAB book 2879.)

high-performance graphics—refers to graphics applications which stress speed and color.

image file—a binary file on diskette, hard disk, or virtual disk, which contains a graphic image. In BASIC the commands BSAVE and BLOAD are used to save and retrieve image files, respectively. Image files often used the extensions PIC and BIN.

indirection—generally, the act of addressing a variable in memory; but specifically the indirection operation (*) which is used in C to declare a pointer. See pointer.

include file—a text file which is merged into the user's source code at compile time. An include file is usually a file which contains declarations and definitions, called a *header* file.

increment—to increase by a specific amount.

inline code—a section of computer code which does not jump to any subroutines to assist it in completing its assigned tasks. Inline code generally executes quicker than modular code.

instance—an occurrence of a graphical entity in a drawing.

instancing—creating a complex 2D or 3D model by multiple occurrences of the same entity at different locations in the drawing.

integer—a whole number with no fractional parts or decimal point. An integer is normally considered to require two bytes of storage. C signed integers (**int**) range from $-32,768$ to $32,767$. C unsigned integers (**unsigned**) range from 0 to $65,535$. A signed long integer (**long**) ranges from $-2,147,483,648$ to $+2,147,483,647$. An unsigned long integer (**unsigned long**) can represent values from 0 to $4,294,967,295$.

interactive—accepting input from, and returning feedback to, the user of the computer.

interactive graphics—relating to a computer program which creates or modifies a graphical display in response to user input. (Also refer to the Author's books concerning BASIC programming: *High Performance Interactive Graphics*, TAB book 2879; and *Supercharged Graphics*, TAB book 2959.)

interpreter—a program that executes another program one line at a time. IBM BASICA and GW-BASIC are examples of interpreters.

iterative—repetitive.

iterative full screen animation—the rapid sequential display of previously-saved graphics pages for the purpose of producing animation. The number of pages available is limited by system RAM or by graphics adapter display memory. Also called frame animation. (Also refer to the Author's books concerning BASIC programming: *High-Speed Animation & Simulation For Microcomputers,* TAB book 2859; and *Supercharged Graphics,* TAB book 2959.)

keyword—see *token.*

library—the file that contains modules of object code, which comprise the functions (subroutines) available for use by the user's C program. The library which is a built-in component of QuickC and Turbo C is called the cone library.

license—the right to use an intellectual property such as a book, software program, musical recording, painting, et cetera. Copyright is the right to copy an intellectual property, which is rarely included in software licenses.

light pen—a pencil-shaped pointing device, through which the microprocessor reads a pixel location for use by the applications program.

line clipping—deletion of a part of a line or graphic which exceeds the physical range of the display screen or viewport.

line styling—using a series of pixel attributes to generate dotted or dashed lines. Also refers to dithering.

LISP—an interpreted, high level programming language used in artificial intelligence applications. LISP is an acronym for list processing language. LISP works on symbols rather than numbers.

local variable—same as static variable. See also global variable.

lock-up—a program failure which results in execution of garbage code. The user can regain control only by a warm reboot (CTRL-ALT-DEL) or a cold restart (power off then power on). See also *hang* and *crash.*

logical operators—**&&** and ¦¦ , which perform logical operations on bytes being compared. **&&** is used to logically AND two types (the resulting evaluated bits will be on only if both respective bits were on). ¦¦ is used to logically OR two bytes (the resulting evaluated bits will be on if either of the respective bits were on).

LOGO—an interpreted, high level language used for education purposes, especially the teaching of geometry and logical thinking.

loop—the iteration or repetition of a group of program instructions.

MASM—an acronym for macro assembler: an assembly language compiler capable of including separately created modules into the finished program. IBM Macro Assembler and Microsoft Macro Assembler are the industry standards.

MCGA—an acronym for multicolor graphics array, which is the proprietary graphics adapter used in the IBM Personal System/2 8086-based personal computers.

medium memory model—an arrangement of RAM for a C program whereby data is limited to 64K but the size of executable code is limited only by available memory. The QuickC compiler uses only the medium memory model.

memory-mapped video—an arrangement whereby the bit contents of an area of RAM correspond directly to the pixels on the display screen. Sometimes used to mean bit map.

memory model—one of the arrangements which C uses to set up memory space for executable code and data. See medium memory model.

menu—a series of options presented on the display screen from which the user is to choose.

menu bar—the horizontal graphic from which pull-down menus are positioned.

page flipping—quickly putting a different graphics page on display for the purpose of creating animation or simulation. Page flipping is used in frame animation and in real-time animation. (Also refer to the Author's books concerning BASIC programming: *High Performance Interactive Graphics,* TAB book 2879; and *Supercharged Graphics,* TAB book 2959.)

paintbrush program—an interactive graphics program which emphasizes artistic creativity of design and color in the resultant image.

pan—to move a graphic to the left or to the right.

parameter—a value which a function (subroutine) expects to receive when it is called. Also called an *argument.*

PASCAL—a compiled, high level programming language used mainly for business applications. PASCAL is noted for its highly structured programs and its ability to teach programming skills. TURBO PASCAL has created a large user base for this language on personal computers.

PC—an acronym for personal computer. A personal computer is powerful enough for serious business, scientific, engineering, and graphics applications, yet inexpensive enough to permit individuals to purchase it. PC can mean a PC, an XT, an AT, a PS/2, or any personal computer compatible with these models. Personal computer is synonymous with microcomputer.

pel—IBM's acronym for picture element, called a *pixel* by nearly everyone else. A pixel is the smallest addressable graphic on a display screen. See pixel.

personal computer—see PC.

ping-pong animation—another name for dynamic page flipping animation.

pixel—an acronym for picture element, called a pel by IBM. A pixel is the smallest addressable graphic on a display screen. A pixel is comprised of a red dot, a green dot, and a blue dot, each of which is excited by the electron guns of the cathode ray tube. The medium resolution graphics mode on IBM personal computers contains 320 pixels across by 200 rows down. The enhanced high resolution graphics mode on an EGA contains 640 pixels across by 350 rows down. VGA graphics modes are available at 640×480 resolutions.

plane equation—a vector formula which describes the qualities of a plane surface, including the location of a given point relative to the surface of the plane. Plane equations are useful for hidden surface removal. (Also refer to the Author's books concerning BASIC programming: *High Performance Interactive Graphics,* TAB book 2879; and *Supercharged Graphics,* TAB book 2959.)

pointer—a variable that contains the address of another variable. See null pointer.

pop-up menu—a menu that is created as an island on the screen, unconnected to any other graphics.

pragma—A user-defined directive that instructs a C compiler to insert specialized routines into the object code in order to check for conflicting memory addresses (pointers) and stack overflow at run-time.

PROLOG—an interpreted, high level language used for artificial intelligence applications and database management systems.

prototype—the initial declaration of a function (subroutine) in a C program, usually containing the return type and argument list of the function.

pull-down menu—a menu which is appended to a menu bar, as if it were being pulled down from the menu bar.

PUT—the BASIC command used to place a previously-saved graphic array on the display screen.

QLB—QuickC library: describes the memory-resident library which a user can create in order to use C functions not contained in QuickC's core library. A QLB file is loaded by the QuickC compiler in high memory at compile time and again immediately prior to run-time. User-created assembly language programs can be placed into a QLB file.

radian—a length of arc based upon the relationship between elements of a unit circle.

radix—the base of a numbering system. The radix of the hexadecimal numbering system is 16, and of the decimal system is 10.

RAM—an acronym for Random Access Memory, also called *user memory* and *user RAM*. It is the memory available for use by programs and graphics. When the microcomputer's power is shut off, the contents of RAM are obliterated.

RAM disk—a virtual disk which exists only in RAM memory. See virtual disk.

ray tracing—an algorithm which calculates the illumination level of a model by tracing a ray of light back from the eye to the model and eventually to the light source(s).

real-time—the actual time during which an event occurs.

real-time animation—also called double-buffer page-flipping animation and ping-pong animation. The microprocessor displays a completed image while constructing the next image on a hidden page. The pages are flipped and the procedure continues.

redundancy—unneeded duplication of software or hardware, usually for the sake of protection against unexpected failures.

refresh buffer—the display buffer. The display hardware uses the display buffer to refresh the display monitor (usually at a rate of 60 times per second).

regen—regeneration of a graphic entity, also called *redraw*. The term is used primarily with CAD programs.

relational operators—<, >, <=, >=, ==, and !=, which in C mean less-than, greater-than, less-than-or-equal-to, greater-than-or-equal-to, equal-to, and not-equal-to, respectively. Do not confuse == with =, which is C's assignment operator. A relational operator compare the relationship between two values. Relational operators are often used as decision-making tools.

relocatable—OBJ code which does not contain absolute (hard-coded) addresses. Prior to run-time, the operating system assigns memory offset values for the addresses referenced in the OBJ code.

rendering—adding illumination, shading, and color to a 3D model. Personal computers using a CGA, an EGA, or a VGA can produce fully-shaded 3D solid models by using an illumination matrix and vector math. (Also refer to the Author's book concerning BASIC programming: *High Performance Interactive Graphics,* TAB book 2879.)

replay mode—regeneration of a sequence of interactive events, especially in games programming and simulation programming.

ROM—an acronym for read-only memory. ROM is memory that cannot be changed by the user. Turning off the power supply has no effect on ROM, which uses magnetic technology instead of electric technology to store data.

ROM BIOS—same as BIOS.

run-time—the time during which the program is executing.

run-time library—the file containing C routines that a program requires during execution. See *core library.*

scalar—a mathematical quantity that has quantity but not direction. A *vector* has quantity *and* direction.

SCD—an acronym for standard color display. An SCD is a digital monitor capable of displaying 16 colors at a maximum resolution of 640×200 pixels. See also analog and ECD.

screen buffer—the area of memory which is being displayed on the screen, usually located at address B8000 hex on the CGA and at addresses A0000 hex on the EGA and VGA. The location of the screen buffer can be changed on the VGA and EGA by selecting a different graphics page. The location of the screen buffer cannot be changed on the CGA.

scroll—to move a graphic or alphanumeric character upwards or downwards across the display screen.

segment—a block of computer memory whose length is 64K or less.

semantics—the study of the meanings of signs, symbols, and tokens. See semiotics.

semiotics—the study of the function of signs, symbols, and tokens in natural languages, artificial languages, and computer languages. See also semantics and syntactics.

sequential-evaluation operator—in C the sequential-evaluation operator (,) is used to separate a series of sequentially evaluated expressions.

SFX—sound effect(s).

shading—adding the effects of illumination, shadow, and color to a 3D model. Sometimes called rendering. (Also refer to the Author's books concerning BASIC programming: *High Performance Interactive Graphics*, TAB book 2879; and *Supercharged Graphics*, TAB book 2959.)

shift operators—$<<$ and $>>$, which shift the bits in a byte to the left or to the right.

SIMULA—a compiled, high level language used for simulations. SIMULA is an acronym for simulation language.

simulation—a programming attempt to imitate a real-world event in real-time mode.

simulator—a program that imitates a real-world event in real-time.

sine—the sine of an angle in a right triangle defines the relationship between the hypotenuse and the side opposite.

small memory model—an arrangement of RAM for a C program whereby the code and data are limited to one segment.

SMALLTALK—a compiled, high level language used for simulation and the teaching of thinking skills.

snap—the size of movement of a crosshair cursor in a CAD program.

SNOBOL—a compiled (and interpreted), high level language used for manipulating non-numerical characters.

software sprite—see graphic array and bitblt.

software sprite animation—see graphics array animation and bitblt.

source code—program instructions written in the original programming language. A program listing is a human-readable version on paper of the program source code.

stack—a single-ended queue in memory, where values are stored and retrieved on a First-In, Last-Out basis (FILO).

statement—an instruction in the program source code. Sometimes called an expression.

static variable—a variable which is available to only the subroutine (function) in which it occurs. Also called a *local* variable. See also *global* variable.

stream—the flow of data to or from a file (or other output device).

structure—a set of items groups under a single name. The elements may be of different types. In an array, the elements must be of a similar type.

stub—see *do-nothing* routine.

subroutine—subordinate, self-contained portion (or module) of a program designed to perform a specific task. A subroutine is called a *function* in C, a *procedure* in assembly language, a *subprogram* in QuickBASIC and Turbo BASIC, and a *module* in Modula-2.

surface normal—a line which is perpendicular to the surface of a plane in a 3D environment. The illumination level of a surface can be derived by comparing the surface normal to the angle of incidence of incoming light rays. (Also refer to the Author's book concerning BASIC programming: *High Performance Interactive Graphics*, TAB book 2879.)

syntactics—the study of the relationship between signs, symbols, and tokens and the people who use them.

syntax—the grammar to be used with a programming language.

system overhead—the amount of time the microcomputer allocates to general housekeeping functions instead of executing programs or generating graphics.

3D—three-dimensional graphics, consisting of width, depth, and height. In microcomputer graphics, 3D images are usually described by x,y,z coordinates.

2D—two-dimensional graphics, consisting of width and height. In microcomputer graphics, 2D images are usually defined by x,y coordinates.

toggle—to change from one possible state to another, as in a program which defines a toggle key on the keyboard. Some programs define a flag variable which can be toggled on or off in order to affect program flow during run-time.

token—a group of characters which is the basic element recognized by a C compiler. Also called a *keyword*.

touch-screen—a display screen which is made sensitive to finger touch by means of an electronic matrix.

trackball—a pointing device similar to a mouse, except the ball is located on the top surface of the device, meant to be activated by moving the palm of the hand over the ball.

trigonometry—a branch of mathematics concerned with the relationship of two sides opposite a specific angle in a right-angle triangle. Sine and cosine are particularly useful for 3D microcomputer graphics.

turnkey system—a computer system consisting of hardware, software, user's guides, system documentation, installation, support, service, and training. Often used to describe high-performance graphics workstations.

type—attribute. For example, an integer variable is of type int.

type cast—the conversion of a value from one type to another type.

unary operator—an operator that manipulates a single variable. C provides the following unary operators: logical NOT (!), bitwise compliment (~), arithmetic negation (−), indirection (*), address-of (&), and unary plus (or arithmetic increment) (+).

union—a C structure which allocates the same memory space to different variables. The variables are often of different types.

user-servile—describes a program which has been designed to serve the needs of the user, as opposed to programs which require the user to adapt in order to use the program.

utility program—a program used as a tool, designed to perform a utilitarian task or organizing type of function. For example, a program which dumps the contents of a screen buffer to a printer is a utility program.

variable—a quantity whose value can change during program execution. X and Y are variables, but 23 is a constant.

vector—a mathematical value that has quantity direction. A scalar value has only quantity.

VGA—the propriety graphics adapter in the IBM Personal System/2 series of 80286 and 80386-based microcomputers. The VGA provide CGA, MCGA, and EGA graphics modes, in addition to its enhanced modes of 640×480 16-color and 320×200 256-color. VGA graphics are supported by QuickC and by Turbo C.

view coordinates—the x,y,z coordinates that describe how a 3D model will appear to a hypothetical viewer after rotation and translation. The view coordinates must be converted to display coordinates prior to being displayed on the monitor. (Also refer to the Author's books concerning BASIC programming: *High Performance Interactive Graphics,* TAB book 2879; and *Supercharged Graphics,* TAB book 2959.)

viewport—a rectangular portion of the display screen which becomes a mini-screen within the larger area of the whole display screen. A viewport is therefore a subset of the display screen.

virtual disk—a simulated disk which exists only in RAM memory. Also called a RAM disk. Because no physical disk drives are involved, reads and writes to the disk are much faster. All data contained in a virtual disk is obliterated when the microcomputer is turned off.

virtual screen—a written-to graphics buffer which is not the display buffer. A written-to, hidden graphics page is a virtual screen, although the term is usually reserved for buffers which are much larger than the screen buffer. Panning and scrolling of graphics can be achieved by sending carefully selected portions of the virtual screen to the screen buffer.

visibility—describes whether or not a function or a variable can be used by other parts of a program.

visible page—the graphics page currently being displayed. Called the display page by QuickC.

void—undefined.

walk-through—frame animation of a 3D architectural model which simulates a walk-through by the viewer.

window—a viewport of the display screen. Often used to describe the logical relationship between the display screen and the world coordinates in 3D graphics programming.

wire-frame drawing—a skeletal drawing of an object created by drawing only the edges of surfaces, not the surfaces themselves. The object is depicted as transparent. No effort is made to conceal surfaces or lines which should be hidden.

witness lines—lines which connect a graphic entity to the dimension lines which describe it (in a CAD drafting program).

world coordinates—the raw x,y,z coordinates which describe the shape of an object. World coordinates are rotated and translated to produce view coordinates, which describe how a 3D model will appear to a hypothetical viewer. View coordinates are converted to 2D display coordinates before being displayed on the monitor. (Also refer to the Author's books concerning BASIC programming: *High Performance Interactive Graphics*, TAB book 2879; and *Supercharged Graphics*, TAB book 2959.)

written-to page—the graphics page to which the microprocessor is currently writing, also called the active page.

ABOUT THE
AUTHOR

Lee Adams is a computer consultant and software author specializing in high performance graphics, animation, and 3D computer aided design. He creates graphics software in C, assembly language, and BASIC. He has 18 years of experience in visual communications, including television animation, and has taught classes in perspective drawing, graphic design, and advertising illustration.

Lee Adams is the author of TAB's three bestselling books about BASIC graphics programming: *High Speed Animation and Simulation for Microcomputers* (#2859); *High Performance Interactive Graphics: Modeling, Rendering and Animating for IBM PCs and Compatibles* (#2879); *Supercharged Graphics: A Guide to Writing Interactive Graphics Software on Personal Computers* (#2959).

Lee Adams welcomes mail from readers. Write to him in care of Reader Inquiry Branch, Editorial Department, TAB BOOKS Inc., P.O. Box 40, Blue Ridge Summit, PA, USA 17214-9989. Include your area code and telephone number if you want a spoken reply. Please allow three weeks for your correspondence to reach the author.

Index

Index

A

absolute coordinates (see world coordinates), 157
achromatic colors, 100, 101
active page, 207
addressable portion of graphic screen, 126, 127
advanced graphics functions, 61-66
  block graphics, 65
  drawing on hidden page, 64
  halftoning (bit tiling), 62
  line dithering (line styling), 62
  page copying, 63
advanced techniques, 149-155
  graphics database for, 149
  saving screen images to disk, 150-154
  sound effects as, 154-155
airbrushed backgrounds, 127, 128
  demonstration program for, 137-142
  foreground graphics same color as, 129
  Turbo C program for, 413-417
ambiguous layout, 94, 96
ambiguous shapes, 91, 92
analog display monitor, 11, 12, 28, 29
analogous harmony, 102
analytic programs, 5
AND logical operator, 249
animated design graphics, 235-246
  rotating 3-D image program for, 235-246
animated educational grahics, 222-234
  hovering hummingbird program for, 222-234
  preparation for, 222

animation
  arcade-style, 300
  bitblt, 6
  block graphic, 8
  frame, 6, 205-246
  graphic array, 8
  hidden page, 8
  page, 207
  ping pong, 9
  real-time, 6
  snapshot, 249
applications, 4, 5, 6
arcade-style animation (see real-time animation), 300, 304-313
  dot-matrix print-out of, 305
  keyboard controls for, 307
  managing ricochets in, 304
  ricocheting ball program for, 309-313
  sound effects in, 308
  travel zones in, 307
  Turbo C program for, 468-472
  vertices of playing field in, 306
area fill, 59, 60
arithmetic operators, 45
arrays, 50-51
  block graphic storage using, 250
  elements in, 50
  variables in, 51
ASCII, 360
assemblers, 360
assembly language graphics driver, 56
assembly language graphics routines, 360-365
  BIOS interrupts in, 364

C memory models and, 361
  interface to, 361
  local variables in, 363
  near and far calls in, 361
  OBJ file in, 363
  passing parameters to, 361
  required software tools for, 360
assignment operators, 46
AUTOEXEC.BAT file, 70, 71

B

backgrounds, 126-142
  3-D, 126
  addressable portion of screen for, 126
  airbrushed, 127
  borders for, 130
  sculpted, 126
bar charts, 174-175
BIOS routines, 68, 78
  interrupts, assembly language, 364
  C programs and, 53, 54
bit block transfer (bitblt), 8, 249
bit plane, 13
bit tiling (see halftoning), 62
bitblt animation, 6, 8, 247-296, 332
  applications for, 250
  array storage of, 250
  block graphics in, 65
  caricatures, 258
  educational software, 285-296
  effect of different logical operators on, 251
  entertainment software using, 258-273
  fundamental concepts in, 8

logical operators and, 249
practical techniques for, 249-257
program listing for, 356-359
PSET logical operator for, 250-255
simulation software in, 274-284
Turbo C program for, 493-496
utility program for, 256-257
block graphics (see bitblt animation)
borders, 130, 131
branching instructions, 48-49
breakout border, 130
built-in graphics functions, 56
business graphics, 170-194
  animated (see frame animated business
    graphics), 212
  animated business chart, 212-221
  animated business chart, Turbo C
    program, 429-435
  characteristics of, 170
  charts as, 171
  demonstration program in 2D, 176-183
  demonstration program in 3-D, 184-194
  emphasis in, 170
  grid lines in, 174
  grouping in, 172
  labels in, 174
  scale in, 172, 173
  simplicity of design in, 170
  spacing in, 172, 173
  tick marks in, 174
  Turbo C chart program for, 423-429

C

C compiler, xviii
  communication with, 51
  compilation phase in, 35
  edit phase in, 35
  four conceptual phases of programming
    with, 33
  link phase in, 35
  operation of, 35-36
  productivity profile choices with, 34
  programming with, 32-33
  run-time phase in, 36
C language
  graphics in, 3
  interface to assembly language for, 361
  memory management and, 31, 38
  power of, 32
  program control in, 44
  program structure for, 43
  software advantages for, 31
  speed of, 32
C programs
  arrays in, 50-51
  BIOS routines with, 53, 54
  branching instructions in, 48-49
  clipping routines for, 146
  communicating with C compiler through,
    51-52
  control in, 44
  fundamental layout of, 54
  graphic routine summary for, 331-359
  graphics portability of, 51
  loop control in, 47-48
  operators in, 45
  QuickC running of, 73-74
  rotation-translation-projection   formula
    for, 160

structure of, 43, 44
syntax portability of, 51
Turbo C running of, 81
variables in, 49-50
calls, near and far, 361
caricature(), 260
caricatures, bitblt animated, 258, 259
cartesia coordinates (see world
    coordinates), 157
center of interest, 90, 91
centering text, 94, 96
CGA____MODE, 75, 83
CHAR FILL, 106
char variable, 49
chart
  animated, Turbo C program for,
    429-435
  business graphic use of, 171
  frame animated, 212-221
  Turbo C program for, 423-429
chroma, 100
chromatic colors, 100, 101
CLEARDEVICE, 58, 83
clearing screen, 58
CLEARSCREEN, 58, 75
clipping routines, 145
  typical C program, 146
  viewports as, 143
code segment, 70, 80
color, 99-115
  achromatic vs. chromatic, 100
  advanced psychology of, 110
  analogous harmony of, 102
  circle (wheel) of, 101
  complementary harmony in, 103
  demonstration program using, 108-115
  equation chart for, 104, 105
  hardware selections for, 99
  harmony among, 95, 101
  potential applications for, 111
  scales for, 103, 104
  shades, tones, and tints in, 100
  shading matrices for, 106
  split-complement harmony in, 103
  terminology used in description of, 100
  wheel for mixing, 94, 101, 102
  wise use of, 94
color/graphics adapter (CGA), xiv, 3, 11
  assembly language routines for,
    382-395
  color palettes for, 99, 100
  display memory of, 19
  frame animation page locations for, 210
  graphics modes available on, 11
  hidden page animation on, 300
  multibit-per-pixel display memory for, 16
  saving screen image to disk on,
    program listing for, 342-347
  saving screen images to disk on,
    153-154, 331
command-line compilers, 34
COMMAND.COM, 68, 78
compact memory model, 38
companion disk, xiv
compilation phase, C compiler, 35
compilers (see C compilers), 32
complementary harmony, 103
computer aided design (CAD), 5
computer aided engineering (CAE), 5

computer aided learning (CAL), 5
computer aided manufacturing (CAM), 5
computer aided styling (CAS), 5
computer requirements, xiv
concepts, 3-9
CONFIG.SYS file, 70, 71
contrast, 95, 97, 127
contrast drawings, 195, 196
control, program, 44
coordinate axis system, defining height,
    width, and depth with, 156
coordinates
  absolute, 157
  cartesian, 157
  database and dynamic, 116
  device-independent, 157
  model space, 157
  view, 157
  xyz, 157
coords(), 119

D

data segment (DS), 70, 80
database coordinates, 116
database managers, 6
declarations, 73, 82
DEFINE, 52
design graphics, animated, 235-246
design, 85-204
DETECTGRAPH, 83
deviation column chart, 175
device-independent 640×480 template,
    89
device-independent coordinates, 157
device-independent programs, 24
directives, 52
display buffer, 249
display controller, 14
display memory
  320×200 16-color mode, 21
  320×200 256-color mode, 22
  640×200 16-color mode, 17
  640×350 16-color mode in, 19
  640×480 16-color mode, 20
  CGA, 19
  EGA, 19
  hardware compatibility chart for, 15
  mapping in, 16
  multibit-per-pixel, 16
  multiplane-per-pixel, 13
  system map for IBM/IBM compatible, 18
  VGA, 19
display options, 3-D image, 158
display page, 207
  real-time animation, 299
display screen, 88
  template to, 87
DOS, 34, 68, 78
dots and dashes, 62
drawing lines (see line drawing), 58
drawing template (see template), 87
DRAW____BG, 275
dropshadow, 117
dull effect, 110
dynamic coordinates, 116
  Turbo C program for, 404-408
dynamic keyboard input, real-time
    animation, 300

E

edit phase, C compiler, 35
editors (see integrated editors), 39
EDLIN editor, 360
educational graphics, frame animated, 222-234
educational software, bitblt animated, 285-296
  simulated clockface, 285
EGA___ECD___MODE, 75, 83
EGA___SCD___MODE, 75, 83
elliptical border, 130
emphasis, 92, 93
  business graphics and, 170, 171
enhanced color display (ECD) monitor, 12, 28, 29
enhanced graphics adapter (EGA), xiv, 3, 10-12
  assembly language routines for, 366-381
  color palettes for, 99
  display memory of, 19
  frame animation page locations for, 209
  graphics modes available on, 13
  hidden page animation on, 299
  memory map of, 20, 21, 23
  multiplane-per-pixel display memory in, 13
  saving screen image to disk, program listing for, 333-338
  saving screen images to disk on, 150-153, 331
entertainment software, 258-273
  animated caricature program for, 261-273
environment, integrated programming, 33,
error messages
  QuickC, 76-77
  Turbo C, 83-84
  Turbo C, spurious, 399
error trapping, 52
Essential Graphics, 34
EXE files
  QuickC, 77
  Turbo C, 84
executive module, 43
executive routine, 43
exponential notation, 50

F

far call, 361
far heap, 70, 80
fclose instruction, 153, 154
features, 36
fetching, keystroke, 53
field size, 110
file control blocks, 68, 78
filmy/atmospheric effects, 110
flight simulation, 314-329
  3-D line clipping for, 316
  animation loop for, 318
  demonstration program for, 317-328
  flight maneuvers in, 314
  full acrobatic loops in, 315
  further reading on, 318
  keyboard controls for, 314
  keyboard routine for, 318
  terrain grid for, 315, 318

Turbo C program for, 472-482
use of integers in, 318
float variable, 50
floating point numbers, 50
FLOODFILL, 59, 62, 106, 127
flowchart, 36
fopen instruction, 152, 153, 154
for/next loop, 44, 47
formulas, personal computer 3-D imaging, 158
frame animated business graphics, 212-219
frame animation, 6, 8, 205-246 332
  business graphics using, 212-219
  CGA page location for, 210
  charts, 212-221
  compatibility and portability of, 211
  design graphics, 235-246
  educational graphics, 222-234
  fundamental concepts of, 7
  memory move for, 208
  optimization of, 211
  perceived movement in, 209
  practical techniques for, 207-211
  process for, 207-209
  program listing for, 348-352
  Turbo C program for, 487-497
  use of display page in, 207
  use of hidden page in, 207
  utility program for, 209-211
  VGA and EGA page locations for, 209
frames, 8
frames (see borders), 130
free memory, 70, 80
fully-shaded models, 158, 160
functions (see also subroutines), 44, 52
  advanced graphics, 61-66
  area fill, 59
  clearing screen, 58
  drawing lines, 58
  fundamental graphics, 57
  returning to text mode, 61
  writing text on graphics screen, 59
fwrite instruction, 153, 154

G

GETIMAGE, 66
GETVIDEOCONFIG, 75
goto instruction, 48
graphic array animation (see bitblt animation)
graphic arrays, 249, 250
  menu management using, 253
graphical user interface, 314
graphics
  applications for, 4, 5, 6
  benefits of using, 4
  C language for, 3
  combining text and, 98
  first steps in, 9
  getting started in, 6
  key concepts for, 3-9
  modes, 12
  program portability in, 23
  text vs., 3
graphics adapters, xiv, 10-12
  color selections available in, 99
  establishing graphics mode for, 57

hardware compatibility chart for, 15
manufacturers and specifications for, 25
multibit-per-pixel display memory, 16
multiplane-per-pixel display memory, 13
operation of, 13
QuadEGA ProSync, 26
QuadEGA+, 25
QuadVGA, 27
standard color palette for, 29, 100
standards for, 25
graphics control code, 45
graphics database, 149-150
  numeric arrays to management of, 149
graphics mode
  configuration module for, 332
  configuration module, program listing for, 338-342
  establishment of, 57
  Turbo C program for, 482-485
graphics programming environment, 1-40
graphics tools, 56-67
GRAPHICS.LIB, Turbo C, 80
GRAPHICS___SETUP, 75, 83
gray shadings, 104, 105
grid lines, 174
grid template (see template), 88
grid(), 318
grouping, 172

H

halftoning, 62, 63
  airbrushed backgrounds using, 127, 128
  gray shades and, 104, 105
  shading matrices for, 106, 107
  Turbo C program for, 399-403
hardware, 10-30
  color selections available in, 99
harmony
  analogous, 102
  color, 101
  complementary, 103
height, width, and depth, coordinate axis system for, 156
hidden page animation, 8, 64, 65, 207 299
  CGA, 300
  EGA, 299
  VGA, 299
hidden surface removal, 3-D images, 159
high-level language, 32
highlighting, 195
hot zone (see center of interest), 90
hovering hummingbird, 222, 234
  Turbo C program for, 436-444
hue, 16, 100
  Turbo C program for, 399-403

I

if/then instruction, 44, 48, 83
illumination, 3-D images, 161
IMAGE___BUFFER, 152, 153, 154
IMAGE___FILE, 153, 154
INCLUDE, 52, 73, 82
INITGRAPH, 58
initializing variables, 73, 82
int variable, 49
integrated editors, 39
integrated programming environments, 33

intensity, 100
interface
  C-language to assembly language, 361
  graphical user, 314
interrupt vectors, 68, 78
IN____BETWEEN, 308
iridescent effect, 110, 111

J

justification, 94-96

K

kernel code, 68, 78
keyboard(), 75, 83, 318

L

labels, 174
Lambert's Cosine Law, 161
languages, levels of, 32
LEFT____ARENA, 308
length, 152, 154
libraries, 56
  third-party graphics, 34
  Turbo C, 80
light sources, 161
line dithering, 62, 63
line drawing, 58, 59, 195-196
  animation of, 274-284
  selecting algorithm for, 89
line styling, 62
line-clipping, 144
  3D, 316
  algorithm for, 146
  logic flowchart for, 147
  typical C program, 146
LINETO, 58, 59, 89
link phase, C compiler, 35
local variables, 363
logic flowchart, 36
logical operators, 46
  bitblt animation and, 249, 251
  graphical effect of (bitblt), 252
  multicolor graphics with, 255
long variable, 49
loop control, 47-48
loops
  for/next, 47
  goto instruction, 48
low-level language, 32
luminous effect, 110
lustrous effects, 110

M

main routine (module), 43
main(), 43, 52, 75, 83
mapping (see display memory), 16
margins, 94, 95, 96
master routine, 43
math control code, 44
mathematical operators, 46
MCGA____MODE, 83
medium memory model, 38
memory management, 38
  advantage of C-language in, 31
memory map
  EGA, 20, 21, 23
  QuickC, 68-70
  Turbo C, 78, 79
  VGA, 20-24

memory models, 38
  assembly language routines and, 361
memory move, 208
menu management, graphic arrays for, 253
metallic effect, 110
MetaWindow, 34, 56
Microsoft C version 5.0, xviii, 34
model space coordinates (see world coordinates), 157
modeling, 156, 157
  translation, rotation, and projection formulas for, 157
models, 6
modes, 12, 13
  320×200 16-color, 21
  320×200 256-color, 22
  640×200 16-color, 17
  640×350 16-color, 19
  640×480 16-color, 20
  establishing, 57
  hardware compatibility chart for, 15
MODE____FLAG, 76, 83
modular programming, 44
monitors
  analog display, 11-13, 28
  enhanced color display, 12, 28
  hardware compatibility chart for, 15
  multiscanning, 11-13, 28
  raster display, 28
  standard color display, 11, 12, 28
  transistor-transistor (TTL), 13
  types of, 27
movedata instruction, 152, 154
MOVETO, 58, 59, 61
moving objects (see translation), 157
multibit-per-pixel display memory, 16
multicolor graphics, logical operators for, 255
multicolor graphics array (MCGA), xiv, 10, 11
  graphics modes available on, 12
multiplane-per-pixel display memory, 13, 16
multiscanning monitor, 11, 12, 28, 30

N

near call, 361
neutral colors, 100
noise(), 154
numeric array, 50
  managing graphics database with, 149

O

OBJ file, assembly language, 363
operators, 45-47
  arithmetic, 45
  assignment, 46
  logical, 46
  logical, bitblt animation and, 249
  mathematical, 46
  relational, 45
optimizing frame animation, 211
Options menu (TC), 80
OR logical operator, 249
outp instruction, 152
OUTTEXT, 61

P

page animation (see frame animation), 207
page copying, 63, 64
pageflip(), 302
painting (see area fill), 59
panoramic views, world coordinates for, 146
parameter passing, assembly language, 361
parentheses, routines and subroutines designated by, 43
ping pong animation (see real-time animation), 9
pitch, 158, 161
plane equation methods, 160
PLANE____LENGTH, 152, 153, 154
pointilism (see stipple drawings), 195
portability, 51
pragmas, 52
process control code, 44
program analysis
  QuickC, 74-76
  Turbo C, 82-83
program control codes, 44
program segment prefix (PSP), 68, 78
programming, 41-84
  concept and features in, 36
  cycle of, 36-37
  developing code for, 36
  flowcharts for, 36
  integrated environment, 33
  memory models for, 38, 39
  modular, 44
programming tools, 43-55
programs
  3-D images, 162-169
  airbrushed backgrounds, 137-142
  animated business chart, 212-221
  animated caricature, 261-273
  bitblt animation source code, 356-359
  bitblt animation utility, 256-257
  bouncing rectangles real-time utility, 302-303
  business graphics, 2D, 176-183
  business graphics, 3-D, 184-194
  CGA assembly language routines, 382-395
  compatibility of, 23
  device-independent, 24
  dynamic keyboard input routine, 301
  EGA and VGA assembly language routines, 366-381
  frame animation source code, 348-352
  frame animation utility, 209-211
  graphics mode configuration module, 338-342
  hovering hummingbird, 222-234
  hues, tones, and shades, 111-115
  real-time animation source code, 353-355
  realistic illustration, 196-204
  ricocheting ball, 309-313
  rotating 3-D image, 235-246
  saving screen image to disk, CGA, 342-347
  saving screen image to disk, VGA or EGA, 333-338
  screen drawing, 120-125
  sculpted backgrounds, 131-137

simulated clockface, 285-296
Turbo C 3-D image, 417-423
   airbrushed background, 413-417
   animated business chart, 429-435
   arcade-style animation, 468-472
   bitblt animation, 493-496
   business chart, 423-429
   dynamic coordinates, 404-408
   flight simulation, 472-482
   frame animation, 487-493
   graphics adapter configuration, 482-485
   hovering hummingbird, 436-444
   hues and halftones, 399-403
   rotating 3-D model, 444-452
   sculpted background effect, 409-413
   simulated clock face, 458-468
   sound effects, 486-487
   walking stick figure, 452-458
   walking stick figure, 278-284
project management software, 5
projection formulas, 157, 159
prototyping, 98
PSET logical operator, 249
   bitblt animation and, 250
pseudocode, 36
psychological effects of color, 110
PUTIMAGE, 66

Q

QLB library, 70
   contents of graphics-oriented, 72
   creation of, 72
   QuickC, 71-73
QuadEGA ProSync graphics adapters, 26
QuadEGA+ graphics adapter, 25
QuadVGA graphics adapter, 27
QuickC, xviii, 34
   common error messages in, 76-77
   compiling data in, 70
   creating EXE files, 77
   data segment (DS) in, 70
   DOS environment for, 70
   loading, 68
   program analysis in, 74-76
   programming environment for, 37
   QLB library of, 70-73
   running program in, 73-74
   stacks in, 70
   syntax incompatibility with Turbo C and, 53, 66, 67
   system memory map of, 68-70
   text buffer in, 70
   two floppy disk drives, programming environment, 37
   use of, 68-77
QUIT____PGM, 75, 83

R

ragged right/left margins, 95
range column chart, 175
raster display monitors, 28
real numbers, 50
real-time animation, 6, 8, 9, 297-329, 332
   bouncing rectangles utility for, 302-303
   dynamic keyboard input in, 300
   flight simulation in, 314-329
   fundamental concepts of, 9
   practical techniques for, 299-303
   program listing for, 353-355

run-time performance of, 302
   two forms of, 300
realistic illustration, 195-204
   demonstration program for, 196-204
   preparation for, 196
   styles of, 195
relational operators, 45
rendering, 156
RESTORECRTMODE, 61, 83
ricochets, arcade-style animation, 304
RIGHT____ARENA, 308
roaming a database, 144
roll, 158, 161
rotation, 157, 158, 159
rotation-translation-projection formula, 160
routine, 52
   parentheses designation of, 43
   summary of C, 331-359
run-time performance, real-time animation, 302
run-time phase, C compiler, 36

S

savescrn(), 152, 153
SAVE____ARRAYS, 260, 275
saving screen images to disk, 150-154
   CGA, 153-154, 331
   VGA and EGA, 150-153, 331
scale, 172, 173
   color, 103
scaling factors, 143
screen division, 91
screen drawing, 116-125
   demonstration program for, 117-125
   dynamic and database coordinates for, 116
   program analysis for, 119
   program flow for, 118
   program listing for, 120-125
screen layout, 87-98
   ambiguity in, 91, 94
   center of interest in, 90
   color use in, 94
   combining text with graphics in, 98
   contrast in, 95
   drawing template for, 87
   emphasis with, 92, 170
   fundamentals of, 90
   grouping in, 172
   prototyping in, 98
   scale in, 172
   screen division for emphasis in, 91
   simplicity of design in, 170
   spacing in, 172
   template to display screen in, 87
   text in, 94
   text sizes in, 97
   using device-independent 640×480 template for, 89
   visual balance in, 92
   visual center in, 90
sculpted backgrounds, 126
   demonstration program for, 131-137
segread instruction, 153
SETACTIVEPAGE, 65
   frame animation and, 207
SETCOLOR, 58, 61
SETFILLMASK, 62, 106
SETFILLPATTERN, 62, 106

SETLINESTYLE, 62, 63
SETTEXTCOLOR, 61
SETTEXTPOSITION, 61
SETVIDEOMODE, 57, 58, 61, 75
SETVISUALPAGE, 65
   frame animation and, 208
shades, 100
shading
   3-D images, 161
   matrices, 106, 107
shadowing, 195
simplicity of design, business graphics and, 170
simulated clock face, 285-296
   Turbo C program for, 458-468
simulation software, 274-284
   walking stick figure, 274-284
simulations, 6
snapshot animation (see bitblt animation), 249
software, xviii, 30-40
   C-language, 31
software sprite, 249
solid models, 158, 160
sound effects, 154-155, 332
   Turbo C program for, 486-487
sound(), 154, 308
source code, 36, 52
sourceoffset, 152, 154
sourceseq, 152, 154
spacing, 173
spinning objects (see rotation), 157
split-complement harmony, 103
sprite, software, 249
stack segment, 70, 80
stacking, 93
standard color display (SCD) monitor, 11, 12, 28, 29
stipple drawings, 195, 196
struct variable, 53, 73
subroutines, 52
   functions as, 44
   parentheses designation of, 43
   passing parameters to (assembly language), 361
subset viewports, 144
surface normal, 161
syntax
   incompatibility between QuickC and Turbo C, 53, 67
   logic errors in, 76, 84
   portability of, 51
   Turbo C graphics, 397

T

targetoffset, 152, 154
targetseg, 152, 154
template, 87, 88
   device-independent 640×480, 89
   display screen from, 87
   ratio formulas for, 90
terrain grid, flight simulation, 315
text
   centering, 94
   combining graphics and, 98
   coordinates for, 60
   good screen layout for, 94, 96
   graphics screen writing of, 59

graphics vs., 3
justifying, 94
margins for, 94
returning to mode of, 61
text buffer, 70, 80
text editors (see integrated editors), 39
text mode, 61
text sizes, 97
third-party graphics libraries (see libraries), 34
thumbnail sketches, 87
tick marks, 174
tint scale, 104
tints, 100
tones, 100
tools, 41-84
translation, 157, 158, 159
transparency effect, 110
Turbo C, xviii, 34, 78-84
  3-D image program for, 417-423
  3-D rotation model program for, 444-452
  airbrushed background effect program for, 413-417
  animated business chart program for, 429-435
  ANSI adaptations for programs in, 396
  arcade-style animation program for, 468-472
  bitblt animation program for, 493-496
  business chart program for, 423-429
  code segment of, 80
  common error messages in, 83-84
  compiling data with, 80
  creating EXE files with, 84
  data segment in, 80
  demonstration programs for, 396-496
  DOS environment for, 80
  dynamic coordinates program for, 404-408
  flight simulation program for, 472-482
  frame animation program for, 487-493
  graphics adapter configuration program, 482-485
  graphics library in, 82

graphics syntax in, 397
hovering hummingbird program for, 436-444
hues and halftones program, 399-403
loading, 78
memory map of, 78, 79
program analysis for, 82-83
programming environment for, 37
project file in, 396
running program in, 81
sculpted background effect program for, 409-413
simulated clock face program for, 458-468
sound effects program, 486-487
spurious error messages in, 399
stack segment in, 80
syntax incompatibility with QuickC and, 53, 66, 67
text buffer in, 80
two floppy disk drives, programming environment, 38
walking stick figure program for, 452-458
TurboHALO, 34, 56

U

unsigned char variable, 49

V

value, 100
variable frequency display monitors (see multiscanning monitors), 30
variables, 49-50
  arrays and, 51
  initializing, 73, 82
  local, 363
  unsigned, 49
vertex, 160
VGA____MODE, 75, 83
video graphics array (VGA) xiv, 3, 12
  assembly language routines for, 366-381
  color palettes for, 99

display memory of, 19
frame animation page locations for, 209
graphics modes available on, 14
hidden page animation on, 299
memory map of, 20-24
multiplane-per-pixel display memory in, 13
saving screen image to disk, program listing for, 333-338
saving screen images to disk on, 150-153, 331
view coordinates, 157
viewports, subset, 144
visual balance, 92, 93
visual center, 90
  physical center vs., 91
void, 73, 82
volume effect, 110

W

walking stick figure, 274-284
  dot-matrix print-out of, 277
  program listing for, 278-284
  Turbo C program for, 452-458
window mapping, 117, 144
windowing routines, 143
windows and viewports, 143-148
wireframe model, 160
world coordinates, 144
  3-D images with, 156-157
  defining of, 157
  panoramic views with, 146
  ratio formulas for, 90
written-to page (see hidden page), 207

X

XOR logical operator, 249
xyz coordinates, 117, 157
X____RES, 75, 83

Y

yaw, 158, 161
Y____RES, 75, 83